ISOBEL DOOLE, ROBIN LOWE & ALEXANDRA KENYON

INTERNATIONAL MARKETING STRATEGY

ANALYSIS, DEVELOPMENT AND IMPLEMENTATION

SEVENTH EDITION

❖ CENGAGE
Learning™

Australia • ... • United States

**International Marketing Strategy,
7th Edition**
Doole, Lowe and Kenyon

Publisher: Annabel Ainscow

Commissioning Editor: Abbie Jones

Content Project Manager: Melissa Beavis

Manufacturing Buyer: Elaine Bevan

Marketing Manager: Amanda Cheung

Typesetter: MPS Limited

Cover design: Adam Renvoize Creative

Front cover image: Koya979/Shutterstock inc

For product information and technology assistance,
contact **emea.info@cengage.com**.

For permission to use material from this text or product,
and for permission queries,
email **emea.permissions@cengage.com**.

British Library Cataloguing-in-Publication Data
A catalogue record for this book is available from the British Library.

ISBN: 978-1-4737-2370-2

Cengage Learning EMEA
Cheriton House, North Way, Andover, Hampshire, SP10 5BE
United Kingdom

Cengage Learning products are represented in Canada by Nelson Education Ltd.

For your lifelong learning solutions, visit **www.cengage.co.uk**

Purchase your next print book, e-book or e-chapter at
www.cengagebrain.com

Printed in China by RR Donnelley
Print Number: 01   Print Year: 2015

To Andrew, Rob, Libby and Will

Sylvia, Jonathan, Catherine, Simon, Ben and Edward

Steve, Sylvia and Peter

BRIEF CONTENTS

CONTENTS

PART I

ANALYSIS   1

PART III

IMPLEMENTATION 297

11 PRICING FOR INTERNATIONAL MARKETS   371

12 TECHNOLOGY ENABLED SUSTAINABLE INTERNATIONAL MARKETING   409

LIST OF FIGURES, TABLES, ILLUSTRATIONS AND MANAGEMENT CHALLENGES

LIST OF FIGURES

LIST OF TABLES

LIST OF ILLUSTRATIONS

LIST OF MANAGEMENT CHALLENGES

PREFACE

Introduction

Markets and marketing are becoming ever more international in their nature and managers around the world ignore this fact at their peril. To achieve sustainable growth in markets that are becoming increasingly global, or merely to survive in domestic markets that are increasingly attacked by international players, it is essential that organizations understand the complexity and diversity of international marketing. Their managers must develop the skills, aptitudes and knowledge necessary to compete effectively around the globe.

This new revised edition of *International Marketing Strategy* continues to meet the needs of the international marketing student and practitioner in an up-to-date and innovative manner. It recognizes the increasing time pressures of both students and managers and so strives to maintain the readability and clarity of the previous editions, as well as providing a straightforward and logical structure that will enable them to apply their learning to the tasks ahead.

The book continues to incorporate new, significant and relevant material with learning innovations that ensure its continued status as the best-selling UK text on international marketing strategy.

Structure of the book

As in previous editions, the book is divided into three main subject areas – analysis, strategy development and implementation – each of which has four chapters. For each chapter the learning objectives for the reader are stated at the outset and these then lead to the key themes of the chapter, which are explored in the text. Boxed 'Illustrations' throughout the text enable the reader to focus on the key issues and discuss the practical implications of these issues for international marketing strategy development. Boxed 'Management Challenges' in each of the chapters provide examples of the kind of practical dilemmas faced by international marketing managers in their everyday operations. Throughout the book we highlight a number of continuing and emerging themes in the management of international marketing. We provide the opportunity to explore the different mindsets of many types of businesses that depend on international markets for their survival and growth: from small poor farmers, to born global innovative technology businesses, to the global brand giants.

Success in international marketing is achieved through being able to integrate and appreciate the interaction between the various elements of the international marketing strategy development process and this is addressed in two ways. First, at the end of each chapter one or two case studies are included. While the main focus of the chapter 'Case Studies' are on integrating a number of the themes of the chapter, the reader should also draw on his/her learning from the chapters that have gone before to give a complete answer. Second, at the end of each part there is a more comprehensive 'Directed Study Activity' for the reader that focuses on international marketing strategy development. At the end of Part I this activity is concerned with analysis, at the end of Part II with strategy development and at the end of Part III with implementation. The format for these study activities is similar so that the three Directed Study Activities, when added together, integrate all the learning from the book and provide a practical and comprehensive exercise in international marketing strategy development for the reader.

New for this edition

All the chapters have been revised and updated to ensure the inclusion of the latest developments in international marketing and in response to the changing focus of international marketing and the new challenges posed by the new patterns of developments in global markets. For this reason we provide many examples of international marketing and innovation in the newly emerging economies of Africa, particularly South Africa, and the Middle East, adding to the examples of development in Asian markets that we also include and build further on the website. We also explain the increasingly global impact of events, such as natural disasters, conflict, the global banking crisis and technological changes on the strategic development and implementation plans of international organizations, large or small.

In Chapter 1 we have included a full section introducing sustainability in an adapted SLEPTS approach to examining the environmental influences on international marketing. Sustainability is about considering the environmental impact of everything we do. This means encouraging a holistic way of thinking in our responses to the global marketing challenges we identify, and assessing the impact of our global marketing strategies – socially, economically and environmentally – in our approach to ensuring sustainability. This is central to the values of responsible international marketing and a theme that we highlight at various stages of strategy development in the chapters of this book.

The global economic crisis sparked a contraction in the volume of global trade and in recent years world trade volume suffered the sharpest decline in more than 70 years. The implications of this changed landscape are discussed in Chapter 2 where we examine the international trading environment and discuss the institutions that aim to influence world trade. Chapters 5 and 6 on international marketing in SMEs and global firms, have been expanded to include a section examining the skills base needed by global managers, the implications of the strategy development issues, how some companies are born global rather than grow internationally, and the age-old mantra that marketers must understand their target market and not assume all consumers, or workforces, are the same. Further examples of international companies from emerging markets provide the basis for discussion of the different contexts faced and the alternative growth strategies.

Customers around the world are becoming more comfortable with the use of technology, such as social media and mobile computing, and we highlight this in a number of different business to business and business to consumer situations throughout the chapters of the book, particularly recognizing the different geographic, economic, social and cultural contexts that new social media and mobile computing has impacted upon. This is examined particularly in the chapters in Part III of the book where we focus on implementation issues. Chapter 12 focuses on this further when we examine how social media, machine2machine technology and sustainability issues, not only support and enable international marketing communications, but also change the process by which the future communication and marketing strategies of organizations in international markets are formulated.

The majority of the Case Studies, Illustrations and Management Challenges are new or updated. We have endeavoured to ensure the material we use reflects a global perspective and have included practical examples from across the world. For this edition we have included a number of our new Case Studies, Illustrations and Management Challenges from North and South Africa and the Middle East, and other emerging countries, in response to the advice and suggestions from reviewers, tutors and students. The authors have focused on responding to the needs of readers who are developing their international marketing skills in Europe, the Americas, Asia and Africa or other parts of the world. Moreover, we believe that organizations operating in these countries face some of the most significant and interesting international marketing challenges today and are developing the most novel solutions. Each Illustration and Management Challenge has questions highlighting specific issues that should be considered in the context of both the industry it focuses on and the area of the world it is spotlighting.

The Directed Study Activity (DSA) is an innovative section at the end of each part with the objective of encouraging readers to integrate their learning from the chapters and the parts. The DSA at the end of Part I highlights the rapid development of the mobile phone services market in Africa and uses this scenario as a backdrop for examining trading infrastructure issues, consumer behaviour issues and examining the development of a latent and exciting market. We focus in DSA 2 on the companies from emerging markets that are challenging the more established players and encourage readers to explore the alternative strategies adopted by these companies to expand their activity. We also encourage readers to consider those companies from emerging markets that have made substantial progress towards becoming global players during the last few years.

In DSA 3 we focus on the opportunities for growth for established consumer brands in emerging markets but also provide the opportunity to consider the contexts that could provide new competition for those global brands.

By obtaining and analyzing data through secondary sources, typically through the Internet, the reader is able to proceed through the steps of the international marketing strategy process, thus acquiring further knowledge and using this opportunity to practise a number of their international marketing skills.

How to study using this book

The aim of the book is for readers to have an accessible and readable resource for use both as a course book and for revision. The text is also recommended reading for students of the CIM qualifications.

It has a clear structure which is easy for the reader to follow, thus making it ideal for incorporation into a course delivered in a 12-week teaching semester. Its geocentric view of international marketing, with examples of good practice in competing internationally from around the globe, makes it ideal for use with courses with multicultural students.

International Marketing Strategy has been developed to help the reader learn, understand and practise a number of elements of the international marketing strategy process. The process involves the analysis of a situation, development of a strategy against a background of a number of strategic options, and the implementation of the chosen option. It is important to recognize that there is not one 'right' strategy, because success is ultimately determined by many factors and, besides, it will usually take a number of years before the strategy can be seen finally as a success or failure. Therefore, this book provides a framework, within the parts and chapter structure, in which to understand and evaluate the factors that should be taken into account (and which should be dismissed too) in building an international marketing strategy.

Structure of the book

Parts

The three parts focus on the topics of analysis, strategy development and implementation. Each part contains an introduction to the four chapters that have been grouped together.

Readers should realize that these groupings of chapter topics within parts are primarily to provide a clear structure and layout for the book. In practice, however, there is considerable overlap between analysis, strategy development and implementation topics. For example, product strategy and market entry are considered by organizations in some situations to be implementation issues, and technology might be used to support analysis, set the overall international marketing strategy, or support implementation.

Part I Analysis   Part I focuses on analyzing the international marketing environment. It provides an introduction to how the international marketing environment influences how firms operate. It explores the changing nature of the environment and explains the structures that support and control international trade. Also considered are the social and cultural influences on customer buying behaviour in international markets.

Frameworks and processes that provide the means to systematically identify and evaluate marketing opportunities and carry out market research across the world are explained.

CASE STUDIES AT THE END OF EACH CHAPTER

PART I ANALYSIS

Chapter 1

Tesco in China When Tesco entered the Chinese market in 2004 it claimed to be putting the customer at the heart of the business through an empathy with cultural and consumer behaviour, but in 2014 the majority of its loss making business was sold to a Chinese state run operation. This case looks at the international marketing lessons to be learnt from the venture.

Going international? You need a language strategy Marketing internationally means communicating with customers, employees, investors and supply chain operators in a common language, but this inevitably means communicating in many different languages. This case explains the need for developing a language strategy and how it can be implemented.

Chapter 2

Export tourism increases the host country's GDP Exporting tourism can make a significant contribution to GDP both for developed and less developed countries and this case explores the tourism value chain and how domestic companies can benefit from promotion and mega events targeted at international tourism.

The mobile phone services market in Africa Penetration of mobile phones is high in many but not all African countries and this case explores the economic and political factors driving the market growth. However, as well as identifying significant consumer benefits and attractive opportunities for firms in the market, this case also looks at the associated risks.

Chapter 3

Islam, Ramadan and the tent business in the Middle East Lavish tents and marquees have long been a mainstay of the corporate events industry during the holy month of Ramadan in the Middle East. This case looks at two UAE-based companies,

Al-Baddad International and Harlequin Marquees & Event Services which had to look at expanding internationally in order to maintain sales in the global downturn.

Cultural challenges in the Turkish ice cream market Turkey is seen as a cultural bridge between East and West. Ice cream consumers in Turkey are influenced by enduring local traditions, but also welcome global products. This case explores the cultural issues that domestic and international ice cream marketers should consider in developing their marketing strategy.

Chapter 4

How do Spike Games segment the global mobile phone gambling market? Spike Games is a business that provides the 'feel of the casino/slot machine' to the mobile phone. This case study explores in detail how the firm has developed a segmentation strategy and in doing that considers the criteria that are country-based and global segment descriptors.

Cultural segmentation map Despite the ever expanding global marketplace, consumers are not homogeneous. Differing values, by country, are presented in this case study. Differences are mapped showing which countries have traditional values and self-expression values, and which have secular rational values and survival values.

Directed Study Activity 1 – International marketing planning: Analysis

In this DSA we spotlight the rapid development of the mobile phone services market in Africa and use this scenario as a backdrop for examining trading infrastructure issues, consumer behaviour issues and examining the development of a latent and exciting market.

PART II STRATEGY DEVELOPMENT

Part II explains the international marketing strategy options available for small- and medium-sized firms and also the largest organizations that will enable them to compete effectively in global markets. The factors that affect the choice of strategy are considered as well as the challenges that are posed to the managers of these strategies.

A key decision for most organizations is which market entry method to use to exploit the market opportunities from the many options available. This is then followed by the selection and development of the products and service strategy that determine the portfolio that will be offered to customers.

Chapter 5

Gripple connecting with international markets For an SME manufacturer of fastening devices for the agricultural and construction sectors that is innovative but has limited resources, the challenge is to further build on its international success by choosing the most promising markets, explaining the use of its products to customers, seeking out the key decision makers and avoiding the pitfalls of international marketing.

Pin it, share it, desire it, sell it Pinterest is a fast growing social media platform where SME e-tailers have the opportunity to provide a shop window to promote their products. This case looks at the benefits Pinterest offers to SMEs and how they should plan their presence on the platform to reach a global audience.

Chapter 6

BMW of the future – super cars or super gadgets? Continued growth for BMW high performance cars depends upon its success in targeting wealthy customers in emerging markets. But will technology advances, such as driverless cars, result in new competitors such as Google and Apple emerging to attack the traditional car markets?

Re-shoring: rethinking global reach Outsourcing of manufacturing and services offshore has been common practice for many firms, largely based on reasons of cost saving. However, many organizations have been rethinking this strategy. This case considers the pros and cons of re-shoring and when it is an appropriate strategy.

Chapter 7

Boost Juice: healthy drink = healthy growth Boost Juice is an Australian provider of healthy, freshly squeezed juices and smoothies and wants to become the world's most loved brand! This case explores how it has achieved success in its international markets

and considers the key factors for franchising to be an effective business model.

When joint ventures go wrong Unforeseen factors cause major problems in promising mergers between companies from developed and developing countries. The case study focuses particularly on Danone's problems in China and looks at where the management made mistakes by not appreciating the different mindsets and cultural differences in managing collaborative working with a Chinese entrepreneur.

Chapter 8

Lego playing with its strengths This case study learns lessons from the global toymaker's limited success with diversification and explores Lego's approach to building its brand when challenged by a new generation of consumers, global market changes and the growth of technologically based competitors.

Accor inseparable services: Online and face-to-face Around the world the Accor brand has developed an excellent reputation for service in the hospitality sector. This case explores the importance of all the elements of the marketing of hospitality services and looks at how other organizations might learn from studying Accor's integrated approach.

Directed Study Activity 2 – International marketing planning: Strategy development

Future global players examines the different starting points and means used by newcomers from developing economies to build the global competitive capability necessary for them to compete with the more established competitive firms from developed countries.

PART III IMPLEMENTATION

Part III deals with the international communication, distribution and pricing strategies that support the introduction and development of the business in the various worldwide markets. The different local market factors that affect implementation are considered. These factors may allow the associated implementation programmes and processes to be standardized across different markets but, frequently, it is necessary to adapt the strategies to suit local needs.

Technology plays a key enabling role in international marketing strategy implementation. It supports the programme and process delivery and also provides opportunities for creativity that allow innovative firms to gain competitive advantage.

Chapter 9

Etihad Airways: Scoring global brand recognition Etihad Airways is a global player in travel but it is building its global brand in other ways too. It has used sponsorship of Manchester City football club to help raise global recognition of its brand and this case explores how pursuing many sport-related marketing activities is helping to further consolidate its position.

Greenpeace – global campaigner Greenpeace must balance the need to create awareness, which often requires shock tactics, with the need to raise funds and best leverage its resources, which are limited when compared to corporates and governments. This case explores how it must communicate effectively by adopting and effectively integrating a variety of traditional offline and online media to appeal to its various target audiences.

Chapter 10

Distribution channels in the Asian insurance market Whereas the Asian insurance market was traditionally dependent on distribution through agents, it is now rapidly diversifying and this case looks at how an integrated distribution strategy can be developed using a range of intermediaries and channels.

Poor packaging = damage = lost profits This case looks at how the use of inappropriate packaging by the smallest rural farmer to the largest multinational can prove costly in terms of financial loss, waste of resources and environmental impact, and what can be done to specify more sustainable materials.

Chapter 11

Countertrade and bartering Bartering involving moneyless exchange of goods and services makes up a significant proportion of world trade. This case explores three examples of its use in education, product placement and online word of mouth exchange, and considers the pricing and non-financial benefits of bartering.

Torque plc Torque, a supplier of car components faces a number of challenges in costing and pricing its products for global markets. This case considers the alternative costing and pricing models it is using and their relative merits in addressing these challenges.

Chapter 12

Heart problems? Wearable tech could save your life Enabling consumers to be technology connected through the 'Internet of things' offers huge potential benefits. This case looks at the use of Wireless Body Area Network (WBAN) to monitor patients and rapidly provide information and alerts to medical staff. The case also looks at sharing personal information and the concerns of many people about privacy.

Unilever: Redefining product policy for a global future As a well-established international marketer for more than a century, Unilever has demonstrated how the many aspects of its international strategy must be continuously refreshed to meet the changing needs and expectations of its stakeholders. This case explores the various dimensions of its strategy and considers what the focus should be for the future.

Chapters

After a brief introduction to each chapter the learning objectives are set out: these should provide the focus for study. To help to reinforce the learning and encourage the reader to explore the issues more fully, the chapters contain a number of additional aids to learning.

Illustrations

The illustrations that have been provided are not present just to reinforce a key issue or learning point that has been discussed within the chapter: the questions that have been added are intended to enable the reader to reflect upon the deeper and broader implications too and thus provide a further opportunity for discussion. Our aim is that the settings for the illustrations be as diverse as possible, geographically, culturally, by business sector, size and type of organization, in order to try to help the reader consider the situations described from alternative perspectives.

Management Challenges

The management challenges included emphasize the point that there are few simple and straightforward management decisions in international marketing. Organizations and managers often face difficult problems that require a decision. The management challenges within a chapter provide the opportunity for the reader to identify those factors that should be taken into account in coming to the decision and, hopefully, consider rather more creative ideas that lead to decisions and solutions that add greater value.

Case Studies

The case studies provide the opportunity for the reader to carry out more comprehensive analysis of key chapter topics before deciding what strategic decisions or plans should be made. These case studies can also be used in the classroom so that analysis and discussions can take place following further research into the topic under investigation. These short cases provide only limited information and, where possible, readers should obtain more information on the case study subject from appropriate websites in order to complete the tasks. The reader should start with the questions that have been supplied in order to help guide the analysis or discussion. After this, however, the reader should think more broadly around the issues raised and decide whether these are indeed the right questions to ask and answer. International markets change fast and continuously, and new factors that have recently emerged may completely alter the situation.

Directed Study Activities

At the end of each of the three parts of the book we have included a directed study activity (DSA). Their purpose is to integrate the four chapters that make up each of the parts. More importantly, however, is that as a whole the three activities provide a framework for planning an international marketing strategy and give the opportunity for readers to consider the practical issues involved in developing, planning and implementing an outline international marketing strategy. The objective of these activities is to provide a vehicle through which the reader is able to develop practical skills in research, analysis, evaluation and strategy development. In completing these activities you will need to synthesize the various strands and themes explored throughout the book and apply them to a practical situation.

ID, RL, AK

ABOUT THE AUTHORS

Isobel Doole

Isobel is Professor of International Marketing and Assistant Dean at Sheffield Business School, Sheffield Hallam University. She is an experienced marketing professional and senior academic in international marketing and in the international competitiveness of small firms. With her co-author Robin Lowe she has built an international reputation through the highly successful textbooks *Strategic Marketing Decisions* and *International Marketing Strategy*. She is a senior examiner for the Chartered Institute of Marketing and has acted as an expert advisor on a number of governmental committees.

Robin Lowe

Robin is a Marketing and Management Consultant. Through his research, consultancy and policy development work in international trade, innovation and entrepreneurship, Robin has made a major contribution to government policy and business support. He also has considerable experience of consulting and training with multinationals around the world, including IBM, Microsoft, AstraZeneca, Renault Nissan, Huawei and Batelco. He is the joint author of several bestselling texts in international marketing, innovation and entrepreneurship.

Alexandra Kenyon

Alexandra is Senior Lecturer at the School of Events, Tourism and Hospitality at Leeds Beckett University. Alexandra was an FP7 European Commission Expert Evaluator and is an Editor for the *Journal of Advertising Research*. Alexandra also has knowledge and experience of empirical research and evaluation of matter congruent with the meetings and events industry and social media marketing for MPI Dallas, US and the social responsibilities of licensed retail outlets for National Pubwatch.

ACKNOWLEDGEMENTS

Inevitably, in the task of writing this textbook we have had help, support and valuable contributions from many people. We would especially like to thank our colleagues from Sheffield Hallam University, Leeds Beckett University and other universities who have contributed a number of case studies and illustrations. We would also like to thank case study contributors for their invaluable contributions to the digital support resources which accompany this book.

We are indebted to our students from many countries and the managers of many businesses, who have freely given their time to share their expert knowledge of international niche marketing. Also the managers in many larger companies, who have discussed with us the challenges they face in global marketing. Over the years they have all helped to shape and influence our view of international marketing strategy.

The team at Cengage Learning have always encouraged us and we are grateful for their professionalism in turning the manuscript into its finished form.

The publisher would like to thank the following reviewers for their insightful feedback:

Tabani Ndlovu, Nottingham Trent University, UK

Paul Riegen, Hogeschool van Amsterdam, Netherlands

Lesley Viney, University of Bedfordshire, UK

CENGAGE
Learning®

Digital Support Resources

All of our Higher Education textbooks are accompanied by a range of digital support resources. Each title's resources are carefully tailored to the specific needs of the particular book's readers. Examples of the kind of resources provided include:

- A password protected area for instructors with, for example, a testbank, PowerPoint slides and an instructor's manual.

- An open-access area for students including, for example, useful weblinks and glossary terms.

Lecturers: to discover the dedicated lecturer digital support resources accompanying this textbook please register here for access: login.cengage.com.

Students: to discover the dedicated student digital support resources accompanying this textbook, please search for **INTERNATIONAL MARKETING STRATEGY** on: cengagebrain. co.uk.

AIMS AND OBJECTIVES

Knowledge and an understanding of the markets in which companies operate are important for all business activities. In international markets, because of geographical distances and the complexities of operating in a number of disparate markets where risk and uncertainty are high, the need for knowledge and understanding becomes of paramount importance. It is this issue that is central to Part I of this book. The chapters in this section concentrate on helping the reader generate a greater understanding of the concepts of the international marketing process and the international environment within which companies operate. It aims to extend the range of understanding in order to enable the reader to deal with international marketing situations and to develop the skills to analyze and evaluate non-domestic markets, which in turn will enable their firms to compete effectively in world markets.

In Chapter 1 we focus on the international marketing environment. The book uses the SLEPTS approach to understanding the complexities of the environmental influences on international marketing, thus enabling the reader to acquire an appreciation of the complexities of marketing on an international basis. We examine what is meant by international marketing and introduce the reader to the international market planning process. We also examine the reasons for success and failure in international marketing strategies and the characteristics of best international marketing practice.

In Chapter 2 the focus is on gaining an understanding of the international trading environment. We first examine, at a macro level, the development of international trading structures and the changes in trading patterns, as well as reviewing the major international bodies formed to foster world trade. The evolution of trading regions is analyzed and the implications to international marketing companies assessed.

In Chapter 3 we take a fairly detailed look at the social and cultural influences in international marketing. The components of culture are examined together with the impact of these components on international marketing. We then look at how cultural influences impact on buyer behaviour across the globe both in consumer markets and in business-to-business markets and discuss methods that can be used to analyze cultures both within and across countries.

In Chapter 4 the focus is on the identification and evaluation of marketing opportunities internationally. Segmentation of international markets is discussed, and how to prioritize international opportunities. The marketing research process and the role it plays in the development of international marketing strategies are also examined. The different stages in the marketing research process are discussed, with particular attention being paid to the problems in carrying out international marketing research in foreign markets and coordinating multi-country studies.

CHAPTER 1

AN INTRODUCTION TO INTERNATIONAL MARKETING

LEARNING OBJECTIVES

After reading this chapter you should be able to:

- Explain and use the SLEPTS factors to assess international markets

- Discuss the differences between export marketing, international and global marketing

- Understand the criteria required to evaluate a company's international marketing strategy

- Appreciate the key steps in the international marketing planning process

INTRODUCTION

Managers around the globe are recognizing the necessity for their companies and organizations to develop the skills, aptitudes and knowledge to compete effectively in international markets.

The fact that the world economy is open and interdependent, the globalization of consumer tastes and the unabated expansion of mobile Internet applications which can be downloaded to smartphone to perform all kind of feats from social networking to online banking, all increase the interdependency and interconnections of country economies across the globe. The need for managers to develop the skills to maximize the opportunities such technological developments bring, impacts on companies of all shapes, sizes and sectors.

In this chapter, readers will be introduced to the concepts of international marketing, enabling them to acquire an appreciation of the complexities of marketing on an international basis and how this activity differs from operating purely in domestic home markets. In the following sections we will define international marketing, examine the important trends in the global marketing environment, and introduce the reader to the international marketing strategy development and international marketing planning process.

The strategic importance of international marketing

The world trade in merchandise exports continues to grow to US$18.8 trillion and world trade in commercial services in exports rose to US$4.6 trillion. It is almost impossible to visualize such large amounts of money; however, it does serve as an indication of the scale of international trade today.

The current global marketplace consists of 7.2 billion people which is expected to rise to 9.6 billion by 2050 and could rise to 27.5 billion by 2100, should fertility levels stay the same as they are now (United Nations 2013). However, it is predicted that fertility levels in less developed countries will fall which means there will be 10.9 billion by 2100 according to the latest projections by the United Nations (2013). They go on to say, however, that some countries, such as Germany, Cuba and Japan, will not contribute to the global population increase, as their populations are shrinking, as shown in Figure 1.1. Generally it is expected that some countries in Europe will see a decline in population, such as Germany, however, the number of migrants moving into Germany is expected to increase (UNICEF 2015).

The last few years have also seen a worldwide increase in personal wealth. Wealth per adult rose by 8.3 per cent suggesting that an average adult's wealth is US$56 000, with Swiss adults enjoying US$587 000; yet for some countries in Central Africa and South Asia adult wealth is below US$5000. Similarly, the percentage share of the world's total wealth is not equally distributed, with North America and Europe combined accounting for a 67.1 per cent share, whilst Africa and India combined account for a 2.5 per cent share. Nevertheless, generally there is an increase in global wealth which brings a higher demand for goods and services. Increasing affluence and commercial dynamism from nations such as China, Brazil and countries across Eastern Europe, means that consumers actively seek choice, with the result that globally competition is intensifying as companies compete to win the battle for disposable income.

Population growth and increased affluence together have helped create a global youth culture which account for approximately 30 per cent of the population globally. In many countries, more than half the population is pre-adult, creating one of the world's biggest single markets, the youth market. Everywhere adolescents project worldwide cultural icons: Coca-Cola, Apple iPhones and iPads, Xbox and Starbucks. Social networking: Facebook, Twitter and blogs are all now commonplace creating a one-world youth culture market that potentially can exceed all others as a premier global market segment. Parochial, local and ethnic products may not satisfy the international culture and identity young people seek.

Older consumers are also increasingly transnational in their consumer identity. They drive globally produced cars, take worldwide holidays, watch programmes from across the globe on television, use globally

FIGURE 1.1   Population of the world 1950–2100, according to different projections and variants

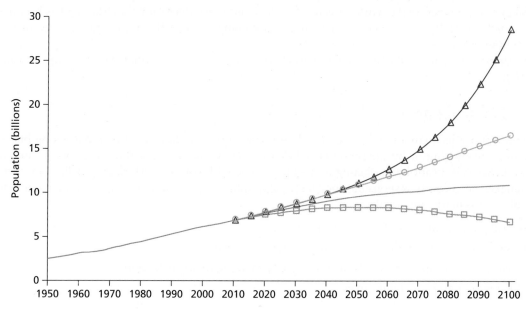

developed technology and are increasingly plugged into the online digital media technology previously only used by the younger generation. On the supply side, transnational corporations are increasing in size and embracing more global power. The top 500 companies in the world account for 70 per cent of world trade and 80 per cent of international investment. Total sales for multinationals are now in excess of world trade, which gives them a combined gross product of more than some national economies.

To strategically position themselves for global competitiveness, companies are consolidating through mergers, acquisitions and alliances to reach the scale considered necessary to compete in the global arena. At the same time, there is a trend towards global standardization, as companies strive for world standards for efficiency and productivity. Figures for 2014 show that worldwide mergers and acquisitions (M&A) reached an all-time high of US$3.6 trillion, overtaking a peak shown in 2007. And with over a third of businesses worldwide considering growing their businesses through M&A there will be many international marketing opportunities riding on the back of that (Consultancy UK 2015). An interesting example in the tourism industry comes from Etihad Airways (2015) which has recently invested over €560 million in Alitalia to help it become the premium Italian airline that it once was.

In the telecommunication market the French company Altice is an example of an organization growing its business both locally and cross-border. Last year Altice acquired SFR, a domestic French-based mobile communication company, and this year they are engaging in a cross-border deal with Portugal Telecom SGPS (PT SGPS). Other organizations look further afield; with some seeing Turkey as a good place in which to do business. The Commercial Bank of Qatar looked to Turkey as part of their international strategy and joined forces with Alternatifbank AS in Turkey with an acquisition of over 70 per cent. The Japanese company Panasonic also entered Turkey when they acquired Viko, an organization that supplies electrical wiring equipment. Panasonic was not only interested in acquiring a local company to make and supply wires for its household electronic equipment, it sees this strategic move as an opportunity to break into the Russian and African markets. Panasonic are not the only Japanese organization to expand internationally. Suntory, a drinks manufacturer, researched potential businesses in the US and bought Beam Inc., known for its Jim Beam bourbon whiskey. Japan has a shrinking population, which is one of the reasons that Panasonic and Suntory are looking to different regions to sustain and grow their business.

The global marketplace is no longer the summation of a large number of independent country markets but much more multilateral and interdependent: economically, culturally and technically. Ownership of companies, money and information moves anywhere in the world, the ease of transactions and transmissions being facilitated by the convergence of long distance telecoms, cuts in the cost of electronic processing and the exponential growth in Internet access.

The combination of these forces has meant that all companies need to develop a marketing orientation which is global in nature and that companies need managers who have the skills to analyze, plan and implement strategies across the world. It is for these reasons that international marketing has become such a critical area of study for managers and an important component of the marketing syllabus of business faculties in universities.

So perhaps now we should turn our attention to examining exactly what we mean by international marketing.

What is international marketing?

Many readers of this textbook will have already followed a programme of study in marketing but, before explaining what we mean by international marketing, let us reflect for a few moments on our understanding of what is meant by marketing itself. The Chartered Institute of Marketing defines marketing as the 'Management process responsible for identifying, anticipating and satisfying customer requirements profitably'. Thus marketing involves:

- focusing on the needs and wants of customers
- identifying the best method of satisfying those needs and wants
- orienting the company towards the process of providing that satisfaction
- meeting organizational objectives.

In this way, it is argued, the company or organization best prepares itself to achieve competitive advantage in the marketplace. It then needs to work to maintain this advantage by manipulating the controllable functions of marketing within the largely uncontrollable, external marketing environment made up of SLEPTS factors, i.e: Social, Legal, Economic, Political, Technological and Sustainable.

How does the process of international marketing differ? Within the international marketing process the key elements of this framework still apply. The conceptual framework is not going to change to any marked degree when a company moves from a domestic to an international market; however, there are two main differences. First, there are different levels at which international marketing can be approached and, second, the uncontrollable elements of the marketing environment are more complex and multidimensional, given the multiplicity of markets that constitute the global marketplace. This means managers have to acquire new skills and abilities to add to the tools and techniques they have developed in marketing to domestic markets.

International marketing defined

At its simplest level, international marketing involves the firm in making one or more marketing mix decisions across national boundaries. At its most complex, it involves the firm in establishing manufacturing/processing facilities around the world and coordinating marketing strategies across the globe. At one extreme there are firms that opt for 'international marketing' simply by signing a distribution agreement with a foreign agent who then takes on the responsibility for pricing, promotion, distribution and market development. At the other extreme, there are huge global companies such as Ford with an integrated network of manufacturing plants worldwide and who operate in some 150 country markets. Thus, at its most complex, international marketing becomes a process of managing on a global scale. These different levels of marketing can be expressed in the following terms:

- *Domestic marketing*, which involves the company manipulating a series of controllable variables such as price, advertising, distribution and the product/service attributes in a largely uncontrollable external environment that is made up of different economic structures, competitors, cultural values and legal infrastructure within specific political or geographic country boundaries.

- *International marketing*, which involves operating across a number of foreign country markets in which not only do the uncontrollable variables differ significantly between one market and another, but the controllable factors in the form of cost and price structures, opportunities for advertising and distributive infrastructure, are also likely to differ significantly. It is these sorts of differences that lead to the complexities of international marketing.

- *Global marketing management*, which is a larger and more complex international operation. Here a company coordinates, integrates and controls a whole series of marketing programmes into a substantial global effort. Here the primary objective of the company is to achieve a degree of synergy in the overall operation so that by taking advantage of different exchange rates, tax rates, labour rates, skill levels and market opportunities, the organization as a whole will be greater than the sum of its parts.

This type of strategy calls for managers who are capable of operating as international marketing managers in the truest sense, a task which is far broader and more complex than that of operating either in a specific foreign country or in the domestic market. In discussing this, Sarathy *et al.* (2006) comment that: 'The international marketing manager has a dual responsibility: foreign marketing (marketing within foreign countries) and global marketing (coordinating marketing in multiple markets in the face of global competition).'

Thus, how international marketing is defined and interpreted depends on the level of involvement of the company in the international marketplace. International marketing could therefore be:

- Export marketing, in which case the firm markets its goods and/or services across national/political boundaries often without any adaptations to the goods and/or services. Generally, exporting begins with neighbouring countries that have similar laws, regulations and consumer culture.

- International marketing, where the marketing activities of an organization include activities, interests or operations in more than one country and where there is some kind of influence or control of marketing activities from outside the country in which the goods or services will actually be sold. Sometimes markets are typically perceived to be independent and a profit centre in their own right, in which case the term multinational or multidomestic marketing is often used.

■ Global marketing, in which the whole organization focuses on the selection and exploitation of global marketing opportunities and marshals resources around the globe with the objective of achieving a global competitive advantage.

The first of these definitions describes relatively straightforward exporting activities, numerous examples of which exist. However, the subsequent definitions are more complex and more formal and indicate not only a revised attitude to marketing but also a very different underlying philosophy. Here the world is seen as a market segmented by social, legal, economic, political, technological and sustainable (SLEPTS) groupings.

In this textbook we will incorporate the international marketing issues faced by firms, be they involved in export, international or global marketing.

For all these levels the key to successful international marketing is being able to identify and understand the complexities of each of these SLEPTS dimensions of the international environment and how they impact on a firm's marketing strategies across their international markets. As in domestic marketing, the successful marketing company will be the one that is best able to manipulate the controllable tools of the marketing mix within the uncontrollable, external environment. It follows that the key problem faced by the international marketing manager is that of coming to terms with the details and complexities of the international environment. It is these complexities that we will examine in the following sections.

The international marketing environment

The key difference between domestic marketing and marketing on an international scale is the multidimensionality and complexity of the many foreign country markets a company may operate in. An international manager needs a knowledge and awareness of these complexities and the implications they have for international marketing management.

There are many environmental analysis models which the reader may have come across. For the purposes of this textbook, we will use the SLEPTS approach and examine the various aspects and trends in the international marketing environment through the social/cultural, legal, economic, political, technological and sustainability dimensions, as depicted in Figure 1.2. In this edition we have added a sustainability dimension. Sustainability is about considering the impact of everything we do, be it sympathy for the biodiversity of a region in which we want to construct a factory, or the human rights of the workforce. This means encouraging a holistic way of thinking in our responses to the global marketing challenges we identify and assessing the impact of our marketing strategies – socially, economically and environmentally – in our approach to ensuring sustainability over the longer term.

Social/cultural factors

The social and cultural influences on international marketing are immense. Differences in social conditions, religion and material culture all affect consumers' perceptions and patterns of buying behaviour. It is this area that determines the extent to which consumers across the globe are either similar or different and so determines the potential for global branding and standardization.

A failure to understand the social/cultural dimensions of a market are complex to manage, as McDonald's found in India. It had to deal with a market that is 40 per cent vegetarian, has an aversion to either beef or pork among meat-eaters and a hostility to frozen meat and fish, but with the general Indian fondness for spice with everything. To satisfy such tastes, McDonald's discovered it needed to do more than provide the right burgers. Customers buying vegetarian burgers wanted to be sure that these were cooked in a separate area in the kitchen using separate utensils. Sauces like McMasala and McImli were developed to satisfy the Indian taste for spice. Interestingly, however, these are now innovations they have introduced into other markets.

FIGURE 1.2   Factors influencing international markets

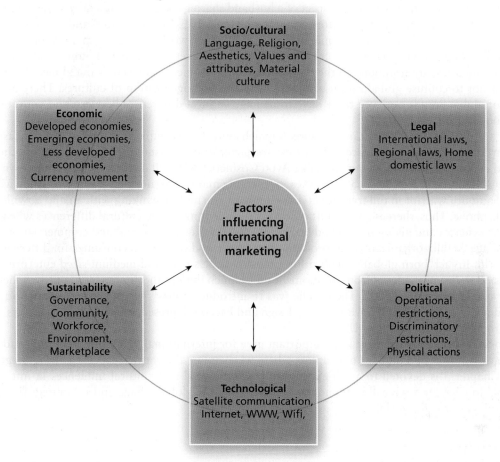

Cultural factors

Cultural differences and especially language differences have a significant impact on the way a product may be used in a market, its brand name and the advertising campaign.

Initially, Coca-Cola had enormous problems in China as Coca-Cola sounded like 'Kooke Koula' which translates into 'A thirsty mouthful of candle wax'. They managed to find a new pronunciation 'Kee Kou Keele' which means 'joyful tastes and happiness'.

Companies that have experienced similar problems in Germany include Irish Mist which introduced its drink brand and Estee Lauder who exported liquid make-up called Country Mist. The problem word was Mist which is a German slang word for 'manure' in Germany.

Pepsi Cola had to change its campaign 'Come Alive With Pepsi' in Germany as, literally translated, it means 'Come Alive Out of the Grave'. In Japan, McDonald's character Ronald McDonald failed because his white face was seen as a death mask. Products launched in France have not always been successful. When Apple launched the iMac in France they discovered the brand name mimicked the name of a well established brand of baby laxative – hardly the image they were trying to project. An actual baby product by Gerber is sold in many countries, but not in France, as Gerber means 'vomit' in French.

Operating effectively in different countries requires recognition that there may be considerable differences in the different regions. Consider northern Europe versus Latin Europe, the northwest of the USA versus the south, or Beijing versus Taipei. At the stage of early internationalization it is not unusual for firms to experience what appear to be cultural gaps with their counterparts in the countries they are expanding into, be it the West going East or the East going West. A campaign by Camay soap which showed a husband washing his wife's back in the bath was a huge success in France but failed in Japan, not because it caused offence, but because Japanese women viewed the prospect of a husband sharing such a time as a huge invasion of privacy.

On the other hand, some commentators argue there are visible signs that social and cultural differences are becoming less of a barrier. The dominance of a number of world brands such as Apple, Coca-Cola, McDonald's, Nike and Google etc., all competing in global markets that generally transcend national and political boundaries, are testimony to the convergence of consumer needs across the globe. However, it is important not to confuse globalization of brands with the homogenization of cultures. There are a large number of global brands but even these have to manage cultural differences between and within national country boundaries.

There are also a number of cultural paradoxes which exist. For example, in Asia, the Middle East, Africa and Latin America, there is evidence both for the westernization of tastes and the assertion of ethnic, religious and cultural differences. Companies like Avon Cosmetics who sell directly through their own distributors are well placed to exploit such paradoxes in emerging markets. In northern Kenya you may well come across a Samburu warrior in full traditional dress doing online mobile banking with an app downloaded to his mobile phone. Thus, there is a vast and sometimes turbulent mosaic of cultural differences when buying, sharing experiences and giving product advice in the global village. The social and commercial online borderless village enables organizations to promote their goods and services to consumers in different regions of the world. In fact 'born global' organizations, mostly niche small- and medium-sized enterprises, begin with a vision to *be* international from the moment they launch their brand. Stereo Skis launched their brand of water skis in Norway in 2007. Their niche was to introduce a new type of sport to the world, mixing snow and water skiing. Their innovative idea, design and Facebook presence soon led to customers in many other European countries and the US.

The social/cultural environment is an important area for international marketing managers and we will return to this subject in a number of chapters where we examine the various aspects of its strategic implications. Chapter 3 is devoted to a full examination of the social and cultural influences in international marketing. In Chapter 5 we will examine the forces driving the global village and its strategic implication to companies across the world.

Social factors

Growth and movement in populations around the world are important factors heralding social changes. Of the world's population, 80 per cent live in developing countries; by 2025 this is likely to reach 85 per cent. Asia has the greatest population with 4.3 billion people, which accounts for 60 per cent of the world's population. China and India together form 37 per cent of the world's population which means approximately two out of every five people live in China and India. However, while world population is growing dramatically, the growth patterns are not consistent around the world.

By the end of the twenty-first century Africa's population is predicted to almost treble with countries such as Zambia and Burundi increasing five-fold. African countries are likely to grow economically, in part because of the growth in the working population (see Illustration 1.1). China's population will rise much more slowly, resulting in a population of 1.38 billion by 2050. Over the same period India's population is predicted to be 1.68 billion which means that India will have more inhabitants than China. The year India surpasses China's population is predicted to be 2028. Overall, there will be a decline in the number of countries with large families. Generally, it is expected that some countries in Europe will see a decline in population, although there will be some increases in population, such as in Germany where increase is due to migration.

There are also visible moves in the population within many countries, leading to the formation of huge urban areas where consumers have a growing similarity of needs across the globe. Nowadays, 50 per cent of the world's population lives in urban areas, with many now living in megacities (United Nations 2014). In 1950 there were only two megacities: Tokyo with 12.3 million people, and New York with 11.3 million people living within the city. Now there are 22 megacities, all with at least 10 million people living within them. Tokyo is predicted to have the highest population of residents by 2030 with a staggering 37.2 million people. New York, once one of the top mega cities is being overtaken by cities in India and China (United Nations 2014). Table 1.1 shows the ten megacities of the world and the projections for the future. This has

ILLUSTRATION 1.1

International marketing strategy – Choppies enters Africa

The World Bank suggests that 11 out of the 20 fastest growing global growth countries are in Africa. Botswana already has a successful international retailer called Choppies which has 67 stores in its home market, 23 in South Africa and 13 stores in Zimbabwe. Choppies has been growing its grocery supermarket since it opened its first store in 1986. Strategic plans are in place to expand further in South Africa and Zimbabwe in the short term and further develop its business in Tanzania and Zambia during the next few years.

The openair bustling street markets of Zambia are very important for people in this region. Culturally, the market is a place to socialize and talk to friends and vendors. More covered stores are being introduced and more businesses are choosing Zambia.

Ramchandran Ottapathu of Choppies is one of those businesses. Ottapathu said: *'If you take the formal retail penetration in Zambia, it's still under 20 per cent. Over 80 per cent is still informal market. So that leaves a lot of opportunity for us to expand.'*

Choppies convenience and grocery stores will be a different experience from the open, informal street shopping familiar to most citizens of Zambia. Nevertheless, Choppies are confident Zambia is a strategic opportunity.

Question

1 What do you see as the major opportunities and threats for Choppies wishing to develop in the African market?

Source: IGD Retail Analysis (2015) Choppies sets out 2015 expansion plans www.retailanalysis.igd.com/Hub .aspx?id=23&tid=3&nid=13468 (accessed 5 January 2015).

Table 1.1   The world's ten megacities

Urban Agglomeration	Country or area	Population (thousands)		
		1990	2014	2030
Tokyo	Japan	32 530	37 833	37 190
Delhi	India	9 726	24 953	36 060
Shanghai	China	7 823	22 991	30 751
Ciudad de México (Mexico City)	Mexico	15 642	20 843	23 865
São Paulo	Brazil	14 776	20 831	23 444
Mumbai (Bombay)	India	12 436	20 741	27 797
Kinki M.M.A. (Osaka)	Japan	18 389	20 123	19 976
Beijing	China	6 788	19 520	27 706
New York-Newark	United States of America	16 086	18 591	19 885
Al-Qahirah (Cairo)	Egypt	9 892	18 419	24 502

Source: United Nations (2014) *World Urbanization Prospects*. New York: United Nations.

powerful implications for international marketing. These cities will be markets in themselves. Urban dwellers require similar products (packaged conveniently and easy to carry). Similarly, they demand services, reliable bandwidth and transportation of all kinds, together with modern visual communications. It also means for any incoming company that customers are accessible. They are identifiable and firms can communicate with them efficiently via supermarkets, advertising and other marketing communication tools.

Legal factors

Legal systems vary both in content and interpretation. A company is not just bound by the laws of its home country but also by those of its host country and by the growing body of international law. Firms operating in the **European Union** are facing ever-increasing directives which affect their markets across Europe. This can affect many aspects of a marketing strategy – for instance advertising – in the form of media restrictions and the acceptability of particular creative appeals (see Illustration 1.2). Product acceptability in a country can be affected by minor regulations on such things as packaging and by more major changes in legislation. In the USA, for example, the MG sports car was withdrawn when the increasing difficulty of complying with safety legislation changes made exporting to that market unprofitable. Kraft Foods sell

ILLUSTRATION 1.2

Online music piracy

Around 95 per cent of music downloads worldwide are illegal. The top five countries that have the most illegal music downloads are US, UK, Italy, Canada and Brazil. There is no international law that deals

specifically with this issue and whilst consumers may not fully understand copyright law they know downloading music for free is immoral. Many consumers, especially teenagers and college/ university students, click and download from a growing number of sites assuming that it is a very low risk act and there is difficulty in finding and punishing consumers. Ed Sheeran sold 1.2 million albums worldwide. There were also 8 million illegal downloads of his songs. This means that Ed Sheeran, his musicians, the people that create his album covers and the marketing team do not receive any royalties from those 8 million downloads. Canada is trying to stop consumers from downloading music illegally. In 2015 consumers will receive a message directly from their Internet Service Provider asking them to stop downloading music illegally. Copyright lawyers in Canada are also requesting consumers to pay $3000 to prevent further very expensive legal action. Other countries in the world have a similar process. However, introducing domestic laws and action will not stop the international law-breaking activity of illegal music downloads.

Question

1 What would be the advantages and disadvantages of implementing international law to prevent music piracy and enable businesses and artists to receive the royalties they deserve?

Source: www.bbc.co.uk/news/technology-19599527 (accessed 30 January 2015).

a product called Lifesavers, which is very similar to the Nestlé Polo brand, in many countries. Using EU law, Nestlé attempted to stop the sale of Lifesavers in the EU purely to protect their market share.

It is important, therefore, for the firm to know the legal environment in each of its markets. These laws constitute the 'rules of the game' for business activity. The legal environment in international marketing is more complicated than in domestic markets since it has three dimensions: (1) local domestic law; (2) international law; (3) domestic laws in the firm's home base.

- ■ *Local domestic laws*. These are all different! The only way to find a route through the legal maze in overseas markets is to use experts on the separate legal systems and laws pertaining in each market targeted.

- ■ *International law*. There are a number of international laws that can affect the organization's activity. Some are international laws covering piracy and hijacking, others are more international conventions and agreements and cover items such as the International Monetary Fund (IMF) and World Trade Organization (WTO) treaties, patents and trademarks legislation and harmonization of legal systems within regional economic groupings, e.g. the European Union.

- ■ *Domestic laws in the home country*. The organization's domestic (home market) legal system is important for two reasons. First, there are often export controls which limit the free export of certain goods (e.g. military items) and services to particular marketplaces; and second, there is the duty of the organization to act and abide by its national laws in all its activities, whether domestic or international.

It will be readily understandable how domestic, international and local legal systems can have a major impact upon the organization's ability to market into particular overseas countries. Laws will affect the marketing mix in terms of products, price, distribution and promotional activities quite dramatically. For many firms, the legal challenges they face in international markets are almost a double-edged sword. Often firms operating internationally face ethical challenges in deciding how to deal with differing cultural perceptions of legal practices.

In many mature markets they face quite specific and, sometimes, burdensome regulations. In many European countries environmental regulations and laws mean a firm is responsible for the retrieval and disposal of the packaging waste it creates and must produce packaging which is recyclable, whereas in many emerging markets there may be limited patent and trademark protection, still evolving judicial systems, non-tariff barriers and instability through an ever-evolving reform programme. In 2015 there was instability when Russia boycotted trade with the US and some European countries because of the political war over Ukraine.

China earned notoriety in the past for allowing copyright infringements and blatant piracy. However, this is now changing. Some governments are reluctant to develop and enforce laws protecting intellectual property, partly because they believe such actions favour large, rich multinationals. Anheuser Busch (USA) and Budvar (Czech Republic) have been in constant litigation over the right to use the name Budweiser in the European Union and both companies have recently been legally deemed the right to use it.

Piracy in markets with limited trademark and patent protection is another challenge. One of the biggest challenges faced internationally is the use of unlicensed, therefore pirated, software. Forty-three per cent of PC software that is installed is done so without a licence and the commercial loss amounts to US$62.7 billion (BSA 2014). Over 80 per cent of PC software installed in Venezuela, Indonesia and Vietnam is unlicensed, and due to the very high number of electronic PCs and Tablets in the US and China, the unlicensed value is over US$18 000 million.

India is regarded by many firms as an attractive emerging market beset with many legal difficulties, bureaucratic delay and lots of red tape. For example, pairs of shoes cannot be imported which causes huge problems for shoe manufacturers who need to import shoes as production samples. By separating the pairs and importing each shoe to a different port, importers of shoes are using a loophole in the law and trying to overcome this problem. Companies such as Mercedes Benz, Coca-Cola and Kellogg have found the vast potential of India's market somewhat hard to break into. Its demanding consumers can be difficult to read and local rivals can be surprisingly tough. Political squabbles, bureaucratic delays and infrastructure headaches are also major obstacles.

Economic factors

It is important that the international marketer has an understanding of economic developments and how they impinge on the marketing strategy. This understanding is important at a world level in terms of the world trading infrastructure such as world institutions and trade agreements developed to foster international trade; at a regional level in terms of regional trade integration; and at a country/market level. Firms need to be aware of the economic policies of countries and the direction in which a particular market is developing economically in order to make an assessment as to whether they can profitably satisfy market demand and compete with firms already in the market.

Among the 196 countries in the world, there are varying economic conditions, levels of economic development and Gross national income per capita (GNIpc). Gross national income in the world is US$70 trillion (purchasing power parity, or ppp). However, it is not shared equitably across the world and the range across the globe is enormous. Qatar, with the highest figure has a GNIpc (ppp) of US$128 530 and Macao SAR, China is second with US$112 230. The lowest figures are for the Democratic Republic of Congo at US$740 and the Central African Republic at US$600. Perhaps more startling is the claim of Credit Suisse (2014) that states the richest 1 per cent of people in the world actually own over 48 per cent of global wealth. Such disparities of incomes set particular challenges for companies operating in international markets in terms of seeking possible market opportunities, assessing the viability of potential markets as well as identifying sources of finance in markets where opportunities are identified but where there is not capacity to pay for goods.

Another key challenge facing companies is the question as to how they can develop an integrated strategy across a number of international markets when there are divergent levels of economic development. Such disparities often make it difficult to have a cohesive strategy, especially in pricing.

The Economist 'Big Mac' Index 2015 (Figure 1.3) is a useful tool which illustrates the difficulties global companies have in trying to achieve a consistent pricing strategy across the world. It provides a rough measure of the purchasing power of a currency. UBS, a bank in the USA, uses the price of the Big Mac burger to measure the purchasing power of local wages worldwide. It divides the price of a Big Mac by the average net hourly wage in cities around the world. Fast-food junkies are best off in Chicago, Toronto and Tokyo, where it takes a mere 12 minutes at work to afford a Big Mac. By contrast, employees must toil for over two hours to earn enough for a burger in Mexico City, Jakarta and Nairobi. This causes problems for McDonald's in trying to pursue a standard product image across markets. Priced in US dollars, a Big Mac in Switzerland would cost US$7.40, in Colombia US$3.34 whereas in Ukraine it would be US$1.20.

FIGURE 1.3   An alternative Big Mac index – how many minutes to earn the price of a Big Mac?

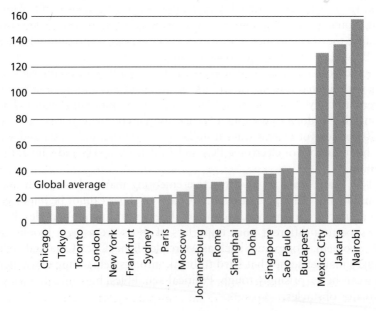

In order to examine these challenges further we divide the economies into developed economies and least developed economies.

The developed economies

The developed economies of the top 10 export traders are China, US, Germany, Japan, Netherlands, France, Republic of Korea, United Kingdom, Hong Kong and the Russian Federation and they account for 52 per cent of the export trade. They are also the main importers with only Italy replacing the Russian Federation in the top 10 importers. For many firms this constitutes much of what is termed the global market. Even though many companies call themselves global, most of their revenues and profits will be earned from these markets. The developing countries have grown in their international focus with more than half of their total exports sent to other developing countries, the most significant being 35 per cent of the exports being sent to developing Asia. This leads some commentators to argue that most competition, even in today's global marketplace, is more active at a regional level than a global level. It is from these developed economies that the global consumer with similar lifestyles, needs and desires, emanates. However, emerging markets are now becoming increasingly economically powerful and moving up the ranks, especially such countries as Brazil and India and China.

The emerging economies

Brazil, Russia, India and China (the BRIC economies), are no longer considered to be the only emerging economies. Mexico, Indonesia, Nigeria and Turkey, known as the MINT economies, are countries that marketing managers of global brands have started doing business with. In these countries there is a huge and growing demand for everything from automobiles to mobile phones and all are viewed as key growth markets where there is an evolving pattern of government-directed economic reforms, lowering of restrictions on foreign investment and increasing privatization of state-owned monopolies. All these rapidly developing economies herald significant opportunities for the international marketing firm.

Such markets often have what is termed a 'dual economy'. Usually there tends to be a wealthy urban professional class alongside a poorer rural population. Income distribution tends to be much more skewed between the 'haves' and the 'have nots' than in developed countries. The number of Chinese and Indonesian people that earn less than US$2 per day has reduced dramatically with a general increase in the middle earners.

Least developed countries

This group includes underdeveloped countries and less developed countries. The main features are a low GDP per capita, a limited amount of manufacturing activity and a very poor and fragmented infrastructure. Typical infrastructure weaknesses are in transport, communications, education and healthcare. In addition, the public sector is often slow-moving and bureaucratic.

It is common to find that least developed countries (LDCs) are heavily reliant on exporting raw materials and these products are the main export earners. In the Democratic Republic of Congo for instance, their exports comprise of copper (56 per cent), cobalt (21 per cent) and petroleum (14 per cent). In addition, three-quarters of LDCs depend on their main trading partner for more than one-quarter of their export revenue. The risks posed to the LDC by changing patterns of supply and demand are great. Falling commodity prices can result in large decreases in earnings for the whole country. The resultant economic and political adjustments may affect exporters to that country through possible changes in tariff and non-tariff barriers, through changes in the level of company taxation and through restrictions on the convertibility of currency and the repatriation of profits. In addition, substantial decreases in market sizes within the country are probable.

A wide range of economic circumstances influences the development of the less developed countries in the world. Some countries are small with few natural resources and for these countries it is difficult to start the process of substantial economic growth. Poor health and education standards need money on a large scale, yet the pay-off in terms of a healthier, better-educated population takes time to achieve. At the same time, there are demands for public expenditure on transport systems, communication systems and water control systems. Without real prospects for rapid economic development, private sources of capital are reluctant to invest in such countries. This is particularly the case for long-term infrastructure projects and, as a result, important capital spending projects rely heavily on world aid programmes. Marketing to such countries can be problematic, as in the case of KickStart in Management Challenge 1.1.

MANAGEMENT CHALLENGE 1.1

How do you sell to subsistence farmers in Africa?

KickStart International is a US non-profit organization that sells irrigation systems to subsistence farmers in Africa. The customers are hard to reach. They live hours from major cities and many are illiterate. Even though they are a non-profit organization, KickStart needs to build brand loyalty which is difficult in a market where there is a lack of trust in a foreign company. The other dilemma is, given the levels of illiteracy, how do they educate the farmers to use the equipment and how do KickStart get their message across given the small budget they have for such activities?

Question

1 How should KickStart approach this market?

Currency risks

While we have examined economic factors within markets, we also need to bear in mind that in international marketing, transactions invariably take place between countries, so exchange rates and currency movements are an important aspect of the international economic environment. On top of all the normal vagaries of markets, customer demands, competitive actions and economic infrastructures, foreign exchange parities are likely to change on a regular if unpredictable basis. World currency movements, stimulated by worldwide trading and foreign exchange dealing, are an additional complication in the international environment. Companies that guess wrongly as to which way a currency will move can see their international business deals rendered unprofitable overnight. Businesses that need to swap currencies to pay for imported goods, or because they have received foreign currency for products they have exported, can find themselves squeezed to the point where they watch their profits disappear.

In Europe, the formation of the European Monetary Union (EMU) and the establishment of the Single European Payments Area (SEPA) led to greater stability for firms operating in the market. The formation of the European Monetary Union and the introduction of the single currency across Europe had important implications for company strategies which we will discuss in Chapter 2, when we examine regional trading agreements, and in Chapter 11, when we look at pricing issues in international marketing.

Political factors

The political environment of international marketing includes any national or international political factor that can affect the organization's operations or its decision making. Politics has come to be recognized as the major factor in many international business decisions, especially in terms of whether to invest and how to develop markets.

Politics is intrinsically linked to a government's attitude to business and the freedom within which it allows firms to operate. Unstable political regimes expose foreign businesses to a variety of risks that they would generally not face in the home market. This often means that the political arena is the most volatile area of international marketing. The tendencies of governments to change regulations can have a profound effect on international strategy, providing both opportunities and threats. The economic impact of violence and conflict amounts to 11.3 per cent of global GDP as well as declining trade, communications and business and consumer trust. The World Peace report shows Syria, Afghanistan, South Sudan, Iraq and Somalia as places of instability and unrest. The instability in the Middle East and the continued threat of global terrorism have served to heighten firms' awareness of the importance of monitoring political risk factors in the international markets in which they operate. Lesser developed countries and emerging markets pose particularly high political risks, even when they are following reforms to solve the political problems they have. The stringency of such reforms can itself lead to civil disorder and rising opposition to governments. Political risk is defined as a risk due to a sudden or gradual change in a local political environment that is disadvantageous or counter-productive to foreign firms and markets.

The types of action that governments may take which constitute potential political risks to firms fall into three main areas:

- *Operational restrictions.* These could be exchange controls, employment policies, insistence on locally shared ownership and particular product requirements.

- *Discriminatory restrictions.* These tend to be imposed on purely foreign firms and, sometimes, only firms from a particular country. Economic sanctions were put in place during the crisis in Ukraine. During that time Russia responded by banning food imports from several EU countries: US, Norway, Canada and Australia. They have also imposed bans on imports from Libya and Iran in the past. Such barriers tend to be special taxes and tariffs, compulsory subcontracting or loss of financial freedom.

- *Physical actions.* These actions are direct government interventions such as confiscation without any payment of indemnity, a forced takeover by the government, expropriation, nationalization or even damage to property or personnel through riots and war. The Argentine government seized Spanish oil company Repsol's assets in the country in 2012, claiming it had failed to invest to meet internal demand. Two years later Repsol agreed compensation of US $5 billion, half of its initial claim, and withdrew from the country (BBC 2014).

Investment restrictions are a common way governments interfere politically in international markets by restricting levels of investment, location of facilities, choice of local partners and ownership percentage. Recent decisions by certain Latin American countries to compel foreign investors to renegotiate their investment contracts on sanction of expulsion, introduced considerable uncertainty for companies operating in the region. When Microsoft opened its Beijing office, it planned to use its Taiwan operations to supply a Mandarin language version of Windows. The government not only wanted such an operating system to be designed in China but also insisted on defining the coding standards for Chinese characters' fonts, something Microsoft had done independently everywhere else in the world. In a flurry of meetings with officials, Bill Gates argued that the marketplace, not the government, should set standards. But the Chinese electronics industry threatened to ban Windows and President Jiang Zemin personally admonished Gates to spend more time in China and 'learn something from 5000 years of Chinese history'. Gates sacked the original management team and promised to cooperate with Beijing (Bloomberg Business 1996).

The **World Trade Organization** has led negotiations on a series of worldwide agreements to expand quotas, reduce tariffs and introduce a number of innovative measures to encourage trade among countries. Together with the formation of regional trading agreements in the European Union, North and South America and Asia, these reforms constitute a move to a more politically stable international trading environment. An understanding of these issues is critical to the international marketing manager, which is why in Chapter 2 we examine in some detail the patterns of world trade, the regional trading agreements and the development of world trading institutions intended to foster international trade. In Chapter 4 we will examine in some detail the procedures, tools and techniques which can help the analysis and evaluation of opportunities across such markets.

The political and economic environments are greatly intertwined and, sometimes, difficult to categorize. It is important, however, that a firm operating in international markets assesses the countries in which it operates to gauge the economic and political risk and to ensure it understands the peculiarities and characteristics of the market it wishes to develop (see Illustration 1.3).

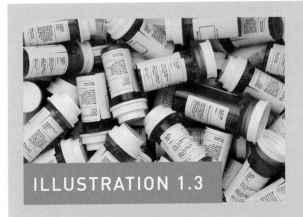

ILLUSTRATION 1.3

Sproxil born global to help us live longer

Counterfeiting is a global problem. Consumers are extremely disappointed when they buy a high-end luxury item via the Internet only to find they have bought a fake. Losing money on a handbag or watch is one thing but buying fake medicine can cost lives. Counterfeit medicine is dangerous for patients as up to 700 000 people die each year from buying fake anti-malaria medicine and tuberculosis drugs.

The multi-million dollar problem is worldwide; worse in emerging countries, and is a drain on businesses and international regulatory bodies. Sproxil is a brand protection service organization in emerging markets with headquarters in the US. Born global is at the very heart of Sproxil, they saw an important niche in the market and developed technology to solve an international problem. Sproxil opened their first local office in Nigeria 12 months after they launched their business and now have offices in Ghana, Pakistan and India. They help businesses, be they global or local, to protect their brands and to help consumers ensure they are buying legitimate medicines and drugs. Consumers at point of purchase text (free of charge) the products on-pack ID number and an immediate reply shows if the product is legitimate or fake. Sproxil has branched out into verifying branded cosmetics, fast moving consumer goods (FMCGs) and electrical goods.

Question

1 Many organizations are born global. What factors enable them to do this?

Source: www.sproxil.com

Technological factors

Technology is a major driving force both in international marketing and in the move towards a more global marketplace. The impact of technological advances can be seen in all aspects of the marketing process. The ability to gather data on markets, management control capabilities and the practicalities of carrying out the business function internationally have been revolutionized in recent years with the advances in electronic communications.

Satellite communications, the Internet and the World Wide Web, client–server technologies, ISDN and cable as well as email, faxes and advanced mobile phone applications have all led to dramatic shrinkages in worldwide communications.

Shrinking communications means, increasingly, that in the international marketplace, information is power. At the touch of a button we can access information on the key factors that determine our business. Multiple channels supply news 7 days a week, 24 hours a day. Manufacturers wanting to know the price of coffee beans or the relevant position of competitors in terms of their share price or new product activity have it at the touch of a button.

As mobile technology renders landline cables and telephone lines redundant, developing countries have abandoned plans to invest in land-based communication. They have bypassed terrestrial communication systems, enabling them to catch up with and, in some cases overtake, developed countries in the market-place. In emerging economies consumers are jumping from no telephone to the latest in global communications technology. Wireless application protocol (WAP) technology allows online services to be available to mobile phone users on the move, wherever they happen to be in the world. The use of Global System for Mobile Communications (GSM) technology enables mobile phone operators to determine the location of a customer globally to send them relevant and timely advertising messages.

British Airways operates its worldwide online operations from Mumbai: everything from ticketing to making an 'exceptional request' facility, such as wheelchair assistance needed for a passenger can be managed from the centre in India. The ease of hiring computer-literate graduates by the hundred, who are intelligent, capable, keen and inexpensive to hire, as is local property to rent, has enabled India to build a global advantage in this rapidly developing industry.

The Internet and the World Wide Web (www)

The Internet and the access gained to the World Wide Web has revolutionized international marketing practices. Airlines such as easyJet and Ryanair have helped completely change the way we book our airline reservations. Alibaba Group with headquarters in China set up an online only business-to-business (B2B) facility to enable small Chinese exporters and manufacturers sell their goods internationally. Firms ranging from a few employees to large multinationals have realized the potential of marketing globally online and so have developed the facility to buy and sell their products and services online to the world.

An estimated 3 billion people – some 42 per cent of the global population – are Internet users. However, for many this will be through public-based Internet services in cafes etc. Online retailing is soaring especially through global Business-to-Business (B2B) sales which are predicted to rise to $6.7 trillion over the next five years (Forest and Sullivan 2014). Major growth is due to the fact that many multinational and international businesses are completing more and more transactions with their supply chain online. The amount of business completed online far outstrips Business-to-Consumer (B2C); however, more consumers than ever before are using mobile smartphones, tablets and PCs to browse and shop for goods and services online.

The Internet has meant huge opportunities for small- and medium-sized enterprises (SMEs) and rapid internationalization for many. It has enabled them to substantially reduce the costs of reaching international customers, reduce global advertising costs and made it much easier for small niche products to find a critical mass of customers. Because of the low entry costs of operating as an online business it has permitted firms with low capital resources to become global marketers, in some cases overnight. There are, therefore, quite significant implications for SMEs which will be examined further in Chapter 5, where we discuss in some detail the issues in international marketing pertinent to SMEs.

For all companies, the implications of being able to market goods and services online have been far reaching. The Internet has led to an explosion of information to consumers, giving them the potential to source products from the cheapest supplier in the world. This has led to the increasing standardization of prices across borders or, at least, to the narrowing of price differentials as consumers become more aware of prices in different countries and buy a whole range of products via social media such as Facebook and Twitter. In B2C marketing this has been most dramatically seen in the purchase of such things as financial services, flights, holidays, music downloads and books. Social media communication activities connect end-users and producers directly, reducing the importance of traditional intermediaries in international marketing (i.e. agents and distributors) as more companies have built the online capability to deal direct with their customers, particularly in B2B marketing. To survive, such intermediaries have begun offering a whole range of new services, the value added element of their offering no longer being principally in the physical distribution of goods but rather in the collection, collation, interpretation and dissemination of vast amounts of information. The critical resource possessed by this new breed of 'cybermediary' is information rather than inventory. The Internet has also become a powerful tool for supporting networks both internal and external to the firm. Many global firms have developed supplier intranets through which they source products and services from preferred suppliers who have met the criteria to gain access to their supplier intranets. It has become the efficient new medium for conducting worldwide market research and gaining feedback from customers.

Thus the Internet produces a fundamentally different environment for international marketing and requires a radically different strategic approach affecting all aspects of the marketing process. Not all forays into Internet marketing have been successful. Many early dotcom high growth companies became 'dot. bombs' when they failed to sustain their early promise. Levi Strauss stopped its Internet selling operation after finding the cost of servicing returned goods was greater than the revenue generated from new sales.

The dual technological/cultural paradox

On the one hand commentators view technological advancement and shrinking communications as the most important driving force in the building of the global village where there are global consumers who have similar needs. On the other hand, to access this global village a person invariably needs a command of the English language and access to the latest technology. In many markets we stumble against the paradox that while in some countries there is a market of well-educated and computer-literate people, in other countries the global electronic highway has completely bypassed them.

Despite all that has been said in previous sections, many developing and emerging markets are characterized by poor, inadequate or deteriorating infrastructures. Essential services required for commercial activity, ranging from electric power to water supplies, from highways to air transportation and from phone lines to banking services, are often in short supply or unreliable. For those reasons less than 42 per cent of the population are Internet users in many countries including Ukraine, Cambodia, Burundi, Zimbabwe, Pakistan, Syria, Peru, Cuba and the Philippines.

The huge population shifts discussed earlier have also aggravated the technical infrastructure problems in many of the major cities in emerging markets. This often results in widespread production and distribution bottlenecks, which in turn raises costs. 'Brown outs', for instance, are not uncommon in the Philippines, even in the capital city Manila, where companies and offices regularly lose electric power and either shut down in those periods or revert to generators. Fragmented and circuitous channels of distribution are a result of lack of adequate infrastructure. This makes market entry more complicated and the efficient distribution of a product very difficult. Pepsi Cola in Eastern Europe has a large number of decentralized satellite bottling plants in an attempt to overcome the lack of a distribution infrastructure.

The reader will find that we examine the impact of the Internet on the relevant marketing practices and processes as we move through the chapters of the book. Chapter 12 of this edition is devoted to examining the implications for the international marketing strategies of companies of such trends in the technology environment.

Sustainability factors

In considering the environmental challenges to international marketing we also need to take heed of numerous reports that warn of the danger to future prosperity if current overconsumption of natural resources is left unchecked. More than three-quarters of the world's people live in countries where national consumption has outstripped biological capacity. Human demands, sometime created by marketers, measure nearly a third more than the Earth can sustain over time. There is increasing proof of sea levels rising, temperatures warming and uncertain effects on forest and agricultural systems. There is growing evidence of increased variability and volatility in weather patterns which are expected to have a significant and disproportionate impact in the developing world, where the world's poor remain most susceptible to the potential damages and uncertainties inherent in a changing climate.

It is feared by some that as global economic wealth increases, global natural wealth and diversity continue to decline. There is concern that indigenous and national culture and languages can be eroded by the strength of globalized brands. It is also argued by some analysts that globalized markets leave many economically behind. Some countries have been unable to take advantage of globalization of markets and their standards of living are seen to be dropping further behind the richest countries. The gap in income within countries also gives an indication of the state of the nation; South America and the Caribbean region have narrowed the inequality earnings gap by increased investment in education. In China due to so many people moving from rural to urban areas, the inequality earnings gap has widened creating a poorer rural population and a wealthier urban population. Generally, inequality in both developed and developing countries has widened because the wealthier minorities have just got richer.

As responsible global marketers, when considering environmental issues we need to ensure in our strategic thinking that we respond to all the issues we have raised in the previous sections with ethical and socially responsible business practices that are sustainable in terms of their environmental, societal and economic impact (see Figure 1.4). This involves ensuring in any global marketing action plan we maximize the positive impacts of global marketing while minimizing the negative; whether social or environmental – local, regional or global.

Sustainability interfaces with global marketing through the social and ecological consequences of marketing activities. Sustainability involves ensuring the social, cultural, economic, political and environmental aspects of a global marketing strategy are integrated.

FIGURE 1.4   Holistic model of sustainability in global marketing

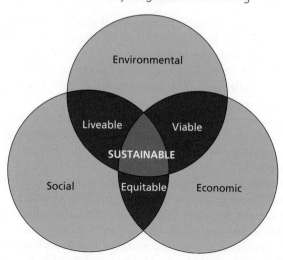

The rise in ethical consumerism and green brands that identify themselves as ethical, has led to a rise in ethic-based decisions across global markets, enabled by increased understanding and information about business practices across the globe. Large corporations now see it as a priority that they are regarded as socially responsible global citizens who are working ethically and improving the ethical standards of their industry.

Sustainability is about considering the environmental impact of everything we do. This means encouraging a holistic way of thinking in our responses to the global marketing challenges we identify and assessing the impact of our global marketing strategies – socially, economically and environmentally – in our approach to ensuring sustainability. This is central to the values of responsible international marketing strategies and a theme that we will return to at various points as we go through the different stages of strategy development in the chapters of this book.

The greatest legacy for the future that we can create is in the perspectives we take and the skills we use as marketing practitioners. While our global marketing strategies need to be innovative and build global competitiveness, we need also to make sure any strategies we develop are grounded in socially and environmentally sustainable business practices. Global marketing strategies should promote sustainable growth, balance prosperity across the world economies and protect our shared global environment. We hope readers of this book developing international marketing strategies will also make sure we all protect our world environmental capital and manage our global market growth creatively, responsibly and ethically.

Differences between international and domestic marketing

As we have seen in the previous sections, there are many factors within the international environment which substantially increase the challenge of international marketing. These can be summarized as follows:

1 *Culture*: often diverse and multicultural markets
2 *Markets*: widespread and sometimes fragmented
3 *Data*: difficult to obtain and often expensive
4 *Politics*: regimes vary in stability – political risk becomes an important variable
5 *Governments*: can be a strong influence in regulating importers and foreign business ventures
6 *Economies*: varying levels of development and varying and sometimes unstable currencies
7 *Finance*: many differing finance systems and regulatory bodies
8 *Stakeholders*: commercial, home country and host country
9 *Business*: diverse rules, culturally influenced
10 *Control*: difficult to control and coordinate across markets.

The international competitive landscape

A major difference for managers operating on international markets is the impact all these currents and cross-currents have on the competitive landscape. In fact Nyaga (2014, p. 685) stated 'a company's long-term success is driven largely by its ability to maintain sustainable competitive advantage and keep it'. The task of achieving this in a competitive environment where firms are subject to local, regional and global competition can be immensely challenging. This is especially so if indigenous local competitors are supported by the government of the country.

Across international markets, advanced countries are seeing significant competition from both emerging markets and less developed countries which are exploiting modern technology and their own low labour costs to compete in markets no longer so protected by tariff walls. The birth of global brand names is no longer the domain of the West.

The complexity of competition is also heightened by the strategic use of international sourcing of components by multinationals and global firms to achieve competitive advantage.

Given the nature of the challenges and opportunities identified above and the speed of change within the international environment, this means that substantially different pressures are being placed upon management than if they were purely operating in domestic markets. It follows from this that the manager of international marketing needs a detailed knowledge and understanding of how traditions and social behaviour impact on a firm's international marketing operations (see Illustration 1.4).

Perlmutter (1995) identified nine cross-cultural management incompetences which lead to failure across a spread of country markets. He defined these core incompetences as: 'the bundle of activities and managerial skills that are mismatched in a great variety of countries where firms do business'.

ILLUSTRATION 1.4

Porsche's social media challenges

After social and political unrest, Bahrain is settled and has a strong identity as a country with many commercial opportunities. The economy is mainly built on petroleum exports, banking and finance. The country has a well-developed modern infrastructure and tourism is booming, particularly when the Formula One is held at Bahrain's Grand Prix track. Global brands need to develop their cross-cultural knowledge and gather information about the traditions and social behaviour of Bahrainis to ensure they succeed in penetrating a new market. There are 1.3 million people in Bahrain and many already have high-end luxury cars as average earnings in Bahrain are high. More than 98 per cent of Bahrainis have Internet access and over 33 per cent use Facebook; smartphone penetration and app usage is very high. Socializing is important and status is often shown through dress and goods.

When the Porsche Boxster was launched in Bahrain the social media activities were left in the hands of Middle Eastern marketers who know the consumer better than the German brand owner. One of the social media launch campaigns enabled new Boxster owners to have their names painted on their car. The campaign gained over 8.7 million Facebook advert impressions which meant on average each Bahraini clicked the advertisement four times! To continue with the opportunity to show their status and wealth, the Porsche team includes many Facebook messages and there are three to four Porsche meetings per month where owners socialize.

Question

1 Why is it important for marketers to collect cultural information and data before entering a new market?

Source: Broers, A. and Warman, M. (2014) *Porsche Centre Bahrain's 'Be A Part of Our History' Porsche Boxster*, Warc Prize for Social Strategy Issue: Entrant, 2014.

The first three are interrelated and relate to the failure to be market driven.

1 Inability to find the right market niches.

2 Unwillingness to adapt and update products to local needs.

3 Not having unique products that are viewed as sufficiently higher added value by customers in local markets.

4 A vacillating commitment. It takes time to learn how to function in countries such as Japan.

5 Assigning the wrong people. Picking the wrong people or the wrong top team in an affiliate.

6 Picking the wrong partners. There is a list of difficulties in building alliances; a main limitation is picking partners who do not have the right bundle of capabilities to help reach the local market.

7 Inability to manage local stakeholders. This includes incompetence in developing a satisfactory partnership relationship with unions and governments.

8 Developing mutual distrust and lack of respect between HQ and the affiliates at different levels of management.

9 Inability to leverage ideas developed in one country to other countries worldwide.

If mistakes are not to be made in your marketing strategies it is essential to ensure that the company has a robust and rigorous approach to its international marketing planning processes. Approaches to achieving this will be discussed in the following sections.

The international market planning process

In international marketing the very complexity of handling the diverse range of factors that must be considered make planning and control a difficult activity to carry out satisfactorily. For large global companies, the problem becomes one of how to structure the organization so that its increasingly complex and diverse activities around the world can be planned and managed effectively, its goals can be achieved and its stakeholders' expectations satisfied.

In this section we look at the international marketing planning and control process and consider how managers can respond to the challenges posed in the previous sections by ensuring they have robust strategy development and market planning processes.

The planning process

The planning process is the method used by the management of the firm to define in detail how it will achieve its current and future strategic aims and objectives. In doing this, it must evaluate the current and future market opportunities, assess its own current and potential capabilities and attempt to forecast how those changes over which it has no control might help or hinder its efforts to reach its objectives.

The international planning process must allow the company to answer the following three marketing questions.

1 Where is the company now?

2 Where does it want to go?

3 How might it get there?

These questions are fundamental for the majority of businesses whether they are large or small, simple or complex, and they emphasize the firm's need to prepare for the future to ensure its own survival and growth within the increasingly competitive international environment. There is an implication in these questions that the future is likely to be significantly different from the past, so planning is inevitably about forecasting and implementing change which determines the very nature and future direction of the organization.

The starting point of the planning process for any company is to set long-term goals and objectives which reflect its overall aspirations. These goals cannot be set in isolation, however, as the company's history and current levels of success in its different country markets are usually major determinants of its future. Other factors, too, over which the company has little control in international markets, such as the economic and political situation of the countries in which it is operating, the response of the competition and the diverse background, behaviour and expectations of its customers, all have a major impact upon the company's operations and will have a significant effect on determining whether or not it will meet its goals.

Too many firms, particularly smaller ones, fail to prepare contingency plans to cope with the unexpected and, in some cases, even the predictable events in international markets: they are often surprised and unprepared for success too. When unexpected events occur, many companies too easily ignore the plan and develop new strategies as they go along. While it may be possible to survive in a relatively uncomplicated domestic environment by reacting rapidly to new situations as they arise, it is impossible to grow significantly in international markets, as an overly reactive management style is usually wasteful of opportunities and resources.

In international markets, planning and control is essential for both day-to-day operations and the development of long-term strategies in order to manage the differences of attitudes, standards and values in the extended parts of the organization and avoid the problems of poor coordination and integration of the diverse activities. The plans which are developed must be sufficiently flexible to cope with unfamiliar cultures, rapidly changing political, economic and competitive environments, and the effects of unexpected events which affect global companies in one way or another throughout the world on an almost daily basis.

As a company moves into international markets, having previously been marketing solely to domestic markets, the processes of planning and control remain largely the same, but the complexity of the process increases dramatically. In a domestic situation misunderstandings between different departmental managers can be relatively quickly sorted out with a face-to-face discussion, but in the international situation this is much harder and often impractical. More impersonal communications, along with longer lead times, different cultures and the use of different languages, result in seemingly inconsistent and often negative attitudes in international managers.

Major evolutionary stages of planning

As most companies move gradually into international markets they go through the major evolutionary stages of planning: the unplanned stage, the budgeting stage, the annual business planning and the strategic planning stage.

The unplanned stage: In its early stages of international marketing, the company is likely to be preoccupied with finding new export customers and money to finance its activities. Frequently business is very unpredictable and is consequently unplanned, so that a short-term 'crisis management' culture emerges.

The budgeting stage: As the business develops, a system for annual budgeting of sales, costs and cash flow is devised, often because of pressure from external stakeholders such as banks. Being largely financial in nature, budgets often take little account of marketing research, product development or the longer term potential of international markets.

Annual business planning: Companies begin to adopt a more formalized annual approach to planning by including the whole of the business in the planning review process. One of three approaches to the process of international market planning generally emerge at this stage:

1 *Top-down planning*: This is by far the simplest approach, with senior managers setting goals and developing quite detailed plans for middle and senior staff to implement. To be successful, this clearly requires the senior managers to be closely in touch with all their international markets and for the business to be relatively uncomplicated in the range of products or services offered. It has the advantage of ensuring that there is little opportunity for misinterpretation by local managers, but the disadvantage of giving little opportunity for local initiative. Most of the strategic decisions at Google are taken in the US, Alibaba Group in China, Samsung in the Republic of Korea and Vodafone in the UK.

2 *Bottom-up planning*: In this approach the different parts of the company around the globe prepare their own goals and plans and submit them to headquarters for approval. While this encourages local initiative and innovation, it can be difficult to manage as the sum of the individual parts that

make different demands on resources, financial returns and marketing profiles rarely add up to a feasible international development plan.

3 *Goals down, plans up*: In an attempt to benefit from the positive elements of the first two approaches, this third approach is based upon senior management assessing the firm's opportunities and needs, setting corporate global objectives and developing broad international strategies. Financial goals are then set for each part of the company, which has the responsibility for developing individual strategies and plans to achieve these targets. For this approach to work effectively the senior management generally allows considerable flexibility in the way that the goals are achieved by the component parts of the firm around the globe. This approach is adopted particularly by companies that have a very diverse portfolio of businesses and products.

The strategic planning stage: So far, the stages discussed have been concerned with relatively short-term planning (one to two years), but for many aspects of international marketing such as new market entry, growth strategies and brand management, much longer-term planning is essential. By developing strategies for a five-year timescale, it is possible to avoid short-term, highly reactive and frequently contradictory and wasteful activity. The annual marketing plan then becomes a more detailed version of the five-year strategic plan which can be rolled forward year on year.

The obvious benefits of strategic planning are that all staff can be better motivated and encouraged to work more effectively by sharing a vision of the future. There are, however, potential dangers too. Long-term strategic plans often fail to cope with the consequences of unexpected events, either environmental or political. There is often confusion between managers over what are strategic issues and what are operational tactics. What a manager in a foreign subsidiary might consider to be a strategic issue, such as achieving a substantial market share increase in the country, might be regarded as an operational matter by a senior manager at the headquarters, which does not consider success in that particular country a priority for the company.

The international marketing planning process

There are a number of elements in the international marketing plan, as detailed in Figure 1.5.

FIGURE 1.5   Aspects of international marketing planning

Stakeholder expections
- Shareholders, customer, host government, employees in each country, pressure groups

Situation analysis
- Evaluation of the environment and individual markets

Resources and capabilities
- Individual small business unit strengths and weaknesses analysis
- Capability to deal with threats and opportunities

Corporate aims and objectives
- Financial, market, area, brand and mix objectives

Marketing strategies
- Growth strategies
- Standardization and adaptation

Implementation of the plan
- Individual SBU and marketing mix plans
- Regional, global or multidomestic integration

Control and feedback
- Setting relevant standards, measuring performance, correcting deviations

Stakeholder expectations   The complexities of the international marketing environment mean another major difference for companies competing on international markets is that the company has many more organizations and people who have a stake in how they conduct their business, and so consequently many more stakeholders whose differing expectations they have to manage. The ability of a company to pursue its chosen marketing strategy is determined to a large degree by the aims and expectations of the stakeholders, who directly or indirectly provide the resources and support needed to implement the strategies and plans. It is important to clearly identify the different stakeholder groups, understand their expectations and evaluate their power, because it is the stakeholders who provide the broad guidelines within which the firm operates. Figure 1.5 identifies the typical stakeholders of a **multinational enterprise**. Body Shop, the environmentally conscious UK toiletries retailer, is always likely to have problems balancing the widely differing pricing and profit expectations and environmental concerns of its franchisees, customers and shareholders.

While the senior management of the firm aim usually to develop and adopt strategies which do not directly oppose these stakeholder expectations, they do, of course, frequently widen or alter the firm's activities due to changes in the market and competition. Moreover, a wide range of stakeholders influence what multinational enterprises (MNEs) do by giving greater attention to the political, commercial and ethical behaviour of the organizations, as well as taking more interest in the actual operation of the business and the performance and safety of the products. As a result of this, companies need to explain their strategies and plans to shareholders through more detailed annual reports to staff through a variety of briefing methods and to pressure groups and the community in general through various public relations activities, particularly when their activities have an impact on the local environment or economy. In international marketing it is particularly important that the firm addresses the concern of its host country stakeholders, who may be physically and culturally very distant from the headquarters.

Particular attention should be paid to the different expectations of the stakeholders and their power to influence the firm's strategic direction. Given the different expectations of the firm's stakeholders it is inevitable that conflicts will occur. For example, shareholders usually want a high return on their investment and may expect the firm to find countries with low production costs, but the workers in these countries want an adequate wage on which to live. It is often the firm's ability to manage these potential conflicts that leads to success or failure in international marketing (see Figure 1.6).

FIGURE 1.6   Some typical stakeholders of multinational enterprises

International pressure groups are another important stakeholder MNEs have to manage. Global communications and the ability of the Internet to draw together geographically dispersed people with shared interests have led to the growing power of globally based pressure groups. Such has been the success of a number of these, it is now the case that pressure groups are seen by many global operators as one of the key stakeholders to be considered in international strategy decision-making. The role of pressure groups in global markets tends to raise awareness of issues of concern. Among those that have received wide press coverage affecting international marketing strategies are:

- the Greenpeace efforts to raise awareness to threats on the environment
- the anti-globalization lobby demonstrating against the perceived dark global forces they see manifested in the World Trade Organization
- the anti-child labour movement
- exploitation of factory workers.

Retailers including Gap and H&M have recently been accused of exploiting workers in factories in Bangladesh (Paige 2013). Workers often started work at 7.00am and continued until 10.30pm; other retailers including Lidl were also reported to pay Bangladeshi workers around $19 for a 10 hour day.

One of the main roles of international public relations is to try to manage the expectations and aspirations of pressure groups and all the stakeholders of a company. In international marketing one of the key responsibilities is to establish good practice to respond to publicity generated by pressure groups on issues where they have been seen not to meet stakeholder expectations.

Situation analysis

Situation analysis is the process by which the company develops a clear understanding of each individual market and then evaluates its significance for the company and for other markets in which the business operates. As the international business environment becomes more competitive, dynamic and complex, there is a greater need for individual managers to be aware not simply of their immediate situation, but also of the possible impact of changes taking place in surrounding areas too. Individual national markets can be both surprisingly similar and surprisingly dissimilar in nature, and it is important to understand these linkages and the implications of the changes which take place. Chapters 2 and 3 give the reader a detailed insight into the factors to consider in carrying out a situational analysis of the international marketing environment.

The processes and procedures for segmenting international markets and carrying out the necessary research to build the situational analysis are examined in some depth in Chapter 4.

A detailed analysis of each of these factors as they affect both the local and international market environments is necessary in order to forecast future changes. The most frequently adopted approach by firms is to extrapolate past trends. However, with so many factors to consider and the increasing frequency with which unexpected events seem to occur, it may be extremely difficult and misleading to build up one all-embracing vision of the future. Firms are responding to this uncertainty by developing a series of alternative scenarios as the basis of the planning process. An effective and robust strategy needs to contain contingency plans to deal with a variety of situations in which the company might find itself.

Resources and capabilities

In stressing the need to analyze and respond to external forces over which even global companies have little control, there can be a temptation among some managers to believe that the current capabilities of the organization are inadequate when facing the future. A more thorough analysis of the firm's situation is needed and the SWOT framework (analyzing the firm's strengths, weaknesses, opportunities and threats) is appropriate for this purpose. It is important, therefore, to audit not just the most obvious company weaknesses, but also the strengths of the company, which are often taken for granted but which are really its source of competitive advantage. This is particularly important in international markets as, for example, customer and brand loyalty may be much stronger in certain markets than others, and products which may be at the end of their life in the domestic market may be ideal for less sophisticated markets. SWOT analysis should, therefore, be carried out separately on each area of the business by function, product or market and focus upon what action should be taken to exploit the opportunities and minimize the threats that are identified in the analysis. This will lead to a clearer evaluation of the resources that are available or which must be acquired to ensure the necessary actions are carried out.

Knowledge management

The increasing globalization of business, particularly because it is being driven by information technology, has led many firms to re-examine what contributes to their global competitive advantage. They have recognized that it is the pool of personal knowledge, skills and competences of the firms' staff that provides its development potential, and they have redefined themselves as 'knowledge-based' organizations. Moreover, these firms have acknowledged that they must retain, nurture and apply the knowledge and skills across their business if they wish to be effective in global markets. The growth potential can only be exploited if the firm becomes a learning organization in which the good practice learned by individual members of staff can be 'leveraged', transferred and built upon throughout its global activity.

Corporate objectives

Having identified stakeholder expectations, carried out a detailed situation analysis and made an evaluation of the capabilities of the company, the overall goals to be pursued can be set. It is important to stress that there is a need for realism in this, as too frequently corporate plans are determined more by the desire for short-term credibility with shareholders than with the likelihood that they will be achieved. The objectives must be based on realistic performance expectations rather than on a best case scenario. Consideration must also be given to developing alternative scenarios so that realistic objectives can be set and accompanied by contingency plans in case the chosen scenario does not materialize.

The process adopted for determining long-term and short-term objectives is important and varies significantly depending on the size of the business, the nature of the market and the abilities and motivation of managers in different markets. At an operational level, the national managers need to have an achievable and detailed plan for each country, which will take account of the local situation, explain what is expected and how performance will be measured. For most companies the most obvious international strategic development opportunities are either in increasing geographical coverage and/or building global product strength. This is discussed in much further detail in Chapter 5 from the viewpoint of the SME and in Chapter 6 from the viewpoint of globally based organizations. Management Challenge 1.2 helps you consider this question from the viewpoint of fast food firms trying to grow their global business.

Marketing strategies

Having set the objectives for the company, both at the corporate and subsidiary level, the company will develop detailed programmes of the marketing strategies and activities which will achieve the objectives. Decisions will need to be made as to how the company will segment and target its international markets. How will it position itself in different international markets? How will it add value to its efforts through its product portfolio, communications, distribution and pricing strategies? It is this that is at the heart of the following chapters of this book as we take the reader through the detailed considerations in developing an international marketing strategy. A central concern in marketing strategy development for international markets is the dilemma facing all international managers as to how far they can standardize marketing strategies in different country markets. This essential question will be examined as we go through different aspects of international marketing strategy development and implementation.

Implementation of the marketing plan

Having agreed the overall marketing strategy, plans for implementation are required at a central and local subsidiary level. Firms usually allocate resources to individual subsidiaries on a top-down basis, but this needs to be modified to include the special allocations made to enable foreign subsidiaries to resource

MANAGEMENT CHALLENGE 1.2

How to start a business in Bolivia

Bolivia is a Latin American country with a population of 10 million. It is a lower income country where the people have a GNI per capita of US$2550. Starting a business in Bolivia is time consuming and bureaucratic due to legal requirements being slow and cumbersome. However, the current President Evo Morales has introduced new laws, frameworks and incentives to encourage domestic and foreign investment. One area of Bolivia that is proving attractive to investors is Santa Cruz, which is one of the fastest growing cities in the world. It is young and vibrant, it is the main business centre in Bolivia, yet culturally it has many museums, art

and cultural centres. Investment has been made in many high-tech private health clinics as well as local fashion brands. The city has also attracted a major international brand, namely KFC, which has opened two restaurants in Santa Cruz. There are high hopes for Santa Cruz as it already provides 35 per cent of the gross domestic product for Bolivia and of all the foreign investment that comes to Bolivia, Santa Cruz receives 40 per cent. With a 365-day sunny climate, it seems Santa Cruz is a city of infinite possibilities.

Question

1 As marketing manager for Santa Cruz, how would you promote your city to other international brands?

Source: Brauch, M. D. (2014), Opening the door to foreign investment? An analysis of Bolivia's new investment promotion law, published in *Investment Industry News*, 11 August 2014. Available from: www.iisd.org/itn/2014/08 /11/opening-the-door-to-foreign-investment-an-analysis-of-bolivias-new-investment-promotion-law/ (accessed 3 March 2015).

specific market opportunities or difficulties encountered in particular markets. Agreement is reached through a process of discussion between the operating department and management levels. Detailed budgets and timescales can then be set for all areas of marketing including those outside agencies (such as marketing researchers, designers and advertising agencies), in order to ensure that their contributions are delivered on time and within the budget. Some allowance must be made for those activities which might be more difficult to estimate in terms of cost or time, such as research and development of new products.

We have, so far, emphasized the need for careful, detailed and thorough preparation of the plan, but it is essential that the plan is action oriented and contains programmes designed to give clear direction for the implementation, continuous evaluation and control of all the firm's marketing activity. The plan must, therefore, be: *strategic*, by fulfilling the corporate and marketing objectives and coordinating the individual strategic business unit (SBU) plans; *tactical*, by focusing upon individual SBU marketing activities in each country; and *implementable*, by detailing the individual activities of each department within the SBU.

The control process

The final stage of the planning process is setting up an effective system for obtaining feedback and controlling the business. Feedback and control systems should be regarded as an integrated part of the whole planning process, and they are essential in ensuring that the marketing plans are not only being implemented but are still appropriate for the changing international environment.

There are three essential elements of the control process:

1 *Setting standards*: The standards that are set need to be relevant to the corporate goals such as growth and profits reported by financial measures, return on capital employed and on sales, and non-financial indicators, e.g. market share. Intermediate goals and individual targets can be set by breaking the plan down into measurable parts which when successfully completed will lead to the overall objectives being achieved. The standards must be understandable, achievable and relevant to each local country situation.

2 *Measuring performance against standards*: To obtain measurements and ensure rapid feedback of information, firms use a variety of techniques, including reports, meetings and special measurements of specific parts of the marketing programme, such as cost–benefit analysis on customers, product lines and territories or marketing audits for a thorough examination of every aspect of marketing in a particular country. They also use benchmarking, which allows comparisons of various aspects of the business, such as efficiency of distribution, customer response times, service levels and complaints, with other companies that are not necessarily from the same business sector.

3 *Correcting deviations from the plan*: Perhaps the most difficult decisions that must be made are to determine when performance has deviated sufficiently from the plan to require corrective action to be taken either by changing the plan or the management team charged with the responsibility of carrying out the plan.

A checklist of the essential elements of the international marketing plan is summarized in Figure 1.7.

FIGURE 1.7   Essential elements of the international marketing plan

---

Does the plan contain:

International analysis

- assumptions about the world economy and the environment trends in the principal markets?
- details of historical performance (sales, cost, profitability)?
- forecast of future performance based on (a) an extrapolation of the past (b) alternative scenarios?
- identified opportunities and threats?

Company capability assessment

- analysis of the company strengths, weaknesses and future capabilities in comparison with local and international competition?

International mission statement with:

- long-term aims and objectives and the strategies to achieve them?
- one year marketing objectives and individual strategies (for example, budgets, brand objectives and development of personnel)?

Operational plans

- detailed country by country forecasts and targets?
- detailed country by country plans for all marketing activities and coordination with other functions (for example, manufacturing)?
- an explanation of how country plans will be integrated regionally or globally if appropriate?

Contingencies and controls

- a summary of the critical factors for success?
- an assessment of the likely competitor response?
- a contingency component for when things do not go to plan?
- a control process for feedback, evaluation and taking corrective action?

Reasons for success

Michael Czinkota (2011) suggests the firms operating in the international environment succeed when they *manage, learn and be pro-active* about the global marketplace at micro and macro levels. Gathering and analyzing crucial information enables firms to respond and develop strategies. The firms that do well will base their success largely on the early identification of the changes in the boundaries of markets and industries in their analysis of their international marketing environment. Management foresight and organizational learning are, therefore, the basis of a sustainable competitive advantage in global markets.

Firms are increasingly vulnerable to losing valuable personal assets, because of the greater mobility of staff, prevalence of industrial espionage and the security risks and abuse associated with the Internet. Moreover, with the increase in communications it is becoming more difficult to store, access and apply the valuable knowledge that exists among the huge volume of relatively worthless data that the company deals with. Consequently, effective knowledge management is now critical for success. This means having online database systems that facilitate effective data collection, a cloud computing capability, storage in data warehouses and data mining (the identification of opportunities from patterns that emerge from detailed analysis of the data held).

Successful global operators use the knowledge gained to assess their strengths and weaknesses in light of their organizational learning and ensure they have the company capability and resources to respond to their learning in order to sustain their competitive advantage. This is particularly important in international markets as, for example, customer and brand loyalty may be much stronger in certain markets than others, and products that may be at the end of their life in the domestic market may be ideal for less sophisticated markets. In the dynamic international markets, therefore, if a firm is to succeed it must develop the ability to think, analyze and develop strategic and innovative responses on an international, if not global, scale.

Characteristics of best practice in international marketing

It is apparent, therefore, that firms and organizations planning to compete effectively in world markets need a clear and well-focused international marketing strategy that is based on a thorough understanding of the markets which the company is targeting or operating in. International markets are dynamic entities that require constant monitoring and evaluation. As we have discussed, as markets change so must marketing techniques. Innovation is an important competitive variable, not only in terms of the product or service, but throughout the marketing process. Countertrading, financial innovations, networking and value-based marketing are all important concepts in the implementation of a successful international strategy.

The challenge, then, of international marketing is to ensure that any international strategy has the discipline of thorough research and an understanding and accurate evaluation of what is required to achieve the competitive advantage. Doole (2000) identified three major components to the strategies of firms successfully competing in international markets:

- A clear international competitive focus achieved through a thorough knowledge of the international markets, a strong competitive positioning and a strategic perspective which was truly international.
- An effective relationship strategy achieved through strong customer relations, a commitment to quality products and service and a dedication to customer service throughout international markets.
- Well-managed organizations with a culture of learning. Firms were innovative and willing to learn, showed high levels of energy and commitment to international markets and had effective monitoring and control procedures for all their international markets.

SUMMARY

- In this chapter we have discussed the growing strategic importance of international marketing and examined the issues associated with successfully competing in international markets. The chapter examines the main differences between domestic and international marketing, the different levels at which international marketing can be approached and the more complex and multidimensional uncontrollable elements of the international marketing environment.

- We have examined the major aspects of the SLEPTS factors in the international marketing environment. The environments in which international companies must operate is typically characterized by uncertainty and change – factors which, taken together, increase the element of risk for international marketing managers.

- It has been suggested that marketing managers need to have a properly planned approach to any international activity because, without this, the costs and likelihood of failure are likely to increase. We examined the international marketing planning and control process and considered how managers can respond to the challenges posed in the international marketing environment by ensuring they have robust strategy development and market planning processes.

- The reasons for success and failure on international markets were examined and it was suggested the firms operating globally that succeed are those that perceive the changes in the international environment and are able to develop strategies which enable them to respond accordingly. Management foresight and organizational learning are, therefore, the basis of a sustainable competitive advantage in global markets.

- The reader has been introduced to many of the concepts that are important to the international marketing management process and will have gained an understanding of the issues to be addressed. All the various aspects of the international marketing strategy process introduced in this chapter will be examined in more detail in the following chapters. In Chapter 2 the international trading environment and the trends and developments in trading patterns will be examined.

KEYWORDS

world trade	cultural paradoxes	World Trade Organization
international trade	European Union	emerging economies
global youth culture	piracy	multinational enterprise
export marketing	gross national income	globalization
international marketing	purchasing power parity	
global marketing	least developed economies	

CASE STUDY 1

Tesco in China

Tesco entered China in 2004. At the time the senior management team boldly claimed that understanding the local culture, shopping habits and needs of local customers featured high on the agenda of their expansion strategy into China. At the time China was viewed by Tesco as their most important and fastest growing overseas operation and they invested heavily in their new venture, more than in any other foreign market as they battled to become established against the other international competition from Walmart and Carrefour.

Tesco focused their business in three regions: in the east of the country, including Shanghai; the north, including Beijing; and the south, including Guangzhou. Ken Towle, Tesco China president, had a very ambitious long term plan aiming to open more new retail space in China than they had built up in the UK. Tesco China intended to invest £2 billion and by 2016 have a property empire of 80 self-built shopping centres, many of them boasting skyscrapers full of apartments, cinemas and gyms.

They did have initial success and more than 50 000 shoppers turned out for the opening of the Qingdao Centre, which was described as feeling a lot more 'local' than the standard foreign hypermarket, with much noise and bustle and the sale of live turtles and fresh stingray adding to the atmosphere.

However, somewhere it all went wrong and in 2014 Tesco announced that it was to merge its now unprofitable operation into a state-run company as a minority partner. Tesco's partner, state-owned China Resources Enterprise Ltd, would be an 80 per cent partner, with Tesco taking just a 20 per cent stake.

Many commentators saw this as a humiliating retreat for the British retail giant and rather than a strategic move, a simple attempt to limit their losses.

An initial cause of Tesco's demise was seen to be its initial market entry strategy in 2004 where it attempted to build the market independently of partners. Many international investors have found it impossible to launch into China without some sort of joint venture with a Chinese partner or partners. In China, relationship building with suppliers, distributors and regulators has to be an essential part to any strategy.

However, the main cause of its inability to build a strong presence in the market was seen to be its cavalier attitude to the Chinese market and its assumption it could replicate its UK strategy in China. The senior management seemed to have a staunch belief that what worked in the UK would work in China and so ignored key cultural differences and tried to replicate a strategy that had served them well in the UK.

Food the world over is closely linked to the social and cultural heritage of a country and Tesco was seen to ignore basic Chinese cultural principles. For example, Tesco's Chinese name 'le gou' translates to 'happy shopping' which was seen by the Chinese consumer to ignore the association to family values so important to the Chinese culture especially in association to food.

The Tesco Club Card also failed to translate to the Chinese market. Their Club Cards just did not appeal to Chinese consumers very much and so failed to tie consumers into the Tesco shop and build a loyal customer base.

Problems with suppliers and regulators, and soaring costs for rent and labour, were also cited as key reasons behind Tesco's failure.

However, on a more strategic level, Tesco appear to have neglected due consideration of brand positioning or repositioning. With established and entrenched international competitors such as Walmart and Carrefour, Tesco had difficulties establishing themselves with a similar brand positioning strategy as their other international competitors.

Tesco unfortunately learnt what many other retailers have learnt before them, that taking a successful retail brand from one country to another is complicated and requires extensive research, huge investment and is fraught with difficulties.

Questions

1 Evaluate the reasons behind Tesco's difficulties in establishing in China.

2 What lessons can you offer to managers trying to develop strategies for international markets?

Sources: *Daily Mail City Focus:* Thorniley, T. 11 January 2010. www.retail-week.com/topics/international/international-analysis-learning-from-tesco-how-not-to-fail-abroad /5064503.2015.

Adapted by: Kate Morse, Sheffield Hallam University

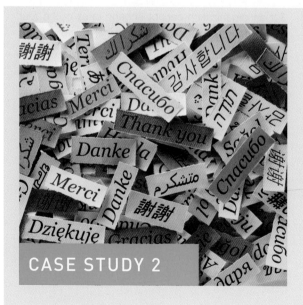

CASE STUDY 2

Going international? You need a language strategy

One of the ways to ensure an organization is successful when it enters the international arena is to have a language strategy. The marketing manager provides a common language with customers, employees, investors and supply chain operators promoting issues including the organization's brand values, its sustainability credentials and promotional offers. Additionally, the marketing manager will be communicating with multiple international marketing agencies to ensure advertisements on television, websites and Twitter are interesting and compelling to their respective local consumer market. To do all this successfully organizations need a language strategy;

yet at the moment not many global brands have a cohesive language strategy.

To engage in a cohesive international language strategy an organization must engage with the following four elements:

1 Choose a lingua franca; also known as the trade language. The lingua franca is the chosen adopted language by organizations that work within a community that does not have a shared language. Therefore a lingua franca is used when organizations have international teams working in countries outside the business's home country and also with traders along the supply chain. The most used lingua franca languages are English, Spanish, Arabic, Chinese and Swahili.

2 Have a policy to provide foreign language training and/or hire expatriates that can speak the lingua franca and also another language in countries where the organization does business.

3 Provide all employees with cultural awareness training specifically highlighting differences and similarities in countries where the organization does business.

4 Have a communication strategy so that consumers see and can engage with the organization in their preferred language.

Organizations that do not engage in a cohesive language strategy are inefficient. The reason inefficiencies occur is because unrestricted multilingualism, with no common language or cultural understanding, causes confusion, misinterpretation, alienation and friction. These inefficiencies occur between employees and traders particularly when working across borders. It also causes tension which leads to a disjointed, disorganized business. Having said that, not all businesses have the funds or expertise to develop and engage with a language strategy.

Marketing managers of international brands such as IBM know their consumer markets. They know they do business in many consumer markets outside their home country's borders so the lingua franca they choose is English. However, IBM also does business in eight other countries. Therefore, they have a policy of hiring someone that knows at least one of the languages native to the eight countries in which

they do business, as well as the lingua franca. Other members of staff at IBM are also trained in foreign languages and cultural awareness so they can engage with overseas colleagues and markets. A coherent language strategy is not only crucial for organizations that have international teams in cross-border trade; it also permits successful mergers and acquisitions and standardization of processes/regulations under a shared vision. It also enables employees to work closely with local markets and traders where a local language is best suited.

In addition to employees and traders, the international marketing manager must consider the 'always connected' consumers. Whilst it is true that many households speak more than one language, consumers state they are more likely to engage with and buy from brands when communication messages are presented in their preferred language.

The Accor hotel brand clearly has a language strategy. Accor communicates with their customers, who incidentally come from 92 countries across the world. They translate over 20 million words per year to communicate effectively with their consumers in their preferred language. Communications take place on many traditional advertising channels as well as on social media platforms.

Questions

1 What are the benefits and weaknesses of a language strategy to an organization?

2 What are the benefits of a language strategy to the consumer?

3 If an organization cannot engage in all of the four elements of the language strategy immediately, which of the elements should they develop first?

Sources: Neeley, T. and Kaplan, R.S. (2014) 'What's your language strategy', *Harvard Business Review*, *92*(9), 70–76; Wakefield, M.A. (2014) SDL millennial study reveals language strategy is critical to enhancing customer experience success, published in SDL on 23 June 2014. Available from www.sdl.com/about/news-media/press/2014/sdl-millennial-study-reveals-language-strategy-is-critical-to-enhancing-customer-experience-success.html (accessed 21 June 2015).

DISCUSSION QUESTIONS

1 What are the major environmental influences which impact on international marketing? Show how they can affect international marketing strategies.

2 Using examples, examine the reasons why marketing strategies fail in international markets.

3 Identify three major global pressure groups. Examine how they have influenced the international marketing strategies of particular firms.

4 What skills and abilities are necessary requirements for an effective international marketing manager? Justify your choices.

5 How can marketing managers accommodate the multiplicity of international markets into a cohesive international marketing strategy and plan?

REFERENCES

1. www.bbc.co.uk/news/world-latin-america-27549309 Spanish oil company Repsol ends operations in Argentina. bbc news online 23 May 2014.

2. Bloomberg Business (1996) Microsoft's long march, published in Bloomberg Business, 23 June 1996. Available from www.bloomberg.com/bw/stories/1996-06-23/microsofts-long-march (accessed 20 June 2015).

3. BSA (2014) The Compliance Gap, BSA Global Software Survey. Washington: BSA.

4. Consultancy.uk (2015) Grant Thornton: One third of firms plan to grow via M&A, published 16 April 2015. Available from www.consultancy.uk/news/1827/grant-thornton-one-third-of-firms-plan-to-grow-via-ma (accessed 13 August 2015).

5. Credit Suisse (2014) *Global Wealth Databook*. Switzerland: Research Institute.

6. Czinkota M.R. (2011) 'International information cross-fertilization in marketing', *The Future of Global Business* 83–85.

7. Doole, I. (2000) 'How SMEs learn to compete effectively on international markets', PhD paper.

8. *The Economist* (2015) The Big Mac index, published 22 January 2015. Available from www.economist.com /content/big-mac-index (accessed 2 March 2015).

9. Etihad Airlines (2015) Alitalia and Etihad Airways finalise €1758 million investment deal. Available from www.etihad .com/en-gb/about-us/etihad-news/archive/2014/alitalia-and-etihad-airways-finalise-1758-million-investment-deal /(accessed 19 June 2015).

10. Forest and Sullivan (2014) Defining our future. Are you ready? Available from www.marketresearch.com/Frost-Sullivan-v383/Future-B2B-Online-Retailing-8683456 /(accessed 13 August 2015).

11. Nyaga, M.N. (2014) 'The role of lending design on sustainable competitive advantage among deposit taking sacco's in Kenya'. *Strategic Journal of Business & Change Management*, 1 (2) 685.

12. Paige, J. (2013) Bangladesh clothing workers still exploited, five months after factory fire, Panorama investigation finds, published in *The Independent*, 23 September 2013. Available from www.independent .co.uk/news/world/asia/bangladesh-clothing-workers-still-exploited-five-months-after-factory-fire-panorama-investigation-finds-8833102.html (accessed 3 February 2015).

13. Perlmutter, M.V. (1995) 'Becoming globally civilised, managing across culture', Mastering Management Part 6, *Financial Times*, 1 December.

14. Sarathy, R., Terpstra, V. and Russow, L.C. (2006) *International marketing*, 9th edn. Dryden Press.

15. UNICEF (2015) www.esa.un.org/MigGMGProfiles /indicators/files/Germany.pdf.

16. United Nations (2013) World Population Projects The 2012 Revision. New York: United Nations.

17. United Nations (2014) World Urbanization Prospects. New York: United Nations.

CHAPTER 2

THE WORLD TRADING ENVIRONMENT

LEARNING OBJECTIVES

After reading this chapter you should be able to:

- Discuss the effects and implications of the factors impacting on world trade

- Explain the key trends in the major regional trading blocs around the globe

- Understand the role of the major world institutions that foster the development of multilateral free trade across the world

INTRODUCTION

International marketing takes place within the framework of the world trading environment. If the reader is to have the skills necessary to develop international marketing strategies, some understanding of the parameters of the world trading environment in which they operate is needed.

In this chapter we examine the development of world trade in recent years and the international trading environment in the context following the global financial crisis in 2008–09. We will analyze the growth and changing patterns of world trade and discuss the institutions that aim to influence world trade.

We will also look at the changing regional trading blocs and the implications these have on trading structures around the globe.

World trading patterns

The world economy consists of over 196 nations with a population of 7.2 billion and a gross domestic product (GDP) output totalled around US$72.6 trillion. Each year, for the last ten years, the global GDP has grown, although there was a fall in global GDP in 2009 due to the global financial crisis. The World Trade Organization (WTO) estimates world trade exports merchandise to almost total US$19 trillion; with the US, China and Germany leading the way, whilst trade in commercial services is currently estimated to be about US$4.5 trillion.

Together, Asia, North America and the European Union (EU) account for 81 per cent of world trade. Figure 2.1 highlights the major trade flows between the three points of what has become known as Ohmae's triad (2005) after the Japanese writer who first coined the phrase.

However, such figures mask the potential of future market opportunities. Of the world's population, 85 per cent live in emerging markets and it is likely that by 2020 the emerging markets will contribute to 65 per cent of the global economic growth. The International Monetary Fund (IMF) showed that emerging market economies were strong during the years 2000–2012; however, the economic growth is now declining. This means that the growth forecasts in countries such as Brazil, Russia, India and China considered to be the four biggest emerging economies (now known as BRICs after being grouped together under the acronym by Goldman Sachs) need to be altered.

The GDP of China which had grown by 8.3 per cent in 2014 is now declining and Brazil's growth rate is declining from their 2000–2012 rate by just over 2 per cent. Nevertheless, Brazil, India and China still produce, and will continue to produce, a very high proportion of goods and services needed worldwide. Other countries that need to be considered, as outlined in Chapter 1, are Mexico, Indonesia, Nigeria and Turkey (MINT), all emerging markets, with population growth and the opportunity to develop their

FIGURE 2.1 Seven merchandise trading states

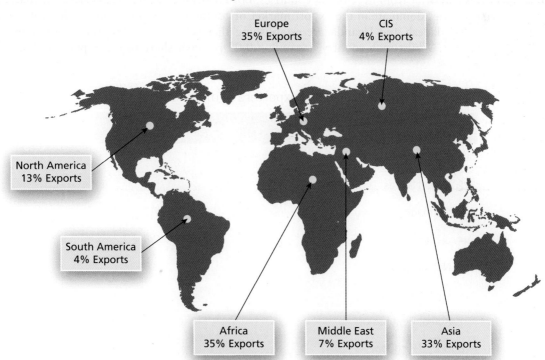

- World merchandise Export Trade is US$19 trillion
- CIS = Commonwealth of Independent States

Source: Kenyon, A.J. (2014), World Trade Organization.

productivity levels and work competitively on a global scale. However, according to the CIA Factbook (2010), measured on a purchasing power parity (ppp) basis, none of the BRIC or MINT country's relative currency value is as favourable as Qatar, Liechtenstein, Macau, Bermuda and Singapore.

The Next Eleven (or N-11) are 11 countries – Bangladesh, Egypt, Indonesia, Iran, Mexico, Nigeria, Pakistan, the Philippines, South Korea, Turkey and Vietnam – identified by Goldman Sachs investment bank as having a high potential of becoming the world's largest economies in the twenty-first century. The bank chose these states due to their promising outlooks for investment and future growth. This of course is a much longer term prediction, time itself will tell how accurate that prediction turns out to be.

In global trade, emerging economies are now major players; their share of world exports has jumped from 20 per cent in 1970 to nearly 50 per cent. Rising exports give countries more money to spend on imports. Over the next decade it is expected that one billion new consumers will enter the global market-place as incomes in emerging countries across Asia and Africa rise further and households start to have more disposable income to spend on non-essential goods.

The global downturn has helped reduce global imbalances in trade. The top three exporters account remains at 27 per cent of total exports, just as it was in 2009. China remains the single largest exporter in the world, with the US overtaking Germany as the second largest exporter (see Table 2.1).

This is a huge development. China did not even warrant a place in the Top 10 table in the 2001 edition of this textbook. By the 2003 edition it had moved up to sixth place and third position in the 2008 edition, giving some indication of the trajectory of the growth of its economy. In this edition the Republic of Korea (as opposed to South Korea) has moved from ninth position in the 6th edition of this book to seventh position in this edition. The Russian Federation has now begun to trade beyond its borders and has entered the top 10 world exporters at number 10.

While China is now the world's biggest exporter of merchandise exports, there are many other ways of reviewing different types of goods and services that are exported. For example, the US accounts for 18.7 per cent of world exports in commercial services which puts it far in front of any other competitors. Ireland is the biggest exporter of computer services from developed countries at 22.17 per cent, with India as the biggest exporter from developing countries, not far behind, with a 19.89 per cent share; this shows that two countries dominate in the export market of computer services. From the least developed countries (LDC), Bangladesh and Uganda are establishing themselves as competitors in the computer services export market. Whilst each country has only a 0.02 per cent share of the export market it will

Table 2.1   The Top 10 world exporters in merchandise, 2013

Country	% Share
1. China	11.7
2. United States	8.4
3. Germany	7.7
4. Japan	3.8
5. Netherlands	3.6
6. France	3.1
7. Korea, Republic of	3.0
8. United Kingdom	2.9
9. Hong Kong, China	2.8
10. Russian Federation	2.8

Source: www.wto.org

ILLUSTRATION 2.1

A simple slice for the hectic lifestyles of men and women: South Africa's innovative manufacturing export

The Republic of South Africa's vision for the future is to enable their citizens to reach their full potential through employment. The Department of Trade and Industry (dti) is marketing South Africa's globally competitive economy and the excellent skills base of their citizens to aid the export market. The reason for this is exports have reduced by 4 per cent to US$93 billion. One of South Africa's strategic objectives is to grow its manufacturing sector to help grow the export trade.

An innovative product Eyeslices® created by Kerryne Krause-Neufeldt, an entrepreneur and scientist, is one manufacturing innovation that is helping to grow the export market of South Africa. Eyeslices® are for men and women who have busy lifestyles and was seen by Kerryne to fill a gap in the market. Their eyes look red, overtired and have dark circles, making the young business professionals look older and more stressed than they are. Using products from Mother Nature the traditional remedy for 'overtired' eyes was to lay down and put cucumber slices over the eyes. Now with twenty-first century science and a lot of innovative flair, Kerryne Krause-Neufeldt has produced Eyeslices® to reduce the hectic lifestyle eye problems. The Cyrogel technology for the product was licensed and the product was marketed, launched and sold out in two hours. Eyeslices® are now available in many high class Spa and Wellness Clinics worldwide including Maha Desert Resort Dubai, Malinowy Zdroj Wellness Clinics in Poland and Trump Towers, New York. Eyeslices® continue to be manufactured in South Africa and are exported to 20 countries worldwide.

Question

1 South Africa has a lot of manufacturing know-how and creative skills such as crafts, fashion and textiles. What are the opportunities and challenges that face South Africa's strategic objective to boost manufacturing exports?

Sources: Eyeslices.com; Department of Trade and Industry, South Africa; World Trade Organization.

---

be interesting to review this percentage share in future editions. See Illustration 2.1 for details of another way of reviewing exports.

The UK's share of global merchandise exports has declined appreciably over the past 30 years. Compared with a 7.5 per cent share in the 1980s, the UK currently accounts for only 2.9 per cent. The Netherlands and France remain fifth and sixth in the Top 10 world exporter list, however, their percentage share has reduced. Another European country that was part of the Top 10 world exporters list was Italy; in 2009 Italy was seventh but by 2013 it had dropped to eleventh place.

Future prospects

The global economic crisis sparked a 12.2 per cent contraction in the volume of global trade in 2008/09 and world trade volume suffered the sharpest decline in more than 70 years. However, world trade has begun to grow, and is expected to continue to grow year on year in the next decade.

In the same period the world GDP fell by 2.2 per cent. The global economic crisis originated in the financial sector in the USA. At the core, there appears to have been unsound lending practices by financial institutions, notably in the private mortgage lending sector, and unsatisfactory risk management practices. The contagion seems to have spread worldwide, causing an unprecedented credit squeeze as interbank lending came to a virtual halt. Consequently, businesses in many countries have faced liquidity squeezes and consumers have cut back their expenses. Worldwide GDP growth was at 2.4 per cent in 2000 and rose to 5.0 per cent in 2007. During the global recession growth declined rapidly; however, during 2015 growth is predicted to be picking up again to around 3.5 per cent.

Table 2.2 examines the annual percentage change in GDP and consumer prices (inflation). In the 6th edition of this book China's growth was 8.3 per cent; now it is 7.9 per cent. Whilst the growth rate has reduced, China continues to have the leading growth rates in terms of GDP among the larger economies. From the African nations, Rwanda retains the lead with a growth rate of 7.5 per cent. Adjusted for ppp its annual output has grown by an average of nearly 5 per cent per annum. Foreign investment into Africa is double that going into India and has grown nine-fold since 2000 to just under US$90 billion. Table 2.2 shows South Sudan to be the country with the highest growth. However, the rapid growth is not organic. Due to civil war, suspension of oil sales and a high government debt, inflation during 2012 rose to 79.5 per cent. Now that oil sales, their main income, have begun again South Sudan's growth rate has improved. South Sudan is aiming to maintain its stability and improve businesses opportunities so that its growth and inflation rate can become organic.

Table 2.2   Percentage change on previous year in real GDP and consumer prices

Country	Growth rate (%)*	Inflation rate (%)
Angola	5.6	8.9
Argentina	3.5	20.8
Australia	0.4	2.4
Brazil	2.3	6.2
China	7.7	2.6
Egypt	1.8	9.0
France	0.3	0.9
Germany	0.5	1.6
Greece	−3.8	−0.8
India	3.2	9.6
Indonesia	5.3	7.7
Japan	2.0	0.2
Libya	−5.1	3.2
Mexico	1.2	4.0
Netherlands	−0.8	2.5
Nigeria	6.2	8.7
Poland	1.3	1.0
Russia	1.3	6.8
Rwanda	7.4	5.9
Saudi Arabia	3.6	3.7
Sweden	0.9	0.0

Table 2.2   Continued

Country	Growth rate (%)*	Inflation rate (%)
South Africa	2.0	5.8
South Korea	2.8	2.8
South Sudan	24.7	1.7
Sudan	3.9	25.0
Turkey	3.8	7.6
UK	1.8	2.0
USA	1.6	1.5
United Arab Emirates		1.3
Venezuela	1.6	56.0

Source: CIA (2015) World Factbook. Available from www.cia.gov/library/publications/resources/the-world-factbook/geos/zi.html (accessed 13 August 2015).

*Inflation rate (consumer prices)

It is not just a country's GDP that is important to consider, China and Russia exhibit strong and healthy balance of payment surpluses. The US, however, has just released its figures and shows a huge trade deficit (US$41 752 million), as does India. According to Table 2.3 firms are likely to have difficulties in such markets as Venezuela, Argentina and Sudan where inflation is in excess of 20 per cent. However even countries

Table 2.3   Balance of trade

Country	US$ million
Argentina	73
Brazil	−2842
China	60 619
Egypt	−2603
India	−6847
Indonesia	738
Mexico	−3248
Russia	15 047
Thailand	−457
Taiwan	15
USA	−41 752
Venezuela	6811

Source: Trading Economics (2014) Balance of Trade. Available from www.tradingeconomics .com/country-list/balance-of-trade (accessed 3 January 2015).

that offer potentially attractive market opportunities, such as two of the MINT countries (Indonesia and Nigeria) could be problematic given they currently have inflation rates of 7.7 and 8.7 per cent respectively. The African nations identified are of particular interest given the potential opportunity they present for market development and growth.

The reasons countries trade

International trade is a vital part of world economic activity but it is not a new phenomenon. While the growth of international trade has accelerated in the past 40 years, it goes back much earlier and has been developing throughout the ages since the time when barter was used.

The great growth period for trade was in the eighteenth and nineteenth centuries when many of today's important trading links were forged and developed.

A major source of many of the conflicts in the nineteenth century was the desire by nations to win the right to trade in foreign markets. One of the reasons why Great Britain went to war with Napoleon was to open the French markets to our newly industrialized nation. The colony of Hong Kong and the associated New Territories, returned to China in 1997, were acquired by the UK in the early nineteenth century for trading purposes.

The reasons why nations trade are many and varied: the two key explanations are based on the theory of comparative advantage and the international product life cycle.

The theory of comparative advantage

The rationale for world trade is based largely upon Ricardo's theory of comparative advantage. At its simplest level, the theory suggests that trade between countries takes place because one country is able to produce a product at a lower price than is possible elsewhere. An illustration of this is provided by the way in which Japanese companies such as Sony and Hitachi came to dominate the European television market. Their strategy was based upon higher product quality, better design and, more importantly for our purposes here, the lower prices that were made possible by far greater economies of scale and better manufacturing technology than was currently being achieved by the European producers.

It is this notion of relative cost that underpins world trade; in other words, countries concentrate on producing products in which they have a comparative advantage over their foreign competitor countries.

How comparative advantage is achieved

A comparative advantage can be achieved in a variety of ways:

- *Sustained period of investment*: This may well lead to significantly lower operating costs.
- *Lower labour cost*: A firm operating internationally may locate a manufacturing plant in an emerging economy to take advantage of the lower labour costs there. The average hourly rate of pay in Denmark is as high as US$35, in the US it is US$23. Lower hourly rates of pay are made in Greece where on average workers earn US$13, in Brazil around US$6, but in the Philippines it is only US$1.50. Many developed countries complain of the disadvantage this creates for them in trying to compete in international markets. This competitive disadvantage is further compounded by the government subsidies and support given in such countries.
- *Proximity to raw materials*: This is another way to achieve comparative advantage as has been the case with Australia's reserves of coal and mineral ores.
- *Subsidies to help native industries*: When the US announced increased wheat subsidies to US farmers, they outraged the Australian and Canadian wheat farmers who saw it as a direct attack on their international markets. Without comparable government support, they felt they were unable to compete with US wheat in these markets.

■ *Building expertise in certain key areas*: This is another way to achieve comparative advantage. The Japanese identified biotechnology as a key area where they have comparative strength and so have targeted it as a priority research area.

Some countries use international trade to acquire a comparative advantage, buying in highly developed products and so speeding up their development. There are, however, some fundamental requirements to gain competitive status. Schwab (2014) states that to be competitive within the world's marketplace, countries need to be stable, productive and sustainable supported by basic foundations. With that in mind he, together with the World Economic Forum, provided a Global Competitive Index based on 12 Pillars of Competitiveness. The 12 Pillars of Competitiveness are split into three stages:

ILLUSTRATION 2.2

The 5th 'essential importer' phase of the international product life cycle

Importing food into Japan

Culture has many definitions, but one that defines us is the food we eat, why we eat it, its traditions, when we eat it and with whom. The food import and export market is therefore significant. The four biggest importers of food are the EU, US, China and Japan.

Japan, as the fourth biggest importer of food, is known for its unique foods including sushi, pickled vegetables and sashimi, often accompanied with rice. Japan is also known for its soups and stews such as miso and sukiyaki and its teppanyaki style of cooking, all of which can be washed down with warm or cold sake, often known as rice wine. The perfect presentation of food and the amazing artistic sweet food industry help identify the Japanese food culture. Despite Japanese food being healthy and of high quality the citizens of Japan are starting to favour western diets.

Japan is not self-sufficient in feeding it citizens. Currently, Japan produces only approximately 40 per cent of the nation's food. Therefore, 60 per cent of food, particularly western-style food, is imported. Food importers not only provide competition for domestic suppliers (the 5th distinct phase of Japan's international product cycle) they are essential to keep the Japanese population fed. One of the reasons the 'essential importers' (the 5th distinct phase of the international product cycle) are necessary is because younger generations have moved from farming communities to employment in the cities of Japan. This means that there are currently only 2.6 million farmers to support 125 million Japanese citizens and clearly this is unsustainable. More importantly, the average age of the Japanese farmer is 65 years; demonstrating a career in agriculture is of no interest to the younger Japanese citizen.

Question

1 The Japanese government has set a strategy to increase food self-sufficiency from the current 40 per cent to 50 per cent by 2020. What would you recommend for the Japanese government?

Source: United Nations (2012) Future of food in Japan www.ourworld.unu.edu/en/future-of-food-in-Japan

Stage 1. Basic Requirements   The Factor Driven Pillars are the foundations; without these a country cannot be a major competitor in the international market. The pillars are:

1 *Institutions* – honest and fair interconnected public and private administrative legal networks, working with government to improve the economy.
2 *Infrastructure* – developed telecommunication, uninterrupted power supplies and transport systems.
3 *Stable Macro-environment*
4 *Health and Primary Education* – healthy citizens contributing to the business and skills economy. Primary education for all.

Countries engaging in the Basic Requirements of Stage 1 include Bangladesh, Nicaragua and Tanzania. Once the Basic Requirements are in place, a country can start to become more effective through Efficiency Driven activities; in doing so they become more competitive within the world marketplace.

Stage 2. Efficiency Driven

5 *Higher Education and Training* – Secondary and tertiary (Undergraduate degree to Doctor of Philosophy) education; together with continuous work-based training.
6 *Goods Market Efficiency* – A range of services and goods enabling a balance between supply and demand. Open market to encourage foreign investment.
7 *Labour Market Efficiency* – Equal gender and age opportunities together with potential for promotion or movement within and/or across economic activities.
8 *Financial Market Efficiency* – Solid banking sector. Efficient risk and investment activities.
9 *Technology Readiness* – Communication and information technology enabling cross-border and/or national research and business opportunities.
10 *Market Size* – Includes both domestic and international market size/potential.

Countries engaging in the efficiency dimensions of Stage 2 include Albania, Indonesia and Peru.

Stage 3. Innovation Driven

11 *Business Sophistication* – Countries known to create quality, brand leading products and services with modern, unique production and distribution mechanisms.
12 *Innovation* – Research and Development, design and creation of technological and scientific products and services.

Countries at Stage 3 which are high in innovation with complex business include China, Qatar and UK.

The international product life cycle

The theory of comparative advantage is often used as the classic explanation of world trade. Other observers, however, believe that world trade and investment patterns are based upon the product life cycle concept. Writing from an American perspective, Vernon and Wells (1968) suggested that on an international level, products move through four distinct phases:

1 US firms manufacture for the home market and begin exporting.
2 Foreign production starts.
3 Foreign products become increasingly competitive in world markets.
4 Imports to the USA begin providing significant competition.

These distinct phases are still used today to outline the international product cycle. This cycle begins with the product being developed and manufactured, for example, in the US for high-income markets, subsequently being introduced into other markets in the form of exports. The second phase begins to emerge as the technology is developed further and becomes more easily transferable. Companies in other countries then begin manufacturing and, because of lower transportation and labour costs, are able to undercut the American manufacturers in certain markets.

The third phase is characterized by foreign companies competing against US exports which, in turn, leads to a further decline in the market for US exports. Typically, it is at this stage that US companies either begin to withdraw from selected markets or, in an attempt to compete more effectively, begin investing in manufacturing capacity overseas to regain sales.

The fourth and final stage begins when foreign companies, having established a strong presence in their home and export markets, start the process of exporting to the US and begin competing against the products produced domestically.

It is these four stages, Vernon suggests, that illustrate graphically how American automobile firms have found themselves being squeezed out of their domestic markets having enjoyed a monopoly in the US car market originally.

Although the product life cycle provides an interesting insight into the evolution of multinational operations, it should to be recognized that it provides only a partial explanation of world trade as products do not inevitably follow this pattern. First, competition today is international rather than domestic for all goods and services. Consequently, there is a reduced time lag between product research, development and production, leading to the simultaneous appearance of a standardized product in major world markets. Second, it is not production in the highly labour-intensive industries that is moving to the low labour-cost countries, but the capital-intensive industries such as electronics, creating the anomalous situation of basing production for high-value, high-technology goods in the countries least able to afford them. Nor does the model go very far in explaining the rapid development of companies networking production and marketing facilities across many countries. Thus, global business integration and sharing of R&D, technological and business resources is seen as a more relevant explanation of today's world trade.

Barriers to world trade

Marketing barriers

While countries have many reasons for wishing to trade with each other, it is also true to say that all too frequently an importing nation will take steps to inhibit the inward flow of goods and services.

One of the reasons international trade is different from domestic trade is that it is carried on between different political units, each one a sovereign nation exercising control over its own trade. Although all nations control their foreign trade, they vary in terms of the degree of control. Each nation or trading bloc invariably establishes trade laws that favour their indigenous companies and discriminate against foreign ones.

Thus, at the same time as trade has been developing worldwide, so has the body of regulations and barriers to trade. The WTO lists the technical barriers to trade that countries use in their attempts to protect their economy from imports. The main protagonists are seen as the USA, Italy, France and Germany.

However, the major barriers to trade are becoming increasingly covert, i.e. non-tariff barriers which are often closely associated with the cultural heritage of a country and very difficult to overcome. The complex distribution patterns in Japan are one such example. Thus, while Japan is seen not to have many overt barriers, many businesses experience great difficulties when trying to enter the Japanese market. In Russia recently 167 500 Motorola handsets were seized at a Moscow airport. They were alleged to have been smuggled, to be counterfeit, to violate a Russian patent and to be a danger to public health. As a result some 50 000, it was claimed, were destroyed by the Interior Ministry, but surprisingly, a large number of Motorola phones appeared on the Russian black market. Whatever the rights and wrongs of the intentions, trade distortion practices can provide nightmare scenarios for the international marketer. It is thus important to be aware of the practices of the countries being targeted and the types of barriers companies face. Trade distortion practices can be grouped into two basic categories: **tariff** and **non-tariff barriers**, as illustrated in Figure 2.2.

Tariff barriers   Tariffs are direct taxes and charges imposed on imports. They are generally simple, straightforward and easy for the country to administer. While they are a barrier to trade, they are a visible and known quantity and so can be accounted for by companies when developing their marketing strategies.

FIGURE 2.2   Market entry barriers

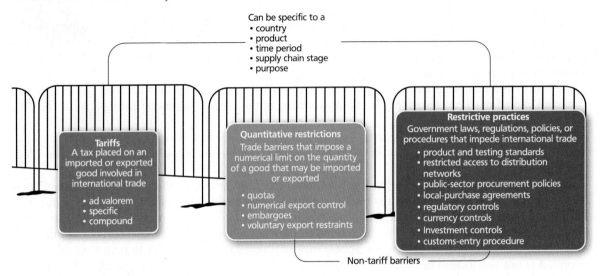

Tariffs are used by poorer nations as the easiest means of collecting revenue. The Bahamas, for example, has a minimum import tax of 30 per cent on all goods, and some products are taxed even higher. Illustration 2.3 gives an example of India's use of tariffs to try and protect its developing industries but also encourage foreign investment.

Tariffs are often imposed to simply protect the home producer, as in the US and Australia. Both of these countries have high tariff walls for certain industries they wish to protect – for example, agricultural products. The trend towards the lowering of tariff barriers across the globe in recent years (the average tariff is now 5 per cent whereas in 1945 it was 45 per cent), together with the opening up of new markets to foreign investment, notably Asia and South America, has greatly complicated the decision for many companies as to where to place manufacturing facilities.

These trends have made global production much more possible, but it has also reduced the need for many overseas plants. Markets that previously demanded local production facilities because tariff levels made importing prohibitive can now be supplied from non-domestic sources.

A good example of these dynamics can be seen in Australia in the automotive sector. Tariffs on imported cars have fallen from 57.5 per cent to 5 per cent. Japanese manufacturers, therefore, found they no longer needed to have plants in Australia to serve the market.

Tariffs can take many forms, as can be seen in Figure 2.2. The most common, however, are:

- *Specific*: Charges are imposed on particular products either by weight or volume and usually stated in the local currency.

- *Ad valorem*: A straight percentage of the import price.

- *Discriminatory*: In this case the tariff is charged against goods coming from a particular country, either where there is a trade imbalance or for political purposes.

Non-tariff barriers   In the past 40 years, the world has seen a gradual reduction in tariff barriers in most developed nations. However, in parallel to this, non-tariff barriers have substantially increased. Non-tariff barriers are much more elusive and can be more easily disguised. The effect can, however, be more devastating because they are an unknown quantity and are much less predictable.

Non-tariff barriers take many different forms:

- Increased government participation in trade is one that is gaining more dominance and which is used by nations to gain competitive advantage, as in the case of the US wheat subsidy previously discussed.

- Customs entry procedures can also impede trade. These take many forms: administrative hold-ups, safety regulations, subsidies and differing technical standards are just a few. To import goods into

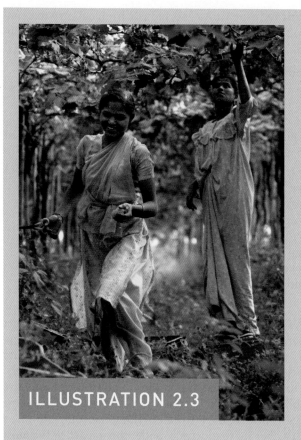

ILLUSTRATION 2.3

Indian wine: Protected or not protected?

It is predicted that 10 per cent of the population in India drink wine; this means the target market is 125 million people. However, wine production in India has just started to increase again after a sharp decline in production, following the Mumbai terror attacks in 2008. There are over 65 wineries in India. Currently, wine production is 11.5 million litres per year which equates to 1.3 million cases of wine. Around 85 per cent of these are located in Maharashtra, Nashik, Pune, Baramati and Sangli and between them are the top five Indian players (Château Indage, Sula, Grover, Vinsura and Reveilo). The increase in younger Indian citizens drinking wine and the growth in tourism means there is a positive outlook for Indian wineries.

As there is such a large target market, wineries in France, Australia and Italy have become interested and are now the top three importers of wine to India. The amount of wine imported worldwide to India is low at 4.4 million litres equating to 490 000 cases.

One of the reasons that wine imports to India are low is the high tariffs of 150 per cent and legislative barriers which means there are huge obstacles to foreign wine producers. In addition to the 150 per cent custom tariff, foreign importers also have to pay 4 per cent special additional tax, 1 per cent customs landing charge and a 5 per cent clearing house fee. The high taxes mean that a bottle of wine needs to be sold at a price at least ten times its production/marketing/distribution cost. The Indian wine industry is in favour of the wine taxes for foreign importers of wine as they argue it gives them an opportunity to develop their businesses and gain a good reputation without having to compete with global brands. The government also introduced protection tariffs to give domestic firms opportunities to grow.

More recently, however, the Indian government increased the VAT tariff on domestic Indian wine from 70 per cent to 150 per cent. This now makes domestic Indian wines as expensive, if not more expensive, than foreign wine brands. This strategy no longer protects the local wineries who are now competing head to head with global wine brands on a price basis.

Question

1 In light of the Indian experience, evaluate the arguments for and against the use of tariffs on the Indian wine industry.

some economic regions, businesses experience 'bloated border bureaucracy'. To import goods into high income countries, on average, seven documents are required, which are all signed by three administrative departments, which means border delays are around 14 days. However, importing goods into Sub-Saharan Africa is much more bureaucratic as, on average, 13 documents are required, each signed by 30 administrative departments, which means border delays last around 60 days.

Therefore, the need for customs modernization and harmonization has become a priority for companies who find their operations severely hampered by 'bloated bureaucratic' requirements and administrative delays at borders and which are likely to get worse as economic globalization gathers pace.

Clearly the extent of customs delays and bureaucratic red tape varies enormously from country to country but everywhere there is a need for governments to take account of business needs for simple, transparent, coordinated and harmonized customs procedures.

■ Quantitative restrictions such as quotas are another barrier. These are limits on the amount of goods that may enter a country. An import quota can be more restrictive than a tariff as there is less flexibility in responding to it. The Japanese car industry faced quotas both in Europe and the US and so developed manufacturing capacity in these markets as a means of overcoming the barriers. The US also imposes quotas on imports from China. However, China, according to the US, has been transhipping products through other ports such as Hong Kong in order to circumvent the quotas.

■ Financial controls were last seen in the UK in the mid-1970s but have been used recently in Mexico and South America where high inflation and lack of **hard currency** required stringent monetary controls. This is probably the most complete tool for the regulation of foreign trade as it gives the government a monopoly of all dealings in foreign exchange. A domestic company earning foreign exchange from exporting must sell it to the national bank and, if goods from abroad need to be bought, a company has to apply for foreign exchange. Thus foreign currency is scarce. The **International Monetary Fund** has placed stringent controls on several countries, in particular, Indonesia, Brazil and Argentina. The latter countries especially have huge external debts which are viewed as unsustainable.

Countries practising exchange controls tend to favour the import of capital goods rather than consumer goods. The other major implication to companies operating in foreign markets is the restrictions on repatriating profits in foreign currency, requiring either countertrade dealings or the use of distorted transfer prices to get profits home (see Chapter 11 on pricing issues).

Non-tariff barriers become much more prevalent in times of recession. In the US and Europe we have witnessed the mobilization of quite strong political lobby groups, as indigenous industries which have come under threat lobby their governments to take measures to protect them from international competition.

The last major era of protectionism was in the 1930s. During that decade, under the impact of the most disastrous trade depression in recorded history, countries around the world adopted high tariffs and abandoned their policies of free trade. In 1944 there was a reaction against the high tariff policy of the 1930s and significant efforts were made to move the world back to free trade. In the next section we will look at the global institutions that have been developed since that time to foster world trade and provide a trade climate in which such barriers can be reduced.

In the 1930s world trade was at low ebb, protectionism was rife and economies were strangling themselves. Several initiatives were born, primarily out of the 1944 Bretton Woods conference, to create an infrastructure that fostered trading relations. These initiatives fell into three areas:

■ *Need for international capital*: the International Bank for Reconstruction and Development (IBRD).

■ *International liquidity*: International Monetary Fund.

■ *Liberalization of international trade and tariffs*: General Agreement on Tariffs and Trade, which became the World Trade Organization.

International Bank for Reconstruction and Development (IBRD)

The World Bank, officially called the International Bank for Reconstruction and Development, was founded together with the International Monetary Fund (IMF) in 1944. The World Bank began operating in June 1946 and membership of the Bank is open to all members of the IMF. Currently, there are 188 member countries. The Bank is owned and controlled by its member governments. Each member country subscribes to shares for an amount relative to its economic strength. The largest shareholder in the World Bank at the moment is the United States.

The World Bank is a vital source of financial and technical assistance to developing countries around the world. They help governments in developing countries reduce poverty by providing them with money and technical expertise they need for a wide range of projects – education, health, infrastructure, communications, government reforms and for many other purposes. Most recent Bank lending to developing countries by the IBRD and its sister organization the International Development Agency (IDA) totalled just under US$47 billion. The IDA is the part of the World Bank that helps the world's poorest countries. Established in 1960, IDA aims to reduce poverty by providing interest-free credits and grants for programmes that boost economic growth, reduce inequalities and improve people's living conditions. The IDA complements the International Bank for Reconstruction and Development (IBRD) which serves middle-income countries with capital investment and advisory service.

The scope of the Bank's operations has increased phenomenally during the past two decades. It now provides more than five times as much financial help to developing countries than it did 20 years ago. The Bank provides support for a wide variety of projects related to agriculture, education, industry, electricity, rural development, tourism, transportation, population planning, urban development, water supply and telecommunications. The Bank lends money only for productive purposes and gives serious consideration to the prospects of repayment before granting the loan.

While the countries who are members subscribe to the share capital of the World Bank, it relies mainly on private investors for its financial resources through borrowing in various capital markets. In this way, private investors become involved in the development efforts of developing countries. Since the IBRD obtains most of its funds on commercial terms, it charges its borrowers a commercial rate of interest. Loans are usually repayable over a 20-year period.

This has led to what has been euphemistically termed the 'debt crisis'. Many of the poor developing countries, recipients of large capital loans, are finding it impossible to meet the burden of debt facing them. Some of this debt is unpayable when the interest on the debt is greater than what the country produces. However, in some cases this is what is known as 'odious debt', debt incurred by undemocratic countries and misspent. Spokespersons often request rich countries to 'write off' the debt of poorer countries. But lending to poor countries has increased by 60 per cent from US$11.4bn (£7.1bn) a year in 2009 to US$18.5bn in 2013 (The Guardian 2014). The World Bank Group provides debt relief to the poorest countries through the HIPC Initiative and the Multilateral Debt Relief Initiative (MDRI). The Initiative calls for the voluntary provision of debt relief by all creditors, whether multilateral, bilateral or commercial, and aims to provide a fresh start to countries with a foreign debt that places too great a burden on export earnings or fiscal revenues.

However, since the global banking crisis the level of debt has become a heavy burden to a number of major exporting countries as well as developing countries. It was expected, following the banking crises, that some of the major developed economies would strategically choose to reduce their debt over the last few years. This did not occur. Indeed no major economy reduced its debt. To further show the effect that the banking crises had on the world's economy, 14 countries have actually increased their debt-to-GDP percentage ratio including Japan, Portugal and Greece. See Table 2.4 for information regarding the 12 highest debt-to-GDP per cent ratio countries.

Following the Great Depression in the 1930s and the accumulating years of monetary devaluation and exchange rate difficulties, the United Nations realized that there was a need to help poorer countries obtain fair loans and opportunities for growth. The International Development Association (IDA) was established in 1960 to help meet this need. It was made an affiliate of the World Bank and was to be administered in accordance with the Bank's established methods. The IDA makes soft loans of about US$7 billion annually. Almost all are granted for a period of 15 years without interest, except for a small charge to cover administrative overheads. Repayment of loans does not start until after a ten-year period of grace. Both the IDA and the IBRD lay down stringent requirements that have to be met before any loans are granted. In many cases this has meant that in order to be granted the investment the countries have had to make quite hard political decisions in order to achieve the balanced budget required. In some cases this has led to severe hardship and social disorder, for which the institutions have been severely criticized.

International Monetary Fund (IMF)

The objective of the IMF was to regain the stability in international exchange rates that had existed under the gold standard. Although the system of pegged rates failed to keep up with the growth in international trade, the functions of the IMF have continued to develop.

Table 2.4   Debt-to-GDP ratio

Rank	Country	Debt-to-GDP ratio[1] %
1	Japan	400
2	Ireland	390
3	Singapore	382
4	Portugal	358
5	Belgium	327
6	Netherlands	325
7	Greece	317
8	Spain	313
9	Denmark	302
10	Sweden	290
11	France	280
12	Italy	259

Source: McKinsey Global Institute (2015), 'Debt and (not much) Deleveraging', McKinsey & Company.

[1]Includes debt of households, non-financial corporations, and government; 2015 data for advanced economies and China; 2013 data for other developing economies.

The main function is to provide short-term international liquidity to countries with **balance of payments deficit** problems, enabling them to continue to trade internationally. The IMF, with its 188 members, provides a forum for international monetary cooperation enabling the making of reciprocal agreements among countries and the monitoring of the balance of payments positions of countries. Thus, it serves to lessen the risk of nations taking arbitrary actions against each other, as happened before it came into being, and it can also sound a warning bell for nations with potential liquidity problems.

The IMF's seal of approval is, for emerging markets, essential to attract foreign investment and finance. It is also a precondition of financial assistance from the Fund. Georgia, Ukraine, Hungary, Iceland, Latvia, Pakistan, Turkey and Sri Lanka have all been recent recipients of IMF funding. Earlier this decade Brazil and Argentina were recipients of the Fund's largest-ever loans. The countries which are currently the biggest borrowers are Greece, Portugal, Ireland and Ukraine. The IMF experienced a sharp decline in its lending business in recent years until the present global financial crisis led to a resurgence in lending. Its role has also started to change as it took on the global role of examining policies that underpin prosperity and poverty and tries to guide nations to the former. In 2014 the Group of 20 (G20) empowered the IMF by making it the key lending institution for crisis-affected countries in need of balance of payments support. As a result, the IMF's lending portfolio has increased over the past year and the cumulative amount of money pledged is US$ 1.0 trillion billion.

The World Trade Organization

The predecessor of the World Trade Organization (WTO) was the General Agreement on Tariffs and Trade (GATT). Established in January 1948, it was a treaty not an organization, with the signatories being contracting parties. The WTO began and continued with eight trade liberalization 'rounds'. These entailed tens of thousands of tariff concessions on industrial goods and covered trade flows worth hundreds of

MANAGEMENT CHALLENGE 2.1

Do high debts mean high risk?

Following the world banking crisis, governments had to reassure the world that their country was economically viable. Table 2.4 gives a ranking of the top 12 debt-to-GDP ratio by country.

their citizens' pension fund. Singaporean's household debt is at 15 per cent. The Singaporean government recently capped the amount of money its citizens can borrow, either through loans or credit cards. Singapore's corporate debt is high for two specific reasons. First, many foreign banks and other financial organizations have chosen Singapore in which to set up a regional headquarters; second, many of them and also businesses in the Asia region raise debt in Singapore and use the money to expand internationally.

Greece's government debt is high as public spending has soared over the last 7 to 10 years.

Sources of debt	Debt-to-GDP %	Total	Real economy debt change, 2007–14 by %		
			Government	Corporate	Household
Singapore	382	129	22	92	15
Greece	317	103	70	13	20

Singapore and Greece have high debt-to-GDP percentage ratios. Underlying the debt-to-GDP percentage ratio are three main sources of debt, which show the real economy debt change (2007–14) by per cent, government debt, corporate debt and household debt. An increase in real economy debt change provides the underlying notion of whether a high debt-to-GDP percentage means the country is at risk or is not at risk. Take for example Singapore and Greece, both have a high debt-to-GDP percentage, however, how Singapore and Greece's debt changed between 2007 and 2014 helps to determine if the country is at risk or not.

Singapore's government debt is 22 per cent. This debt is low and is mainly money put aside for

Additionally, government employees, of which there are many in Greece, received a large salary increase (almost double). Greece has low household and corporate debt.

Questions

1 Compare and contrast the different types of debt that make up the total real economy debt change, 2007–14 by percentage.
2 Compare and contrast the real economy debt change of Singapore and Greece.
3 Which country has a high debt but is of low risk?

Source: McKinsey Global Institute (2015), 'Debt and (not much) Deleveraging', McKinsey & Company.

billions of dollars. In all, 23 countries participated in the 1948 opening round when 45 000 tariff concessions were agreed, covering US$10 billion worth of trade. Under the first eight GATT rounds, the average tariff on manufactured products in the industrial world fell from around 45 per cent in 1947 to under 5 per cent. This has been an important engine of world economic growth which, in turn, has stimulated further increases in world trade. Signatories to these treaties account for well over 90 per cent of world trade.

More recently the WTO has increased its focus to adapt to current worldwide issues. The Fourth Global Review of Aid for Trade provided an agenda for future discussions 'post 2015'. The WTO now engages members to discuss value chains between countries, particularly how developed countries can engage with the LDCs (Least Developing Countries) in goods and services, and share knowledge and help with infrastructure and skills. The WTO currently has 160 members and another 24 countries, including China, Ukraine and Turkey who have observer status.

The WTO generally encourages discussion and participation in multilateral trade and most-favoured-nation status which obliges each signatory to the treaties to grant the same treatment to all other members on a non-discriminatory basis. It has evolved regulations which it has tried to enforce through its adjudicatory disputes panels and complaints procedures. Since its start in 1995, over 400 disputes have been through the dispute settlement mechanism of the WTO. The USA, the EU, China and India have been its biggest users. Last year major WTO members including the EU and the USA launched 77 complaints against China with a value of about US$10 billion, 40 per cent of the complaints coming from India. Most of the cases against China are related to its cost advantage of cheap labour costs. India recently announced a six-month ban on imports of toys from China in a move that has been seen by observers to be aimed at protecting Indian manufacturers from cheaper Chinese imports. The most notable disputes between the USA and China have been over copyright, piracy and the use of brand names. Between the USA and the EU it has often been over quotas and the enforcement of regulations. The USA considers the EU's refusal to approve genetically modified (GM) foods illegal under the WTO trade rules and launched a formal complaint against them. Barring US producers from exporting GM crops to the EU is estimated to cost US producers several hundred million dollars a year. Interestingly, however, the WTO has recently allowed the EU to impose up to US$4 billion of tariffs against America as recompense for a US foreign tax sales break which the WTO has deemed an illegal subsidy. However, India has also been at odds with the USA and Europe over their developing wine industry as Illustration 2.3 illustrates.

The main aim of the WTO is to promote a free market international trade system. It promotes trade by:

- working to reduce tariffs
- prohibiting import/export bans and quotas
- eliminating discrimination against foreign products and services
- eliminating other impediments to trade, commonly known as non-tariff barriers.

WTO are continuing to liberalize trading rules and labour equalities in a number of areas, including agricultural subsidies, textiles and clothing, services, technical barriers to trade, trade-related investments and rules of origin.

Over three-quarters of the WTO members are developing countries. The Doha Round (2001) was dubbed the Development Round as it specifically aimed to ease trading restrictions for these countries. It is estimated that developing countries face trade barriers four times those applied by rich countries to each other. These barriers reduce export earnings by US$100 billion per annum. Two of the main problem areas for negotiators are the international trading of textiles and agriculture, which accounts for 70 per cent of developing countries' exports. Average tariffs for textiles are 15–20 per cent compared to an average of 3 per cent for industrialized goods. In the EU and the USA agricultural subsidies amount to US$1 billion per day, six times the annual amount spent on aid by these two regions.

Progress towards the WTO's objectives has been seriously stalled several times. One of the main problems has been the USA's unease due to the developing countries refusal to open up markets to the extent demanded. Of equal concern to the developing countries is the refusal by the USA to reduce the trade-distorting subsidies which developing countries view as leading to the unlawful dumping of produce from the USA onto global markets. Of equal concern is the EU's refusal to reduce the agricultural tariffs which block developing countries from EU markets.

It is believed by some that during the 50 years of global economic expansion under the auspices of GATT, despite the long-term commitments to multilateral trade and all the work to develop a free multilateral trading system across the world, what we have in reality are a series of giant **trading blocs**. We will explore some of the more important ones in the next section.

The development of world trading groups

The formation of the European Monetary Union in 1999 was, perhaps, the most significant trading bloc to be formed. When the **Single European Market** was formed in 1993, the United States effectively became the second largest market in the world. Given the rise of the economies of China and India, the question that interests many observers of the global competitive battles now being fought, is who will dominate the global markets of the future? There is a fear that the world economy may divide into three enormous trading blocs dominated by the world's major trading regions, the EU, NAFTA and China/East Asia, rather than a world of multilateral free trade, particularly if the implementation of the Doha Declaration does not fully succeed. Some commentators argue that national economies are becoming vulnerable to the needs of the trading blocs within which trade is free, currencies are convertible, access to banking is open and contracts are enforceable by law. While this scenario may be a long way from the present position, we are already seeing the growing strength of trading blocs such as the North American Free Trade Association (NAFTA), **Association of South East Asian Nations (ASEAN)** and the European Monetary Union.

In this section we will examine in detail the regional trading blocs that are emerging, but first let us examine different forms of trade agreements.

Forms of market agreement

There are nine levels of market association ranging from limited trade cooperation to full-blown political union (see Table 2.5). At the lower level of association, agreements can be purely for economic cooperation in some form, perhaps a decision to consult on or coordinate trade policies. At the next level of cooperation, there will be the development of trade agreements between countries on either a bilateral or multilateral basis. Often these are for a particular sector – for example the multi-fibre agreement on textiles. Sometimes such agreements, especially trade preference ones, will act as a forerunner to closer ties. As far as formal trade groupings are concerned, there are five major forms: free trade areas, customs unions, common markets, economic unions and political unions.

Free trade area

The free trade area type of agreement requires different countries to remove all tariffs among the agreement's members. Let us assume that there are three nations – A, B and C – that agree to a free trade area agreement and abolish all tariffs among themselves to permit free trade. Beyond the free trade area A, B and C may impose tariffs as they choose. The EEA (European Economic Area) formed between the EU and EFTA (European Free Trade Area) and the LAFTA (Latin American Free Trade Area) illustrate the free trade area type of agreement, as does NAFTA, the agreement between the USA, Canada and Mexico, and the Asian Free Trade Area (AFTA).

Customs union

In addition to requiring abolition of internal tariffs among the members, a customs union further requires the members to establish common external tariffs. To continue with the example (countries A, B and C), under a customs union agreement B would not be permitted to have a special relationship with country X – A, B and C would have a common tariff policy towards X. Prior to 1993, the EC was, in reality, a customs union. Both the Economic Community of Central African States (ECCAS) and the Economic Community of West African States (ECOWAS) have the objective of being a customs union. **Global System of Trade Preferences Among Developing Countries (GSTP)** is a system allowing for preferential trade between developing countries. The main purpose of the GSTP was, and still is, to help developing countries cooperate economically and discuss ways to develop trade through open and fair negotiations; to the benefit of all.

Common market

In a common market type of agreement, not only do members abolish internal tariffs among themselves and levy common external tariffs, they also permit free flow of all factors of production among themselves. Under such an agreement, countries A, B and C would not only remove all tariffs and quotas among themselves and impose common tariffs against other countries such as country X, but would also allow capital and labour to move freely within their boundaries as if they were one country. This means that, for example, a resident of country A is free to accept a position in country C without a work permit.

The European Union is essentially a common market, with full freedom of movement of all factors of production. Similarly, the Andean nations in South America have formed ANCOM, the Central American

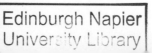

Table 2.5 Main types of trade associations

Type	Description	Degree of policy harmonization among members	Common external tariff	Free movement of capital and people	Example
Economic cooperation	Broad agreement for consultations on and possible coordination of economic trade policies	None/very low	No	No	Canada–EC framework agreement, APEC
Bilateral or multi-lateral trade treaty	Trade regulation and often, but not necessarily, liberalization in one or more specified sector(s)	Low	No	No	The Peru, Chile Accord
Sectoral free trade agreement	Removal of internal tariffs in a specified sector may include non-tariff barrier reduction	Medium (within specified sector(s))	No	No	The multi-fibre agreement
Trade preference agreement	Preferred trade terms (often including tariff reduction) in all or most sectors, possibly leading to free trade area	Low/medium	No	No	South African Development Cone (SADC)
Free trade area (or agreement)	Removal of internal tariffs and some reduction of non-tariff barriers in all or most sectors	Medium	No	No	ASEAN, NAFTA
Customs union	Free trade area but with a common external tariff, harmonization of trade policy toward third countries	Medium/high	Yes	Possibly	**ECOWAS & EECSA** **ECOWAS** COMESA, ANCOM, CACM Mercosur
Common market	Customs union, but with provisions for the free movement of capital and people, removal of all trade barriers, elaborate supranational institutions, significant harmonization of internal market structure and external policies				European single market
Economic union	Common market, but with integration of monetary policies, possibly common currency, significant weakening of national powers of member states	Very high	Yes	Yes	European Monetary Union **CEMAC**
Political	Full or partial federalism, including sharing of powers between supranational institutions and national governments	Highest	Yes	Yes	Would resemble federal states (e.g. US, Canada, Germany)

nations have grouped themselves as CACM, the Caribbean community have formed CARICOM and Southern Africa have formed the Common Market for Eastern and Southern Africa (COMESA).

Economic union

Under an economic union agreement, common market characteristics are combined with the harmonization of economic policy and member countries are expected to pursue common fiscal and monetary policies. Ordinarily this means a synchronization of money supply, interest rates, regulation of capital market and taxes. The Economic and Monetary Community of Central African States (CEMAC), has the objective of being an economic union. In effect, an economic union calls for a supranational authority to design an economic policy for an entire group of nations. This is the objective of the European Monetary Union.

Political union

This is the ultimate market agreement among nations. It includes the characteristics of economic union and requires, additionally, political harmony among the members. Essentially, it means nations merging to form a new political entity: Germany and the USA are perhaps the closest examples historically. Yugoslavia, which was created after the First World War, was a political union, as was the Soviet Union, although neither of these still exist.

Figure 2.3 shows the major trading regions to have developed significantly in the past decade, together with their member countries. In the following sections we will examine these major trading groups and the developments they have undergone.

FIGURE 2.3 Regional trading areas of the world

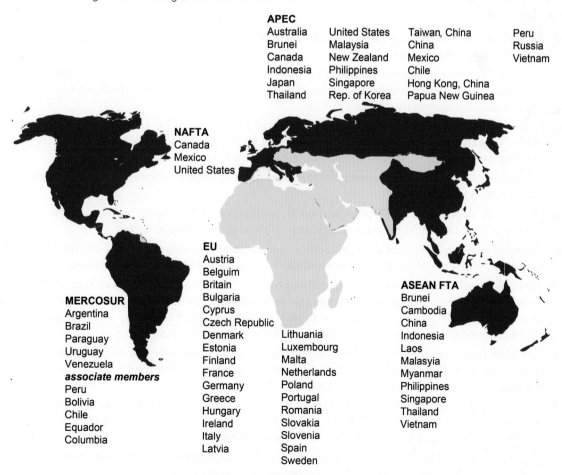

APEC

Australia	United States	Taiwan, China	Peru
Brunei	Malaysia	China	Russia
Canada	New Zealand	Mexico	Vietnam
Indonesia	Philippines	Chile	
Japan	Singapore	Hong Kong, China	
Thailand	Rep. of Korea	Papua New Guinea	

NAFTA
Canada
Mexico
United States

MERCOSUR
Argentina
Brazil
Paraguay
Uruguay
Venezuela
associate members
Peru
Bolivia
Chile
Equador
Columbia

EU
Austria
Belguim
Britain
Bulgaria
Cyprus
Czech Republic
Denmark
Estonia
Finland
France
Germany
Greece
Hungary
Ireland
Italy
Latvia
Lithuania
Luxembourg
Malta
Netherlands
Poland
Portugal
Romania
Slovakia
Slovenia
Spain
Sweden

ASEAN FTA
Brunei
Cambodia
China
Indonesia
Laos
Malasyia
Myanmar
Philippines
Singapore
Thailand
Vietnam

The European Union

Since 1987 and the signing of the Single European Act, Europe has undergone momentous changes, the key among these being:

- the creation of the EU and its single market
- formation of the European Monetary Union (EMU)
- the expansion of the European Union (EU) to include members of the European Economic Area (EEA) and Central, Eastern and Southern Europe.

The Single European Market

The formation of the European Union meant that the EU became the largest trading bloc in the world with an estimated population of over 500 million people (2011), making it a powerful competitive force in the global markets. This, of course, was the key objective of the moves towards unification and the formation of the single market across the union. In the early 1980s it was recognized that if European companies were to compete successfully in the increasingly interdependent and global economy, a free and unbridled large internal market was necessary. This would enable companies to develop the critical mass needed to compete globally. The highly fragmented and restricted European market was seen as a major barrier to the ability to compete in global markets.

The EU was formed as a result of the signing of the Single European Act in 1986 which created, within Europe, 'an area without internal priorities in which the free movement of goods, personal services and capital is ensured in accordance with the provision of the Treaty of Rome'.

The key changes were:

- *Removal of tariff barriers*: A single customs check at all intra-EU borders enabling goods and services to move freely across Europe.
- *Removal of technical barriers*: A major impediment to trade was the differing and complex standards required in each country. Harmonization of these standards has paved the way for product standardization throughout Europe.
- *Public procurement*: Public procurement amounts to 17 per cent of EU GNP; in the past only 2 per cent of which went to foreign suppliers. By opening up the market to all European suppliers and by ensuring its enforcement, it is estimated that 17.5 billion Euros are saved per annum.
- *Free movement of labour and workers' rights*: Nationals of member states now have the right to work in other member states.
- *Opening up of professions*: Through mutual recognition of qualifications, professionals in certain categories have their qualifications recognized by other member states.
- *Financial services*: The opening up of banking, insurance and investment services through the introduction of a single banking licence and the harmonization of banking conditions.
- *Transport, haulage and coastal cabotage*: Road haulage permits and quotas have been abolished. A more competitive air transport industry is also being pursued, as is unlimited cabotage for transport through the EU. Trucks are now allowed to pick up goods in any EU country and drop them off where required without the bureaucracy of permits and border documentation.
- *Company law*: Several European developments in the area of company law are taking place in the fields of takeover bids, health and safety, cross-border merger, etc. The road to greater control from Brussels is now becoming especially apparent in this area.
- *Fiscal barriers*: There are many EU variations of fiscal policies, e.g. VAT. The UK has a standard rate of 20 per cent but VAT rates vary across the EU from 7 per cent in the Canary Islands to 27 per cent in Hungary. Moves are being made to reduce these disparities.
- *The environment*: The European Environment Agency was established to try to provide an integrated and Europe-wide policy for environmental protection.

Most analysts agree that the formation of the EU has greatly enhanced market opportunities for European companies. Since its formation it is estimated to have created about 2.5 million jobs and generated prosperity equivalent to 1 trillion Euros. As a result of its formation, there is a potential home market of 500 million consumers for companies within its walls. Intraregional trading among EU members accounts for 75 per cent of all trade. With such interdependency, it is little wonder that so much effort has been put into completing the unification. However, 15 or so years on, while most goods are now crossing Europe's national borders with little or no hindrance, the liberalization of trade in services has not made the same progress. Europe's service providers are hindered by all sorts of petty bureaucratic rules, often justified on health, safety or consumer protection grounds, which discourage them from entering new European markets. In some cases, the European Commission has itself hampered progress by granting certain industries exemptions from the normal rules of fair competition, although these exemptions are starting to be undone.

European Monetary Union

The idea of a single European currency had been around since the early 1960s. As trade between member countries increased, various attempts were made to stabilize exchange rates. Previous systems such as the **Exchange Rate Mechanism** (ERM) attempted to create monetary stability through a system of fixed and floating exchange rates. This proved, however, to be incapable of coping with capital flows, which resulted in problems for sterling and the lira in September 1992, with the remaining currencies also facing problems the following year. Pressure for further integration in the Community resulted in the move to monetary union and a single European currency. This created the **Economic and Monetary Union (EMU)**, sometimes called the Eurozone as countries within the zone all use the Euro as a domestic currency. Britain and countries such as Sweden and some recent members to the EU are not members of the Eurozone. Firms from these countries however, trading in the European Union, are affected by the Euro and economic activity in the Eurozone. Companies not in the Eurozone have to convert their customer invoices and accounts, credit notes and prices into Euros. Company computer systems for customer and/ or supplier accounts have had to be adapted to deal with Euros as many companies who operate across Europe follow a strategy of pricing all products in Euros. For instance, many retailers such as Marks and Spencer and Zara price in sterling and the Euro in the UK.

Strategic implications

The EMU was not just a monetary event, but one that has had a serious impact on the real economy. Prices and wages became transparent; consumers now shop around for the best deals; middlemen try to exploit any prevailing regional price differences and margins everywhere are now coming under pressure.

The competitive environment is viewed by many as being tougher under the EMU. The development of the EMU in Europe affected companies both inside and outside the Eurozone, but companies operating inside the Eurozone have had to adjust more quickly than companies operating outside it.

Global European companies such as Hewlett Packard, BMW, Daimler-Benz and Siemens for example, use Eurozone pricing policies. Pharmaceutical companies introduce new drugs across the EU at a single pan-European price. The banks have been significant losers in terms of the business of buying and selling European currencies. The formation of the Single European Payments Area (SEPA), discussed in Chapter 11 has further impacted on the margins previously achieved by European banks. The biggest difference, however, has not been between industries but between efficient, flexible companies and those that have stuck to their old national ways and found it difficult to compete in the new open and competitive landscape.

Companies that have concentrated on their national markets have been particularly vulnerable to takeover or extinction at the hands of their more far-sighted European competitors. Those businesses already used to competing internationally have had a strong advantage. As sources of supply widen, specializations based on national talents have developed further. French and German companies, for example, run call centres from Dublin, where multilingual Irish operators (or continental expatriates) provide advice or take orders over the telephone more cheaply and flexibly than would be possible in the companies' home countries. Another effect of the single currency has been to open the European market for those small and medium-sized companies who have previously concentrated on their domestic customers. It has been estimated that currency fluctuations and the costs of dealing with them previously deterred a third of small and medium-sized German companies from venturing abroad. Many who did export concentrated exclusively on countries where currencies were informally linked to the Deutschmark, such as Austria and the Netherlands.

Widening European membership

Enlargement of the European Union has happened at several stages of its development over the past 50 years, and there have been four previous enlargements.

In 1993 the European Council adopted the Copenhagen Criteria for admission to the EU. These require that member countries attain the following:

- Stable institutions guaranteeing democracy and the rule of law.
- A functioning market economy, as well as the capacity to cope with the competitive pressure and market forces within the EU.
- The ability to fulfill membership obligations, including adherence to the aims of political, economic and monetary union.

To date 12 countries from Southern, Central and Eastern Europe have joined the EU. Turkey and Macedonia are in the application stages of accession.

The 12 new member states of Central and Eastern Europe have enjoyed a higher average percentage growth rate than their Western European counterparts since joining the EU. The reasons for this include government commitments to stable monetary policy, export-oriented trade policies, low flat-tax rates and the utilization of relatively cheap labour. It is reasonable to expect such a differential to continue in the medium term and as such the member states of Central and Eastern Europe may be where the exciting market opportunities are in Europe. Illustration 2.4 discusses one such example.

However, given that the EU is now a tariff free trade area, the inclusion of Central Europe makes the disparities between the wealth of members more pronounced. Denmark is one of the wealthiest countries of the 27 EU members with a GDP *per capita* of US$59 832. This compares to a GDP *per capita* in Portugal of US$21 733, Poland of US$12 877 and Bulgaria of US$7499. The EU average is US$32 600. Clearly this poses challenges for marketers trying to establish a consistent marketing position across the European Union.

The Free Trade Area of the Americas

The North American Free Trade Area (NAFTA) consisting of the US, Canada and Mexico, is regarded as the world's richest single market, with a combined population of 444 million people and has a combined economy of over US$17 trillion. Together the NAFTA members account for 34 per cent of the world's GDP.

The main provisions of the NAFTA agreement aimed to:

- Eliminate tariffs on manufactured goods.
- Eliminate tariffs on 57 per cent of the agricultural produce from Mexico.
- Harmonize and streamline customs procedures and bureaucracy.
- Liberalize telecommunications, transport, textiles, banking and finance.
- Establish a NAFTA trade commission to settle trade disputes.

The attractive feature of NAFTA is that by virtue of the fact that Mexico is at a different stage of economic development from the US and Canada, the gains through specialization have been relatively large, allowing the US to specialize in more complex products that are intensive in their use of knowledge, technology and capital equipment.

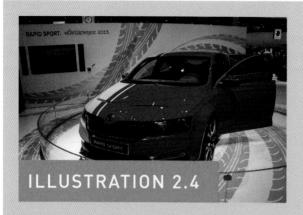

ILLUSTRATION 2.4

Škoda: From shameful to stardom

The Czech word Škoda means pity or shame so on seeing a passing Škoda car, Czechs used to say 'there goes a shame' – and nobody would argue much. Today, Škoda Autos has completely overhauled its image and is one of the star businesses in the Czech Republic. Škoda's mantra is to be innovative but ensure new ideas, technology and production are for the benefit of the customer under the 'Simply Clever' aim.

Škoda is unique in the Czech Republic as it is the only car manufacturer that produces and develops cars. The investment, and of course international sales, makes Škoda the largest production company in Central and Eastern Europe according to Deloitte CEE TOP 500.

However, it is not just about building cars that makes Škoda so popular. The brand image has won the 'Rhodos Award for Image in non-food manufacturing'.

Prof. Dr H.C. Winfried Vahland, chairman of the board of management, states that one of the key elements that make Škoda successful is Škoda's hardworking team; all 25 000 of them from engineers to marketers and patternmakers to designers. The proof in that statement shows in their impressive list of awards:

1st in the Czech Top 100

'Best Industry Employer'

'Top Automobile Industry Employer'

'Best Career Website'

Škoda is also keen to invest time and money in graduates from domestic universities where they gained 2nd place with the Czech Republic Graduate Barometer and the Best Presentation at Job Fairs.

Behind all the glitz and positive news, unfortunately, there are disruptions. Wages in some areas of Škoda are low and workers and their Unions are calling for higher pay rises – or strike action. Further, job layoffs and movement of some jobs to external organizations are also fuelling strike action.

Question

1 Evaluate the reasons for Škoda's success and imminent problems.

Sources: www.praguepost.com; www.deloitte.com; Škoda's Report and Accounts.

The available evidence suggests that this is precisely what has happened. US exports to Mexico of electronic goods, transport equipment and services have increased substantially. Meanwhile, most of the anecdotal evidence about US workers harmed by NAFTA comes from light manufacturing industries and agriculture.

However, it must be said that the scale of change induced by NAFTA is probably quite small relative to other factors impinging on the US economy over the last decade, such as technological change and their foreign policy initiatives.

For many, the creation of NAFTA was a US response to the formation of the single market in Europe. However, for others it has signalled the era of the drive by the US to create a free trade area across the Americas. The **Free Trade Area of the Americas** (FTAA) is a proposed agreement to eliminate or reduce trade barriers among all nations in the American continents (except Cuba) and involves negotiations with the Central American Common Market, the Andean Community and Mercosur. Spearheaded by the United States, the FTAA was intended to unite Latin America and North America in one broad trade accord. However, there is opposition and a number of Latin American and the Caribbean nations have formed The Bolivarian Alliance for the Peoples of Our America (ALBA) in opposition to the FTAA. The ALBA aims to achieve regional economic integration of its members. They use a virtual trading currency called the Sucre and eventually aim for this to become a hard currency. Mercosur is an important trading region for the EU. Discussions began officially in Madrid in 2010 and in 2013 the EU became Mercosur's first trading partner. The benefit of the partnership is two-way: the main exports from Mercosur countries are from agriculture whilst on the flip side the EU's main export to Mercosur is machinery and transport equipment. Overall, 20 per cent of Mercosur's trade is with the EU. Together the trade between EU-Mercosur is €110 billion (European Commission 2014).

The Asia Pacific Trading Region

Asia Pacific Economic Cooperation

The Asia Pacific Economic Cooperation (APEC) is essentially a forum among 21 member economies who border on the Pacific. Thus, it includes the NAFTA member states, Russia, China and Japan, as well as the founding father Australia, New Zealand, ASEAN nations and Peru and Chile in South America. APEC members account for approximately 40.5 per cent of the world's population, approximately 54.2 per cent of world GDP and about 43.7 per cent of world trade.

The APEC forum has worked to reduce tariffs and other trade barriers across the Asia–Pacific region, with the aim of creating efficient domestic economies and increasing exports. Key to achieving APEC's vision are what are referred to as the 'Bogor Goals' of free and open trade and investment in the Asia–Pacific region. It has three key objectives:

■ to develop and strengthen the multilateral trading system across APEC
■ to increase the interdependence and prosperity of member economies
■ to promote sustainable economic growth in the region.

Some members of the group would like an Asia–Pacific trading bloc to emerge because they fear being excluded from traditional US markets.

Combining FTAA, East Asian and Australasian countries into one Asia–Pacific bloc would mean that nearly 70 per cent of their trade would be intraregional. However, there is marked resistance among Asian members of APEC to an enhanced role of the group. The US is giving a high priority to the APEC grouping and intends to forge closer trade and investment ties across the Pacific.

The Asia–Pacific region has the fastest growth in the world. Asia is the principal export region for US products. Trans-Pacific trade is 50 per cent greater than its transatlantic trade and more than 40 per cent of US trade is now in the Asian region. To foster this growth, the United States supports a more active APEC. It is from this region too that a number of the new global brands are emerging, as discussed in Illustration 2.5.

The members of the Association of South East Asian Nations (ASEAN) – Thailand, Indonesia, Singapore, Brunei, Malaysia, the Philippines, Vietnam, Myanmar, Cambodia and Laos – plan to complete the formation of the ASEAN free trade zone (AFTA) by 2015 and form an Asian Economic Region by 2020.

ASEAN is already well on the way to creating a largely tariff-free market of 580 million people, nearly one-tenth of the global population. The goal is to increase 'the region's competitive advantage as a production base geared for the world market'. The primary mechanism for achieving this is the Common Effective Preferential Tariff (CEPT) scheme, which established a schedule for phased tariff reductions to a rate between 0–5 per cent. Total trade of the ASEAN members is now US$1 trillion and they have a combined GDP of US$1.5 trillion.

However, some observers are sceptical about the potential development of AFTA. Geographical distances and cultural and political disparities have meant that previous attempts at closer economic integration have failed. These nations are keenly competitive and some members have not kept to agreements to lower trading restrictions. ASEAN has also failed to support action against its rogue state of Myanmar, thus making many doubt the political will of the group. Where EU and NAFTA integration has been based on treaties, in Asia so far it has been based on market forces, the chief of these being the region's fast rate of growth. Asia accounts for about a third of world production. Increasingly growth is also coming from intra-Asian trade, which recent estimates have put as high as 45 per cent.

ILLUSTRATION 2.5

Developing global brands from the Republic of Korea

The Republic of Korea has become a leading country in terms of exports with a 3 per cent share of the world's merchandise export trade (See Table 2.1) making it the 7th biggest exporter. Once a poor country, the Republic of Korea has invested in electronics, developing their own global brands that are sold both domestically and internationally. Currently, the two highest ranked brands in Korea are Samsung and Hyundai.

Samsung is the number one brand in Korea and in 2014 it was ranked 18th in the FT Global 500 companies. Samsung is the largest semi-conductor manufacturer brand. It manufactures many consumer electronic devices including TVs, computers, microwave ovens and communication devices. Often over 50 per cent of products manufactured in the Republic of Korea are sold domestically, but they are clearly gaining recognition and sales worldwide.

The Republic of Korea's most famous communication device is the Samsung Galaxy Smartphone. Domestically, the Samsung Galaxy outsells it main rival, Apple's iPhone. The Samsung Galaxy S6, launched in 2015 at the MWC (Mobile World Congress) was tipped to be the Number 1 Smartphone. Continuous innovation and creativity at Samsung keeps journalists and consumers anticipating the next 'big revolution and evolution'. Samsung's brand helps enforce Korea's country brand as one that is a hub of cutting edge ideas, technology and design.

The Republic of Korea's second best brand is Hyundai, ranked 150 in the FT Global 500 Companies. Hyundai produces high-end luxury cars, SUVs, low-cost cars, together with trucks and commercial vehicles. Whilst Hyundai sells cars in 180 countries mostly through dealerships, their largest target market is in China and India. One of the reasons Hyundai is gaining popularity is their dedication to the brand's aim, which is 'New Thinking, New Possibilities'. With that aim in mind Hyundai continuously challenge and revolutionize car technology, particularly in their low-cost car range.

Questions

1 Evaluate the environmental factors that are fuelling the growth of the super brands Samsung and Hyundai.

2 How could other developing countries grow based on the Republic of Korea's model presented here?

Sources: www.samsung.com; www.hyundai.com; www .ft.com

ASEAN-China Free Trade Area (ACFTA)

A significant development in the progress of ASEAN has been the formation of the China-ASEAN Free Trade Area in 2010. The new free trade area brought together the ASEAN countries and China to create a trading bloc with a combined population of 1.9 billion, a combined GDP of up to US$6 trillion and total trade volume of US$4.5 trillion.

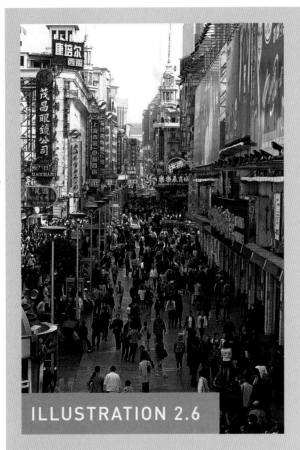

ILLUSTRATION 2.6

China and India: The technology challenge

China is now the third largest buyer of hi-tech goods and services in the world, behind America and Japan. China and India make an interesting contrast in their technological development. They have roughly the same population, but China spends 2.5 times as much on technology as India. China is the world's largest mobile phone market with some 800 million mobile phone users, and has the second largest market for PCs. India has some 545 million mobile phones, enough to serve about 45 per cent of the population, but only about 366 million people or 31 per cent of the population have access to improved sanitation. China has around 384 million Internet users compared with 51 million in India. The two countries are adopting technology at different paces and in different ways.

A further difference is that China's manufacturing strength means hi-tech gear is available locally at low cost, whereas India must import it. India has focused more on software and services, which can be delivered via networks without bureaucratic interference, unlike China which has focused on competing in physical goods. However, India is seen as playing an invaluable role in the global innovation chain. Motorola, Hewlett-Packard, Cisco Systems, Google and other tech giants now rely on their Indian teams to devise software platforms and the tech hubs are in such places as Bangalore. These companies are spawning companies producing their own chip designs, software and pharmaceuticals at an exhilarating pace of innovation.

Question

1 Compare and contrast the opportunities and challenges of competing in the market for a high tech product in India and China.

Source: www.economywatch.com 2010; www.in.reuters.com/.

Barriers to developing a cohesive trading region   While an Asian trading bloc may never have the cohesion of either Europe or America as the fastest-growing economic region in the world, any move towards integration will be watched closely by international competitors. There are particular barriers to developing a liberalized Asian trading bloc. First, there is a huge diversity among the nation states, not just culturally but in historical, religious and economic terms. Japan currently has a GDP per capita of US$39 400, whereas the figure for Myanmar is just US$462. Politically, the countries embrace very different systems. Vietnam and Laos have communist dictatorships, Myanmar and Thailand have military juntas and Brunei is an absolute monarchy. In a number of countries the institutions are either non-existent or too weak to ensure the economic fairness necessary to sustain the progress to regulation of markets and trust in the rule of law which is crucial to any commercial relationship. Furthermore, the geographical area is huge and there are no natural groupings of nation states. Management Challenge 2.2 focuses on the opportunities and challenges that Rwanda poses to companies trying to develop a presence in East Africa.

MANAGEMENT CHALLENGE 2.2

Small businesses help Rwanda recover

Rwanda has received considerable international attention due to the 1994 genocide, in which an estimated 800 000 people were killed. Since then the country has made a recovery and is now considered as a model for developing countries. For example, Rwanda's growth has improved in consecutive years at 4.6 per cent (2013) to 6.5 per cent (2015); and is forecast to grow to 7.1 per cent by 2017.

However, political oppression, lack of free speech and poverty often seem to tarnish the country's positive growth data, but citizens of Rwanda are growing in confidence and are taking care of themselves and their communities. Green activists have persuaded the population that plastic bags damage the environment – so much so they are banned from shops and confiscated at airports. Community action groups are forming to ensure local citizens clean their streets and make their parks and green spaces beautiful and, more importantly, the business dreams of citizens are becoming reality.

Christine Mbabazi began her fashion business in her bedroom in Rwanda's capital city of Kigali. She wanted to promote beautiful African fabric, demonstrating one of the cultural influences of 'what is Africa'. So Christine began designing and sewing for her Christine Creative Collection. Now, through determination she has a boutique on the high street selling both formal and fun clothes.

Cephas Nshimyumuremyi, a science teacher, gained his idea of producing skincare soaps and jellies when he was teaching children at his local school. During an experiment in one of his classrooms Nshimyumuremyi showed that science + natural ingredients = bacteria exterminated. He thought about the experiment and wondered if he could add business to the equation. He did, and now Nshimyumuremyi has his own company called Ubruranga Products that provides skincare creams and jellies that kill bacteria and provide healthy, clear skin for people in Rwanda. To keep traditional Rwandan medicine alive, Nshimyumuremyi uses natural ingredients used by traditional healers.

Both business entrepreneurs were successful. They had issues like any other business person, local or international, in that they had to choose their target market carefully, and package and promote their goods and services. Advertising in Rwanda is very much more localized, however, there are no producers of small packages and plastic bottles that Nshimyumuremyi needed for his creams and jellies. Therefore, even micro businesses often have to import supplies from neighbouring countries.

Question

1 What opportunities and challenges have the Rwandian business entrepreneurs seen and overcome?

Sources: www.cnn.org; CNN (2015) Can you start a successful business with just $10? This man did. www.edition.cnn.com/2015/02/11/africa/uburanga-skincare-rwanda/ (accessed 25 March 2015); CNN (2014) From bedroom to boutique: Handmade fashion with a Rwandan heart www.edition.cnn.com/2014/11/27/world/africa/christine-creative-collections-rwanda-fashion/ (accessed 25 March 2015).

SUMMARY

- In this chapter we have discussed the major developments in international trade. The world economy consists of over 196 nations with a population of 6.8 billion and an output (GDP) totalling US$61 trillion (ppp). World trade in merchandise totals US$12 trillion and trade in services is currently estimated by the WTO to be about US$4 trillion.

- In the last 50 years multilateral trade has flourished and a number of institutions have been developed to foster international trade. The World Bank, the IMF and the WTO all play important roles in ensuring a multilateral and fair international trading environment. It is important for the reader to have an understanding of how they may impact on the international marketing strategy of a company.

■ The major trading regions around the globe are at different stages and their continuing development has been discussed. The creation of the EU and the formation of the Economic and Monetary Union (EMU) have changed the competitive landscape across the globe radically. Other areas are now formally developing as trading regions with free trade areas emerging in Asia, the Pacific and the Americas. Some commentators believe this is moving world trade to a more regionally focused trading pattern.

■ In recent years there have been substantive changes in the global competitive structures as emerging markets strengthen their economic foundations and regional trading areas become more cohesive. The BRIC economies, Brazil, Russia, India and China are viewed as the star performers in emerging economies.

■ The centre of gravity and dynamism of the Asia–Pacific economy in the past decade has been China. China is developing the potential to dwarf most countries as it continues its rapid development and speedy economic growth. Commentators are interested to see whether it is China or India that will dominate the global trading structures of the twenty-first century.

KEYWORDS

Next Eleven (or N-11)

trade deficit

international product life cycle

comparative advantage

tariff

non-tariff barriers

hard currency

International Monetary Fund

World Bank

International Development
    Association (IDA)

balance of payments

trading blocs

Single European Market

Association of South East Asian
    Nations (ASEAN)

Asian Free Trade Area (AFTA)

Global System of Trade
    Preferences Among
    Developing Countries (GSTP)

Exchange Rate Mechanism

Economic and Monetary Union

Free Trade Area of the Americas

CASE STUDY 1

Tourism: Export Australia,
London and Uganda:
It increases the host
country's GDP

Exporting a country's historic culture, beautiful beaches or amazing city museums through advertising encourages tourists to visit and spend their tourism pound. Both the tourist and the money they spend whilst visiting, indirectly helps increase the country's GDP. To encourage tourists it is also important for governments to invest in the tourism infrastructure to ensure tourists can travel easily and safely whilst enjoying a variety of experiences, attractions and cultures.

Australia recently invested in the tourism infrastructure and this has assisted in increasing the number of tourists from New Zealand, USA, China, Singapore, Malaysia, Hong Kong, India and Germany. One recent government investment, of US$10 million, gave Australia 'Approved Destination Status' for the benefit of Chinese tourists. The Approved Destination Status provides Chinese people with the advantage of choosing government certificated guided tours around the host country of Australia. The benefit of marketing

FIGURE 2.4   Tourism value chain

Accommodation + Food and beverage + Souvenirs and entertainment + Transportation + Excursion services = Indirect contribution to GDP

and investing in Approved Destination Status for the Chinese market has paid off. In Australia during 2013–14 over A$5 billion was spent by Chinese tourists. This was an increase of over 16 per cent on that spent in the previous year. It is projected that the number of Chinese tourists will increase and the amount of money they spend will also increase to approximately A$8.5 billion. Exporting Australia and increasing the number of tourists visiting Australia is of significant indirect benefit to its GDP because tourists contribute to the Tourism value chain. The tourism value chain includes five key areas where tourists spend money and indirectly contribute into a country's GDP, as shown in Figure 2.4 above.

As Figure 2.4 shows, exporting a country as a tourism destination indirectly affects many different businesses. Boutique hotels or bed and breakfast owners will provide accommodation for tourists, small businesses such as taxi firms will transport tourists around the city and pubs or restaurants will feed hungry tourists. The tourist pound will, therefore, indirectly contribute to the host country's GDP.

The United Kingdom (UK) states that the value of its tourism is £126.9 billion which is 9 per cent of the country's GDP. In employment terms, when more tourists arrive in the host country they spend money on accommodation, transport, entertainment, or indeed any area within the tourism value chain; they also help increase the number of people who are directly or indirectly employed in the tourism trade. For example, tourists that eat in hotels, restaurants, cafés or pubs contribute to the number of employed people in agriculture as the more tourists there are, the more food needs to be harvested by the British farmer. The more tourists that visit the UK's football museums,

the more tour guides are needed. The fastest growing employment sector in the UK is tourism and more significantly tourism was one of the main industries that helped support the UK's economy during and following the global banking crises.

Exporting a country for tourists is just one way of increasing a nation's GDP. Exporting a country's ability to host a mega event such as a the Olympics, as London did for the 2012 Games, also provides opportunities for domestic organizations to benefit as there is an influx of tourists contributing to the tourism value chain before, during and after the mega event. If businesses along the tourism value chain benefit, so does the contribution to the host country's GDP.

Exporting tourism is definitely not a marketing or business strategy for developed countries only. The least developed countries (LDCs) are also experiencing benefits from the tourism pound. Uganda historically had coffee as its highest exported product. However, Uganda as a tourism destination has removed coffee as the biggest export earner; now the biggest export earner is the tourist pound.

Questions

1 What are the benefits of the tourism value chain?

2 For a LDC of your choice what areas of the tourism value chain could you promote to the international tourist?

3 From your findings from question 2 what businesses would benefit and how?

Sources: www.austrade.gov.au; www.ons.gov.uk

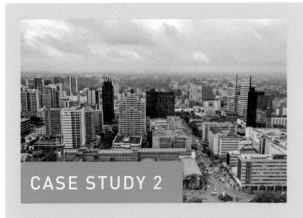

CASE STUDY 2

The mobile phone services market in Africa

The average penetration of mobile phones in Africa is almost 66 per cent. Gabon, the Seychelles and South Africa now boast almost 100 per cent penetration. Only five African countries – Burundi, Djibouti, Eritrea, Ethiopia and Somalia – still have a penetration of less than 10 per 100 inhabitants.

Popular mobile services include money transfers which allow people without bank accounts to send money by text message. Many farmers use mobiles to trade and check market prices. Besides sending money and paying for goods, they check balances, buy mobile airtime and settle utility bills.

In most of Africa, only a fraction of people have bank accounts – but there is huge demand for cheap and convenient ways to send money and buy prepaid services such as airtime. In Kenya, a pilot scheme called M-Pesa is being used to disburse and pay microloans by phone. Meanwhile, Celpay is offering platforms for banks and phone companies in Zambia and Congo. Interestingly, it has inspired a shift in banking services across the world. Operators in other countries have been doing their best to catch up.

However not all potential consumers are ready to make the leap. Many think banking is too expensive and complicated, and helping new customers become financially literate takes time. The technology remains a problem in some cases, with downloads requiring dozens of text messages. Several rival platforms are still in the fight, but so far those that emphasize simplicity and ease-of-use over state-of-the-art technology and security have made the greatest strides. A lot also hangs on putting the right laws and regulations in place. They need to be tight enough to protect vulnerable users and discourage money laundering, but open enough to allow innovative mobile banking to grow.

However, the main barrier to further expansion remains the cumbersome regulatory frameworks. Taxes can also act as a barrier, particularly import duties on handsets or special mobile communications surcharges. The mobile industry has been seen as a cash cow by governments in some countries who have used its popularity for generating tax revenues but haven't invested in the infrastructure for its growth. To expand coverage into rural and remote areas, government support will be required.

Rural areas in some countries are also often economically unattractive for operators to invest in. This is usually not due to a lack of demand but rather to lack of basic infrastructure. The roads in Africa can be notorious, the infrastructure under-developed and the continent has more than its fair share of conflicts and crises.

The cost of making calls and sending texts in Africa is also relatively high and many of its countries are poor. A 'digital divide' also persists in terms of Internet access and broadband speed. Governments need to address this situation and bring the continent more meaningfully online if the industry is to expand.

Questions

1 Analyze and evaluate the economic and political influences that will impact on the growth of the mobile phone services market in Africa.

2 What do you see as the major risks to an international company wishing to compete in this industry sector in the African market?

Sources: www.reuters.com; www.news.bbc.co.uk; www.economist.com; www.guardian.co.uk

DISCUSSION QUESTIONS

1   Identify barriers to the free movement of goods and services. Explain how barriers influence the development of international trade.

2   What do you consider to be the macro forces impacting on the development of world trade? Show by examples how they are changing the nature of international business.

3   To what extent do you agree with the view that the open global market no longer exists but simply consists of closed trading regions within which trade now moves freely?

4   How has the emergence of China as a major global competitor impacted on global marketing?

5   Recent mega mergers in the pharmaceutical and media industry are becoming increasingly evident. What is the rationale behind such mergers and how will it lead to global competitive advantage?

REFERENCES

1.   Agtmael, A. (2007) *The emerging markets century*, Simon and Schuster.
2.   Dicken, P. (2007) *Global shift – mapping the changing contours of the world economy,* 5th edn. Sage.
3.   European Commission (2014) Countries and Regions, Mercosur www.ec.europa.eu/trade/policy/countries-and-regions/regions/mercosur/ (accessed 20 March 2015).
4.   Griffin, R.W. and Pustay, M.W. (2009) *International business*, 6th edn. Pearson/Prentice Hall.
5.   *The Guardian* (2014) Poor nations 'pushed into new debt crises'. Available from www.theguardian.com/business/2014/oct/10/poor-nations-debt-crisis-developing-countries (accessed 20 March 2014).
6.   Schwab, K. (2014) 'The Global Competitiveness Report 2013–2014, Geneva', *World Economic Forum*.
7.   Vernon, R. and Wells, L.T. (1968) 'International trade and international investment in the product life cycle', *Quarterly Journal of Economics*, May.

USEFUL WEBSITES

www.economist.co.uk

www.news.ft.com/

www.imf.org

www.wto.org

www.oecd.org

www.cia.gov/library/publications/the-world

www.google.com/publicdata/directory

www.un.org

www.worldbank.org

CHAPTER 3

SOCIAL AND CULTURAL CONSIDERATIONS IN INTERNATIONAL MARKETING

LEARNING OBJECTIVES

After reading this chapter you should be able to:

- Discuss and evaluate social and cultural factors impacting on an international marketing strategy
- Understand the cross-cultural complexities of buying behaviour in different international markets
- Assess the impact of social and cultural factors on the international marketing process
- Carry out a cross-cultural analysis of specified international markets

INTRODUCTION

Markets in countries around the world are subject to many influences, as we saw in Chapter 1. While it is possible to identify those influences common to many country markets, the real difficulty lies in understanding their specific nature and importance.

The development of successful international marketing strategies is based on a sound understanding of the similarities and differences that exist in the countries and cultures around the world. The sheer complexity of the market considerations that impinge on the analysis, strategic development and implementation of international marketing planning is a major challenge.

In this chapter we will examine the social and cultural issues in international marketing and the implications they have for strategy development.

Social and cultural factors

Social and cultural factors influence all aspects of consumer and buyer behaviour, and the variation between these factors in different parts of the world can be a central consideration in developing and implementing international marketing strategies. Social and cultural forces are often linked together. While meaningful distinctions between social and cultural factors can be made, in many ways the two interact and the distinction between the various factors is not clear-cut. Differences in language can alter the intended meaning of a promotional campaign and differences in the way a culture organizes itself socially may affect the way a product is positioned in the market and the benefits a consumer may seek from that product. A sewing machine in one culture may be seen as a useful hobby; in another it may be necessary to the survival of a family.

Kotler (2015) included such things as reference groups, family, roles and status within social factors. While this is a useful distinction from the broader forces of culture, social class and social factors are clearly influenced by cultural factors. Take the example of the family, which is an important medium of transmitting cultural values. Children learn about their society and imbibe its culture through many means, but the family influence is strong, particularly during the early formative years of a child's life. Furthermore, the way in which family life is arranged varies considerably from one culture to another. In some cultures the family is a large extended group encompassing several generations and including aunts and uncles, while in other cultures the family is limited more precisely to the immediate family of procreation, and even then the unit might not be permanent and the father and mother of the children might not remain together for the entirety of the child-rearing process. Thus, social and cultural influences intertwine and have a great impact on the personal and psychological processes in the consumer and buyer behaviour and, as such, play an integral part in the understanding of the consumer in international markets. Toys'R'Us found quite distinct differences in the type of toys demanded in their various international markets. Whereas US children preferred TV and movie-endorsed products, Japanese children demanded electronic toys, South East Asian children wanted educational toys, and the more conservative cultures of the European markets expected a choice of traditional toys.

It is not feasible to examine all the social or cultural influences on consumer and buyer behaviour in one chapter, neither is it possible to describe all the differences between cultures across the world. In the first section we will highlight the more important sociocultural influences which are relevant to buyer behaviour in international markets. In the following section we will focus on developing an understanding of the components of culture, its impact on consumer behaviour and the implications for international marketing strategies. We will then discuss the methodologies which can be used to carry out cross-cultural analysis to enable comparisons to be made across cultures. Finally, we will examine business-to-business (B2B) marketing and the impact of culture in these types of markets.

What is culture?

Perhaps the most comprehensive definition of culture is that of Matsumoto and Van de Vijver (2010) who said culture '*Is a unique meaning and information system, shared by a group and transmitted across generations that allow the group to meet the basic needs of survival by coordinating social behaviour to achieve a viable existence and to transmit successful social behaviours.*' (p.5) Or perhaps, more appropriately: '*. . . it's just the way we do things around here*'. In relation to international marketing, culture can be summed up as: '*The sum total of learned beliefs, values and customs that serve to direct consumer behaviour in a particular country market.*'

Thus, culture is made up of three essential components:

Beliefs: A large number of mental and verbal processes which reflect our knowledge and assessment of products and services.

Values: The indicators consumers use to serve as guides for what is appropriate behaviour. They tend to be relatively enduring and stable over time and widely accepted by members of a particular market.

Customs: Overt modes of behaviour that constitute culturally approved or acceptable ways of behaving in specific situations. Customs are evident at major events in one's life, e.g. birth, marriage, death, and at key events in the year, e.g. Christmas, Ramadan, Hanukkah, Chinese New Year, etc.

Such components as values, beliefs and customs are often ingrained in a society and many of us only fully realize what is special about our own culture – its beliefs, values and customs – when we come into contact with other cultures. This is what happens to firms when they expand internationally and build up a market presence in foreign markets: often the problems they face are a result of their mistaken assumption that foreign markets will be similar to their home market and that they can operate overseas as they do at home. Frequently in international markets the toughest competition a firm may face is not another supplier but the different customs or beliefs as a result of cultural differences. This means that for a company to succeed in that market they often have to change ingrained attitudes about the way they do business. The beliefs and values of a culture satisfy a need within that society for order, direction and guidance. Thus, culture sets the standards shared by significant portions of that society, which in turn sets the rules for operating in that market.

Hofstede *et al.* (2010) identify a number of layers within a national culture.

Layers of culture

- A national level according to one's country which determines our basic cultural assumptions.
- A regional/ethnic/religious/linguistic affiliation level determining basic cultural beliefs.
- A gender level according to whether a person was born as a girl or as a boy.
- A generation level which separates grandparents, parents and children.
- A social class level associated with educational opportunities, a person's occupation or profession.

All of these determine attitudes and values and everyday behavioural standards in individuals and organizations.

Given such complexities, market analysts have often used the 'country' as a surrogate for 'culture'. Moreover, culture is not something granted only to citizens of a country or something we are born with, it is what older generations set in place for us and what popular culture, through advertisements and television, helps us to learn and grow in our environment. Similar environments provide similar experiences and opportunities and hence tend to shape similar behaviours.

Terpstra *et al.* (2012) identify eight components of culture which form a convenient framework for examining a culture from a marketing perspective (see Figure 3.1).

FIGURE 3.1   A cultural framework

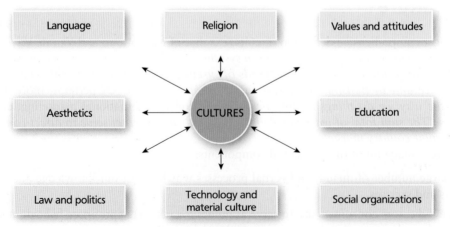

Source: Terpstra, V., Foley, J. and Sarathy, R. (2012). *International marketing*. Naper Press.

The components of culture

Education   The level of formal primary and secondary education in a foreign market will have a direct impact upon the sophistication of the target customers. A simple example will be the degree of literacy. The labelling of products, especially those with possibly hazardous side-effects, needs to be taken seriously for a market that has a very low literacy rate. Imperial Chemical Industries (ICI) markets pesticides throughout the world: in developed countries its main form of communication is advertising and printed matter. In developing countries they rely heavily on training and verbally based educational programmes to get their message across.

Social organization   This relates to the way in which a society organizes itself: how the culture considers kinship, social institutions, interest groups and status systems. The role of women and caste systems are easily identifiable examples – if the firm has a history of successfully marketing to 'the housewife/ homemaker', life is more difficult in a culture where women have no social status at all. House ownership is another example. In Switzerland the majority of people rent rather than own their houses and expect to rent property with domestic appliances already installed. Even these domestic appliances are often leased by the landlord rather than owned, meaning the attitude to property ownership is very different to that found in other Northern European cultures.

Technology and material culture   This aspect relates not to materialism but to the local market's ability to handle and deal with modern technology. Some cultures are using natural sources, such as solar panels and wind turbines, to provide heating and lighting for their homes. This technology is not just for advanced western countries. Some families in Africa who have never had electricity before are using solar technology. Some cultures find servicing cars and trucks on a yearly basis astounding as they only pay attention to their cars when they are broken. In instances such as these the international organizations are often faced with the choice of either educating the population (expensive and time-consuming) or de-engineering the product or service (difficult if you have invested heavily in product development).

Law and politics   The legal and political environments in a foreign market are usually regarded as consequences of the cultural traditions of that market. Islamic law such as Sharia law is generally based on the traditions and guiding principles from the Muslim holy book, the Qur'an, the guidance known as the Hadith provided by the prophet Muhammad and the Islamic scholars' judgments known as fatwas. Legal and political systems are often a simple codification of the norms of behaviour deemed acceptable by the local culture. This aspect was dealt with in some detail in Chapter 1. **Cultural sensitivity** to political issues in international markets is of the utmost importance. Thus, an advertisement for the Orange mobile phone network in Ireland with the strapline 'The future's bright, the future's orange', clearly did not have any awareness of political and sectarian sensitivities surrounding the 'Orange Order' marches that take place in Northern Ireland.

Aesthetics   This covers the local culture's perception of things such as beauty, good taste and design, and dictates what is acceptable or appealing to the local eye. A firm needs to ensure that use of colour, music, architecture or brand names in their product and communications strategies is sympathetic and acceptable to the local culture. For the unwary, there are many, many traps in this area. Pepsodent tried to sell its toothpaste in the far reaches of East Asia by emphasizing that it 'whitens your teeth'. Unfortunately they did not realize there was a practice among local natives in some areas of chewing betel nuts to blacken their teeth to make them attractive. Colour can mean completely different things in different cultures and brand colours sometimes do not travel well because of this, as we can see in Illustration 3.1.

Values and attitudes   The values consumers from different countries place on things such as time, achievement, work, wealth and risk-taking will seriously affect not only the products offered but also the packaging and communication activities. The methods used by a firm to motivate its personnel are also strongly influenced by the local culture and practice. Encouraging local sales forces to sell more by offering cars and more money, for example, may not work in all cultures.

ILLUSTRATION 3.1

Beware of colour in marketing communications

Colours immediately evoke instinctive associations of meaning buried within our subconscious or from learnt experiences. What is important for the international marketer is to understand that people from different cultures attach feelings and emotions to the same colour. This is because colours often have deep symbolic meanings based on traditions and histories. Therefore across cultures association of colour has evolved discretely.

Consider the colours white, green and red. These colours evoke several distinct feelings and associations to people in different cultures.

White is considered a natural, pure and happy colour to people in the UK, US, Australia and New Zealand. For Bedouin people, white symbolizes joy and fertility. However in Japan white is associated with death.

Green is associated by people in Belgium, the UK and US as envy due to Christian ethics set down over 1500 years ago. Yet in China, green is associated with trustworthiness.

Red is another colour which has many meanings. It means love in many cultures including Korea. In China, red is also considered to be a lucky colour, whilst in some African countries red represents death and mourning. In many western cultures red has become a colour that symbolizes love. Red is a significant colour on St Valentine's Day where the colour represents romance. This symbolism is something which marketing has played a significant role in creating through the use of red in packaging, red heart-shaped gifts, advertising messages and flowers.

Continuing with the idea of love and romance, a wedding day is a very special day. Planning and organizing the wedding can take many months, if not years, but one of the most important purchases associated with a marriage is the wedding dress of the bride. The colour of the wedding gown is a reflection of tradition associated with the bride's culture. Red is often the colour of the bride's dress in China to bring good luck. Red is also the traditional colour worn by brides in India. In the UK and US the bride's dress is often white to signify purity and happiness. The picture represents the style of clothes worn at an Indonesian wedding. It is very common for the bridegroom to wear white in religion/traditional rituals because it symbolizes 'pureness'. The bride's family have roots from Solo, Central Java, therefore the Batik skirt and ornaments represent the Solo region of Indonesia.

An understanding of colour is just one of the cultural sensitivities that marketers need to research and understand before they enter new markets.

Question

1 What cultural sensitivities have you come across that you think marketing managers should research before they enter a new market?

Religion   Religion is a major cultural variable and has significant if not always apparent effects on marketing strategy. For example, the identification of sacred objects and philosophical systems, beliefs and norms as well as taboos, holidays and rituals is critical for an understanding of a foreign market. Religion, for example, will affect the food that people eat and when they eat it, as well as their attitudes to a whole range of products from deodorants to alcoholic drink. Therefore, products such as Laughing Cow, a cheese spread made in Kentucky as part of Bel Brands USA, cannot be exported to India under that brand name, as the cow is a sacred animal.

In some countries religion is the most dominant cultural force. For instance, in Islamic markets such as Saudi Arabia, no violation of religion by advertising and other promotional practices, no matter how insignificant, will go unnoticed or unpunished either by the government or the consumer. This can cause problems for advertisers. Shaving advertisements cannot be shown if the male actor shows too much of his chest. In many European countries a married woman wears her wedding ring on her left hand. However in Norway, Austria, Poland, Netherlands and some parts of Denmark, women wear their wedding ring on their right hand. Advertisements showing a mother and her baby must ensure the wedding ring is worn on the correct hand as in some European cultures it would show that the baby is born to an unmarried mother which for them is taboo.

Comparative ads are banned as, according to the laws of Islam, pegging one product against another diminishes the sense of unity and social community. Companies operating in these markets need to understand the difference between three key terms: *Haraam, Halal* and *Makruh*.

Haraam are subjects or things that are absolutely unlawful and strongly prohibited in Islam, such as alcohol and cheating. These taboo subjects are banned in advertising and other promotional activities in countries such as Saudi Arabia, Kuwait and Iran. *Halal* is the opposite to *Haraam* and is a term designating any object or an action which is permissible to use or engage in, according to Islamic law. The term is commonly used to designate food seen as permissible according to Islamic law. *Makruh* are subjects which are seen as distasteful: they are discouraged in Islam but are not banned. Smoking is not forbidden in Islam but it is highly discouraged.

Language   Language can be divided into two major elements: the spoken language of vocal sounds in patterns that have meaning, and silent language, which is the communication through body language, silences and social distance. This is less obvious but is a powerful communication tool. To many commentators language interlinks all the components of culture and is the key to understanding and gaining empathy with a different culture. In the following section we will examine the different components of language.

MANAGEMENT CHALLENGE 3.1

Silent language – non-verbal communication

Non-verbal communication includes many factors from how people greet each other, their facial expressions, their body language, and even how people listen to each other. Body language is considered to be clearer than verbal language, but only if the body language is understood. Like verbal language, body language can project cultural specific communication messages. It is vital to be aware of these non-verbal aspects of communication as various cultures express themselves differently through hand gestures, eye movements and the reason why they smile. Therefore, incorrect use of non-verbal communications in a business setting or in an advertisement could confuse or insult others and even break the governing laws of a country. Take for instance the way people greet each other. In some East and South East Asian countries people greet each other without touch. They place their hands together, a 'wai', and bow to greet the other person. In western culture a handshake is the common greeting. Whereas, in many Southern and Eastern European countries people kiss each other on the cheek as a greeting. Kissing as a greeting is viewed by many South Asian people as an intimate act; something which should not take place in public. Kissing in public in Arabic countries such as Saudi Arabia is forbidden and people can be arrested and imprisoned for breaking the law.

Question

1 What do you think are the dos and don'ts of carrying out business or creating advertisements for international companies?

Language and culture

Spoken language   Spoken language is an important means of communication. In various forms, e.g. plays and poetry, the written word is regarded as part of the culture of a group of people. In the spoken form the actual words spoken and the ways in which the words are pronounced provide clues to the receiver about the type of person who is speaking.

Chinese is spoken as the mother tongue (or first language) by three times more people than the next largest language, English. However, Chinese is overtaken by English when official language population numbers are taken into account. However, the official language is not always spoken by the whole population of a country. For example, French is an official language in Canada but in some areas Canadians have little or no fluency in French. English is often, but by no means always, the common language between business people of different nationalities (See Case Study 2 in Chapter 1).

Speaking or writing in another language can be a risky activity (see Illustration 3.2). In any communication message, particular attention needs to be paid when translating from one language to another. The

ILLUSTRATION 3.2

Language and meaning – lost in translation

The English language is often used in communication signs around the world. However, many signs produce funny or unusual translations.

Visitors to a zoo in Budapest were asked 'Not to feed the animals. If you have any suitable food, give it to the guard on duty.'

At a Kenyan zoo visitors were asked 'Please do not put your hand in orphan's mouth or risk losing a finger.'

In cities retailers often produce interesting advertisements:

A Bangkok dry cleaner to potential customers: 'Drop your trousers here for best results.'

Pee Cola available in Ghana does not necessarily sound appetising.

A Hong Kong dentist claims to extract teeth 'By the latest Methodists'.

Airports often present some interesting communication messages to international travellers:

'Delayed due to some reasons'.

For mothers and babies 'Baby diaper exchange'.

And for emergencies 'If you are stolen, call the police at once'.

To encourage travellers to recycle their plastic water bottles there are waste bins provided: 'Liquid abandoned place'.

And for all other waste use the bin entitled: 'Poisonous and evil rubbish'.

And finally, to encourage kindness, international travellers are requested to:

'Please look after oldster and child'.

And give foreign currencies in the charity box 'for especially difficult children'.

Question

1 Consider any communications signs or advertisements that you have seen. What 'meaning' have you seen that has been lost in translation?

Sources: *Daily Mail*, *Lonely Planet* and *The Sunday Times*.

creative use of copy to gain attention and to influence comprehension of the target audience can result in a clever use of words. However, inadequate translation often results in clumsy errors. In Germany a 'General Motors' advertisement mentioned a 'body by Fischer' which became 'corpse by Fischer'. This is clearly a straightforward translation error, directly resulting from the mistranslating of the word 'body'. The Hertz company's strapline, 'Let Hertz put you in the driving seat', became 'Let Hertz make you a chauffeur'. Instead of communicating liberation and action as intended, this translation provided an entirely different meaning, implying a change of occupation and status. In India an advertisement for the milky drink Horlicks was translated into Tamil as '20 men asleep under the tree'.

Language of social media marketing   The choice of language to use for company websites, Facebook page and mobile apps is also problematic for companies operating across many borders. Should it be multilingual, thus incurring greater costs in ensuring its sustainability, or should it be in one language? The top three languages used on the Web are English with around 30 per cent, Chinese 23 per cent and Spanish 8 per cent. English is a widely spoken language throughout the world.

Managers have previously assumed that English is the international language of the Internet. While this was so in the early days, according to Forrester Research, Web contact time is doubled on sites localized for language and culture. Japanese businessmen, for example, are three times more likely to conduct an online transaction when addressed in Japanese. The US consultancy Global Reach estimates that for every US$2 million a US site generates from domestic sales, another US$1 million is lost when non-Americans do not easily understand the website. Currently over 55 per cent of websites use English as their only language or the language of their main landing page. However, this number is likely to change as more local websites are being set up by even the smallest business. It is predicted more Chinese, Russian and Indonesian websites will be created thus changing the dominant social media marketing language.

A preferred solution for many companies is to build the main website capability to offer a multilingual website, localized to the language and cultural sensitivities of the market. A global brand then needs to centralize the message, translate it and colloquialize it. Another reason for localization is to ensure a company is compliant with local regulations. In France, for instance, consumers enjoy a one-week grace period after they receive an online purchase. In Germany, comparative advertising is banned on the Web and in China, clients' companies may find their websites are monitored by the Chinese government.

The same issue of course is faced by advertisers on social networking sites, as seen in Illustration 3.3.

Silent language   Silent language is a powerful means of communication and the importance of non-verbal communication is greater in some countries than others. In these cultures people are more sensitive to a variety of different message systems. Silent language examines the many influences we face each day, influences that are silent in that they are not verbal but that are quite loud in terms of the effects they have on our development, our relationships and so on. Many of these influences are cultural, attitudes and behaviours we inherit from our cultural heritage and learning. Understanding the cultural similarities and differences is essential when leading a new workforce in a difference country or persuading new consumers to try a different brand (Goman 2011). As different cultures speak different verbal languages so does our culture give rise to differences in the silent languages used to communicate. The silent language factors that are important in international marketing include attitudes to time, which influences the importance of being on time, and attitudes to space, which impacts on the conversational distance between people. What is universal, however, is that silent language provides subliminal messages giving people a clear way to analyze whether or not the person they are working with or speaking to is credible and trustworthy, likeable or nervous. And when trusted friends are a social insurance it is very important for international marketers to be able to interpret the very varied silent language.

Silent languages are particularly important in sales negotiations and other forms of business meetings. They will, in addition, influence internal communications in companies employing people from different countries and cultures.

Difficulties can arise even between cultures which are geographically close to each other but have different perceptions of language. The word concept in English translates into 'an abstract idea; a general notion', whereas *konzept* in German translates more into a 'plan or programme'. German and English executives could meet with hugely varying expectations if a conceptual discussion was on the agenda.

ILLUSTRATION 3.3

There's an APP for that

Businesses and consumers are using mobile apps on smartphones and tablets more and more. In fact, in 2013 mobile app downloads amounted to 82 billion worldwide and the figure is expected to rise to 200 billion app downloads per year by 2017. Whilst the main app downloads are games, weather and social media sites such as Facebook and news, global brands realize that if their consumers are using mobile apps they need to find innovative ways to connect.

Many global retail brands have mobile apps which are really useful for consumers who, in two taps of the app, can locate stores nearby or contact the customer service team and business 24 hours a day, 7 days a week. Therefore, retailers are investing in mobile apps to grow their business. Traditionally, international retailers who wanted to grow their business would open a new store, on a new high street. However, the traditional growth model is outdated because consumers are no longer visiting the high street as often. The modern consumer chooses to buy groceries to clothes, medicine to music, via their smartphones and tablets.

Question

1 The Tesco mobile app provides an innovative experience to appeal to online consumers. How important do you think mobile apps are for international organizations?

Source: Portio Research (2013) Mobile Factbook Report available from www.portioresearch.com

Cultural learning   The process of enculturation, i.e. learning about their own culture by members of a society, can be through three types of mechanism: *formally*, through the family and the social institutions to which people belong; *technically*, through the educational processes, be it through schools or religious institutions; and *informally*, through peer groups, advertising and various other marketing-related vehicles.

This enculturation process influences consumer behaviour by providing the learning we use to shape the toolkit of labels, skills and styles from which people construct strategies of action, e.g. persistent ways of going through the buying process.

The process of acculturation is the process international companies need to go through to obtain an understanding of another culture's beliefs, values and attitudes in order to gain an empathy with that market. As we have seen, culture is pervasive and complex and it is not always easy for someone outside a given culture to gain an empathy with that market.

Having examined the main components of culture and the various important dimensions, we will now look at how culture impacts on consumer behaviour.

Culture and consumer behaviour

There are several important ways in which the various components of culture influence a consumer's perception, attitude and understanding of a given product or communication and so affect the way a consumer behaves in the buying process. Jeannet and Hennessey (2006) identify three major processes through which culture influences consumer behaviour – cultural forces, including religion, history, family and language; cultural message including symbols, morals and knowledge; and consumer decision process including selecting, prioritizing wants and decision making.

Culture is seen as being embedded in elements of society such as religion, language, history and education (cultural forces). These elements send direct and indirect messages to consumers regarding the selection of goods and services (cultural message). The culture we live in determines the answers to such questions as: Do we drink coffee or juice at breakfast? Do we shop daily or on a weekly basis? and in doing so affects the consumer's decision process.

The body of theory on which our understanding of **consumer behaviour** is based comes predominantly from the USA. Therefore, Usunier and Lee (2012) argue that the means by which international marketing managers understand consumer behaviour is flawed because the theoretical principles on which we base our understanding do not necessarily hold true across different cultures. There are some important assumptions which international marketers need to question when applying western theoretical principles to consumer behaviour across international markets such as:

1 Does Maslow's hierarchy of needs remain consistent across all cultures?
2 Is the buying process in all countries an individualistic activity?
3 Are social institutions and local conventions the same across all cultures?
4 Who, within the family, does the consumer buying process include? And is this consistent across cultures?

Does Maslow's hierarchy of needs remain consistent across all cultures?

Culture influences the hierarchy of needs (Maslow 1970) on two levels. First, the axiom that one need must be satisfied before the next appears, is not true for every culture; and second, similar kinds of needs may be satisfied by different products and consumption types.

For example, in some less developed countries, a consumer may go without food in order to buy a refrigerator and, therefore, satisfy the dominant need of social status before physical satisfaction. A study identified that self-esteem needs were most important to Chinese consumers, and physiological needs the least important. Physiological needs include food, water, shelter, etc., self-esteem needs include prestige and success.

In building a presence in the Chinese market, companies would need to target consumers with high self-esteem needs by linking a product such as credit cards to success in business, or beer to success in sporting activities.

Likewise, similar kinds of needs may be satisfied in very different ways. For example, to a Hindu the need for self-realization does not necessarily imply material consumption, as in western cultures, but in fact abandoning all worldly possessions.

Is the buying process in all countries an individualistic activity?

Many western buying behaviour models are primarily based on individual purchases with reference to family decision making in the context of husband and wife decisions. They assume buying decisions are focused on an individual's decision-making process. In Asian or Arabian cultures a family may be a complex structure and an individual would need to take into account all members of the family in making major purchase decisions, so the decision making is generally of a more collectivist nature. See Illustration 3.4 for more details regarding shopping behaviour in collectivist cultures.

Are social institutions and local conventions the same across all cultures?

Institutions such as the state, religious institutions, trade unions and the education system also influence consumer behaviour.

The UK company Rompa©, which serves the market for people with learning disabilities, found enormous cultural differences across their European market due to the varying influences the national institutions had on how charities and social institutions should be organized. In Germany the market was highly organized and strongly supported financially by the state. In Spain the state lottery was the prime benefactor of major national charities, whereas in Italy the church was the major benefactor, with very little involvement by the state.

ILLUSTRATION 3.4

How cultural dimensions influence shopping behaviour

Teenagers are often targeted by global and local brands as they have significant influence on the world economy, the choices parents make and they can become loyal customers of the future. During their teenage years young people begin to take more control away from their parents, form their own identity and become more self-aware. What teenagers buy and what they wear is a crucial part of their lives, therefore shopping becomes an important leisure activity.

Teenagers from the USA are from an individualistic background. They are generally quite low on uncertainty avoidance. When shopping the US teenagers want to show their individualism, they want to stand out from the crowd, they like to take risks with their choices and enjoy novel and interesting clothes. Whilst US teenagers seek peer approval they still want to remain individuals and see shopping as a recreational event.

French teenagers are quite different. They are higher on the individualistic scale than US teenagers and much higher on the uncertainty avoidance which means French teenagers seek approval from their peers much more than US teenagers. In fact French teenagers have a very strong desire to 'fit in' and want their friends to agree that their shopping purchases are correct. So much so that it is recommended that marketers should ensure the physical spaces in fashion changing rooms are bigger so that friends can approve purchases before it is too late.

Question

1 Hofstede's cultural dimensions can be considered by marketing managers in many other situations. What situations do you think consumers may behave differently in because of the cultural dimensions and what should marketing managers do about this?

Source: An, D. (2014) 'Tangibilizing services through visual tangible cues in corporate websites: a six-country cross-cultural analysis'. *Journal of Services Marketing*, *28* (7), 566–579.

Who, within the family, does the consumer buying process include? And is this consistent across cultures?

There are many inconsistencies in the buying processes across cultures around the globe. Three aspects which are particularly pertinent to our discussion are the differences in the level of consumer involvement, the perception of risk in a purchase and the cognitive processes of consumers.

Consumer involvement

The Chinese are seen as having a low level of involvement when purchases are for private consumption but a high level of involvement when they are buying products for their social or symbolic value. Since the Chinese greatly value social harmony and smoothness of relationships within the extended family, the social significance of products is highly important, be it to express status, gratitude, approval or even disapproval.

Perceived risk

The level of risk consumers associate with a purchase varies enormously across cultures, and as such it is an important variable in consumer behaviour. It will determine whether a consumer will go for the comfortable purchase or is willing to try new products and services. Risk incorporates three components: physical, financial and social.

Whereas in some countries, *physical risk* may be important (e.g. the fear of Ebola or AIDS), others may be more sensitive to *social risk* and the loss of social status if a wrong buying decision is made (i.e. the Chinese fear of losing face). *Financial risk* closely relates to the level of economic development in a country. It is likely to be less in the more affluent economies where if a wrong purchase decision is made the financial hardship suffered may not be so profound.

The level of brand loyalty found in a market is also closely related to the perception of risk. There are huge variations in attitudes to brand loyalty across different cultures. In the US the standard buyer behaviour is that of disloyalty. A consumer will shift from one brand to another because it is standard behaviour to test several competitive products and so foster price competition. Thus, in the US it is relatively easy for a new entrant to persuade Americans to try their product, but much harder to get them to keep buying it. Similarly in Poland consumers are not loyal to supermarkets. They will collect leaflets and coupons providing details of special offers and shop at the store which provides the best value.

In other cultures, consumers are more fundamentally loyal, less brand-conscious and not so used to cross-product comparisons. In Australia and South East Asia buyers have a greater need for brand security, are less confident with regard to trying unknown products and so are less willing to take risks. See Management Challenge 3.2 which shows consumer strategies to limit perception risks.

MANAGEMENT CHALLENGE 3.2

What's the risk?

When purchasing a family skiing holiday, choosing a birthday present for a 6-year-old child or deciding which university to attend, consumers are often worried about the potential financial, social and physical risks involved. When purchasing products or services, consumers have strategies to reduce the potential risks, such as staying loyal to a brand or reading expert reviews and searching through magazines. Another strategy that consumers use is to simply ask advice and recommendations from friends and family members. Consumers use Word of Mouth (WOM) recommendations on a regular basis because it helps to decrease the fear of risk. To further lower the perceived risks consumers turn to Facebook, Twitter, Trip Advisor and other online community sites where 'friends' can provide Word of Mouth advice and recommendations.

Organizations such as the Belgian fashion brand Kipling, or Just Eat the world's leading online takeaway ordering service, recognize the value of word of mouth; so much so, that they reward happy consumers. Happy customers that endorse products and services are worth more than messages in print magazines. Viewing photographs and reading online reviews provides consumers with sufficient Word of Mouth information to reduce many perceived financial, social and physical risks.

Question

1 What online photographs and reviews have you used and how did this help reduce your perceived risks?

Source: *Marketing Week*, 'How to get fans to cheer your brand on', 10/09/2014.

Cognitive style

Western consumer behaviour models assume a logical buying process with rational steps, including the formation of awareness, the searching for information, reviewing the information, evaluating alternatives and finally making a choice. Sometimes by attacking traditional cognitive styles advertisers have had surprising success.

Many authors argue that internationally there are many different models of the buying process. Asian consumers tend to have a quite different cognitive style to western consumers. The Chinese as well as the Japanese have a more synthetic, concrete and contextual orientation in their thought patterns, as opposed to the Americans who tend to have a more analytical and abstract decision-making process. Thus, culture not only impacts on how we behave as consumers but on the whole decision-making process.

Analyzing cultures and the implications for consumer behaviour

As we have seen in previous sections, there are many social and cultural influences which determine our values, beliefs and customs and combine to form a **cultural identity** which in turn influences the process of decision making when buying products. All these aspects need to be examined to understand the consumer in any international market.

Blackwell *et al.* (2006) suggest the following steps should be undertaken when analyzing consumer behaviour in international markets. They propose that if a company is to fully empathize with a culture they must pose a series of questions about buyer behaviour, culture and the suitability of various marketing communications approaches for that culture. These steps consist of:

- *Determine relevant motivations in the culture.* What needs are fulfilled with this product in the minds of members of the culture? How are these needs presently fulfilled? Do members of this culture readily recognize these needs?

- *Determine characteristic behaviour patterns.* What patterns are characteristic of purchasing behaviour? What forms of division of labour exist within the family structure? How frequently are products of this type purchased? Do any of these characteristic behaviours conflict with behaviour expected for this product? How strongly ingrained are the behaviour patterns that conflict with those needed for distribution of this product?

- *Determine what broad cultural values are relevant to this product.* Are there strong values about work, morality, religion, family relations and so on that relate to this product? Does this product denote attributes that are in conflict with these cultural values? Can conflicts with values be avoided by changing the product? Are there positive values in this culture with which the product might be identified?

- *Determine characteristic forms of decision making.* Do members of the culture display a studied approach to decisions concerning innovations, or an impulsive approach? What is the form of the decision process? Upon which information sources do members of the culture rely? Do members of the culture tend to be rigid or flexible in the acceptance of new ideas? What criteria do they use in evaluating alternatives?

- *Evaluate promotion methods appropriate to the culture.* What role does advertising occupy in the culture? What themes, words or illustrations are taboo? What language problems exist in present markets that cannot be translated into this culture? What types of sales staff are accepted by members of the culture? Are such sales staff available?

- *Determine appropriate institutions for this product in the minds of consumers.* What types of retailers and intermediary institutions are available? What services do these institutions offer that are expected by the consumer? What alternatives are available for obtaining services needed for the product but not offered by existing institutions? How are various types of retailers regarded by consumers? Will changes in the distribution structure be readily accepted?

Self-reference criterion

As we have discussed, it is of crucial importance when examining foreign markets that the culture of the country is seen in the context of that country. It is better to regard the culture as different from, rather than better or worse than, the home culture. In this way, differences and similarities can be explored and the reasons for differences can be sought and explained. The differences approach avoids the evaluative and often superior approach based on one's own self-reference criterion.

'Self-reference criterion' (SRC) characterizes our unconscious reference to our own cultural values when examining other cultures. Usunier and Lee (2012) suggest a four-step approach to eliminate SRC:

1 Define the problem or goal in terms of home country cultural traits, habits and norms.
2 Define the problems or goals in terms of the foreign culture, traits, habits and norms.
3 Isolate the SRC influence in the problem and examine it carefully to see how it complicates the problem.
4 Redefine the problem without the SRC influence and solve for the foreign market situation.

The process of enculturation to gain empathy with a foreign country market is not an easy one. It requires:

■ *Cultural empathy*: the ability to place yourself in the position of the buyer from another culture. In this way a strong attempt is made to understand the thinking approaches, the decision-making process and the interactions between this and the cultural and other forces influencing the buyer.
■ *Neutrality*: the ability to identify the differences that exist without making value judgements about 'better' or 'worse' cultures. Inevitably, self-reference will exist. If the focus is placed on differences rather than superiority, the chances of achieving accurate cross-cultural analysis are increased.

To ensure they achieve this, companies follow a number of policies. They may recruit foreign staff at their head office, collaborate with local firms when entering a new market or they may put managers through acculturation programmes. Guinness, the makers of Ireland's famous stout, understood the importance of avoiding SRC in developing their knowledge base of the new international markets in which they were operating, so they ensured they had a management team in each market which was truly multinational, as well as including managers with a local knowledge of Ireland, its landmarks and the history of Guinness stout.

Cross-cultural analysis

So far our discussions have been concerned primarily with understanding what is meant by culture, examining its components and surveying its influence on consumer behaviour and how that differs across cultures.

However, strategists and students of international marketing need to move beyond this and endeavour to develop ways to compare and contrast consumers, market segments and buyers across cultures. In today's global environment where culture is becoming increasingly deterritorialized and each culture is penetrated by the influences of other cultures, this is becoming increasingly complex as a research task. Cultural influences are much more diffuse and opaque than previously. This means that cultural analysis does not necessarily equate to country analysis and any research design must account for such complexities.

International marketers must decide the relevant cultural segments/grouping for analysis and then need appropriate frameworks or conceptual schemata to enable comparisons to be made and contrasts and similarities to be drawn across cross-cultural groupings.

For the most part, cross-cultural classification approaches tend to be either mere lists or incredibly theoretical complex structures. There is a recognized lack of a universal, broadly generalizable framework within which to visualize cross-cultural analysis. The contextual approach and the work of Hofstede *et al.* (2010) is used by many researchers as the basis for methodologies of cross-cultural analysis. A further framework has been developed through the GLOBE programme which focuses on cross-cultural leadership attributes. In the following sections we will examine how these concepts can be used by firms in attempting to analyze consumer behaviour across cultures and will then highlight some further frameworks which readers may find useful.

The high/low context approach

The main thesis of the contextual approach to analyzing culture is that one culture will be different from another if it understands and communicates in different ways. Languages are therefore seen as the most important component of culture.

The language differences between some cultures will be large and therefore there will be marked differences in their cultures. Language and value differences between the German and Japanese cultures, for instance, are considerable. There are also differences between the Spanish and Italian cultures but they are much less; both have languages based on Latin, they use the same written form of communication and have similar although not identical values and norms.

In different cultures the use of communication techniques varies. In some languages communication is based on the words that are said or written (spoken language). In others, the more ambiguous elements such as surroundings or social status of the message-giver are important variables in the transmission of understanding (silent language). Hall (1997) used cultural dimensions to classify cultures into what he referred to as 'low context cultures' and 'high context cultures'.

- *Low context cultures* rely on spoken and written language for meaning. These are cultures where people tend to have many connections but of short duration or for some specific reason. In these societies, cultural behaviour and beliefs may need to be spelled out explicitly so that those coming into the cultural environment know how to behave. Senders of messages in low context cultures encode their messages expecting that the receivers will accurately decode the words used to gain a good understanding of the intended message. Germany, Switzerland, UK and the USA are viewed as low context cultures. These cultures have a high explicit content in their communications.

- *High context cultures* are those cultures where people have close connections over a long period of time. Many aspects of cultural behaviour are not made explicit because most members know what to do and what to think from years of interaction with each other. High context cultures use and interpret more of the elements surrounding the message to develop their understanding of the message. In high context cultures the social importance, knowledge of the person and the social setting add extra information and will be perceived by the message receivers. Saudi Arabia, Japan, Asia and South America are seen as high context cultures. These cultures have subtle and complex ways of communicating with people according to their age, sex and the relative and actual social positions of the people conversing.

The greater the contextual difference between those trying to communicate, the greater the difficulty firms will have in achieving accurate communications. Table 3.1 outlines the communication differences between low and high context cultures.

Hofstede's cultural dimensions

Hofstede (2010) was primarily interested in uncovering differences in work-related values across countries. He identified five dimensions of culture: individualism, power distance, uncertainty avoidance, masculinity and Confucianism. These dimensions, he argued, largely account for cross-cultural differences in people's belief systems and behaviour patterns around the globe.

Individualism

Individualism (IDV) describes the relationship between an individual and his or her fellow individuals in society. It manifests itself in the way people live together, for example in nuclear families, extended families or tribes, and has a great variety of value implications. At one end of the spectrum are societies with very loose ties between individuals. Such societies allow a large degree of freedom and everybody is expected to look after his or her own self-interest and possibly that of the immediate family. Societies of this type exemplify high individualism (high IDV) and display loose integration. At the other end are societies with very strong ties between individuals. Everybody is expected to look after the interests of their in-group and to hold only those opinions and beliefs sanctioned by the in-group which, in turn, protects the individual. These 'collective' (low IDV) societies show tight integration. Hofstede identified highly individualistic countries as the USA, Great Britain and the Netherlands. Collectivist countries were Colombia, Pakistan and Taiwan. The mid-range contains countries such as Japan, India, Austria and Spain.

Table 3.1 Communication styles in low and high context cultures

Factor	High context culture	Low context culture
Overtness of messages	Many covert and implicit messages, with use of metaphor and reading between the lines.	Many overt and explicit messages that are simple and clear.
Locus of control and attribution for failure	Inner locus of control and personal acceptance for failure.	Outer locus of control and blame of others for failure.
Use of non-verbal communication	Much non-verbal communication.	More focus on verbal communication than body language.
Expression of reaction	Reserved, inward reactions.	Visible, external, outward reaction.
Cohesion and separation of groups	Strong distinction between ingroup and outgroup. Strong sense of family.	Flexible and open grouping patterns, changing as needed.
People bonds	Strong people bonds with affiliation to family and community.	Fragile bonds between people with little sense of loyalty.
Level of commitment to relationships	High commitment to long-term relationships. Relationship more important than task.	Low commitment to relationship. Task more important than relationships.
Flexibility of time	Time is open and flexible. Process is more important than product.	Time is highly organized. Product is more important than process.

Source: Straker, D. (2008) *Changing Minds: in Detail*, Syque Press.

Power distance

Power distance (PDI) involves the way societies deal with human inequality. People possess unequal physical and intellectual capacities which some societies allow to grow into inequalities in power and wealth. However, some other societies de-emphasize such inequalities. All societies are unequal but some are more unequal than others. The Philippines, India and France score relatively high in power distance. Austria, Israel, Denmark and Sweden show relatively low PDI scores, while the United States ranks slightly below midpoint.

Combining power distance and individualism reveals some interesting relationships (see Figure 3.2). Collectivist countries seem to show large power distance but individualist countries do not necessarily display small power distance. For example, the Latin European countries combine large power distance with high individualism. Other wealthy western countries combine smaller power distance with high individualism. It is interesting to observe that in Hofstede's sample, almost all developing countries tend to rate high on both collectivism (low individualism) and power distance. Of the countries Hofstede studied, only Costa Rica combined small power distance with high collectivism (low individualism).

Uncertainty avoidance

Uncertainty avoidance (UA) reflects how a society deals with uncertainty about the future, a fundamental fact of human existence. At one extreme, weak UA cultures socialize members to accept and handle uncertainty. People in such cultures tend to accept each day as it comes, take risks rather easily, do not work too hard and tolerate opinions and behaviour different from their own. Denmark, Sweden and Hong Kong all rated low in UA. The other extreme – strong UA societies – fosters the need to try to beat the future, resulting in greater nervousness, aggressiveness and emotional stress. Belgium, Japan and France ranked relatively high in uncertainty avoidance while the United States scored somewhat below midpoint.

FIGURE 3.2   Power distance/individualism dimensions across culture

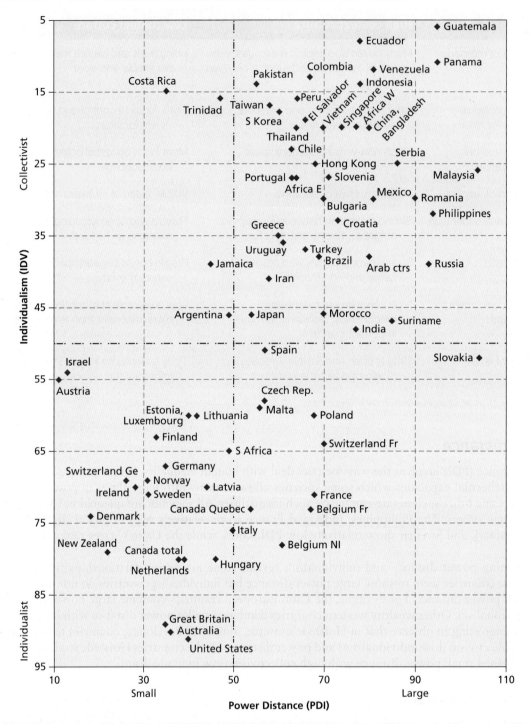

Source: Hofstede, G., Hofstede, G.J. and Minkov, M. (2010) *Cultures and Organizations: Software for the Mind: Intercultural Cooperation and Its Importance for Survival*, 3rd edn. McGraw Hill. Reproduced with permission.

Masculinity

Masculinity (MAS) deals with the degree to which societies subscribe to the typical stereotypes associated with males and females. Masculine values stress making money and the pursuit of visible achievements: such societies admire individual brilliance and idolize the successful achiever, the superman. These traditional masculine social values permeate the thinking of the entire society, women as well as men. Hofstede's research indicated that within his sample, Japan, Austria, Venezuela and Italy ranked highest in masculinity.

In more feminine societies, both men and women exhibit values associated with traditionally feminine roles such as endurance and an emphasis on people rather than money. Societal sympathy lies with the underdog, the anti-hero rather than the individually brilliant. Sweden, Norway, the Netherlands and Denmark rank as some of the most feminine societies studied by Hofstede. The United States scored fairly high on the masculinity dimension, placing it near the top one-third.

An assertive salesperson would be better accepted in a highly masculine culture such as Austria than in Denmark's more feminine culture. The level of masculinity also explains part of the perception that business people have of each other. In feminine countries where relationships are more highly valued, the supplier–client relationship is seen much more as a partnership than in more masculine cultures. Thus, the affective aspects of the business relationship are seen as of vital importance, particularly in negotiations as we will see in the section on cross-cultural negotiating later in this chapter.

Confucian dynamism

The Confucian dynamism dimension assesses cultures on the degree they are universalistic or particularistic. Universalistic cultures believe that what is true and good can be determined and defined and can be applied everywhere. Particularistic cultures evolve where 'unique circumstances and relationships are more important considerations in determining what is right and good rather than abstract rules'(Hofstede 2010). Confucian philosophy traditionally pervades Chinese culture. Its major characteristics include a strong bias towards obedience, the importance of rank and hierarchies and the need for smooth social relations. Within Confucian ethics, four basic relations were: between ruler and those ruled, father and son, husband and wife, and friend and friend. Everyone is expected to know where they stand in the hierarchy of human relations and one's place carries with it fixed standards of how one behaves towards others.

Culture/communication typologies

A number of writers have developed frameworks that can be utilized for cross-cultural analysis which have built on the above work. In this section we will discuss the communication typologies and the relationship between the cultural dimensions identified by Hofstede and the adoption of new products.

Communication typologies

Four verbal communication typologies were suggested by Gudykunst (2005) which can be used as a basis for cross-cultural analysis. These are as follows:

1 *Direct vs indirect* refers to the degree of explicitness of the verbal message of a culture. The Chinese use the indirect style, often hiding their real feelings and being more concerned with group harmony and the feelings of others. The use of the indirect style refers to the high context culture and Hofstede's collective dimension.

2 *Elaborative vs succinct* reflects the quantity of talk that people feel comfortable with in a particular culture. The succinct style is where quantity of talk is relatively low. This reflects high uncertainty avoidance and a high context culture. Elaborative styles may be used more in low context cultures where the spoken language is of greater importance, as in the US.

3 *Personal vs contextual* contextual style focuses on the role of the speaker and the role of relationships. The role and hierarchical relationship of the parties in conversation will be reflected in the form of address and words that are used. This type of communication reflects high power distance, collectivism and high context cultures such as Japan.

4 *Instrumental vs affective* defines the orientation of the speaker. In the affective verbal style the speaker is process orientated. There is concern that neither the speaker nor the receiver will be put in an uncomfortable position. The speaker also listens to and closely observes the receiver in order to interpret how the message is being taken. This is a reflection of a high context collective culture, such as South East Asia.

Such typologies may influence the receptiveness of consumers across cultures to humour in advertising. We explore this in Illustration 3.5.

Hofstede's cultural dimensions vs rate of product adoption   Singh (2006) suggests that particular dimensions of culture are critical in determining whether consumers of certain cultures are likely

ILLUSTRATION 3.5

Humorous advertisements – Would Polish advertisements make you laugh?

Cultural differences and their dimensions should be considered in all aspects of marketing. Advertising, in particular, must not be neglected as it reflects and influences consumers and is the most pervasive paid-for social communication. The question international brands ask is, can advertisements cross borders? More importantly would consumers from different cultures enjoy a humorous advertisement in the same way? These questions have been debated and researched many times.

The conclusion is different cultures enjoy different types of humour. In the UK humour in advertisements is often ridiculous, 'way over the top' from reality. Additionally, UK advertisers use word-play that deliberately makes words and phrases ambiguous but amusing. In France advertisers use jokes to gain attention and please audiences. Advertisements in Thailand are considered to be very creative and popular with consumers who enjoy the black humour and slapstick that represents Thai behaviour. Clearly, humour is something which is not always transferable.

In some cultures for example, humour can be seen as a sign of aggression or dominance. And a smile, often seen as a fun ice breaker between actors in advertisements, is not necessarily a sign of approval or humour with Chinese or Malaysian consumers. Furthermore, ethnic or gender-related humour is still acceptable in some parts of the world such as areas of Europe; but it should be avoided in the USA.

Another aspect that is discussed over and over again is whether humour should be used in advertisements for 'serious products'. Serious products include funerals, mortgages and life insurance. The reason for the debate is that using humour or including celebrities that are comedians may trivialize the serious product or service being offered. Despite that, since the privatization of many major sectors in Poland and the transition from a Communist to post-Communist society, all Polish banks' campaigns include celebrities; often comedians and humour.

PKO Bank Polski is the largest bank in Poland, and one of the oldest. It is interesting to note that PKO Bank has spent over 110 million zloty (over £22m) on humorous advertising, the highest amount of money spent of all the Polish financial institutions. All of their advertisements contain humour and Szymon Majewski, a comedian and chat-show host. Generally the types of humour used by PKO Bank include slapstick, clownish, surprise and irony. Like many other brands the humour contained in PKO Bank's advertisements include many situations and circumstances that only Polish people would understand and find funny.

Question

1 Evaluate the implications of using humour in advertising international brands.

Source: Beata Szymańska-Waczyńska, Alexandra J Kenyon and Eamonn Judge.

to easily adopt new products or services, or not. Essentially he measured the propensity of a culture to innovate and found that cultures characterized by a small power distance, weak uncertainty avoidance and masculinity are more likely to be innovative and accept new product ideas than cultures where there was a large power distance, strong uncertainty avoidance and more feminine traits exhibited. Equally he suggested that cultural dimensions were also linked to the preferred type of communication. Individualistic cultures are more likely to be swayed by more impersonal channels, whereas collectivist cultures are more likely to be swayed by interpersonal communications. Heineken tapped into the need for social acceptance to avoid uncertainty in collectivist cultures in their innovative campaign in Asia. They built a perception of popularity by asking staff in bars selling Heineken to leave bottles on tables by not pouring full beers into glasses and not collecting the empties. Suddenly little green bottles were seen everywhere and it didn't take long for customers to start asking for that particular brand.

Globe programme   The GLOBE (Global Leadership and Organizational Behaviour Effectiveness) programme is an extensive research project, which has built on previous studies of cultural divergences and patterns. It is working to integrate previous research to develop one single platform to carry out cross-cultural analysis on leadership attributes. Across 62 countries, the GLOBE programme investigates how cultural values are related to organizational practices, conceptions of leadership, the economic competitiveness of societies and the human condition of its members. The programme identifies the following nine cultural dimensions:

- uncertainty avoidance
- power distance
- collectivism – in-group (family and organization)
- collectivisim – society (societal and organizational institutions)
- gender egalitarianism
- assertiveness
- future orientation
- performance orientation
- humane orientation.

Social and cultural influences in business-to-business marketing

Much of the discussion relating to the influences of social cultural factors on international marketing assumes a market for predominantly fast-moving consumer goods where decisions are made on either a family or individual basis. Yet a considerable proportion of exports relates to industrial goods and services where companies are primarily concerned with company-to-company or business-to-business marketing and dealing, therefore, with primarily organizational or even government buyers. The question we now need to address is how relevant the social/cultural factors we have been discussing are to these types of markets.

In business-to-business marketing there are essentially two types of buyers: organizations and governments. In this section we will highlight some of the social/cultural influences on these types of buyers which are particularly relevant to international marketing. Following this we will discuss the impact of culture on cross-cultural negotiating styles and the practice of gift-giving in international business relationships.

Organizational buyers

Business buying decisions are influenced by decisions about technology, the objectives and tasks of the company, the organizational structure of the buying company and the motivations of people in the company. The technology decision is an interesting area. Some companies rely on their own internal capability to produce solutions to problems they need to solve in the areas of technology and how to manufacture the product. However, Japanese companies have encouraged their suppliers to help them by providing technological improvements. This approach is now influencing business practices across the world. The US adversarial approach of developing a precise buying specification and then challenging supplying firms to win the contract by providing the best deal is now less common.

Culture at the organizational level can play a significant part in the way in which the various roles are enacted. When it comes to international encounters, humour for instance can be a double-edged sword. The dangers of a joke backfiring are increased when the parties concerned do not share a common culture. Different cultures have different beliefs and assumptions which determine when humour is considered appropriate, what can be joked about and even who can be joked with. Attitudes to uncertainty, status and the sanctity of business influence the extent to which humour is allowed to intrude on proceedings.

There are a number of different corporate cultural characteristics in European countries which influence buyer behaviour. The French have a hierarchical system of management with a strong tendency to centralism; consequently it is often difficult for sales people to reach the top manager as that individual may well be buffered behind half a dozen assistants. Spanish and Italian decision making tends to be highly autocratic and based on the model of the family; decision making is shared with systems that tend to be informal. The German position is influenced by earned respect for formal qualifications and technical competence. Leadership depends upon respect rather than subservience.

Government buyer behaviour

In many countries the government is the biggest buyer, far larger than any individual consumer or business buyer. Governments buy a wide range of goods and services: roads, education, military, health and welfare. The way in which governments buy is influenced by the extent to which public accountability in the expenditure of public money is thought important.

It has been estimated that 20 per cent of the gross domestic product (GDP) of the European Union is controlled through the value of purchases and contracts awarded by the public sector. In the US approximately 30 per cent of the gross national product (GNP) is accounted for by the purchases of US governmental units. For some companies their international business comprises government buyers in different countries. It is important, therefore, to understand the government buying processes.

Usual forms of buying procedure are the open tender and selective tender. In open bid contracts, tenders are invited against a tight specification, and contracts are usually awarded to the lowest-price bid. Selective tender contracts are offered to companies who have already demonstrated their ability in the area appropriate to the tender. Only those companies on the selective tender list will be invited to tender. As with open tender, the lowest price is often used to adjudicate the bids.

In the European Union specific rules have been drawn up in an attempt to remove the barriers between potential suppliers of government contracts from different countries of the EU. Suppliers from all EU member states should have an equal opportunity to bid for public authority contracts and public works contracts must be advertised throughout the EU.

The business-to-business buying process

In the B2B buying processes the various types of buying are classified into three different classes of buying: straight re-buy, modified re-buy and new task.

A straight re-buy represents the bulk of the business buying. The buy signal is often triggered through information systems when stock levels reach a predetermined replenishment point. The modified re-buy indicates a certain level of information search and re-evaluation of products/services and supplies before the purchase is made. The new task represents an area of considerable uncertainty in which the company needs to make decisions about what it wants, about performance standards and about supplier capabilities. The new task, particularly if the purchase is of major importance to the company, will involve senior management and might take a long time to complete.

The way in which a company manages each of the buy classes will be influenced by cultural factors. Companies with a strong ethnocentric orientation may limit their search to suppliers from their own country. For more internationally oriented companies, the country of origin effect will distort information collection and appraisal. The influence of established relationships in cultures in which personal contacts and relationships are important will act as a barrier to companies which operate in a more formal way.

Relationship marketing is very important in business-to-business marketing, where companies may gain competitive advantage not necessarily from the product but through the added value they have built because of their relationship. This is especially important in markets such as China. The Chinese rely heavily on personal relationships in business dealings. It is important for foreign companies to understand the dynamics of these relationships (known as *guanxi*). There is a saying in Chinese, 'If you do not have a relationship you do not exist'.

Personal selling and negotiation between the buyer and seller as they go through the interaction process in order to build a business relationship which is mutually beneficial is an important part of international marketing. It is in this process of negotiation and relationship building that cultural factors have their greatest impact.

The role of culture in negotiation styles

Culture can be a major determinant in the success or failure of business negotiations. In Saudi Arabia business may look informal and slow paced, but in negotiations a businessman would be grossly insulted if they were expected to negotiate with a representative rather than the top person. Indian negotiators bargain much longer and tend to be much more competitive and persistent in trying to maximize their gains.

However, some commentators suggest that while a lack of understanding of the cultural differences in negotiation styles may be a major cause of negotiation failure, awareness of cultural differences may not be a major factor in negotiation success, unless that awareness is accompanied by a deeper understanding of how culture impacts on the whole negotiation process. A negotiation process (Graham and Sano 1989) can be broken down into four stages:

1 Non-task discussion
2 Task-related exchange of information
3 Persuasion
4 Concession and agreement.

The first stage, *non-task discussion*, describes the process of establishing rapport between members of the negotiation teams. Japanese negotiators would spend considerable time and money entertaining foreign negotiating teams in order to establish a rapport, whereas US executives saw the delays as frustrating and the money spent as wasteful. GEC Alsthom sales executives found karaoke sessions very useful when negotiating with the North Koreans for a contract for high-speed trains between Seoul and Pusan. The firm understood from the outset that the first stage of negotiations needed to include a broad range of activities, such as singing, to help establish a rapport on which the relationship could be built.

The *task-related exchange of information stage* describes the exchange of information that defines the participants' needs and expectations. Well over 90 per cent of all large Japanese companies and most of the smaller ones use a decision-making process called *ringi*. The system is based on the principle that decisions are made only when a consensus is reached by the negotiating team. Proposals are circulated among the negotiating team for each to affix their own personal seal of approval. Without the group's approval, which takes a long time to acquire, no proposal will be accepted. What may appear to US negotiators as stalling tactics is often simply the different process by which the Japanese reach a decision.

The *persuasion stage* for US executives is the one that consumes time, whereas for Japanese negotiators who have previously taken the time to understand each other's expectations, it is seen as unnecessary. Japanese negotiators may, as a result, remain silent. This is not because they do not agree with the proposal but because they are either waiting for more information or, for them, agreement has been reached and therefore negotiations are complete.

This often leads to misunderstanding at the *concession and agreement stage*. An extension of the Japanese preference for establishing strong personal relationships is their dislike for the formal western-style contract. A loosely worded statement expressing mutual cooperation and trust developed between negotiating parties is much preferred. The advantage of these agreements is that they allow a great deal of flexibility in the solution of unforeseen problems, whereas western negotiators may feel the need to bargain to the end and do not see their job as complete until they have actually obtained a signature. Table 3.2 gives an interesting summary of differences in buyer–seller negotiating styles in selected countries.

Table 3.2   Differences in buyer–seller relationships styles

International market	Climate	Importance of relationships	Process	Decision making
United States	Sometimes viewed as an aggressive or confrontational climate	Of less importance. Focus is on achieving desired results	Ordered process where each point is discussed in sequence	Can be either an individual or group decision process
Canada	Positive, polite climate. Hard sell will not work here	Of less importance. Focus is on achieving desired results	Ordered process where each point is discussed in sequence	Can be either an individual or group decision process
Latin America	Positive and hospitable climate	Personal, one-on-one relationships very important	Relationship building through socialization will precede negotiations	Decisions are usually made by a high-level individual
United Kingdom	Traditional, polite climate. Hard sell will not work here	Of less importance. Focus is on achieving desired results	Ordered process where each point is discussed in sequence	Can be either an individual or group decision process
Germany/Austria	Rigid, sober climate	Low. Germans remain aloof until negotiations conclude	Systematic process with emphasis on contractual detail	Even the most routine decisions are made by top-level officials
France/Belgium	Formal, bureaucratic climate. Hard sell will not work here	Formal, arm's-length relationships with attention to etiquette	French teams use argument to generate discussion	Usually a group process headed by a senior negotiator
Japan	Formal polite climate with many idiosyncratic nuances	Great importance. Long-term relationships are what matter most	First all general items are agreed on, then details are discussed	A total group process with all levels involved in the final decision
China	Bureaucratic climate with an abundance of 'red tape'	Very important. Traditional, cultural courtesies are expected	Discussions are long and repetitive. Agreements must be in writing	Usually a group process headed by a senior negotiator
Russia	Bureaucratic climate with an abundance of 'red tape'	Low. Russians will remain reserved until negotiations conclude	Cumbersome process due to bureaucratic constraints	Usually a group process headed by a senior negotiator

Source: Lewin, J.E. and Johnston, W.L. (1997). 'Managing the international salesforce'. *Journal of Business and Industrial Marketing*. 12 (3/4).

Usunier and Lee (2012) suggests a number of ways to minimize cultural impact in negotiations in order to build effective transcultural relationships:

■ *Adaptation.* In international business meetings, people who do not appear to feel the need to adapt may be considered indolent: 'Those who adapt are aware of differences, whereas those to whom others adapt remain unaware'. Usunier and Lee (2012).

■ *Interpreters.* Be aware that interpreters influence meaning. They may translate better from one language into another than in the opposite direction. The loyalty of interpreters needs to be considered. Are they more in favour of one party than the other? Should you use your own interpreter? Should you use several interpreters to reduce stress errors and bias?

■ *Cultural blocks.* Not everything will translate – it is not possible to translate meaning exactly for all elements in an interpretation. Culture-specific elements will block some attempts at translation.

■ *The stereotype.* Avoid negative stereotyping which is likely to increase negotiation conflicts and difficulties.

■ *Intercultural preparation.* Good prior preparation in intercultural understanding is a necessary investment to improve international business effectiveness.

Ethical issues in cross-cultural marketing

Cultural sensitivity is often at the heart of the ethical dilemmas that managers face when operating in international markets. There are few, if any, moral absolutes and few actions for which no one can provide reasonable justification. Almost every action can be justified on the basis that it is acceptable in one particular culture. In thinking about ethics managers need to be aware that simply defining what is ethical by the standards, values and actions from their own culture may be insufficient in satisfying all the stakeholders of a multinational enterprise. What is often seen as an acceptable business practice in one culture can be seen as ethically questionable in another. The SRC effect discussed earlier is particularly relevant to the discussion of how cultural sensitivities impact on what is an ethical business practice. Managers from different cultures will always be able to challenge, for instance, the US, African or Japanese perspective of what is ethical.

The ethical challenges facing international marketing managers are many. In recent years such issues as environmental abuse, the use of child labour, poor working conditions and the low levels of pay in Third World factories have received particular attention. Western consumers choosing brands look for reassurance that the product has been produced in what they see as a socially responsible manner. Some clothing brands such as Primark, Nike and Gap have suffered adverse publicity when it has become known that child labour has been used to produce their products. Some brands have made valiant attempts to ensure ethical standards in their international operations, but often it is not the brand that is wholly to blame but their supply chain (See Illustration 3.6). This means international businesses must not only act responsibly themselves but ensure all parts of their supply chain does so too.

Consumers globally are becoming well informed through better education and faster and more effective communications. Increasingly, therefore, they are able to question the actions of multinational enterprises, as we saw in the discussion of the role of pressure groups in Chapter 1. For their part, while the largest multinationals are extending their influence within the global markets, they are becoming more vulnerable to criticism. Over the past few years, quality and service have improved considerably, but now firms are increasingly expected to ensure that their behaviour is ethical and in the interests of the global community which makes up their market.

However, international marketing executives operating across cultures will find themselves facing moral and ethical dilemmas on a daily basis on a wide range of issues when faced with the ethical dilemmas operating in countries where bribery and corruption are endemic.

Bribery and corruption

An integral part of conducting business internationally is the practice of gift-giving. However, in many western countries such practice is seen as bribery/corruption and is tightly regulated and controlled. Business gift-giving – or bribery, depending on your point of view – if improperly executed, could stop

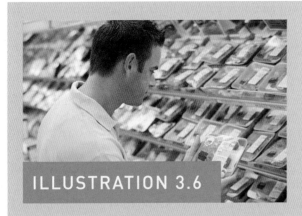

ILLUSTRATION 3.6

Ensuring ethical standards in international operations

During 2013 the 'Horsemeat Scandal' in Europe took away consumer trust in the food that we eat. During routine checks of food processing plants by the Food Safety Authority of Ireland, DNA from horsemeat was found in products that were packaged and sold as beef. Further investigations showed that other products including beef burgers contained pork (but pork was not included in the list of ingredients contained within the food item). Immediately, supermarkets such as Aldi and Lidl withdrew products from their shelves that had been bought from the food processing plant, and so did Burger King who had also purchased contaminated products.

The scandal has many implications on a global scale. Businesses often source meat, fish, fruit and vegetables directly from source or from export supply chain businesses. Buying directly from a source includes purchasing apples from an orchard in France

or chickens from a local organic, freerange farm. However, a great deal of food sourcing comes through a very long supply chain. For example, a batch of meat identified in the horsemeat scandal began at a slaughterhouse in Romania. The horsemeat was packaged and labelled as beef and purchased by a business from Luxembourg. The meat was then traded by two businesses, the first from Holland and the second from Cyprus. The meat was then purchased by a French company that processed the meat which was then sold to the Irish food processing plant. This demonstrates the journey that meat, fish, fruit and vegetables can take before arriving on our supermarket shelves or in restaurants.

The trading of meat in this way often occurs because of an international low-priced competitiveness marketplace.

Including horse and pig meat in products that are sold as beef has implications on consumer sensibilities; be that religious or cultural.

Further problems occur for consumers and medical associations when drugs are given to horses and chickens that may be harmful to consumers. Drugs are given to horses to reduce infection and to chickens to make them fatter and produce more meat per chicken. KFC has seen sales of their chicken products go down in China by over 30 per cent since it was published in national media that drugs were being injected into chickens; locally this was known as the 'fatter chicken scandal'.

Question

1 How should global companies resolve the ethical dilemmas identified above?

sensitive negotiations and ruin new and potential business relationships. German and Swiss executives tend to feel uncomfortable accepting gifts, which they view as bribes, as they will not want to be seen as being under obligation to the other party. However, business gift-giving in many cultures is an important part of persuasion. In cultures where a business gift is expected but not given, it is an insult to the host.

Cultures that view bribery as an acceptable business practice tend to fall into the high context category. In such a culture the communication style is more implicit, non-verbal and more reliant on hidden cues in the context of personal relationships. In Japan, for example, a highly developed and affluent society, gift-giving practices are widespread in the business culture. Refusing to participate in gift-giving in such cultures can cause bad feeling and misunderstandings between business clients. In high context cultures, financial inducements are often seen as important steps in bringing a person into the inner circle of a business relationship or to strengthen the relationship between a buyer and a seller.

By contrast, people in low context cultures rely on explicit contracts, communication is more formal and explicit, and negotiations based on a more legalistic orientation. Laws applying to bribery tend to be very well laid out. In some cultures, all business gifts will be viewed as illegal bribes; conversely, other cultures view gifts, pay-offs and even bribes merely as a cost of business. Bribery and corruption are part of the commercial traditions of many parts of Asia, Africa and the Middle East. Transparency International, a global counter-corruption watchdog, ranks Somalia as the most corrupt country, followed closely by Afghanistan and Myanmar. To many international marketing managers operating in those markets, how to respond to the demand for a bribe could be a problematic ethical dilemma. It can sometimes be very difficult to empathize with the cultural values of another country if they challenge your own personal morals.

Piracy

Piracy has been a particular problem to the global music and software industry.

Different cultures have varying perspectives on piracy. The US courts take a very stringent view and prosecute offenders that are caught. In China and India views on intellectual property rights are much more difficult to define. The International Intellectual Property Alliance claims that despite now being members of the WTO piracy is still a big problem in China.

In China, Havoscope estimate at least US$26 billion-worth of goods sold each year inside the country are counterfeit. However, according to Fox News the Chinese authorities are now cracking down on product piracy, in just three months in 2011 they arrested 3001 people, confiscated huge amounts of pirated products and closed some 300 websites selling counterfeit and fake goods.

Worldwide sales of counterfeit goods are estimated by Havoscope to be in the region of US$532.93 billion. Over 5.5 billion cigarettes, or 20 per cent of all cigarettes sold in South Africa, are either smuggled or counterfeit cigarettes. Procter and Gamble estimates that 10–15 per cent of its revenues are lost each year to counterfeit products. The Ukraine now exports counterfeit optical discs, Russia markets counterfeit software, Paraguay markets imitation cigarettes. Counterfeit pharmaceuticals are routinely marketed to countries unable to afford the expensive products of the authentic drug companies; often these are substandard, or have fake labels. It is estimated by the World Health Organization that between 5 and 7 per cent of drugs sold are counterfeits, with potentially fatal consequences. As discussed in Chapter 1, Sproxil report that fake anti-malarial and tuberculosis drugs alone account for over 700 000 reported annual deaths.

American industries lose US$200–250 billion a year to counterfeiting. The fact that many global manufacturers have moved their production to low-cost bases around the world is seen by some to have opened the floodgates to counterfeiting. The global brands have been able to take advantage of low labour costs but gave insufficient attention to securing intellectual property rights in such countries. In today's markets, where so much of the added value of a product is in its brand identity, counterfeiters have been able to exploit consumers' expectations of quality and service with counterfeit products. Brands such as Louis Vuitton, Nike, Microsoft, Gucci and Prada are among the most counterfeited of global brands.

Much of the problem stems from cultural attitudes to the rights of anyone to own intellectual property. The Chinese have argued that if all ideas were copyrighted they should be able to patent the compass, ice-cream, noodles and many other products they have given to the world. Recently Starbucks won a high profile case against a Chinese company using the Chinese version of its name, the court ruling that the company had the sole right to its name in both English and Chinese. The French cognac company Hennessey also won a piracy case in China against two companies copying its brand and selling it as French cognac brandy, even though it was produced and bottled in China. In Europe, the European Commission has proposed new rules to harmonize member states' legislation on IPR enforcement. This has been particularly important because the EU embraced new members from Eastern Europe, where counterfeiting is a serious problem in some countries.

Although nations and organizations often provide ethical guidelines on bribery, counterfeiting, etc., ultimately international managers have to make decisions based on their own personal views of what is and is not ethical. Managers need to form a view when operating across different cultures as to what constitutes ethical decision making within an organization. Managers need to reflect on what constitutes ethical behaviour, how decisions will be viewed by stakeholders and the perceived and real impact upon the organization of making a decision that breaches ethical standards. Central is the importance the company places on the need for an ethically responsible approach to their operations in the global markets.

Companies are increasingly of the view that organizational behaviour considered to be unethical can decrease a firm's wealth, while behaviour considered by stakeholders to be ethical can enhance a company's competitive advantage on global markets. Attempting to take an ethically responsible decision, though, could mean the loss of perhaps an efficient and cheap source of supply or in some cases the loss of a potential deal. Any decision would need very careful consideration.

The consequence of an ethically responsible approach would involve increased resources and attention being applied to a number of areas, such as:

- The increased need for accurate and timely information.
- Increased attention to press, public reaction and global pressure groups.
- Closer relationships with stakeholders and members of the supply chain to ensure all interests are taken into consideration.
- Being prepared, when serious risks are identified, to take positive and constructive action.

SUMMARY

- The influence of social and cultural factors in international marketing is complex and often extremely difficult for a firm operating in foreign markets to analyze and understand. In today's global environment, where culture is becoming increasingly deterritorialized and each culture is penetrated by the influences of other cultures, the issue of examining and understanding cultural sensitivities is becoming increasingly complex.

- If the firm is operating across a number of markets, finding consistent methods of analyzing their cross-cultural markets poses particular challenges. The cultural dimensions of Hofstede, the contextual classification of cultures and the GLOBE programme dimensions are three frameworks that can be used.

- This chapter has focused on developing an understanding of the components of culture and how these components impact on consumer beliefs, values, attitudes and purchasing behaviour.

- Culture also affects the way that business is carried out in different markets. Culture underpins the legal structure of a country and ethical attitudes to decision making and the acceptability of bribes, etc. Managers need to form a view when operating across different cultures as to what constitutes ethical decision making within an organization and what constitutes ethical behaviour.

- Culture has a significant impact, therefore, on the international marketing strategies of firms, both in consumer and business-to-business markets. In this chapter the reader should have acquired an awareness of the possible methods that can be used to categorize differences across cultures to enable a cross-cultural analysis to be carried out. In Chapter 4 we go on to look at the methods of analyzing and researching international markets.

KEYWORDS

social and cultural factors	non-verbal communication	cross-cultural
beliefs	enculturation	low context cultures
values	attitude	high context cultures
customs	consumer behaviour	individualism
cultural sensitivity	perception of risk	ethical challenges
silent language	cultural identity	piracy
spoken language	self-reference criterion	

CASE STUDY 1

Islam, Ramadan and the tent business in the Middle East

Ramadan represents one of the five pillars of Islam, which all Muslims are expected to follow, the other four are 'Faith' or *Shahadah*; 'Prayer' or *Salah*, 'Charitable Giving' or *Zakah* and the 'Pilgrimage to Makkah' or *Hajj*. The month of Ramadan is a time for spiritual reflection and prayer. Ramadan is usually observed in the ninth month of the Islamic lunar calendar and is one of the most important months for Muslims as it is believed this is the month that the Qur'an was first revealed to the Prophet Mohammed. During this month all healthy Muslims fast from sunrise to sunset when they must refrain from all food, drink, gum chewing, tobacco use and any kind of sexual contact.

Muslims believe their good actions bring greater reward during these 30 days because the month has been blessed by Allah. 'Fasting' reminds Muslims of the suffering of the poor who often don't get to eat well. During the 'holy month' of Ramadan, most Muslims tend to wake up just before sunrise to have a meal or *Suhoor*. They will then not be able to eat or drink until sunset when it is traditional to open the fast with a date (date palm as it is believed that the Prophet Mohammed broke his fast with such a fruit) and then proceed to have the *Iftar*. Certain individuals and/or groups hold *Iftar* parties (where they prepare lots of food and then invite people round to eat). Ramadan has both spiritual and physical significance. It often lasts between 29 to 30 days, depending on the sighting of the new moon, which marks the celebration of *Eid El Fitr*. Prior to this final day of celebration, tents and/or marquees are traditionally put up by the privileged to cater for the less privileged in the spirit of *charitable giving* during this sombre and sober month.

In the Middle East and North Africa (MENA), lavish tents and marquees have long been a mainstay of the corporate events industry during the holy month of Ramadan. However, recently due to the financial crisis the marquee business has suffered as the main players have started re-strategizing their marketing activities. In the Arabian Gulf region and the United Arab Emirates (UAE) in particular, a complete tent costs anything between AED200 000 and AED250 000 (approx. £33 000–£42 000) to set up.

While the tent business is fast becoming a crowded market in the UAE, two players are worth elaborating upon: *Al-Baddad International* and *Harlequin Marquees & Event Services*. Both of these firms have started to look further afield in order to maintain sales following the economic downturn – in so doing they have adopted different international marketing strategies. In the case of the first firm, *Al-Baddad International* (henceforth *Al-Baddad*), it is a subsidiary of Al-Baddad Global, established in Abu Dhabi in 1971 (the same year the country attained independence from Great Britain) by the late Hajj Hassan Al-Baddad. The firm claims to be a leading provider of innovative mobile halls and prefabricated buildings in the MENA region. Among its main products are outdoor solutions, exhibitions, conferences, weddings, special events, private occasions, festivals, camps, warehouses and temporary accommodations. Since its founding, *Al-Baddad* has continually built a business across the MENA region with Egypt and Libya being the most recent markets (see Table 3.3). The firm also lays claims to leadership in mobile halls and tents in the region – manufacturing large quantities of tents and prefabricated buildings all year round through a company known as 'Al-Baddad Capital'.

Al-Baddad's marketing strategy has revolved around three key themes: 'explore, create, and always adopt new techniques and innovations to keep its solutions ahead of the curve', as it strives to guarantee its place among the top suppliers in its industry both regionally and internationally. As one of the key players in the MENA, it nonetheless faced the challenge of a downturn in business due to a decline in corporate sponsorship and so needs to think through how it might expand into new markets. Commenting on how they fared in 2010, Bilal Hamdan, the company's marketing manager remarked that:'. . . this year we were more creative'. This creativity underlined the company's marketing strategy including offering hotels price discounts in exchange for their branding to be displayed at the venues. The firm also considered

Table 3.3   Al-Baddad branches worldwide

Year of entry	City/country	Year of entry	City/country
1971	Abu Dhabi (UAE)	2001	Riyadh (Saudi Arabia)
1989	Al-Ain (UAE)	2002	Jeddah (Saudi Arabia)
1989	Sharjah (UAE)	2005	Ras Al-Khaimah (UAE)
1992	Dubai (UAE)	2005	Kuwait
1996	Qatar	2009	Damman (Saudi Arabia)
1996	California (USA)	2010	Egypt
1997	Jordan	2010	Libya

Source: Official website of Al Baddad. Available online at: www.albaddadintl.com/aboutus.htm

cultural events and other opportunities across the MENA region having observed that some hotels had decided to opt for the structures they had set up for the FIFA World Cup.

In the case of the second firm, *Harlequin Marquees & Event Services* (*Harlequin* henceforth), the firm was established in 1998, many years after Al Baddad, and claims to be at the 'forefront of Gulf hospitality', catering for all the usual events – from product launches to gala dinners amongst others. *Harlequin* also boasts Arabesque-themed solutions in its opulent *Ramadan Majlis* (an Arabic term meaning 'a place of sitting' used to describe various types of special gatherings) tents. *Harlequin Marquees* is part of the Arena Group, which is split into four trading divisions across the world (Arena Americas, Arena UK & Europe, Arena Middle East & Asia, Arena Overlay) – with a presence in seven cities (Abu Dhabi, Bangkok, Dammam, Dubai, Kuala Lumpur, Riyadh, Singapore) across five countries (Saudi Arabia, UAE, Malaysia, Singapore and Thailand). In the Middle East & Asia Division, there are four separate trading companies of which *Harlequin* is the UAE operating arm (others include Arena Tents Saudi Arabia; Asia Tents Arena, Malaysia; and Arena Event Services, Singapore).

During the holy month of Ramadan, *Harlequin* provides a variety of structures, interiors and furniture to hotels, private and corporate clients across the Arabian Gulf region (notably in the UAE and Saudi Arabia). The firm also claims to create bespoke interiors in both traditional and contemporary styles, with hundreds of items of furniture and accessories perfect for Ramadan including Moroccan tables and

poufs, low level lounge-seating, Arabic rugs, lanterns and Omani pots. In recent years it has also provided structures for *Iftar* and *Suhoor*, as well as canopies for *Sheesha* (smoking water pipes) at 5-star locations including the Ritz-Carlton, the Fairmont Bab Al Bahr, The Westin (both in Dubai and Abu Dhabi), Sofitel, the Grand Hyatt, and the Habtoor Grand Hotel.

Founder, Carmen Clews, a former employee of Britain's Royal Air Force air traffic control team, partnered with Charlie Wright to guide the full-service event design and rental company into a 45-employee operation that claims to have some of the world's biggest blue-chip companies as its clients. Indeed, the creative enterprise of designing '*modern Arabia*' event environments, complete with frosted arabesque pattern tent windows and white LED-lit 'star' fabrics, satisfies *Harlequin*'s hunger for unique challenges. The firm also considers itself adept at leveraging its marketing strategy – i.e. a patient player in a crowded market. As sources at the firm once pointed out, 'We have to be extra careful, taking nothing for granted and never assuming anything.' But while embellishing the virtue of such patience, the management acknowledges the need for a bit of impulsiveness – 'Acting immediately on ideas that feel right', is something that has got *Harlequin* where they are today. Since its launch in 1998, the firm's outstanding quality, service and contribution to the events sector has been recognized through numerous awards in 2006/2007:

- 2006 Lloyds TSB Small Business Awards Winner
- *Special Events Magazine* 2006 Gala Awards
- *Special Events Magazine* 2007 Gala Awards

Table 3.4   Top companies under category 'Tents & Tarpaulins'

Al Baddad International	Emirates Tents & Tensile Structure
Al Saba Tents LLC	Al Daiem Tents IND. LLC
Citiscape LLC	Alain Tents
Dubai Coast Trading LLC	Al Aydi Tents & Metal Ind
Mehler Tex.nologies Middle East Trading LLC	Al Hamra Shades Industries LLC
Electra Events & Exhibitions (LLC)	Roza Tents LLC
Al Mumtaz Tents & Canopies LLC	Al Safa Tents Fix
Al Mumtaz Tents Co LLC	Structurflex Middle East Contracting LLC
Qaryat Al Saba Tents LLC	Life Way Tents L.L.C
Al Arab Trading (FZE)	Rahal Green Technology

Source: *Arabian Business,* www.arabianbusiness.com/photos/20-must-try-ramadan-tents--509436.html

However, as the previous case, *Harlequin* has seen a downturn. According to Camilla Quinn, the client services manager of *Harlequin*, 'We're finding that the main reason hotels have pulled out this year has been because they've not been able to get the sponsorship.' Another member of the company's management team stated, 'We had four clients who were all quite far down the line with putting structures up, but they were all based on receiving corporate sponsorship. With all four of them it fell through at the last minute and they all completely pulled their Ramadan tents.'

While both *Al Baddad* and *Harlequin* have been making major strides across the MENA, it is worth adding that there are other players in the market (see Table 3.4 for a brief summary), among which *Electra Events & Exhibitions* (henceforth *Electra*) established in Dubai in 1992, is worth elaborating upon. Electra was originally an electrical contracting firm before transforming and venturing into the exhibition stand contracting market and in 2003 was taken over by Jean-Charles Durand, *Electra*'s current CEO. Since then, *Electra* has enjoyed tremendous growth and the company is now a leading provider of exhibition stands and exhibitions management, event contracting, tent and marquee rental solutions and decor and furniture rental in the MENA. As a result of this growth, *Electra* opened two additional branches in Abu Dhabi in 2010 and Doha in 2012.

Electra is led by a management team with combined 20 years' of experience in the exhibition stands contracting industry in the MENA. Its team of more than 500 experts includes designers, architects, engineers, project managers, carpenters, painters, upholsterers, electricians, logisticians, drivers and more who all work in-house, deliver the latest European standards and practices, and have been trained to operate its state-of-the-art machinery and equipment. The firm provides a customized approach to corporate stand contracting, and specializes in exhibition stands working directly with exhibitors to provide a complete design, prototype and building service. It also provides full decor and furniture rental service for exhibition stands and events, comprising of both off-the-shelf and custom-made upholstery solutions. From its three locations in Dubai, Abu Dhabi and Doha, *Electra* has built an industry-wide reputation for delivering creative, high-quality and responsive services – leveraging its strategy of keeping 'everything in-house!' According to sources at the firm, 'keeping our exhibition stand, tent rental and furniture rental services in-house allow us to have a wide range of expertise at our fingertips [. . .] having a group of more than 500 in-house experts that trust, respect each other and are used to working together, we can ensure that our clients benefit from a completely integrated service that will be delivered on time.' The firm also attributes its success to facilities and not just people, 'Our facilities and equipment play an essential role. Our 15 000m² premises are equipped with state-of-the-art machinery and European equipment [that] can create just about anything in any shape or size, from near seamless wooden jointing to precision-cut steel struts.' The firm also boasts 'A dedicated logistics department with a fleet of vehicles that allows [it] to offer a peerless choice of diverse tent and marquee rental solutions.'

A final notable player in the market is *Wicked LLC* (henceforth *Wicked*), which was conceived in 2007 to address the UAE's lack of indoor event and entertainment venues. By selecting unique, flexible and exciting structures that could be easily and quickly assembled a 'Wicked Venue' can be created virtually anywhere. Operating across the MENA from its Dubai head office (Jebel Ali Industrial 2) *Wicked* now provides a host of services related to the temporary structure industry, including tents, canopies, flooring, air conditioning, power distribution, interior design and fit out, audio visual, landscaping amongst others.

Questions

1 Discuss how *Al Baddad* and *Harlequin Marquees* have adapted their microenvironment in response to the turbulent macroenvironment within which they operate.

2 Compare and contrast the international marketing mix strategies adopted by *Al-Baddad* and *Harlequin Marquees*.

3 How do these compare with *Electra* and *Wicked*?

4 To what extent would you agree with *Electra*'s claim of offering a 'peerless choice of diverse tent and marquee rental solutions'?

5 Is there any room for another player to launch into this market? Why or why not?

Sources: Bundhun, R. (2010) 'Now is the summer of our discount tent', Abu Dhabi: *The National Newspaper*, Business Section, 2 September; Daniyah Hafiz (2008) 'What is Ramadan?' BBC Lancashire, UK (5 September 2008). Online at: www.bbc.co.uk/lancashire/content/articles/2006/10/09/ramadan_feature.shtml (Accessed 3 September 2010); Harlequin Marquees (no date) Official website of *Harlequin Marquees & Event Services.* Online at www.harlequinmarquees.com/; Huda (about.com) Ramadan Information. Online at: islam.about.com/od/ramadan/tp/ramadan-hub.htm

Author: Nnamdi O. Madichie, PhD. Canadian University of Dubai.

CASE STUDY 2

Cultural challenges in the Turkish ice cream market

Turkey is situated at the meeting point of South Eastern Europe and South Western Asia. It is bordered by Bulgaria to the northwest, Greece to the west, Georgia to the northeast, Armenia, Iran and Nakhchivan to the east, and Iraq and Syria to the southeast. Turkey considers itself both European and Asian, and cherishes this diversity and the Turkish people regard themselves as a cultural bridge between the East and the West.

Turkish people have a famous reputation of being hospitable, polite and extremely professional. They love to meet new friends and think nothing of spending half the day talking to a complete stranger while putting the world to rights but at the same time they tend to work extremely hard and stay at work for long hours.

Turkey has a large and youthful population, the 12–24 age group accounts for 31 per cent of the population. Armed with a rising spending power this segment of the market offers a dynamic consumer base for a range of consumer products including ice cream. BMI Research expects ice cream sales to rise by 28 per cent in the next three years. The country's hot climate, increasing urbanization, a growing middle class, its young population and increasing exposure of the youth market to packaged ice cream brands are all seen as key ingredients fuelling the growth. According to Euromonitor, per capita ice cream consumption was under 0.5 litres per annum in 1990 and expected to grow to 2.8 litres per capita by 2017.

However in Turkey the consumption of ice cream also has a strong cultural heritage. Since ancient times the Turkish people kept the winter snow from melting by storing it in mountain crevices which they covered with twigs. Come summer, they brought it up from its storage place, put it in bowls and ate it with stewed fruit, drizzling it with molasses. This sweet, called 'karsambac', is regarded as the ancestor of today's ice cream. More recently, the traditional Turkish Maras ice cream, which is hung on a butcher's hook and cut with a knife, is believed to have been made since the eighteenth century. Maras ice cream contains salep (powdered orchid root) and can be eaten with knife and fork. It is believed to originate from the city and region of Maraş and hence is also known as Maraş ice cream. Dondurma is another traditional ice cream commonly sold from both carts and store fronts where the mixture is churned regularly with long-handled paddles to keep it workable.

Yet despite such traditions the leading player in the ice cream market is Unilever Sanayii ve Ticaret Turk AS with a market share of 74 per cent. This leading position is due to the company's well-known and highly popular brands such as Cornetto and Magnum and extensive distribution network. Also the company is very active in terms of successful new product launches and advertising campaigns. Secure in the market's future growth, Unilever invested US$128 million into a new ice cream production facility in Turkey in 2014. Domestic companies Dinamik Gida (Alaska) in Istanbul and Izmir Sutlu Mamulleri (Memo) in Izmir have only a small share of the market. Other international companies are now starting to build strong positions in the market. The global food company Nestlé, the US-based ice cream parlour chain Cold Stone Creamery, and other international companies all operate in the Turkish market.

However for companies entering the Turkish ice cream market there are a mixture of modern and traditional cultural challenges to consider. Some Turks adhere to a belief that cold foods, such as ice cream, will cause illnesses such as sore throats and the common cold; such people hold that the consumption of warm liquid while consuming ice cream is needed to counteract these effects. There is also a belief that ice cream is not an all year round dessert but simply something to be enjoyed in warm weather. Around ninety per cent of ice cream consumption is between May and October. For many of the youth population ice cream brands are part of a trait of conspicuous consumption where social face, prestige and image are influential variables in their purchasing habits and their brand choice.

Questions

1 Evaluate the cultural considerations for a foreign company entering the ice cream market in Turkey.

2 What advice would you give to a company if they are to build a competitive position in this market?

Sources: BMI Research, Growth in Turkish ice cream sector, Food and Drink Insight, Jan 2014; Euromonitor International, Country Report, Ice cream in Turkey, Jan 2015; www .en.wikipedia.org/wiki/Dondurma (accessed June 2015).

DISCUSSION QUESTIONS

1 Discuss the view that culture lies at the heart of all problems connected with international marketing.

2 What is culture? Is it important for international marketers to take account of it or is globalization going to make it a thing of the past?

3 Given the cultural sensitivities to ethical dilemmas, can there ever be a global harmonization of ethical business practices in international marketing?

4 How do social and cultural influences impact on international business negotiations? Using examples, advise a company preparing for cross-cultural negotiations.

5 It has been suggested that firms from developed countries should market to developing countries by establishing partnerships in a neighbouring developing country. Explain the reasons behind such a proposition and the implications for a firm developing a globalization strategy.

REFERENCES

1. Blackwell, R.D., Miniard, P.W. and Engel, J.L. (2006) *Consumer Behaviour*, 9th edn. The Dryden Press.

2. Goman, C.K. (2011) *The Silent Language of Leaders: How Body Language Can Help – or Hurt – How You Lead*. USA: John Wiley & Sons.

3. Graham, J.L. and Sano, Y. (1989) *Smart Bargaining: Doing Business with the Japanese*. New York: Harper Business.

4. Gudykunst, W.B. (2005) *Cross-cultural and Intercultural Communication*, Sage Publications.

5. Jeannet, J.-P. and Hennessey, H.O. (2006) *Global Marketing Strategies*, 2nd edn. Houghton Mifflin.

6. Kotler, P. (2015). *Principles of Marketing: Value Edition*. Prentice Hall.

7. Maslow, A.H. (1970) *Motivation and Personality*, 2nd edn. Harper and Row.

8. Matsumoto, D. and Van de Vijver, F.J.R. (2010) *Cross Cultural Research Methods in Psychology (Culture & Psychology)*. Cambridge.

9. Terpstra, V., Foley, J. and Sarathy, R. (2012). *International Marketing*. Naper Press.

10. Singh, S. (2006) 'Cultural differences in and influences on consumers propensity to adopt innovations', *International Marketing Review*. 23(2) 173–91.

11. Usunier, J.-C and Lee, J.A. (2012) *Marketing Across Cultures*. Harlow: Pearson Education Limited.

CHAPTER 4

INTERNATIONAL MARKETING RESEARCH AND OPPORTUNITY ANALYSIS

LEARNING OBJECTIVES

After reading this chapter you should be able to:

- Appreciate the key roles of marketing research in international marketing

- Understand the concepts and techniques to identify and evaluate opportunities internationally

- Build a market profile analysis of a foreign country market

- Discuss the difficulties and issues that arise in developing multicountry primary research studies

INTRODUCTION

Discussions in previous chapters have illustrated the highly risky and complex environment in which the international marketing manager operates. If a company is to survive in the international marketplace, it is important that it searches for methods to reduce the risk of making a wrong decision as far as possible.

This is why **marketing research** is so fundamentally important to the international marketing process, for while it cannot help a manager reduce risk to the point of zero, it can ensure that the starting point for decision making is knowledge, rather than guesswork. Lack of knowledge of foreign markets is one of the first major barriers an international marketing manager will encounter. An effective marketing research strategy is the first step in overcoming that barrier.

The purpose of this chapter is to examine the place of marketing research in international strategy and the contribution it makes to the decision-making process. We will, therefore, be examining such concepts as the role of marketing research and opportunity analysis in international markets and the building of an international marketing information system. We will also examine some of the aspects of primary marketing research in international markets and discuss the practicalities and problems in implementing multicountry studies.

The role of marketing research and opportunity analysis

Marketing research can be defined as the systematic gathering, recording, analysis and interpretation of data on problems relating to the marketing of goods and services.

The role of research is primarily to act as an aid to the decision maker. It is a tool that can help to reduce the risk in decision making caused by the environmental uncertainties and lack of knowledge in international markets. It ensures that the manager bases a decision on the solid foundation of knowledge and focuses strategic thinking on the needs of the marketplace, rather than the product. Such a role is, of course, necessary in all types of marketing.

In international marketing, because of the increased uncertainties and complexities in world markets, the capacity to ensure a systematic planned process in the research and the use of secondary information, prior to field research, is of paramount importance if quality information is to be obtained. The research process (Malhotra *et al.*, 2013) consists of six key stages. These steps are the logical process for any research study to go through in its implementation and will be relevant for all research studies:

1   *Defining the problem.* It is important to decide what information is needed and set the objectives of the research, ensuring it is both commercially worthwhile and that the objective is feasible and achievable. Discussions with key stakeholders, decision makers and reviewing current secondary data is also fundamental in defining the problem. From the discussions the **Research question** evolves.

2   *Developing the approach to be taken.* The planning phase will concern itself with timescales, resources to carry out the work, the expertise required to meet the objectives and the decision as to whether a qualitative or quantitative approach is to be taken.

3   *Designing the research.* In designing the research, strategy consideration will be given to the different action steps that need to be taken. Ensuring full use of secondary data sources will be important, as will the use of a pilot study to ensure the development of an effective and meaningful questionnaire.

4   *Carrying out the field work.* Decisions as to how the questionnaires will be administered (telephone, mail, online, personal interviews) or where focus groups will take place will be made, as well as decisions as to who will do the work and what resources, including mobile devices or recording equipment, are required.

5   *Analyzing the data.* The data analysis stage will need to take full account of the objectives of the research and the client's needs. Many researchers will argue that the methodology to be used should be decided in the first stages of the research planning as it will impact on the questionnaire design and how the interviews are administered. Completing data analysis includes rigor in coding and transcription.

6   *Preparing the report and presentation.* The report and presentation are the researcher's outputs and vital in establishing the credibility of the research methods used and the validity of the findings of the research. See Illustration 4.1 for details of how different research questions are answered based on the same activity.

The role of international marketing research

The ability for research to deliver fast and yet sensitively analyzed results across a range of different countries in today's global markets is crucial for competitive success. In the past decade, we have seen the speed of business increase substantively with the global diffusion of computers, digital technologies and instant global telecommunication. Instant communication has become the standard across global markets, which means that marketing research has a critical role in feeding into decision makers' time-sensitive insights and changes in market behaviours around the globe. As such, the Internet has transformed the way we find information on our customers and track our markets worldwide. Social media analysts can provide selective, dynamic and up-to-date information to a larger number of users or individuals enabling marketers to save on the expensive research costs of collecting data from different countries. Companies worldwide

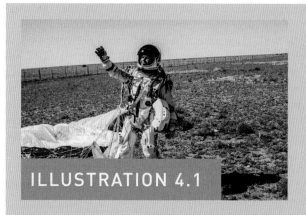

ILLUSTRATION 4.1

Science + Global Research = Red Bull Sales

Malholtra's research process is used in many different ways and it could be used by scientists and Red Bull when researching one activity.

Let us suggest a research question for scientists:

'Can a human being travel faster than sound?'

And for Red Bull:

'Can Red Bull increase its average number of YouTube subscribers from 2000 per day to 87 000 during a sponsored event?'

The scientists and Red Bull chose different research approaches and different ways to analyze data but they both researched one activity.

The activity was Red Bull's Stratos Jump when Felix Baumgartner leapt out of a balloon that was floating 128 100 ft up in the sky. This is equal to almost four times higher than Mount Everest, the equivalent of 24 miles or 39 km high! The jump from such a high stratosphere took 9 minutes and 3 seconds to complete and during the 'death defying leap' Felix reached a maximum velocity of 833.9 mph (1342 km/h). By reaching that velocity Felix became the first skydiver to travel faster than the speed of sound. Data was collected using speed monitors and second-by-second speeds were collected, analyzed and verified by the Federation Aeronautique Internationale (FAI). Therefore, the research question for the scientists was answered. Was Red Bull's research question answered?

Thirty-five cameras filmed the historic Red Bull Stratos Jump and eight million people watched it 'live'. Red Bull filmed and made many short documentaries, live streaming, YouTube videos and many photographs. The films and photographs were placed on many social media platforms. The research data that Red Bull collected and analyzed was the social media activity of their fans worldwide.

Red Bull began to analyze their data from the day of Felix's jump. Data showed that Red Bull's Facebook page received 900 000 interactions via posts on their wall. Out of the 900 000 they also analyzed an impressive 83 000 shares. To answer their research question: Red Bull's average number of YouTube channel subscribers rose from 2142 to an amazing 87 801 on the day Felix jumped from the balloon. On top of the global data collected from Facebook and YouTube, Red Bull were able to drill-down to sales by country of their energy drink following the jump. They analyzed sales data and discovered that new markets were acquired since the jump (South Korea, Japan, India and Brazil) and sales rose by 7 per cent in the US.

Question

1 How did the scientists and Redbull use the research process?

Source: Christopher Ratcliffe (2014) econsultancy.com

are able to get information that was previously impossible or too expensive to come by if they have access to the Web. This is now available 24 hours a day, often at a reasonable cost and sometimes free of charge. This is hugely beneficial to smaller companies for whom accessing up-to-date information used to be a huge barrier to competing internationally. Now SMEs have the power of information giving them access to new markets worldwide.

The development of better decision tools and decision support systems and of globally based research supplier networks has in turn led to an increase in the usage of continent-wide and worldwide online surveys which often transcend national boundaries. The development of specialist global niche marketing research strategies and a rapid increase in the rate and spread of product innovation, with which research must keep pace, have all meant that the old days of slow-moving local or national marketing research studies are long gone. In just a short time span the Internet has transformed all areas of marketing research simply because it allows the researcher to make instant connections to multiple sources of competitive and customer information. This enables the researcher to mine for customer information and competitor information, and permits marketers to monitor customer activity across the globe with great ease. The use of social network sites to carry out global marketing research is also expanding rapidly. UK shoppers spent an estimated £107 billion online in 2014, and the growth is around 11 per cent increase year on year. Worldwide the ecommerce (including retail sales) topped $1 trillion and this is expected to more than double by 2017, according to eMarketer. The consumer and B2B behaviour has created an information explosion ready to be explored to identify trends and opportunities. The availability of online databases and Web-enabled information sources has transformed the nature of international marketing research and the role it plays in the marketing process. Global internet networks enable companies across the globe to build the ultimate in customization strategies or 'one-to-one' marketing plans. It is estimated that over three-quarters of revenue for marketing research agencies is derived from online research. Equally, the role of the marketing researcher has become much more closely aligned with the decision-making processes of organizations.

Research into international market issues can incorporate three major roles:

- *Cross-cultural research*: The conducting of a research project across nation or culture groups.
- *Foreign research*: Research conducted in a country other than the country of the commissioning company.
- *Multi-country research*: Research conducted in all or important countries where a company is represented, Terpstra *et al.* (2012).

This does not in any way convey the enormity of the task involved in developing an international market intelligence system which would be sufficient to provide the information necessary to make sound international marketing decisions. Such an information system would not only have to identify and analyze potential markets, but also have the capacity to generate an understanding of the many environmental variables discussed in the previous three chapters. Many levels of environmental factors will affect international marketing decisions, from macro-level economic factors to political–legal factors, as well as the micro market structures and cultural factors affecting the consumer. It is a truism of international marketing that by competing in countries around the world uncertainty is generally greater and the difficulties in getting standardized information are also greater. The lack of market knowledge is the greatest obstacle to companies; without it they fail. Therefore, access to such knowledge makes it possible for the internationally experienced company to extend its activities to new markets and succeed.

As such, the role of the international market researcher is to provide an assessment of market demand globally, an evaluation of potential markets and of the risks and costs involved in market entries, as well as detailed information on which to base effective marketing strategies.

To achieve this, the researcher has three primary functions to carry out:

1 Scanning international markets to identify and analyze the opportunities.
2 Building marketing information systems to monitor environmental trends.
3 Carrying out primary marketing research studies for input into the development of marketing strategies and to test the feasibility of the possible marketing mix options, both in foreign country markets and across a range of international markets.

In the next three sections we will examine each of these in some detail.

Opportunity identification and analysis

Scanning international markets

There are 196 countries in the world (including Taiwan and the Vatican City). Even a large multinational corporation would find it difficult to resource market development in all these countries. Thus, the first task for the researcher is to scan markets to identify which countries have the potential for growth. International markets are scanned primarily at this stage to identify countries that warrant further research and analysis; hence the researcher will look for countries that meet three qualifying criteria:

1 *Accessibility.* If a company is barred from entering the market, it would be an ineffective use of resources to take research further. The scanning unit would assess such things as tariffs, non-tariff barriers, government regulation and import regulations to evaluate the accessibility of the market. Japan is still seen as a highly profitable market, but it is viewed by some as inaccessible due to the perception of the difficulties involved in overcoming trade barriers.

2 *Profitability.* At this level the researcher would assess factors that at a macro-level could render the market unprofitable – for example, the availability of currency, the existence of exchange regulations, government subsidies to local competition, price controls and substitute products. Many countries in Africa are fully accessible, but companies question the ability of trade partners in some of these countries to pay. The extra risk of non-payment reduces the profit return calculations of those markets.

3 *Market size.* An assessment is made of the potential market size to evaluate whether future investment is likely to bear fruit.

The specific indicators a company will look for tend to be very product- and market-specific. Thus a hand tool manufacturer in the north of England specializing in tools for woodworking craftsmen would look for evidence of a hobby market (accessibility), high levels of disposable income (profitability) and large numbers of educated, middle-aged men with leisure time (market size). In Management Challenge 4.1 the reader is asked to consider the specific indicators that Apple includes when developing their country growth portfolio.

MANAGEMENT CHALLENGE 4.1

Apple re-thinking growth opportunities

Apple was founded in 1976 and has remained a brand that is highly innovative and respected by consumers in many countries. Its main products are Macintosh computers, the iPod, iPhone, iPad and iTunes. The marketing growth strategies of Apple have been threefold. First, the culture at Apple headquarters is to innovate, constantly improve and always challenge convention by bringing art and sensual experiences to hitherto functional objects. Second, their retail outlets synchronize with this and enable consumers to interact with the product in open, friendly, highly-desirable locations, where personal setup areas and free training classes are available. Their consumer strategy includes the APPLE acronym: Approach. Probe. Present. Listen. End. This ensures consumers leave the store knowing their new Apple product will become an asset in their day-to-day lives. Third, Apple is an esteemed brand that has not deviated nor stretched its brand to include low cost items. Interestingly, their consumers are price *insensitive* and will camp outside stores when new products are launched so they can be the first to try out new technologies and designs.

Apple is interested in developing its country portfolio where there are highly desirable shopping locations, not street markets or bazaars, but fashionable, high-end retail high streets, consumers with high disposable incomes and excellent Internet retail. Apple is growing in previously untapped places such as Turkey and Brazil. Apple have recently opened their first stores in Turkey and Brazil as these developing countries have the necessary ingredients and numbers of wealthy consumers who will want to own premium, globally branded products.

Question

1 In scanning global markets which other countries with specific indicators are important for Apple to include when developing their country growth portfolio?

Having identified those opportunities, the researcher will need to make an assessment of their viability for further investigation. In principle, there are three types of market opportunities:

1 **Existing markets.** Here customers' needs are already serviced by existing suppliers; therefore, market entry would be difficult unless the company has a superior product or an entirely new concept to offer the market.

2 Latent markets. In this type of market there are recognized potential customers but no company has yet offered a product to fulfil the latent need. As there is no direct competition, market entry would be easier than in existing markets as long as the company could convey the benefits of its product to the market. Coca-Cola and Pepsi Cola dominate the global market. Qibla Cola, however, has tapped into a latent market by targeting consumers who do not want to buy a western global brand. They launched their cola not on its product benefits but as an alternative for consumers around the globe who oppose western policies in the Middle East and who wish to support ethical causes. Qibla also gives 10 per cent of all profits made to good causes.

3 Incipient markets. Incipient markets are ones that do not exist at present but conditions and trends can be identified that indicate the future emergence of needs that, under present circumstances, would be unfulfilled. It may be, of course, that existing companies in the market are positioning themselves to take advantage of emerging markets but at present there is no direct competition. Management Challenge 4.2 asks you to think about an innovative creation of a bank for a market poorly serviced in Bangladesh.

MANAGEMENT CHALLENGE 4.2

An incipient market hoping to be discovered

Some of the world's poorest people need help. The help they need is not always charitable donations but help to get them out of poverty through employment. Muhammad Yunus saw that the people in Bangladesh's rural areas were suffering. Yunus could have given a donation, but instead he decided to form a bank to help the poorest of people have the opportunity to form a business or buy products to sell through micro-credit. Being an economist, Yunus realized that if his idea was sustainable there was a 4-billion-people **latent market** around the world based on the consumer target market of those with an annual per capita income below $1500 (purchasing power parity). And as these people were desperately poor with limited prospects, no existing bank network would lend money to them. The only networks available to these people were predatory moneylenders. Yunus could have researched all possible banking models to provide the most appropriate solution. However, he did not do that. Nor did he recruit researchers to engage Bangladeshi people in surveys and focus groups. What Yunus did was spend time speaking face-to-face with people in the poorest villages; enjoying tea with them at road-side huts, debating a range of ideas and jointly forming solutions over the dinner table. Grameen Bank (the translation of *gram* is *village* or *rural*) was formed and the first micro-credit of $27 was shared between 42 women who made bamboo furniture. The bank products and services are available in other rural poor areas in countries worldwide including: Columbia, Guatemala, Ghana, Philippines and Kenya. For Grameen Bank there was no direct competition by major banking networks for people in poverty; only predatory moneylenders.

Question

1 What secondary data and primary data did Yunus use to help him formulate a new banking product for this latent market?

Source: www.grameenfoundation.org/

The nature of competitive products can be analyzed in a broadly similar way, with three distinct product types: competitive products, improved products and breakthrough products. A competitive product is one that has no significant advantages over those already on offer; brands often promote specific, but minor, elements of the product as their USP (unique selling point; or proposition) to try to differentiate products that are essentially very similar. An improved product is one that, while not unique, represents an improvement upon those currently available; improvements often come with pricing offers or new technological advances. A breakthrough product, by way of contrast, represents an innovation and as such, is likely to have a significant competitive advantage.

The level and nature of competition that a firm will encounter can, therefore, be analyzed by relating the three types of market demand to the three types of competitive products. This is illustrated in Figure 4.1

FIGURE 4.1   Nature of competition and level of market development

Types of market					
Product	**Existing**	**Latent**	**Incipient**		Low
Competitive	'Me too' little advantage	Classic market gap	Possible long-term advantage		
Distinctive	Ease of market entry	No direct competition	Market development needed		Cost
Truly innovative	High competitive advantage	First mover advantage	Markets need to be identified		High

Low   High

Risk

and can be used as a basis for determining first, whether market entry is likely to succeed, and second, whether the company possesses any degree of competitive advantage. This, in turn, provides an insight into the nature of the marketing task needed. In saying this, however, it needs to be emphasized that this sort of insight provides an initial framework for analysis and nothing more. What is then needed is a far more detailed assessment of the degree of competitive advantage that the company possesses.

Obviously the greatest opportunities, together with the greatest risk and potential for profit, are in the identification of incipient markets. The problem is that because markets do not yet exist there is no market data. Researchers, therefore, use analytical techniques to make sure they identify and recognize conditions in incipient markets, thus enabling their companies to develop strategies by which to be first into the market. Consider the Management Challenge 4.2 and the high risks that had to be considered by Grameen Bank's founder in Bangladesh's incipient market. In the research techniques used, the basic principle is to compare, contrast or correlate various factors in the market under study with some external variant to identify similarities within the market or with other markets, thus assessing whether the right conditions exist for a market to emerge.

Some of the key techniques used are now discussed.

Demand pattern analysis

In this technique, it is assumed that countries at different levels of economic development have differing patterns of demand and consumption. By comparing the pattern of demand in the country under study with the pattern of demand in an established market when the product was first introduced, a broad estimate of an incipient market can be achieved.

Multiple factor indices

This assumes that the demand for a product correlates to demand for other products. By measuring demand for the correlated product, estimates of potential demand can be made. For example, a manufacturer of frozen foods may make an assessment by measuring the number of houses with freezers. Not all market potential indexes are developed from a single comparison; some are combinations of several factors, occasionally as many as 20. Many of these indexes are developed by particular companies or industries to measure market potentials for their products in a given country where the market is seen as incipient. Multiple market indexes are designed to measure the relative potentials of different markets for a particular product. Such indexes have the advantage of taking into account several factors that influence the sales of the given product and so help the company identify potential markets.

Analogy estimation

Analogy estimation is used where there is a lack of market data in a particular country. Analogies are made with existing markets comparing and contrasting certain ratios to test for market potential. This technique is based on the theory of diffusion of innovation. It assumes that the innovation in the new market will diffuse and develop in much the same manner in all other markets around the world. This technique arouses mixed levels of enthusiasm, since experiences of using it across international markets have been variable. In addition, it is an expensive technique to implement and doubts have been expressed about the accuracy of its forecasts in a world of instant communication and global launches, and failures, of new products. Those who have used it typically adopt one of two approaches:

- A cross-section approach, where the product market size for one country is related to some appropriate gross economic indicator in order to establish a ratio. This ratio is then applied to potential countries under analysis to estimate the potential for the product's market size in those countries.
- A time-series approach based on the belief that product usage moves through a cycle. Thus one assumes that the potential countries under analysis will follow the same pattern of consumption as a more advanced economy, albeit with a predetermined time lag.

Macrosurvey technique

This method is essentially anthropological in approach and can help companies to establish themselves early in emerging countries with obvious long-term marketing benefits. The technique is based on the notion that as communities grow and develop, more specialized institutions come into being. Thus, one can construct a scale of successively more differentiated institutions against which any particular country can be evaluated to assess its level of growth and development and its market potential.

These techniques highlight the importance of **comparative research** and regular market screening if incipient demand is to be identified at an early stage. However, the value of several of the techniques does rest upon the assumption that all countries and their consumption patterns will develop along broadly common lines. If firms are to make effective use of many of these techniques, the assumption of common economic development patterns must stand. Increasingly, however, evidence is emerging to suggest that global commonality does not exist to this degree and there are strong arguments for companies grouping country markets for the purposes of this sort of comparative analysis.

Risk evaluation

As previously stated, incipient markets offer the greatest opportunity for profit potential, but as Figure 4.1 shows risks are high.

The risk factor in opportunity analysis cannot be over-estimated. Sometimes political risk itself can be the most important determining factor to the success or failure of an international marketing campaign. In the markets where opportunities have been identified, researchers need to make an assessment first as to the type of risk apparent in that market (political, commercial, industrial or financial), and second as to the degree of that risk. Matrices such as the one identified in Figure 4.2 can be useful in carrying out such assessments.

Over recent years marketers have developed various indices to help assess the risk factor in the evaluation of potential market opportunities. Nowadays a number of such indices are readily available online. The Knaepen package, an OECD sponsored classification, and the Business Environment Risk Index (BERI), are perhaps two of the most well-known ones.

World Economic Forum

The World Economic Forum provides an annual indication report of the competitiveness of countries. Their report ranks the competitiveness performance of 144 economies based on the 12 competitiveness factors (see Table 4.1).

FIGURE 4.2   The four-risk matrix

Country						
Risk level Risk type	A Low	B Moderate	C Some	D Risky	E Very risky	F Dangerous
Political						
Commercial						
Industrial						
Financial						

There are many factors used in calculating the competitiveness of each country. The pillars in Table 4.1 show the 12 pillars of competitiveness. Pillars 1–4 indicate factor driven competitive elements, pillars 5–8 provide factors demonstrating a country's competitiveness in efficiency and the final 9–12 pillars show how innovative a country is. Countries that are ranked high in all pillars such as Switzerland and Singapore show they are a highly competitive country, advanced in research and development, have an excellent infrastructure and present themselves on the world stage as having an efficient financial market. Countries ranked low in competitiveness include Guinea, Chad and Yemen as they are not highly innovative, and don't have an high proportion of their population engaged in higher education and training. The interesting information provided in this report for marketers and businesses is the change in rankings. Countries that move up the rankings in efficiency and innovation are clearly showing they have the potential for international organizations to consider for future growth opportunities.

The Knaepen Package

The Knaepen Package is a system for assessing country credit risk and classifying countries into eight country risk categories (0–7). It measures the country credit risk, i.e. the likelihood that a country will service its external debt. The classification of countries has two basic components:

1 the Country Risk Assessment Model (CRAM), which produces a quantitative assessment of country credit risk; and

2 a qualitative assessment which considers political risk, commercial and other risk factors not taken into account in the CRAM model.

Table 4.1   Competitiveness factors

12 Pillars of competitiveness		
1. Institutions	5. Higher education and training	9. Technology readiness
2. Infrastructure	6. Labour market efficiency	10. Market size
3. Macroeconomic environment	7. Goods market efficiency	11. Business sophistication
4. Health and primary education	8. Financial market efficiency	12. Research and development innovation

Source: World Economic Forum, 2014.

The final classification is a consensus decision of country risk experts who meet several times a year. These meetings are organized so as to guarantee that every country is reviewed whenever a fundamental change is observed and at least once a year. The list of country risk classifications is published after each meeting.

Business Environment Risk Index (BERI)

The BERI provides country risk forecasts for 140 countries throughout the world and is updated three times a year. This index assesses 15 environment factors, including political stability, balance of payments volatility, inflation, labour productivity, local management skills, bureaucratic delays, etc. Each factor is rated on a scale of 0–4 ranging from unacceptable conditions (0) to superior conditions (4). The key factors are individually weighted to take account of their importance. For example, political stability is weighted by a factor of 2.5. The final score is out of 100 and scores of over 80 indicate a favourable environment for investors and an advanced economy. Scores of less than 40 indicate very high risk for companies committing capital.

The main value of subscribing to such indices is to give companies an appreciation of the risk involved in opportunities identified. There are a number of organizations around the globe who publish country risk ratings – Standard and Poor, the OECD, *The Economist* and Moodys – so information on risk evaluation is readily available to the Internet researcher.

Major global corporations such as IBM, Microsoft and ICI have specialist political risk analysts monitoring environmental trends to alert senior managers to changes and developments which may affect their markets.

International marketing segmentation

At the scanning stage, the manager researching international markets is identifying and then analyzing opportunities to evaluate which markets to prioritize for further research and development. Some framework is then needed to evaluate those opportunities and try to reduce the plethora of countries to a more manageable number. To do this, managers need to divide markets into groups so they can decide which markets to prioritize or even to target.

Market segmentation is the strategy by which a firm partitions a market into submarkets or segments likely to manifest similar responses to marketing inputs. The aim is to identify the markets on which a company can concentrate its resources and efforts so that they can achieve maximum penetration of that market, rather than going for a market-spreading strategy where they aim to achieve a presence, however small, in as many markets as possible.

The Pareto law usually applies to international marketing strategies with its full vigour. The most broadbased and well-established international firms find that 20 per cent of the countries they serve generate at least 80 per cent of the results. Obviously these countries must receive greater managerial attention and allocation of resources. The two main bases for segmenting international markets are by geographical criteria (i.e. countries) and transnational criteria (i.e. individual decision makers).

Geographical criteria

The traditional practice is to use a country-based classification system as a basis for categorizing international markets. The business portfolio matrix (Figure 4.3) is indicative of the approach taken by many companies. In this, markets are classified in three categories.

The business portfolio matrix

Primary opportunity These markets indicate the best opportunities for long-term strategic development. Companies may want to establish a permanent presence and so embark on a thorough research programme.

FIGURE 4.3 Business portfolio matrix

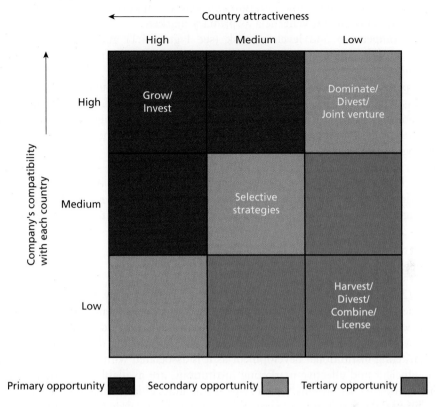

Source: Harrell, G.D. and Keifer, R.D. (1993) 'Multinational market portfolio in global strategy development', *International Marketing Review* 10(1), Emerald Insight; Campbell, D., Edgar, D. and Stonehouse, G. (2011) *Business Strategy: An Introduction*. Hampshire: Palgrave.

Secondary opportunity These are the markets where opportunities are identified but political or economic risk is perceived as being too high to make long-term irrevocable commitments. These markets would be handled in a more pragmatic way due to the potential risks identified. A comprehensive marketing information system would be needed.

Tertiary opportunity These are the catch-what-you-can markets. They will be perceived as high risk and so the allocation of resources will be minimal. Objectives in such countries would be short term and opportunistic, some companies would give no real commitment. No significant research would be carried out.

Figure 4.3 illustrates the business portfolio matrix. The horizontal axis evaluates the attractiveness of each country on objective and measurable criteria (e.g. size, stability and wealth). The vertical axis evaluates the firm's compatibility with each country on a more subjective and judgemental basis. Primary markets would score high on both axes.

This is a particularly useful device for companies operating in a portfolio of markets to prioritize market opportunity. Ford Tractor carried out such an analysis of key markets. In assessing market attractiveness they explored four basic elements:

1 market size
2 market growth rate
3 government regulations; and
4 economic and political stability.

Competitive strength and compatibility were defined in the international context and such factors as market share, market representation, contribution margin and market support were examined. Using this analysis they identified Kenya, Pakistan and Venezuela as primary markets.

The nature of competition and levels of risk (see Figure 4.1) and the business portfolio matrix (Figure 4.3) have a lot in common regarding risk, need for research and ways to identify countries in which to do business.

Equally, a company may use the BERI index, Hofstede's cultural dimensions or the Knaepen package as a basis for classifying countries. Whatever measurement base is used, once the primary markets have been identified companies then normally use standard methods to segment the markets within countries using such variables as demographic/economic factors, lifestyles, consumer motivations, geography, buyer behaviour, psychographics, etc.

Thus the primary segmentation base is geographic (by country) and the secondary bases are within countries. The problem here is that depending on the information base, it may be difficult to fully formulate secondary segmentation bases. Furthermore, such an approach can run the risk of leading to a differentiated marketing approach which may leave the company with a very fragmented or concentrated international strategy.

Infrastructure/marketing institution matrix

Sheth and Arma (2005) suggest international markets be categorized by the country's infrastructure and marketing institutional development. A country's infrastructure development refers to roads, telecommunication, legislative bodies, open and free justice systems, etc. Infrastructure development is usually associated with economic development. The availability of media efficiency of the distribution channels are used as indicators for marketing institutional development as it is associated with competitive marketing offerings, i.e. competitive, efficient and effective marketing institutions, are available to marketers in countries with highly developed marketing institutions, which generally includes efficient and effective distribution channels.

Using these dimensions (see Table 4.2) countries can be classified as (1) Developed infrastructure and developed marketing institutions, e.g. the US, UK and Scandinavia. (2) Developed infrastructure but restricted marketing development, e.g. Japan and Germany. Examples of marketing development restrictions are countries that have time restrictions on when the store can be open (e.g. Germany) or restrictions on the size of stores (e.g. Japan). (3) Low levels of infrastructure development but have developed marketing institutions such as retailers and media, e.g. India and Mexico. The last category has low infrastructure development and low marketing institutional development. Typically these are countries that have not

Table 4.2   Infrastructure/marketing institution matrix

| | | Infrastructure | |
		Developed	Restricted
Marketing institutions	Developed	e.g. UK, Scandinavia, US	e.g. India, Mexico
	Restricted	e.g. Japan, Germany	e.g. Indonesia, Vietnam

developed efficient and effective distribution systems due to geography (e.g. Indonesia) or legal restrictions (e.g. Vietnam).

A major drawback with the country-based approach is that countries do not buy products, consumers do. Global markets, therefore, need to be understood in terms of groups of buyers who share the need and desire for a product and the ability to pay for it, not just those who share a national border (as is the case in Illustration 4.1). If companies are to establish brand positions across a number of international markets, an increasingly common strategic goal, then they need to use a segmentation strategy that enables them to build a consistent brand position across those markets. If a company is to try to achieve a consistent and controlled marketing strategy across all its international markets, it needs a transnational approach to its segmentation strategy. If the basis for global market segmentation is one that cuts across national boundaries, then marketing strategies can be developed that will work for similar segments around the globe.

Transnational segmentation

Buyers in any particular segment seek similar benefits from and exhibit similar behaviour in buying a product. According to Hassan and Stephen (2005), although these consumers may live in different areas of the world and come from very different backgrounds and value systems, they have commonalities in association with a given global brand. To achieve a transnational approach to segmentation therefore, a country as a unit of analysis is too large to be of operational use. An alternative approach is to examine the individual decision maker (*ibid*. 2005). Key bases for segmentation would include such variables as value systems, demographic, psychographic and behavioural criteria.

Demographic variables have obvious potential as cross-national segmentation criteria. The most commonly used variables include sex, age, income level, social class and educational achievement. Frequently use is made of a battery of demographic variables when delineating transnational market segments.

Psychographic segmentation involves using lifestyle factors in the segmentation process. Appropriate criteria are usually of an inferred nature and concern consumer interests and perceptions of 'a way of living' in regard to work and leisure habits. Critical dimensions of lifestyle thus include activities, interests and opinions. Objective criteria, normally of a demographic nature, may also be helpful when defining lifestyle segments. Research International, when researching the transnational segments of young adults globally, divided them into four broad categories. 'Enthusiastic materialists' are optimistic and aspirational and to be found in developing countries and emerging markets like India and Latin America. 'Swimmers against the tide', on the other hand, demonstrate a degree of underlying pessimism, tend to live for the moment and are likely to be found in Southern Europe. In Northern Europe, the US and Australasia consumers are the 'new realists', looking for a balance between work and leisure with some underlying pessimism in outlook and, finally, the 'complacent materialists' are defined as passively optimistic and located in Japan.

Behavioural variables also have a lot of potential as a basis for global market segmentation. In particular, attention to patterns of consumption and loyalty in respect of product category and brand can be useful, along with a focus on the context for usage. Variables such as the benefit sought or the buying motivations may be used. Behaviourally defined segments may be identified in terms of a specific aspect of behaviour which is not broad enough to be defined as a lifestyle. Papadopoulos and Martin (2011) recommend behavioural elements of consumers be included in segmenting the market. Therefore, it may be more useful to include International Marketing Selection (IMSel) by behaviours such as 18–24-year-olds from Scandinavian countries that like skiing, or 24–35-year-olds from the sub-continent that take a pilgrimage to Mecca.

Mosaic Global

One of the trends enabling segmentation using individualistic characteristics to become a feasible strategy for many companies, is the development of geodemographic databases. One such database is the Mosaic Global from Experian. Mosaic Global is a single, consistent classification providing insight and understanding on the demographics, lifestyles and behaviour of 880 million people from the world's most prosperous economies including North America, Europe and Asia Pacific.

It is based on the idea that the world's cities share common patterns of residential segregation. Each have their enclaves of metropolitan strugglers, suburbs of career and family, and communities of sophisticated

ILLUSTRATION 4.2

Global and glocal segmentation research

PSA Peugoet Citroën, the French car manufacturer, operates around the world; currently concentrating on China, Brazil, Argentina, Chile, Mexico and Russia. For these markets minor specification changes are needed for their classic Peugeot 508, together with full transformations of the Peugeot 207 which for the South American market is part car, part pick-up truck.

However, PSA Peugoet Citroën does not just sell cars – it sells emotions and feelings that surround the cars, such as French style, chic and *joie de vivre*. As outlined in Chapter 3, culture and traditions influence people in different countries when making purchasing decisions. Therefore, PSA Peugeot Citroën investigated global and glocal segmentation trends.

Consumers the world over have a bond with their car. Universally strong bonds occur if the car satisfies the following needs:

Usage: Does this car provide the functionality and suitability for the driver's needs, e.g. boot/trunk that fits golf clubs/shopping, fuel economy?

Experience: Will this car satisfy individual and/or family needs?

Image: Do the values and qualities of this car's brand match and demonstrate the personality and identity of the people that purchase this car?

Consumer bonds such as these are global. However, PSA Peugeot Citroën and other international brands need to identify specific characteristics of people in different countries and segment them in order to be successful. And this is *glocalisation,* where a *global* brand understands the characteristics of the local consumer.

As stated above, China is a country that PSA Peugeot Citroën is investing in. After considerable research, particularly qualitative research, it was discovered there are six dominant consumer segments in China:

1　*The Conservatives* – these people are older, rural citizens.

2　*The Solos* – intellectual people whose Chinese traditions and culture remain strong and China's open market and economy changes do not affect their own activities.

3　*The Followers* – as the name implies they follow the current economic trends and behavioural changes.

4　*The Bad Boys* – these are people who have dual lives: part with the dominant Chinese culture applied to them externally and from their parents, and part libertarian, where they enjoy the image and culture of a relaxed and fun modern society.

5　*The Social Creepers* – this category identifies people who continue to better themselves and to achieve the norms of those people at the next level of society's hierarchy.

6　*The Pioneers* – confident people who admire and stay embraced to China for its grand past and culture and are full of pride to see the opportunities for personal as well as country growth in the new China.

Question

1 Do you think the six consumer segments would be similar in other countries?

2 How can PSA Peugeot Citroën use these customer segments in its marketing strategy?

Sources: Merza, A., Laetitia, R., Becker, C. and Zheng, X. (2014) Working on socio-cultural dynamics and customers' segmentation from local to global: An application case on well-being, health and Generation Z. *ESOMAR Asia Pacific*, Jakarta, May 2014.

)ourhoods that display strong similarities in terms
; of where they are found. The result is a classifica-
with a set of distinctive demographic and lifestyle
d by the classification.

:ountry and across the 29 countries in which it
. ..., .he system gives the researcher the ability to iden-
tify the type of people using certain products and services and to identify at a local level where the similar
geodemographic types are, thus acting as an aid to the segmentation of markets and the identification of
primary and secondary markets. Retailers are amongst the biggest users of geosegmentation not only when
deciding on the location of new stores but by generating a better understanding of their customer profiles.
All they need is the address of their customers and then by adding the cluster codes to every customer
address they are able to define, group and describe the types or segments of their customers, assess their
products' performance, decide site location and measure market performance by segments.

In Europe with an ageing population there is a growing interest by companies in senior retirees with
disposable income and differing service requirements to the younger population. Financial services, health
care providers as well as mobility equipment suppliers and housing developers, all use geosegmentation to
aid their segmentation and targeting strategies. Mosaic Global will also be of use in identifying the sample
in a research survey and for building lists in a direct marketing exercise.

Despite the attractiveness of using individualistic characteristics, it is apparent there is strong potential
for significant differences in the patterns of consumer behaviour within **global segments** derived using this
method. Also, international similarities in lifestyle and behaviour do tend to be specific, and relevant primarily to specialist products and niche markets.

Hierarchical country – consumer segmentation

To overcome some of the above problems, a compromise approach would be to implement a procedure for
global segmentation which integrated features of both processes.

Hassan and Stephen (2005) propose a hierarchical approach to global market segmentation that takes
into account country factors but also incorporates individual behaviourist characteristics into a segmentation strategy that helps companies develop cross-national segments to allow for a global positioning
strategy.

On this basis the marketing strategy would build on the premise that world markets consist of both
similarities and differences and that the most effective strategies reflect a full recognition of similarities and
differences across rather than within markets. Thus, companies competing internationally should segment
markets on the basis of consumers, not countries. Segmentation by purely geographical factors leads to
national stereotyping. It ignores the differences between customers within a nation and ignores similarities across boundaries. Colgate and Palmolive reached such a conclusion when carrying out an analytical
review of their own segmentation strategies, and now use the hierarchical approach.

Any global segmentation strategy needs to be carried out in stages:

1 Identify those countries that have the infrastructure to support the product and are accessible to the company.

2 Screen those countries to arrive at a shorter list of countries with the characteristics that make the market attractive, e.g. a frozen dessert manufacturer may say that for a market to be attractive they need to have at least five million refrigerators per market.

3 Develop mini-segments within these countries based on factors such as:

   ■ information search behaviour
   ■ product characteristics required.

   The outcome of this process would be a series of mini-segments within qualified countries.

4 The development of transnational segments begins by looking for similarities across segments. Factor analysis of the behavioural patterns of these segments would enable managers to understand the characteristics of the demand of each segment as regards marketing mix issues. Each mini-segment would, therefore, be rated on several strategic factors in terms of potential response.

5 Cluster analysis is then used to identify meaningful cross-national segments, each of which, it is thought, would evoke a similar response to any marketing mix strategy.

It is argued that this approach would enable marketers to design strategies for cross-national segments and so take a more consumer-orientated approach to international marketing. In prioritizing markets, companies would use consumers as their primary base. Some writers argue that companies still need a secondary segmentation stage to identify the key countries where these transnational segments can be found.

The market profile analysis

Analyzing foreign country markets

Having completed the scanning stage, the researcher will have reduced the number of potential countries to a feasible list requiring further research. The researcher needs then to systematically evaluate the markets identified and to build an analytical picture of the foreign country markets. This is primarily the role of the market profile analysis.

In building a market profile, the objective of the company is first, to develop a cost-effective information flow between the environment in which the company operates and the head office decisionmakers and, second, to use a consistent approach to facilitate cross country comparisons.

Using the 12C environmental analysis model in Table 4.3, this can help the researcher achieve these two objectives. The information input into the 12C analysis will help the researcher to draw up a market profile analysis, as shown in Figure 4.4.

The objective of a market profile analysis is to enable the company to use the environmental information to identify opportunities and problems in the potential marketing strategies. For example, the fact that television advertising is prohibited in a country will have major implications for a promotional strategy.

It is this type of detailed assessment that helps companies determine the degree of competitive advantage they may possess and the most appropriate method of market entry. Using consistent frameworks also enables the researcher to make cross-country comparisons much more easily.

Sources of information

In building an MIS (marketing information system; also marketing intelligence system), companies would utilize a variety of information services and sources. The starting point for most international researchers in the UK is UK Trade and Investment. This government department helps businesses export and grow

Table 4.3   The 12C framework for analyzing international markets

Country
- general country information
- basic SLEPTS data
- impact of environmental dimensions

Concentration
- structure of the market segments
- geographical spread

Culture/consumer behaviour
- characteristics of the country
- diversity of cultural groupings
- nature of decision making
- major influences of purchasing behaviour

Choices
- analysis of supply
- international and external competition
- characteristics of competitors
- import analysis
- competitive strengths and weaknesses

Consumption
- demand and end use analysis of economic sectors that use the product
- market share by demand sector
- growth patterns of sectors
- evaluation of the threat of substitute products

Contractual obligations
- business practices
- insurance
- legal obligations

Commitment
- access to market
- trade incentives and barriers
- custom tariffs

Channels
- purchasing behaviour
- capabilities of intermediaries
- coverage of distribution costs
- physical distribution
- infrastructure
- size and grade of products purchased

Communication
- promotion
- media infrastructure and availability
- which marketing approaches are effective
- cost of promotion
- common selling practices
- media information

capacity to pay
- pricing
- extrapolation of pricing to examine trends
- culture of pricing
- conditions of payment
- insurance terms

Currency
- stability
- restrictions
- exchange controls

Caveats
- factors to be aware of

FIGURE 4.4   Market profile analysis

overseas, and provides a variety of support services to such organizations. The majority of western nations have similar government-sponsored organizations helping exporters to develop information on international markets.

Some reports have been critical of the deficiencies in the provision of market intelligence by government departments and of firms' abilities to use this information. The main criticisms are:

- Information is non-specific to particular industries.
- Firms experience problems with the bureaucratic nature of some government services.
- Data is often in a form which is unsuitable for the company's needs, or too general to be of use.
- Services have been available only in the capital city.
- Inadequate publicity about the information and services available.

Other institutions that offer advice and information to companies researching international markets include:

- business libraries
- university libraries
- international chambers of commerce
- UK Trade and Investment: national and regional international marketing intelligence centres
- local business links
- embassies
- banks
- trade associations
- export councils
- overseas distributors
- overseas sales subsidiaries
- foreign brokerage houses
- foreign trade organizations.

Online databases

As previously stated in an earlier section of this chapter, one of the main developments in the availability of secondary information for international markets is the plethora of web-based information sites, online databases, company customer response management (CRM) databases and online research services.

Online databases are systems which hold computerized information which can be accessed through the Internet, making a wide range of information available from an online database to a manager in a matter of seconds. Information can be transmitted from anywhere in the world instantaneously, bringing obvious benefits.

There are numerous advantages in using online databases. They are regularly updated – two or three times per day – and are therefore much more current than traditional printed sources. Retrieving information online is much more cost-effective than manual searching and is considerably faster. Online databases can be accessed 24 hours a day, seven days a week. You also retrieve – and consequently pay for – only the information you want.

Online data sources can also be a solution for carrying out cross-cultural marketing research when primary data collection is prohibitive due to its cost. Marketing information globally is now becoming much more consolidated as global organizations develop databases that are excellent for cross-country comparisons and for accessing global market information. Table 4.4 gives examples of some of the globally based online databases that managers wishing to carry out comparative studies or globally based marketing research may find useful.

Table 4.4 Online databases

Company information	
Marketing Database:	243 million business records globally in over 196 countries
Kompass Global B2B Portal:	10 million companies in 70 countries
DataStream:	Financial data on companies worldwide
Extel:	Worldwide company and market information
Predicast:	Overview of market and technology company data
Trade data	
Google public data:	Large global publicly available data sets
WTO gateway:	World Trade Organization data sets
Reuters:	Global market data
UN Comtrade:	Global merchandise trade statistics
Global Trade Information Services:	International merchandise trade data
Croners:	Comprehensive guide to exporting goods in over 200 export markets
Eurostat:	Detailed statistics on the EU countries
IMF/World Bank/UN:	World trade statistics
Market information	
MINTEL:	Global market and consumer data
Business Monitor International:	Analysis, ratings, rankings and forecasts covering 200 global marketing companies across 24 different industries
CIA World Factbook:	Profiles of countries and territories around the world
Euromonitor:	International market intelligence
Profound/MAID:	Full text market research reports

Organizations in developing countries are increasingly using online computerized databases for their market research work as they become better equipped with telecommunication facilities. The type and volume of trade information available through online databases has expanded dramatically over recent years, with new databases of interest to business and trade organizations continuously being introduced to the market.

The use of the Internet for marketing intelligence, therefore, is one of the most important ways in which connectivity can improve a firm's ability to develop international markets. Buying or commissioning market research reports can be a prohibitively expensive business. For a fraction of the cost, and in some cases free of charge, much of the same information can be gathered electronically. Given the time and expense associated with the collection of primary data, the use of web-based online databases are now central to building marketing information on international markets. However, researchers do need to be wary when using such databases and ensure they fully evaluate the credibility and worthiness of the data they obtain from such sources to ensure the accuracy and validity. The volume of relevant international marketing information available on the Internet is too extensive to describe in detail in this chapter, but includes numerous online newspapers and journals, an extensive list of individual country and industry market research reports, trade lists of suppliers, agents, distributors and government contacts in a large number of countries, details on host country legislation covering imports, agency agreements, joint ventures, etc.

Some of the best sites for undertaking general country screening and international marketing research include:

- Brand data: www.brandchannel.com; www.gbrands.com; www.globalstrategies.com
- BusinessWeek: www.businessweek.com
- The Economist: www.economist.com
- European Union: www.europa.eu
- Google: www.google.com/publicdata
- UK Trade and Investment: www.uktradeinvest.gov.uk
- UK Chambers of Commerce: www.britishchambers.org.uk
- United Nations: www.un.org
- World Bank: www.worldbank.org
- World Fact Book: www.cia.gov/cia/publications/factbook
- World Trade Organization: www.wto.org

These are just a few examples of the large number of websites which provide access to sources of international trade and marketing data as well as other useful services.

Problems in using secondary data

In carrying out marketing research internationally, problems arise by virtue of the very nature of the number and complexities of the markets being investigated. While the use of secondary data is essential in international marketing research, the reader needs to be aware of its limitations and some of the problems that occur in using secondary data.

Perhaps the most frequently discussed issue is the availability and accessibility of quality secondary information in international markets. The collection of secondary data concerning the economy and the business infrastructure in some countries varies in quality and consistency, and evaluation of secondary data is critical for international marketing research. Different countries, even for internationally based statistics, may report different values for a given statistic, such as GDP, because of differences in the way the unit is defined. Measurement units may not be equivalent across countries and the accuracy of secondary data may also vary from country to country. Business and income statistics are affected by the taxation structures and the extent of tax evasion. Population censuses may vary in frequency and year in which the data is collected.

One of the reasons for the distortion of data in some countries is the political considerations of governments. The International Labour Organization found the actual unemployment rate in Russia was 10 per cent rather than the officially reported 2 per cent. The Indian government estimates that India's middle class numbers 250 million but, according to a recent survey of consumer patterns conducted by the National Council of Applied Economic Research in Delhi, the Indian middle class probably totals 100 million at best and there is much stratification among them. This problem might be solved by obtaining authentic data from international organizations such as the OECD, EU, World Bank, etc.

The inconsistencies which can be found in the classification of various types of data in various countries are also a problem when carrying out any comparative analysis across markets. Terpstra *et al*. (2012) say that the most important problem associated with the secondary data, especially in developing countries, is its scarcity. A further problem which can be quite misleading is the timeliness of the collected secondary data: it might have been collected several years earlier and never updated and is therefore outdated and of little value for future planning. Thus it can be a problem when accessing online databases where the year the data actually refers to may be a few years before the actual publication date. This may result in the researcher being misled into thinking they are viewing current data.

Many countries attempt to attract foreign investment by overstating certain factors that make the economic picture look better. On the other hand, some countries understate certain factors, making the economic situation appear worse in order to attract foreign aid.

The Asia–Pacific market is an important market and so obtaining reliable information in this region is of crucial importance for many companies. INSEAD surveyed one thousand managers of European companies operating in the Asia–Pacific region, and found that only in Japan and Singapore were companies able to easily access data that was viewed as being of a reliable quality. In China, Taiwan and Vietnam data was not trusted by researchers. Even though Japanese data was relatively accessible, there were still difficulties due to the fact that the information was over-abundant and so it was difficult to select and interpret the relevant data or to give it any practical application.

None of the limitations discussed above should devalue the importance of secondary data in international marketing research. For many smaller companies lacking the resources to carry out primary research in markets which are geographically distant, it may be the only information to which there is relative ease of access (see Illustration 4.3).

ILLUSTRATION 4.3

Taking some of the legwork out of primary research

One of the stages in the marketing research process is called research design. During this stage it is important to choose the research instrument, be it a survey or an interview guide for a focus group. If a survey is chosen one of the many ways the survey can be distributed is to a panel of experts on a research panel.

Mark Bidou launched Maximiles (later known as Bilendi) in Paris in 1999 as an organization that provided a panel of experts that would answer survey questions. The business has grown so much that there are offices in UK, France, Germany, Spain, Italy, Austria, Switzerland and North Africa. Bilendi also belongs to a network of full service agencies for survey requests outside Europe and North Africa.

To date there are over 1.8 million panel member experts available to answer surveys, watch videos or complete bespoke 'quick polls'. The main benefit of using Bilendi is to reach high-target consumers by age, gender, country of residence, leisure activities, behaviour or education level to name just a few.

Bilendi has been used to send surveys to over 1200 people in South Africa, UK, US, China, India and Germany about their experiences at business conferences. To ensure only experts were questioned, panel members were only able to complete the survey if they had been to a conference within the last 12 months. Translation services are made available for the German and Chinese panel members as they prefer to answer surveys in their own language.

High street retailers and transnational supermarkets also use panel members to gauge the reactions of panel experts to advertising and price promotions. Businesses are able to provide their own survey to niche, high-target consumers so that they can react to the responses and stay ahead of competitors.

Panel members receive bonus points to complete a survey or watch a video. Points are spent on high-ticket brands such as Sony, Disney, John Lewis, easyJet and Lego.

Question

1 What are the strengths and weaknesses for using panel member experts in primary research?

Source: www.bilendi.com

FIGURE 4.5   Flowchart of the marketing research process

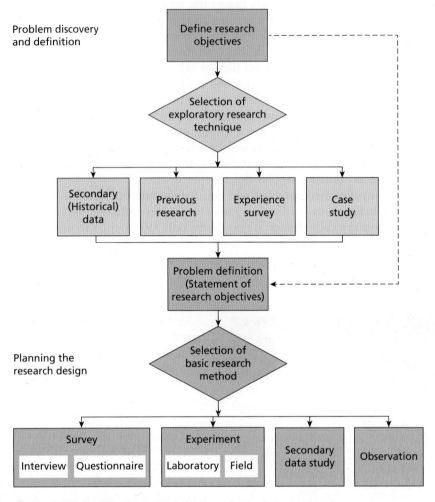

Source: Babin, B.J. and Zikmund, W.G. (2016) *Essentials of Marketing Research*, 6th ed., Cengage Learning.

Primary research in international markets

We have discussed scanning international markets to identify potential market opportunities and the building of market information systems from which the market profile analysis is formulated. So far we have only discussed obtaining information from secondary sources. It is unlikely that a researcher will be able to obtain the information for input into a marketing information system from secondary sources alone. Having exhausted these sources the researcher will need to embark on the collection of primary data to obtain the information required.

In the following sections we will discuss the issues facing the researcher which should be considered when endeavouring to carry out primary research studies. To do this we use the seven-step framework (Malhotra *et al.* 2013) depicted in Figure 4.5.

Problem discovery and definition report

The precise definition of the marketing research problem is more difficult and more important in international marketing research than in domestic marketing research. Unfamiliarity with the cultures and environmental factors of the countries where the research is being conducted can greatly increase the difficulty of obtaining accurate findings. Often there are no clear geographical boundaries to the market you are trying to investigate which can make the design of the research problematic. Other issues occur when developing markets push in front of developed markets, once again showing the time-series approach assuming developing countries will follow the same pattern cannot always be observed.

On a practical level, the differences in climate and infrastructure create problems. A survey on floor cleaning products across Europe would have to take account of the fact that Scandinavians have wooden floors, there are lots of tiled and stone floors in the Mediterranean, and in the UK many houses have carpets.

Many international marketing efforts fail not because research was not conducted but because the issue of comparability was not adequately addressed in defining the marketing research problem. This is why, as we saw in Chapter 3, it is so important to isolate the impact of self-reference criteria (SRC) and the unconscious reference to our own cultural values when defining the problem we are attempting to research in international markets.

Developing an innovative approach

It is important in international marketing research to maintain flexibility in the approach you may have in the initial stages of the research. In the first stage of primary research, companies often use informal means to gather preliminary information and extensive use is made of the network of contacts available to the company both at home and abroad. It is unlikely that a full understanding of the foreign market will be obtained without visiting that market to gain information first hand. The first steps in doing this would be by networking and obtaining information through relatively informal means such as networking consortia or multi-client studies. United Bank Ltd in Management Challenge 4.3 was looking for such an innovative approach.

Networking

The use of contact networks to build information is vitally important because of the sometimes prohibitive cost of carrying out detailed market research studies overseas. Before any detailed studies are undertaken, trade contacts need to be fully explored.

MANAGEMENT CHALLENGE 4.3

Money? What money? It's branchless, moneyless banking

The United Bank Limited UK has just launched its money transfer service to Pakistani people living in the UK who want to send money to family members back home. The money is transferred within minutes to their loved ones who are not able to get online or don't live near ATMs. This transfer method cuts out expensive agent fees.

However, another arm of United Bank Limited is already popular with over 3.5 million account holders in Pakistan. Mobile-money in Pakistan is very popular from bank transactions to savings via mobile apps. This way of dealing with money flourished when

Pakistan's government-to-person (G2P) payment system for social cash transfers became digitized. The government digitized system produced a branchless banking industry. On the back of that United Bank Limited launched a money-mobile service called Omni which became a very popular bank used by the extraordinarily mobile-money savvy population. Behavioural changes have also occurred with the introduction of mobile-money in Pakistan. Known as a nation that tended to keep their savings 'hidden' at home, Pakistanis are now confident to use Omni to deposit even small amounts of money as well as financial transactions. Mobile-money is prevalent in Pakistan; it has grown faster than in some more developed countries.

Question

1 What other products and services could be adopted more quickly in developing countries than developed countries? And why is that?

Source: www.gsmaintelligence.com

In order to find solutions to the many international marketing research problems, improvisation in international research is essential.

Most companies will make extensive use of their existing networks to build the market profiles and develop information bases. These could be agents, distributors, licensees, joint venture partners or other companies operating in the country under investigation.

Consortia

Marketing research consortia enable the comparison of data across different cultures and aid international marketing research efforts. Consortia are used by companies as a way of overcoming the difficulties involved in gathering data and establishing contacts in foreign markets. Essentially a group of companies will come together to research a particular market area in which they have a common interest. The advantages are:

- The consortium is more visible in the foreign market.
- It is more likely to enjoy the support of the home export promotion organization.
- It achieves economies through the joint use of export facilities both at home and in foreign markets.
- It increases the resources available to support the research operation.

However, if a company is to join a consortium, then it has to be prepared to have its autonomy reduced; this fact alone is the major reason most consortia fail. There also has to be a strong reason to join together for the relationship to develop. Nevertheless, by the pooling of resources, consortia are very useful in giving companies the resources needed to acquire knowledge on markets. Often agencies will offer **Omnibus studies** which have much the same benefits (see Illustration 4.4).

Due to the problems and considerations we have discussed above, it may be that detailed research studies will only be carried out in markets where the market viability is seen to be positive and when detailed consumer/market information is required to develop marketing strategy. The cost of primary field research can be high and so it will only be carried out after all other sources have been investigated.

A survey carried out by INSEAD of European companies operating in the Asia–Pacific region showed that companies perceived the most significant sources of information as being personal contacts of the companies themselves, whether these were customers, other business relationships or their own market surveys.

A second tier of usefulness was then identified as consisting of other direct sources such as government contacts and contacts with competitors or trade associations. Finally, there was a third tier comprising publicly available information such as newspapers and magazines. This information may be widely read but relatively little weight seems to be given to its strategic value. The importance of directly collected information seems to confirm the view that business in Asia depends more heavily on the creation of a network of relationships than on analysis of hard data collected through surveys or other published information.

The collection of primary data

The cost and effort of collecting primary data in new markets is far higher than that of collecting such data in the domestic market. This is particularly the case in developing countries where no marketing research infrastructure or experience is available. Primary research in these circumstances would entail substantial investment costs in developing basic information relating, for example, to sampling frames or trained qualified interviewers. This, of course, reinforces the importance of secondary data for research purposes and the need for a systematic planning process when embarking on a primary research project.

Organizing the research study

There are two major organizational questions which the international marketing manager will need to address:

- Should the research be carried out by foreign local subsidiaries or should all marketing research be centralized at headquarters?
- Should the fieldwork be carried out in-house or by an agency?

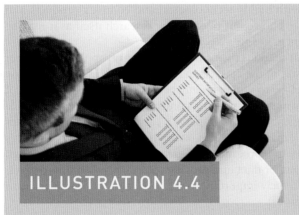

ILLUSTRATION 4.4

Sharing the cost – Omnibus surveys

Omnibus studies have the advantage of enabling the client to participate in large surveys with focused questions at much less expense than would be the case otherwise. A significant growth in this type of field research has been seen in the past few years, particularly as more companies have become operational on international markets. An omnibus is a syndicated survey where several businesses can buy as few or as many questions as they wish for a fixed cost per question. The cost per question varies dependent upon how specialized the omnibus members are. A general panel member is any person over the age of 18. Specialist omnibus members include small business omni-panels and college omni-panels.

OmniPulse is one US business that enables organizations to add between 3 and 10 questions onto their survey. Questions can include simple yes/no questions or more complex attribute ratings, ranking questions to open-ended questions. Ipsos MORI is a UK company that provides Omnibus opportunities for organizations that would like to explore the thoughts and feelings of people aged 11–16. Surveys take place in UK schools including topics such as charities, political and social trends, faith, aspirations and leisure time. Additionally, Ipsos MORI offer international omnibus surveys which include questions from hardware and software companies who would like to understand the growing trend in local and online gaming, the size of the gaming market and the personal profiles of the gamers.

Omnibus surveys are available for all, be it major international organizations who benefit from the weekly omnibus surveys delivered to 50+ countries for year-on-year trends, or SMEs that want to understand a single market.

Question

1 Identify a number of examples where omnibus studies could be used as a primary marketing research tool in international markets.

Sources: Omnipulse www.researchnow.com; IPSOS- MORI www.ipsos-mori.com

Centralization vs decentralization

If a centralized approach is adopted, then decisions have to be made regarding the specific responsibilities of the operating unit and what managerial arrangements should exist between the unit and headquarters staff. Further to this, decisions have to be taken as to what relationship is to exist between the local research staff who are ultimately responsible to headquarters and the local line management.

If a decentralized approach is chosen, then arrangements have to be made for research findings to be transferred from one operating unit to another. There is also the question of who has the overall responsibility for administering and overseeing the market research budget to ensure that resources are not wasted by a possible duplication of research effort.

Such issues are complex and are also related to overall organizational issues, which are examined in some depth in Chapter 5. In this chapter we will concentrate our discussion on the decision as to whether the company should carry out international research itself, or involve independent research agencies.

In-house or agency

Whether a company chooses to do all the research in-house or to use an agency will largely be determined by factors such as company resources, market expertise and product complexity.

If a company operates in a specialist B2B market with highly technological and complex products and has significant experience in the market, it may have no choice but to carry out research itself as it may be difficult to find an agency with the necessary competence.

However, if the company is operating in the consumer markets then a different scenario applies. Consumer research may require an established field force and the size of the markets may mean that a research company with field work resources is needed. A priority could well be to obtain an independent objective assessment of a foreign country; this could require specialist interviewing skills which a company alone might not be able to resource and thus would require the services of an agency. If the company is carrying out a **multi-country study** and needs a consistent research approach across all markets, then an international agency with resources across markets may be much more able to handle the research programme. Often, however, research in foreign markets may require a local firm to do the field work, gather data and provide some analysis and interpretation. The selection and use of a foreign firm may be extremely important to the success of the whole project.

In choosing an agency, a company has six basic options:

- A local agency in the market under investigation.
- A domestic agency with overseas offices.
- A domestic agency with overseas associate companies.
- A domestic agency which subcontracts field work to an agency in the market under investigation.
- A domestic agency with competent foreign staff.
- A global agency with offices around the world.

Which solution is best for the researcher will depend on a number of factors: the ease of briefing the agency; supervising and coordinating the project; the probability of language problems arising; the requirements of specialist market knowledge; the standard of competence required; and the budget available.

Thus, no single option is universally the best to select. It is primarily dependent on the budget available, the requirements of the research, the expertise within the company and, of course, the market under investigation. In a research study in Saudi Arabia the UK agency wished to maintain control and coordination of the project. However, western interviewers would have had little success in eliciting meaningful information from Saudi businessmen. Therefore, it was decided to employ a Cypriot field work agency to translate the questionnaire into Arabic and carry out the interviews etc. This led to certain control and communication problems, but it was the only realistic methodology to obtain the required information.

It may often be the case that in a multi-country study a combination of agencies are used. A typical multi-country study will go through the following steps:

1 The project is discussed at length with the client.
2 The field work agencies in each country are selected.
3 The questionnaire is designed centrally.
4 The questionnaire is translated locally and the translation is checked centrally.
5 The questionnaire is piloted locally.
6 The questionnaire is finalized centrally.
7 The interviewers are briefed locally by an executive of the central company.
8 The field work is carried out locally.
9 The coding and editing plan is provided for the local agencies.
10 The edited and coded questionnaires are returned to head office.
11 A coding and editing check is carried out centrally.
12 Computing and analysis are carried out centrally.

Research design

In formulating a research design, considerable effort is needed to ensure that the methods used will ensure comparability of data. In order to handle problems such as cultural bias in research design and interpretation of data etc., perspectives of researchers from different countries and cultures could be incorporated in the process so that the bias is minimal. However, this method will only work if there are no major problems of communication between researchers from different environments. If this is not the case, there is a possibility that some other kind of unknown bias might be introduced into the research process which could be even more harmful. A study of the cultural and social values and the method of conducting research in the host country could play an important role in facilitating the process of international marketing research.

One of the first factors to consider in developing a research design is the reliability and validity of the secondary data used. As we have previously discussed, the accuracy of secondary data varies enormously across countries. This means that the database being used to develop primary research may be inaccurate or highly biased, or lack the capability to make multi-country comparisons.

Further to this, the research design needs to incorporate methods which will be feasible in the foreign country markets, as well as allowing the international researcher to obtain meaningful and relevant findings.

For example, in India there is a highly variable literacy rate across the country and across genders. According to www.india.gov, the literacy rate in the country is 65 per cent, 75 per cent for males and 54 per cent for females. However, in some rural areas it is much lower. In Bihar there is a literacy rate of 47 per cent, in Jammu and Kashmir it is 55 per cent. There are hundreds of languages and there can be very real fears that the interviewer, in some rural areas, is a government inspector in disguise. In such a scenario, a researcher would have problems throughout the research process in establishing the basic sample, designing the questionnaire and applying analytical techniques. However, India also has a rapidly growing affluent and educated middle class that in absolute terms is larger in size than the total population of any Western European country.

Social and cultural factors are one of the most important issues which affect the process of international marketing research. In collecting primary data, the researcher needs to consider the issues facing them in evaluating the possible methods under consideration.

In this context, qualitative research, survey methods, questionnaire design and sampling considerations are particularly important.

Qualitative research

Because the researcher is often unfamiliar with the foreign market to be examined, qualitative research is crucial in international marketing research. In the initial stages, qualitative research can provide insights into the problem and help in developing an approach by generating relevant research questions and hypotheses, models and characteristics which influence the research design. Thus, qualitative research may reveal the differences between foreign and domestic markets. It may also help to reduce the psychological distance between the researcher and the respondent. In some cases, the researcher must rely on qualitative research because secondary data may not be available. Some problems associated with qualitative techniques in developing countries are such things as accessibility (different concept of time), sampling (extended demographic factors such as religion and tribal membership), shorter span of attention and less familiarity with abstract thinking.

Focus groups can be used in many settings, particularly in newly emerging markets where there is scant data and companies are trying to establish the cultural sensitivities in the market to their products and services. In some cultures, such as in the Middle or Far East, people are hesitant to discuss their feelings in a group setting. In these cases, in-depth interviews can be used.

The use of projective techniques is sometimes appropriate. Association techniques (word association), completion techniques (sentence completion, story completion) and expressive techniques (role playing, third-person technique) involve the use of verbal cues and so are all good cross-cultural research techniques.

Survey methods

There are several issues to consider in evaluating the various interviewing methods available.

Online surveys   As the Internet achieves greater penetration even in less developed markets, online surveys are now becoming predominant globally. Speed of execution, the obtaining of timely responses, ease

ILLUSTRATION 4.5

The use of social networks to understand global consumer opinion

It is clear that businesses are encouraging consumers to spread positive messages about their business when on Facebook, Twitter, Instagram and of course through blogs. What international businesses often do not do is engage directly with consumers and ask for feedback and opinions. In fact many organizations do not have a social media space specifically allocated for customer feedback and even fewer businesses have strategic aims and objectives to gather feedback and opinions from their online community. This is despite thousands of dollars or euros being spent on focus groups and discussions with their 'off-line' community.

One global organization that does understand the value of their consumer feedback and opinions is Starbucks. With over 38 million likes on Facebook they must be doing something that is working.

MyStarbucksIdea.force.com is a dedicated web-based feedback, share and vote page. Starbucks' global community is encouraged to suggest new ideas and share opinions that are not only read by 'other fans' but are regarded as valuable, insightful and timely feedback from consumers. The suggestions include ideas and opinions such as 'free gift cards' for loyal Facebook likers to opinions about gluten-free food or recommendations for more recycling ideas. New product development ideas about Coffee and Espresso account for over 44 500 suggestions, over 14 000 experience ideas are posted encouraging Starbucks to enable local artists to display their paintings, and thousands of involvement ideas suggesting loyalty cards 'go global' for use by frequent, overseas travellers.

Question

1 Identify the main advantages and disadvantages of using social networks to understand consumers in global markets.

of interview and speed of analysis are all major benefits to international marketing researchers. Globally access to the Internet is still scarce in some countries and in others subject to government controls. This could mean potential bias in both the sampling and in the answers given by respondents.

As more of us share personal information online through sites like Facebook, Pinterest and Linkedin, companies are using these networking sites as a means of contacting customers. This gives them the opportunity to analyze consumption patterns, examine behavioural targeting, cost effective online product testing and as a means of building direct contact with the consumer to access a plethora of information. Illustration 4.5 shows how Starbucks gathers research data with fans across the world.

Telephone interviewing With the setting up of global call centres, Internet telephony and the collapse in the price of international telephone calls, multi-country studies are now often conducted from a single global location and are now much cheaper and easier to control. Most telephone data collection is conducted through CATI (Computer aided telephone interviews) which are cost-effective as well as reliable.

CATI/telephone surveys are the most effective method of collecting data from global customers as it can be organized from one location and administered globally. In the US, Canada and Europe, the telephone has achieved almost total penetration of households. In most developing nations, such as across Africa however, mobile phones are more prevalent than landlines and it could be that only a few households have telephones. Even in countries like Saudi Arabia, where telephone ownership is extensive, telephone directories can be incomplete and out of date.

Therefore, telephone interviews are most useful when employed with relatively upscale consumers who are accustomed to business transactions by phone, be it mobile or landline, or consumers who can be reached by phone and can express themselves easily.

Mail interviewing   Because of the rise of the online survey the use of mail interviews internationally has declined dramatically. However, in countries where literacy is high and the postal system is well developed and where there are still problems in terms of access to the Internet, mail surveys still continue to be used. In Africa, Asia and South America, however, the use of mail surveys and mail panels is low because of illiteracy and the large proportion of population living in rural areas.

No questionnaire administration method is superior in all situations. Table 4.5 presents a comparative evaluation of the major modes of collecting primary data in the context of international marketing research.

Questionnaire design

The questionnaire or research instrument should be adapted to the specific cultural environment and should not be biased in terms of any one culture. This requires careful attention to each step of the questionnaire design process. It is important to take into account any differences in underlying consumer behaviour, decision-making processes, psychographics, lifestyles and demographic variables.

The use of unstructured or open-ended questions may be desirable if the researcher lacks knowledge of the possible responses in other cultures. Unstructured questions also reduce cultural bias because they do not impose any response alternatives. However, unstructured questions are more affected by differences in educational levels than structured questions. They should be used with caution in countries with high illiteracy rates.

The questions may have to be translated for administration in different cultures. A set of guidelines has been proposed by Brislin (2001) for writing questionnaires in English so that they can be easily translated. These include:

- use short and simple sentences
- repeat nouns rather than using pronouns
- avoid metaphors
- avoid adverbs and prepositions related to place and time
- avoid possessive forms
- use specific rather than general terms
- avoid vague words
- avoid sentences with two different verbs if the verbs suggest different actions.

The problems of language and translation were discussed in Chapter 3 and equally apply in marketing research. A translation of a questionnaire might be grammatically correct but this does not necessarily mean that it is conveying the appropriate message. For example: value for money is not a common phrase in Spain; the equivalent phrase is 'price for product'. In the Middle East 'payment' is a transactional word; it refers to repaying a debt and so would be inappropriate in the context of purchasing a product.

Another problem is that countries sometimes have more than one official language: a decision has then to be made as to what the most appropriate language is. In Malaysia and Singapore, for instance, consumer surveys regularly employ three languages (English, Malay and Chinese). An interviewer may need a command of several languages or dialects to undertake field work. In Pakistan, the official language is Urdu, but most of the official work in government departments is done in English. However, most local

Table 4.5   Advantages and disadvantages of different survey approaches

Characteristic	Door-to-Door Personal Interview	Mall Intercept Personal Interview	Telephone Interview	Snail Mail Survey	E-mail/Internet Survey
Speed of data collection	Moderate	Fast	Very fast	Slow	Fastest
Geographic flexibility	Limited to moderate	Confined mostly to urban and suburban areas	High	High	High (worldwide)
Respondent cooperation	Moderate in getting an answer. Excellent once respondent agrees to participate	Good in agreement to respond. Moderate cooperation thereafter	Difficult to get an answer. Good cooperation thereafter. Varies landline versus cell	Moderate all the way around	Low from general population but high when hot button issue presented or sample is a computer panel
Versatility of questioning	Quite versatile	Extremely versatile	Limited versatility, particularly for cell calls	Not versatile; requires highly standardized format	Good versatility for logical branching and respondent assignment
Questionnaire length	Long	Moderate	Moderate for landline and short for cell	Moderate but varies depending on incentive	Moderate but varies depending on incentive
Item nonresponse rate	Low	Medium	Medium	High	Software can assure none
Possibility for respondent misunderstanding	Low	Low	Average	High	High
Degree of researcher or interviewer influence on responses	High	High	Moderate	Lowest	Low with exceptions depending on data source

Table 4.5 Continued

Characteristic	Door-to-Door Personal Interview	Mall Intercept Personal Interview	Telephone Interview	Snail Mail Survey	E-mail/Internet Survey
Supervision of interviewers	Moderate	Moderate to high	High, especially with central location interviewing	Not applicable	Not applicable
Anonymity of respondent	Lowest	Moderate	Low	Highest	Moderate
Ease of callback or follow-up	Difficult	Most difficult	Easy	Easy, but takes time	Difficult if respondents are unknown. Easy if sample drawn from e-mail list
Cost	Highest	Moderate to high	Low to moderate	Low	Low to moderate depending on potential cost of access to sample
Special features	Visual materials may be shown or demonstrated; extended probing possible	Taste tests, product trials, viewing of marketing materials possible. Ideal for representing population of mall/shopping centre shoppers	Fieldwork and supervision of data collection are simplified. Distinction must be made between landline and mobile/cell phone calls	Respondent may answer questions at own convenience; has time to reflect on answers	Streaming media software allows use of graphics and animation as well as random assignment to experimental conditions

Source: Babin, B.J. and Zikmund, W.G. (2016) *Essentials of Marketing Research*, 6th edn, Cengage Learning.

nationals who understand English also usually understand Urdu. There is also a particular segment of social class in the country which prefers English to Urdu in their daily routines. Should the researcher use English or Urdu?

The literal translation of a questionnaire can pose problems. A different language is not just a matter of different spellings but of different linguistic concepts. This is why translation agencies recommend back translation into the original language. This identifies and corrects many of the problems faced in simple translation. The technique of 'decentring' in translation, where the material is translated and retranslated each time by a different translator, also minimizes mistakes being made.

Sample frame

The problems of obtaining valid sampling frames tend to be more complicated in researching international markets. It might be difficult or even impossible to obtain a reliable sampling frame. Due to problems associated with the validity and reliability of secondary data in some countries, experience and judgement need to play an important part in constructing the sample where there is no reliable database. It may mean that accepted techniques of marketing research in developed countries cannot always be directly transferred, even to other developed countries where data might have to be collected through less formalized methods. This applies especially in countries lacking a marketing infrastructure where, unless sufficient care is taken in selecting the sampling frame, the sample chosen will invariably be distorted.

Field work

Interviewee bias
The major problems in field work are errors caused through bias in the interviewing stage of the process which can mean that reliable multi-country studies where results can be compared and contrasted across different countries are sometimes difficult to achieve.

Different cultures will produce a varied response to interviews or questionnaires. For example, purchase intentions for new products frequently peak in Italy because Italians have a propensity to over-claim their likelihood to buy, whereas German results are much closer to reality. If Germans say they will buy a product they probably will.

Another problem is that in some countries it is not possible for the female members of a household to respond personally to a survey. In such countries, mail or online surveys for researching the female market might obtain a much better rate of response.

In some countries the rate of response of a particular segment of society might be quite low due to tax evasion problems, with respondents unwilling to provide any information which gives an idea of their economic status (Terpstra *et al.* 2012). Even within the same country, different social classes of customers could have differing responses to marketing research techniques. In some cultures the respondent may cause bias by attempting to please the interviewer and give the answers they think they want to hear. This happened to BSN in Japan. The French conglomerate carried out a study in Japan to find out people's attitudes to yogurt. The results indicated that the Japanese were becoming much more westernized in their food and eating habits and that there was a potential market for yogurts. BSN launched their products, set up distribution and invested heavily in promotion. However, the sales were disappointing. Follow-up research showed that the questions used in the original research were too simplistic to elicit accurate responses. The Japanese were far too polite to reply NO to a question. Therefore the responses to yes/no questions were highly misleading. Likewise, they did not wish to offend westerners by criticizing the usage of a spoon as an eating implement.

Interviewer bias
Interviewer biases are often due to communication problems between the interviewer and respondents. Several biases have been identified in multicultural research, including rudeness bias, 'I can answer any question' bias, courtesy bias, sucker bias, hidden premises bias, reticence–loquaciousness bias, social desirability bias, status difference bias, racial difference bias and individual group opinion bias (Malhotra and *et al.*, 2013).

Extensive training and close supervision of the interviewers and other field staff may be required to minimize these biases.

The selection ... country research. ... recruit and ... esirable as ... te for the

..., in preparing ...ers'? These are ...t be a problem at ... sampling or a problem of translation ... questionnaire.

Second is the issue of how to ensure comparability of data across cultures. Some researchers prefer to standardize data to ensure comparability. In contrast, others prefer statistics based on non-standardized data on the basis that this allows a truer comparative analysis.

Report preparation and presentation

In any research study there is the chance of cultural bias in the research findings. International research often involves researchers from one cultural environment conducting research in another cultural environment, or communicating with researchers from another cultural environment. In international research situations, effective communication between the respondents and the researcher is essential to avoid problems of misinterpretation of the data. The phenomenon of cultural self-reference criteria is cited as a possible cause of the misinterpretation of data and can lead to a systematic bias in the findings. The reader is referred to the discussion in Chapter 3 and the discussion on the steps that can be taken to remedy self-reference criteria.

Some agencies follow the practice of always ensuring foreign market studies are written in the local language and include interpretation as well as analysis. The nuance can then be discussed with the translator.

Face-to-face debriefings with agencies and researchers are also a good way to synthesize the results from multi-country surveys and form coherent conclusions through open discussions with representatives who have participated in the research across a range of countries.

Continuous research   In this chapter, in order to discuss the relevant issues in a logical manner, we have used the six-step research design framework. It is perhaps important to stress, however, that international market research, while expensive, is by no means a 'one-off' activity. In today's dynamic environment where changes occur almost on a daily basis in some rapidly growing markets (e.g. India and China), it is important that research be on a continuous basis to ensure a company keeps ahead of its competition.

SUMMARY

- In this chapter we have examined the three main roles of the international marketing researcher: scanning international markets, building up market profiles and carrying out primary research across global markets. The rise of the Internet has impacted critically on the role of international market research and led to the development of better decision tools and the development of globally based research supplier networks and global databases.

- International research is, in many cases, a complex, expensive and time-consuming task and evidence suggests that for these reasons many international firms fail to research markets to the extent that is really necessary. The consequences of this are significant in terms of both missed opportunities and the failure to meet existing and developing market demand.

- The issues relevant to the identifying and analyzing of opportunities across the globe were discussed and the problems involved in categorizing and segmenting international markets identified. Several models used in the segmentation process of international markets were presented.

- Within this chapter, we illustrated the strategic importance of opportunity analysis and the contribution that market research can make to the decision-making process.

- In examining the international marketing research process the six-step research design framework was used. It was suggested that many international marketing efforts fail not because research was not conducted, but because the issue of comparability was not adequately addressed in defining the marketing research problem. The importance of self-reference criteria (SRC) was discussed and at each of the six stages the relevant issues for the international marketer highlighted.

KEYWORDS

marketing research	market segmentation	online databases
research process	pareto law	websites
cross-cultural research	differentiated marketing	secondary data
marketing information	transnational	primary data
existing markets	segmentation	omnibus studies
latent markets	global segments	multi-country study
incipient markets	market profile analysis	qualitative research
comparative research		

CASE STUDY 1

How do Spike Games segment the global mobile phone gambling market?

Spike Games developed a whole new business by transferring the 'feel of the casino/slot machine' to the mobile phone. Mobile phones provided a platform to deliver casino-style games. Initially games had to be pushed to a player's phone using SMS push messaging. After the advent of the iPhone touch sensitive device, delivery and play became much easier (as US companies, both Apple and Google decided to not allow gambling apps on their app stores).

In the early days, market research showed there were few companies delivering fruit machine-style games on mobile phones. Closer inspection of their games revealed the games were basic and designed from the perspective of a games designer rather than a fruit machine designer. Estelle research also estimated that the mobile gambling market was set to rise rapidly to US$50 billion by 2020. The market for mobile gambling games therefore had huge growth potential. Spike Games was able to deliver superior quality games compared with its competitors, bringing the feel of playing on the Las Vegas slots to the mobile phone. Games could be played any time, anywhere; on the way to work on the bus/train, waiting in the bus queue, etc. Competitors, however, had a few years' foothold in the market, acquired key partners and had begun to establish a mobile casino brand.

The mobile gambling market was split into a number of sectors providing different style games. The lottery and bingo style games, more traditional fruit machine/casino games including roulette and blackjack, skills-based games such as quiz games, points for prizes games and non-gambling games such as just for fun slot machines where players paid just for the download to their pho...

...y to design high-quality games based on superior software design.

'I'd been to a number of gambling conferences including International Casino Exhibition (ICE) in London and Global Gaming Expo in Las Vegas; our games were raising eyebrows from international contacts, I knew at that point our games could go global.' Rob Anderson the CEO reported.

Spike Games sold their mobile casino package to industry intermediaries around the globe who could reach the 'mobile gambler'. Therefore, as a business to business operation, Spike Games needed to consider how to segment the global markets to identify companies with the largest penetration of potential mobile phone gamblers. This meant understanding:

a the profile of the mobile phone gambling game player around the world; and

b which companies could best reach those players globally.

Spike Games sold their mobile casino games via a website where players downloaded games directly to their mobile phones. This meant they had to identify which companies would want to operate their own mobile casino. In principle anybody could set up their own mobile casino, however, given that Spike Games revenue streams would be based on a percentage of gambling revenues, their target customers needed to have access to a large database of potential mobile gambling games players. Which companies had access to such a large database of potential players? How should they best be identified and reached? Would online casinos look for a mobile arm to their operations, or would entrepreneurs with sufficient revenues want to manage their own mobile casino? The latter would need a heavily supported promotional campaign to build a large enough database to capture a percentage of mobile phone gamblers.

Given the 'virtual' nature of the product and its user, i.e. the online mobile casino and the mobile gambler, Spike Games had a difficult decision to make in trying

...same income, age brackets or life-stage segments? It was more likely that the mobile phone gambler was a niche customer located in different countries across the world.

Geography was only an issue in terms of gambling legislation. Players could be global but legislation was not. Culture and legal issues played a big role in the gambling sector. Many gambling-style companies were basing operations offshore, or had to acquire expensive gambling licences. Legislation was continually changing. The US enforced the wire act with regard to internet gambling which made it an offence to gamble online. In 2007 the UK expanded the 1968 gambling act to encompass Internet gambling. As Britain is part of the EU it was forced to accept licences from other jurisdictions many of whom had low tax advantages. Eventually Britain followed many other European states and created the point of consumption tax which meant that if a company wanted to take a bet from a British citizen then they would need to have a UK licence.

Spike Games knew it had the right combination of expertise in games and software design and experience in the fruit machine sector. It only needed to find the best way to reach the mobile gambling game player around the globe and identify the best route to the market ensuring it did not breach gambling legislation.

Questions

1 Critically evaluate the arguments for and against the use of country by country versus global market segment descriptors as bases for the segmentation of the global mobile phone gambling market.

2 How can Spike Games develop a global segmentation strategy that could be used as the basis for a global marketing plan?

3 Advise Spike Games on how they should research the global opportunities to better understand the market for mobile gambling.

Source: Alexandra Anderson, Sheffield Hallam University

CASE STUDY 2

Cultural segmentation map

We have been exploring the social and cultural considerations that organizations who want to grow internationally must research. We have also reviewed databases that supply a wealth of information about the business world be it B2B, global or international. Further, there are many secondary research databases which show the complex range of influences that guide consumers to behave, purchase and express themselves. A constant, year-on-year review of these databases is essential as the world has changed dramatically over the last 30 years and continues to change at a rapid rate. This change is brought on by social, legal, economic, political, technological and sustainability (SLEPTS) transformations which, in turn, provide new opportunities for businesses.

At the heart of any business is the consumer. Therefore, to research the growth in populations, merging cultures, migration and the fact that millions of consumers may all be viewing one social media space – at the same time – makes it top priority for

FIGURE 4.6   Cultural segmentation map

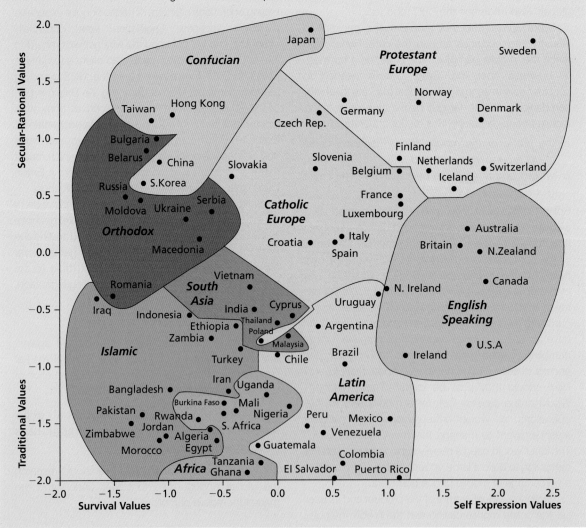

marketers. Therefore, it is crucial that marketers review existing research databases that show how consumer's behavioural, cultural priorities and aspirations can change over time.

One database, the World Values Survey (WVS), enables marketers to review a cultural map of people's views and beliefs from 100 countries. Such a high number of countries researched means countries from the very poor to the very rich are included. The map shows there are two cross-cultural variations that are distinguished by different deep-set values. The values shown vertically are **Traditional values** versus **Secular rational values** and on the horizontal axis there are **Survival values** versus **Self-expression values**.

Traditional values are shown where citizens consider religion and the family are important. The parent/child relationship is very strong and there is great respect for authority figures.

Citizens from **secular-rational value** countries have very different beliefs and values to the traditional value dimensions. Citizens in secular-rational values tend to be less religious, live on a more level basis with authority figures and accept that civil partnerships, divorce and abortion are part of their society's way. Data collected through the WVS shows that 84 per cent of Zimbabwean citizens consider religion to be a very important aspect in their life. In Romania 51 per cent of people think that religion is very important, whereas only 8 per cent of Swedish people think that way. This shows that citizens of Zimbabwe have high traditional values and Sweden has high secular-rational values.

The values shown on the horizontal axis consider the different dimensions of **survival values** against **self-expression values**. As the name implies, people who think survival values are important need personal physical security, money and economic survival. However, self-expression values needs go beyond

survival and include equal rights for men and women and the protection of environments so that future generations can enjoy them. The WVS collects data asking citizens from Jordan and the Netherlands to consider the following scenario: 'if jobs were scarce' would they agree that a man should have the job rather than a woman? Just 7 per cent of citizens from the Netherlands agreed with this scenario; however 81 per cent of people from Jordan agreed that men should have more rights to a job if jobs were scarce. Self-expression countries such as the Netherlands believe in equal rights, whereas people from Jordan or other survival countries are less inclined to believe in equal rights for men and women.

These are just some examples of the data collected from thousands of people around the world. To understand the beliefs and values of people the world over WVS asks many questions; from those about leisure time to politics, membership of charitable organizations to confidence in their government and whether they are a nervous or imaginative person. WVS even asks people questions about the quality of air and roads in their hometown.

Questions

1 In what ways can knowing the beliefs, values and motivations of people throughout the world help marketers?

2 How could marketers use the knowledge gained from the WVS to decide which country their organization should develop business relations with?

3 There are many reasons why is it important for marketers to know whether citizens of a country have traditional values or secular rational values; what are they?

Source: World Values Survey, www.worldvaluessurvey.org

DISCUSSION QUESTIONS

1   What are the problems in carrying out multi-country studies? As an international market researcher, how would you avoid these dangers?

2   Many companies are looking to emerging markets in their internationalization programmes. What are

the problems in researching these markets? How, if at all, may they be overcome?

3   Identify the principal methods that companies might use in assessing and reviewing opportunities across international markets. Suggest the alternative means by which firms can prioritize and segment international markets.

4   As firms become more global so does their requirement to gather global information. Outline the key categories of a global information system and explain their relevance.

5   Citing specific examples, show how the spread of the Internet has impacted on international market research. What are the problems and limitations of using web-based research?

REFERENCES

1.   Brislin, R.W. (2001) *Understanding Cultures' Influence on Behaviour*, 2nd edn. Harcourt.

2.   Hassan, S.S. and Stephen, H.C.T. (2005) 'Linking global market segmentation decisions with strategic positioning options', *Journal of Consumer Marketing,* 22(2) 81–9.

3.   Malhotra, N.K., Birks, D.F. and Wills, P. (2013). *Essentials of Marketing Research*. Pearson.

4.   Papadopoulos, N. and Martín Martín, O. (2011). 'International market selection and segmentation: Perspectives and challenges'. *International Marketing Review*, 28(2) 132–149.

5.   Sheth, J. and Arma, A. (2005) 'International e-marketing: Opportunities and issues', *International Marketing Review,* 22(6) 611–22.

6.   Terpstra, V., Foley, J. and Sarathy, R. (2012). *International Marketing*. Naper Press.

7.   World Economic Forum (2014) The Global Competitiveness Report 2014–2015. Available from www3.weforum.org /docs/WEF_GlobalCompetitivenessReport_2014-15.pdf (accessed 2 February 2015).

DIRECTED STUDY ACTIVITIES

An introduction

Successful international marketing is about taking a planned approach to analysis, strategy development and implementation. The chapters of this book focus upon providing the underpinning knowledge to support the process of planning an international marketing strategy. The purpose of the three directed study activities at the end of each of the three parts of the book is to integrate the four chapters that make up each of the parts. More importantly, however, is that as a whole, the three activities provide a framework for planning an international marketing strategy and give the opportunity for readers to consider the practical issues involved in developing, planning and implementing an outline international marketing strategy.

Learning Objectives

On completing the three integrated learning activities you should be able to:

- Analyze critically the international marketing environment of a given company situation.

- Apply relevant concepts and models to each of the development stages of an international marketing strategy.

- Make clear links between analysis and the chosen response. The issues identified in the analysis should lead directly to the development and implementation of a strategy.

- Develop a realistic and cohesive international marketing strategy.

The aims of the directed study activities (DSAs) therefore are much wider in scope than the short case studies found at the end of each chapter. The objective is to provide a vehicle through which the reader is able to develop practical skills in research, analysis, evaluation and strategy development. In completing these activities you will need to synthesize the various strands and themes explored throughout the book and apply them to a practical situation. To complete each of the activities the reader must move well beyond the boundaries of the textbook, researching new material and exploring the interplay of the concepts discussed in the text and possible solutions to the practical problems identified in each activity.

Each DSA depicts very different scenarios.

Part 1: We spotlight the rapid development of the mobile phone services market in Africa and use this scenario as a backdrop for examining trading infrastructure issues, consumer behaviour and cultural issues and examine the development of a latent and exciting market.

Part 2: We identify a number of companies from emerging markets that are developing as global brands competing against entrenched western global players. How do such companies compete effectively against existing global competitors, and how can they ensure they build a sustainable competitive advantage?

Part 3: Yum brands has a portfolio of some of the best known fast food brands. Due to changes in the market environment, customer expectations and competition, it must use creative approaches in implementing its international marketing strategies to maintain its growth.

In each of the activities a series of questions is posed, together with suggestions on how to get started, a framework depicting the key factors to consider in completing the task, and suggested websites you may find useful.

Additional observations are also made that will assist you in addressing the key issues and how you could develop the activity further.

In all the activities we have provided only outline information on the scenarios. A key skill in international marketing is *finding* information about international markets, analyzing it, deciding what is most important and preparing a structured, logical rationale for the decisions that must ultimately be made. In each activity, therefore, you will need to seek information outside of the case to complete the task. Much of the information you can use is available online. You should not have to approach staff in the organizations depicted for further information to complete the task.

INTERNATIONAL MARKETING PLANNING: ANALYSIS

Introduction

In this activity we explore the development of the mobile phone services' market in Africa and the attendant challenges and opportunities faced in its development by companies trying to develop a marketing strategy across the region to enable them to become globally competitive. We explore the international marketing opportunities and challenges companies face in this market.

The mobile phone services' market in Africa, especially Southern Africa, can be defined as a latent market with huge growth potential. However, there are huge challenges in terms of lack of infrastructure and the ability of many in the market to pay, which mean it is a highly challenging market. Anyone entering the market needs to develop a thorough understanding of the complexities of the African marketing environment in which they are competing and decide how to segment the market, which segment to target and how to develop a positioning strategy to achieve competitive leverage. Increasing global competition in this market necessitates greater innovation, not just in products and services, but in all aspects of the operation. To understand such issues we need to build the skills to research, analyze and evaluate how such factors impact international strategy development. We hope the reader will develop these skills in this activity.

Learning Objectives

On completing this activity you should be able to:

- Identify and analyze international market opportunities and challenges
- Use appropriate conceptual frameworks to develop a market profile analysis
- Identify sources of information, methods of information collection and methods of information

analysis suitable for international marketing operations

- Understand the complexities of researching international markets and be able to identify possible solutions

The scenario: Market information

In a world where more people have access to mobile phones than to flushing toilets, telecommunications operators in search of growth are naturally drawn to countries where phone usage is still low. Yet fixating on so-called penetration rates – the number of mobile subscribers as a percentage of the population – can be a mistake. For example the Egyptian operator Orascom entered what, on that measure, was the ultimate growth market, North Korea. Two years later, the mobile penetration rate there was still barely above 0 per cent.

Operators have had better luck in Africa. Penetration across the continent will reach 50% of subscribers by 2020 from 2 per cent a decade ago. Africa is in the grip of a mobile phone revolution. In the past 15 years, subscribers in sub-Saharan Africa have risen from 72 000 to 329 million (GSMA 2015). While many rural villagers huddle around paraffin lamps as darkness falls, neon lights come to life as they illuminate the mobile phone masts proliferating across the African landscape.

According to Mobile Africa, the number of mobile phone subscriptions far exceeds fixed-line subscriptions. The International Telecommunication Union reckon that more Africans have begun using phones in the past decade than in the whole of the previous century! Use of mobile phones is increasing at an annual rate of 7 per cent, more than twice the global average.

Ten years ago Africa was dubbed 'the hopeless continent'. Since then its progress has been remarkably hopeful. Thanks to rising living standards, the middle class in Africa has tripled in the last 30 years and the continent's working-age population will double from 500 million today to 1.1 billion in 2040.

Africa's annual output is growing by approximately 5 per cent (adjusted for purchasing power parity), twice as fast as in the previous ten years and faster than the global average. Foreign direct investment to the region increased from US$10 billion to US$88 billion – more than India (US$42 billion) and, even more remarkably, catching up with China (US$108 billion). The Boston Consulting Group notes that the revenues of Africa's 500 largest companies (excluding banks) have grown at an average of 8.3 per cent a year over the past decade.

Consumer goods companies ranging from western giants such as Procter & Gamble to emerging market car companies such as China's Great Wall and India's Tata Motors are pouring into Africa. Foreign firms are starting to use Africa as a base for manufacturing as well, as labour costs in India and China rise.

The mobile phone market has been an integral part of this growth.

In Africa, average penetration of mobile phones stands at nearly half the population, and in North Africa it is almost two-thirds. Gabon, the Seychelles and South Africa now boast almost 100 per cent penetration. Only five African countries – Burundi, Djibouti, Eritrea, Ethiopia and Somalia – still have a penetration of less than 25 per 100 inhabitants.

Uganda, the first African country to have more mobiles than fixed telephones, is cited as an example of cultural and economic transformation. Penetration has risen from 0.2 per cent ten years ago to 30 per cent now, with operators making huge investments in infrastructure, particularly in rural areas. Given their low incomes, only about a quarter of Ugandans have a mobile subscription, but street vendors offer mobile access on a per-call basis. They also invite those without access to electricity to charge their phones using car batteries.

Popular mobile services include money transfers, allowing people without bank accounts to send money by text message. Many farmers use mobiles to trade and check market prices.

Company information

Companies continue to invest heavily in this market. Forecasts suggest around US$100 billion will be invested over 7 years by companies such as France Telecom and Bharti Airtel who paid US$10 billion for a group of African mobile companies and recently acquired Zain Africa. Bharti, India's largest mobile phone company, is aiming to more than double the number of mobile phone users in Africa. In Africa it intends to pursue the low-cost outsourced business model of operations that has served it so well at home.

The Indian operator segments Africa by language and has divided its operations in Africa into three separate divisions to meet their needs. These divisions include Bharti Anglophone (comprising the English-speaking nations – Ghana, Kenya, Malawi, Sierra Leone, Tanzania, Uganda, Zambia), Bharti Francophone (comprising the French speaking nations – Burkina Faso, DRC, Chad, Congo B, Madagascar, Niger, Gabon), while Nigeria, the continent's largest market, will be a separate unit.

There are also a number of strong more local brands such as Essar Telecom which offers services under the 'Yu' brand in Kenya. However, others such as Warid have been acquired by Bharti Airtel as industry consolidation takes place.

Internet technologies

Mobile Internet technologies play a very important role in making Internet services available to many in Africa. Africans are using them for more than calling their friends and family, many are using them to do their banking. About half a million South Africans now use their mobile phones as a bank. For these new banking customers both the mobile phone and the whole system of banking are new to them.

Besides sending money to relatives and paying for goods, they check balances, buy mobile airtime and settle utility bills. Traditional banks offer mobile banking as an added service to existing customers, most of whom are quite well off. Wizzit, and to some extent First National Bank (FNB) and MTN Banking, are chasing another market: the 16 million South Africans, over half of the adult population, with no bank account. Significantly, 30 per cent of these people do have mobile phones. Previously ignored as the bottom of the pyramid and of little commercial importance to the large corporations, such customers are now being courted. Wizzit hired and trained over 2000 unemployed people, known as Wizzkids, to drum up business. It worked: eight out of ten Wizzit customers previously had no bank account and had never used an ATM.

People using advanced technology to manage their finances had until now depended on the archaic system of barter. They have leapfrogged telephony technology and jumped from dealing only in cash or barter to the world of cellular finance. A simplified kind of account called Mzansi has been launched to reach the non-banking customers, and portable banks and ATMs have been rolled out in townships and in the countryside.

In most of Africa, only a fraction of people have bank accounts – but there is huge demand for cheap and convenient ways to send money and buy prepaid services such as airtime. In Kenya, a pilot scheme called M-Pesa is being used to disburse and pay micro-loans by phone. Meanwhile Celpay is offering platforms for banks and phone companies in Zambia and Congo. In countries like Somalia, with chaotic conditions, cash transfers by phone will be a bonus.

By clicking a few keys on a mobile phone, money can be zapped from one part of Kenya to another in seconds. For urban migrants sending money home to their villages, and for people used to queuing at banks for hours to pay bills or school fees, the M-Pesa money-transfer service, operated by Safaricom, Kenya's largest mobile operator, is a godsend. It is used by 17 million people, or over half the population, and transfers the equivalent of almost 50 per cent of Kenya's GDP each year. The most ambitious is Africa's biggest operator, MTN, which is rolling out mobile-money schemes in several African countries. Together with five other providers it has opened up the Ugandan market where users of the service have increased from 10 000 to 19 million in 7 years.

Market challenges

There are many difficulties on the way. Not all potential consumers are ready to make the leap. Many think banking is too expensive and complicated, and helping new customers become financially literate takes time. The technology remains a problem in some cases, with downloads requiring dozens of text messages. Several rival platforms are still in the fight, but so far those that emphasize simplicity and ease-of-use over state-of-the-art technology and security have made the greatest strides. A lot also hangs on putting the right laws and regulations in place. They need to be tight enough to protect vulnerable users and discourage money laundering, but open enough to allow innovative mobile banking to grow.

However the main barrier to further expansion remains the cumbersome regulatory frameworks. Countries with similar economic circumstances but with a liberalized market generally show higher penetration rates. Taxes can also act as a barrier, particularly import duties on handsets or special mobile communications surcharges. The mobile industry has been seen as a cash cow by governments in some countries who have used its popularity for generating tax revenues but haven't invested in the infrastructure for its growth. To expand coverage into rural and remote areas, government support will be required.

Rural areas in some countries are also often economically unattractive for operators to invest in. This is usually not due to a lack of demand but rather to lack of basic infrastructure. The roads in Africa can be notorious, the infrastructure under-developed and the continent has more than its fair share of conflicts and crises.

The cost of making calls and sending texts in Africa is also relatively high and many of its countries are poor. In South Africa and Kenya, running a mobile phone costs the average user 5 per cent of a monthly income. Yet in countries such as Malawi and Central African Republic, average monthly mobile costs are as much as 50 per cent of average monthly earnings. Big chunks of some markets remain unreachable because of this.

A 'digital divide' also persists in terms of Internet access but this is changing too as Internet penetration has passed 20 per cent in Africa. Because of the lack of availability of fixed lines, mobile broadband accounts for 90 per cent of Internet subscriptions and so Internet access in Africa is much more dependent on the penetration of smartphones.

References

www.reuters.com

www.news.bbc.co.uk

www.timesofindia.indiatimes.com

www.economist.com

www.guardian.co.uk

GSMA (2014) The Mobile Economy Sub-Saharan Africa 2014 Accessed at http://www.gsmamobileeconomyafrica.com/GSMA_ME_SubSaharanAfrica_Web_Singles.pdf Accessed 7 October 2015

The task

1 Analyze and evaluate the major environmental influences that will impact on the growth of the mobile phone services market.

2 Building on the results of your analysis from Question 1, and with reference to a company of your choice, draw up a market profile analysis for the area.

3 Propose and justify an effective segmentation strategy of the African market that will form the basis on which a company of your choice can build a regional marketing strategy. This should form the basis on which the company you have chosen can enter and develop the market.

4 For the company referred to in Question 2, show how the company should develop some of the segments identified. In doing so, you will need to fully appraise them of the challenges and problems they will face and how they should respond to these challenges.

Useful websites

www.southafrica.net

www.allafrica.com

www.gamos.org

www.news.bbc.co.uk

www.globaldashboard.org

www.wto.org

www.ita.doc.gov/tradestats

www.worldbank.com

www.foreign-trade.com

Getting started

In international markets it is exceedingly difficult to obtain a comprehensive understanding of the relevant market environment. Africa is particularly difficult due to the scarcity of reliable data. In tackling the task it is useful to categorize the elements of the environment into social and cultural, legal, economic, political and technological forces (SLEPT).

In the increasingly global marketplace, companies are trying to identify methodologies for segmenting and evaluating international markets that transcend national and cultural boundaries. You are asked to develop a segmentation strategy. It is important here to remember that simply segmenting the market on a geographical basis will be too simplistic and not form a basis on which the company can build a regional strategy. You will need a hierarchical approach where your segmentation strategy has several steps and can incorporate the multidimensional aspects of a global niche segment.

It is important in building a market profile analysis to develop a systematic method for building a market information on the markets you have prioritized. The 12C framework is a useful tool when developing profiles of international markets. Finally, you need to think through the implications of your research and consider the issues the analysis has highlighted and the implications for developing a strategy. Of particular importance, examine these issues in the light of possible resources/cultural/management constraints that the company you choose may face.

In summary, therefore, the framework shown in Table I provides a guide to the key factors that need to be considered in tackling the task identified.

The way forward

After reading Part II of this textbook you may wish to return to plan the next stage of your strategy. The most important issue is deciding how quickly the firm should develop internationally and how – country by country, concentrating on a particular segment or seeking a regional presence distribution. You should define a strategy that builds upon the firm's competitive advantage, identifying a positioning strategy that meets the needs of the target segment you have chosen. Then you should identify the criteria that will determine the choice of market entry.

After reading Part III you will be in a position to define the implementation plan and make decisions on the marketing mix elements, relationship building and supply chain management. You can identify how management and technology systems might support the international expansion. Finally, you will be able to identify the monitoring and control systems that will be used.

Table I Key factors to consider

The element of the plan	Some concepts, models and issues to be addressed
Environment	• The global SLEPT factors, including political and economic issues and socio/cultural factors affecting the opportunities for the firm
	• The changing global trends in competition and customer expectations that impact on business
	• The international challenges to be met

The element of the plan	Some concepts, models and issues to be addressed
Home and possible international markets	• The level of market development and competitive structures • Prioritization of markets using country attractiveness and latent assessment of markets • Commercial, home, host country stakeholder expectations and ethical issues
Company capability	• SWOT, competitive advantage • Products: international product life cycle, knowledge and capability
Segmentation	• Basis of segmentation/criteria for global segmentation/global niche possibilities • Hierarchy of segmentation
Market information	• Market profile analysis and the information systems, data collection and management to support it • Market and environmental risk and potential commercial opportunity using the 12C framework
Strategic options	• Potential strategic alternatives for the company • The challenges faced and potential responses to the issues identified in the analysis • The resource constraints

PART II: STRATEGY DEVELOPMENT

AIMS AND OBJECTIVES

Having identified and analyzed the opportunities that exist within international markets in the first section of the book, we now turn our attention to the ways in which firms can use international marketing to develop their international business in order to exploit these opportunities profitably. The focus in Part II is on developing an international marketing strategy that is appropriate for the firm, given the environment and market context in which it is working, the firm's capability and the ambition of its management. Throughout the section we emphasize the importance of the mindset of the management of the firm in planning their international marketing and take decisive action to deal with the challenges posed by the business and market context, analyzed in section 1.

The first chapter in Part II, Chapter 5, concentrates on the international marketing strategies of small- and medium-sized enterprises. The discussion ranges from firms taking their first steps in international markets or marketing, to international customers from their home base, to those dynamic small firms that have the ambition and capability to grow quickly to become the major global players of the future.

When we think of globalization it is the very largest firms in the world that come to mind. Chapter 6 is concerned with the global strategies of the firms that operate within a global context and build brands that are instantly recognizable. Their global strategies aim to appeal to customers worldwide and ensure that as many customers as possible choose their products and services.

For any firm moving into a new international market the key step is to decide which market entry method should be chosen in order to achieve the best outcome from the investment that is made.

In Chapter 7 we discuss the factors that firms must consider in selecting an appropriate market entry method.

In Chapter 8 we consider the product and service management strategy and focus upon the need to have a constantly evolving portfolio of products and services that meet the current and future needs of global customers.

INTERNATIONAL NICHE MARKETING STRATEGIES FOR SMALL- AND MEDIUM-SIZED ENTERPRISES

LEARNING OBJECTIVES

After reading this chapter you should be able to:

- Appreciate the nature and types of international marketing undertaken in the SME sector
- Compare the different strategic approaches and mindsets of SMEs in international marketing
- Understand the factors affecting SME international strategic management
- Identify the characteristics of the different stages of international development of SMEs
- Be able to evaluate the factors for success and failure in SME international marketing

INTRODUCTION

Small- and medium-sized enterprises (SMEs) have always been significant creators of wealth and employment in domestic economies, but are a less powerful force outside their home territory, usually because of their limited resources. Indeed many SMEs, despite what may be obvious business capability, never move into international markets at all. However, for reasons which will be explored in this chapter, SMEs have growth potential, both in fast-growing business sectors that involve applying new technology, and in market niches where innovation in mature industry sectors can lead to new opportunities. In less developed markets entrepreneurs can play a vital role in countering poverty by creating new businesses to employ local people. The impact of these SMEs in regenerating the economy can increase considerably if they can gain access to international markets.

In this chapter we discuss the factors which influence the patterns of international development of small- and medium-sized firms, including the strategic options available to them and the particular problems they face in implementing their strategy. We also emphasize the different mindsets of SMEs needed to exploit their business situation.

The traditional model of SME internationalization is exporting, in which goods are manufactured in one country and transferred to buyers in other countries, but many SMEs are involved in a broader range of international marketing activity and it is for this reason we observe many international niche marketing companies. Small service providers generate revenue from customers in foreign markets either by providing services from the home country which customers can access wherever they are situated (for example, information and advice supplied via the Internet) or by providing services in the firm's home country, and requiring the customers to visit (for example, tourism, training and education residential courses).

Increasingly, large firms are finding that operating on a global scale often makes them inflexible and unresponsive to fast-changing markets, with the result that smaller, more entrepreneurial firms with an innovative idea, can compete globally in their chosen niche market from the start (born globals). To be successful all these international market approaches require an understanding of the factors affecting international marketing and what capabilities are needed to grow the business internationally.

The SME sector and its role within the global economy

A number of definitions of the small- and medium-sized firm sector exist, but the most commonly used terms relate to the number of employees in the company. The European Union (EU), for example, defines SMEs as those firms employing less than 250 staff. (Note: in the US an SME is defined as having fewer than 500 employees.) The EU's SME definition can be broken down further by including micro-firms as having less than 10 employees, small firms with less than 50 employees but more than 10 employees, and medium firms that equate to between 50 and 249 employees.

This characterization, however, effectively includes 99 per cent of all firms in Europe and accounts for roughly over 65 per cent of employment and, because it includes sole operators as well as quite sophisticated businesses, is not particularly useful for segmenting the smaller firms sector.

In this chapter, therefore, the review of smaller firm international strategies is not restricted to firms with a specific number of employees, but instead focuses on those issues that apply to businesses in general which have the mindset to think and act like small- and medium-sized enterprises. The reason for adopting this stance is that a garment-making firm with 250 employees has a very restricted capacity to internationalize, whereas a 250-employee financial services or computer software company could be a significant international player. Many quite large companies take business decisions within a small group of major shareholders or senior managers in much the same way that the family owners of small firms take decisions. Many of the fastest-growing international firms grow rapidly through the 250 employee ceiling without making significant changes to their international strategic approach or management style. Our discussion, therefore, relates to issues affecting firms which could not be described as large multinational enterprises (MNEs) with the global power to dominate their sector, but we do consider some of the implications for firms growing from being SMEs to global players. Additionally, as outlined in Chapter 1, there are many SMEs that are born global, and yet whilst having a small number of employees are in fact micro-multinationals. See Illustration 5.1 for details.

SMEs can be vulnerable to changes in the competitive environment and there are high failure rates. Because of globalization, the liberalization of trade policies and removal of protectionism and most trade barriers, virtually all firms are part of the global market, simply because their suppliers, customers and competitors are likely to be global players. In practice, however, many SMEs do remain focused on the domestic market, which may soon become over-supplied and this may be one reason why many firms fail to grow. Only a small percentage of SMEs, perhaps less than 5 per cent, grow significantly and an even smaller percentage have the ambition to become international traders.

Despite this the SME sector is increasingly recognized as a creator of wealth and employment because over the last 20 years many large firms have periodically downsized by reducing their workforce, rationalizing their operations and outsourcing their activities, often to smaller firms. Public sector organizations have also increased their outsourcing and in many countries this has left the small- and medium-sized firms sector as the only significant growing source of wealth and employment.

The role of SME internationalization in economic regeneration

Encouraging entrepreneurship is seen by many experts and the European Commission as the route to future prosperity for emerging markets (see Illustration 5.1). It can be argued that growing the private business sector helps put money in people's pockets, increases domestic demand, generates tax revenues

ILLUSTRATION 5.1

Sonetel: A European born global micro-multinational SME

The heading for this illustration seems almost too good to be true. Can a newly formed company be 'born global' and have enough resources to be a multinational company on Day 1?

Henrik Thomé, the CEO and Founder of Sonetel is an entrepreneur who is driven by projects that 'change the world'. Henrik Thomé identified a niche market that had a consumer market worldwide. Fellow entrepreneurs also wanted to expand internationally but were deterred by the high communication costs that international businesses often encounter. Therefore, Henrik Thomé developed Sonetel which is a very low cost digital telephone network for other micro-multinational SMEs.

Sonetel provides a local telephone number for micro-multiinational SME businesses so that consumers, from different countries, can use the local telephone number when placing orders or asking for help.

International businesses want to provide a 'local presence' for their new consumers despite their head office being thousands of miles away. Consumers

that use a local telephone number perceive a local presence. More importantly, the benefit for the consumer is that they pay local prices for the telephone call. Research shows that consumers trust businesses that have a local telephone number as they feel the business demonstrates commitment. The business also benefits as the cost of purchasing a local telephone number from Sonetel can be as low as $1 per month. Further, internal calls between business colleagues; no matter where they are in the world, are free. Sonetel also allows incoming calls to mobile phones, which means colleagues can answer consumer telephone calls whilst on the move.

Sonetel operates in 196 countries, with 416 417 companies using the telephone services. Expansion has recently taken place in Turkey, Colombia, the Virgin Islands, Brazil and Mexico. Due to expansion the CEO felt it necessary to increase his team to keep up with demand. He expanded his team by 50 per cent and now Sonetel has 24 employees.

Sonetel is just one successful digital SME. However, with 65 per cent of European employees working for an SME, the European Commission has acknowledged the potential for SMEs to explore and provide digital technology for large data, social, mobile and cloud storage solutions. At present the European Commission is stimulating interest for digital entrepreneurship through finance and knowledge exchange.

Questions

1 How did the external environment help Sonetel become successful?

2 Why has the European Commission identified SME growth potential in the digital technology sector?

Sources: Sonetel (2015) www.sonetel.com (accessed 1 April 2015); European Commission (2015) Growth: Stimulating Digital Entrepreneurship www.ec.europa.eu/growth/tools-databases/dem/monitor/project-description (accessed 1 April 2015).

and reduces dependency on international aid. Indeed there is considerable debate about the proportion of international aid that should be used for alleviating hunger, addressing basic health care and education, and improving a country's infrastructure, as opposed to supporting and promoting business creation and development.

In practice, however, it can be argued that it is those SMEs that trade internationally which are most important. SMEs that market their products and services in the domestic economy often grow at the expense of other domestic SMEs because of the relatively limited home market. However, export markets offer seemingly unlimited scope for SMEs to grow and have the effect of importing jobs and foreign currency, so creating wealth in the domestic economy. Of particular significance in less developed countries, as we shall see in Chapter 7, is the first 'level' of international market entry strategies. This includes domestic purchasing in which the international customer purchases products from the emerging market SME in its home country. Examples would include a supermarket sourcing fruit or coffee shop chains sourcing coffee beans from African farmers. In Chapter 7 we discuss this in more detail.

The challenges for SMEs from less developed countries

Small organizations from emerging markets are often severely disadvantaged in international marketing. For example, small farmers from poor countries are frequently exploited by aggressive multinational retailers who ruthlessly use the global competition among small organizations. The poor negotiating position of the farmers and the perceived demand from consumers for low prices forces down the prices paid to farmers to one which is so low that it results in workers living below the poverty line. Although the multinational retailers sign up to ethical social corporate responsibility principles, many fail to behave ethically in their everyday transactions and there are many stories of unacceptable behaviour.

Fairtrade and the protection of the interests of farmers   The Fairtrade organization (www.fairtrade.org) was developed to promote ethical consumption to both businesses that buy products from farmers and for consumers who choose brands that include the Fairtrade label. It is an independent consumer label which appears on products as an independent guarantee that disadvantaged producers in the developing world are getting a better deal, fair prices for their products and decent working conditions.

For a product to display the Fairtrade mark it must meet international Fairtrade standards. These standards are set by the international certification body Fairtrade Labelling Organizations International (FLO), which inspects and certifies them. They receive a minimum price that covers the cost of sustainable production and an extra premium that is invested in social or economic development projects. Fairtrade principles include:

- direct purchasing from producers
- transparent and long-term trading partnerships
- cooperation not competition
- agreed minimum prices to cover the costs of production, usually set higher than market minimums
- focus on development and technical assistance via the payment to suppliers of an agreed social premium (often 10 per cent or more of the cost price of goods)
- provision of market information; and
- sustainable and environmentally responsible production.

Fairtrade now has 1.4 million farmers and workers in 1140 certified producer groups in 74 countries and with Fairtrade turnover reaching in excess of €5 billion the programme has certainly been successful (Fairtrade International 2014).

There are arguments for and against the Fairtrade principles. The major argument against Fairtrade is that it acts as a kind of subsidy and creates artificially high prices which can then encourage the creation of surpluses. In practice, the key step is connecting the farmers better with their distant markets, helping them to develop their market knowledge, build their export or processing capability, or to diversify to meet newly identified demand. Fairtrade provides examples including coffee growers developing citrus or macadamia nuts, banana farmers moving into other premium tropical produce, or investment in alternative income-generation projects such as ecotourism, as well as support for community health and education programmes.

Infrastructure weaknesses   The challenges for international marketers from emerging markets are huge. Many of the emerging countries have difficult geography and terrain with remote areas and an inhospitable climate. Many have a poorly developed infrastructure and suffer unreliable and often poor quality supplies of utilities, such as energy, water and power. Fixed line telecommunications and transport are slow and unreliable. Usually there is an overly bureaucratic and inefficient financial and business support infrastructure. The informal economy is huge in less developed countries (LDCs) and, in addition, bribery and corruption are rife at all levels. War and terrorism can have a devastating long-term effect on trade.

However, organizations from emerging markets can and do succeed in building their businesses despite these challenges if they can connect with their market and thus build the knowledge and capabilities to compete. For example, simply knowing what the actual international market price is for their products, rather than relying for price information on a buyer or a third party, is crucial and can have a huge impact on the viability of a small organization. By enabling a real time connection with international market information that bypasses incomplete, unreliable and out-of-date infrastructure, mobile computing could bring about the next 'industrial revolution'. It is also important for these SMEs to understand the value contributions of the supply chain, identifying changing customer demands and expectations, market trends, understanding what quality standards are required and knowing how to meet them and appreciating the power of branding to raise the perception of the products.

In countries that have a small, unsophisticated domestic market these issues may not be so significant, but in international markets the goods and services must compete with those from other countries, even though they may be cheaper or unique. This poses the problem of the customers' perceptions of the quality of their goods and service. What is acceptable in a local emerging market may not be acceptable to consumers in a developed country. While the obvious route to the international market is by becoming a contract manufacturer or grower, the Internet offers further potential. To address the imbalance in power between the supplier and major international customers, improved networking of small growers and manufacturers can help. However, Illustration 5.2 shows that even when Fairtrade principles are adhered to there are price wars.

Government support

We have explained the potential contribution of entrepreneurs and SMEs to the regeneration of national economies in terms of jobs, and wealth creation through internationalization and the challenges they face. It is hardly surprising, therefore, that governments in developed and developing countries encourage SMEs to internationalize by running export promotion programmes providing support and advice.

Governments often provide support in the form of resources and advice but at significantly different levels, ranging from help with documentation, comprehensive country market information, export credit guarantees, trade missions and, in some cases, target country representative offices. The Organization for Economic Cooperation and Development (OECD 2009) emphasize the need for policymakers to be more concerned with determining what assistance might be useful in helping firms to become more marketing orientated and focused on satisfying customer needs by improving quality, service and specifications to meet international standards and becoming more effective in conducting business overseas. While help with language training is usually available, it is cultural training in both the social and business culture that is often more important. In South Africa, Proudly South African (www.proudlysouthafrican.co.za) is an initiative of the National Economic Development and Labour Council (Nedlac) and is supported by organized business, organized labour, government and the community to encourage firms to achieve the high standards necessary to compete against international competition and in foreign markets. Illustration 5.1 also shows that the European Commission, with discussions from EU members, feel that entrepreneurs should be encouraged to provide digital solutions. In addition, governments also support exporting from particular regions of the

ILLUSTRATION 5.2

Price wars at the checkout – unfair practice towards Fairtrade banana farmers

One of the principles of Fairtrade is to ensure farmers are part of a price-protected scheme which means they receive an agreed minimum price for their produce. The minimum price enables farmers not only to have a fair and stable income from their produce, but it also provides money to support their own long-term sustainable development. Further, a Fairtrade premium goes towards a range of community projects, often in their area.

Bananas are one of the UK's favourite fruit. Over 20 years ago it was considered a premium product as each banana cost around 22p at the supermarket. However, the cost of a banana has halved with bananas currently costing around 11p each. Interestingly, bananas are one of the food items that have gone down in price when other basic food items, such as eggs and milk, have increased in price, by just under 80 per cent over the same period.

Price promotions and/or continuous price reductions at supermarkets have made banana farmers nervous. Some banana farmers are feeling they may be squeezed out of the marketplace. Others are at an even more critical point and are deciding to change their crop to a product which is more price stable and has more long-term sustainable prospects. Naturally, if there are fewer banana farmers the banana will become a premium product again as the cost of bananas, for the retailer, would increase substantially. The big question then would be . . . 'Will consumers pay high prices for a fruit that has been very affordable for so long?'

All UK supermarkets battle over advertising headlines. Many popular advertising headlines include cut-price food items, including bananas. And when one supermarket announces a cut-price food item the other supermarkets tend to follow. They do this because supermarkets don't want their customers to feel 'left out'. When this happens a price war begins.

The banana price wars at UK supermarkets are also down to the retailer's supply chain activity. Currently 5 billion bananas are sold in the UK; only a third of those bananas are bought from Fairtrade farmers. In the UK only supermarkets Sainsbury, the Co-op and Waitrose sell Fairtrade bananas exclusively; other supermarkets in the UK do not. Due to heavy worldwide demand even Fairtrade banana farmers are selling some of their produce on the open market, which means some of their bananas are not sold under the Fairtrade price-protected system. Therefore, some of the banana farmers may have to sell their produce at prices well below the protected Fairtrade minimum price.

The Fairtrade Foundation (UK) considered the plight of the millions of banana farmers worldwide who were not being treated fairly. Their campaign 'Make our Bananas Fair' raised awareness and produced a petition, backed by 70 000 supporters, which was presented to the Secretary of State for Business requesting government intervention. Government listened to the socially responsible and ethical plea and recently introduced very high fines to supermarkets operating in the UK that are found to be treating their suppliers unfairly.

Questions

1 Why should global companies, such as supermarkets, support their extended supply chain and what are the benefits?

2 Why should governments intervene when global companies do not treat their extended supply fairly?

Sources: *The Guardian* (2014) Banana price war requires government intervention, says Fairtrade Foundation, www.theguardian.com (accessed 4 April 2015); Fairtrade Foundation (UK) (2015) 'Make Bananas Fair', www.fairtrade.org.uk (accessed 4 April 2015).

country or support particular sectors that have exhibited the greatest growth potential. For example, the South African Department of Trade and Industry supports a number of sectors including agro-processing, chemicals, electronics and textiles.

The OECD suggest the role of private sector organizations, such as chambers of commerce, could be enhanced citing a number of examples, as well as public sector agencies, such as local authorities, local business support agencies, banks and accountants, which also provide SMEs with a range of services to support their international marketing activity. The support activities should focus particularly on addressing the barriers to internationalization by, for example, redressing managerial capacity barriers and also providing a wide range of actions to support the motivating factors.

Management Challenge 5.1 is concerned with the role of marketing in stimulating business in some of the poorest countries, but also prompts the broader question about how to get the best value from public money provided by governments to small firms.

We know that SMEs play different roles in the global economy, they have different ambitions and exploit different types of opportunity. It is this diversity that leads to SMEs adopting different approaches to international development.

MANAGEMENT CHALLENGE 5.1

International marketing helping social enterprises

For the most part in this book we discuss international marketing as it applies to private sector organizations and occasionally we refer to the larger global charities, such as Oxfam and Save the Children.

In practice, the for-profit and not-for-profit sectors converge in the area of social entrepreneurship. There has been unprecedented interest from public, private and charitable organizations and companies in addressing the problems of Africa, for example through UN initiatives, interventions by companies and campaigns, such as Make Poverty History.

The Skoll World Forum on Social Entrepreneurship founded by Jeff Skoll, the first president of eBay, suggests that such initiatives do not work and that the people in the country can succeed in business provided a longer-term view of investment is taken.

The principles of international marketing are fundamental and can be applied to all aspects of the work of campaigning, interventions and generating success for small firms in the poorest parts of the world.

Question

1 How can marketing help people in the poorest parts of the world?

Source: www.skollfoundation.org/

The nature of SME international marketing strategies

In exploiting these opportunities to generate revenue from international markets SMEs have a number of alternative strategies which provide a useful method of categorization of SME internationalization.

- *Exporting* is primarily concerned with selling abroad domestically developed and produced goods and services.
- *International niche marketing* is concerned with marketing a differentiated product or service overseas, usually to a single customer segment, using the full range of market entry and marketing mix options available.
- *Domestically delivered or developed niche services* can be marketed or delivered internationally to potential visitors.

■ *Direct marketing including electronic commerce* allows firms to market products and services globally from a domestic location.

■ *Participation in the international supply chain* of an MNE can lead to SMEs piggybacking on the MNE's international development. This may involve either domestic production or establishing a facility close to where the MNE's new locations are established in other countries.

Exporting

The emergence of global competition and the opening up of international markets has stimulated many firms to embark on the internationalization process; for many of them, exporting is the first significant stage. Exporting has been the most popular approach adopted by firms to enter and penetrate foreign markets as it requires less commitment of resources, has little effect on the firm's existing operations and involves low investment and financial risks. Leonidou *et al.* (2007) identify the factors stimulating smaller firms to export. However, exporting, when defined as the marketing of goods and/or services across national and political boundaries, is not solely the preserve of small- and medium-sized businesses, nor is it a temporary stage in the process of internationalization for many firms. Many companies, both large and small, do not progress beyond the stage of relatively limited involvement in international markets.

Motivation

In OECD (2009) there are references to a large volume of literature covering exporting, including export stimuli, barriers to exporting and promotion programmes. Despite the wide variation in the contexts in which the research was carried out some broad conclusions can be reached.

The research primarily focuses on proactive stimuli but it is also important to recognize that motivations to export can also be reactive too. Two examples of reactive strategies are:

1 If a product has reached maturity or is in decline in the home market, the company may find new foreign markets where the product has not reached the same life cycle stage and which, therefore, offers potential for further growth.

2 Companies may seek new markets abroad to utilize their production facilities to their full capacity.

In these circumstances companies may well embark on marginal pricing and sell at lower prices on the export markets, seeking only a contribution to their overall cost for their home base market.

The following are reactive stimuli:

■ adverse domestic market conditions

■ an opportunity to reduce inventories

■ the availability of production capacity

■ favourable currency movements

■ the opportunity to increase the number of country markets and reduce the market-related risk

■ unsolicited orders from overseas customers.

To reduce risk, OECD (2009) identify proactive stimuli for exporting as growth motives, including profits, an increased market size, a stronger market position and market diversification. If a company sees only limited growth opportunities in the home market for a proven product it may well see market diversification as a means of expansion. This could lead to the identification of new market segments within a domestic market, but it may well lead to geographic expansion in foreign markets. Thus, companies try to spread risks and reduce their dependence on any one market. Equally the firm may identify market gaps.

The proactive company with knowledge assets, including the management's previous international experience and capability, innovation capability, unique products or services, resources and a well-managed marketing information system, will identify foreign market opportunities. This could, of course, be by undertaking formal structured research. Proactive companies, however, highlight the importance of networks, supply chain links and social ties, through immigrant communities in global markets.

The following are proactive stimuli:

- attractive profit and growth opportunities
- the ability to easily modify products for export markets
- public policy programmes for export promotion
- foreign country regulations
- the possession of unique products
- economies resulting from additional orders.

And certain managerial elements including:

- the presence of an export-minded manager
- the opportunity to better utilize management talent and skills
- management beliefs about the value of exporting.

Barriers to internationalization

Many companies with export potential never become involved in international marketing, and a series of export studies have found that it is often a great deal easier to encourage existing exporters to increase their involvement in international markets than to encourage those who are not exporting to begin the process. The reasons given by companies for not exporting are numerous. The biggest barrier to entry into export markets for these companies is the fear that their products are not marketable overseas: consequently they become preoccupied with the domestic market. Other SMEs believe that because of the particular nature of their business sector, their domestic market continues to offer the best potential for market growth or market share growth and is not so vulnerable to international competition, so a domestically focused strategy makes the best use of their resources.

The OECD (2009) have summarized a large number of recent research studies into the SME internationalization barriers. The following are the areas which are identified:

- Shortage of working capital to finance exports.
- Inadequate knowledge of overseas markets and lack of information to find and analyze markets.
- Inability to contact overseas customers, including finding the right partner, the right representation and suitable distribution channels.
- Lack of managerial time, skills and knowledge, including differences in managers' perceptions and psychological barriers to internationalization.

There is significant risk too because SMEs have little influence over environmental change and recession often leads to many business casualties. SMEs can over-extend themselves financially by growing internationally too quickly. If there is a downturn in demand they may not be able to generate sufficient cash and profits to service their debt and often end up being taken over or going bankrupt.

Illustration 5.3 shows how a global company shares its knowledge of exporting with SMEs in Africa which increases motivation and sustainability.

Non exporters tend to highlight issues such as the perceived bureaucracy associated with international markets and trade barriers, whereas experienced exporters tend to believe that these problems should be addressed through managerial proactivity, for example, by training staff and seeking expert assistance. A number of studies suggest other factors that might be specific in some contexts. In addition studies in Nigeria by Okpara and Kabongo (2010) or by DHL (2014) added other barriers to the above including factors such as poor infrastructure, limited utilities, poor payment systems, corruption and bureaucratic bottlenecks, particularly at customs.

ILLUSTRATION 5.3

Win:Win:Win through DHL knowledge exchange with Botswana SMEs

Over 95 per cent of businesses in Africa are small- and medium-sized enterprises (SMEs), Cull and Beck (2014). Africa is progressing well in terms of its exports from some direct investors from China and from its own SMEs. In fact its exports to countries around the world grew faster than those of some other regions. Unfortunately the exports are mainly dominated by primary commodities, such as oil, iron and gas, which account for the majority of exports from African countries (IMF 2015). However, one country that is gaining positive ground within the African region is Botswana. Botswana has three key exports: diamonds, beef and tourism. And with two recently introduced items on the political agenda, namely Botswana's Economic Diversification Drive and The National Export Strategy (OECD 2014) it will be interesting to see if the country will increase its merchandise exports in the next few years.

One major growth area within the Botswana economy is small- and medium enterprises (SMEs). Botswana's SMEs have a considerable number of employees in many regions across the country, which in turn contributes between 30 to 45 per cent of Botswana's GDP. Yet the SMEs exports are limited due to lack of knowledge, financial resources, unclear distribution channels and few intermediaries. However, DHL Worldwide has stepped in to fill those gaps.

SMEs can discover the export opportunities available to them through DHL, either online, through books or face-to-face with local DHL employees. SMEs are encouraged to contact Mokgethi Magapa, DHL Express Botswana country manager, who will help them understand their potential and go global.

This is a Win:Win:Win situation for SMEs, Botswana and DHL. It is beneficial for SMEs to improve and grow their business; it will also help the SMEs to expand into international markets which in turn will help Botswana's GDP and merchandise exports. And for DHL? Charles Brewer, managing director for DHL Express Sub-Saharan Africa explains the benefits for DHL best by saying: 'In facilitating trade in and out of Botswana with the rest of the world, we intend to contribute meaningfully in making the country more successful and assist in the economic diversification drive, focused on international express delivery.' (Botswana Gazette 2014) .

Questions

1 What steps can small firms take to increase their international export opportunities?

2 How can other countries and SMEs benefit from knowledge exchange?

Sources: Botswana Gazette (2014) SMEs to underpin Africa's growth, www.gazettebw.com/smes-to-underpin-africas-growth-dhl-md/ (accessed 30 March 2015); Botswana Gazette (2014) BancABC helps SMEs realize their full potential, www.gazettebw.com/bancabc-helps-smes-realize-their-full-potential (accessed 30 March 2015); OECD (2014) Economic Outlook Africa 2014, www.oecd-ilibrary.org (accessed 3 April 2014).

Niche marketing   Having identified the motivations and barriers to exporting it is tempting to conclude that many exporters are characterized by being product-oriented – selling abroad the products and services that are successful in the domestic market. Moreover, exporters often seem to throw away their successful domestic marketing strategies in international markets, preferring instead to delegate their marketing to agents and distributors. In doing this they seem to overlook the alternative market entry and marketing mix strategies that are available to them, opting instead for a strategy of least involvement. In many cases this approach may meet the exporting firm's immediate objectives, especially if, for example, they are simply seeking to offload excess production capacity, but it does not provide them with a sound basis for substantially increasing their international market presence.

Table 5.1 The difference between exporting and international niche marketing

Marketing strategy	Exporting selling production capacity	International marketing meeting customer needs
Financial objective	To amortize overheads	To add value
Segmentation	Usually by country and consumer characteristics	By identifying common international customer benefit
Pricing	Cost based	Market or customer based
Management focus	Efficiency in operations	Meeting market requirements
Distribution	Using existing agents or distributor	Managing the supply chain
Market information	Relying on agent or distributor feedback	Analyzing the market situation and customer needs
Customer relationship	Working through intermediaries	Building multiple level relationships

Source: www.unctad.org © UNCTAD, © United Nations 2000–2011.

By contrast, **international niche marketing** occurs where firms become a strong force in a narrow special-ized market of one or two segments across a number of country markets. Having a customer-focused niche strategy, SMEs target specific markets that have a specific need. SMEs of this kind often use networks to gain new target markets and satisfy existing ones and it is the commitment and regular communication that enables customer-focused niche SMEs to specialize internationally (Hagen *et al.* 2012). They also confirm some of the issues that Brown and McDonald (1994) explain when considering the development opportu-nities listed in Table 5.2.

Table 5.2 International niche marketing – development opportunities

To sustain and develop the niche the firm must:
Have good information about the segment needs
Have a clear understanding of the important segmentation criteria
Specialize based on customer-focused needs
Understand the value of the product niche to the targeted segment(s)
Provide high levels of service
Commitment and communication
Carry out small scale innovations
Seek cost efficiency in the supply chain
Maintain a separate focus, perhaps, by being content to remain relatively small
Concentrate on profit rather than market share
Evaluate and apply appropriate market entry and marketing mix strategies to build market share in each country in which they wish to become involved

Sources: Hagen *et al.* 2012; Brown and McDonald 1994.

As outlined in Table 5.2 international niche marketing is ideal for SMEs as segments are often very small or too specialized to attract large competitors. True niche marketing does not include well known brands or companies that are minor players in a mass market offering undifferentiated products. Therefore, for the international niche player to be successful the product or service must be distinctive (highly differentiated), be recognized by consumers and other participants in the international supply chain and have clear positioning. International niche marketing is vastly different from SMEs exporting internationally on a more standardized/undifferentiated approach.

Niche marketing of domestically delivered services

In the travel industry domestic firms such as hotels, tour operators and leisure attractions generate foreign earnings for the country by attracting visitors. International destination marketing of cities such as Prague, the wildlife reserves of Botswana and countries such as Vietnam is increasingly important for economic success in certain areas. It is usually undertaken by relatively small organizations such as tourist boards that represent a huge network of dependent providers of accommodation, catering, leisure activities and experiences. Their role is becoming increasingly important as the economies of the destinations become ever more dependent on tourism, and competition between destinations and the number of potential visitors increase.

With increased international travel and improved access to worldwide communications, a much wider range of services is being offered to visiting customers. Examples include the provision of education, specialized training, medical treatment, sports, cultural and leisure events, and specialist retailing such as luxury goods. For example, around 435 500 students (UK Council for International Student Affairs 2015) from outside the UK come to study at higher education institutions in the UK and many more study at colleges and private language schools. The British Council supports the international marketing efforts of what are largely independent institutions.

Clearly these activities lead to wealth and jobs being generated in the local economy in much the same way as with exporting and niche marketing. The international marketing strategy processes and programmes are similar too, in that the products and services must meet the requirements of, and be promoted to, international customers. Consequently, issues of standardization and adaptation of the marketing mix elements are equally important. The additional challenge is that the benefits obtained from the service provided must be unique and superior and thus outweigh the benefits to the consumer of their locally available services, as well as the cost of travel that the customers will incur in the purchasing and consumption process.

In addition to the services designed to be offered to individuals in both consumer and business-to-business markets, a whole range of additional services which fall into this category of being domestically delivered are concerned with developing solutions for opportunities or problems identified abroad. These might include technology developments, such as research into new drugs, trial and testing facilities, software development and product and packaging design services.

There are many examples of research and development companies, such as Imagination Technologies and ARM in computer microchip design that licence their new technologies to customers around the world.

Importing and reciprocal trading

Importing is clearly the opposite process to international marketing and as such might be seen by governments as 'exporting' jobs and potential wealth. However, the purpose of considering importing here is to highlight the nature of international trade as it is today. Rarely do supply chains for products and services involve solely domestic production and delivery. There has been a substantial increase in outsourcing, not only by large firms but by SMEs too.

Exporting and importing have become inextricably linked so that the challenge is one of adding value to imported components and services, no matter where they are sourced, so that they can then be re-exported in order to meet the international customers' needs effectively and profitably.

Importing activity can also considerably enhance a company's potential to network, leading ultimately, perhaps, to reciprocal trading in which, as a result, the supplier might take other products or services in return from the customer.

Foreign direct investment   It might be concluded from this that raising the level of value-adding supply chain activity in a particular country is the ultimate aim of governments. Most governments take this further by encouraging foreign direct investment (FDI) by multinationals in the belief that as well as aiding the economy through increasing employment and tax revenues, the MNEs' operations will benefit the indigenous SME supply sector by:

- providing additional B2B sales opportunities for the SME suppliers to provide components, subcontracted fabrication work and non-core services as part of the MNE's supply chain; and
- setting and establishing higher international quality standards among the suppliers, which will then enable them to better compete in international markets.

The danger with FDI is that MNEs will only maintain their operations in a particular country while it is financially advantageous. When the MNE finds a lower labour cost country location for its operations it will move on. Many countries have found that low-cost assembly-type manufacturing or call centre operations can be easily relocated with the associated loss of jobs and tax revenues. While the government can take action to encourage continuing high levels of FDI through financial incentives, ensuring a well-educated and flexible workforce, an efficient, responsive and flexible SME supply chain will also be a significant factor in MNE location decisions.

Direct marketing and electronic commerce

Cross border direct marketing and, in particular, electronic commerce continues to grow as customers become more confident in buying goods from abroad. Direct marketing offers the benefits of cutting out other distribution channel members such as importers, agents, distributors, wholesalers and retailers, by using a variety of communications media, including post, telephone, television and the Internet. For SMEs' suppliers these allow borders to be crossed relatively easily with limited investment and risk, and without the SMEs having to face many of the barriers already highlighted in this chapter. Illustration 5.4 shows how a website, www.etsy.com provides a platform for small craftwork businesses to gain access to global customers.

Direct marketing also has a number of disadvantages. Despite the range of media available, communicating can still be problematic as personalization of the communication is essential for direct marketing success. In cross-border direct marketing there is always the danger of cultural insensitivity and language mistakes in the communications. Many of the following comments apply to both traditional direct marketing using physical media and electronic commerce, but we have focused on online trading as it is this method that has had the most impact on SME internationalization.

If customers speak different languages then it may be necessary for online retailers to have multilingual websites. This can add cost in setting up and servicing the website. The continued growth of online retailers may depend on selling to international customers who do not speak the home country language. Moreover, because of the need to manage large numbers of customers it is necessary to use databases which must be up-to-date, accurate and be capable of dealing with foreign languages. Even an incorrectly spelt name can be insulting to the recipient.

The Internet provides smaller firms with a shop window and also the means of obtaining payment, organizing and tracking shipment, and delivery. For some products and services it can provide the means by which market information can be accumulated and new ideas collected, developed and modified by customers and other stakeholders.

Electronic commerce has led firms to redefine their business and it can also be a business in its own right. For example, many electronic commerce services take the form of information transfer and this can become the basis of the product or service itself, for example, specialist advice on personal finance, travel and hobbies.

As well as being a route to market in its own right in the form of direct commerce, the Internet as an interactive marketing information provider has an increasingly important role in each of the above international niche marketing strategies.

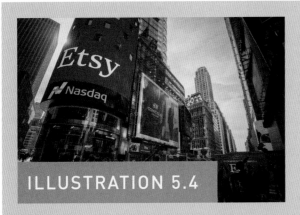

ILLUSTRATION 5.4

Online community selling space for SMEs

Etsy is a global marketplace for SME retailers set up in 2005. Its philosophy was to provide a space for a global community of SME entrepreneurs and enable them to start trading immediately with a buying community. The idea certainly appealed to individual crafts people, especially SMEs that had only one employee! Within a very short time a vast array of handmade items became available from silk paintings to pottery vases, avant-garde furniture to play-gyms for cats. Etsy began as an SME, now, 10 years on, it has grown and employs over 600 people. However, Etsy is still an exciting place for other SMEs to open an online shopfront within minutes. Currently there are over 1 million sellers and nearly 20 million buyers – both of which are growing daily.

One of Etsy's successful businesses is Maya Honey based in Slovakia. Maya Honey supply glass and ceramic beads to be made into jewellery and lamps. They certainly have an international portfolio of consumers as their products are bought by other retailers and individuals around the world. To date they have had over 70 000 sales and stock 2500 items – all on display via their Etsy shopfront. Maya Honey recommends other Etsy sellers should be active on all social media platforms to direct traffic to their Etsy online shopfront. It is also recommended by Maya Honey that customer questions are answered promptly and details of delays or delivery costs be clear – but their most sound advice to engage with customers and be thoughtful of their needs.

Timothy Adam is another Etsy success. Adam has made 1977 sales and has 9200 Etsy admirers. Adam's Etsy online shopfront includes links to his Facebook page (3000 likes) and his Twitter feed (38.3k followers). Clearly he is following Maya Honey's advice by engaging in social media platforms. Adam's passion is bringing 'metal to life' and he has found Etsy a successful way to promote and distribute his product; something he was struggling with in Ohio, US. Consumers from around the world can buy Adam's copper chairs or metal jewellery. His Etsy online shopfront also allows potential customers to read reviews from his other buyers. Therefore, potential customers can check his craftsmanship but also purchase something interesting and unique.

Question

1 What are the advantages and disadvantages for crafters of a niche sales platform like Etsy?

Sources: Etsy.com; Timothy Adam (2015) www.etsy.com/uk/shop/TimothyAdamDesigns; Maya Honey (2015) www.handmadeology.com/the-etsy-success-formula-be-patient-be-active-be-kind/

The Internet offers the benefits to SMEs of real time communications across distances and the levelling of the corporate playing field, leading to more rapid internationalization as well as achieving competitive advantage by:

- creating new opportunities
- erecting barriers to entry
- making cost savings from online communications
- providing online support for inter-firm collaboration, especially in research and development, as an information search and retrieval tool
- the establishment of company websites for marketing and sales promotion; and
- the transmission of any type of data including manuscripts, financial information and computer-aided design/computer-aided manufacture (CAD/CAM) files.

There are some disadvantages, especially the relative ease with which it is possible to become flooded with electronic messages (spam) and orders. While this may be manageable for certain products and services where production volumes can easily be increased or decreased, sales feasts and famines can cause havoc where production capacity is less flexible.

As advanced search engines become more sophisticated it is essential (and expensive) to make sure that the firm's offer is listed on the first page of search results for key words. The implications of this are that instead of marketing being essentially passive in electronic commerce, the marketing input required in designing websites needs to become increasingly sophisticated in promoting the products, providing interactive product design, development and safe payment arrangements. Technical and customer service support, and initial customer segmentation and targeting, are increasingly important to the delivery of an effective, focused business. Thus, while many SMEs see the Internet as a low-cost distribution channel, the greater competition and more sophisticated versions of electronic commerce make it more difficult for SMEs to compete. SMEs frequently face the dilemma of how to cope with powerful competitors. For example, dealing with niche markets used to be problematic for MNEs because of the difficulty of managing millions of small transactions, so SMEs could operate with more freedom in their chosen niche. Now, however, information and communications technology allows MNEs to more cost-effectively manage relatively small volumes and values, making them more competitive in niche markets.

The advent of e-business and the Internet appears, therefore, to offer the benefits to SMEs of being able to ignore borders and make more direct interaction possible between international SMEs and their customers. However, Servais, Madsen and Rasmussen (2007) explain that even 'born global' SMEs use the Internet only to a limited extent to sell their products and as a tool to support existing relationships. Considerable opportunities exist therefore for more creative direct marketing by SMEs.

The nature of international development

The internationalization process differs enormously depending on whether the company first serves the domestic market and later develops into foreign markets (adaptive exporter), or is expressly established from its inception to enter foreign markets (**born global**). Adaptive and born global exporters differ in a variety of ways, including their respective market assessment processes, reasons for international market involvement, managerial attitudes and the propensity to take risks. Successful born globals are seen to overcome their distinctive challenges with flexible managerial attitudes and practices, Solheim (2012).

Many exporting firms, especially in high-technology or industrial markets, internationalize through their **network** of relationships. Firms in any market establish and develop relationships through interactions with other individuals and firms, leading the parties to build mutual trust, respect and knowledge. Kulmeier and Knight (2010) explain that it is the quality of the relationships in four dimensions:

- communication
- co-operation
- trust; and
- commitment

that are critical. Internationalization of the firm, therefore, becomes a consequence of the interaction between the firms in the network they have formed. The network of business relationships comprises a number of different stakeholders – customers, customers' customers, competitors, supplementary suppliers, suppliers, distributors, agents and consultants – as well as regulatory and other public agencies. In any specific country, different networks can be distinguished. Any or all of these relationships may become the conduit for the internationalization of a company. In these cases the internationalization process of a company is more aptly visualized as a series of multilateral cycles rather than a linear process (see Figure 5.1).

Thus, the internationalization process manifests itself by the development of business relationships in other countries:

- Through the establishment of relationships in country networks that are new to the firm, i.e. international extension.

FIGURE 5.1   The multilateral aspects of the internationalization process

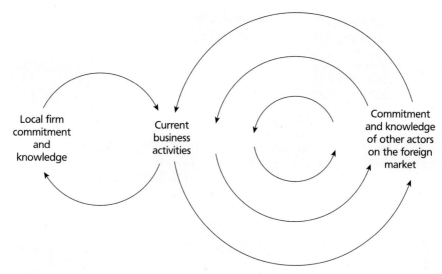

Source: Johannson J. and Vahlne J.E. (1992) 'The Mechanism of Internationalization', *International Marketing Review*, Emerald Insight.

- Through the development of relationships in those networks, i.e. penetration.
- Through connecting networks in different countries, i.e. international integration.

Relationship and network building are especially important in the fast changing, global environment, but particularly in high technology industries. Studies of the internationalization process of small hi-tech firms indicate that some of these companies follow the traditional internationalization patterns, while others behave differently. They go directly to more distant markets and rapidly set up their own subsidiaries. One reason seems to be that the entrepreneurs behind those companies have networks of colleagues dealing with the new technology. Internationalization, in these cases, is an exploitation of the advantage created by networking and may benefit from external facilitation.

Crick and Crick (2014) found that internationalization strategy formation for high performing SMEs is not always planned. In fact, due to the managers networks, closeness to consumers and experiences opportunities are often seen but not expected. Therefore, the nature of SME niche business can often seem unplanned, but it is the very nature of being able to react to consumer needs that makes SMEs for niche products successful.

Balabanis and Katsikea (2003) explain the further dimensions and add that there is some evidence to suggest that an entrepreneurial approach, which involves risk-taking, being proactive and innovative in developing strategies, is useful in international marketing development.

Geographic development of SMEs

For SMEs, country market selection and development of market share within each country are particularly important for growth. Given their limited resources and narrow margin for failure it is vital that their method of country market development is effective. The various patterns of SME international development are shown in Figure 5.2.

The conventional approach is for new companies to test the viability of their products in the domestic market before spreading internationally, but we have already indicated that a number of firms become international players almost immediately after they have been formed, either because they are born global or they operate within a common regional market. The different patterns of international spreading are now discussed.

FIGURE 5.2   Geographic development of SMEs

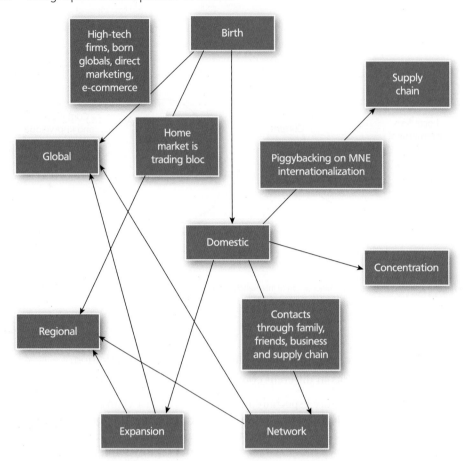

Market expansion and concentration

The conventional view of country selection is that from a sound domestic base SMEs develop either by choosing between expanding into many markets, gaining a superficial presence and accepting a low overall market share, or concentrating their marketing activities in a small number of markets in which they can build a significant market share. The research in this area is inconclusive about the precise reasons why firms adopt one strategy or another.

Katsikeas and Leonidou (1996) found that market concentrators tend, in general, to be smaller firms, because of their greater interest in export profitability and lesser concern with export sales objectives. Typically they make regular visits overseas and this appears to play a key role in their strategy for penetrating the market. Concentrators experience more problems associated with product adaptation to the needs of their customers, but pricing and their marketing organization needs present less of a problem.

Market expanders tend to be larger firms who are more concerned with export sales objectives, do more export marketing research and have greater overall market share expectations. They place less emphasis on profitability, personal visits are less important and they perceive fewer product adaptation-related problems. E-commerce businesses are typical market expanders.

Where the domestic market is redefined

The lowering or removal of barriers between countries and the move, for example, in the EU to the harmonization of standards, the removal of tariff barriers, reduction of non-tariff barriers and the introduction of a common currency within a regional trading bloc mean that SMEs are more likely to be active in more than one country market because the regional market is considered to be their domestic market. This is particularly the case, for example, in mainland Europe where there are no additional costs in travelling to a neighbouring country and, often, a common language may be used.

Where the SME international development is the result of networking

Many SMEs adopt what appears to be a rather unsystematic approach to country market selection. Their patterns of development tend to be the result of a network approach where the selection of the market is not merely made on the relative attractiveness of the markets and their match with the company capability, but rather on the reduction of the risk of entering unknown markets by working with individuals or companies they know. International development through using existing networks of contacts is more typical of Asian firms than SMEs from western countries.

Internationalizing through networking using a small business management model still provides entrepreneurs with the means of achieving security, often because it allows fast adaptation in a rapidly changing world. Through a global network many small units can come up with a variety of solutions at an acceptable level of risk.

Entrepreneur and family networks

Globally there is a need to move away from a managed economic system to a more international entrepreneurial society. The move has already started and as stated above SMEs and entrepreneurs are creating economic growth for developed as well as developing countries. The Global Entrepreneurial Index is also identifying this movement. Currently, for investors in technology, the top five entrepreneurial city hubs in which to do business are in London, Berlin, Eindhoven, Budapest and areas within Lithuania (Coleman 2015). The top three countries which have the biggest gains are United Arab Emirates, Latvia and Lithuania. Developing countries still have a long way to go, but their drive for entrepreneurship is now taking shape.

Another network that needs to be included here is entrepreneurial family networks. Nueno (2000) explains that the Chinese can be effective entrepreneurs. While 1 per cent of the population of the Philippines is ethnic Chinese, they control 40 per cent of the economy; half the economies of Indonesia and Thailand are controlled by 4 per cent and 10 per cent ethnic Chinese respectively, and in Malaysia two-thirds of the economy is controlled by ethnic Chinese.

They operate effectively within a family network and, because the Chinese are spread throughout the world, they can lay the foundations for stronger links among businesses across borders as a network of entrepreneurial relationships. As we indicated earlier, in practice most SMEs operate within a network of personal contacts, but this is much more formalized in some cultures, such as the Chinese, because it is based on *guanxi* and the obligation to return favours. The Confucian tradition of hard work, thrift and respect for one's social network provides continuity, and the small network-based enterprises bound by strong cultural links are well suited to fast-changing markets. Illustration 5.5 explains the impact of family groups on international trade and gives an example of the effect of family feuds.

Networking and relationship marketing are now emphasized as key components of most SME internationalization strategies.

Where the SME is born global

Some SMEs market their products and services globally from birth or soon after because the customer segment or competition is global (especially in high technology, breakthrough products) or because the distribution method is global, for example, direct marketing and telecommunications-based international marketing (e.g. Internet). A survey for the Global Entrepreneurship Monitor (2014) found that many of the developed countries (US, UK, Spain, Germany, Norway, Latvia) are innovation-driven economies, confirming the finding of the Global Entrepreneurial Index. Countries such as Botswana, Bolivia and the Philippines are factor-driven economies, showing that these countries are identified as being 'early stage entrepreneurs',

ILLUSTRATION 5.5

Family networking

Success in Asia still runs on power, prestige, influence, favours given and received, family fortune and connections. Without these even the simplest deal can come unstuck for no obvious reasons. For example, the Chinese, Japanese, Koreans and Indians have their own special connections and their business styles come down to trust and credibility – who vouches for whom.

There are six big economic groups in Asia that are growing fast as a result of networking. These are:

- Japanese *keiretsu* company connections.

- Koreans with *chaebol* conglomerates.

- Mainland Chinese with party and military links.

- Ethnic or overseas Chinese with their stored wealth, extended family, dialect and guild connections.

- The emerging *pribumi* and *bumiputera* (indigenous) business leaders of Indonesia.

- Malaysia with their political connections; the Indians with their family dynasties.

It is networking on a grand scale that provides the basis of the international operations as there are an estimated 57 million Chinese and 18 million Indians that are living abroad. A Singaporean Chinese trader may have family connections in Taiwan, Hong Kong, Guandong, Fujian or Vietnam that can provide legal, banking and support services when moving across borders.

A small group of families also control the Indian economy and are successfully developing their global businesses. However, it is internal family disagreements that are their major concern. For example, the giant conglomerate, Reliance Industries was built as a rags-to-riches story over decades by Dhirubhai Ambani. After he died his sons, Anil and Mukesh fell out over the direction of the company. By 2005 they could no longer work together and their mother brokered a demerger into two groups. But the feud continued with Mukesh blocking Anil's telecom group's efforts to merge with South Africa's MTN. A dispute followed regarding gas prices and ended in court. Anil won and Mukesh appealed the ruling, but the oil ministry stepped in when it realized how damaging it was for the government when two wealthy men were seen to be fighting over the resources that should belong to the country.

The traditional power of the mainland Chinese dynasties was disrupted during the communist era and new dynasties will be created.

In the West many of the old, great family business dynasties have declined in importance and given way to the new entrepreneurs who have exploited new technologies, such as Rupert Murdoch of News International, which includes Sky. Perhaps such organizations are creating new family dynasties.

Question

1 To what extent do you expect the old family groups to be the future successes and to what extent do you expect the new groups that have created their wealth through new technologies to succeed them?

---

therefore, they have not yet fully embraced an international orientation. See Illustration 5.5 above. Further, these countries have low export sales and limited experience of selling online to international consumers; as a consequence this also identifies them as being in the early stages of entrepreneurialism. Few US entrepreneurs, for example, have high international orientation of over 25 per cent of their customers, whereas three-quarters have a small percentage of international customers. Interestingly, Eastern European countries tend to have high international orientation.

A number of studies of born global firms have been made in different country contexts. Mort and Weerawardena (2006) explain that the new concept of international entrepreneurship has followed research into born global firms and highlighted the importance of relationships and networking in enabling the identification and exploitation of market opportunities and facilitating the development of knowledge-intensive products. Harris and Wheeler (2005) focus on the role of the entrepreneur's interpersonal relationships in the internationalization process and explain that strong, deep relationships are developed in wide social/personal and business situations that do not just provide information and access to networks but, more importantly, can be influential in directing strategy and can lead to the transformation of the firm.

Kalinic and Forza (2012) examine the differences between born global firms/international new ventures (INVs) SMEs and those SMEs that *gradually* develop into international markets; they conclude that they do exhibit different characteristics. Born globals/INVs have a managerial vision from the start of their business, whereas SMEs that gradually move to international markets do so when they have a significant, well developed, home base. Further born global/INV businesses have a clear niche-focus, are highly innovative and proactive in their strategic international development from inception. This is a more dynamic approach than the SMEs that react to opportunities internationally as time goes on and are less innovative because of that. Management views the world as its marketplace from the outset whereas INVs' management see foreign markets as adjuncts to the domestic market and hence typically focus on regional markets. The majority of born globals are formed by active entrepreneurs and tend to emerge as a result of a significant breakthrough in some process or technology. They may apply cutting-edge technology to developing a unique product idea or to a new way of doing business. The products and services that born globals sell directly involve substantial value added and the majority of such products may be intended for industrial use. They do not compete on price.

Several trends have given rise to the emergence of born global firms:

- The increasing role of niche markets, especially in the developed world. As markets mature, products increasingly become commodities, and SMEs respond by identifying sub segments of customers that require a more specialized or customized product or service.

- To compete with large, powerful MNEs smaller firms must specialize. However, while the demand from a domestic niche market may be very small, the global demand can sustain an SME that is prepared to supply the niche on a worldwide basis.

- Recent advances in process technology mean low-scale batch production can be economical and new technologies mean that SMEs can compete with large firms to produce sophisticated products.

- Communications technologies allow SMEs to manage across borders and information is more readily accessible to everyone. It is now much less expensive to go international than it was just 20 years ago.

- Quicker response time, flexibility and adaptability to foreign tastes and specific customer requirements give these firms an immediate competitive edge.

- SMEs can gain access to funding and support, benefit from joint research programmes and technology transfer and employ cross-border educated managers more easily than ever before.

- Increasingly, international business is facilitated through partnership with foreign businesses – distributors, trading companies, subcontractors and alliances – allowing new specialist firms to participate in global networks more easily than before.

Supply chain internationalization

The pattern of **internationalization** of firms that are part of the **supply chain** of an MNE is usually determined by the international strategy adopted by the MNE. In a continual effort to achieve focus and operational efficiency, firms constantly think about what are their core competences and answer the question 'what business are we in?'. The response to this question leads MNEs to identify those components and services that were part of the overall product offer but which they regarded as being peripheral to their business. As a result of this, many decide to outsource more of their supplies, either from MNE specialist component makers and service providers, or from SMEs that have exploited these new opportunities to grow.

The reasons for MNEs to **outsource** can be summarized as follows:

- It reduces the capital requirements of the business (the supplier rather than the MNE invests in new processes and facilities).
- It overcomes the difficulty of developing quickly and maintaining in-house knowledge in many different specialist knowledge areas.
- It improves flexibility, as some firms are better equipped and can carry out small production runs, special designs and development tasks more quickly.
- The MNE can take risks in more peripheral activities where their expertise is weak, stopping the firm from falling behind in the effectiveness of its non-core operations.
- The economies of scale of suppliers may make components much cheaper through outsourcing rather than from in-house supplies.
- The expertise of business support service providers, for example in transport and delivery systems, cannot be matched.
- Downsizing without outsourcing can lead to management resources becoming too stretched and unfocused.

The disadvantages of outsourcing are:

- *Loss of know-how* – Western businesses in many sectors have outsourced manufacturing to Asian firms who have subsequently opened up as competitors.
- *The costs of managing the outsourced supplies* – Managing outsourced components and services does require time and technical expertise and, particularly in the case of IT, there have been some difficulties of integrating the service with the firm's primary strategic objectives.

Both large and smaller firms have been the beneficiaries of this increased outsourcing but for smaller firms there are particular challenges. These include:

- The need to become closely linked with one or two major customers, upon which the SME is almost entirely dependent for survival and success.
- Internationalization is driven by the demands of the MNE. Failure to follow their product or market development demands may result in the loss of all the business as the MNE will seek alternative suppliers.
- They are under continual pressure to make operational efficiencies and design improvements in order to offer even better value for money.
- Concentration on developing the relationship with the MNE may lead to the firm becoming relatively weaker in external marketing, putting the firm at a disadvantage if it needs to find new customers when difficulties occur. Management Challenge 5.2 suggests another way of rethinking which country would be best when outsourcing the production side of the business.

The advantages for SMEs are:

- The opportunities to learn from working with the MNE. This is likely to improve the smaller firms' strategic and operational management systems, communications and purchasing efficiency.
- They get greater business security through reliable and predictable ordering while the customer is successful.
- The opportunity to focus on production and technical issues rather than being diverted by the need to analyze changes to the market, customer and competition to the same degree.

Developing relationships

The key to success in working within the supply chain of an MNE is developing an effective relationship which can build upon the advantages and minimize the disadvantages of cooperative working between

MANAGEMENT CHALLENGE 5.2

Outsourcing production: Points to consider

Costs matters, particularly to MNEs and SMEs when they wish to expand the production side of their business. This is especially important if the business strategy is also to reduce production costs. With this strategy in mind many businesses consider moving production to a new international host country where costs may be lower than those in their home country.

In the past, China has been seen as an excellent choice for businesses. Indeed, the low wages of China's factory workers has helped many businesses reduce their production costs. However, recent activities may not make China as attractive as it used to be. For example, Chinese factory workers have seen a fourfold increase in their wages over the last 10 years. Additionally, China's recent Yuan appreciation and fluctuations have left businesses thinking carefully about choosing China.

Mexico could be high on the list of possibilities as it already has a strong manufacturing reputation. The workforce has received only a twofold wage increase, as opposed to the much higher wage increase in China. Additionally, Mexico has seen a decrease in energy prices. Eastern Europe is also attractive as they have a very good production reputation. Workers in Eastern Europe have recently been striking for better pay and received it. Some Eastern European countries, such as Poland, have a strong currency and stable exchange rates due to its flourishing economy. This does enable Polish factories to demand and expect to receive higher prices for their outputs than they have in the past.

Two other attractive countries in terms of low wages are Brazil and Russia which makes them attractive to SMEs and MNEs. However, the reputation both countries have in terms of corruption and politics may tarnish the cost benefit opportunity low wages offer.

Questions

1 What are the main factors that SMEs and MNEs should consider when outsourcing the manufacturing side of the business to a new host country?

2 What research do you suggest the marketing manager completes before recommending a country to complete the production and manufacturing side of the business?

Source: *The Economist* (2014) When cheap is not so cheap, www.economist.com (accessed 31 November 2014).

firms which may have some business objectives in common, but also may have a number of differences. As more SMEs become involved in international supply chains, the ways in which relationships between smaller suppliers and the MNE differ between western and Asian styles of management become particularly significant.

The western way of arranging sourcing is a competition-based approach and has the advantage of a much sharper focus on cost reduction, profit and individual creativity. The Asian approach is more cooperative-based and includes ensuring that more than one strong supplier is available, expertise is shared and built upon, and the competitive focus is always on the much larger market opportunity.

Over the past few years the number of cooperative arrangements between western and Asian styles within one supply chain has increased and, as a result, arrangements which could be described as a combination of the two have been developed in which longer-term contracts have been agreed in order to maximize the cooperation between the MNE and supplier, but without the insistence on sharing information with the losing contractor, which was often a feature of the Asian approach.

International strategic marketing management in SMEs

Having considered the various categories of SME internationalization and the nature of SME international development, we now turn to the factors which influence the international marketing management of SMEs. The McKinsey 7S framework, shown in Figure 5.3, is useful for discussing the elements.

FIGURE 5.3   McKinsey 7S framework

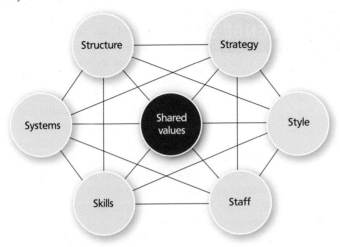

Source: McKinsey 7S framework, Thomas J. Peters and Robert H. Waterman (1982) *In Search of Excellence*, Warner.

The McKinsey 7S framework

The first three elements – strategy, structure and systems – are considered to be the hardware of successful management and as such can be implemented across international markets without the need for significant adaptation. The other four – management style, staff, skills and shared values – are the software, and are affected by cultural differences. Often it is the management of these aspects of the business that highlights good management in the best firms and relatively unimpressive management in poorer performing firms. It is quite obvious too that it is these elements of the framework which can vary considerably from country to country and provide the most significant challenges for SMEs developing from their home base into an organization with involvement in a number of different countries.

The characteristics of these four software elements are:

1 *Style*: In organizations such as McDonald's, it is the consistency across the world of the management and their operational style that is one of the distinguishing features of the companies. For SMEs the management and operational style frequently reflects the personality, standards and values of the owner, and is often maintained as the firm matures, as is the case with Richard Branson of Virgin and Steve Jobs of Apple.

2 *Skills*: The sorts of skills that are needed to carry out the strategy vary considerably between countries and also over time as the firm grows rapidly and new strategies and systems are introduced. As the levels and quality of education of staff may vary considerably too, an effective human resource development strategy can be important to identify and build the necessary skills.

3 *Staff*: The people that are recruited around the world need to be capable, well trained, and given the jobs that will best allow them to make use of their talents. Recognition of the contributions of the staff, the criteria for advancement, acceptance of appraisal and disciplinary processes vary considerably between countries.

4 *Shared values*: Despite the fact that staff come from different cultural backgrounds there is a need for employees to understand what the organization stands for, where it is going and to share the same organizational values.

The first part of the next section on international strategic management focuses broadly upon the 'hardware' and the second part on the 'software' of the McKinsey 7S framework.

The generic marketing strategies for SME internationalization

While there are an infinite number of individual implementation strategies that an SME might adopt, the generic marketing strategies provide a useful starting point.

Segmentation, targeting and positioning

The principal approach to marketing strategy development follows three stages, normally referred to as segmentation, targeting and positioning (STP marketing):

1 Identification of the various segments that exist within the sector, using the various segmentation methods which we discussed in Chapter 4. It is important for the SME to define cross-border segments with clearly identifiable requirements that it is able to serve.

2 The firm must then target the segments which appear to be most attractive in terms of their size, growth potential, the ease with which they can be reached and their likely purchasing power.

3 In seeking to defend and develop its business the firm needs to position its products or services in a way that will distinguish them from those of its local and international competitors and build up barriers which will prevent those competitors taking its business.

Competitive strategies

In order to create the competitive advantage necessary to achieve growth, Porter (1990) suggests that firms should adopt one of the following three generic competitive strategies. However, each poses particular challenges for SMEs in international markets:

1 *Cost leadership* requires the firm to establish a lower cost base than its local or international competitors. This strategy has typically been adopted by companies that are located in countries that are component or service providers and have lower labour costs. As a result of their limited financial resources, however, SMEs that adopt a low-cost strategy spend little on marketing activity and are vulnerable to either local firms or larger multinationals temporarily cutting prices to force the firm out of the market. Alternatively, changes in currency exchange rates or other instability in the economic climate can result in newer, lower priced competitors emerging.

2 *Focus*, in which the firm concentrates on one or more narrow segments and thus builds up a specialist knowledge of each segment. Such segments in the international marketplace are transnational in nature and companies work to dominate one particular segment across a number of country markets. Typically this strategy necessitates the SME providing high levels of customer and technical service support, which can be resource intensive. Moreover, unless the SME has created a highly specialized niche, it may be difficult to defend against local and international competition.

3 *Differentiation* is achieved through emphasizing particular benefits in the product, service or marketing mix, which customers think are important and a significant improvement over competitive offers. Differentiation typically requires systematic incremental innovation to continually add customer value. While SMEs are capable of the flexibility, adaptability and responsiveness to customer needs necessary with this strategy, the cost of maintaining high levels of differentiation over competitors in a number of international markets can be demanding of management time and financial resources.

Many SMEs base their international strategy on the generic strategy which has given them competitive advantage in domestic markets and then attempt to apply this same successful strategy in international markets. American and Chinese firms benefit from having a huge domestic market. By contrast, SMEs from emerging markets and from countries with smaller domestic markets often have to export merely to find enough customers to enable them to survive.

Growth strategies

Typically SMEs have limited resources and so need to make difficult decisions about how to use these resources to grow the business. As long ago as 1957 Ansoff identified four growth strategies – product penetration, market development, product development and diversification – that still guide marketers today; growth strategies are shown in Figure 5.4. Following a product penetration strategy

FIGURE 5.4   Ansoff growth matrix

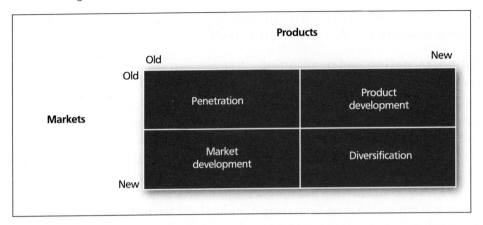

is appropriate if a company has an existing portfolio of products and a presence in its target markets, which offer considerable potential expansion of sales. The resources available to the company under these circumstances can be best used in concentrating on doing more of what is already being done well.

Diversification, on the other hand, is a strategy used in international markets in situations where demand for the company's existing products is falling rapidly (for example, in recent years in the defence industry), where resources are available but would not generate an acceptable return if used on existing activities. Also, in the case of firms run by entrepreneurs, the owner can often become bored with the firm's current activities and seeks out new challenges by developing a new product for a new market.

For most companies the most obvious strategic development opportunities are in increasing geographical coverage (market development) – which is discussed in Chapter 7 – and product development – which is discussed in Chapter 8 – perhaps by further differentiating a current product or applying their current technology to a new application. However, these options compete for resources and firms have to choose which approach will generate a greater return on investment.

The factors which affect the choice of an SME's international marketing strategy

Figure 5.5 indicates a number of the factors which influence the choice and development of an SME's international strategy. Particular issues include environmental trends, the market and industry structure, the customer requirements from different countries, the nature and intensity of local and international competition, and the degree to which the SME can defend its niche. In SMEs, however, specific company factors are particularly important in the decision. These include the resources available, the products and services that have been developed and the firm's attitudes to international development and management of risk. These will result in the firm adopting a specific approach to individual country selection as the strategy develops.

Market factors

The most significant factor inherent in SMEs is their relatively small size and lack of power in most international markets in which they wish to be active. This puts them at a disadvantage with local competitors and MNEs, as they often lack the management resources to spend on researching new markets, the contacts necessary to quickly develop effective distribution of their products and sufficient financial resources to enable them to compete with the promotional spend of their competitors and thus be strong enough to withstand a 'price war'.

FIGURE 5.5 Factors affecting SME internationalization

At the same time smaller size means that SMEs can offer customers the benefits of a more personal service from the firm's owners or senior managers, faster decision making and, usually, a greater willingness to listen. Of course, the SME must work out how to profit from international market developments by building on these potential strengths.

The SMEs' challenge is to communicate some unique selling propositions to their customers and create other competitive advantage dimensions, thus building barriers to entry around the niche that they have identified in order to stop attacks by competitors. There are a number of ways that this can be done.

First, underpinning any product/service offer must be a significant improvement in customer added value – there is little point in SMEs trying to market 'me-too' products internationally.

Second, if the product is a technical or design breakthrough it should be protected wherever possible by patent or copyright. It is worth saying, however, that if the patent is challenged, the costs of fighting a court case, particularly in a foreign country, can be prohibitive for an SME with limited resources.

Third, the firm must exploit any creative way of shortcutting the route to market, for example by convincing experts or influential participants in the supply chain of the value of the product offer so they might recommend it, or by gaining exposure for the product at important events or in highly visible places. Some SMEs are using e-commerce to achieve some of these objectives: as a direct route to their international customers, to improve their efficiency in an international supply chain and to achieve greater effectiveness through collaboration with other SMEs.

Fourth, instead of using the traditional exporting routes to market such as agents and distributors, alternative methods of market entry, for example using licensing, franchising or joint ventures, can increase the diffusion of the product or service into the market more cost-effectively. Finally, more SMEs are now cooperating with other firms – a customer, competitor or a firm engaged in a complementary activity.

Company factors

Only a minute proportion of the world's SMEs can be characterized as fast growth organizations and become the multinational enterprises of the future. The sole objective of many businesses, such as the corner shop, the market trader and the car mechanic is to look for sufficient business from the domestic market to survive.

The smaller size and entrepreneurial approach of SMEs offers the advantages of flexibility and adaptability to new demands placed on them, speed of response to new opportunities and, usually, very focused management. However, SMEs lack adequate planning skills and are often unwilling or unable to devote sufficient time and finances to the research and development of new business opportunities and this can result in wasted effort and some expensive failures.

Frequently SMEs have insufficient knowledge of the culture, market structure and business practices of new markets. The response of SMEs to international marketing is affected by their perceptions of this risk. At one extreme the SME will be deterred from becoming involved at all. At the other extreme the risk-taking SME will experiment with international marketing, perhaps with very little preparation, believing that the firm will be able to respond quickly enough to deal with any difficulties that emerge. More cautious SMEs will attempt to assess and manage the risks involved by evaluating the market opportunity and planning their use of management operations and financial resources to enable a cost effective internationalization approach to be developed.

Underlying the diversity in the range of a firm's attitudes to risk are the owners' ambition for the firm and how this fits with the firm's capabilities. To be successful the firm needs a vision of its international future which can be delivered using capabilities and resources that already exist, but also include those that can be acquired over a realistic timescale. It is often the case that successful SMEs are those that are able to clearly recognize the threats and opportunities in each marketplace, correct their weaknesses and build upon their strengths. SMEs that are unsuccessful in internationalizing are those that do not understand how their market is changing and what new resources and skills are needed, or are unwilling or unable to acquire them.

It is worth saying that many SMEs are so dominated by their owner that they become almost the personification of the owner, whose opinions, knowledge and attitudes determine the strategies adopted and decisions made. Usually decision making is well thought-through with the owner being aware, understanding and managing the risks of working in an unfamiliar market, but sometimes owners lacking international expertise make decisions that can be irrational and even foolhardy.

Country selection

High levels of existing competition in developed countries make market entry challenging for SMEs. At the same time the new high growth emerging markets offer opportunities for SMEs to develop their specialized niche products and services.

Increasing amounts of investment are now focused on the new emerging markets. The most adventurous SMEs recognize the need to be an early market entrant: thus, for some, the most promising markets for their specialized products and services are in Africa and South America but, at the same time, they are also the most risky.

Cui *et al.* (2014) suggest SMEs that choose to develop and grow internationally select countries based on whether they are using an *exploitation* strategy or an *exploration* strategy. Essentially SMEs that choose the exploitation strategy choose new host countries that are similar to their home country in terms of the legal framework and the way organizations do business with one another. Additionally, SMEs will choose host countries where the general culture and behaviours of citizens are similar to those of their home country. Overall, there is familiarity between the home country and the new host country. This strategy gives the SMEs the opportunity to exploit and draw upon their existing success, extend the product life cycle of

FIGURE 5.6   SME – international country selection strategy

their products and benefit from economies of scale. If all these elements are equal the marketing mix can remain standardized between the home country and the host country. However, if there is a great deal of unfamiliarity in an SME's home country and the new host country it has chosen to develop and grow, then the SME will have used the exploration strategy. Unfamiliarity between home and new host countries will mean there are different political issues, economic development structures may not be congruent, the way to conduct business and formalize agreements will have unfamiliar processes and timeframes, and so on. Nevertheless, many SMEs choose the exploration route if they wish to research, evolve and develop their products and services with new consumer markets. During the research and development stage in the new host country it is likely that through gaining knowledge of the host country's needs and wants, products and services will need to be adapted to accommodate for different needs and wants. One of the benefits of choosing the exploration strategy is that it gives opportunities to gain competitive advantage due to the adapting current practice to the demands/requests of a new target market.

Figure 5.6 shows the differences between the two strategies and likens them to Ansoff's growth matrix (see Figure 5.4).

As shown in the table in Figure 5.6 there are two strategies that SMEs could take when considering which country to enter into as part of their growth plans. Figure 5.7 shows the different international country selection strategy visually, considering an SME from the UK.

Systems and support networks   Typically, SMEs tend not to have sophisticated systems and support networks for managing their international operations as is the case for large firms. Of course, advances in technology and the lower cost of IT systems, discussed in Chapter 12, are enabling SMEs to develop more advanced systems than they have had in the past. However, SMEs tend to rely on more informal, 'soft' systems and support networks that are based on personal contacts with family, friends, other business managers and officials for support, advice, information and knowledge.

FIGURE 5.7   Exploration and exploitation strategy

⟶ Shows exploitation strategy
- - - - ➤ Shows exploration strategy

Organization structure

As an SME increases its involvement in international markets, so it needs to set up an **organization structure** that will enable the leadership and management to support, direct and control its often widespread and growing organization effectively.

Sarathy *et al.* (2006) have identified some of the variables which might influence the decision:

- size of the business
- number of markets in which it operates
- level and nature of involvement in the markets
- company objectives
- company international experience
- nature of the products
- width and diversity of the product range; and
- nature of the marketing task.

For a firm starting out in export markets, the decision is relatively simple. Either its international business is integrated within the domestic business or separated as a specialist activity. Setting up a separate export department allows greater independence to look specifically at international marketing opportunities.

However, this could indicate a less or more important activity and could, as a result, create conflicts between domestic and international market demands and ineffective use of company resources. As the company develops further, it is faced with deciding how its international operations should be organized, for example by area, by product and by function. Figure 5.8 and Figure 5.9 show typical organizational structures along geographic and product lines. Organization by function is only really appropriate for smaller companies with relatively simple product ranges.

As the firm grows it may decide to establish control in different ways – for example, it may wish to control branding and corporate identity issues centrally through the use of international product managers. At the same time it might wish to control the profitability of the business by having a senior executive in each individual country. In this way, the firm operates as a matrix structure within which individual managers might be responsible to different senior managers for different activities.

Skills, capability and the stages of internationalization   Having discussed the alternative categories of international marketing and the strategies which SMEs adopt, we now turn to the process of

FIGURE 5.8 Product structure

SME internationalization and the factors which lead to success and failure. In looking at a cross-section of firms it is possible to find some firms with different mindsets regarding international trade. These include those that are taking the major step from being a solely domestic company to generating their first revenue from foreign country sales, others that are moving from the early stages of internationalization to a point where international marketing is totally integrated as part of the firm's activities, and a limited number of firms which are still small but have become confident world-class marketing companies.

The first step Firms typically approach involvement in international marketing rather cautiously, as the first step towards what may appear to them to be a rather unpredictable future. For small- and medium-sized

FIGURE 5.9 Geographic structure

firms in particular, exporting remains the more promising alternative to a full-blooded international marketing effort, since it appears to offer a degree of control over risk, cost and resource commitment.

The further internationalization of the firm is the process in which the enterprise gradually increases its international involvement. This evolves in an interplay between the development of knowledge about foreign markets and operations on one hand and an increasing commitment of resources to foreign markets on the other. Market knowledge and market commitment are assumed to affect decisions regarding the commitment of resources to foreign markets and the way current activities are performed. Market knowledge and market commitment are, in turn, affected by current activities and operational decisions.

Thus, firms start internationalization by going to those markets that they can most easily understand. There they will see opportunities, perceive low market uncertainty and gain experience – as they go through the internationalization process they will enter new more challenging markets where there is greater psychic distance. Psychic distance is defined in terms of factors such as differences in language, culture, political systems, etc., which disturb the flow of information between the firm and the market. This means that as the companies' market knowledge grows so does their commitment, which in turn affects the type of strategy they use.

More advanced stages of internationalization   As companies increase their international involvement so improvements occur in the organization, management and attitudes of those companies. Longer-term resources are committed and international business becomes part of the strategy rather than a tactical opportunity. Greater involvement in export marketing leads to better training and development, higher research and development expenditures, improvements in quality control, lower perceptions of risk and reduced costs of doing business, all of which leads to increased performance.

Figure 5.10 provides a staged approach to conceptualizing the internationalization process based on a composite of various writers' ideas. Firms can be characterized as being at one of the stages shown.

For many firms the internationalization process of companies is not a gradual incremental process but a series of step changes. There may be a number of factors which might initiate a step change, for example, an unexpected product or market success, the recruitment of a new chief executive, serious failure leading to a reassessment of the business, loss of markets, the changing expectations of stakeholders, owners impatient for a more substantial return on their investment or business or family connections keen to share in the SME's success.

Grimes, Doole and Kitchen (2007) developed profiles of the internationalizing firms and it is possible to use this to characterize firms at each stage of internationalization.

The passive exporter   The passive exporter tends to lack any international focus, and perceives export markets as having a high hassle factor. Many passive exporters are relatively new to the export business, often reacting to unsolicited orders, and tend to see their market as essentially home based.

FIGURE 5.10   Levels of internationalization

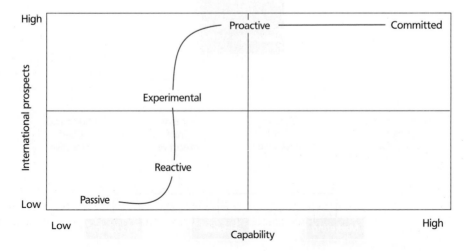

Such firms do not carry out research or invest in export promotion campaigns and have little direct contact with foreign companies. Firms at this stage perceive little real need to export and have no plans to do so in the future.

The reactive exporter The reactive exporter sees export markets as secondary to the domestic markets but will put effort into dealing with key export accounts. Although they do not invest heavily in attracting export orders, once they have done business with a foreign customer they will follow up for repeat orders.

Such firms may have started to promote their export capacity and be starting to visit overseas clients. However, they have only a basic knowledge of their markets and are still undecided about their future role as an exporter.

The experimental exporter The experimental exporter is beginning to develop a commitment to exporting and starting to structure the organization around international activities. They are in regular contact with key accounts and are beginning to develop alliances with export partners to build better products and services by using information from their successful markets.

Although they would prefer not to, such firms are prepared to make product adaptations to suit overseas customer needs and may have appointed dedicated export staff to look after this part of the business.

The proactive exporter The proactive exporter is focused on key export markets, and devotes substantial amounts of time and resources to entering and developing new markets. Regular market assessment in the form of desk research and using partners' information is carried out, and promotional materials are produced in a number of foreign languages.

Senior management regularly visit key accounts to maintain healthy relationships with clients and exporting may account for up to 50 per cent of turnover. Exporting opportunities are welcomed and seen as crucial to the business.

The well-established exporter The committed exporter knows that exporting is integral to the business and sees the domestic market as just another market. The majority of the turnover is generated through international trade and significant amounts of time are spent on this activity, with senior and middle managers frequently visiting customers.

Investment in training is substantial as skills are needed in-house and thinking on export markets is both short-term tactical and longer-term strategic, with regular reviews of the overall mission and plan of action. Networks abroad provide excellent information and quality assured partners deliver on time, every time.

The firm's movement from one stage to the next, for example from reactive to experimental, experimental to proactive and proactive to world class, therefore, is not gradual. Each of these step changes requires a coordinated strategy to improve the performance of the firm. Doole, Grimes and Demack (2006) explored the management practices and processes most closely associated with high levels of export capability: from this ten benchmarks of international marketing practice are identified (Figure 5.11) which indicate the most critical areas of the firms' management skills. Closer examination of the nature of these benchmarks reinforces the idea that successful international marketing is a predictor of fast growth. Further analysis suggests three key areas that SME international marketers need to focus on to ensure success:

1 Developing the characteristics of a learning organization.
2 Developing effective relationships.
3 Having a clear international competitive focus.

Learning organization A culture of innovation and learning throughout the firm is a common feature of successful firms that compete internationally. There is clear commitment from the top with senior management intent on building knowledge assets, and time and resources are invested in learning at all levels.

FIGURE 5.11   Characteristics of successful international business-to-business marketers

Successful international business-to-business marketers:
1 Have a clear competitive focus in international marketplaces and a specific directional policy as to where the top management intend taking the firm.
2 Have high levels of repeat business and operate tight financial controls in export markets.
3 Have the tenacity and the resilience to face challenges and drive through change.
4 Have a perception that risk indicates a problem to be solved, not an insurmountable barrier.
5 View themselves as international niche marketers, not necessarily as good exporters.
6 Fully invest in ensuring they have thorough knowledge of the international markets in which they operate.
7 Are able to exploit distinctive product advantages in international markets.
8 Are strongly committed to supplying quality products and services to all their customers wherever they are in the world.
9 Build close relationships throughout the supply chain and invest in maintaining regular communications with their overseas partners.
10 Have a well-defined communications strategy and invest in good quality promotional materials.

Source: Isobel Doole's PhD thesis (2000).

Investment in skills development enables the firms to be flexible in overcoming barriers and to be persistent in the face of difficulties. High levels of emotional energy are invested in the firm and staff are innovative and willing to learn. A shared vision and a sharing of experiences among internal partners are also key elements of the successful organizations' commitment to learning. Tight financial measurement and performance are seen as crucial.

Effective relationships   Firms who compete successfully in international markets build close relationships, not only with customers but with others throughout the supply chain. Effective relationships are crucial and sometimes the focus of successful organizations. Competitive advantage may not be the product itself, but the added value given to the product and the ability to exploit opportunities by the close, meaningful and regular communication with customers, increasingly through e-commerce.

A commitment to quality procedures, a quality mission and the use of quality-assured intermediaries are seen as vital. Service reliability is key to the firm's relationships and underpins its contribution to the supply chain.

Clear competitive focus   Firms establish a clear and truly international focus, demonstrating a strong competitive position in a precisely identified market. Many successful firms adopt niche marketing strategies based on a clear mission statement and a planned development strategy.

Other features usually include clearly differentiated products, strong brand positioning and high levels of flexibility in adapting products to suit particular markets.

A thorough knowledge of markets is built up through innovative and informal means of collecting information and through focused research capability, concentrating resources where they are of most use. Most successful companies have primary markets which account for at least 30 per cent of their export turnover.

International entrepreneurship and fast growth

There are a small number of firms which achieve hypergrowth through commercially exploiting a revolutionary idea, innovative business method or adopting a marketing strategy which simply leaves all the competitors behind. While some of these firms succeed as a result of a new technical or scientific invention, more important is the entrepreneurial flair needed to exploit the idea commercially. Some of the greatest successes are, therefore, associated with individual entrepreneurs who have the vision, determination, ability and ambition to succeed.

MANAGEMENT CHALLENGE 5.3

PayPal: Is it trying to tell Malaysian SMEs something?

PayPal is the most well known and well used online payment platform. Consumers use PayPal for many online purchases including items from ebay.com, bookings from Hotels.com, Jet2.com and Trainline.com. Consumers can even load up their Starbucks card on the move using PayPal.

PayPal is a fantastic payment device for SMEs, particularly those that do business internationally. Alex Cheong, founder of web2ship.com is a business-to-business merchant from Malaysia who states he is very happy with PayPal. Like many merchants fraud and security of monetary transactions are high on the list when trading internationally. PayPal's secure mechanisms make Alex and his consumers feel safe. But using PayPal is not just a payment tool, it is a research tool. The recent Cross Border Insights report from PayPal showed that online exports year-on-year (YoY) have increased dramatically.

Take, for example, Malaysian overland exports to Singapore and China. Exports have increased to Singapore by 5.1 per cent YoY and China by 9.2 per cent YoY. Contrast those figures with online exports and a different picture emerges: Singapore online exports 38 per cent YoY and China 58 per cent YoY. It is clear online export sales are growing at a much faster rate than overland export sales. This is good news for SMEs who are considering international growth and for existing businesses who should cement relations with their current stock of consumers. The boom is also steered by the government of Malaysia's initiatives which support local businesses. That mixed with consumer confidence in shopping directly from merchants internationally adds to the boom. With 143 million active PayPal accounts worldwide Malaysian SMEs could certainly benefit from this boom.

Questions

1 What are the benefits of comparing export sales by overland and online segments?

2 How could SMEs in other countries benefit from the online export boom experienced in Malaysia?

Source: *SME Magazine Asia* (2014) Export data is showing e-commerce is heating up export trade, 2 April 2014, www.smemagazine.asia (accessed 3 April 2014).

The secret of high growth

For many firms high growth in revenue and profits is the ultimate goal, but this challenge is set against a global background of ever-greater competition and the increasing expectations of customers. During times of recession or more intense competition some firms still manage to grow at a spectacular rate. It is by studying these firms that the drivers of fast growth in SMEs can be identified.

Kim and Mauborgne (2005) explain that it is necessary to find market areas that are uncontested (like the blue ocean of uncontested waters). Slower growth firms typically focus upon the competition by benchmarking and seeking to meet the customers' (slightly) increased expectations. Their goal is to outperform their rivals, usually by offering a little more value for a little less cost. The competitive response from the rivals is to do the same and, inevitably, this leads to a cycle of small-scale leapfrogging. A lot of blood is spilled (red ocean) as rivals try to damage each other!

Becoming embroiled within this competitive scenario initiates a pattern of strategic behaviour which is, in fact, opposite of that which is associated with growth. Firms become reactive, drawing in resources to respond to the short-term competitive actions, and have no time or resources to think about the sorts of products and services that are needed for the future on a worldwide basis. Without this creativity the firms fall back on imitating competitors, believing the competitors' actions to be right for the market, rather than really exploiting the changes taking place in their customers' needs and wants.

By contrast, high growth firms leave the competitors to fight among themselves and, instead, seek to offer customers a quantum leap in value. The question that they need to pose is not what is needed to beat the competition but rather what is needed to win over the mass of customers. The implications of this are that it is necessary to challenge the conventional wisdom and assumptions of the industry about the basis on which firms compete and what customers value. An additional bonus from challenging the way the industry does things is that if the firm thinks on an international scale it can also lead to large cost savings as unnecessary operations are cut out. If the benefits really lead to a step change in value they will be perceived as such by customers all round the world.

Cirque du Soleil was a small organization that challenged the ideas that circuses are for children and should have animals, which are expensive to keep. For many it is also unethical to keep animals in captivity. Instead they created a spectacular show for adults which focuses on a combination of performance, art and music and has quickly become a worldwide phenomenon with 4000 employees.

In starting to change the way the firm thinks about its competitive strategy, it should address the following questions:

- What factors that your industry takes for granted should be eliminated?
- What factors that your industry competes on should be reduced well below the standard?
- What factors that your industry competes on should be raised well above the standard?
- What factors should be created that your industry has never offered?

By finding answers to these questions the firm can create new markets and new expectations for customers in existing markets. The Apple iPod, low-cost airlines (South West Airlines, easyJet and Ryanair), online communities (YouTube and Twitter) and mobile phones (Nokia) show how providing a quantum leap in value to customers can reward the innovators. Typically it is smaller firms that are not weighed down by the industry traditions and standards that challenge conventional wisdom. If the ideas are sufficiently innovative and appealing they will create new international niche opportunities.

Shared values   The core advantages of SMEs and main factors for success are their innovative capability, responsiveness, adaptability and flexibility, which enable them to avoid direct competition from larger competitors. These values, which must come from senior management, must be shared and encouraged throughout the organization. They must also be underpinned by good strategic planning and management.

Due to the small scale of operations of SMEs, staff around the world often relate closely to and communicate regularly with the owner or senior manager of the SME, so it is often the personal values of the owner and their view of how the products and services should be marketed that become the shared values of the organization.

The reasons for failure   Many SMEs fail to reach their full potential because they do not manage effectively the international marketing and operational activities that are critical for international success. These factors include:

- Failure to scan the international environment effectively.
- Overdependence on one product.
- The ease with which larger, more powerful competitors or a number of smaller local competitors can copy the idea.
- Failure to respond to worldwide changes in customer needs.
- Failure to plan financial resources.
- Failure to plan for fluctuation in currency values.
- Failure to manage and resource both market and operations expansion.
- The prohibitive cost of enforcing patents and trademarks in foreign courts which may favour local firms.

One of the possible consequences of niche marketing is that success in one international market segment may lead to complacency and overdependence on that market as discussed in Illustration 5.6, or the erroneous belief that the firm has built up barriers to entry which will prevent the entry of potential competitors. Against

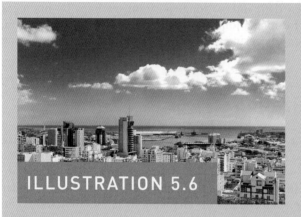

ILLUSTRATION 5.6

SME failure – Is it always their fault?

Mauritius and China are continents apart in terms of size, infrastructure and culture. However, they have had very good relations in the past with embassies in each partner's capital, assisting cooperation in areas of technological and scientific research. Currently, however, Mauritian SMEs are hurting because of the cheap imports from China.

Mauritius has a liberal approach to trade. It has been an export-orientated country for over 40 years and the Mauritian economy has benefited from this, boasting a host of export categories including apparel at 46.7 per cent of their exports, sugar (20 per cent), machinery/transport equipment (18 per cent) jewellery and precious stones (5 per cent).

Export-wise the main trading partners of Mauritius are the European Union where 62 per cent of their exports reach, with US receiving 10 per cent and South Africa receiving 8 per cent. China is not a main export destination, receiving only 0.3 per cent of goods from Mauritius, a figure which has been decreasing rapidly over the years.

On the import side, Mauritius has three main partners. Collectively, countries from the European Union import the most at 25 per cent, India 20 per cent and China 14 per cent. China's imports have increased at an unanticipated rate over the years and it is predicted that they will overtake India as Mauritius' number 1 country importer. Not only are SMEs in Mauritius hurting because of the Chinese import phenomenon, it is also the amount of textiles and manufactured products that are imported that is making SMEs suffer.

One industry affected by the Chinese import phenomenon is the footwear industry. Recently, Bankers Shoes began importing Chinese footwear as this strategy was cheaper than continuing to manufacture shoes in their own factory. In light of this, local production has gone down from 500 pairs per day to 50 and the workforce has diminished from 57 employees to 38. The footwear industry was also affected following the Mauritian government's decree to waiver customs duty on imported footwear.

Questions

1 Why have SMEs in Mauritius failed?

2 What advice would you give to SMEs in Mauritius?

Sources: Ancharaz, V. and Tandrayen-Ragoobur, V. (2013) 'Red dragon China and small Mauritius' trade links: an in-depth analysis', *Journal of Chinese Economic and Foreign Trade Studies*, 6(3), 119–144; African Business (2013) 'SMEs swim against cheap imports', No. 402, 109.

powerful global competitors the barriers are often an illusion. The product may be superseded by an even better idea from a competitor or, alternatively, larger competitors can often gain business with an inferior product simply because of their greater promotional power or their control over the distribution channels.

Because of the often ad hoc, unplanned way that SMEs develop internationally they underestimate the level of resourcing that is needed in both time and money, the difficulties and delays that may arise and consequently the length of time it takes to reach profitability in new foreign markets. The investment that is needed is frequently greater than the firms expect and they often fail to negotiate a suitable arrangement with their bank or other funders before difficulties emerge.

The main danger associated with international niche marketing is that the income stream is often dependent upon one single product or service idea, or a very limited product portfolio. Given the capacity of competitors to copy product ideas, the firm must be absolutely sure that it has built in some unique competitive advantage such as a strong brand, unique technology or reliable business contacts to sustain it against the competition.

Creative SMEs find alternative ways to strengthen their international position, perhaps by finding a different way of expanding. This can be achieved by forming a joint venture or alliance with another firm, contracting out production to a firm with spare capacity, licensing the product or process, or even agreeing to be taken over.

The future of SME internationalization

There are many pitfalls for an SME that is active in international markets. For some SMEs the greatest risk is internationalizing at all, particularly if they have no definable source of competitive advantage and little understanding of international marketing. However, with increasing globalization, firms such as these are no longer able to hide their inefficiency or lack of creativity in the domestic market as they will come under attack from international competitors. The global environment and the changing dynamics in markets can be equally challenging.

Almost as risky is operating as a traditional exporter – selling excess capacity into markets about which the SME has little or no information and with which its managers have little cultural empathy. Manufacturing SME exporters from developed countries struggle to compete with companies from emerging markets which have lower labour costs. However, small low-cost manufacturers in emerging markets are coming under pressure from manufacturers from less developed countries that can undercut their prices. For SMEs that are innovative and ambitious, are prepared to embrace new technology, use new routes to market and find new innovative ways of doing business, there are opportunities for success on a scale never before envisaged, provided they are willing to learn, have a clear competitive focus and a strong network of connections. For the most successful there is often an alternative opportunity to sell out, for example, Innocent Smoothies by Coca-Cola, Pret à Manger by McDonald's, Ben and Jerry's by Unilever and Seeds of Change by Mars.

SUMMARY

- SMEs have always been involved in international marketing but now have greater opportunities to develop internationally and create wealth and employment for their domestic economy. New technology allows smaller firms to access information and communicate internationally in a way that was not possible before.

- Successful SME international marketers are those that build relationships with individuals and organizations that can help them understand the nature and value of the competitive advantage that they possess, and learn from their own experiences and those of others.

- The principles of international marketing can be applied to all categories of SME international activity, ranging from exporting manufactured goods, through e-commerce to marketing domestic attractions to tourists. However, SMEs use different ways of internationalizing and selecting countries for market entry from an incremental selection of countries, based on market potential or a network of contacts, through to high technology businesses that are 'born global'. This depends upon the context in which the firm is internationalizing.

- The chosen SME internationalization strategies are underpinned by generic marketing strategies but are often also affected by the management's perception of the barriers in the environment, the support that is provided in the domestic country and the specific market factors that affect their business sector.

- The stage of international development that the SME has reached reflects the company's capability, and the confidence and attitude of the senior management to internationalization. It usually shows how the SMEs have utilized their inherent strengths of flexibility, adaptability, innovative capability and speed of response in developing their markets.

- There are a number of factors that lead to success and failure for SME international development, but the most significant factor is the ability of SMEs to offer customers a quantum leap in value by innovating throughout the marketing process.

KEYWORDS

small- and medium-sized enterprises

born global

micro-multinationals

domestically delivered or developed niche services

electronic commerce

barrier to entry

international niche marketing

reciprocal trading

network

market concentrators

market expanders

internationalization

supply chain

outsource

7S framework

generic marketing strategies

organization structure

stages of internationalization

CASE STUDY 1

Gripple connecting with international markets

SMEs are typically highly innovative, but usually lack the necessary power and resources to dominate supply chains and so must find partners to work with. As a niche producer of wire joiners and tensioners, researching and selecting target markets overseas and finding the best way to market and sell their products is not an easy task for Gripple Ltd.

Established by Hugh Facey in 1988, Gripple expanded from its humble surroundings in Sheffield, UK, to become an SME with offices in both Europe and the US. In 2000 Gripple Europe was established in the Alsace region of France, followed by Gripple Inc. near Chicago in the US. As an employee-owned company and with innovation core to their continued success, Gripple in turn began to support budding entrepreneurs in different sectors. The company has won four Queen's Awards in the UK and is one of a select group of businesses to have secured an award

in each of the scheme's categories – innovation, international trade and sustainable development.

The 'Gripple' is a unique fastening device and has no direct competition; twisted wire rope and traditional anchor systems are alternative products, but Gripple has a unique offering for suspension solutions. Their principal sectors are agriculture and construction; the former a traditional market for Gripple and for which the original idea of the 'Gripple' was born, the latter where innovation within the company opened up new and exciting opportunities. As a mature market for Gripple, opportunities in the agricultural sector are pursued via their traditional routes to market using longstanding distributorships. The construction sector is however a complex one; the key purchasers and key decision makers are located within different organizations in the supply chain. Contracting construction companies will project manage turnkey projects, tendering for public and private sector contracts. Architects work with engineers, who in turn demand products and services with exacting requirements.

Gripple locates partners whose products are directly linked to the Gripple product. Take, for example, the provision of light fitting suspension systems in hospitals located in markets prone to earthquakes (the seismic solution sector for Gripple). Once the build is complete Gripple seeks to partner complementary original equipment manufacturers (OEMs) such as the lighting companies. However, each sector and each geographical market supply chain can work in different ways. Gripple has a number of questions to answer in evaluating the potential of international market opportunities. Who funds the construction of hospitals in different geographical markets? Who decides on the final design? Which tier of supplier should Gripple focus on for their market entry strategy?

In 2009, Eric Laroche joined Gripple and wanted to introduce a systematic approach to their international market selection. He tasked a graduate in the company to create an international market selection tool which could rank each geographic market using a range of criteria.

'We identify key criteria, we weight them, find out what is important to us, and we go with a hit list of countries.'

Armed with this 'hit list' Gripple go to market and validate their information. Once validated, entrance into that market is then dependent on the quality of the partnerships they develop and if the potential business matches their expectations from research, they invest in placing people on the ground. In their key markets of Europe, US and India the latter stage of this process is based on locating people in the market who know the Gripple culture, having worked in the organization in the UK for a number of years. However, when Gripple has tried to enter new markets such as Brazil, using just local contacts, they have been less successful.

Questions

1 How can you select potential overseas markets where your innovation is unheard of and what criteria would you use in Gripple's international market selection tool to select potential markets?

2 How would you locate the key decision makers in sectors that have complex supply chains?

3 What steps might you take to educate the sector and market in the use of your product?

4 How could you apply your strategy to the civil construction sector in Brazil?

CASE STUDY 2

Pin it, share it, desire it, sell it

Worldwide consumers are engaging with many social media platforms, and retailers must ensure they are active where their consumers are present. Pinterest is one of those platforms where SME e-tailers have the opportunity to provide another shop window, 'free of charge', promoting their products. Pinterest is in addition to the SME e-tailers website, Instagram, Facebook page and Twitter feed. What is crucial for business is that Pinterest boards and pins give SME e-tailers the opportunity to become part of their consumer's personal life. Enid Hwang, Pinterest's company community manager, states Pinterest is a very personal and intimate virtual platform where consumers choose what they want to view, pin and repin.

Pinterest has only been active for 5 years and already it has over 79 million users (almost double the number of users since 2014) and the numbers are expected to keep growing with the male segment growing faster than the female segment. There are over 50 billion picture pins with personal pinboards entitled 'Shoes I Want' to 'Woodwork DIY' and 'Things to do in Montenegro'. Generally Pins are categorized into shopping and leisure categories called, for example, 'Wedding Cakes' or 'Clothes to Buy for Holidays'. E-tailers categorize folders and populate the folder with Pin It pictures that provide a visual bookmark for the consumer and a promotional tool for the e-tailer.

WeMakeWebsites is a London-based company that is hugely successful in the Shopify e-commerce world. Two of their top tips (see text) for SME e-tailers provide an insight into how to communicate a brand, its values and ethos through Pinterest.

The example SME e-tailer used in this case study is Up Knörth based in Vancouver, British Columbia. Up Knörth provides high quality, rugged outdoor, sustainable and durable clothes and accessories for men and women who have a keen environmental conscience.

Tip 1. Tell a story

It is recommended that SME e-tailers like Up Knörth tell a story on Pinterest through pictures that encompass the brand's values, lifestyle, desirable products and places. The story-telling objective is to ensure pinners understand how the Up Knörth brand fits with the pinners' lifestyle. Up Knörth does this with PinBoards. PinBoards include items of their own products together with PinBoards entitled Cabin design, Camping, Adventuremobile and Growing. Each PinBoard shows pins of how their products and their values fit the values of pinners that also enjoy rugged, outdoor adventures and care for the environment.

Tip 2. Contribute and get discovered

Pinterest is all about providing appealing pictures of products and lifestyles. Pin It pictures on Up Knörth's PinBoards are beautiful, inspiring and desirable. The products for sale are included but there are 1287 pins of log cabins either taken by the Up Knörth team or Pin Its of cabins in Norway pinned from fantasticnorway. no and of a rustic cabin pinned from lostonabacroad.

tumblr.com. All their log cabin pictures were repinned or liked by Up Knörth's 141 986 followers. Contributing beyond Up Knörth's own products attracts and engages followers and helps them understand the brand and what its values are.

These tips help a business such as Up Knörth stay connected and build further networks. More importantly, Pinterest Boards stimulate enquiries and click-throughs to the e-tailers website, blog, Facebook and other social media platforms. Up Knörth blog about environmental issues, produces video diaries of travel adventures in wild and wonderful places as well as suggesting minimalistic DIY ideas (using recycled materials of course) and Nordic recipes including Dill and salt-cured Salmon.

Questions

1 What are the advantages of using Pinterest for SMEs?

2 What strategies should SMEs use when planning to begin using Pinterest?

3 Why does Up Knörth include a range of PinBoards?

4 How important is Pinterest for an SME's communication strategy?

Sources: Columbus Despatch (2015) Pinterest drawing wider audience $11 billion social-media hub hopes to corner market on brainstorming, www.dispatch.com (accessed 6 April 2015); WeMakeWebsites (2015) Blog: How to Use Pinterest to grow your Business, wemakewebsites.com /blog (accessed 6 April 2015); Up Knörth (2015) Pinterest Board, www.pinterest.com/upknorth/

DISCUSSION QUESTIONS

1   How can the smaller business compensate for its lack of resources and expertise in international marketing when trying to enter new markets?

2   Why is international niche marketing likely to be a superior approach to export selling?

3   As the leader of a rock group you have had moderate success in your home country but have noticed that you seem to be gaining fans in different countries. As you have not been signed up by a recognized music company, how might you exploit your popularity internationally?

4   How does the mindset of a proactive international marketer differ from a reactive marketer?

5   Small international marketing firms do not have the resources to carry out market research systematically. What advice would you give to a Danish renewable energy firm that wishes to enter the Southern African market?

REFERENCES

1. Ansoff, I. (1957) 'Strategies for diversification', *Harvard Business Review*, 35(5): 113–24.

2. Balabanis, G. and Katsikea, E.S. (2003) 'The relationship between environment, export strategy development approaches and export performance', *Proceedings of the Annual Conference of the Academy of Marketing Science*, Washington DC, 26, 17–18.

3. Brown, L. and McDonald, M.H.B. (1994) *Competitive marketing strategy for Europe*, Macmillan.

4. Crick, D. and Crick, J. (2014). 'The internationalization strategies of rapidly internationalizing high-tech UK SMEs: Planned and unplanned activities', *European Business Review*, 26(5), 421–448.

5. Cui, A.P., Walsh, M.F. and Zou, S. (2014) 'The importance of strategic fit between host–home country similarity and exploration exploitation strategies on small- and medium-sized enterprises' performance: A contingency perspective', *Journal of International Marketing*, 22(4), 67–85.

6. Cull, R. and Beck, T. (2014) Policy Research Working Paper 7018 'SME Finance in Africa', World Bank Group.

7. DHL Botswana (2015) Country Profile www.dhl.co.bw/en/country_profile/key_facts.html

8. Doole, I., Grimes, A. and Demack, S. (2006) 'An exploration of the management practices and processes most closely associated with high levels of export capability in SMEs', *Marketing Intelligence and Planning*, 24(6).

9. Fairtrade International (2014) Monitoring the scope and benefits of Fairtrade, 6th edn, www.fairtrade.org.uk (accessed 4 April 2015).

10. Global Entrepreneurship Monitor (2009) 'Adult Population Survey (APS) Global Entrepreneurship Monitor', accessed at: www.gemconsortium.org.

11. Grimes, A., Doole, I. and Kitchen, P.J. (2007) 'Profiling the capabilities of SMEs to compete internationally', *Journal of Small Business and Enterprise Development*, 14(1): 64–80.

12. Hagen, B., Zucchella, A., Cerchiello, P. and De Giovanni, N. (2012) 'International strategy and performance – Clustering strategic types of SMEs', *International Business Review*, 21(3), 369–382.

13. Harris, S. and Wheeler, C. (2005) '"Entrepreneurs" relationships for internationalization: functions, origins and strategies', *International Business Review*, 14(2): 187–207.

14. IMF (2015) Sub-Saharan Africa Navigating Headwinds, published April 2015, International Monetary Fund.

15. Kalinic, I., and Forza, C. (2012). 'Rapid internationalization of traditional SMEs: Between gradualist models and born globals', *International Business Review*, 21(4), 694–707.

16. Katsikeas, C.S. and Leonidou, L.C. (1996) 'Export marketing expansion strategy: differences between market concentration and market spreading', *Journal of Marketing Management*, 12.

17. Kim, W.C. and Mauborgne, R. (2005) 'Blue ocean strategy: how to create uncontested market space and make competition irrelevant', Harvard Business Press.

18. Kulmeier, D.B. and Knight, G. (2010) 'The critical role of relationship quality in SME internationalization', *Journal of Global Marketing*, 23(1), Jan.

19. Leonidou, L.C., Katsikeas, C.S., Palihawadana, D. and Spyropoulou, S. (2007) 'An analytical review of the factors stimulating smaller firms to export: implications for policy makers', *International Marketing Review*, 24(6), 735–70.

20. Mort, G.S. and Weerawardena, J. (2006) 'Networking capability and international entrepreneurship', *International Marketing Review*, 23(5): 549–72.

21. Nueno, P. (2000) 'The dragon breathes enterprising fire', In S. Bailey and F. Muzyka, *Mastering entrepreneurship*, FT Prentice Hall.

22. OECD (2009) 'Top barriers and drivers to SME internationalization', Report by the OECD Working party on SMEs and Entrepreneurship, OECD.

23. OECD (2014) Economic Outlook Africa 2014, www.oecd-ilibrary.org (accessed 3 April 2014).

24. Okpara, J.O. and Kabongo, J.D. (2010) *International Journal of Business and Globalisation*, 5(2), 169–87.

25. Porter, M.E. (1990) *Competitive Advantage of Nations*, Free Press.

26. Sarathy, R., Terpstra, V. and Russow, L. (2006) *International Marketing*, 9th edn. Dryden Press.

27. Servais, P., Madsen, T.K. and Rasmussen, E.S. (2007) 'Small manufacturing firms involvement in international e-business activities', *Advances in International Marketing*, 17: 297–317.

28. Solheim, Erling Magnus. (2012) 'The internationalization process of born global companies: A study of born globals without prior internationalization experience', Unpublished. NTNU School of Entrepreneurship.

29. UK Council for International Student Affairs (2015) 'International student statistics: UK higher education', www.ukcisa.org.uk (accessed 2 April 2015).

CHAPTER 6

GLOBAL STRATEGIES

LEARNING OBJECTIVES

After reading this chapter you should be able to:

- Appreciate the various aspects of globalization and be able to compare and contrast the alternative global strategies

- Evaluate the factors that determine a firm's choice of global strategy

- Identify the challenges that firms, particularly from emerging markets, face in developing a global presence

- Appreciate the role of branding in globalization

- Understand the factors affecting global marketing management

INTRODUCTION

Having discussed the nature of international development in smaller firms we now consider the global marketing strategies of the largest firms that compete on a worldwide basis. The largest firms have the mindset of achieving **globalization** as the route to maximizing performance by introducing, where possible, standardized marketing programmes and processes to enhance efficiency and competitiveness. At the same time, they adapt certain operational activities to local needs in order to achieve effectiveness by maximizing short-term revenue generation. The problem that such firms face is exactly which aspects of their international activity to standardize and which to adapt because the decisions are often context specific and are affected by the particular factors which drive change within their particular industry. This leads to firms adopting a variety of global strategies, from those that are very similar from country to country to those that are substantially different in each country in which the firm operates and this substantially increases complexity. In the past global marketing has been dominated by firms from developed countries, such as Coca-Cola, McDonald's and Microsoft but an increasing number of firms such as LG and Samsung, from recently emerging markets, have become global players too. As the balance of economic power in global markets shifts further to the BRIC countries, many more firms from those markets are poised to continue the trend.

In this chapter we start by reviewing the dimensions of the concept and drivers of globalization, before considering the alternative strategic approaches and the factors that drive strategic choice. This discussion is then followed by an examination of the strategy implementation issues that multinational enterprises (MNEs) might face in managing their global business and building their global presence, with particular emphasis on global branding. We end the chapter with a discussion of the issues that must be addressed in order to manage global marketing effectively.

The alternative views of globalization

Over the past two decades the term globalization seems to have led to a polarization of views. For some, globalization is associated with opportunity, the removal of barriers to prosperity for all countries of the world and greater exposure to, and understanding of, different cultures. Others see globalization, capitalism and MNE activity as the same thing. They believe global companies dominate international business, ruthlessly exploit the countries' resources and adversely influence the economy and culture of every country, moving their operations from country to country according to which offers the lowest wage rates. Thus, they have no thought for those who lose their jobs or the well-being of those who are paid extremely low wages. In the last few years the actions of global companies have been blamed for a number of world problems, such as the banks for the subprime mortgages and the resulting recession of 2008, and BP for the Gulf of Mexico disaster.

In practice globalization is about progress towards an, as yet, undefined goal and few companies, even those with the most familiar brand names, are truly global. Table 6.1 lists the biggest firms in the world by revenues. It shows that seven of the top ten companies by revenue are in the oil and gas industries and each are strongly dependent on a large domestic market and a few additional key markets in other countries. This becomes clearer by contrasting this with Table 6.2, which shows the top 20 transnational companies (TNC) ranked by foreign assets. UNCTAD (2010) provides a measure of the real **transnationality** of multinationals by identifying an index of transnationality (TNI), which is an average of the measures of transnationality (foreign to total assets, sales and employment). This, perhaps, provides a more accurate picture of the most transnational companies ranked this time in order of TNI (Table 6.3). The reason that this list is different from Tables 6.1 and 6.2 is that firms from the US have a huge domestic market in which to grow before embarking upon international, then global activity (note the positions of the US firms). By contrast, firms from smaller countries have always had to internationalize simply to grow.

Table 6.1   Top 10 companies in the world by revenues

Rank	Company	Revenues (billion)	Country	Industry
1	Wal-Mart Stores	$469.2	United States	Mass Merchants
2	Royal Dutch Shell	467.2	Netherlands	Integrated Oils
3	China Petroleum & Chemical	433.2	China	Integrated Oils
4	Exxon Mobil	420.7	United States	Integrated Oils
5	BP	375.6	United Kingdom	Integrated Oils
6	PetroChina	347.9	China	Integrated Oils
7	Toyota Motor	267.0	Japan	Automobile OEM
8	Volkswagen	247.8	Germany	Automobile OEM
9	Total	234.4	France	Integrated Oils
10	Chevron	222.6	United States	Integrated Oils

Overview

Bloomberg ranked 67 260 publicly listed companies based on revenue for their latest fiscal year. The top are displayed.

Methodology

For all companies on this list except Walmart Stores, which reported 2013 results, figures are for 2012.

Source: Top 10 revenue worldwide companies, last updated June 2013, Bloomberg. Reproduced with kind permission.

Table 6.2   The top 20 non-financial transnational companies: index of transnationality ranked by foreign assets

Ranking by:				Assets	
Foreign assets	Corporation	Home economy	Industry[a]	Foreign $m	TNI[b] (Per cent)
1	General Electric Co	United States	Electrical & electronic equipment	331 160	48.8
2	Royal Dutch Shell plc	United Kingdom	Petroleum expl./ref./distr.	301 898	72.8
3	Toyota Motor Corporation	Japan	Motor vehicles	274 380	58.6
4	Exxon Mobil Corporation	United States	Petroleum expl./ref./distr.	231 033	62.6
5	Total SA	France	Petroleum expl./ref./distr.	226 717	79.5
6	BP plc	United Kingdom	Petroleum expl./ref./distr.	202 899	69.7
7	Vodafone Group Plc	United Kingdom	Telecommunications	182 837	88.9
8	Volkswagen Group	Germany	Motor vehicles	176 656	58.6
9	Chevron Corporation	United States	Petroleum expl./ref./distr.	175 736	59.3
10	Eni SpA	Italy	Petroleum expl./ref./distr.	141 021	71.2
11	Enel SpA	Italy	Electricity, gas and water	140 396	57.3
12	Glencore Xstrata PLC	Switzerland	Mining & quarrying	135 080	82.8
13	Anheuser-Busch InBev NV	Belgium	Food, beverages and tobacco	134 549	93.3
14	EDF SA	France	Utilities (Electricity, gas and water)	130 161	34.0
15	Nestlé SA	Switzerland	Food, beverages and tobacco	124 730	97.1
16	E.ON AG	Germany	Utilities (Electricity, gas and water)	124 429	73.3
17	GDF Suez	France	Utilities (Electricity, gas and water)	121 402	55.2
18	Deutsche Telekom AG	Germany	Telecommunications	120 350	61.9
19	Apple Computer Inc	United States	Electrical & electronic equipment	119 918	59.6
20	Honda Motor Co Ltd	Japan	Motor vehicles	118 476	74.3

(a) Industry classification for companies follows the United States Standard Industrial Classification as used by the United States Securities and Exchange Commission (SEC).
(b) TNI, the Transnationality Index, is calculated as the average of the following three ratios: foreign assets to total assets, foreign sales to total sales and foreign employment to total employment.
Source: From World Investment Report 2014: Annex Tables © 2014 United Nations. Reprinted with the permission of the United Nations.

Table 6.3 The top 20 non-financial transnational companies ranked by index of transnationality

TNI[b]	Corporation	Home economy	Industry[a]	TNI[b] (Per cent)
1	Nestlé SA	Switzerland	Food, beverages and tobacco	97.1
2	Anglo American plc	United Kingdom	Mining & quarrying	95.9
3	Anheuser-Busch InBev NV	Belgium	Food, beverages and tobacco	93.3
4	British American Tobacco PLC	United Kingdom	Food, beverages and tobacco	91.0
5	Linde AG	Germany	Chemicals	91.0
6	Barrick Gold Corporation	Canada	Gold mining	89.2
7	SABMiller PLC	United Kingdom	Food, beverages and tobacco	89.1
8	ArcelorMittal	Luxembourg	Metal and metal products	89.0
9	Vodafone Group Plc	United Kingdom	Telecommunications	88.9
10	WPP PLC	United Kingdom	Business services	87.8
11	Diageo PLC	United Kingdom	Food, beverages and tobacco	85.8
12	Koninklijke Philips Electronics NV	Netherlands	Electrical & electronic equipment	84.7
13	Hon Hai Precision Industries	Taiwan Province of China	Electrical & electronic equipment	84.4
14	AstraZeneca PLC	United Kingdom	Pharmaceuticals	83.6
15	Volvo AB	Sweden	Motor vehicles	83.5
16	Hutchison Whampoa Limited	Hong Kong, China	Diversified	82.9
17	Glencore Xstrata PLC	Switzerland	Mining & quarrying	82.8
18	Unilever PLC	United Kingdom	Diversified	80.8
19	Fiat S.p.A.	Italy	Motor vehicles	80.2
20	BG Group plc	United Kingdom	Oil and gas field exploration	79.8

(a) Industry classification for companies follows the United States Standard Industrial Classification as used by the United States Securities and Exchange Commission (SEC).
(b) TNI, the Transnationality Index, is calculated as the average of the following three ratios: foreign assets to total assets, foreign sales to total sales and foreign employment to total employment.
Source: From World Investment Report 2014: Annex Tables © 2014 United Nations. Reprinted with the permission of the United Nations.

The most dominant TNCs still come from developed economies and are typically from the motor, petroleum and telecommunications sectors. However, the TNCs from developing countries (top 20 in Table 6.4) are now gaining a significant presence. An increasing number of TNCs from emerging countries will appear in the top 100 in the world as emerging markets grow.

There is no doubt that the world's largest firms seek a worldwide presence. Driving this acceleration of global MNE activity appears to be increased competition which Sjobolom (1998) suggests is being brought about by four forces: changes in consumer expectations; technological change; deregulation; and regional forces.

Table 6.4   Top 20 companies from developing countries: index of transnationality ranked by foreign assets

Ranking by:				Assets	
Foreign assets	Corporation	Home economy	Industry[a]	Foreign US$bn	TNI[b]
1	Hutchison Whampoa Limited	Hong Kong, China	Diversified	85 721	80.9
2	CITIC Group	China	Diversified	78 602	17.1
3	Hon Hai Precision Industries	Taiwan Province of China	Electrical & electronic equipment	65 471	84.3
4	Petronas - Petroliam Nasional Bhd	Malaysia	Petroleum expl./ref./distr.	49 072	39.2
5	Vale SA	Brazil	Mining & quarrying	45 721	44.5
6	China Ocean Shipping (Group) Company	China	Transport and storage	43 452	48.9
7	China National Offshore Oil Corp	China	Petroleum expl./ref./distr.	34 276	18.6
8	América Móvil SAB de CV	Mexico	Telecommunications	32 008	49.4
9	Lukoil OAO	Russian Federation	Petroleum and natural gas	31 174	42.8
10	Cemex S.A.B. de C.V.	Mexico	Non-metalic mineral products	30 730	80.1
11	Petróleos de Venezuela SA	Venezuela, Bolivarian Republic of	Petroleum expl./ref./distr.	27 462	18.2
12	Samsung Electronics Co., Ltd.	Korea, Republic of	Electrical & electronic equipment	26 077	26.9
13	Singapore Telecommunications Ltd	Singapore	Telecommunications	25 768	63.5
14	Hyundai Motor Company	Korea, Republic of	Motor vehicles	25 443	25.6
15	Jardine Matheson Holdings Ltd	Hong Kong, China	Diversified	24 284	57.9
16	Sabic – Saudi Basic Industries Corp.	Saudi Arabia	Petroleum expl./ref./distr.	23 540	51.9

Table 6.4   Continued

Ranking by:				Assets	
Foreign assets	Corporation	Home economy	Industry[a]	Foreign US$bn	TNI[b]
17	Gazprom JSC	Russian Federation	Petroleum and natural gas	23 425	24.0
18	Wilmar International Limited	Singapore	Food, beverages and tobacco	23 088	75.5
19	China Resources Power Holdings Company Ltd	Hong Kong, China	Energy	22 938	99.9
20	Tata Motors Ltd	India	Automobile	21 575	59.2

(a) Industry classification for companies follows the United States Standard Industrial Classification as used by the United States Securities and Exchange Commission (SEC).
(b) TNI, the Transnationality Index, is calculated as the average of the following three ratios: foreign assets to total assets, foreign sales to total sales and foreign employment to total employment.
Source: From World Investment Report 2014: Annex Tables © 2014 United Nations. Reprinted with the permission of the United Nations.

Globalization and standardization

In seeking to compete successfully in increasingly globalized markets, multinational enterprises realize that a precondition of long-term growth is a worldwide presence. In previous chapters we have discussed the nature of global markets and a fundamental question is whether global markets require standardized products. Decades ago a number of writers such as Elinder (1961) and Levitt (1983) debated whether or not this would result in globally standardized products and services.

So far, there are few examples of product and service offers which have been completely standardized across the world and are probably limited to those sold over the Internet in the business-to-business sector. Some of the most widely available products which might be considered to be standardized in fact are substantially adapted. You can taste the Coca-Cola variants from around the world at the museum in Atlanta and try the different McDonald's menus as you travel. Computer companies use different language options in their service manuals. American baseball has the World Series competition in which only North American teams take part, in contrast to the soccer World Cup in which 204 teams applied to take part. The concept of globalization, therefore, is often characterized by contradictions, such as the need to standardize some elements of the marketing mix while, at the same time, accepting the need to respond to local needs and tastes by adapting the product or service. Some believe that the true nature of globalization is encapsulated in the phrase 'think global, act local', in which there is an acknowledgement of the need to balance standardization and adaptation according to the particular situation. Even this concept is challenged because it implies that the starting point for the strategy is based on a standardized marketing mix. For many MNEs the alternative – 'think local, act global' – may be more appropriate given that it implies focusing on local needs, but taking the opportunity, whenever feasible and appropriate, to standardize elements of the marketing mix and globalize support services. Against this background the word globalization is associated in a very imprecise way with many different aspects of the international marketing strategy process.

The drivers of globalization

Although globalization may be difficult to define satisfactorily, there are a number of drivers of globalization that can be used to explain its impact and discuss its implications:

- market access
- market opportunities

- industry standards
- sourcing
- products and services
- technology
- customer requirements
- competition
- cooperation
- distribution
- communication and information
- the company's strategy, business programmes and processes.

ILLUSTRATION 6.1

ebay China: Didn't think local

ebay Inc. is a global commerce online platform company with its head office in San Jose, California. There are over 33 500 people working for ebay in 32 countries worldwide. The company is extremely successful and is ranked among the worldwide 100 most valued brands and with 128 million active users of ebay it is a retail shopping experience than consumers enjoy. ebay is set to continue its expansion into many more countries.

China is one of the BRIC countries that multinational companies are still investigating as the 'next big thing' in their international strategic marketing plans. All have large untapped markets. China is thought to be particularly interesting as it has over 1 billion citizens, but more importantly, has a growing tech-savvy middle class with money to spend. Therefore, ebay could not resist choosing China in which to do business. ebay bought EachNet, an existing

Chinese online marketplace and changed the name to ebayChina. However, after 2 years ebay announced the company's exit from China.

The main reason ebayChina failed was because ebay Inc. expected to use their standardized format, which was highly successful in 32 countries, and roll it out in China. However, culturally Chinese buyers and sellers want to form 'swift *guanxi*' which is a personal relationship before making transactions. The personal relationships formed with buyers and seller is highly prized and 'swift *guanxi*' could not take place between buyers and sellers through ebayChina.

This does not mean online retail is unbearable for Chinese consumers. On the contrary, Chinese consumers are very active within online retail spaces particularly when 'swift *guanxi*' can take place. taobao.com (part of the Alibaba Group) is a Chinese-based company that knows about 'swift *guanxi*' and they have incorporated instant messaging between buyers and sellers so that personal relationships can easily and quickly be formed. taobao.com has a 96 per cent share of the online retail marketplace in China.

Questions

1 What mistakes did ebay make?

2 What market research recommendations would you make to ebay to help future success when entering into new countries?

Source: Ou, C. X., Pavlou, P. A. and Davison, R. (2014). 'Swift guanxi in online marketplaces: The role of computer-mediated communication technologies', *MIS Quarterly*, 38(1), 209–230.

Globalization of market access has increased as the number of inaccessible markets has reduced following the political changes that have opened up markets, for example in Central and Eastern Europe and China, to much greater MNE involvement. While these 'new' markets have become more accessible, firms entering them usually face difficult problems invariably establishing their global products there because of the differences in social and business culture and the lack of a reliable infrastructure, the unfamiliar and unpredictable legal framework and the varying standards and values of business practice, which often lead to corruption. While these markets offer attractive growth prospects, many western global firms have shown themselves to be ill-equipped to exploit these opportunities. Initially they were unwilling or unable to 'go it alone' in these markets, which were unsophisticated by developed country standards, and found it necessary to form partnerships with local firms, with mixed results.

In the short period since these markets have opened up many local companies have experienced phenomenal domestic growth which has enabled them to build a platform from which they themselves can become global players.

Market access is also being improved by the increasing regionalization, resulting from the growth of trading blocs. Firms are reinforcing this effect by helping to reduce inter-country barriers and thus improve market access by operating more standardized pan-regional marketing programmes and processes such as product development and advertising. Indeed the market access challenges for global companies now relate not so much to externally imposed barriers but to internal management issues faced by competing in emerging markets against increasingly sophisticated competitors.

Globalization of market opportunities has increased with the continued deregulation of certain sectors, such as financial services where the traditional barriers between the various parts of an industry, such as banking, insurance, pensions, specialist savings, mortgage and loan suppliers, are being broken down. This has enabled supermarket groups to enter many market sectors, including financial services and pharmacy product retailing.

Removal of sector barriers has resulted in mergers or alliances of firms to form larger and more powerful groups which can offer a complete range of products or services to their customers in the sector. For such MNEs, the power base may be a large domestic or regional market, as has been the case with a number of mergers in financial services or in automobiles. As will be discussed later, Daimler (Germany) and Chrysler (USA), merged in 1998 to create a more comprehensive product range in their industry sector but this failed, leading Daimler to sell Chrysler, but then embark on an alliance with Renault.

The privatization of government-owned utilities such as electricity, gas and telephone is leading to industry restructuring where previously there were monopolies with tight operating restrictions. This is allowing firms to compete in geographic areas and industry sectors from which they have previously been excluded.

The UK has allowed foreign ownership of many key state assets, for example six of its main airports are owned by a consortium led by Grupo Ferrovial, a Spanish firm, which includes South Korea's national pension service as a major investor. Owners of its utilities include EDF and GDF Suez (French) EON (Germany), RWE (Germany) Iberdrola (Spain), Macquarrie (Australia) and communications include Telefonica (Spain), Hutchinson Whampoa (Hong Kong), France Telecome and Deutsche Telecom (Germany), (Arnott, 2010).

A major condition of the Greek bailout in 2015 that involved loans of 86 billion euros was that the country should sell 50 billion of the country's assets, one-fifth of its annual GDP. However, previous attempts to sell assets had proved problematic, for example, the sale of the seaside site of the former Athens airport for 915 million euros (Campbell, Chrysoloras and Benedetti-Valentini 2015).

Globalization of industry standards is increasing as technical operating standards, professional rules and guidelines are being adopted more widely, primarily due to the harmonization of regulations within trading blocs, but more generally around the world as a result of the increased mobility of experts and advisers, and the wider use of quality standards, such as ISO 9000. It is a precondition of supplying major customers that firms operate to certain product and service standards that can be recognized regionally and globally.

The largest MNEs are expected to work to ethical standards that cover such diverse areas as employment, environmental protection and unfair competition. As a result, MNEs demand that their staff work to exacting company standards. Professional staff are usually also regulated by national bodies and so greater regional harmonization is affecting standards of behaviour and performance. Despite this there is a long way to go. It has proved difficult for governments and regulators to agree and introduce standards for financial services to reduce a risk of a repeat of the banking crisis in 2008.

FIGURE 6.1   The benefits of global sourcing

- *Cheaper labour rates*. Fashion and clothing marketers obtain supplies from low labour rate countries such as China, Indonesia, Costa Rica, Vietnam and Latin America. There can, however, be problems of product quality and criticism of unethical behaviour as these firms resort to 'island hopping' to the new lower labour rate areas that result from changes in local country economic development, or their contractors may employ child labour.

- *Better or more uniform quality*. Certain countries and companies have competitive advantage over others as suppliers because of the local availability of materials and skills.

- *Access to the best technology, innovation and ideas*. Firms search the world to identify a particular research or design centre which might offer the specialist expertise they require. For example, Nissan set up design facilities in California and Microsoft has established research facilities close to Cambridge University in the UK.

- *Access to local markets*. Developing stronger links with a country through sourcing can help to generate new business in that country. For example, the aircraft maker Boeing has opened up the market in China following its decision to purchase components there.

- *Economies of scale advantages*. Where the location of a manufacturing or distribution operation is convenient to supply a whole region it can lead to significant cost advantages.

- *Lower taxes and duties*. Certain countries may offer tax advantages to manufacturers and low rates of duty when shipping goods to the customer. The relocation of some higher added value activities can help by spreading currency risk.

- *Potentially lower logistics costs*. Global transport and warehousing companies use IT more effectively to control product movement and inventory.

- *More consistent supply*. Some foods would be restricted because of seasonality if steps had not been taken to arrange supplies from countries with different growing seasons.

Globalization of sourcing has increased as companies search the world for the best and cheapest materials, components and services rather than rely on local suppliers. Figure 6.1 identifies the benefits of global sourcing.

Illustration 6.2 explains that new country destinations are being found for outsourcing.

The major risks in global sourcing are in dealing with countries where there might be political, economic and exchange rate risks. There are also specific risks associated with an individual supplier that might use the knowledge gained and power which results from a strong position in the supply chain to become a competitor. As increasing numbers of scientists and engineers are being trained in China, India and Central and Eastern Europe, so outsourcing of research and development now to these countries will lead to increased competition from there in the future. Quality and service provided by the supplier can be critical and if not managed can begin to affect the reputation of the customer. An example of this is shown in Management Challenge 6.1. What is crucial is that the MNE must retain its competitive advantage and not outsource its supplies to the point where it gives away all its technical and commercial secrets, power in the market or risks supply quality problems. This potential danger needs to be managed by purchasers improving their supplier–purchaser relationships or, perhaps, even forming longer-term strategic alliances. The additional benefit of better supplier–purchaser relationships can be improved communications and the avoidance of some unnecessary supply chain costs resulting from inadequate specifications, misunderstandings about quality and generally poor management. As we will see later, the Internet has made the development of international supply chains easier but has also changed their nature.

Globalization of core products and services. More and more products are reaching the mature phase of their product life cycle and this is leading to greater commoditization of products and services. Consumers see very little difference between the offerings of many competing suppliers as they become less loyal to a single brand. The increased speed at which new innovations can be copied by other competitors means that core benefits can no longer be a point of differentiation between competitors. MNEs are responding

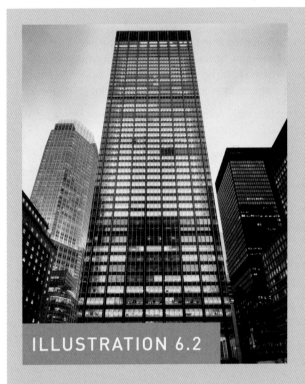

ILLUSTRATION 6.2

JP Morgan: Taking the outsourcing plunge

JP Morgan is the third richest conglomerate in the world and is a global leader when it comes to investment banking, financial transaction processing, private equity, commercial banking and asset management. Clearly they are a multinational company in themselves and they also research market dynamics, in all sectors, to inform other multinational organizations. With over 200 years' experience, JP Morgan offers first class business-to-business services. To do that they employ the best people and by giving the best service they have benefitted and have an ever expanding business portfolio. However, there is a downside to that which is an equally expanding administration workload. Therefore, JP Morgan took an unprecedented plunge into unchartered waters of outsourcing. It goes without saying that JP Morgan completed an extensive cost/benefit analysis of outsourcing their administration services; as opposed to keeping these services in-house. Extensive research was done to satisfy JP Morgan that outsourcing will provide the exceptional levels of service their consumers enjoy.

JP Morgan completed their research and decided to outsource administration services. The crucial benefit for JP Morgan is that it will enable them to focus on their core competencies. Their primary workforce will play to their strengths: investing money and giving finance-based advice. Further benefits of outsourcing include reduced costs, continuity of service and working with a dedicated high-quality administration team that can provide a speedier and more flexible service than can be achieved in-house.

JP Morgan had to choose a business 'somewhere in the world' that they would be able to trust, as their multibillion pound business would be in jeopardy if JP Morgan chose a poor quality organization. Therefore, JP Morgan started to shop around. The first place businesses can look when choosing to outsource is The Global Services Location Index. The Index provides businesses, such as JP Morgan, with details as to which countries are offering and are successful in service provision. The top two countries in the Global Services Location Index are:

1 India, known for business process outsourcing, IT services and voice services.

2 China which has a reputation for business process outsourcing and IT services.

However, JP Morgan chose Sri Lanka, which is 16th in the Index. Sri Lanka at 16th place in the Index has gone up five places from the previous year's Index. Sri Lankans are known for being highly educated, talented and having technical skills. Not only have JP Morgan chosen Sri Lanka to outsource some of their business, Google, Nokia and the London Stock Exchange have also chosen Sri Lankan organizations to look after some of their service needs.

Question

1 What do you consider to be the key factors for outsourcing?

Sources: JP Morgan (2013) Why Outsource Now? www .jpmorgan.com/cm/BlobServer/is_why_outsource_now .pdf?blobkey=id&blobwhere=1320605420032&blobhead er=application/pdf&blobheadername1=Cache-Control&b lobheadervalue1=private&blobcol=urldata&blobtable=Mu ngoBlobs (accessed 12 April 2015). Kearney, A.T (2014) Global Services Location Index A Wealth of Choices: From Anywhere on Earth to No Location at All, www.atkearney .com/documents/10192/5082922/A+Wealth+of+Choices .pdf/61c80111-41b2-4411-ad1e-db4a3d6d5f0d

MANAGEMENT CHALLENGE 6.1

Toyota: Are they STILL growing too fast?

In the 6th edition of this book we reported that Toyota was trying to enter into so many different markets that the quality brand name suffered. The reason for this was in 2006 when 2.2 million vehicles were recalled to correct faults that included problems with their hybrid car, tyres bulging and possibly bursting in their small pick-up, and the possibility that air bags would not inflate in a crash. Four years later, Toyota was still putting quantity and expansion first and in 2010 it had to recall around 10 million vehicles for various faults including faulty floor mats, sticking accelerator pedals, braking software problems and steering malfunctions. The Toyota name, whose brand values are reliability, safety and quality, was severely tarnished. Investigations showed that by outsourcing so many products to meet Toyota's international expansion demand, quality standards had fallen.

President Akio Toyoda, grandson of the founder of the company, has decided enough is enough. What he means by that is 1. Enough cross-border expansion, 2. Enough 'big is best' mentality. Akio Toyoda realized that the ethos of the company had changed, the "workforce" were mainly robots and there is no heart or craftsmanship in the cars. This global company will not set up any new car manufacturing plants for 3 years, expansion is on hold. Robots are taking a back seat and skilled, experienced workers will become masters in crafting cars, improving production lines and reducing waste, all of which is underlined by **quality**. Currently over 100 Toyota manual, not robotic, intensive workspaces are in operation. Learning and skills are being developed within the workspaces in the hope that each fully trained member of staff will become a *Kami-sama* – Japanese for Gods – which is what the workers were called when he began working as a novice for Toyota. With the improvements to quality and automation, targets have been set for the future to sell more than 10 million vehicles. The hope is that a deceleration of big expansions, improved skills and quality workmanship will mean that Toyota will never be blamed again for 13 deaths because of faulty ignition switches.

Question

1 What are the lessons that Toyota has learned by recognizing it was growing too fast?

Sources: Trudell, C. Hagiwara, Y. and Jie, M. (2014) 'Toyota returns to focusing on craftsmanship; workers tapped for new ideas on improving manufacturing process', www.driving.ca (accessed 14 April 2015); Maynard, M. and Fackler, M. (2006) 'A rise in defects at Toyota puts its reputation at stake', *New York Times*. 5 August.

to this and gaining competitive advantage over local competition by differentiating their products through developing their marketing and customer service capability in the form of the brand image, higher levels of service or better technical support.

Globalization of technology. Technology is converging within and between industries, with similar processes and ideas being used, for example, in telecommunications, information technology hardware and software, and entertainment and consumer electronics. This means that new multifunctional products and services cross the traditional boundaries between the industry sectors. New technologies are adopted around the world at ever greater speeds. In many industries this is being driven by a small number of global players that have the market power to change the ways of working and generate sufficient demand from customers to make the wider application of the ideas more cost-effective. In this way the globalization of technology is contributing very significantly to the competitive advantage of the MNEs that are able to market products in a number of industry sectors because they have developed effective distribution channels and international promotion.

Globalization of customer requirements is resulting from the identification of worldwide customer segments, such as teenagers with similar worldwide tastes in music, fashion and fast food, and the very rich, who live the celebrity lifestyle and buy the most expensive fashion brands, fly first class or hire their own plane, stay at the same luxury hotels and own super performance cars. No matter where they originate they consume the same products and services. With industries becoming more globalized, the demands placed on the business support services, such as advertising agencies, accountants, law firms and consultants, are converging too. Customers in both the consumer and business-to-business markets are demanding and getting what they perceive to be added value global products and services which better meet their changing needs than those they have been used to receiving from national companies.

Globalization of competition between industry giants tends to result in the same fight being replicated in each corner of the world, with MNEs using largely similar competing product or service offers. Traditional national firms have been outmanoeuvred by aggressive fast-growing international competitors who are far better at exploiting technical changes and other globalization effects and winning customers with more sophisticated marketing. They are also able to cross-subsidize their activities between countries, so helping them to gain an unfair advantage over local competition.

Mature industries, as well as new technology sectors, are being affected by global competition. For example, while the majority of the top ten chemical companies are European, there is increasing competition particularly from Asian companies, which have different cost structures and systems of industry regulation. Success in these component and raw material industries has traditionally been dependent upon the product portfolio, the relationship with customers and the levels of technical service and support provided. Increasingly, the fact that these are components in the supply chain of branded consumer products means that successful suppliers must carry out more effective marketing to members of the supply chain that are closer to the customer.

Globalization of cooperation. To compete in all the major world markets it is necessary to make available huge financial resources, often outside the scope of individual firms. This is leading to the formation of alliances between major MNEs, members of a supply chain or between firms with complementary activities. The Japanese *keiretsu* go further in that they are formal organizations between banks, manufacturers and trading companies with cross-share ownership, and have the huge resources necessary to build businesses in the major world markets. This has enabled them to make investments over a number of years to establish a dominant long-term market position in a particular industry.

Globalization of distribution is occurring, first, as the supply chain becomes increasingly concentrated on fewer, more powerful channel distributors, retailers and logistics companies; second, as e-business technology dominates the exchange and transfer of data and the whole process of product and service transactions, including methods of product and service selling, ordering, customizing, progress chasing, payment arrangement and delivery confirmation; and third, as logistics become a source of competitive advantage, for example in retailing, having contributed to the international success of Walmart, Ikea and Tesco. For many organizations it can be argued that a global approach to distribution means organizing according to factors such as proximity to the population and transport infrastructure, rather than country borders.

Globalization of distribution is particularly important for companies such as Amazon that use e-commerce, as they must be able to make transaction and logistics arrangements to enable them to provide high levels of service and efficiency to customers, wherever they are located.

Globalization of communication and information. Major changes in telecommunications and information technology have had three effects. First, global communications such as satellite and cable TV, and the World Wide Web have made it essential that MNEs develop a consistent worldwide corporate identity and brand image. As consumers travel physically or virtually by way of the media or World Wide Web, they are exposed to communications and advertising originating from MNEs from many parts of the world. Consistency of the communication is vital for reinforcing brand familiarity, quality and values.

Second, digital technology is driving the localization and individuality of communications, for example through the proliferation of local TV channels, on-demand video and television and the continued development of the Internet, which allows greater exposure for individual communications. These developments go further than simply improving the accessibility of the traditional one-way communications with customers by adding a two-way, interactive dimension to the firms' relationships with their global customers. And clearly a three-way, interactive dimension is business to consumers, consumers to business and consumer to consumer.

Third, the explosion of social media through websites such as Facebook and Twitter, means that much more discussion of the MNE's activities takes place outside the influence and control of the company. Thus while the globalization of communications leads to global access for customers, the need to integrate communications is becoming ever more difficult to manage.

Globalization of the company's strategy, business programmes and processes. The result of these globalization effects is to pose challenges to firms to achieve both improved global operational efficiency and greater

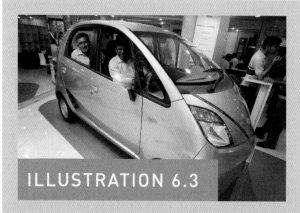

ILLUSTRATION 6.3

Conglomerate from India spreading its wings to the UK

Tata is a major conglomerate with many international companies under its umbrella. Each company works independently, having their own board of directors, challengers and strengths. However, all companies work to satisfy their stakeholders and bring quality of life to their community, a key quality of the Tata group. In total there are 32 publicly-listed Tata enterprises including Tata Motors, Tata Steel, Tata Consultancy Services, Tata Power, Tata Global Beverages, Tata Chemicals, Indian Hotels and Tata Teleservices.

Tata Motors is one of its most innovative arms of the group. Over 50 years ago an Engineering and Research Centre was formed at the Tata Motors campus in Pune, India. The research and development team was young, fresh and full of ideas, but lacked experience. During their early years Tata Motors operated under a 'licence raj' system where the government directed businesses regarding what they manufactured and where. Now the Indian government's mantra is 'Make in India', something that Tata Motors is showcasing through Pune's 6000 strong team of designers and engineers equipped with state of the art tools working on 50 engine platforms and 250 variants of vehicles. No longer are the engineers and designers stripping down engines from Mercedes Benz and

rebuilding them better and cheaper. Now Tata Motors is providing new technologies, applying sustainable and green principles whilst improving cost efficiencies that other motor engineers are looking to replicate. Interestingly, the Tata conglomerate does not research and design amazing new products in India, they choose to work in countries known for their expertise and experience.

Tata Group chairman emeritus Ratan Tata and the new chairman Cyrus P. Mistry recently visited the University of Warwick campus in Coventry to lay the foundation stone for a new £150 million Engineering and Research Centre (ERC). This National Automotive Innovation Centre (NAIC), the largest in Europe, is designed to provide the global market, through cutting-edge technology, with a state of the art automotive innovation centre, planned as the largest research facility of its kind in Europe, to create the next generation of vehicles for the global market. Once again, as they did in Pune, investment is being made in an Engineering and Research Centre where academia and industry are working together; this time across borders and not only are they providing high-tech solutions but tens of thousands of jobs. The ERC spans a 33 000 sq m complex and will provide space for 1000 engineers, designers and academics. The jobs will enable people to come in from apprenticeship level to senior managers.

When choosing where Tata Motors should expand internationally the UK was selected because of its long history of excellence in car manufacturing. Tata Motors are helping to build and strengthen the UK's reputation in this area.

Question

1 What are the key issues that Tata faces as it progresses to becoming a global company?

Sources: Tata enterprises www.tata.com (accessed 13 April 2015); *The Economic Times* (India) Ratan Tata launches automotive innovation centre in UK www.economictimes .indiatimes.com/articleshow/46600484.cms?utm_source= contentofinterest&utm_medium=text&utm_campaign=cppst (accessed 13 April 2015).

global market effectiveness. The global firm's response to managing the complexity of international marketing must include developing an all-embracing global strategy supported by effective marketing programmes and processes that will integrate the various disparate activities of the firm's far-flung strategic business units.

In considering each of these areas of globalization in turn it is possible to identify business sector examples in which the globalization trend is relatively advanced and others in which it is in its early stages. For example, accountancy and associated consultancy is dominated by four major players, whereas until the late 1990s retailing could be regarded as a largely national or, at most, subregional activity with few examples of retailers active in more than five or six countries. The challenge for global companies is to lead the development towards globalization in industry sectors where there is the greatest potential for growth. However, there is no guarantee that by simply being globally active in an industry sector a firm will benefit. Firms must be able to manage the environmental threats and exploit their market opportunities by building global competitive advantage. Illustration 6.3 shows how a firm from an emerging country has become a global player and is investing and expanding into a developed country.

Alternative strategic responses

It is against the background of the trend towards globalization and the need to build a worldwide presence that firms must develop strategic responses which are appropriate to their situation and are feasible to implement. For MNEs, the question may be how to rationalize their activities to gain greater focus and effectiveness. For firms that have progressed through the early stages of expansion into new country markets, as we discussed in the previous chapter, the next stage is to decide whether or not to progress further and, if so, what strategy they might adopt to enable them to manage their involvement in many countries. Underpinning the growth strategy in either case must be some fundamental decisions about the product portfolio and expansion into new country markets.

The international competitive posture

The level of geographic development and product strength determine the strategic options available to a company. Gogel and Larreche (1989) identify four types of competitors along the two dimensions of product range and geographic coverage, as shown in Figure 6.2. The position of a company on the international competitive posture matrix will determine the strategic options that organizations can consider when deciding upon their international strategy.

   Kings. Because these firms have a wide geographic coverage and strong product portfolio they are in a strong competitive position. They have been able to expand geographically and have not dispersed their resources into weak products. They are in the best position to have an effective global strategy and are the true global companies.

   Barons. These companies have strong products in a limited number of countries. This makes geographic expansion attractive to them unless their domestic and close-by markets are large and untapped in

FIGURE 6.2   The international competitive posture matrix

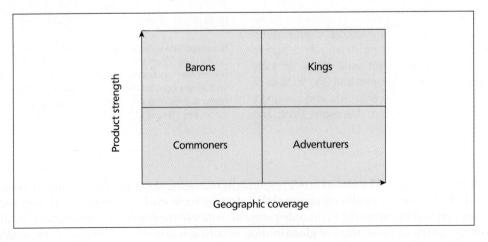

Source: Gogel and Larreche (1989).

which case there is little need for international expansion. However, without domestic growth opportunities barons can be attractive to companies wishing to supplement their own product strength and therefore they may be takeover targets.

Adventurers. These have been driven to expand geographically, but they lack a strong portfolio. They are vulnerable to an increasing level of global competition. Their challenge is to consolidate their product position by focusing on internal product development, acquisition or by eliminating products to concentrate on a narrower portfolio in a classic global niche strategy.

Commoners. Commoners have a product portfolio with relatively weak international potential and narrow geographic coverage. They may have benefited from legal barriers protecting them from intense competition in their existing markets. They are likely acquisition targets, and before any geographical expansion they need to build their product portfolio. A likely international strategy could be one of supplying own-brand products to retailers.

Increasing geographic coverage and product strength means competition for resources and each quadrant of the matrix reflects the trade-offs that may become necessary. The position of a firm on the matrix reflects how it has been able to balance its resources between consolidation and expansion of geographic coverage and product strength. Technology companies such as Microsoft were initially adventurers, marketing their operating system widely before building up their product range to become the 'kings' they are today. Companies from Asian markets frequently are 'barons', developing a strong product range and building their home or close regional markets before developing internationally.

Global strategy drivers

The fundamental driver of a global strategy is whether the market allows significant global standardization of the marketing activity or whether substantial adaptation is needed to address local differences and expectations. The challenge for global firm strategy development is to maximize the efficiency and effectiveness of their operations. While having a completely standardized marketing offer, products, services, communications, etc. would be very efficient, for most companies it would not maximize effectiveness in revenue generation, given the differing needs of customers from different countries and cultures. The second driver is what orientation the company adopts – in other words how it sees itself in the global market.

Before looking at the market factors it is useful to consider the company orientation, shown in Figure 6.3.

The **standardization** and **adaptation** drivers lead to the worldwide strategy options illustrated in Figure 6.4 with, at one extreme, the concept of a multidomestic approach in which the firm has a completely different strategy for every single market and, at the other extreme, a global approach in which everything in the marketing activity is standardized in all countries. In addition, an ethnocentric firm that is very focused on the domestic market might seek to export its home market model with few modifications. In practice, firms adopt a combination of standardization and adaptation of the various elements of the marketing management programmes and processes by globalizing some elements and localizing others. In broad terms it is possible to categorize a firm's strategic development as multidomestic, global or regional, a third strategy in which separate, but largely standardized marketing strategies are implemented across a region of the world.

The largest, most complex companies in the world use a combination of all these strategies. A transnational approach is one in which the firm has a standardized identity and corporate values throughout the firm but delivers its strategic objectives through composite strategies which contain elements of multidomestic, regional and global strategies. The global marketing strategy is influenced significantly by the supply chain decisions relating to location of operations and outsourcing arrangements.

Zou and Cavusgil (2002) identify three perspectives of global marketing strategy: the standardization perspective, the configuration perspective and the integration perspective. The global firm locates its supply chain activities in those countries where they can be carried out most efficiently. Components are then transferred to another country for assembly, before the highly standardized finished goods are exported to the countries in which they will be sold, supported by largely standardized marketing. Global firms then integrate their activities and competitive moves to enable them to become major players in all major markets. Increased outsourcing makes these tasks more challenging as success depends on customer requirements being met on time.

FIGURE 6.3   Company orientation in global strategy development

Global orientation	Focus
Ethnocentric	Because the domestic market is considered to be the most important, the company adopts home country standards and values, and assumes that the marketing offer in the home country will be acceptable in new country markets. Standardized products and services are typically designed for the domestic country and exported. The brand usually reflects the domestic country image.
Polycentric	Each country market is unique and the marketing offer is designed to meet the individual needs of the customers of each country. Typically a country manager would ensure that the products and services are adapted locally and the brand is developed to incorporate cultural differences. This would typically result in a multi-domestic strategy.
Regiocentric	Developing a regional strategy as the geographic market focus, for example, a company might develop a product and service portfolio for Europe, or for Southern Africa. The organization gives the regional managers considerable autonomy but the regional focus can leave missed opportunities to standardize.
Geocentric	This is the global or transnational company that sees the entire world as a potential market. The strategy adopted focuses on one global customer segment that requires a globally standardized product or service. Alternatively a geocentric company develops a transnational strategy that uses a strategy based on a standardized identity and well communicated values but then integrates standardized and adapted elements of the marketing offer to efficiently meet the diverse needs of customers.

Standardizing the various elements of the marketing process has the aim of scale economies and experience curve effects in operations, research and development, and marketing, and concentrating value chain activity in a few country locations to exploit comparative advantage and so improve efficiency. The experience curve effect or learning curve relates to the relationship between experience and efficiency.

FIGURE 6.4   Alternative worldwide strategies

Standardization and adaptation

The challenge facing firms with aspirations to become truly effective global players appears to be turning widespread international presence into global competitive advantage. The critical success factor in achieving this is to offer added value for global customers by providing them with benefits that are significantly better than those provided by the competitors, particularly local competitors. The benefits can be tangible, for example a global product, such as Intel processors, that are broadly the same worldwide, or intangible, for example a brand such as Rolex that is recognized worldwide. At the same time they must aggressively seek cost efficiencies that will enable the firm to offer better value for money than their competitors.

In practice, firms manage these apparently incompatible requirements by using strategies that are appropriate to their own situation, and striking a balance between the different degrees of standardization or adaptation of the various elements of international marketing process.

In general:

- Marketing objectives and strategies are more readily standardized than operational marketing decisions.
- Within the marketing mix, products are most easily standardized, promotion less so and distribution and pricing only with difficulty.
- The more operational the decision the more likely it is to be differentiated.

Consequently the elements of marketing management should be seen as being at different points of a continuum of standardization, where the product and service image is generally easier to standardize than individual country pricing.

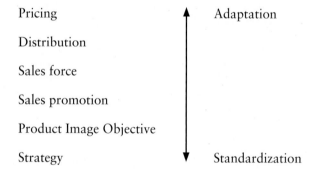

Pricing — Adaptation

Distribution

Sales force

Sales promotion

Product Image Objective

Strategy — Standardization

Of course, as Akgün *et al.* (2014) state some businesses will both standardize *and* adapt elements of their marketing mix keeping the product brand name standardized but adapting on-pack promotions or colour and distribution opportunities dependent upon which country they enter. See Management Challenge 6.2 for an example of a Turkish furniture business's marketing mix challenges.

Globally standardized strategy

A company adopting a global strategic orientation makes no distinction between domestic and foreign market opportunities, seeking to serve an essentially identical customer segment appearing in many countries around the world, and developing global strategies to compete with other global firms. Global marketing can be defined as the focusing of an organization's resources on the selection and exploitation of global market opportunities consistent with and supportive of its short-term strategic objectives and goals.

Global marketing is the realization that a firm's foreign marketing activities, in whatever form they take, need to be supportive of some higher objective than just the immediate exploitation of a foreign market opportunity. Global marketing can, therefore, involve the selection of a country for its potential contribution to globalization benefits, even entering an unattractive market which has global strategic significance – for example, the home market of a competitor. Thus an organization with such a global focus formulates a long-term strategy for the company as a whole and then coordinates the strategies of local subsidiaries to support this.

MANAGEMENT CHALLENGE 6.2

Turkish B2B and their marketing mix

Domestic businesses often feel compelled to expand internationally because their domestic economy is weak and/or unemployment is high, both of which lead to low consumer spend. Alternatively, to take advantage of economies of scale businesses consider it a wise move to make more of the same product and find new consumer marketing internationally. The latter is known as Ansoff's market development growth strategy (See Figure 5.4 in Chapter 5). A Turkish furniture business chose the market development growth strategy as it saw business-to-business (B2B) opportunities outside their domestic market. During the research project they realized that they could standardize some of their marketing mix elements, but adapt others.

The product name, brand and style of furniture items were standardized across international markets. However, the colours of the products needed to be adapted as western European consumers preferred lighter or white furniture, whereas Romanian consumers

preferred much darker colours. The price for the same product was adapted for each international country. The pricing policy was based on a competition-based policy. This meant that the Turkish furniture was costed at a price similar to other furniture of similar standard available in each country. The marketing mix place was adapted too. In some countries, such as France and Greece, the Turkish furniture business could sell direct to independent franchisees. However, in Germany and Austria the Turkish furniture business could only sell to chain stores. Therefore, the distribution B2B network available in each country contributed to the level of standardization or adaptation required. The Turkish furniture business provided standardized advertising material for international stores that sold their furniture on an exclusive basis. However, they did allow the international stores to adapt the advertising material to suit local consumer needs.

Question

1 What are the advantages and disadvantages of the adaptation and standardization of marketing mix elements for the Turkish furniture?

Source: Akgün, A. E., Keskin, H. and Ayar, H. (2014). 'Standardization and adaptation of international marketing mix activities: A case study', *Procedia-Social and Behavioral Sciences*, 150, 609–18.

Many writers have offered views on this issue. For example Levitt (1983) suggested that in order to be competitive in the world market, firms should shift their emphasis from local customized products to globally standardized products that are advanced, functional, reliable and low priced. Buzzell (1968) argued that product standardization has the benefits of (a) economies of scale, (b) faster accumulation of learning through experience that can aid efficiency and effectiveness and (c) reduced costs of design modification.

In summarizing the forces at work in the standardization debate Meffet and Bolz (1993) describe the globalization push and pull factors which are driving marketing standardization, but technology advances over the last two decades have led to counter push and pull factors for customization to meet the needs and expectations of individual and small groups of customers, as we have discussed in previous chapters. The globalization and customization drivers are shown in Figure 6.5. Not only have many barriers to standardization across markets been removed or reduced enabling cost savings to be made, the previously prohibitive additional costs of customization have been hugely reduced by technological advances.

The challenge for firms is to achieve efficiency and effectiveness in delivering marketing programmes and processes. The opportunity to standardize programmes and processes and reduce cost and improve efficiency through economies of scale and the experience effect (or learning curve) is driven by the globalization of customer demand and competition, and the possibility for global players to cross-subsidize markets to increase sales volume (offset losses in one market by profits from other markets). Moreover, globalization of technology means that new products have shorter lives and the rapidly increasing research and development costs require the high costs of innovation to be recovered more quickly, due to the shorter pay back cycles for new products. Rapid diffusion of new products into all possible global markets is necessary.

FIGURE 6.5 Globalization and customization push and pull factors

Source: Meffett and Bolz (1993) in Halliburton and Hunerberg (eds) *European Marketing Readings and Cases,* Addison-Wesley.

Driven by the customization push and pull factors, firms are also focusing on the effectiveness of their marketing by customizing their offer. It is still possible, however, to make cost savings by developing standardized processes. For example, while it may not be possible to or desirable to completely standardize the marketing programmes, such as the product range, advertising campaigns and prices across all markets, it is possible to globally standardize the processes by which the product portfolio is managed, new products are launched, marketing communications are delivered, online and offline advertising space is booked, and how the marketing information system is populated with data and the marketing planning processes are integrated around the world. In this situation some of the globalization drivers such as economies of scale and the experience effect (or learning curve) can be achieved through process standardization.

Market fragmentation has increased and, in practice, global firms have to strike an appropriate balance between the relative advantages of standardization, adaptation to local tastes and customization to individual customer needs. There is little point in standardizing programmes for marketing products and services if consumers reject them.

Multidomestic strategies A company adopting a multidomestic orientation assumes that foreign market opportunities are as important as home market opportunities. However, the company takes the view that the differences between its international markets are so acute that widespread adaptation is necessary to meet market needs and to retain competitive leverage in local markets. Thus, the company essentially follows a differentiated marketing strategy with individual marketing mix strategies in many of their world markets.

For many major businesses there are few benefits to be obtained from widespread standardization of their activities. Consequently a well-organized and managed multidomestic strategy is an effective method for many companies for developing a global business.

An example of an organization which can be accurately characterized as having a multidomestic strategy is Asea Brown Boveri (ABB), discussed in Illustration 6.4.

A key factor in the strategy is encouraging senior managers to be entrepreneurial in responding to local customer needs, industry standards and different stages of economic development.

ILLUSTRATION 6.4

ABB: a new model of global entrepreneurialism – good while it lasted?

ABB was formed by a merger of Sweden's Asea and the Swiss company Brown Boveri. It had customers in the process industries, manufacturing and consumer industries and in utilities (oil, gas and petrochemicals). When chief executive Percy Barnevik was faced with merging two companies with different business cultures and operations, he decided to create a fundamentally different model of how a large MNE could be organized

and managed. He created the new head office in Zurich to make the merger less like a takeover by the Swedes, and started dispersing the two head offices of 6000 staff among a number of frontline units.

He created a head office with 135 staff managing 1300 companies with 5000 profit centres. He cut 90 per cent of headquarters staff by moving 30 per cent into the small business units (SBUs), 30 per cent into free-standing service centres concerned with value-adding activities, and eliminated 30 per cent of the jobs. Similar huge cuts in management were made in the headquarters of the subsidiaries.

The management within the SBUs, which usually had fewer than 200 employees, were given a substantially enhanced role in managing their business. ABB was one of the most admired firms of the 1990s. Bartlett and Ghoshall (2015) said that Barnevik's achievement was combining the contradictions of big and small, local and global, economies of scale and intimate market knowledge to create a truly global organization.

ABB employed 160 000 staff in 100 countries and a large part of their manufacturing was moved away from the developed countries to the developing countries, including Eastern Europe. By employing people in developing countries ABB was in a position to sell further expertise and services as they helped build the countries' infrastructure.

Barnevik was succeeded by Jorgen Centremann in October 2000, but he lasted less than two years as the company's share price halved. ABB missed its profit targets, it nearly ran out of cash as its debts mounted, and in 2002 it made its first loss of US$787 million. The problems were compounded by the threat that a US unit would go bankrupt because of the potential liabilities (capped at US$1.3 billion by a US court) resulting from a number of massive lawsuits involving asbestos.

Question

1 Could the model be blamed for ABB's problems?

Thus, while there are many forces driving companies towards achieving a global strategy through standardizing as many marketing activities as possible, there are also very important prevailing arguments persuading companies that they can also achieve an effective worldwide strategy through a multidomestic approach. These forces are as follows.

Industry standards remain diverse   For many traditional industries such as those based upon engineering and particularly those that involve large investment in plant and equipment, the cost of harmonization of standards is high and the progress to harmonization is slow. The markets for these industries often involve a country's infrastructure, transport and utilities and, consequently, depend on often protracted government spending decisions. Usually in making decisions such as these, governments will give consideration not simply to market factors, but also to the impact on the economy, environment and the electorate's expectations.

Customers continue to demand locally differentiated products Cultural heritage and traditions still play a strong role in areas such as food, drink and shopping. While there are increasing moves to accept cross-border products, there is still resistance in many cultures.

Being an insider remains critically important The perceived country of origin effect of goods still has a bearing on take-up of products, and local manufacturing of goods is frequently necessary to overcome this scepticism. In business-to-business marketing, there is a definite bias in favour of products sourced from particular areas, such as Silicon Valley in the US, and so IT/electronic firms often decide to set up local manufacture there.

A further factor is that companies that make a significant commitment to a country by establishing manufacturing, research and development capability are likely to be consulted by the government as they prepare new legislation. This should result in providing greater opportunities for influencing than would be possible for a company that shows little commitment to the country, perhaps simply exporting to the country.

Global organizations are difficult to manage In finding ways to coordinate far-flung operations, firms have to decentralize and replace home country loyalties with a system of corporate values and loyalties that is acceptable to the firm's staff around the world. For some companies this proves to be problematic and, in some cases, the head office values and culture can be significantly different from those of the workforce. Their desire to impose standardized products with little or no consultation on their country operations is very often seen as arrogant by local staff.

Management myopia Many products and services that are suitable candidates for global marketing are ignored as managers fail to seize the opportunity to build their business in a wider range of markets. On the other hand, products that work well in the managers' home markets are often believed to be acceptable to customers worldwide without being given full consideration. Self-reference criteria often makes it difficult for managers to take other than a narrow, national view of international marketing. Moreover, because there are no guarantees that a business can succeed, the firm must be willing to risk the heavy investment that the move from a multidomestic to a global strategy requires. For some, the resources required and the risks involved are simply too great.

Regional strategy

One of the most significant developments in global marketing strategy is how firms respond to the rise of the regional trading blocs. Even in globalized industries, company strategies are becoming more of a composite of regionally focused strategies and programmes. For many companies, regionalization represents a more manageable compromise between the extremes of global standardization and multidomestic strategies. For example, there are some obvious differences in the challenges of marketing to North America, Africa and South East Asia and different strategies are usually formulated for each region.

However, many firms create regional management for the convenience of creating manageable teams rather than to exploit regional similarities. For example, a number of MNEs create a regional division titled EMEA, which comprises Europe, Middle East and Africa – regions which might be characterized by their differences rather than their similarities.

Regional trading blocs tend to favour their own MNEs, and for those companies located outside the region there can be significant tariff and non-tariff barriers. Public–private sector committees decide on standards, such as car emissions, safety standards and security. By shifting operations and decision making inside the region an MNE can gain advantage from being part of the consultation and decision-making process.

The key to developing effective regional strategies is deciding in what ways the marketing strategy for one region should be differentiated from the others, and being able to respond quickly to threats or opportunities that emerge in the region.

However, while regional strategies are built around the common elements within a region and the distinctiveness of the region, in practice the differences within the region are still huge. Many organizations

MANAGEMENT CHALLENGE 6.3

Go global, stay local

Bernard Anault is the owner of 60 LVMH luxury brands including the iconic Louis Vuitton handbags, Dom Perignon champagne, Bulgari jewellery and Dior fragrances. He and the family business are ranked 13th in Forbes' (2015) World's Billionaires list; based on their net worth of $38 billion. They have the largest share in the European luxury market with US$36.38 billion dollars in sales. With their head office in Paris, Bernard Anault promotes the heritage and culture of French fashion through their luxury brands.

One of LVMH's competitors, Hermes, also has their head office in Paris. Hermes are also a family-run business gaining US$4.48 billion from the European luxury market. Hermes are known for their scarves, fragrances and of course the Birkin and Kelly handbags that have a celebrity A-list following.

Both companies are global 'big luxury' companies whose products are available online, through their own retail stores and concessions in airports and hotels around the world. Products and promotion is standardized; they feel no need for adaptations. Their prices remain high, appealing in the main to the middle and upper socio-economic groups. Both brands are particularly popular in developing countries where such well-known brands clearly signify a person's wealth. Some, however, say that the Louis Vuitton logo is a 'look at me' status driven brand. Others say that Hermes provides status as it often makes consumers wait six months for products to come to market. Nevertheless, both brands hold their value and re-sale value very well – with Hermes Birkin bags often selling for 50 per cent more than the original sale price.

Questions

1 Why can some brands go global, but stay local to their heritage?

2 What are the benefits of this strategy for the businesses and the consumer?

Sources: Forbes (2015) Billionaire List www.forbes.com /profile/bernard-arnault/ (accessed 13 April 2015); *The Economist* (2014) 'Beauty and the beasts' www.economist .com/news/special-report/21635758-think-global-act-artisan -beauty-and-beasts (accessed 13 April 2015).

Think Global and Act Local and develop their product range accordingly. Therefore, the big differences in the country environments and markets require more responsive approaches rather than centralized multi-national management. Companies are taking the opportunity from the formation of regional trading blocs to include regional objectives and plans as a significant part of their worldwide strategy and build on existing, or form new, cooperative trading relationships. Starbucks have understood this concept, often known as glocalization, by offering to not only change the menus to suit consumer variations but they have also brought a different localization feel through the layout of their coffee shops. In US New Orleans the store brings the local spirit into their store by enabling local artists to display their paintings; this has gone down very well with positive feedback on MyStarbucksideas.force.com.

The prime motivation in the formation of the regional trading blocs is to enable indigenous companies to build the critical mass of activity within the home region necessary to enable them to compete effectively in global markets. The European Union, for example, has strived to create collaborative working between participants in a common supply chain, or those offering complementary or competitive products. Where the companies come from different countries, political differences do still arise, particularly if national governments are concerned about the retention of jobs in sensitive industries, such as the defence and airline industries. Airbus is one such consortium in the manufacture of aeroplanes in Europe that has at different times benefited and suffered from political interference.

Transnational strategies   If a firm has sufficient power and resources to exploit all the available opportunities on a worldwide basis, with little need to adapt strategies or involve partners to any great extent, then a simple strategy can be developed. However, many multinationals have a wide range of products and services, some of which might be suited to global and others to multidomestic development.

The successful exploitation of these opportunities might require a much more flexible approach to strategic development; for example, it could involve a number of partners in licensing, joint ventures and strategic alliances as well as wholly owned operations.

Transnational companies integrate diverse assets, resources and people into operating units around the world. Through flexible management processes and networks, transnational companies aim to build three strategic capabilities:

- Global scale efficiency and competitiveness.
- National level responsiveness and flexibility.
- Cross-market capacity to leverage learning on a worldwide basis.

Nistor (2014) and Bartlett and Ghoshal (2015) state that the aims of transnational companies generally use standardized products that are flexible to cope with local consumer needs leading to the firm's global scale efficiency and competitiveness in its totality. This task means the firm needs the ability to recognize market opportunities and risks across national borders. The overall goal is to achieve global competitiveness through a fully integrated strategy and operations. Thus, a transnational approach is not a particular strategy, but a strategic perspective that evolves as firms and the markets in which they operate increase in complexity. Hewlett Packard is a transnational organization because some of its marketing operations and research and development are centralized and standardized, whereas other units operate with a substantial degree of independence. It has a strong corporate identity and some of its promotional themes, for example around e-business, are common throughout the firm. It has also formed strategic alliances with partners in order to carry out certain research and development activities where it is likely to benefit from the participation of partners. In such organizations the implications for strategic development are significant. A transnational strategy that is to achieve global competitive advantage needs to accommodate some, or all of the following:

- Simple and complex individual product and market policies, which may be independent or interdependent.
- Customer segments that are specific and unique to a cross-national niche market so the resultant segments are transnational and valid across borders.
- Working closely with firms that are customers, suppliers, competitors and partners at the same time, but simultaneously ensuring that the values of the company are maintained and demonstrated to the external stakeholders through establishing clear and unambiguous positioning in all markets.
- Maintaining and building meaningful and added value relationships in the supply chain.

International marketing management for global firms

So far in this chapter we have identified the changing trends in the business environment that are leading to increasing globalization and the factors that affect the firms' response to this, particularly in the way they standardize or adapt their marketing programmes and processes. We have shown distinct differences in the way global strategies can be developed to meet individual firms' situations. Implementing these global strategies, however, poses considerable problems and it is to these that we now turn.

As in the previous chapter, it is useful for the discussion to be based loosely upon the McKinsey 7S framework, which includes the hardware elements of strategy, structure and systems and the software elements of management style, staff, skills and shared values. Again we start with the hardware elements of strategy, systems and organization structure.

Global strategy implementation

Global firms have the objective of developing effective business operations in all the major markets in the world in order to maximize their performance. In the past they may well have prioritized the developed economies in North America, Europe and Asia, principally Japan. More recently these firms have developed a significant presence in many more markets. Now the focus for investment has focused on the BRIC countries, Brazil, Russia, India and China. Research and investment will also soon turn to the MINT countries (Mexico, Indonesia, Nigeria and Turkey) as growth prospects look healthy. Countries in the Middle East are seeking to grow and diversify their business activity away from a dependence on oil. They too are gaining a foothold in the other emerging markets of Asia, Africa and South America if they wish to benefit from the anticipated future development.

However, building a **global presence** is hugely expensive, and many firms see no value in expanding globally if their home country or region offers sufficient growth prospects without marketing their products and services in what they might perceive to be higher risk areas. US and Chinese companies have a large domestic market and, despite the rapid growth prospects of other regions of the world, their unfamiliarity often makes them unattractive. Despite this, with growth rates four times as high in Asia as in the rest of the world, almost all the Fortune 500 and leading European companies invest heavily in this area.

Opportunities in emerging markets for global firms

Most multinational enterprises, particularly from developed countries, focus on the customers that are wealthy enough now or will be in the future to purchase their premium goods and services, and companies such as McDonald's and Yum are opening new outlets at unprecedented rates.

However, for many multinationals the very poorest parts of the world appear to be largely economically inactive and offer little opportunity for profitable growth. A small number of MNEs have traded with these countries for many years, often buying and selling raw materials or selling processing machinery, and developing a presence by selling basic products to the consumer and B2B market. Prahalad and Hart (2002) have suggested that there is a pyramid of wealth, shown in Table 6.5, and emphasize that those with the lowest incomes still have the potential to create a significant demand for goods and services if they meet the specific needs of poor consumers and ensure that products and services are marketed to them in a sensitive way. While it might be expected that consumers from emerging markets simply want unsophisticated products, it may well prove a mistake to try to market to emerging markets those products that have reached the end of their life cycle and been replaced in developing countries. The particular situation in an emerging market may require a specific, innovative solution and this may miss out a particular technology development stage.

Hart and London (2005) have identified examples of innovative solutions that include not only products and services that satisfy customer demand but also create new routes to market that are more efficient in these emerging markets. This often requires the MNE to work with partners through less formal channels and networks than they are used to. The resulting solutions, such as lower cost manufacturing techniques, design and distribution can then be marketed to other parts of the world. For example, development of technology and changing economic environments is making MNEs consider new networks as shown in Illustration 6.5.

The instability of emerging markets, crime and corruption are some of the main problems that MNEs have to deal with directly to ensure they protect their staff and reputation; however, their unfamiliarity with these markets makes this difficult, and here too local partners can prove invaluable.

The emergence of MNEs from emerging markets

So far we have focused on strategies of firms that already have a strong presence in developed countries and wish to extend that to emerging markets, but a current feature of global marketing is the emergence of future

Table 6.5 The global pyramid of wealth

	Global population (mn)	Purchasing power (US$)
The wealthy	800	15 000
The emerging middle class	1500	1500–15 000
Low income markets	4000	<1500

Source: Prahalad, C.K. and Hart, S.L. (2002) 'The fortune at the bottom of the pyramid', *Strategy and Business,* 26: 54–67, Booz and Co.

ILLUSTRATION 6.5

The rise of the machines in emerging markets

One of the largest MNEs, General Electric (GE), is investing $200 million in India. GE are building a new factory on 250 000 square feet of Indian land, housing machines imported from Germany and Japan. But this factory is not just a factory; the factory is a SMART factory. What makes it smart is not the fact that the factory is full of the latest hardware and software, it is the way the hardware and software talk to each other that makes this factory smart. The robotics and automated processes talk through a specially devised intranet where big data is shared. The big data then provides the 3D printers with imaging instructions which go on to build anything from a huge wind turbine to a small valve for use by medical surgeons. What is even more exciting is that the smart factory can change its production output using up to 1500 imaging instructions each year. Technology has enabled this unexpected, but long awaited change in manufacturing.

Smart factories such as GE's are currently rare but the idea of them is causing a stir in the manufacturing world. Factories such as these enable MNEs to gain economies of scale which is a major benefit. In the past GE's factories tended to be built with one product in mind: huge investment sitting idle if no orders arrive, as happened during the recent downturn in manufacturing output. Now GE can produce hundreds of different products and appeal to many different markets.

The opportunity to build a brand new multimodel smart factory in India has come about because of the change in the global economy. In the past China has been the dominant force in manufacturing output. The change in the global economy and the decentralization of manufacturing has made MNEs, such as GE, see alternative places to do business.

Question

1 What lessons can be drawn from GE's development into India?

Source: Das G. (2014) 'Rise of the machines', *Business Today*, 15 July.

players. The high growth rates in the BRIC and MINT countries are providing the platforms for the new generation of global players. Bracken (2007) suggests that it will be multinationals from emerging markets that could achieve the greatest growth in the future; as shown by Tata in Illustration 6.3. Developing countries have traditionally depended upon foreign companies to supply job training and know-how and, in exchange, multinationals, usually from western countries, could force concessions from national governments enabling them to build sales in new markets. Globalization and the requirements of a market economy, therefore, reduced the power of national governments. Now the governments of the strongest emerging countries are no longer willing to surrender their home market to foreign companies that exert undue influence in the industry sector and which might delay technology transfer into the developing country and so delay the economic development of the country. The size of the home markets in India and China provides domestic companies with a large base to build the potential multinational companies of the future. China, for example, has decided to develop its own car industry and India, following the removal of central planning and bureaucracy in the 1990s, has created some strong IT outsourcing businesses, such as Wipro, Tata and Infosys.

In emerging markets, volume and low cost have driven the hypergrowth and the ambitions of young managers. Entrepreneurs spot opportunities in other sectors than their own, so a property developer might move into computers (*Economist*, 2010a).

Leggett, (2013) suggests that whilst the BRIC countries have grabbed the attention of MNCs for a number of years, their deceleration is starting to move the major players to ASEAN (Association of Southeast Asian Nations) which includes Malaysia, the Phillipines and Indonesia. However, success stories from these countries may take some time and naturally business success from the BRIC countries will be evaluated to support greater achievements in other developing nations. There is some evidence that this is changing, partly through organic development and partly through acquisition. Tata is meeting the needs of local, first time, middle class consumers through its Nano car development, but has also taken over Citigroup's Global Services outsourcing division. China's BYD in batteries and Huawei, second largest supplier in the world to Ericsson in mobile telecom equipment, equally provide business customers with cost effective solutions. These companies are building their global presence also through acquisition, as discussed at various points (*Economist* 2010b).

Multinationals from developed markets will now have to work harder to access these fast-growing emerging markets as it will prove to be much harder to go it alone and more difficult to exert control over local partners who now see the possibility of developing their own global businesses.

Multinationals from the last generation of emerging markets have already become global players with dominant market shares in western markets. Toyota, from Japan, now close to becoming the leading US car maker, was virtually unknown in the West until 1965, and Samsung from South Korea is vying with Apple for first place in the worldwide mobile phone market.

For firms wishing to build a truly global presence, there are a number of challenges, including:

■ Responding to the changing basis of **competitive advantage**.
■ Increasing **global appeal** by building the **global brand**.
■ Developing sustainable strategies.
■ Creating a global presence by achieving **global reach**.
■ Managing diverse and complex activities across a range of often similar but frequently disparate markets and cultures.

Regardless of which strategy is chosen the Boston Consulting Group certainly recommend that to remain and emerge competitive in the global arena it is essential to understand the global challenges, develop and professionalize practices at all key stages and most importantly drive forward though innovation.

Global appeal and the changing basis of competitive advantage

All major firms today are capable of offering good-quality products and services that offer value for customers, so this is no longer a source of differentiation and competitive advantage as competitors quickly offer lower cost alternatives.

The rapid growth of the Japanese car industry was largely based on value for money criteria, with quality, reliability and performance at a reasonable cost being the basis of the appeal. However, as the Japanese manufacturers, such as Toyota, have continued to develop more sophisticated cars and establish local supply chains, their competitors from the emerging economies, such as Kia and Hyundai, have replaced them in offering cheaper and even better value for money cars. At the same time a number of firms, such as Tata with its Nano, are competing for the very lowest price car segment. The car market is highly competitive and characterized by over-capacity, and it is becoming ever harder for major global players to be consistently profitable. The question is how and where they should compete, particularly against the new players that are identifying new segments. A few of the car makers from the developed countries have substantially improved their quality and reliability and offer designs and brand imagery with better consumer appeal for the most affluent customers in developed and emerging markets.

It is possible to observe similar changes in the information technology industry as cost conscious consumers increasingly expect computer suppliers to offer improved performance, functionality, quality, security and greater reliability as well as becoming more 'user-friendly' – all at considerably reduced prices. To attract affluent consumers, firms must now offer more intangible benefits, including better styling, higher levels of service support and advice, more interesting and appealing software and online services, and a 'cool' brand. The spectacular performance of Apple was the appeal of the iMac, iPod, iPhone and iPad to a design-conscious segment. Consumers are becoming more confident with technology, and are willing to experiment by downloading software and multiple apps from a variety of online platforms.

Consumers are also prepared to mix and match basic with expensive items. The cost of basic clothing sold through supermarkets and stores such as Zara and Primark has fallen dramatically in recent years, making it difficult for retailers to operate in the middle ground between high fashion and low cost. But high fashion – and cost – items, shoes and handbags are also matched with basic items.

In B2B situations, the basis of competitive advantage is also changing and specialty niches are becoming rarer especially when new technology such as 3D printing has a major impact on industry. 3D printing enables big growth opportunities in toys and footwear. The interesting part is not just the fact that technology can print an exact 3D copy of a 'must have' toy but the fact that there would be no shipping or transportation costs (*Strategy and Business*, 2015).

Increasing global appeal by building the global brand

Branding is usually considered within the marketing strategy as part of the product and service policy, and we have addressed the use of brands in international marketing there. Global brands, however, are inextricably tied up with achieving global appeal and building a global presence, so we have included a broader-based discussion of global branding at this point.

Global brand management

Holt, Quelch and Taylor (2004) noted that three decades ago Levitt was arguing that organizations should offer standardized products globally, but now consumers find it difficult to relate to generic standardized products, so firms have adopted 'glocal' strategies in which they have customized product features, selling and marketing to local tastes and instead build their efficiencies on a global scale around 'back office' activities of which customers are unaware.

Holt *et al.* (2004) found that most transnational firms are perceived differently from other firms because of their power, and have suffered from this because they have been major targets for anti-globalization protests. However, most people choose one global brand over another based on three dimensions: quality, indicated by the firms' global stature, the cultural myths and stories created by the firms, and the firms' efforts in corporate social responsibility. In the past for some brands the country of origin of the brand was important as it was often part of the cultural myth, but Holt *et al.* believe that this is no longer important. Indeed the trend for a number of global brands has been to dissociate themselves from their country of origin, for example, British Airways has renamed itself BA, British Petroleum has become BP and Kentucky Fried Chicken has become KFC.

For decades the power of the biggest global brands seemed to increase steadily but their dominant position now seems to be more dependent on success in newer markets and responding to changes in their existing markets.

Khashani (1995) draws attention to changes in a number of factors which affect the performance of the brands:

- Customers are better educated, better informed, more sceptical, more willing to experiment, less brand loyal, much more media aware and have higher expectations of the total package.
- Competition is more aggressive, with more rapid launches of higher quality 'me-too' products.
- Retailers have installed better electronic point-of-sale technology and, as a result, have greater awareness of brand performance. In response to better consumer information, they have introduced better quality private labels.

These changes in the brand market environment have been compounded by weaknesses in brand management, including:

- low investment
- inadequate product development
- poor consumer communication
- an emphasis on quick paybacks rather than long-term brand building
- too little innovation; and
- an emphasis upon small modifications.

For global brand success it is essential to listen to the market and get closer to global customers. It is necessary to be bold, think creatively, set new market and performance standards, and take risks. The aim must be to think globally, launch products and services sequentially and rapidly across markets and build world brands. There are many 'almost great' brands but only a few are truly great.

While the progress of global brands seems to be unstoppable, they do not always succeed. Walmart withdrew from South Korea and Germany in 2006 because financial losses could no longer be tolerated. Despite promising for years that performance could be improved, it never managed a turnaround. In both countries Walmart failed to compete with dominant local companies that were better at catering for local tastes. Moreover, Barbaro (2006) notes that in Germany in the late 1990s Walmart changed the name of its stores from a well known reliable local brand to Walmart, a name that was unfamiliar to local shoppers.

The global development of brands can lead to some dilemmas. Both Google in China and RIM (Blackberry) in the United Arab Emirates and Saudi Arabia, have run into problems of government controls, which can result in the need to compromise on the brand values.

Business-to-business branding   In business-to-business marketing, purchasers and users value the commitment of suppliers to the product and service and benefit from the added value from dealing with a firm. For example, buyers talk about suppliers such as Apple or Vodafone as brands, which lends a sense of authority to the purchasing decision, or users might detail a specific product or service that must be purchased, e.g. an iPhone or the iWath. In some situations there may be benefits which can be gained from cobranding with globally recognized branded components (e.g. Intel microprocessors in computers). This trend is becoming increasingly important as consumers become more influential in the choice of components and services in the supply chain and demand products that contain branded components.

In international business-to-business branding firms use different naming strategies, with some firms concentrating less on corporate brand endorsement and more on the individual brand in the same way as Procter and Gamble and Unilever do in consumer markets. For example, the pharmaceutical product brands Zantac and Tagamet are promoted by GlaxoSmithKline without any obvious association with the manufacturer in the brand name.

Ultimately, the rationale for the existence of brands in business-to-business marketing is the same as in consumer goods marketing – to avoid the commoditization of products, which leads to decisions being based only on price.

Brands are also important in the not-for-profit areas. For example, although the charity sector is fragmented into many thousands of organizations, it is the global charities with well marketed brands, such as Red Crescent/Red Cross, Oxfam and Save the Children, that are the most successful in terms of scale of activities. When major disasters occur it is these organizations that have the resources to cope.

Creating a global presence by achieving global reach

The aim of many MNEs is to dominate their market sector by building a presence in every worthwhile market. However, few firms have the resources to build a strong presence in all the countries in the world and so rely on third parties to enable them to reach into similar markets. Many firms cannot afford to wait until they have built the products, services, image and resources through organic growth within the firm. Instead, they use a wide range of growth, market entry and marketing mix strategies to achieve global reach and these are discussed in later chapters.

Mergers and acquisitions   The rationale for acquisitions and mergers has been that a well-managed company should take over a weaker rival marketer of competing or complementary products in order to achieve higher growth and savings in operating, management and marketing costs.

As market entry methods, acquisition or mergers are used to facilitate access to particular markets. In some business sectors, however, there appears to be a view that it is only by operating on a very large scale on a worldwide basis that customers can receive the level and quality of service that they need. This seems logical in the case of aircraft manufacture where industry consolidation has left only two main players, Boeing and Airbus. Scale economies in accountancy may not be so obvious and, of course, there are still many small accountancy practices, but the global sector is dominated by four companies, Deloitte, KPMG, EY (formerly Ernst and Young) and PricewaterhouseCoopers, whereas there were eight major players in 1989.

Cross-border mergers and acquisitions are becoming increasingly common too, but often do not deliver the expected outcomes, for example, in telecommunications Vodafone (UK) with Mannesmann (Germany), and in automobiles Daimler-Benz (Germany) and Chrysler (US). One of the implications of mergers is the impact upon branding decisions and whether the merged firm will retain two separate brand identities or whether they will merge them. The decision often depends upon whether the senior management believes the brand is important for their particular company or industry sector. Smith (1998) reports research by McKinsey which suggests that there are three routes to brand consolidation:

- Phasing out brands over time, when the strategy is to retain loyal customers who will buy as long as the brand is available.

- Quickly changing some of the branding, which only works well if the firm has control over distribution, advertising and promotion.

- Co-branding to manage the transition, which is the most common approach, used, for example, when Whirlpool bought Philips domestic appliances.

The pitfalls of mergers and acquisitions   There are serious pitfalls associated with mergers and acquisitions, particularly where they involve cross-border ownership and cooperation. Finkelstein (1998) refers to a study of 89 US companies acquired by foreign buyers during the period 1977–90 and found the performance of most of them had not improved within one year.

As well as the obvious organizational challenges that follow from a merger, such as who will be in charge, whose products and services will be offered (or dropped) and where costs savings should be made, particularly if the merger or acquisition was not entirely harmonious, there are the cross-cultural challenges, such as the different ways of doing business in Europe, the US and Asia, different corporate governance, the status and power of different employee and management groups, job security guarantees, government regulations and customer expectations.

Finkelstein (1998) recommends that the integration process should focus on value creation by ensuring employees actually achieve the synergy that is promised before the deal is done, planning in detail how the various cross-border problems will be overcome and developing a clear communication plan to cope with the whole process.

Managing diverse and complex activities across a range of often similar but often disparate markets and cultures

The implications of pursuing a global strategy are that organizations must continually expand into what are likely to be less stable markets, perhaps tertiary opportunities from Figure 4.3 or incipient markets in Figure 4.1. Typically these will be in some way less attractive (at least at the present time) because of the associated political and economic risks of entering less developed markets, more difficult trading conditions and barriers to 'free' trade. By comparison with the firms' existing markets, these emerging markets may demand disproportionately high investment in management time and financial resources as well as involving the firm in considerable additional financial and reputation risk if things go wrong.

The risks associated with specific emerging country market involvement can be substantial however, and include some or all of the following:

- Financial loss associated with inappropriate investment, such as buying unusable assets, being unable to achieve acceptable levels of performance from the purchased assets, losing the assets by misappropriation to the host country government or to partners.

- Damage to the firm's reputation through association with the country, its government and intermediaries, especially where they are seen to be corrupt, engage in unacceptable social or business practices, or have close relationships with other countries or organizations which are considered to be corrupt.

- Litigation arising from offering an unacceptable product and/or service to the country, or becoming involved in questionable business practices.

- Prompting an unexpected international competitor response by attacking a market which it considers to be its home territory.

- Initially making arrangements with joint venture partners, distributors, agents or government agencies to secure entry but which become inappropriate in the medium to long term.

- Damage to the firm's reputation through insensitivity in its operations in the country, when it might be accused of exploiting local labour, the country's resources or causing environmental damage to the country.

The problem for international strategic management in less developed countries is that the 'rule book' that managers rely on in developed countries does not always apply, because business infrastructure and processes are not well established.

Organization structure for transnational firms

While the simple organization structures discussed in the previous chapter are appropriate for managing the international strategies of SMEs, the largest transnational companies, by their very nature, have complex structures that are specific to the firms' context. As a result, organization structures differ from firm to firm.

Most firms operate using a form of matrix structure, but Majaro (1991) distinguished between a macropyramid structure in which companies such as McDonald's exert usually highly centralized control; the umbrella structure in which geographically based SBUs take responsibility for the global strategy of the MNE in specific activities; and the interglomerate, in which the SBUs of companies such as ABB, discussed in Illustration 6.4, and many Asian-owned comprises, such as Hutchison Whampoa, Tata and Guandong Investments, operate as quite independent international businesses.

Systems, processes and control

Given the complexity of international strategic marketing in global firms it is essential that the organization operates effective processes for the management of its complex operations, processes and systems to enable managers to be able to share information effectively.

Control

Control is the cornerstone of management. Control provides the means to direct, regulate and manage business operations. A significant amount of interaction is required between the individual areas of marketing (such as market development, advertising and selling) and the other functional areas (such as human resources, finance, production, research and development).

However, for many firms, control means a separate activity through which senior managers are able to keep a check periodically (weekly, monthly or quarterly) on more junior levels of management, who often see this in terms of being called upon to justify their actions. Feedback and control systems should be regarded as an integrated part of the whole planning process, and they are essential in ensuring that the marketing plans are not only being implemented worldwide but are still appropriate for the changing environment in each country.

There are a number of benefits of an effective strategic control system. It encourages higher standards of performance, forces greater clarity and realism and permits corporate management to intervene when necessary. Moreover, it ensures that the financial objectives do not overwhelm the strategic objectives, encourages clearer definition of responsibilities making decentralization work more effectively and so provides more motivation for managers.

There are three essential elements of the control process:

1 *Setting standards*: The standards that are set need to be relevant to the corporate goals such as:

- growth and profits reported by financial measures, e.g. return on capital employed and on sales; and

- non-financial indicators, e.g. market share.

Intermediate goals and individual targets can be set by breaking the plan down into measurable parts which, when successfully completed, will lead to the overall objectives being achieved. The standards must be understandable, achievable and relevant to each local country situation.

2 *Measuring performance against standards*: To obtain measurements and ensure rapid feedback of information, firms use a variety of techniques, including reports, meetings and special measurements of specific parts of the marketing programme, such as:

- cost–benefit analysis of customers;
- product lines; and
- territories or marketing audits,

for a thorough examination of every aspect of marketing in a particular country. They also use benchmarking which allows comparisons of various aspects of the business, such as efficiency of distribution, customer response times, service levels and complaints, with other companies that are not necessarily from the same business sector.

3 *Correcting deviations from the plan*: Perhaps the most difficult decisions that must be made are to determine when performance has deviated sufficiently from the plan to require corrective action to be taken, either by changing the plan or the management team charged with the responsibility of carrying out the plan. Evaluation of the performance of a particular management team is particularly difficult in international marketing as the performance of a particular SBU can only be compared with its own plan, a plan determined by the headquarters or with the performance of a 'similar' SBU. There are obvious weaknesses in making any of these comparisons, resulting in considerable difference of opinion between the head office and subsidiary.

A key element in the control process is the input from people, both the directly employed staff of the company but also the staff of the other members of the supply chain. Various quality management models, e.g. Total Quality Management, Continuous Quality Improvement and Business Excellence, supported by international standards such as ISO 9000, are used by firms to underpin the control process. Consistency across the firm's global operations can be increased and general improvements made using a variety of techniques:

- Benchmarking against other SBUs within the firm, other firms within the business sector and the 'best in the class' in a particular activity, such as just in time operations control, service centre response rates or delivery performance.
- Identifying good practice wherever in the world it occurs and applying the lessons either in individual SBUs or across the firm.
- Encouraging performance improvement through self-assessment (individuals completing questionnaires and improvement plans alone), peer review (evaluation by staff at the same level) and appraisals completed by more senior managers.

Setting standards to achieve consistency and establishing continuous performance improvement projects throughout the global company can, however, be problematic because of cultural barriers, differences in language and ethical standards causing different levels of motivation, communications problems and misinterpretation of instructions and advice. In addition, different measuring techniques, standards and imprecise reporting procedures and processes, can create difficulties in achieving a meaningful control process.

Return on marketing investment

One of the problems for marketing is the concern that marketing and promotion expenditure is simply seen as a cost to the business with no benefits linked to it. As a key control tool, therefore, measuring the return on marketing investment is essential for any business-to-business or consumer marketing manager looking to improve their ability to produce real results in revenue growth. In much of the traditional marketing activity it is difficult to define the specific benefits that can be attributed to one individual activity.

With online marketing, as we shall see later, it is easier to link the marketing investment with its impact. In practice, firms need to measure the effect of an integrated marketing programme, in order to learn good and bad practice.

Planning systems and processes

The increasingly turbulent environment resulting from more rapid changes in technology, competition, consumer taste and fashion means that the traditional systems and processes for preparing the analysis, strategy development and action plans take too long. Balabanis *et al.* (2004) emphasized that global information systems are needed to enable HQ and subsidiary managers to keep track of environmental changes (opportunities and threats), facilitate the coordination and control of operations in different locations and assist in sharing of new ideas and knowledge.

Timescales must be reduced to make sure that the plan is still relevant when it is being implemented. Consequently, it is necessary to avoid planning that is too general and unfocused and to improve the quality of implementation and the relevance and responsiveness of the process.

As a result of this, increasing emphasis is being placed by MNEs on scenario and contingency planning to take account of things going wrong because of unexpected changes in the environment. Moreover, greater reliance is being placed on expert systems for understanding market changes, carrying out forecasting, resource planning and gap analysis. The plans prepared tend to be based on the understanding that they will be emergent, and will evolve during the timescale of the plan rather than be decided before the time period of the plan begins. The plans may be designed to be incremental, with the start of each new phase being prompted by a change in the environment or by the successful completion of a previous implementation phase.

Building skills in transnational organizations

While the structures outlined provide some general understanding of the alternative methods of organizing the management, they are for most companies an oversimplification. Cagni (2006) explains that old-fashioned, centralized, multinational management is no longer appropriate as it creates a single process overseen from head office. While this creates scale advantages, improved efficiency and the capability to share knowledge, local staff see a loss of autonomy, the creation of an ivory tower for the elite and the disempowerment of local managers, leaving them with less interesting jobs. The structure needs be developed in a way that avoids rigidity as flexibility is needed to respond to the changes in environment and market.

This has implications for the roles of the international marketing manager, as Bartlett and Ghoshal (2015) have concluded. The management of transnational businesses must be highly specialized and understand that there is likely to be a great deal of resistance from consumers that receive highly sanitized, standardized, homogenized products. Global business or product division managers have the responsibility to further the company's global-scale efficiency and competitiveness, but not lose sight of the fact that the consumer may not like the 'one-size fits all' approach. They must combine the strategist skills of recognizing opportunities and risks across national and functional boundaries, be the architect for worldwide resource and asset utilization, and the coordinator of activities and capabilities.

The country manager must play a pivotal role by sensing local customer needs, but also satisfying the host government's requirements and defending the company's market position. The country manager is likely to have objectives that conflict with the business manager and so must be prepared to negotiate to overcome the differences. The functional manager's role is the business environment scanner, cross-pollinator of ideas and champion of specific aspects of the business which are essential for success. The global manager may be required to play a number of roles and no one person can fulfil the required tasks alone. This manager must provide leadership, while acting as the talent scout and the developer of the other levels of management.

As a result, patterns of activity in a transnational company will vary considerably in each new situation. Innovations, for example, should be generated at several locations and in several ways throughout the world, so that the company is not restricted to making centralized decisions. For the past 10 to 20 years, firms such as Shell, Philips and Unilever have used an integrated network approach, with resources and capabilities concentrated in various locations and accessed through the free flow of knowledge, technology, components, products, resources and people. By developing matrix structures, firms can achieve efficiency, responsiveness and the ability to develop and exploit their knowledge and capability for competitive advantage.

As the international operations of firms increase in diversity and tangible ties between the activities become strained, so the nature of the formal systems and organizational structures must change too. Training programmes, career path planning, job rotation, company-wide accounting, evaluation and data-processing systems become more important as part of the shared value system of the firm.

Staff and the problems of international management

Of the potential sources of problems of planning in international marketing, it is the relationship between headquarters and local subsidiary staff that is likely to be the largest single factor. Headquarters staff, as guardians of the overall company strategies, claim to have a far broader perspective of the company's activities and might expect that subsidiary staff should simply be concerned with implementation of the details of the plan. Subsidiary staff claim that, by being closer to the individual markets, they are in a better position to identify opportunities and should, therefore, play a large part in developing objectives and strategies. This situation must be resolved if the planning process is to be effective, so that all staff have a clear idea of their own role in setting, developing and implementing policy, and understanding how their individual contributions might be integrated into the corporate objectives and strategies.

Govindarajan and Gupta (2001) comment on the need to create teams comprised of many nationalities to benefit from the synergies and collective wisdom superior to that of an individual. The failure rate of teams is high – in a survey one third of teams rated their performance as largely unsuccessful – and this is due to lack of trust, with hindrances, even when members speak in the same language, including semantics, accents, tone, pitch and dialects. Mortensen and Beyene (2009) explain that to build trust it is necessary to spend time onsite observing the people, places and norms of the distant locale as this not only leads to direct knowledge of the other but also leads to knowledge of self as seen by the other (reflected knowledge), thus affecting trust through identification, adaptation and reduced misunderstanding.

Sebenius (2002) notes that decision-making and governance processes vary widely not only in terms of legal technicalities but also the behaviour and core beliefs that drive them. The solution is to map out the decision-making process and anticipate problems before they arise.

The difficulties of planning in international markets are further developed by Brandt *et al.* (1980), in a framework of international planning problems, and Weichmann and Pringle (1979), who identified the key problems experienced by large US and European multinationals.

Many companies recognize that for strategies to be successful they must be owned and so staff at all levels must be involved in the marketing planning process. This is becoming more difficult as MNEs have ever greater numbers of their workers employed outside the head office country. As the company grows, therefore, a company-wide planning culture should be developed, with the following objectives:

- Planning becomes part of the continuous process of management rather than an annual 'event'.
- Strategic thinking becomes the responsibility of every manager rather than being restricted to a separate strategic planning department.
- The planning process becomes standardized, with a format that allows contributions from all parts of the company.
- The plan becomes the working document, updated periodically for all aspects of the company, so allowing performance evaluation to be carried out regularly.
- The planning process is itself regularly reviewed and refined through the use of new tools and techniques in order to improve its relevance and effectiveness.

Brett, Behfar and Kern (2006) identify the advantages of multicultural teams in international firms, including deep knowledge of different product markets and culturally sensitive customer service, but also note

ILLUSTRATION 6.6

How global companies thrive thanks to leadership

Philips, a Dutch company is a worldwide success due, in part, to its local leadership and management style. The heart of Philips is to improve the lives of consumers through innovation, health care, lifestyle and lighting. The head office of this global company is in a small town called Eindhoven, 125 km from Amsterdam, Holland's capital. The sales figures for Philips are impressive, but what is unusual about this is that its own domestic market attributes only 10 per cent of total sales. This means that some of their regional subsidiaries provide much higher sales; and with that the region gains high status within the company. The main manager at the regional subsidiary is often an expatriate of Holland, some have even been expatriates of Eindhoven. The reason for this is that all head regional managers must have substantial international experience and empathy with different cultures from around the world. Expatriates, therefore, have often learnt their trade, and the Philip values, working in subsidiaries in Europe, Japan or the US. The international experience and learned leadership skills give the expatriate an understanding of and willingness to accept local workforce and consumer needs. With that, and their innate enthusiasm to be entrepreneurial, they make product changes. However, changes are only made through regular meetings with local managers to ensure there is a balance between Philips corporate ideals and localization.

Another example of the 'joined up thinking' between corporate and local management is seen when discussions take place on technical and marketing functions. Traditions of joint decision making, creating an innovative culture and sharing responsibility for the success of Philips are still in place, despite the company's divergence into new countries where the business hierarchy is not as open as it is in Holland. At all Philips regional subsidiaries local managers and the head regional manager form small working parties that include 'front-line' employees from technicians and operatives to junior managers. The purpose is to listen and share recommendations to invest in new technical and marketing initiatives.

Question

1 What are the main differences in leading a national business compared to a global company?

Sources: Bartlett, C.A. and Ghoshal, S. (2015) 'Organizing for worldwide effectiveness. The transnational solution', Chapter 14 in Buckley, P.J. and Ghauri, P.N. (eds). *International Business Strategy: Theory and Practice*. Routledge

the problems caused when cultural differences affect team effectiveness, direct versus indirect communication, trouble with accents and fluency, differing attitudes to hierarchy and authority, and conflicting norms for decision making. The authors emphasize the need to pinpoint the root cause of the problems, intervene early and see the challenges as stemming from culture rather than personalities.

What makes a good international manager

For many of the most powerful businesses increasing globalization is the future scenario, and the most successful will be managed by people who can best embrace and thrive on the ambiguity and complexity of transnational operations. Using Illustration 6.6 it is interesting to consider the changes in organization culture that take place as a result of globalization.

A number of researchers have emphasized the need for managers to be able to handle national differences in business, including cultural divergence on hierarchy, humour, assertiveness and working hours.

In France, Germany, Italy and a large part of Asia, for example, performance-related pay is seen negatively as revealing the shortcomings of some members of the work group. Feedback sessions are seen positively in the US but German managers see them as 'enforced admissions of failure'.

The **international manager**, therefore, must be more culturally aware and show greater sensitivity, but it can be difficult to adapt to the culture and values of a foreign country while upholding the culture and values of a parent company. The only way is to give managers experience overseas, but the cost of sending people abroad is typically two-and-a-half times that for a local manager, so firms look for alternatives, such as short-term secondments, exchanges and participation in multicultural project teams.

Wills and Barham (1994) believe that international managers require four sets of attributes. They must:

1 Be able to cope with cognitive complexity and be able to understand issues from a variety of complicated perspectives.

2 Have cultural empathy, a sense of humility and the power of active listening. Due to their unfamiliarity with different cultural settings international managers cannot be as competent or confident in a foreign environment.

3 Have emotional energy and be capable of adding depth and quality to interactions through their emotional self-awareness, emotional resilience and ability to accept risk. They must be able to rely on the support of the family.

4 Demonstrate psychological maturity by having the curiosity to learn, an awareness of time constraints and a fundamental personal morality that will enable them to cope with the diversity of demands made on them.

Management culture

There has been considerable discussion about the difference between the Asian and western models of management and the reasons for the differences, such as the elements of a deeply embedded culture and more recent history, for example, the effects on management of working within a centrally planned economy. Deshpandé *et al.* (2004), however, also note the differences between Asian management cultures and suggest that Chinese and Vietnamese firms, emerging from centrally planned economies to some form of market socialism, tend to be bureaucratic. Indian firms tend to be entrepreneurial. Japanese culture is the most consensual and the least entrepreneurial. Hong Kong tends to be about average in that it reflects the mixed Chinese and western influences on its management culture.

They conclude that there are in fact four organizational culture types:

1 Competitive or market culture which is characterized by an emphasis on competitive advantage and market superiority.

2 Entrepreneurial or adhocracy culture which emphasizes innovation and risk-taking.

3 Bureaucratic or hierarchy culture in which regulations and formal structures are important.

4 Consensual or clan culture which emphasizes loyalty, tradition and internal maintenance.

They found that in each country more competitive and entrepreneurial firms perform better and consensual and bureaucratic firms perform worse than their national peers. They also noted that market orientation has a greater effect on performance in Asia and innovativeness has a greater effect in the more industrialized nations.

As the workplace becomes more globalized, having a multicultural team is becoming the norm (Agrawal and Rook 2013). In researching the differences between Asian and western management cultures they found significant differences in key leadership behaviours that relate to implementing company strategy, promoting responsiveness to customers and other stakeholders, fostering respect and understanding in the workforce and handling the pressures of the managerial lifestyle. However, rather than focusing on cultural differences Carlos Ghosn, Chairman and CEO of Renault-Nissan Alliance (Kase, Slocum and Zhang 2011) maintains strength comes from diversity and the richest solutions come when ideas are challenged by colleagues with different perspectives.

Management style and shared values

The different contexts and stages of global development of firms mean that there is no proven right and wrong management style and shared values for the firm. Indeed the shared values, as we have seen earlier, may be the only common aspect of the company that binds the various parts together and may be based upon a long tradition in the firm, built up over many years. This is particularly the case in companies dominated by extended family ownership, such as in many Asian businesses, or where the principles of the founding family of a business are maintained.

What is important to recognize is that although global businesses are complex and diverse, the chief executive can have a major effect on the business. The personality of entrepreneurs such as Ratan Tata, Steve Jobs, Michael Dell and Richard Branson has shaped the management style and shared values of the businesses they have created from their early days.

SUMMARY

- The increase in global business activity has resulted from a number of drivers in the environment, particularly through technological developments. Clearly it is communications and information technology that have had the greatest effect on creating a global marketplace. Firms have also accelerated the move towards greater globalization by developing a worldwide presence and strategy, and offering similar products and services.

- To exploit global markets firms have developed appropriate strategies for their particular situation. These range from multidomestic strategies, in which each market is seen as separate and individual, through to globally standardized strategies in which the firm has identified one global segment with similar needs. In practice, the largest firms are too complex for one simple strategy to be appropriate and so they use a combination of different strategies to build global efficiency, local effectiveness and knowledge assets.

- In the past global trade has been dominated by MNEs from developed countries, but now companies from emerging markets that have built their capability and resources in the domestic market, are becoming global players investing in developed countries too. The competitive advantage that they have built in their home market must then be tested in the global marketplace.

- To succeed globally, firms must build global appeal through globally recognized brands, but also innovate, as the basis of competitive advantage in many industries changes continually.

- An increasingly common feature of transnational strategies is the greater level of cooperation between firms that would otherwise be competitors, customers or suppliers.

- To enable managers to set and control the operations of the business an appropriate organization structure is needed. International managers must also be able to recruit and develop the right staff that will have the skills necessary to deal with the complexity, diversity and conflicting challenges of global business development.

KEYWORDS

globalization	standardization	global brand
transnationality	adaptation	global reach
market access	global presence	business-to-business marketing
global sourcing	competitive advantage	control
World Wide Web	global appeal	international manager

CASE STUDY 1

BMW of the future – super cars or super gadgets?

After carrying out thorough market analysis to identify future growth opportunities, it is important to think about developing an appropriate strategic response to the changing opportunities and threats in the short, medium and long term. As the large traditional American and European vehicle markets were hit by the last recession, strong arguments were made for well-established manufacturers to invest in the world markets that showed the greatest growth prospects as the result of a rapidly growing GDP.

For a number of years business strategists have enthused about opportunities in the BRIC countries (Brazil, Russia, India and China), where fast GDP growth was predicted, and where increasing affluence would create huge demand for consumer goods, but especially for premium products. For example, for some time Russia was the largest volume market for Rolls Royce cars. However, marketing strategies must take account not only of long-term future opportunities, immediate environmental challenges and emerging predictable competition such as local manufacturers, but also of unpredictable, unexpected, non-traditional competitors.

China is the world's largest car market and in 2015 accounted for a fifth of BMW group sales, about 450 000 vehicles. However, as the GDP growth rate began to slow in China the car market started to exhibit more 'normal' behaviour similar to that in traditional markets. Concerns over air quality, congestion and a tightening regulatory regime made for a more challenging market. The regulatory authorities in Beijing and Shenzen initiated restrictions on new car registrations and more cities started to follow.

The Indian economy has been forecast to show similar growth rates to China and eventually become the largest world economy. As a result the Indian car market was expected to show similar patterns of consumption to the Chinese market but for BMW this has not happened. BMW sold just 7500 units a year as the premium car market in India total was only 40 000 compared to that in China of 2 million.

A slowdown in Brazil and other South American countries with economies that depend on the export of commodities turned them into difficult markets. In Russia, the uncertain state of the domestic economy, falling currency exchange rate and political problems significantly and adversely affected consumer spending. At the height of these problems in Russia, Renault Nissan stopped taking orders for some models that used large quantities of imported parts to stem their losses. Moreover, many of the 'Next Eleven' markets that were forecast to break into the 'global big league' were also faltering.

Competition in the car market is also increasing. Established European and Asian manufacturers have thrived as many traditional American car manufacturers hit difficulties and a number of new, cost effective car manufacturers have emerged, particularly from Asia. But some market analysts are suggesting that the US West Coast technology giants, such as Google and Apple, pose the greatest future competitive threat to established car manufacturers with the development of autonomous (driverless) cars.

If autonomous cars drive on the road together, their speed and interaction will have to be regulated and so the size, power and performance of engines would no longer be so critical for success. In-car gadgets would become more important. Google and Apple, who are leaders in such technology, could work with car component suppliers to develop their supply chain, or even form partnerships with existing brands, in a similar way to how Mercedes worked with Swatch, the Swiss watchmaker, to produce the Smart car. They also understand the different infrastructure that might be needed to support autonomous cars.

Most of the established car makers have developed supporting technology for the driverless car – the question for the strategists is which brand of autonomous car will the driver trust?

Questions

1 What are the key opportunities and threats that BMW face in (a) the short term and (b) the long term, and what are the likely timescales?

2 What are BMW's strategic imperatives (the things they must do) to retain and build their competitive position in the car market?

3 How should BMW's strategy differ across regional and country markets?

Source: R. Lea 'BMW's growth story hits a BRICs wall', *The Times*, 2 March 2015, and R. Lea 'US driverless cars threaten German giants', *The Times*, 6 March 2015.

CASE STUDY 2

Re-shoring: rethinking global reach

The benefits of offshoring and outsourcing, global strategies that many MNEs engage in, have been outlined in this chapter. Low wages paid to manufacturing workers or the low land/rents in China and Mexico are two of the cost benefits of choosing offshoring and outsourcing strategies.

However, many MNEs have seen cracks in offshoring and outsourcing strategies. Therefore, MNEs are bringing back product manufacturing and services, such as callcentres to within their shores.

There are many reasons for re-shoring:

Social conscience: Following the world economic crises businesses such as Google, GE and the Ford Motor Company decided to invest in human capital and have brought production and service jobs back to America.

Transportation costs: Rising costs, such as shipping, fuel and associated taxes mean that goods produced in Northern China, Russia or Eastern India have to travel long distances, and thus increase costs per item which in turn reduces profit margins. Other business taxes have also made SMEs and MNEs consider re-shoring. Easybike Group decided to review their offshore

strategy. Easybike Group have now retuned production of their electric bicycles to Saint-Lô in Normandy from China.

Speed to market: Many MNEs know that consumers have a less patient mindset than in the past. Zara, the fast-fashion brand, brought back manufacturing clothing and accessories to Northern Spain. Fast for Zara means that over 60 per cent of fashion items go from 'the drawing board' to retailers in two weeks. Therefore, the Zara brand and their consumers do not want long delivery times, a disadvantage of having manufacturing outsourced or offshore in countries thousands of miles away.

Consumer demand: Many banks, insurance and telecommunication businesses offshored their call centre services. However, consumers protested. Consumers did not feel comfortable when discussing personal financial matters with someone overseas. As long ago as 2006 Lloyds Bank re-shored call centre services back to the UK. More recently the Royal & Sun Alliance MoreThan brand re-shored its call centre from India to Halifax, Sunderland and Liverpool, creating 350 jobs in the UK.

'Made In...': Many consumers also want to buy products and engage in services from and in their own country. The French government, like many others, is keen to show that SMEs and MNEs are supporting France's economy. During 2013 Rossignol began building an ultra-modern factory in Sallanches (Haute-Savoie). Previously a Taiwanese factory produced their skis but now 20 000 pairs of 'Made in France' skis will be produced in Sallanches. By re-shoring Rossignal enables consumers to feel patriotic and contribute more directly to their economy and Rossignol can fly the flag for French innovation. Additionally, Rossignol now feels closer to its consumers, who are mainly European and North American and can respond quickly to technological advancement and consumer needs. 'Made in Britain' clothing ranges have also been introduced to M&S and Debenhams retail stores in the UK.

Quality: Consumers, be they B2B or B2C are increasingly demanding and desire high quality goods and services. Many British manufacturers state providing quality as the key reason for re-shoring retail production. Asos want more quality products made in the UK and Mulberry have announced they want 50 per cent of their bags made in the UK; both organizations are investing in education and training to ensure there are sufficient skilled workers to meet demand.

Narrowing wages gap: This case study began by highlighting that low wages paid in countries such as China and Mexico are one of the benefits of offshoring and outsourcing. Recent times have seen increases in wages in China, Mexico, Turkey and Poland, therefore these countries are less likely to be chosen if MNEs continue to offshore. There is a narrowing wage gap between many countries. However, Bangladesh and the Philippines could still be included in offshoring and outsourcing decisions. However, the calculation of low wages plus high transportation costs may make more businesses re-shore or simply stay within their own shores.

Questions

1 Compare and contrast the advantages and disadvantages of offshoring, outsourcing and re-shoring.

2 What are the main benefits of re-shoring?

Sources: L'Usine Nuvelle (2013) 'Relocalisation en France réussie pour les skis Rossignol', www.usinenouvelle.com/article/relocalisation-en-france-reussie-pour-les-skis-rossignol.N189366 (accessed 14 January 2014); Hawkes, S (2013) 'RSA brings 350 call centre jobs back to the UK', www.telegraph.co.uk/finance/newsbysector/banksandfinance/insurance/10388596/RSA-brings-350-call-centre-jobs-back-to-the-UK.html Telegraph 18 October 2013 (accessed 14 April 2014); KPMG (2014) 'Production's coming home: what companies need to know about re-shoring',www.kpmg.com/global/en/issuesandinsights/articlespublications/consumercurrents/pages/productions-coming-home.aspx (accessed 14 April 2015).

DISCUSSION QUESTIONS

1 What do you consider to be the differences between a global, regional and an international mindset? What are the arguments for and against setting a firm's aim to be a global player rather than a regional or international player?

2 Identify the reasons why international strategies sometimes fail in their objective to build competitive advantage. What capabilities do firms need to compete internationally?

3 What is the rationale behind megamergers and major acquisitions? Using examples, explain the advantages and disadvantages of this approach to achieve global reach.

4 What are the critical success factors in developing a global brand? What must an international firm do for its brand to achieve 'global' status? Give examples to support your opinion.

5 What are the main challenges that are faced by international managers in contributing to the management and control of a global marketing strategy? What advice would you give to a manager with this responsibility?

REFERENCES

1. Agrawal, A. and Rook, C. (2013) Global leaders in East and West –do all global leaders lead in the same way? Insead Business School working paper. Available at www.insead.edu/facultyresearch/research/doc.cfm?did=52985 (accessed online).

2. Akgün, A.E., Keskin, H. and Ayar, H. (2014) 'Standardization and adaptation of international marketing mix activities: A case study', *Procedia-Social and Behavioral Sciences*, 150, 609–618.

3. Arnott, S. (2010) 'Who owns Britain: Watchdog launches first UK stock take', *The Independent*, 15 May.

4. Balabanis, G., Theodosiou, M. and Katsikea, E.S. (2004) 'Export marketing: developments and a research agenda', *International Marketing Review*, 21 (4/5): 353–77.

5. Barbaro, M. (2006) 'Wal-Mart profits falls 26%, its first drop in 10 years', *New York Times*, 16 August.

6. Bartlett, C.A. and Ghoshal, S. (2015) 'Organizing for worldwide effectiveness. The transnational solution',

Chapter 14 in Buckley, P.J. and Ghauri, P.N. (eds). *International Business Strategy: Theory and Practice*. Routledge.

7. Boston Consulting Group (2014) Redefining global competitive dynamics, September 2014. Part of the winning growth series BCG.org.

8. Bracken, P. (2007) Revenge of the domestic tigers. Available from www.strategy-business.com/article/05316 (accessed 19 August 2015).

9. Brandt, W., Hulbert, J. and Richers, R. (1980) 'Pitfalls in planning for multinational operations', *Long Range Planning*, December.

10. Brett, J., Behfar, K. and Kern, M.C. (2006) 'Managing multi-cultural teams', *Harvard Business Review*, 84 (11): 84–91.

11. Buzzell, R.D. (1968) 'Can you standardize multinational marketing?', *Harvard Business Review*, 46 (6): 101–14.

12. Cagni, P. (2006) 'Think global, act European', available at www.strategy-business.com.

13. Campbell, M., Chrysoloras N. and Benedetti-Valentini, F. (2015) Greek bailout rests on asset sale plan that already failed, Bloomberg Business July 13, 2015.

14. Cranfield School of Management (2007) International Assignments. Available from www.som.cranfield.ac.uk/som/news.

15. Deshpandé, R., Farley, J.U. and Bowman, D. (2004) 'Tigers, dragons and others: profiling high performance in Asian firms', *Journal of International Marketing*, 12 (3): 5–29.

16. *Economist* (2010a) 'The world turned upside down', *The Economist*, 15 April.

17. *Economist* (2010b) 'Grow, grow, grow. What makes emerging-markets companies run', *The Economist*, 15 April.

18. Elinder, E. (1961) 'How international can European advertising be?', *International Advertiser* December:12–16.

19. Finkelstein, S. (1998) 'Safe ways to cross the merger minefield, Mastering global business Part 4', *Financial Times*, 20 February.

20. Gogel, R. and Larreche, J.C. (1989) 'The battlefield for 1992: product strength and geographical coverage', *European Journal of Management*, 17: 289.

21. Govindarajan, V. and Gupta, A.K. (2001) 'Building an effective global business team', *MIT Sloan Management Review*, 42(4): 63–71.

22. Hart, S.L. and London, T. (2005) Developing native capability: why multinational corporations can learn from the base of the pyramid, *Stanford Social Innovation Review*, Summer. Available from www.ssireview.org/.

23. Holt, D.B., Quelch, J.A. and Taylor, E.L. (2004) 'How global brands compete', *Harvard Business Review*. 82(9): 68–75.

24. Kase, K., Slocum, A. and Zhang, Y. (2011) *Asian versus Western Management Thinking, Its Culture-bound Nature*, Palgrave Macmillan.

25. Khashani, K. (1995) 'A new future for brands', *Financial Times*, 10 November.

26. Leggett, R. (2013) 'As emerging markets slow, firms search for "new" BRICs', *Harvard Business Review* 28 November 2013 www.hbr.org/2013/11/as-emerging-markets-slow-firms-search-for-new-brics/ (accessed 14 April 2015).

27. Levitt, T. (1983) 'The globalization of markets', *Harvard Business Review*, 61(3): 69–81.

28. Majaro, S. (1991) *International Marketing*, Routledge.

29. Meffet, H. and Bolz, J. (1993) 'Standardization of marketing in Europe needs effort', in C. Haliburton and R. Hunerberg (eds) *European Marketing Readings*, Addison-Wesley.

30. Mortensen, M. and Beyene, T. (2009) 'Firsthand experience and the subsequent role of reflected knowledge in cultivating trust in global collaboration', Working papers Harvard Business School Division of Research, 1–65.

31. Nistor, C. (2014) 'Firms' transnationalization evolution of multinational groups operating in Romania'. *SEA-Practical Application of Science*, (5): 51–58.

32. Prahalad, C.K. and Hart, S.L. (2002) 'The fortune at the bottom of the pyramid', *Strategy and Business*, 26(54): 67.

33. Sebenius, J.K. (2002) 'The hidden challenge of crossborder negotiations', *Harvard Business Review*, 80(3): 76–85.

34. Sjobolom, L. (1998) 'Success lies one step ahead of the consumer, mastering global management', *Financial Times*, 6 February.

35. Smith, A. (1998) 'The conundrum of maintaining image', *Financial Times*, 8 May.

36. *Strategy and Business* (2015) 's+b trend watch: 3D printing's impact on the transportation industry', Spring Issue 78, 19 January 2015

37. UNCTAD (2010) World investment report 2009, UN conference on trade and development Available from www.unctad.org.

38. Weichmann, U.E. and Pringle, L.G. (1979) 'Problems that plague multinational marketers', *Harvard Business Review*, July/August.

39. Wills, S. and Barham, K. (1994) 'Being an international manager', *European Management Journal*, 12(1).

40. Zou, S. and Cavusgil, S.T. (2002) 'The GMS: a broad conceptualization of global marketing strategy and its effect on firm performance', *Journal of Marketing*, 66: 40–56.

CHAPTER 7

MARKET ENTRY STRATEGIES

LEARNING OBJECTIVES

After reading this chapter you should be able to:

- Identify the alternative market entry options available to firms seeking to develop new country markets

- Compare the different levels of involvement, risk and marketing control of these market entry methods

- Understand the criteria for selecting between the market entry options

- Appreciate the advantages and disadvantages of the different market entry methods

- Understand the motivations and challenges of market entry partnership strategies, such as alliances and joint ventures

INTRODUCTION

For the majority of companies, the most significant international marketing decision they are likely to take is how they should enter new markets, and how they will maintain and build their involvement in existing markets to increase their international competitiveness. Having identified potential country, regional and world markets in previous chapters and discussed the development of international marketing strategies in both smaller and global firms, in this chapter we examine the different market entry options open to firms to enable them to select the most appropriate method for their given situation. For most small and medium-sized businesses this represents a critical first step, but for established companies, the problem is how to exploit opportunities more effectively within the context of their existing network of international operations and, particularly, how to enter new emerging markets.

There are advantages and disadvantages with each market entry method. Critical in the decision-making process are the firm's ambition and capability, assessment of the cost and risk associated with each method, and the level of involvement the company is allowed by the government. These factors determine the degree of control it can exert over the total product and service offer and the method of distribution.

There is, however, no ideal market entry strategy and different market entry methods might be adopted by different firms entering the same market and/or by the same firm in different markets. We particularly focus on the collaborative strategies adopted by the very largest firms.

The alternative market entry methods

The various alternative market entry methods are shown in Figure 7.1. They cover a span of international involvement from almost zero in domestic purchasing, when the firm merely makes the products available for others to export but effectively does nothing itself to market its products internationally, to total involvement where the firm might operate wholly-owned subsidiaries in all its key markets. These are approximate relative positions and vary according to the specific situation. E-commerce might be placed in a range of positions depending upon the particular business model adopted. For Facebook and Google it is the complete offer, whereas for the manufacturer of capital equipment it might be simply an information source.

The market entry decision is taken within the firm and is determined to a large extent by the firm's objectives and attitudes to international marketing and the confidence in the capability of its managers to operate in foreign countries. In order to select an appropriate and potentially successful market entry method, it is necessary to consider a number of criteria including:

- The company objectives and expectations relating to the size and value of anticipated business.
- The size and financial resources of the company.
- Its existing foreign market involvement.
- The skill, abilities and attitudes of the company management towards international marketing.
- The nature and power of the competition within the market.
- The nature of existing and anticipated tariff and non-tariff barriers, and other country specific constraints, such as legal and infrastructure limitations.
- The nature of the product itself, particularly any areas of competitive advantage, such as trademark or patent protection.
- The timing of the move in relation to the market and competitive situation.

This list is not exhaustive, as the entry method might be influenced by other factors which are specific to the firm's particular situation. For example, the laws of a host country might prevent a firm from owning 100 per cent of an operation in that country. Trade embargos put in place by the United Nations may prevent a firm entering the country during times of war or terrorism; in the country of origin of the product or service may make market entry inadvisable.

Timing is another particularly important factor in considering entry. For example, emerging markets typically have bursts of optimism and growth often followed by setbacks caused by political or economic factors, or changing customer expectations. The Asian approach of allocating time and resources in the expectation of improved trading conditions in the future has paid off in many emerging markets. Chinese companies are investing heavily in the infrastructure in Africa in exchange for valuable resources and

FIGURE 7.1 Market entry methods and the levels of involvement in international markets

Levels of involvement

Wholly-owned subsidiary
Company acquisition
Assembly operations
Joint venture
Strategic alliance
Licensing
Contract manufacture
Direct marketing
Franchising
Distributors and agents
Sales force
Trading companies
Export management companies
Piggyback operations
Domestic purchasing

assets and in the expectation that the economies of African countries will improve in the near future. This approach contrasts with that of many western companies who seem to invest only when a particular country is about to 'take off', but it may be too late if their Asian rivals are already well entrenched.

Risk and control in market entry

We referred earlier to the fact that one of the most important characteristics of the different market entry methods is the level of involvement of the firm in international operations. This has significant implications in terms of levels of risk and control and is shown in Figure 7.2. Figure 7.2 also shows the four categories of market entry methods: indirect and direct market entry, cooperation and direct investment.

The cost of resourcing the alternative methods usually equates closely to levels of involvement and risk. The diagram does suggest, however, that higher levels of involvement bring greater potential for control over its foreign country marketing activities and also higher potential risk, usually due to the high cost of investment. In practice this is an oversimplification, because firms whose products are marketed internationally through domestic purchasing are at risk of losing all their income from international markets without knowing why, because of their total reliance on their customer's strategy for success.

Partnerships, in the form of joint ventures and strategic alliances, have become increasingly common over the past few years because they are thought to offer the advantage of achieving higher levels of control in market entry at lower levels of risk and cost, provided that there is a high degree of cooperation between companies and that the individual objectives of the partner companies are not incompatible.

In making a decision on market entry, therefore, the most fundamental questions that the firm must answer are:

- What level of control over our international business activities do we require?
- What level of risk are we willing to take?
- What cost can we afford to bear?

In answering these questions it is important to consider not just the level of control, risk and cost, but also the relative importance that the firm might place upon the different elements of its marketing activity. For example, lack of control over certain aspects of the marketing process, such as after-sales servicing which is often undertaken by third party contractors, may affect the reputation and image of a company or brand

FIGURE 7.2   Risk and control in market entry

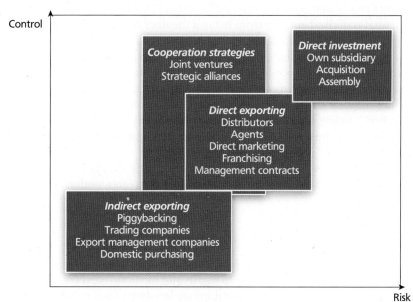

because consumers frequently blame the manufacturer rather than a distributor or retailer for the poor quality of after-sales service that they have received.

Indirect exporting

For firms that have little inclination or few resources for international marketing, the simplest and lowest cost method of market entry is for them to have their products sold overseas by others. The objective of firms which use this method of entry may be to benefit from opportunities that arise without incurring any expense or simply to sell off excess capacity into foreign markets with the least possible inconvenience. Firms such as these often withdraw from this activity as soon as their sales into the home market improve. While indirect exporting has the advantage of the least cost and risk of any entry method, it allows the firm little control over how, when, where and by whom the products are sold. In some cases the domestic company may even be unaware that its products are being exported.

There are four main methods of indirect exporting and these are by using:

1 domestic purchasing
2 an export management company (EMC) or export house (EH)
3 piggyback operations; and
4 trading companies.

Domestic purchasing

Some firms or individuals do not realize that their products or services have potential export value until they are approached by the buyer from a foreign organization, who might make the initial contact, purchase the product at the factory gate and take on the task of exporting, marketing and distributing the product in one or more overseas markets. Examples of this include purchasing beads from the Maasai and cocoa beans from farmers in Africa. Body Shop sourced naturally occurring ingredients for its ranges of toiletries and cosmetics and made domestic purchasing from deprived regions of the world a feature of its marketing activity. Taking a moral stance and demonstrating environmental concern, however, can make the firm a target for detractors. Ben and Jerry's took this route, in sourcing ingredients for their ice cream from community-based suppliers, but when fashions changed and certain ingredients were no longer popular, they were criticized for stopping supply arrangements with community-based social enterprises.

Local subcontractors to original equipment manufacturers (OEMs) fall into this category, as their international market potential is derived entirely from being a member of the OEM's supply chain. While for the manufacturer or supplier domestic purchasing could hardly be called an entry strategy, it does provide the firm with access to and limited knowledge of international markets. However, the supplying organization is able to exert little control over the choice of markets and the strategies adopted in marketing its products. Small firms find that this is the easiest method of obtaining foreign sales but, being totally dependent on the purchaser, they are unlikely to be aware of a change in consumer behaviour and competitor activity or of the purchasing firm's intention to terminate the arrangement. Illustration 7.1 shows how a Chinese wholesale market enables local businesses to gain status in developed countries and provides great benefit to otherwise poor farmers.

If a company is intent upon seeking longer-term viability for its export business it must adapt a more proactive approach, which will inevitably involve obtaining a greater understanding of the markets in which their products are sold.

Export management companies or export houses

Export houses or export marketing companies (EMCs) are specialist companies set up to act as the export department for a range of companies. They can help small- and medium-sized companies to initiate, develop and maintain their international sales. As well as taking orders from foreign buyers, they provide indirect

ILLUSTRATION 7.1

Yiwu: the wholesaler market that doubles as a tourist attraction

One of the fastest-growing markets in the world is for 'single priced items'. The concept has its origins in the US with discount retailers Dollar Tree and Dollar General which started in the 1950s. Supermarkets around the world want to sell items for 99p, 99 cents, 100 yen or one euro and some shops are set up just to sell these items. Consumers want to buy cheap 'things'. They buy cheap things during a recession, but on average consumers buy even more cheap things during boom times. Yiwu Wholesale Market in China is the most spectacular place to buy those cheap things. In fact the United Nations has declared Yiwu to be the biggest wholesale market in the world to buy cheap 'things'. And with over £5 billion worth of business taking place with discount retailers such as Dollar Tree, US, Poundland, UK and Bein Al Qasrain Gifts, 1 to 10 dirham retailers in Dubai, it is clearly a success story. Yiwu has five designated districts, some districts are five floors high! Within the districts there are 20 specialist areas providing over 1.7 million products and within the districts there are over 62 000 sales booths providing small commodity items including plastic flowers, toy trains, hair accessories, football scarves, Christmas decorations (all year round of course), gloves, ties, automobile parts, pet accessories, stationary and cosmetics.

Zheinlain Hongyu Medical Commodity Co. Ltd. is one of the thousands of suppliers showcasing their products at Yiwu. The specialties of Zheinlain Hongyu Medical Commodity Co. Ltd are plasters, bandages and first aid kits which are bought by Poundland. Their success is such that they are building new factories to make and package their products.

Well Knitting is another successful business which has a sales booth at Yiwu showcasing football scarves and hats. The owner, and now very successful businessman, Wu Pengxu, says he 'dresses' football fans worldwide. He makes woolly hats (selling for 32p) and scarves (selling at 80p) for football fans of Manchester United to Preston North End and Chelsea to Exeter City FC. Another successful store is Yiwu Beautiful Flower Co. Ltd that provides accessories for women throughout the world. Of the two million floral hair brooches made, 10 per cent go to the UK. Again retailers like Poundland buy some of their products for as little as 23p.

These success stories come from small businesses using the Yiwu Wholesale Market as 'gateway to the world of buyers'. Some of those business owners were poor farmers, but now they are rich home owners with three cars in their driveway!

Yiwu Wholesale Market is vast and is now surrounded by a staggering number of hotels and restaurants, and of course an international airport. It has been described as a shopper's paradise and awarded the title of 'China's first shopping and tourist area at AAAA level' and thousands of tourists from around the world visit the spectacular Yiwu Wholesale Market.

Questions

1 Who are the target markets for Yiwu?

2 In your opinion why is it successful?

Sources: Yiwu (2015) Link Yiwu. Your buying office in China, www.linkyiwu.com/ (accessed 18 April 2015); Philips, T. (2013) Yiwu, the 'magical' Chinese city supplying Poundland with cheap goods for Britain, www.telegraph.co.uk/news/worldnews/asia/china/9949829/Yiwu-the-magical-Chinese-city-supplying-Poundland-with-cheap-goods-for-Britain.html (accessed 18 April 2015).

access to international market information and contacts. By offering ranges of products from various companies they provide a more attractive overall sales package to foreign buyers, and by carrying a large range they can spread selling and administration costs over more products and companies, and reduce transport costs because of the economies of making larger shipments of goods from a number of companies.

EMCs deal with the necessary documentation and their knowledge of local purchasing practices and government regulations is particularly useful in markets that might prove difficult to penetrate. The use of EMCs, therefore, allows individual companies to gain far wider exposure of their products in foreign markets at much lower overall costs than they could achieve on their own, but there are a number of disadvantages too. The export house may specialize by geographical area, product or customer type (retail, industrial or institutional) and this may not coincide with the suppliers' objectives. As a result of this, the selection of markets may be made on the basis of what is best for the EMC rather than the manufacturer. As EMCs are paid by commission, they might be tempted to concentrate upon products with immediate sales potential rather than those that might require greater customer education and sustained marketing effort to achieve success in the longer term. EMCs may also be tempted to carry too many product ranges and as a result the manufacturer's products may not be given the necessary attention from sales people. The EMC may also carry competitive products which they promote preferentially, again to the disadvantage of a particular firm.

Care is needed in selecting a suitable EMC and resources should be allocated to managing the relationship, monitoring performance and learning more about the markets in which products are being sold in order to seize new opportunities. As sales increase, the firm may wish to manage its own exporting but the transition may not be very easy. First, the firm is likely to have become very dependent on the export house and unless steps have been taken to build contacts with foreign customers and increase market knowledge, moving from using EMCs could prove difficult. Second, the firm could find it difficult to withdraw from its contractual commitments to the export house. Many agreements are based only on the current and short term situation. Third, the EMC may be able to substitute products from an alternative manufacturer and so use their customer contacts as a basis for introducing new competition against the original exporter.

E-business was expected to have a very significant adverse effect on EMCs and even threaten their survival. However, in assessing the impact of e-business Sharma, (2013) found that EMCs are of great benefit to the ever-increasing e-businesses and they certainly have an efficient and effective role by engaging with B2B companies worldwide.

Piggybacking

In piggybacking, an established international distribution network of one manufacturer might be used to carry the products of a second manufacturer. The second manufacturer is able to ride on the back of the existing reputation, contacts and administration of the carrier with little direct investment themselves.

The carrier is either paid by commission and so acts as an agent, or alternatively, buys the product outright and so acts as an independent distributor. There are also advantages in piggybacking for the carrier as they are able first, to carry a wider product range and so present a more attractive sales package to potential buyers and second, to benefit from economies of scale by increasing their revenue without incurring additional costs of marketing, selling administration and distribution.

There can, however, be problems as the terms and conditions of the marketing arrangements are often poorly thought out because piggybacking often starts on a 'try it and see' basis. Either company might become locked into an arrangement that proves unsatisfactory for them, particularly as a firm's strategic objectives change over a period of time. Decisions about such marketing mix issues as branding might not suit both companies, and arrangements for providing technical support and service for products often prove to be a source of disagreement and difficulty.

For smaller firms, piggybacking can work when two products are interdependent, or if the second product provides a service for the first. Larger companies, too, have found it successful, particularly when the rider has experienced some kind of barrier to entering particular markets, or the use of an existing distribution network can provide faster market development.

A form of piggybacking occurs when an MNE moves into an emerging market. This provides the opportunity for their key suppliers, such as advertising, market research and consultancy companies, to set up local offices there.

Trading companies

Trading companies are part of the historical legacy from the colonial days and although different in nature now, they are still important trading forces in Africa and Asia. The United Africa Company, part of Unilever, for example, was once claimed to be the largest trader in Africa.

One of the major benefits of using trading houses is that their extensive operations and contacts allow them to operate in more difficult trading areas. One important aspect of their operations is to manage countertrade activities, in which sales into one market are paid for by taking other products from that market in exchange. The essential role of the trading company is to quickly find a buyer for the products that have been taken in exchange.

Indirect exporting is often a small company's first experience of international marketing: it has the advantages of being a simple and low-cost method of gaining exposure of products in foreign markets without the company first having to gain the necessary expertise in the various aspects of international trading. However, the company has little control over its international marketing activities and is restricted to simply reacting to new situations and opportunities as they arise. It is extremely difficult to build up international marketing knowledge and expertise by marketing at arm's-length, or to develop any significant long-term product and promotional strategies. Moreover, because of the lack of direct contact between the firm and the market, indirect entry approaches are usually perceived as lacking long-term commitment. As a result, customers and other members of the distribution channels are likely to withhold their full commitment to the firm and its products until the firm becomes more involved in the market, by adopting a more direct approach.

Direct exporting

If a company wishes to secure a more permanent long-term place in international markets, it must become more proactive through direct involvement in the process of **exporting**. Indeed, exporting is the most popular approach for firms as it requires less resources, has little effect on existing operations and involves low investment and financial risks (Leonidou, Katsikeas and Samiee, 2002). However, this requires definite commitment from the company and takes the form of investment in the international operation through allocating time and resources to a number of supporting activities. In addition, Helm and Gritsch (2014) state that when marketers clearly understand the key components of the export marketing mix they will significantly reduce uncertainty. The export marketing mix is summarized in Figure 7.3.

The benefits of direct over indirect exporting are that the proactive approach makes it easier to exert more influence over international activities, resulting in a number of specific advantages for the exporter such as greater control over the selection of markets, greater control over the elements of the marketing mix, improved feedback about the performance of individual products, changing situations in individual markets and competitor activity and the opportunity to build up expertise in international marketing.

The disadvantages of direct exporting are that the direct investment necessary is considerable because the whole of the marketing, distribution and administration costs will now be borne by the company. In taking this decision, the company must be quite sure that the costs can be justified in the light of the market opportunities identified. Illustration 7.2 shows how an exporter from an emerging country has a large part to play in the exporting of flowers.

For those firms wishing to change from indirect to direct exporting, or to significantly increase their marketing efforts, the timing can be critical as the extra costs involved can often place a huge financial burden

FIGURE 7.3   The components of the export marketing mix

Product:	selection, development and sourcing
Pricing:	policy, strategies, discount structures and trading terms
Promotion:	corporate promotions and local selling, trade shows and literature
Distribution:	sales force management, agents, distributors and logistics
Services:	market research, training and sales servicing
Finance and administration:	budgets, order processing, insurance and credit control
Technical:	specifications, testing and product quality

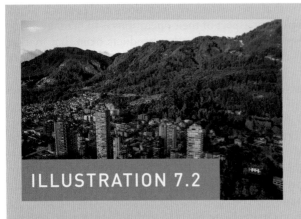

ILLUSTRATION 7.2

Exporting flowers: A blooming business for Columbia

The Netherlands is the world's number one exporter of flower bouquets. They export over 45 per cent of the world's flowers and their flower sales amount to a staggering US$3 813 663 000! However, the second largest exporter of flowers is Columbia with impressive sales of US$1 334 597 000 worth of the world's flowers. The Columbian flower export business began in earnest in the 1960s when the US and Columbian governments set up an 'Alliance for Progress' programme focusing on export trade from Columbia to the US in agricultural produce. Flowers are not the first thing that springs to mind when thinking of agricultural produce. However, Columbia has fine, temperate weather all year round. They have fertile, moist soil and plenty of water making it a perfect place from which to grow and export flowers. Additionally labour is cheap in Columbia.

Columbians are community spirited entrepreneurs and so the many hundreds of flower growers formed the Association of Columbian Flower Exporters (Asocolflores) to pool innovative ideas that would drive their international businesses forward. One of the first collective ideas dealt with the distribution and handling problems associated with their cargos of flowers. During the early years, flowers were transported by airplane. The flowers were transported in the hold, like tourist luggage, and loaded and offloaded by baggage handlers. This process damaged many flowers, which in turn reduced profit margins. Additionally, employing baggage handlers to load and offload their cargo was extremely expensive. Asocolflores improved the distribution process by collectively hiring cargo planes and providing loading and offloading equipment at Miami airport, the first airport that received their cargo of flowers. This improved the distribution process and reduced costs. Flowers, like fruit and meat, are temperature-sensitive items. Therefore, the Columbian entrepreneurs got together and provided cool storage fridges at Bogota and Miami airports in order to keep their flowers fresh for longer periods. These collaborations boosted sales and made Columbia famous for its flowers, and soon the exporters were able to market, promote and sell their flowers through their own importer–distributer companies in Miami and Europe, instead of using expensive brokering houses.

All in all, flower exports from Columbia are blooming, so much so that in Miami, Bogota and Medellin the airports' main cargo is flowers. But Columbian flower exporters do not want to 'stay local'. At present 80 per cent of sales are to the US due to the local proximity and the transportation set-up. Additionally the flower exporters sell to the US under a tax duty-free agreement. However, exporters are finding new markets in Russia, Britain and South Korea.

Question

1 What makes an exporter from an emerging market successful against worldwide competition?

Sources: USDA Foreign Agricultural Service (2015) The history of the Colombian flower industry and its influence on the United States. GAIN Report 6 February; Workman, D. (2014) Flower bouquet exports by country – world's top exports, www.worldstopexports.com/flower-bouquet-exports-country/3307 (accessed 24 April 2015).

on the company. The solution to this is, wherever possible, to make the transition gradually and in a well-planned way, starting with a beachhead or initial landing in one nearby foreign market.

Factors for success in exporting

A considerable amount of research has been carried out into the barriers and motivations for new exporters and the stages of internationalization, and this was discussed in Chapter 5.

Katsikeas, Leonidou and Morgan (2000) concluded that the way exporting performance is assessed is important. The simplest measure is whether firms do or do not export. Measurement of the financial performance of the firm in terms of export sales volume, growth and profitability, and the ratio of export to total sales is useful to measure longitudinal firm performance, but is less useful for comparing firm performance between industry sectors, because the industry sectors may be structured quite differently. Subjective measurements of the performance of the management of the firm are often helpful but pose a problem, too, in their comparability between firms and sectors.

Katsikeas *et al.* (2000) did, however, conclude that a number of factors were important in contributing to successful exporting:

- Commitment of the firms' management.
- An exporting approach in the firm which emphasizes the importance of augmenting and maintaining skills.
- A good marketing information and communication system.
- Sufficient production capacity and capability, product superiority and competitive pricing.
- Effective market research to reduce the psychic distance between the home country and target country market given that it is knowledge that generates business opportunities and drives the international process.
- An effective national export policy which provides support at an individual firm level, and emphasizes the need for knowledge-based programmes which prioritize market information about foreign market opportunities.

They found that the cost of export planning incurred by the firm did not correlate with export performance, and suggested that this might be explained by the fact that a major source of strength in exporting is flexibility and adaptability to export opportunities and the ability to make an immediate strategic response. Moreover, firm size and the managers' experience were not critical factors in export success, but they did recognize that these factors may be the source of the export stimuli in the first place, and could be major determinants of the firm's commitment to exporting and its ability to solve problems.

It is generally accepted, therefore, that in a small business, attitudes and commitment to international expansion are crucial for success, whereas in larger companies other factors can have a bearing on performance. The size of a company can either hinder or encourage international development because of the variations in the capability of the staff for planning, the lack of consistency of information and the degree to which adaptation of the mix is necessary. A number of other factors, such as the types of strategies that are pursued, segmentation, product and pricing can also affect export success.

International marketing of services is more fully explored in Chapter 8, but early stage exporting of services is different from exporting of products. Styles, Patterson and La (2005) found there is limited research into the unique success factors in the sector but report some key success factors, emphasizing appropriate use of the tangible and intangible assets and personnel-related factors where there is high face-to-face contact.

Selection of exporting method

The choice of the specific individual markets for exporting was discussed in Part I of this book, but it is important to re-emphasize that the more subjective factors, such as a senior executive's existing formal or informal links, particular knowledge of culture or language and perceived attractiveness of markets, may well influence an individual firm's decision.

Once individual markets have been selected and the responsibilities for exporting have been allocated, the decision needs to be taken about precisely how the firm should be represented in the new market. Clearly the nature, size and structure of the market will be significant in determining the method adopted. In a large market, particularly if a high level of market knowledge and customer contact is needed, it may be necessary to have a member of the firm's staff resident in or close to the market. This cannot be justified if the market is small or levels of customer contact need not be so high. Alternatively a home-based sales force may be used to make periodic sales trips in conjunction with follow-up communications by telephone, fax and email.

Many other factors will affect the cost–benefit analysis of maintaining the company's own staff in foreign markets, such as whether the market is likely to be attractive in the long term as well as the short term and whether the high cost of installing a member of the firm's own staff will be offset by the improvements in the quality of contacts, market expertise and communications. The alternative, and usually the first stage in exporting, is to appoint an agent or distributor.

Agents

Agents provide the most common form of low-cost direct involvement in foreign markets and are independent individuals or firms who are contracted to act on behalf of exporters to obtain orders on a commission basis. They typically represent a number of manufacturers and will handle non-competitive ranges. As part of their contract they will be expected to agree sales targets and contribute substantially to the preparation of forecasts, development of strategies and tactics using their knowledge of the local market. Agents do not take ownership of the goods but work instead on commission, sometimes as low as 2–3 per cent on large value orders.

The selection of suitable agents or distributors can be a problematic process. The selection criteria might include:

- The financial strength of the agents.
- Their contacts with potential customers.
- The nature and extent of their responsibilities to other organizations.
- Their premises, equipment and resources, including sales representatives.

Clearly, the nature of the agreement between the firm and its agent is crucial in ensuring the success of the arrangement, particularly in terms of clarifying what is expected of each party, setting out the basis for the relationships that will be built up and ensuring that adequate feedback on the market and product development is provided.

There are various sources for finding a suitable agent at low cost to the exporter:

- Asking potential customers to suggest a suitable agent.
- Obtaining recommendations from institutions such as trade associations, chambers of commerce and government trade departments.
- Using commercial agencies.
- Using agents for non-competing products.
- Poaching a competitor's agent.
- Advertising in suitable trade papers.

Achieving a satisfactory manufacturer–agent relationship

To achieve success the exporter–agent relationship needs to be managed by:

- Allocating time and resources to finding a suitably qualified agent.
- Ensuring that both the manufacturer and agent understand what each expects of the other.
- Ensuring that the agent is motivated to improve performance.
- Providing adequate support on a continuing basis including training, joint promotion and developing contacts.
- Ensuring that there is sufficient advice and information transfer in both directions.

Distributors

Distributors buy and stock the product from the manufacturer, organize selling and distribution and so take the market risk on unsold products as well as the profit. For this reason, they usually expect to take a higher percentage to cover their costs and risk.

Distributors usually seek exclusive rights for a specific sales territory and generally represent the manufacturer in all aspects of sales and servicing in that area. The exclusivity, therefore, is in return for the substantial capital investment that may be required in handling and selling the products. The capital investment can be particularly high if the product requires special handling equipment or transport and storage equipment in the case of perishable goods, chemicals, materials or components.

The issue of agreeing territories is becoming increasingly important as in many markets, distributors are becoming fewer in number, larger in size and sometimes more specialized in their activity. The trend to regionalization is leading distributors increasingly to extend their territories through organic growth, mergers and acquisitions. Also, within regional trading blocs competition laws are used to avoid exclusive distribution being set up for individual territories. However, the car industry in the EU was allowed to retain exclusive distribution until block exemption was removed. In anticipation of this Mercedes decided to take over its dealerships in order to retain control.

Other direct exporting methods

There are three other modes of exporting which are considered to be direct: management contracts, franchising and direct marketing, typically online buying.

Management contracts   Management contracts emphasize the growing importance of services, business skills and management expertise as saleable commodities in international trade. Normally the contracts undertaken are concerned with installing management operating and control systems, and training local staff to take over when the contract is completed. Many construction projects, such as the rebuilding of Afghanistan and Iraq, were undertaken in this way.

Other examples of management contracts may be as part of a deal to sell a processing plant as a turnkey operation, in which the capital plant and a management team are provided by the firm to set up and run the plant for the first few months of operation, and then train the local team to take over. With increased privatization and outsourcing of facilities management by public and private sector organizations there is a substantial growth in management contracts and in firms providing these services. Business process outsourcing has become a rapidly increasing international growth opportunity for companies such as Wipro and IBM, who provide a wide range of IT, human resource and operations processing services.

Franchising is a means of marketing goods and services in which the franchiser grants the legal right to use branding, trademarks and products, and the method of operation is transferred to a third party – the franchisee – in return for a franchise fee. The franchiser provides assistance, training and help with sourcing components, and exercises significant control over the franchisee's method of operation. It is considered to be a relatively less risky business start-up for the franchisee but still harnesses the motivation, time and energy of the people who are investing their own capital in the business. For the franchiser it has a number of advantages, including the opportunity to build greater market coverage and obtain a steady, predictable stream of income without requiring excessive investment.

Chan (1994) identifies two types of franchise. With product/trade franchises, for example car dealerships, petrol service stations and soft drinks bottlers, the franchisees are granted the right to distribute a manufacturer's product in a specified territory. Business format franchise is a growing sector and includes many types of businesses, including restaurants, convenience stores and hotels. This type of franchise includes the licensing of a trademark, the system for operating the business and the appearance of the location.

Franchising can take the form of single-unit franchising in which the arrangement is made with a single franchisee, or multi-unit in which the franchisee operates more than one unit. The multi-unit franchisee may be given the responsibility for developing a territory and opening a specified number of units alone or, as is common in international markets, operating a master franchise, in which the master franchisee can sub-franchise to others. See Case Study 1 Boost Juice: Healthy drink = healthy growth for an example of franchise success.

Franchising, be it single or multi-unit business is one of the major success stories in terms of international growth, Duckett (2008) and King *et al.* (2013). Franchising is a basic contractual agreement between the franchisor, the owner of the brand and supporting marketing mix, and a franchisee who invests personal time and money into the franchisors' brand. Internationally, franchisors are able to draw upon the cultural knowledge of appointed franchisees. This is of great benefit when considering service delivery, tastes, local demands, expectations, competitors and of course accessing local suppliers. Local franchisees can make suggestions to a fast food menu such as removing pepperoni from pizza toppings at Pizza Hut, providing more corn in Japanese restaurants, and suggesting that KFC include gravy, peas and pumpkin in Australian outlets. Local competitive knowledge is also helpful so now McDonald's have added spaghetti to the menu to compete more effectively with Jollibee in the Philippines. For the franchisee the major benefit for investing in an international franchise business is to be supported by global brand awareness and advertising.

Currently the top five international franchise companies are SUBWAY®, McDonalds, KFC, Burger King and 7-Eleven (Franchise Direct 2015). These are all US brands, but some other well known franchise brands come from Europe including Europcar, originating from France with 13 600 outlets worldwide and Carrefour, originating from Spain with over 6450 outlets worldwide.

However, SUBWAY® with over 42 000 units worldwide, is one of the largest international franchise business. The length of a franchise with SUBWAY® is 20 years with the opportunity to renew the franchise at the end of this period of time. SUBWAY® are keen to want franchisees to be committed to their brand for the long haul (SUBWAY® (2015)). And the franchisees seem to show their commitment and more as around 70 per cent of new Subway franchise businesses available in the UK are bought by existing franchisees (www.subway.co.uk).

Trading companies have frequently been appointed as master franchisees and, while this has helped to accelerate the growth of franchising, it has also influenced the franchiser's internationalization process. Because of the global power of these trading companies they are able to challenge the franchiser's decisions in the franchise process and have a considerable say in the strategic development of the business. There is an imbalance in power in franchising and Weaver, Frazer and Giddings (2010) noted that four government enquiries took place in Australia between 2006–2008 to try to resolve problems and they conclude that a lack of due diligence and unrealistic expectations increase the likelihood of relational conflict.

Most US hotels are part of branded groups but considerable scope exists in China and India, where hotels remain independent. The group sells off hotels to investment companies but offers franchises and management contracts to ensure a steady flow of bookings.

Direct marketing and online purchasing
Direct marketing is concerned with marketing and selling activities which do not depend for success on direct face-to-face contact. This includes mail order, telephone marketing, television marketing, media marketing, direct mail and electronic commerce using the Internet. We discuss e-commerce developments more fully in Chapter 12. There is considerable growth in all these areas, largely encouraged by increased availability of information and the development of information and communication technology to analyze it and client management systems to manage customer contacts. The changing lifestyles and purchasing behaviour of consumers, and the increasing cost of more traditional methods of entering new markets, are further drivers of this trend. The critical success factors for direct marketing are in the standardization of the product coupled with the personalization of the communication. While technical data about the product might be available in one language, often English, the recipients of the direct marketing in international markets expect to receive accurate communications in their domestic language. International direct marketing, therefore, poses considerable challenges, such as the need to build and maintain up-to-date databases, use sophisticated multilingual data processing and personalization software programs, develop reliable credit control and secure payment systems.

However, it can offer an advantage in entering new markets. Whereas American firms had trouble breaking into the Japanese market, catalogue firms were successful because they were positioned as good value for money for well-known clothing brands, compared to Japanese catalogues which were priced higher for similar quality items.

Direct marketing techniques can also be used to support traditional methods of marketing by providing sales leads, maintaining contact or simply providing improved customer service through international call centres. Where multiple direct channels are used for market entry, it is the integration of channels through effective customer relationship management systems that is essential to ensure customer satisfaction.

Foreign manufacturing strategies without direct investment

Having so far considered market entry strategies that have been based upon the development, manufacture and supply of products and services from the firms' domestic operations, we now turn our attention to strategies which involve production and service supply from overseas plants. Before discussing the alternatives available for ownership and control of overseas operations, it is necessary to consider the factors which may lead a firm to start having its products and services produced in one or more of its international markets.

Reasons for setting up overseas manufacture and service operations

The benefits of overseas manufacturing and service operations are:

Product. Avoiding problems due to the nature of the product, such as perishability.

Services that are dependent for success on local intellectual property, knowledge and sensitivity to the local market.

Transporting and warehousing. The cost of transporting heavy, bulky components and finished products over long distances is reduced.

Tariff barriers/quotas. Barriers to trade, which make the market inaccessible, are reduced.

Government regulations. Entry to some markets, such as Central and Eastern Europe, are difficult unless accompanied by investment in local operations.

Market. Local manufacture and service operations may be viewed more favourably by customers.

Government contacts. Firms are likely to be viewed more favourably if they contribute more to the local economy.

Information. A strong local presence improves the quality of market feedback.

International culture. Local presence encourages a more international outlook and ensures greater commitment by the firm to international markets.

Delivery. Local manufacture and service operations can facilitate faster response and just-in-time delivery.

Labour costs. Production, distribution and service centres can be moved to lower labour cost markets provided there are appropriate skills and adequate information technology infrastructure to maintain satisfactory quality.

For most companies, the cost of setting up an overseas operation is initially much higher than expanding the domestic facility by an equivalent amount, as we indicated earlier in this chapter. While the equipment costs are likely to be similar, and other costs such as labour, land purchase and building may even be cheaper, it is the cost involved in transferring technology, skills and knowledge that normally proves to be expensive and is often underestimated.

Transferring operations from a domestic to an overseas plant reduces the demand on the home plant, which might have traditionally supplied all the firm's overseas markets, and the firm must plan either to quickly reduce the cost of running the domestic plant or find new business to replace the production that has been transferred abroad, otherwise the viability of the domestic plant might be put at risk. Setting up new plants overseas involves large cash outflows and can put a significant strain on the firms' finances. Poor planning, underestimation of costs or unforeseen problems associated with setting up a plant overseas have frequently caused businesses to fail or be vulnerable to takeover.

The reason for locating the manufacturing plant close to the market may be due to the nature of the product but increasingly it is the costs of manufacture (including labour, raw materials and government support) as well as the costs of transport. For many firms, setting up foreign country operations for market entry reasons has prompted them to review their business and frequently resulted in them closing down their domestic operation and transferring labour-intensive activity to lower labour-cost countries.

Regionalization is also having a significant effect on plant location; for example, in the car industry location decisions are being based on a variety of factors, such as the participation of the country in monetary union, the different levels of productivity and the need to be closer to the most attractive potential markets. Mexico has expanded its car manufacturing business within NAFT; see Illustration 7.3 for details of how Mexico is developing that business, possibly toppling China off the top spot for car manufacturing. Hutton (2006) observed that Eastern Europe has become the new Detroit: General Motors, Volkswagen, Audi, Renault Daewoo, Suzuki, Toyota, Peugeot, Hyundai, Skoda and Kia all have factories there. Interestingly, South Korean firms are looking to 'make where they sell' to avoid paying tariffs and high transport costs, but Kia noted that wage rates in Slovenia were one-fifth of those in South Korea. Reversing this trend, however, Hyundai invested US$1 billion in an assembly plant in Alamaba to produce sports utility vehicles and their Sonata model.

Having emphasized that a move into overseas manufacturing and service operations involves high cost and risk, firms can choose between different levels of financial commitment. They can, for example, embark upon foreign manufacturing strategies which do not involve direct investment, such as contract manufacture and licensing agreements, or strategies which do involve direct investment albeit at different levels of cost and risk, for example, assembly operations, **wholly-owned subsidiary**, company acquisition, joint venture and strategic alliances.

Contract manufacture

A firm which markets and sells products into international markets might arrange for a local manufacturer to produce the product for them under contract. Examples include Nike and Gap, both of whom use contract clothing and shoe manufacturers in lower labour-cost countries. The advantage of arranging contract manufacture is that it allows the firm to concentrate upon its sales and marketing activities and, because investment is kept to a minimum, it makes withdrawal relatively easy and less costly if the product proves to be unsuccessful.

Contract manufacture might be necessary in order to overcome trade barriers and sometimes it is the only way to gain entry to a country in which the government attempts to secure local employment by insisting on local production. If political instability makes foreign investment unwise, this may be the best way of achieving a marketing presence without having the risk of a large investment in manufacturing. The disadvantage of contract manufacture as an entry method is that it does not allow the buyer control over the manufacturer's activities.

Outsourcing from contract manufacturers allows firms such as Sara Lee Desserts to be very flexible by supplying differentiated food products for different regional markets and adjusting costs more quickly when necessary. It also has the financial benefit of lower capital employed, but the risks are that the local contractor may not achieve the desired quality levels or may not gain the necessary knowledge to market the product themselves and compete directly with the international marketer. The marketing firm has less control over the conditions in the factory (intentionally or unintentionally). Some years ago Nike and Gap received bad publicity with the sweatshop conditions in plants they used in Asia. More recently Primark was one of the retailers whose products were made in a sweatshop factory that collapsed; 1000 Bangladeshi workers were killed. As a result they had to sever contracts with plants which refused to comply with company standards for wage levels and dreadful working conditions. Primark stepped forward with compensation for the families of those that died.

Two Scottish companies, Young's and Dawnfresh, provide further examples of contract manufacture. They are processors and marketers of shellfish caught in Scottish waters. However, both companies announced that they were closing their processing plants in Scotland with the resulting loss of 190 jobs. Young's decided to ship 120 000 tonnes of scampi 12 000 miles to Thailand for peeling before they make the return journey. Dawnfresh shipped its scampi to China for peeling.

Licensing

Licensing also requires relatively low levels of investment. Organizations involved in the film, television and sports industries, as diverse as Disney, the Olympic Games Committee and Manchester United Football Club, have been particularly successful in licensing the use of brands, characters and themes, generating

MANAGEMENT CHALLENGE 7.1

Peppa Pig: On the road in Brazil

Helped by brother George and Mummy and Daddy pig, Peppa with her characteristic laugh and love of muddy puddles is a popular British preschool cartoon and her adventures are shown in 180 countries. Peppa Pig's owner, Entertainment One and Nickelodeon, the most watched children's channel in the US, agreed a partnership to screen Peppa, surprisingly for American TV keeping the British accents. Entertainment One are now looking to recreate the success in Brazil so Peppa Pig and her friends are on the road in Brazil.

In 2015 Peppa Pig was launched in Brazil and was a phenomenal success. Entertainment One's licensing agent in Brazil is Exim and they certainly know what appeals to their consumer base. Brazilians like a carnival atmosphere and Peppa Pig went on the road and was showcased to adoring fans in twelve malls around Brazil including Rio de Janeiro, São Paulo, Salvador and Londrina. Even before the roadshow,

three million pairs of Peppa Pig shoes had been sold in the eight months ending February 2015. Similarly over a quarter of a million Peppa Pig books and magazines were flying off the shelves. The pre-school age children of Brazil adore Peppa Pig and the TV show has many fans. 100 000 DVDs have also found their way into the homes of Brazilian children. Peppa Pig is a fun product across many media platforms with simple interactive spaces for children on their website. But it was the opportunity to meet Peppa Pig and her brother George, Suzy Sheep, Rebecca Rabbit, Pedro Pony and Danny Dog face-to-face that brought 35 000 fans out of their homes to watch Peppa Pig Treasure Hunt Show.

Question

1 What do you consider to be the key elements of a global TV brand?

Sources: Langsworthy, B. (2015) Entertainment One enjoys 'phenomenal' response to Peppa Pig in Brazil, Licensing Biz, 7 April 2015 www.licensing.biz/news/read/entertainment-one-enjoys-phenomenal-response-to-peppa-pig-in-brazil/041825 (accessed 24 April 2015); A. Mostrous, 'From muddy puddles to global superstar, Peppa is laughing all the way to the bank', The Times, 11 October 2010.

Please note that Peppa Pig facts are correct as of March 2011.

huge sales of licensed products (an example appears in Management Challenge 7.1). It is estimated that the global merchandising industry is worth US$191 billion and instantly recognizable logos or characters are key, with cartoon characters making the most successful brands. The Simpsons is the most successful licensed TV show in history, with sales of more than US$8 billion. It is a form of management contract in which the licenser confers to the licensee the right to use one or more of the following: patent rights, trademark rights, copyrights and/or product or process know-how. In some situations, the licenser may continue to sell essential components or services to the licensee as part of the agreement.

There are a number of reasons why licensing is a useful entry method. Financial and management commitments can be kept low, the high cost of setting up a manufacturing, retailing or marketing subsidiary can be reduced and tariff and non-tariff barriers can be avoided. Licensing is particularly useful, therefore, to deal with difficult markets where direct involvement would not be possible, and where the market segments to be targeted may not be sufficiently large for full involvement.

Licensing usually has a number of benefits for the licenser. The licensee pays for the licence normally as a percentage of sales and thus, as the sales grow, so does the revenue to the licenser. Considerable control exists as the licensee uses the rights or know-how in an agreed way for an agreed quantity of product, and the licensee markets and purchases products for an agreed fee.

For the licensee, there are a number of advantages. For a relatively low outlay, it is possible to capitalize on established know-how with little risk and avoid the high research and development cost associated with launching a new product in many markets. This is particularly important in the industrial market, for example, where licensing of proven technology enables companies to enter markets with products which would be prohibitively expensive to develop.

Problems can occur in licensing if the licenser does not respond to changes in the market or technology, or does not help to develop the market for the licensee. A very capable licensee may have learned so much about the market and product that the contribution from the licenser is no longer required. The licensee too may either be unwilling or unable to develop the market in the way that the licenser would wish. These sources of conflict often arise as a result of the environment, competitors and market demand changing over the licensing period.

Sarathy *et al.* (2006) identify a number of techniques that can be adopted in order to minimize the potential problems of licensing:

- Develop a clear policy and plan.
- Allocate licensing responsibility to a senior manager.
- Select licensees carefully.
- Draft the agreement carefully to include duration, royalties, trade secrets, quality control and performance measures.
- Supply the critical ingredients.
- Obtain equity in the licensee.
- Limit the product and territorial coverage.
- Retain patents, trademarks, copyrights.
- Be an important part of the licensee's business.

Foreign manufacturing strategies with direct investment

At some point in its international development, a stage is reached when the pressure increases upon a firm to make a much more substantial commitment to an individual market or region. The reasons for investment in local operations are:

- *To gain new business*. Local production demonstrates strong commitment and is the best way to persuade customers to change suppliers, particularly in industrial markets where service and reliability are often the main factors when making purchasing decisions.
- *To defend existing business*. Car imports to a number of countries are subject to restrictions and as their sales increase, so they become more vulnerable to locally produced competitive products.
- *To move with an established customer*. Component suppliers or service providers often set up their own local subsidiaries in order to retain their existing business, compete with local component makers and benefit from increased sales.
- *To save costs*. By locating production facilities overseas, costs can be saved in a variety of areas such as labour, raw materials and transport.
- *To avoid government restrictions* which might be in force to restrict imports of certain goods.

See Illustration 7.3 for ways that Mexico is promoting itself to foreign investors.

For most multinationals there is a strong requirement to demonstrate that they have a permanent presence in all their major markets. The actual form of their operations in each market is likely to vary considerably from country to country but they must also reduce their own manufacturing and operations costs through making the supply chain more cost-effective. Some firms, for example, in the shoe and footwear industries obtain component or finished product supplies from the lowest labour cost areas; Ford locates its component suppliers on a manufacturing campus close to its assembly plants.

Assembly

A foreign owned operation might be set up simply to assemble components which have been manufactured in the domestic market. It has the advantage of reducing the effect of tariff barriers, which are normally

ILLUSTRATION 7.3

Mexico: Developing into a big player of manufacturing

The reasons for setting up overseas manufacturing businesses are outlined in this chapter and this Challenge shows those principles.

Mexico's economic outlook is positive: GDP is growing, unemployment rates are reducing and their inflation rates are falling. Export revenue is already valued at US$397.5 billion with the vast majority of that relating to manufacturing of cars, airplane parts, computers and mobile phones. Therefore, the Mexican government is proud and they are not only promoting these facts but showcasing Mexico as a great place in which to do business. So much so they are changing regulations to incentivize manufacturing companies to build production factories in Mexico; which in turn will help unemployment figures stay low and boost local economies.

Volkswagen and Nissan, both worldwide car manufacturing brands, are stepping up their investments in Mexico by building new and/or improved factories. And when big brands such as Volkswagen and Nissan show interest in a country, others will follow. Mazda is increasing its production capacity from 140 000 cars per year to 230 000 cars per year by 2016, and South Korea is investing in Mexico for the first time with the production of their Kia.

In addition to the Mexican government's incentives, labour costs in Mexico are low. China, once heralded as the number one country for car manufacturing is falling out of favour with big brands because of their ever increasing labour costs. With the average wage in Mexico for an unskilled automobile worker being $900 per year less than an equivalent working in China it is no wonder car manufacturers are thinking of turning to Mexico.

Further, there are many excellent skilled assembly workers in Mexico, something which foreign manufacturing investors find attractive as it saves money on intensive training from a zero to low-skilled workforce.

Question

1 What are the benefits and risks for foreign car manufacturers investing in Mexico?

Sources: Kynge, J. (2015) 'Mexico steals a march on China in car manufacturing', *The Financial Times*, 21 April www.ft.com/intl/cms/s/2/0bc33e06-e81e-11e4-894a -00144feab7de.html#axzz3YP0HhhQ3 (accessed 24 April 2015); The Offshore Group (2015) 'Foreign companies continue to invest in Mexico manufacturing', 2 Feb offshoregroup. com/2015/02/09/foreign-companies-continue-to-invest-in -mexico-manufacturing/ (accessed 24 April 2015).

lower on components than on finished goods. It is also advantageous if the product is large and transport costs are high, for example in the case of cars. There are other benefits for the firm too, as retaining component manufacture in the domestic plant allows development and production skills and investment to be concentrated, thus maintaining the benefit from economies of scale. By contrast, the assembly plant can be made a relatively simple activity requiring low levels of local management, engineering skills and development support.

There is an argument that assembly plants do not contribute significantly to the local economy in the long term. In initially attracting Nissan, Honda and Toyota assembly plants, the UK government claimed that many jobs would be created at relatively low cost but critics claimed that the number of jobs created in the assembly plants was not very significant and, unless the components were made locally, little transfer of technology would be achieved and the assembly plants could relatively easily be moved to a new location. In practice as other car manufacturers withdrew from the UK market these Japanese manufacturers became the only major established firms. Both to counter threats such as this and also to generate further employment, countries can take steps to develop the component supply business either by interrupting the

ILLUSTRATION 7.4

HSBC buying problems in the US

If expansion is too rapid it can cause problems. In February 2007 HSBC announced a profits warning, the first in its 142-year history. The unexpected profit underperformance was attributed to Household (renamed HFC and later HSBC Finance Corporation) its US subsidiary which was bought for US$15 billion in 2003. HSBC had to increase its bad debt provision by £900 million when US borrowers failed to make their mortgage repayments. Perhaps most surprisingly, given that HFC was the leading profit generator in the six months to June 2006, there was no American representative on HSBC's main board. However far worse was to come.

HFC was a major subprime mortgage lender and bad debts destroyed the value of the company. Moreover, HFC's credit card loans, with many again in the subprime market, stood at US$49.6 billion, around two-thirds of all HSBC credit card loans, and the credit card operation was forced to write off US$5.4 billion in bad or doubtful loans. 800 HFC branches were closed in an effort to shrink its exposure to the subprime market amid calls for HSBC to walk away from HFC.

Question

1 How can an organization reduce the risk of new market entry?

Sources: P. Aldrick (2007) 'HSBC "to axe loan arm chiefs"', *Daily Telegraph*, 9 February; R. Wachman (2009) 'HSBC faces crisis over us credit cards', *The Observer*, 12 April.

component supply chain through imposition of import or foreign exchange rate restrictions or, as in the case of CzechInvest, the inward investment arm of the Czech Republic, by supporting local component manufacturers who can supply 'just in time'. Coca-Cola uses 50 per cent owned bottling and distribution companies in local countries, supplying them with concentrate to maintain control over the recipes.

Wholly-owned subsidiary

As we indicated in Figure 7.2, for any firm the most expensive method of market entry is likely to be the development of its own foreign subsidiary, as this requires the greatest commitment in terms of management time and resources. It can only be undertaken when demand for the market appears to be assured. Illustration 7.4, however, illustrates the pitfalls of inadvisable acquisition.

This market entry method indicates that the firm is taking a long-term view, especially if full manufacturing facilities are developed rather than simply setting up an assembly plant. Even greater commitment is shown when the R&D facilities are established in local countries too. If the company believes its products have long-term market potential in a relatively politically stable country, then only full ownership will provide the level of control necessary to fully meet the firm's strategic marketing objectives. There are considerable risks too, as subsequent withdrawal from the market can be extremely costly, not simply in terms of financial outlay, but also in terms of the firm's reputation in the international and domestic market, particularly with shareholders, customers and staff.

Company acquisitions and mergers

In the previous chapters we discussed the role of acquisitions and mergers in achieving globalization. Illustration 7.5 demonstrates the justification for using acquisition as a means of strategic development to strengthen a long term position and acquire new talent but also shows that governments can play an important role in the process, and can foil takeover attempts.

ILLUSTRATION 7.5

Facebook acquires on-trend photo-sharing businesses

Facebook has acquired over 40 different businesses since its launch including FriendFeed, Divvyshot and Chai Labs. Facebook did not purchase these businesses for their assets or market share. What they bought was talent inside the entrepreneurs who had set up the innovative and successful business, driven it forward and were future thinkers. Facebook bought talent to add to the existing pioneering culture that they are known for.

Two major photo-sharing businesses were acquired recently, Instagram and WhatsApp. Instagram was bought for US$1 billion; WhatsApp was bought for US$22 billion. The new photo-sharing businesses have been added to Facebook's portfolio of products, with the intention that they will help fulfil Mark Zuckerberg's (chief executive of Facebook) dream of connecting everyone to everybody else through virtual platforms.

Instagram is one of the fastest growing photo-sharing networks with over 300 million monthly active people. There are 70 million photos uploaded, on average, each day. Facebook bought the talent that came with Instagram but they also bought a potential revenue stream. Advertising started to appear on a consumer's Instagram from 2013. Brands are still tentative about this space to advertise as promotions only appear to a highly targeted audience based on an Instagram-er's Facebook profile. So Ben and Jerry's, one of the earliest advertisers on Instagram, only promote their brand to Facebook-ers that like ice-cream. The expected revenue from Instagram has not yet lived up to expectations. However, Facebook will be watching Instagram's performance and with revenues of US$700 million (2015) and projected $5.8 billion (by 2020) it will certainly be a welcome monetizing stream. In addition to Ben and Jerry's, Burberry, Disneyland and GoPro are advertising on Instagram; Facebook, no doubt, will hope other big brands follow.

WhatsApp has 700 million monthly active users. Users are charged a 99p subscription for using WhatsApp after the first year. The plan for WhatsApp is to increase the customer base and increase activity. Ways to monetise the platform will evolve as users and advertisers decide and monitor what WhatsApp's benefits are.

Question

1 What are the benefits and pitfalls of Facebook's acquisitions?

Sources: Fiegerman, S. (2015) Instagram revenue projected to hit $5.8 billion in 2020, analyst says, 19 February mashable .com/2015/02/19/instagram-revenue-estimate-2020/; Facebook.com; Instagram.com

---

The considerable pressure to produce short-term profits means that speed of market entry is essential and this can be achieved by acquiring an existing company in the market. Among other advantages, acquisition gives immediate access to a trained labour force, existing customer and supplier contacts, recognized brands, an established distribution network and an immediate source of revenue. Companies from emerging markets have used acquisition as a fast route to acquiring a globally recognized brand, for example, Lenovo's acquisition of IBM's PC division, Aspen Pharmacare's takeover of Australia's Sigma Pharmaceuticals to acquire market share, or India's Bharti Airtel's acquisition of the African assets of Kuwait's Zain to build its African telecoms business.

In certain situations acquisition is the only route into a market. This is the case with previously state-owned utilities. Many utilities and infrastructure companies in the UK are foreign owned, for example, water companies are owned by Australian investment fund Macquarie, Suez, Vivendi and Bouygues (France),

Union Fenosa (Spain) and YTL (Malaysia), the British Airports Authority by Ferrovial of Spain and electricity companies by EDF of France.

Expropriation is the opposite of privatization and occurs when a government, usually a nondemocratic regime, takes strategic assets from a company, such as an oil well or mine. Even the most powerful companies are unable to stop this and often receive little compensation.

Sometimes the reasons for international business acquisition are, perhaps, not driven by business logic as it seems questionable whether any of the takeovers of British premiership football clubs will make money, starting with Roman Abramovitch's purchase of Chelsea and the Glazer family ownership of Manchester United, even though the marketing opportunities are huge.

An acquisition strategy is based upon the assumption that companies for potential acquisition will be available, but if the choice of companies is limited, the decision may be taken on the basis of expediency rather than suitability. The belief that acquisitions will be a time-saving alternative to waiting for organic growth to take effect may not prove to be true in practice. It can take a considerable amount of time to search and evaluate possible acquisition targets, engage in protracted negotiations and then integrate the acquired company into the existing organization structure.

Another disadvantage of acquisition is that the acquiring company might take over a demotivated labour force, a poor image and reputation, and out-of-date products and processes. All of these problems can prove costly and time-consuming to overcome.

While takeover of its companies is often accepted by government as a way of increasing investment, takeover of companies which are regarded as part of a country's heritage or key to security can raise considerable national resentment if it seems that they are being taken over by foreign firms. A country looking to develop its own technology and manufacturing is likely to believe that acquisition of a domestic company by an MNE is not as desirable as the MNE setting up a local subsidiary. See Management Challenge 7.2 where governments are setting up joint ventures.

Moreover, acquisition by a large international firm is often associated with job losses and transfer of production facilities overseas. In the past few years there has been considerable debate about acquisition and mergers as a method of achieving rapid expansion. The rationale that is used for acquisition is that an ineffective company can be purchased by a more effective company which will be able, first, to reduce costs; second, improve performance through applying better management skills and techniques; and third, build upon the synergy between the two companies and so achieve better results. Many takeovers in the UK and US were financed by huge bank loans justified on the basis that an improvement in future profits would be used to pay the high interest charges. In practice few companies are able to realize the true benefits of synergy. If the other parts of the acquirer's business underperform, for example during a recession, then the acquired company is used to service an increasing debt and is starved of investment.

Some firms use acquisition to focus on their core business and sell off peripheral activities to raise the necessary investment funds for new projects or to plug holes in their finances. As part of its commitment to raise US$30 billion by the end of 2011 to meet the obligations of the Gulf of Mexico oil spill, BP sold assets in many countries around the world.

Cooperative strategies

There are a number of situations in which two or more firms might work together to exploit a new opportunity. The methods that are adopted are joint ventures, strategic alliances and reciprocal ownership, in which two firms hold a stake in each other's business.

Joint ventures

Joint ventures occur when a company decides that shared ownership of a specially set up new company for marketing and/or manufacturing is the most appropriate method of exploiting a business opportunity. It is usually based on the premise that two or more companies can contribute complementary expertise or resources to the joint company, which, as a result, will have a unique competitive advantage to exploit. Table 7.1 shows the contributions of partners from developed and developing countries.

Table 7.1 Who provides what in partnerships between firms from developed and developing countries?

Developed	Developing
Marketing systems	Customer insights
Brands and communication	Land
Financial management	Buildings and equipment
Forecasting	Distribution networks
Planning	Skills
Technology	Low costs
Information systems	Beneficial wage rates
Capital	
Supply chain management	Tax relief
Know-how	Political connections
Human resources	Neighbouring markets
Financial incentives	

Source: Schiffman, L.G. and Kanuk, L.L. (2000) *Consumer Behaviour*, Prentice Hall.

While two companies contributing complementary expertise might be a significant feature of other entry methods, such as licensing, the difference with joint ventures is that each company takes an equity stake in the newly formed firm. The stake taken by one company might be as low as 10 per cent, but this still gives them a voice in the management of the joint venture.

There are a number of advantages of setting up joint ventures. These include:

- Countries, such as the Philippines, try to restrict foreign ownership.
- Many firms find that partners in the host country can increase the speed of market entry when good business and government contacts are essential for success.
- Complementary technology or management skills provided by the partners can lead to new opportunities in existing sectors, for example, in mobile communications.
- Global operations in R&D and production are prohibitively expensive, but necessary to achieve competitive advantage.
- The two companies can share investment costs and risk.
- The firms can learn from each other, particularly how to participate in local markets.

There are, however, some significant disadvantages of joint ventures as a market entry method. As joint venture companies involve joint ownership, there are often differences in the aims and objectives of the participating companies which can cause disagreements over the strategies adopted by the particular companies. If ownership is evenly divided between the participant firms, these disagreements can often lead to delays and failure to develop clear policies. In some joint ventures the greater motivation of one partner rather than another, particularly if they have a greater equity stake, can lead to them becoming dominant and the other partner becoming resentful. Some firms more effectively learn their partners' skills, so in a General

Motors–Toyota joint venture, Toyota learned about supply logistics and managing US staff, whereas GM failed to learn Toyota's manufacturing methods.

The other disadvantages of this form of market entry compared to, for example, licensing or the use of agents, is that a substantial commitment of investment of capital and management resources must be made in order to ensure success. Start-up costs for management and control and developing cultural understanding can be high. Many companies would argue that the demands on management time might be even greater for a joint venture than for a directly owned subsidiary because of the need to educate, negotiate and agree with the partner many of the operational details of the joint venture.

Some experts recommend that a joint venture should be used by companies to extend their capabilities rather than merely exploit existing advantages, and is not recommended if there are potential conflicts of interest between partners. The role of the government in joint ventures can be particularly influential, as it may control access to the domestic market. Moreover, a government may be persuaded to adapt its policy if a firm is bringing in advanced technology or is willing to make a major investment. Most of the major multinationals have increased their involvement in joint ventures, but the implications of this are that it leads to increasingly decentralized management and operations, more closely aligned to transnational operation than to global standardization, in which more centralized control is necessary.

Where joint ventures are used for emerging market entry there is also the possibility of a conflict of objectives which can occur between the international company, which wishes to develop a new market, and the local company which wishes to develop its own foreign markets or withdraw profits from the joint venture to finance other projects.

In analyzing the results of joint ventures in China, Vankonacker (1997) observes that joint ventures are hard to sustain in unstable environments and concludes that more direct investment in China will be wholly-owned, offering Johnson & Johnson's oral care, baby and feminine hygiene products business as a success story. Management Challenge 7.2 shows that joint ventures do not have to take place between two businesses; governments are engaging with the benefits of joint ventures.

Strategic alliances

While all market entry methods essentially involve alliances of some kind, during the 1980s the term **strategic alliance** started to be used, without being precisely defined, to cover a variety of contractual arrangements that are intended to be strategically beneficial to both parties but cannot be defined as clearly as licensing or joint ventures. The Star Alliance of airlines that includes Lufthansa, BMI, Scandinavian Airlines, Singapore Airlines and South African Airways is one example. Bronder and Pritzl (1992) have defined strategic alliances in terms of at least two companies combining value chain activities for the purpose of competitive advantage.

Some examples of the bases of alliances are:

- technology swaps
- R&D exchanges
- distribution relationships
- marketing relationships
- manufacturer–supplier relationships
- cross-licensing.

Perhaps one of the most significant aspects of strategic alliances has been that many involve cooperation between partners that might also be competitors. This can pose problems for the participants, who must be careful about sharing information with their alliance partner but avoid information leakage where the organization may be competing.

There are a number of driving forces for the formation and operation of strategic alliances.

Insufficient resources: the central argument is that no organization alone has sufficient resources to realize the full global potential of its existing, and particularly its new products. Equally, if it fails to satisfy all the markets which demand these products, competitors will exploit the opportunities which arise and become stronger. In order to remain competitive, powerful and independent companies need to cooperate.

Pace of innovation and market diffusion: the rate of change of technology and consequent shorter product life cycles mean that new products must be exploited quickly by effective diffusion out into the market. This requires not only effective promotion and efficient physical distribution but also needs good channel management, especially when other members of the channel are powerful, and so, for example, the strength of alliances within the recorded music industry including artists, recording labels and retailers, has a powerful effect on the success of individual hardware products such as the MP3 player.

High research and development costs: as technology becomes more complex and genuinely new products become rarer, so the costs of R&D become higher.

Concentration of firms in mature industries: many industries have used alliances to manage the problem of excess production capacity in mature markets. Sometimes this leads to takeovers as has occurred in the One World between BA and Iberia.

Government cooperation: as the trend towards regionalization continues, so governments are more prepared to cooperate on high-cost projects rather than try to go it alone. There have been a number of alliances in Europe – for example, the European Airbus has been developed to challenge Boeing, and the Eurofighter aircraft project is a collaborative venture by Britain, Germany, Italy and Spain.

Self-protection: a number of alliances have been formed in the belief that they might afford protection against competition in the form of individual companies or newly formed alliances. This is particularly the

MANAGEMENT CHALLENGE 7.2

Joined-up thinking: Africa and the Gulf

The United Nations (UN) advise that agricultural production including fruit, vegetables, wheat, corn and rice needs to increase by 100 per cent in developing countries. They also advise that in the more developed countries food production needs to increase by around 70 per cent. These increases need to take place by 2050 to feed the world's rising population. Many countries will not be able to achieve the increases that the UN recommends. The main reason for this is because many countries have only small areas of agricultural land, limited farming expertise and more importantly their land is arid. The UAE recognizes it cannot increase its agricultural production to that recommended by the UN. Whilst UAE land is rich in energy reserves, such as oil, they have very limited fresh water supplies and limited land for agricultural growth. Indeed, for many years, the UAE has purchased food from outside its borders.

Parts of North Africa have a history of famine, disease, poverty and hunger. Over 80 per cent of African people live and work on farms and they should, therefore, have abundant crops of fruits, vegetables, cotton, rice and wheat. However, due to low productivity, no investment in technological advances, poor irrigation systems and a chaotic infrastructure, production is very low.

A joint venture has been formed between the Middle East and Africa. The Middle East will provide a multimillion dollar investment in African agriculture. Africa, in exchange for the investment, will feed the Middle East.

Two examples of how this joint venture is working are Qatar and Saudi Arabia. Hassad Food from Qatar has invested US$1 billion in Sudan's agriculture. Sudanese farmers will grow wheat, corn and soya, which will then be exported to Qatar. Saudi Arabia has invested US$2.5 billion in Ethiopia's agriculture. In exchange for the investment Ethiopian farmers will produce rice for Saudi Arabia. The joint venture will be of mutual benefit to both parties.

Questions

1 What are the benefits of joint ventures?

2 Why has the joint venture between the Middle East and Africa been formed?

3 What are the benefits of this joint venture?

Source: Rafaty, M. (2014) View from Middle East and Africa: Can Africa feed the Middle East?, published 14 August 2014, www.fdiintelligence.com/Locations/Middle-East-Africa /View-from-Middle-East-and-Africa-can-Africa-feed-the -Middle-East (accessed 26 April 2015).

case in the emerging global high technology sectors such as information technology, telecommunications, media and entertainment.

Market access: strategic alliances have been used by companies to gain access to difficult markets; for instance, Caterpillar used an alliance with Mitsubishi to enter the Japanese market.

Further benefits to a strategic alliance are shown in Management Challenge 7.3 where businesses need each others' expertise to take their own products to market.

MANAGEMENT CHALLENGE 7.3

Plastic and food: The perfect strategic alliance

KOR Food Innovation was founded by Chef John Csukor and he has an insatiable passion for food. Csukor has been a food innovator and developer for many years. He has many marketing, food production and purchasing talents. Through Csukor's employment in mass catering at Motorola Hospitality Group, Compass Group and Starbucks Coffee Company, he has fed thousands of hungry workers. More recently John Csukor has set up his own business called KOR Food Innovation. KOR Food Innovation helps other businesses design and implement a menu strategy for their workforce; they run focus groups to establish the latest trends in food and/or home-based cooking and even design food product labels. Csukor and his research team made up of dieticians, food designers and fine-dining chefs, develop a range of amazing food that is commercially-ready for hotels, restaurants and supermarkets.

Dupont, original makers of gunpowder, now has many business segments including industrial bio-science, agriculture and performance materials. They found their fame through researching and manufacturing plastic, Polymer and Lycra for sportswear and women's hosiery. One area of their business is to provide plastic covers to protect ready-made food, meats and cheese from bacteria and of course to help keep food fresh for longer periods.

KOR Food Innovation and Dupont have formed a strategic alliance. KOR Food Innovation has designed new meat-based products that need a plastic packaging. The plastic packaging designed by Dupont enables KOR Food Innovation's meat-based products to be cooked in the oven to over 400°F, without the packaging shrivelling and shrinking. The plastic can be used on fresh or frozen meat produce and can go straight to the oven. There are even air-vents in the plastic to release steam and baste the meat based products.

Question

1 What are the benefits of the strategic alliance between KOR International and Dupont?

Sources: Dupont (2013) Data Book; KOR Food Innovation www.korfoodinnovation.com/

As with all entry strategies, success with strategic alliances depends on effective management, good planning, adequate research, accountability and monitoring. It is also important to recognize the limitations of this as an entry method. Companies need to be aware of the dangers of becoming drawn into activities for which they are not designed.

Voss *et al.* (2006) emphasize the importance of cultural sensitivity in cross-border alliances and the implications for trust and quality information exchange.

Minority stake share holdings

In this chapter we have considered many different methods of cooperation between partners. Over the years many firms have taken an equity stake in another firm for a variety of reasons. Russia, for example, restricts foreign ownership to 49 per cent. The main reason is that it is regarded as less risky to build an ownership stake over time to reduce uncertainty in the workforce. Volkswagen took a 31 per cent stake in Skoda and gradually increased this to 70 per cent, the remainder is owned by the Czech government. It might provide the opportunity to influence the strategy of that firm, create a basis upon which to share expertise between the firms or establish a platform that might lead to a more formal business relationship, such as a merger, as well as generating an immediate return on the investment. Renault took a stake in Nissan to save the company from bankruptcy and succeeded in turning the company around by helping it to launch a more attractive and competitive range of cars. Renault then became the recipients of Nissan's expertise in improving quality and production efficiency.

What is quite clear is that global firms are adopting a range of market entry partnership arrangements to maximize their global performance and presence. The businesses are becoming increasingly complex as they embark on joint ventures, with the associated formal responsibilities, strategic alliances, short-term contractual obligations and shareholdings which might be the basis for closer future cooperation.

Inevitably the challenge for management is to manage the various stakeholder expectations and maximize the opportunities that come from synergy and the complementary activity of the partners. To do this it is necessary to select partners that are willing and able to contribute at least some of:

- complementary products and services
- knowledge and expertise in building customer relationships
- capability in technology and research
- capacity in manufacturing and logistics
- power in distribution channels; and
- money and management time.

The management must also deal with the added complexity and potential for conflicts between two quite different partners that arise because of differences in:

- objectives and strategies
- approach to repatriation of profits and investment in the business
- social, business and organization cultures; and
- commitment to partnership and understanding of management responsibilities.

While cooperative strategies promise synergy, the potential for cost saving and faster market entry, it requires considerable management effort to overcome the inherent difficulties and dedication to see the partnerships through to success.

SUMMARY

- For a firm at the start of internationalization, market entry can be regarded as a critical first step which is vital not only for financial reasons, but also because it will set a pattern of future international involvement. It determines not just the opportunities for sales but also a valuable source of market information.

- Market entry methods can be seen as a series of alternatives available to international firms, and a global strategy might utilize a number of different approaches. A firm can make individual decisions based on the factors affecting one specific country or the whole region and choose the most appropriate method for the particular set of circumstances.

- The choice of market entry method should be based on an assessment of the firm's desired involvement in the market and the level of control of its marketing mix in the country, set against the financial and marketing risks.

- For large established companies that already have extensive involvement in international markets, the market entry decision is taken against the background of the competitive nature of the market, the environment, its global strategy and an existing and substantial network of operations.

- The company's competitive strategy is likely to require simultaneous decisions affecting its arrangements in a number of markets in order to improve its competitive position by entering untapped or emerging markets, or expanding its activities in existing markets.

■ In order to achieve these objectives within a very short timescale, rather than relying on organic growth the companies have used a variety of market entry strategies, including joint ventures and alliances, often with competitors. This is leading to increasingly complex operations being created in which companies strive to balance the opposing forces of competitiveness and cooperation, and quite frequently such arrangements fail to deliver the expected benefits.

KEYWORDS

market entry	trading companies	contract manufacture
market involvement	exporting	licensing
risk and control	distributors	acquisitions
indirect exporting	management contracts	joint ventures
domestic purchasing	franchising	strategic alliance
export houses	direct marketing	
piggybacking	wholly-owned subsidiary	

CASE STUDY 1

Boost Juice Be healthy: Boost Juice great for all

Janine Allis, founder and managing director of Boost Juice, one of Australia's most recognized franchises, wants it to be the *world's most loved brand!!* Janine, like many entrepreneurs, endeavours to create a business that is of benefit to its consumers. In the early twenty-first century Australia, in company with most of the developed world, was facing the fact that there was an obesity epidemic. Young and old were eating too much, not exercising and often relying on high calorie/high fat/high sugar diets. Many health ministers and journalists were particularly worried about young people; especially as many global fast food brands had products that were low in vitamins and high in sugar, fat and salt. Janine realised

there was a gap in the marketplace. She discovered that there were no retail outlets that served *healthy fast food.* And this situation was not just in Australia. Janine researched all major countries around the world and discovered that healthy fast food retail outlets for young people to hang-out in and relax were not available . . . anywhere!! In 2000, Janine opened her first Boost Juice outlet in South Australia. The Boost Juice menu was developed by Boost Juice's own nutritionist and naturopaths to provide a selection of healthy, freshly squeezed juices and smoothies.

The target market for Boost Juice is 15–35-year-old males and females but their core target market is 25-year-old females who already live a healthy lifestyle. To cater for their core target market, all drinks are 98 per cent fat free and free of artificial flavours or colourings. Based on what the core market wanted and the product Janine devised, the company's philosophy is all about creating a space for people who want to chill-out with their friends *and* stay healthy. Over the years, the philosophy has not changed; but their product line has increased. Now there are many new drinks and snack items including Banana Bread, Choc Protein Balls and live frozen yogurts. They also have a 'lite' range for consumers who want a lower calorie smoothie. For people that want drinks containing nutrients and antioxidants they have a Green range.

Boost Juice products are not the only thing that makes Boost Juice retail outlets special; they have many carefully planned intangible elements. The intangible elements include the very best in sunshine music for young people, vibrant, bright and cheerful fixtures and fittings, and the *ultimate* warm and friendly welcome. All of which creates a cool, sociable vibe.

Boost Juice now has 350 retail outlets. Janine Allis always had a global vision in mind, as she knew a healthy fast-food outlet was a unique concept worldwide. Now Boost franchisees are juicing in the United Kingdom, Thailand, Indonesia, South Africa, Macau, Chile, Singapore, Malaysia, Germany, the Baltics and India. But she could not go worldwide with just her own money, and did not want to borrow from a bank. Therefore, Janine became a franchisor and offered the vision, brand, products and service philosophy to others as a franchise business.

The cost of a Boost Juice franchise varies dependent upon the location and size of the business.

	Australia	*The Baltics*
Initial investment fee	Approximately $240 000 to $320 000 excluding GST (Boost Australia, n.d.).	Ranging from 40 000 to 50 000 EUR excluding VAT which includes training costs, franchise fee, installation costs, furnishings and equipment expenses (Boost Juice Bars, n.d.).
Franchise fee	Initial franchisee fee of $41 000 for the license (The Franchise Mall, n.d.).	It is included in the initial investment fee.
Ongoing royalty fee	8% of gross monthly turnover, and 3% of gross monthly turnover payable for marketing fees (Boost Australia, n.d.; The Franchise Mall, n.d.).	8% of the monthly net sales, and an additional 3% of the net sales contributed for Boost Juice Marketing Fund (Boost Juice Bars, n.d.).
	South Africa	*Malaysia*
Initial investment fee	Approximately R550 000 to R600 000 excluding VAT. This includes franchise fee, training fee, fitout costs, plant and equipment, and allowance for working capital (Boost Juice Bars, 2014).	Ranging from RM 250 000 to RM 350 000 including franchise fee (iFranchise Malaysia, n.d.).
Franchise fee	R75 000 excluding VAT. This is included in the initial investment fee (Boost Juice Bars, 2014).	RM 65 000 which is already included in the initial investment fee (iFranchise Malaysia, n.d.; Yeong, 2013).
Ongoing royalty fee	Ongoing royalty fee at 8% of gross monthly sales, whereas an additional 4% of gross monthly sales contributed to Boost Juice Marketing Fund (Boost Juice Bars, 2014).	Ongoing royalty fee at 6% (iFranchise Malaysia, n.d.).

Not only has Janine grown her business it certainly seems Boost Juice is attracting attention and winning awards. The awards include:

- National Retailers Association Award – Training/ HR Initiative Award
- A Boost Juice Franchisee – Scott Meneilly – Winner of the Retailer of the Year Award
- Franchise Council of Australia's Multi Unit Franchisees of the Year

- National Retailers Association Awards
- Training/HR Initiative Award
- Westfield Best Food Retailer Finalist (Boost Franchise)
- Individual Achievement Award (Boost Franchise)

Boost Juice is doing incredibly well financially with an increase of 9 per cent of network sales at US$155 million in 2012–2013, compared to $141 million the year before (Greenblat, 2013).

All in all Janine has been an amazing franchisor. She says there are four key principles to being a successful franchisor:

1. Offer the franchisees a profitable businesses.
2. Have happy franchisees – they work hard for themselves, but also for Boost Juice brand.
3. Always remember the buying power the Boost Juice brand has – use that to get the best deals for the franchisees.
4. Make sure the brand is rock solid – clear markets, clear offer – promoted in the right places.

Questions

1 Why has Boost Juice been successful?

2 What are the different costs that a franchisee has to pay?

3 What are the factors that franchisors have to consider when developing their franchising network?

4 Create a recruitment plan to encourage new franchisees to join the Boost Juice network.

Sources: Boost Australia (n.d.) Boost Juice Bars [online]. Available from www.boostjuice.com.au/ (accessed 25 April 2015); Boost Juice Bars (n.d.) Franchise: Frequently Asked Questions [online] Available from www.boostjuicebars.ee /kkk (accessed 25 April 2015); Boost Juice Bars (2014) Steps and Application [online] Available from boostjuice.co.za/wp-content/ (accessed 25 April 2015); Greenblat, E. (2013) Boost Juice looks to upsize in Asia. The Sydney Morning Herald [online] 29 July. Available from www.smh.com.au/business / (accessed 20 December 2014); iFranchise Malaysia (n.d.) Boost Juice Bars Franchise Business Opportunity [online]. Available from www.ifranchisemalaysia.com/ (accessed 26 April 2015); The Franchise Mall (n.d.) Boost Juice Franchise Information [online]. Available from www.thefranchisemall. com/franchises/details/14243-0-boost_juice.htm (accessed 20th December 2015); Yeong, E. (2013) Doubling Boost Juice's presence in Malaysia, Singapore. The Sun Daily [online], 6 November. Available from: www.thesundaily.my /news/874637 (accessed 26 April 2015); YouTube (2014) Top Four Traits of Successful Franchisors: Boost Juice Founder Janine Allis, published 4 Nov 2014 youtu.be/oSUo8ZCotaY (accessed 14 April 2015).

Authors: QiuYuan, Chong and Alexandra J Kenyon Leeds Beckett University

CASE STUDY 2

When joint ventures go wrong

A few years ago the arguments for strategic alliances and joint ventures as international market entry strategies for companies from developed countries entering a developing country seemed clear and compelling. They seemed particularly appropriate for China and in some cases appeared the only way. The theory was that the Chinese company provided access to cheap labour, local regulatory knowledge, knowledge of consumer behaviour and access to what appeared to be a relatively small, high-risk domestic market. The foreign partner provided capital knowledge, access to international markets and the promise of jobs in China. The attraction was that the market was promising, although at the same time it was geographically vast with very complex, contradictory and often invisible rules. Many of the largest companies in the world pursued collaborations of this type with what were then local Chinese companies in the belief that the arrangement would reduce risk but still allow high levels of control over the marketing strategy in China.

In practice many joint ventures and alliances have failed to deliver the original promise, involving companies from just about every industry sector, including Peugeot (cars), Remy Martin (spirits), Foster's (beer), News Corporation (media) and many telecoms firms. Chinese companies originally were keen to receive money, technology and business 'know-how', but they now have global ambitions of their own and do not want to be constrained by a global multinational partner who may want to curtail these ambitions. The joint venture partners frequently argued about the allocations of profits and decisions on investments.

China itself has also changed, having become a member of the World Trade Organization it agreed to be more open in legal matters. As the domestic economy grew more rapidly than anyone expected domestic capital was freely available, with the result that there was little need for money from foreign investors. As the Chinese market became one of the most attractive in the world and sentiment in China became more nationalistic and self-reliant the balance of power shifted between the Chinese and foreign partners, and providing access to China for foreign partners was of much less interest to indigenous companies.

Danone, a French Food multinational, acquired a 51 per cent stake in the Chinese firm Hangzhou Wahaha Beverage and believed they had struck an excellent deal. Wahaha originally knew little about the new business and welcomed a partner. The company was managed by Zong Qinhou, the entrepreneurial founder of Wahaha. He had developed the company from a milk selling stall to China's largest beverage company in 20 years.

Danone had very little success in the Chinese market prior to this joint venture and provided little input to the management of the new company believing they knew best. Without challenge from Danone, Zong was the main decision-maker, and the Confusion culture with its business model of the family reinforced his authority as an autocratic leaders. He was headstrong, did not want to share control, viewed the western model of corporate governance as inefficient and saw Danone as the provider of passive capital. Zong travelled 200 days per year around China testing consumer preferences. Danone could not appoint executives and Zong ended the contracts of high ranking R&D and marketing staff that Danone employed.

The lack of control by Danone allowed Zong to set up parallel companies so displacing profits from the joint venture. He was able use the trademark outside the joint venture because Danone had not challenged a court ruling in the early days of the joint venture. Zong was able to gain sympathy for his dealings outside the joint venture because foreign ownership had become politically sensitive in China.

Zong was able to use the fact that Danone has set up other joint ventures in China with other local companies such as Robust, Aquarius, Mengniu Dairy and Bright Dairy Food and allowed directors to sit on other boards in breach of Chinese law. The companies became involved in an acrimonious public dispute with 30 lawsuits on 3 continents. Chinese society is relationship rather than law driven. The Chinese step outside the law when they feel justified, but Danone came to realize that this becomes a disadvantage when a dispute arises. Danone resolved the problem only by pulling out of its joint venture resulting in a loss of £3 billion of income, around 10 per cent of its worldwide sales. Its other Chinese joint ventures also failed suggesting that Danone simply had not got to grips with the culture.

In interviews with 20 S&P 100 companies Chao, Rinaudo and Uhlaner (2014) found that around 40–60% of joint ventures underperform expectations or fail completely, including many involving firms with significant experience of JV formation. Alliances may be formed for local business reasons when speed is critical, but they still need to be part of a coherent strategy and a disciplined planning process. It is often easier to focus on the financials and business case rather than the more subjective strategic and operational issues. Leadership during the JV formation can become disjointed and the interest and involvement of senior managers of one of the parent companies can decline as their time is taken with unrelated, business problems. The ambitious JV partner can exploit the situation when a JV is failing, often resulting in the creation of a new competitive challenger.

Questions

1 What are the factors that a multinational firm should consider when deciding to use a joint venture as a market entry strategy for a developing country? What are the potential benefits and risks in taking this course of action?

2 Develop an outline international marketing strategy for a joint venture between Danone, a French multinational food company, and a food producer from a developing country. Explain which companies you feel should be responsible for providing the leadership and decision-making for the various activities detailed.

Sources: U. Wassmer, P. Dussauge and M. Planellas (2010) 'How to Manage Alliances Better Than One at a Time', *MIT Sloan Management Review*, 1 April. J. Yao, (2008) 'Why Danone's ventures failed', *International Financial Law Review*, March, 27(3): 46–48.

Chao, J., Rinaudo E. K., and Uhlaner R. (2014) 'Avoiding blind spots in your next joint venture' McKinsey Insights, January 2014. Accessed at http://www.mckinsey.com/insights/corporate_finance/avoiding_blind_spots_in_your_next_joint_venture on 23 Sept 2015.

DISCUSSION QUESTIONS

1   What market entry options does a small firm that has developed specialist security equipment for use at airports have when seeking to develop internationally? Specify what you consider to be the important criteria in deciding the appropriate entry method.

2   As a consultant you have been asked to advise a leisure and hotel complex in Southern Africa on how they should increase the number of international visitors. Explain their options and potential risks, and how they might control the way their offer is marketed, particularly if you have recommended the use of third parties.

3   International marketing of intellectual property, such as technological inventions, creative works, the performing arts and consultancy, provide opportunities and pose particular challenges for market entry. Using examples to illustrate your answer, explain what the opportunities are and identify the specific cross-cultural challenges of marketing this intellectual property internationally.

4   Why is acquisition often the preferred way for companies from emerging markets to establish wholly-owned operations abroad, and what are the limitations of acquisition as an entry method?

5   Explain the alternative approaches to collaboration that firms might adopt in their quest to become global players. What are the advantages of collaboration, and what are the potential pitfalls?

REFERENCES

1.   Bronder, C. and Pritzl, R. (1992) 'Developing strategic alliances: a conceptual framework for successful co-operation', *European Management Journal*, 10(4): 412–421.

2.   Chan, P.S. (1994) 'Franchising: key to global expansion', *Journal of International Marketing*, 2(3): 3–9.

3.   Duckett, B. (2008) 'Business format franchising: a strategic option for business growth – at home and abroad', *Strategic Direction*, 24(2): 3–4.

4.   Franchise Direct (2015) 'Top 100 global franchises – rankings' www.franchisedirect.com/top100globalfranchises/rankings/ (accessed 26 April 2015).

5.   Helm, R. and Gritsch, S. (2014). 'Examining the influence of uncertainty on marketing mix strategy elements in emerging business to business export-markets', *International Business Review*, 23(2), 418–428.

6.   Hutton, R. (2006) 'Eastern Europe the new Detroit', *Sunday Times*, 15 October.

7.   Katsikeas, C.S., Leonidou, L.C. and Morgan, N.A. (2000) 'Firm-level performance assessment: review, evaluation and development', *Journal of Academy of Marketing Science*, 28(4): 493–511.

8.   King, C., Grace, D. and Weaven, S. (2013). 'Developing brand champions: a franchisee perspective', *Journal of Marketing Management*, 29(11–12), 1308–1336.

9.   Leonidou, L.C., Katsikeas, C.S. and Samiee, S. (2002) 'Marketing strategy determination of export performance: a meta analysis', *Journal of Business Research*, 55: 51–67.

10.   Sarathy, R., Terpstra, V. and Russow, L. (2006) *International Marketing*, 9th edn. Dryden Press.

11.   Sharma, V.M. (2013) 'Enhancement of trust in the export management company-supplier relationship through e-business', International Journal of Commerce and Management, Vol. 23: 1, 24–37.

12.   Styles, C., Patterson, P.G. and La, V.Q. (2005) 'Executive insights: exporting services to South East Asia: Lessons from Australian knowledge-based service exporters', *Journal of International Marketing*, 13(4): 104–28.

13.   SUBWAY® (2015) 'Franchise opportunities' www.subway.co.uk/business/franchise/default.aspx (accessed 25 April 2015).

14.   Vankonacker, W. (1997) 'Entering China: an unconventional approach', *Harvard Business Review*, March–April.

15.   Voss, K.E., Johnson, J.L., Cullen, J.B., Sakano, T. and Takenouchi, H. (2006) 'Relational exchange in US–Japanese marketing strategic alliances', *International Marketing Review*, 23(6): 610–35.

16.   Weaver, S., Frazer, L. and Giddings, J. (2010) 'New perspectives on the causes of franchising conflict in Australia', *Asia Pacific Journal of Marketing and Logistics*, 22(2): 135–155.

CHAPTER 8

INTERNATIONAL PRODUCT AND SERVICE MANAGEMENT

LEARNING OBJECTIVES

After reading this chapter you should be able to:

- Understand the nature of international product and service marketing and appreciate the elements that make up the product and service offer

- Evaluate the factors affecting international product and service strategy development both external and internal to the firm

- Explain the issues that affect international product and service management across borders

- Identify the implications of the image, branding and positioning of products and services in international markets

- Understand how innovation contributes to the international product and service strategy

INTRODUCTION

Success in international marketing depends to a large extent upon the value proposition, satisfying the demands of the market and ultimately, on whether the product or service offered is suitable and acceptable for its purpose. More markets are reaching maturity and fewer products can be differentiated by their core benefits and so are becoming commodities. In defining the term 'product', therefore, we include additional elements such as packaging, warranties, aftersales service and branding that make up the total product and a complete package of tangible and intangible benefits for the customer. Services are taking an increasing share of international trade, but managing services internationally poses particular challenges. This is because the delivery of services is so dependent on the context, which is usually influenced by the varying cultural perceptions of what is acceptable service. In both product and service markets increasing customer expectations and competition mean that it is essential for firms to continually add better value through innovation and new product development (NPD). Much of this innovation is related to technological developments.

In this chapter we focus upon some of the key aspects and recent trends of international product policy by considering the changes in the nature of the products and services offered individually and within the portfolio, their relationship with the market and how innovation can create new products and services. Particularly important is the need to provide customers around the world with a satisfactory experience when using the product or service. To achieve this requires a clear understanding of when to meet the similar needs and wants of transnational customer segments and when to adapt to local tastes and requirements.

The nature of products and services

The reason that the majority of companies initially develop international markets is to generate new market opportunities, increase sales of an existing product or service or to offload excess capacity. However, the product must be seen as a bundle of satisfactions, providing people not just with products but with satisfying experiences in terms of the benefits they provide rather than the functions the products perform. These concepts are particularly important in international marketing, because, for example, the growth of such global consumer products as McDonald's 'I'm lovin' it' and Coca-Cola's 'Regret Nothing' cannot be attributable solely to a distinctive taste. Much of their success might be attributed to the aspirations of their international customers to be part of the 'Coca-Cola Culture', by deriving satisfaction from a close association with the product and the brand and also being reminded of the experiences associated with the product such as enjoying music, being with friends or watching sport.

In understanding how products can provide satisfying experiences and benefits for people, it is necessary to clearly identify and understand the motivations of the target consumer and not make assumptions about them.

International product and service marketing

The term 'product' is used in marketing to refer both to physical goods, such as a can of baked beans or a refrigerator, and services such as insurance or a holiday. In fact few products can be described as pure product with no service element – salt is often suggested as approaching a pure product. Education is probably the closest to a pure service. All offers are a combination of product and service components, as shown in Figure 8.1. Before considering the total product 'offer' in more detail, it is important to consider the specific characteristics of services and the challenges they pose in international marketing.

Service characteristics are:

■ **Intangibility:** Services include both tangible and intangible elements. Intangible elements cannot be touched, smelt or seen. An intangible element of a service could be 'magical'. A magical experience is what parents want for their children when they visit a Disney resort. A 'magical' experience cannot be touched, smelt or seen. However, 'magical' can be experienced when children see the Disney characters on parade; receive a big hug from Goofy or when Elsa from the film *Frozen* sings 'Let it go'. Tangible elements of this magical service offer from Disney include the magic castle, costumes of heros and heroines and music. Air transportation has intangible elements such as 'feeling safe' or 'enjoyment'; the tangible elements include food, drink and the in-flight safety video. For car insurance the intangible element is 'peace of mind', the tangible elements are a written policy and a free gift. And for education the tangible elements include a certificate, wearing a cap and gown, having a graduation photograph, all to demonstrate success in education. All the tangible elements are used as reminders and reinforcements of the service in order to confirm the benefit provided and

FIGURE 8.1   The product-service continuum

enhance its perceived value. However, the physical evidence of the service that is offered may be valued very differently by people from different countries and cultures.

■ **Perishability**: services cannot be stored – for example, the revenues from unfilled airline seats are lost once the aircraft takes off. This characteristic causes considerable problems in planning and promotion in order to match supply and demand at busy and quiet times of the day. Perishability is also a problem for events organizers. An event that has only sold 900 of the 1000 tickets for a rock band's gig in Manchester cannot be sold after the gig has taken place; especially as the rock band has moved to Edinburgh for a gig that was a 'sell out'. Therefore, it is also problematic predicting unfamiliar patterns of demand and managing capacity in distant and varied locations.

■ **Heterogeneity**: services are rarely the same, because they often involve interactions between people. For fast food companies this can cause problems in maintaining consistent quality, particularly in international markets where there are quite different attitudes towards and expectations of customer service. The hope is that employees of international brands provide the same quality of service throughout the world. Consumers also expect the same quality of service; and if they receive poor service in Frankfurt the international brand's reputation will diminish.

■ **Inseparability**: the service is created at the point of sale. This means that economies of scale and the experience curve benefits can be difficult to achieve and supplying the service in scattered markets can be expensive. Where the service involves some special expertise, such as pop music, the number of consumers is limited by the size and number of venues that can be visited by the performer. If the fans are in a market which is remote, they are unlikely to see the artist and need other forms of communication, such as videos, website and books, in order not to feel too separated from the performer. Twitter has been used by celebrities to maintain continual contact with their devoted followers. And with Katy Perry, Justin Beiber and Taylor Swift with around 60 million followers each(!) it is clear fans and celebrities find Twitter a useful platform to stay inseparable.

The three additional marketing mix elements
These differences between product and service offers have certain implications for the international marketing mix and, in addition to the usual four Ps for products – product, price, place and promotion – another three Ps for services are added. Because of the importance and nature of service delivery, special emphasis must be placed upon:

■ *People*. Consumers must be educated in order for their expectations of the service to be managed, and employees must be motivated and well trained in order to ensure that high standards of service are maintained. However, because of cultural differences the staff and customers in various countries often respond differently not only to training and education but also in their attitudes to the speed of service, punctuality, willingness to queue and so on. However, firms such as consultancies, advertising agencies or IT management supplying services around the world to an MNE customer, will be expected to maintain the same standards at every country location, but local staff and customers may have different attitudes to service in each. *People* also includes call-centre staff, online 'chat help' contacts and of course all the people that reply to Facebook and Twitter messages. Even though these employees are remote from the consumer they must also be well trained and communicate the brand's values at all times.

■ *Process*. As the success of the service is dependent on the total customer experience, a well-designed delivery process is essential. Customer expectations of process standards vary with different cultures and standardization is difficult in many varied contexts. Frequently the service process is affected by elements for which the service deliverer may be blamed by frustrated customers but over which they have little control. Sports fans might travel to an event at great expense only to experience delays at an airport, excessive policing or bad weather. Although their team may perform well the fans may be reluctant to travel to future matches because of their unsatisfactory overall experience. Process is a key element for restaurants. Some restaurateurs meet and greet their consumers, guide them to the table, provide a menu, discuss the meal options and offer advice on dishes and wines that complement each dish. Other restaurateurs expect their consumers to find their own table, review the menu, pay up-front for drinks and food and collect their own food from the buffet. The process of moving the consumer through their meal experience is very different and demonstrates the difference between high and low-service restaurants. At its most basic the process of customer management should make it easy for the customer to deal with the firm no matter where they are in the world.

■ *Physical aspects*. Many physical reminders, including the appearance of the delivery location and the elements provided to make the service more tangible, can enhance the overall customer experience. Apart from using appropriate artefacts to generate the right atmosphere, constant reminders of the firm's corporate identity help to build customer awareness and loyalty. For example, the familiar logos of Louis Vuitton, Google, BBC and Etihad Airways may give the reassurance necessary for a consumer to use a service in a foreign market.

Low-cost airlines, such as Ryanair (Ireland), Mango (South Africa), Flynas (Saudi Arabia) and Lion Air (Indonesia), have put pressure on the national flag carriers by changing each element of the marketing mix, using their websites to manage most transactions, yield management software to maximize revenue generation rather than price maintenance and charging for every 'extra' after the customer has purchased a seat. There are some specific problems in marketing services internationally. There are particular difficulties in achieving uniformity of standards of the three additional Ps in remote locations where exerting control can be particularly difficult. Pricing, too, can be extremely problematic, because fixed costs can be a very significant part of the total service costs but may vary between locations, for example, in the case of mobile telephony. As a result the consumer's ability to buy and their perceptions of the promised and received service may vary considerably between markets, resulting in significantly different prices being set. Increasingly important in service marketing is the need to provide largely standardized services customized to individual requirements. This clearly poses considerable challenges to international service providers. For example, an MNE might employ an international law firm to protect its interests but the scope for offering a standardized service is limited by the fact that every country has its own different legal system.

There are a number of generalizations that can be made about international marketing of services. Foreign markets present greater opportunities for gaining market share and long-term profits for MNEs if local firms are less experienced in customer management and communication and quality of service delivery. If cultural sensitivity and local knowledge is key then local service companies are likely to succeed. Companies such as Google, eBay and Facebook have lost out to local imitators in China and India. Information technology and the development of expert knowledge networks are the sources of competitive advantage for international service marketers. Due to the high initial cost of financing overseas operations, joint ventures and franchising are rapidly growing entry methods, and frequently the market entry strategy is based on forming alliances or piggybacking as existing clients move into new markets. Government regulations and attitudes to the protection of local suppliers vary considerably from country to country, but more new markets are opening up.

While it might seem appropriate to categorize physical goods as tangible and services as intangible, marketing increasingly appears to be concerned with blurring this distinction. For example, a product such as perfume is not promoted as a complex chemical solution, but instead, as one perfume house executive put it, 'dreams in a bottle'. Many services appear to compete over tangible 'add-ons' as we discussed earlier in this chapter.

The international marketing of service

One of the achievements of the Uruguay Round of negotiations on the General Agreement on Trade in Services (GATS) was to identify four modes of delivery or ways in which services may be exported. This is useful in detailing the nature of international services:

1 *Cross-border trade*, where the trade takes place from one country to another, without the movement of persons. Only the service itself, for example, market research or training, crosses the border electronically (email), by telecommunications (telephone, radio) or by infrastructure (air, rail).

2 *Consumption abroad*, where the customer travels to the country where the service is supplied (tourism, education or training, legal services).

3 *Commercial presence*, where the supplier establishes a commercial presence abroad (banks, construction project offices or warehousing and logistics).

4 *Movement of natural persons*, where the provider of the services crosses the border (arts and culture, recreation and sports).

Any of the four modes constitute trade so long as the local firm is being paid by the foreign firm, no matter where the service is provided.

Illustration 8.1 shows how TripAdvisor has provided an online consumer-generated platform showing open and honest comments of a variety of service industries including hotels, restaurants and resort destinations.

'Invisible' services contribute to all aspects of economic activity. For example, infrastructure services (transport, communications and financial services) provide support to any type of business. Education, health and recreational services influence the quality of labour available, and professional services provide the specialized expertise to increase firms' competitiveness. Services make up an increasing proportion of GDP and are also used to add value to the product offer as outlined in the following section.

ILLUSTRATION 8.1

TripAdvisor: 'You' as brand managers promoting service characteristics

In 2006 *Time* magazine voted 'You' as the most influential person of the year. The reason for this is that social media has placed 'you', the customer, in a powerful position as more and more people share their attitudes and opinions of products and services.

In fact, it can be said that consumers are brand managers for products and services they like; and very honest reviewers for products and services they do not like. This is certainly true for reviewers on TripAdvisor.

TripAdvisor is, in the main, a consumer generated social platform. It was originally produced as a web-based platform for professional hotel reviewers and journalists to upload their advice and opinions, about hotels, for holiday makers.

However, within no time at all, consumers began uploading their own opinions, and later, began ranking and rating hotels, restaurants, resorts, vacation rentals, flights and travel packages.

TripAdvisor is very popular. Currently there are over 200 million TripAdvisor reviewers from 45 countries. There are 4.5 million reviews for hotels, attractions and restaurants on TripAdvisor and there are a staggering 315 million visits to the website each month. This certainly means many consumers are eager to listen to the views and opinions of the user-generated network.

TripAdvisor reviewers, therefore, are like 'brand managers' for a hotel, restaurant or attraction. The reviewers provide fair and honest information about the service characteristics shown earlier in this chapter. They review many things from sleep quality, cleanliness of rooms and lots of added value aspects. Personal experiences are also shared by reviewers. These experiences include the romantic or family fun atmosphere at a restaurant they have visited; fabulous relationships made with waiting staff at a hotel and superb 'taste-bud' popping flavours at the World Curry Week Festival. Reviewers also share negative comments such as the dreadful sewerage smells found around swimming pools or impolite reception staff. All in all the user-generated content provides opinions from people from all walks of life, age and country and with so many hits per months TripAdvisor seems to be the place to visit before choosing many hospitality or leisure venues.

Questions

1 Referring to the characteristics of services, how does TripAdvisor help or hinder consumer's decisions?

2 How can TripAdvisor help or hinder businesses?

The components of the international product offer

In creating a suitable and acceptable product offer for international markets, it is necessary to examine first, what contributes to the 'total' product, and second, decide what might make the product acceptable to the international market. Kotler and Armstrong (2014) suggest three essential aspects of the **international product offer**, which should be considered by marketers in order to meet consumer needs and wants:

1 *Core customer benefits*: the elements that consumers perceive as meeting their needs and providing satisfaction through performance and image. When consumers go to a coffee or tea shop they buy more than a drink. Consumers also buy socialization with their friends, time to chat and exchange news.

2 *Actual products*: the elements most closely associated with the core product, such as features, specifications, styling, branding and packaging. Consumers that use a bank need benefits such as honesty and reliability. The international bank Santander (head office Spain) offers this benefit. The actual core products and attributes include: recognizable logo, staff uniforms (the same world over), savings accounts, mortgages, loans, credit cards and online banking services.

3 *Augmented products*: the additional elements to the core product which contribute to providing satisfaction, and include delivery, after-sales service and guarantees. For Santander augmented products include customer service staff, via phone or email, mortgage and service advisors, pension planning advisors, terms and condition documents providing guarantees for the services and products of Santander.

These elements form the augmented product, an extended version of which is shown in Figure 8.2. Moving down and to the right of the diagram shows the elements that are relatively more difficult to standardize in different country markets.

Having introduced the concept of the total product offer, it is essential to evaluate each aspect of the product in terms of what benefits the consumer might expect to gain and how the offer will be perceived by consumers. This can be done by answering the following six questions for each market:

1 For what purpose has the product been developed and how would the product be used in that country?

2 What distinctive properties does the product have?

3 What benefits is the consumer expected to gain?

FIGURE 8.2   The three elements of the product or service

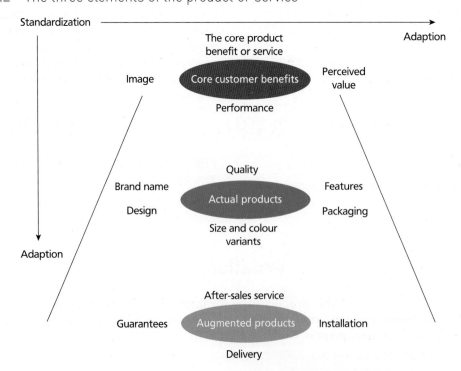

4 How is the product positioned and what image do consumers perceive it to have?

5 Which consumer segments of the total market are expected to buy it, on what occasions and for what purposes?

6 How does the product fit into the total market?

The main issue for a company about to commence marketing internationally is to assess the suitability of the existing products for international markets. As a minimum, a purchaser in an overseas market expects to have a clear explanation of how a product should be used, so the instructions on the domestic packaging usually have to be translated for international markets. Interestingly, one cosmetics marketer found that in some countries customers objected if their language was not printed first on multilingual packs.

The question is, however, to what extent the components of the total product offer can and should be adapted for international markets. In the case of a product where only the packaging needs to be changed, the effect on the overall cost is likely to be minimal, but if more fundamental changes to the product itself are required, because of differences in use or safety regulations, the higher cost might prove prohibitive for a small company. Such problems can be circumvented by taking an alternative market entry approach such as licensing or franchising.

Products, services and value propositions

The distinction between products and services is becoming increasingly blurred. In practice there are few 'pure' products and services and most offerings from firms are a combination of the two but to succeed it is essential they focus on value based marketing, which requires:

- A deep understanding of customer needs and decision-making processes.
- The formulation of value propositions that meet the needs of customers and create a differential advantage.
- The building of long term relationships with customers, so that loyalty and trust is built on the satisfaction and confidence in the supplier.
- The necessary superior knowledge, skills, systems and marketing assets (including brand) to deliver superior value.

At this point it is worth noting that customer expectations are increasing. A value proposition that simply claims to offer a good quality product or reliable service no longer satisfies customers. Customers will be dissatisfied if they do not receive good quality products and service, but they will only be satisfied if they are delighted with the product or service because of some extra benefits that exceed their expectations. Of course, what will delight customers around the world varies considerably. With this in mind it is important to understand and interpret added value and how it is measured is shown in Illustration 8.2.

Factors affecting international product and service management

There are a number of factors that affect the international management of products and services including:

- the balance between standardization and adaptation owing to:
  - cultural factors
  - usage factors
  - legal factors
- product acceptability
- shortening product life cycles
- the effect of different market entry methods
- changes in marketing management
- ethical and green environmental issues.

ILLUSTRATION 8.2

Sit back, relax and enjoy your flight: Value in service organizations

All domestic or international travellers want a safe and stress-free journey. This is particularly important when consumers travel by air to see their friends and family, to attend a meeting or conference or to set off on their annual holiday. Flight passengers expect airlines to provide a safe and secure journey. Passengers also want to enjoy the flight experience; especially if they have paid a lot of money for it! Additionally, they want to feel refreshed and relaxed when they reach their destination.

Airline Excellence Awards are given to the airline which first puts the passenger experience at the heart of their business but also goes above and beyond in terms of their value proposition.

Of course safety of the passengers (and employees) is Number 1. If an airline company wants to be considered for an Airline Excellence Award it must get a Seven Star Rating for safety. To do this the airline has to submit fatality reports; airlines earn points if their fleet of planes has been fatality free for the previous 10 years. Additionally, airlines need to provide safety audit certificates to show they meet the safety standards set by the International Civil Aviation Authority, an agency of the United Nations.

The World Airline Awards announced recently gave top spot for the world's best cabin crew to Garuda Airlines from Indonesia. The service delivered by the cabin crew is rewarded based on hard service and soft service. The hard service includes measurable elements in being efficient with moving passengers on and off the plane, delivering safety details prior to take-off and rigorous attention to detail, particularly with paperwork. The second element, the soft service, refers to the enthusiasm of the staff, their friendly approach to all passengers, their kindness and all-round attitude to their roles and their brand. The Garuda Airline and staff that won this award are very proud of the consistent high levels of service provided each day, every day.

AirlineRatings.com have also announced their awards and put Air New Zealand at the top of the list for the second year running. Air New Zealand has been rewarded for their innovations. They give passengers unbelievable comfort when normally uncomfortable flight seats can be manoeuvred to form a 'sofa in the sky'. Families enjoy this especially when watching an in-flight movie together as it feels like home. The in-flight amenities are also ranked highly containing socks, noise cancelling ear-plugs, lip balm and so on. All this in addition to their friendly, committed staff.

Questions

1 Added value, innovation and safety are important for airlines. What are the challenges for airlines?

2 What do you suggest are the critical success factors that airlines should concentrate on in the future?

Sources: World Airlines Award (2015) The world's best airlines announced at 2014 World Airline Awards www .worldairlineawards.com/(accessed 4 May 2015); Airlineratings .com (2015) Air New Zealand wins 2015 airline of the year, published 2 December 2014 www.airlineratings.com/ (accessed 4 May 2015).

The discussion in Chapter 6 on globalization leads to the conclusion that for the largest companies in the world the benefits of marketing standardized products are very significant indeed, but while firms may be prepared to invest heavily to achieve standardization, in practice, virtually all products must be adapted to some degree. The issue then becomes to what degree their industrial or consumer product or service should be standardized or adapted to the needs of the local market. Even the most obviously global companies achieve only partial standardization of products. For example, while Coca-Cola adopt a global standardized branding strategy, they modify the product for particular customer segments by offering Diet, Light and Caffeine-Free Coca-Cola and altering the sweetness for different national tastes. McDonald's, too, alters its menu in different countries to cater for local tastes and accommodate their health and food safety needs.

All firms must identify the benefit or satisfaction that the consumer recognizes and will purchase. This benefit must provide the basis upon which the company differentiates its products from those of its competitors. For a product such as the mobile phone, when it was first introduced the competitive advantage was a technical breakthrough, the first portable long distance mobile voice communication, and so standardization of the core benefit was possible. As products were copied and developed so new sources of competitive advantage were sought for the mobile phone and this led to standardization of non-core elements of the augmented product, for example, additional functions such as texting, camera facilities, music and video downloading and so on. Fragmentation then occurs as manufacturers choose to differentiate their product in different ways, such as design, greater functionality, a more robust product for rough use or producing a very basic phone that will appeal to specific segments. Also different business models such as 'Pay and Go' accelerated usage. Sometimes, however, the differentiation does not appeal. Vodafone withdrew a very basic phone soon after its introduction because of lack of demand.

The decision for most companies to standardize or adapt is based on a cost–benefit analysis of what they believe the implications of adaptation and standardization might be for revenue, profitability and market share. In normal circumstances, the cost of adaptation would be expected to be greater than the cost of successful standardization. Only if the needs and tastes identified in the target market segment are significantly different and substantial additional business will be generated, can the extra cost involved in making and delivering adapted products be justified. Illustration 8.3 shows how law firms need to adapt to the different practice requirements to gain a foothold in new markets.

While some companies are tempted to adopt a policy of adaptation in order to satisfy immediate demand, others believe that continual exposure to the standardized products will redefine customer needs and ultimately change their tastes, leading to greater market share in the longer term. Summarizing the advantages of product standardization, the company benefits from more rapid recovery of investment, easier organization and control of product management, the possibility to reduce costs through economies of scale, and the experience effect throughout most of the firm's operations, such as production, advertising and distribution.

Product standardization is both encouraging and being encouraged by the globalization trends in markets, including:

1 Markets are becoming more homogeneous.
2 There are more identifiable transnational consumer segments.
3 There is an increase in the number of firms moving towards globalization, so forcing greater standardization throughout industry sectors.

There are some disadvantages of product standardization too; for example, market opportunities might be lost when it is impossible to match very specific local requirements. Some managers of local subsidiaries who are only expected to implement global or regional product policies can become demotivated and miss market opportunities if they are not given the opportunity to be entrepreneurial.

Greater standardization of products makes it easier for competitors to copy at ever-lower prices, but this leads inevitably to standardization within a product category so that consumers are unable to differentiate between competing products, with the result that a 'commodity market' is created. To counter this, competition is focused increasingly upon the augmented product elements. In the family car market, for example, there is very little to choose between the performance, reliability and economy of the main competitors, including Ford, General Motors, Renault, Toyota, Peugeot and Nissan. Against this background, the promotion of individual cars focuses upon design, image, warranties and financing arrangements and rather less on individual performance comparisons. The industry is also continually developing products for subsegments, examples being the Smart car, Toyota Prius hybrid energy source car and sports utility vehicles.

ILLUSTRATION 8.3

Peru: Legal and taxation services globalized using local talent

Baker & McKenzie have a team of 4000 lawyers, tax advisers and economists. The team works within and across borders. Combined they speak 75 languages, come from 55 nationalities and work within one of the 74 offices around the world. Offices are located as far apart as Tokyo (Japan), Tijuana (Mexico), Baku (Azerbaijan) and Brisbane (Australia). The aim of Baker & McKenzie is to expand and share their expertise where they think it is needed. Each time they see a new opportunity in a new country they apply for a licence so that they can invest and set up a business. Alternatively, they acquire an existing business. Either way Baker & McKenzie do not encounter any objections to their request to set up business because they make it clear that whilst they are a global business they want to employ local talent. The talent they want from local employees is their understanding of the country's legal system, their expertise of local taxation and regulations, and their experience of collaborations across borders in legal matters.

Abu Dhabi is one of the places that Baker & McKenzie have invested in. They realized that due to the major growth in the region, cross-border legal advice would be needed for building and land purchases and business acquisitions. They also opened an office in Bahrain to strengthen their brand in the Middle East. More recently, Baker & McKenzie saw opportunities in Burma (Republic of the Union of Myanmar) as their cities were liberalizing, growing and changing. Thus an international business that employs excellent staff from the South East Asia region saw an opportunity for growth in Yangon, a major city in Burma. With an already strong brand presence in South East Asia, choosing to invest in a business in Yangon and employing local talent seemed a natural progression for Baker & McKenzie.

At the other side of the world Baker & McKenzie entered Peru and to ensure they had the best local talent they acquired a very well-established Peruvian practice. Chairman Eduardo Leite stated that globalization of their business will continue and the quest for expansion can only happen if they tap into the expertise of locally qualified lawyers, experts and taxation teams. For services and products it is therefore important to stick with the marketing mantra of 'think global, act local'.

Questions

1 What are the benefits and risks for a law firm entering different markets?

2 Based on Baker & McKenzie what would you recommend other service organizations do in terms of globalization and localization?

Sources: Taylor, M. (2015) Baker & McKenzie adds Grant Thornton partner to Yangon base, published in *The Lawyer* 5 May. Available from www.thelawyer.com (accessed 6 May 2015); Sundar S. (2013) 'Global 20: Baker and McKenzie' published in Law360, 1 August.

Reasons for adaptation of the product

In some instances, product standardization may not be possible due to environmental constraints either through mandatory legislation, because of such reasons as differences in electrical systems, legal standards, safety requirements or product liability, or because the firm believes that the product appeal can be increased in a particular market by addressing cultural and usage factors.

Cultural factors   Certain products and services, such as computers and airline flights, are not culturally sensitive as the benefits they offer are valued internationally. Here the **adaptation** is peripheral to the main benefit, for example, translation of instructions into different languages. Other products and services are more culturally sensitive and might need to be adapted more substantially. Food is a particularly difficult area for standardization, as the preparation and eating of food are often embedded in the history, religion and/or culture of the country. This presents specific problems for fast food firms, for example, where the main ingredients of McDonald's and Burger King, beef and pork, prove unacceptable to many potential customers, and the necessary ingredients for fast food, such as the specific type of wheat for pizza bases, suitable chicken and mozzarella cheese are unavailable, or are of variable quality in certain countries.

One example of service development is Islamic banking, which for many years was regarded as a small niche activity. However, the growing sense of religious identity in the Muslim world together with the significant increase in construction in the Middle East has led to rapid growth in the sector.

Changes are taking place in product acceptance, however. For example, fashion is becoming increasingly globalized and the traditional domination of the fashion industry by western designers is gradually being broken down. Denim jeans infiltrated countries like India which had hitherto only accepted traditional dress. Some people believe that the erosion of the country's traditional heritage and culture, particularly by the media and MNE advertising, is unethical and should be resisted. Others suggest that larger countries such as India and China simply take those international products which serve a particular need and ignore other global products.

Usage factors   The same product might be used in quite different ways in different markets, partly due to the culture of the country, but also due to the geographical factors of climate and terrain. Unilever and Procter & Gamble have a large variety of products adapted and branded for different markets because of the different ways products are used. For example, French people wash clothes in scalding hot water, while the Australians tend to use cold water. Most Europeans use front-loading washing machines, whereas the French use top-loaders. Equipment supplied to armies fighting in unfamiliar and inhospitable climates has often proved ineffective.

Honda found that when they first introduced motorcycles into the US they were unreliable and frequently broke down. Japanese riders were only able to travel short distances, whereas American riders were used to riding the bikes over longer distances and much rougher terrain. Honda quickly realized, however, that Americans and Indonesians were fascinated by their 50cc to 125cc bikes and promoted them instead. Honda quickly became established and were able to introduce better performing larger bikes too.

Legal standards   The standardization of products and services can be significantly affected by legislation. Legal standards are often very country-specific, sometimes because obscure laws have been left unchanged for decades. There have been considerable problems for the European Union in attempting to harmonize standards during the creation of the single market and it took a number of years to achieve agreement on relatively simple products, such as confectionery, jam and sausage.

Lack of precise, reliable, understandable and universally accepted scientific information, for example in food safety (beef, lamb and chicken), serves only to make it more difficult to achieve a satisfactory industry standard. Pharmaceutical companies experience problems in introducing products into different markets, because individual governments have differing standards of public health and approaches to healthcare. Many countries insist that they carry out their own supervised clinical testing on all drugs prior to the products being available on the market and, for example, the instructions and contraindications might need to be changed and agreed with health authorities locally.

Product liability   In the US, over the past few years there has been a considerable increase in litigation, with lawyers seeking clients on a no win–no fee basis. For marketers, particularly those selling potentially life-threatening products such as pharmaceuticals and cars, this demands much greater caution when introducing standard products based on the home country specification. In extreme circumstances litigation can lead to huge financial settlements, for example in cases related to the oil, tobacco and asbestos industries.

Product acceptability

Consumers generally are becoming much more discerning and have greater expectations of all the elements of the augmented product. The manufacturer must take responsibility for controlling the pre- and post-purchase servicing and warranties provided by independent distributors and retailers. The packaging, branding and trademark decisions are becoming increasingly important because the global social media no longer allows mistakes and failures to go unpublicized.

Consumers, too, have different perceptions of the value and satisfaction of products and their view of what is acceptable will vary considerably from country to country. The product usage, production process or service offered may not fit with the culture and environment of the country and the product or service may not be acceptable for its intended use. Certain healthcare services, such as abortion, gambling, banking products and alcohol are unacceptable to some cultures.

Shortening product life cycles

The merging of markets through increasing globalization is leading to greater concentration of powerful suppliers who have the resources to rapidly copy a competitor's product or develop their own products to exploit a new market opportunity. The increasing pace of technology means that a technical lead in a product is not likely to be held for very long, as competitors catch up quickly. This means that product life cycles are becoming shorter, by a third in some cases, and improvements are introduced more frequently; often annually. This must be added to the much higher cost of research, development and commercialization of new products, which places much greater pressures on the firm to distribute the new product throughout world markets as quickly and widely as possible in order to achieve a high return on research and development investment before new products are introduced.

Franchising, joint ventures and alliances

The pressure to exploit new technology and products as quickly and widely as possible has encouraged the rapid expansion of more creative and cost-effective ways of achieving cooperation in research, development and distribution, such as franchising, joint ventures and strategic alliances. As discussed in the previous chapter, while these market entry methods allow less control than total ownership, they do enable firms to develop a wider sphere of activity than they could do alone. Of course, the challenge is to find partners with truly complementary expertise, knowledge and capability.

Marketing management

These trends have led to significant changes in the way that marketing management operates, allowing a more creative approach to be adopted in developing product policy. First, there are a wider range of options available in international marketing management, particularly through innovation and integration of the marketing mix elements which will be discussed later in this book. Second, there have been significant improvements in the tools available for performance measurement, real time data analysis and planning. Third, there are more insightful and widely available sources of information through online marketing research, involving customers, suppliers and the web community in product and service evaluation and innovations, which allow greater power for global brand management. It must be pointed out that success in using these tools requires managers to be more flexible in redefining niche segments and creative in innovating in all areas of the marketing mix. Fourth, with improved internal and external networking, NPD can become much more integrated within the firm's strategies and be capable of more satisfactorily meeting customer needs through the management of supply chain relationships.

Environmental and social responsibility issues

By way of contrast, unscrupulous companies have exploited the different legal controls and lower risks of litigation by sending for disposal hazardous products, such as chemical waste, to less developed countries with lower standards. However, this practice is being increasingly challenged by international pressure groups and is backed up by the United Nations to encourage all countries and companies to consider environmental issues (United Nations 2014).

Concern for environmental issues is becoming greater in many countries and has considerable implications for product policies, but the nature, patterns and strength of interest vary considerably from country to country.

The United Nations state that businesses should engage in environmental issues, take the initiative to support environmental responsibilities and choose environmentally friendly technologies. Additional social responsibility issues that businesses should engage in and be transparent about, through annual reports, press releases and newsletters, include:

Governance: Environmental and social responsibilities should be at the heart of businesses in their mission and vision statements and of course how they 'do business'.

Workforce: all employees, particularly in the service and manufacturing industries, must be given fair and equal rights, be paid a fair wage and receive training and career opportunities.

Advertising and communication: must be honest and truthful.

Supply chain: Businesses should only engage with other organizations that also care for the environment and conduct their business in a responsible manner.

Against this background MNEs and SMEs must respond in an appropriate way to the global and local concerns by taking a more comprehensive approach to dealing with environmental and socially responsible issues by anticipating and, where appropriate, initiating changes. They must also evaluate and manage proactively all the effects on the environment of their operations. See Management Challenge 8.1 to see how global fashion brands must take more care with their supply chain, the workforce and be prepared to communicate speedily and honestly.

Malagasy is a gourmet food company that sells high-quality products to supermarkets. It has partners in Madagascar that produce and package the chocolate, nuts, spices and honey it uses. It is a social enterprise that balances its commercial aims with social and economic objectives. The company realized that with many firms 95 per cent of the final value of a chocolate bar is created outside the country from which the chocolate ingredients originate. However, more value can be retained in the country where the ingredients originated if the finished product is made and packaged in that country – and that is what Malagasy do (Stone 2006).

A number of companies have set corporate strategies which address these issues. Sony, for example, incorporate environmental considerations into the planning of every product, and Ford has adopted the environmental standard, ISO4001 worldwide.

The goal is to achieve environmental excellence with firms such as The Body Shop, 3M, British Telecom, Johnson Matthey, Merck, Norsk Hydro and Rank Xerox taking a strategic approach rather than making *ad hoc* decisions. There are many problems in building environmental considerations into corporate strategy, including the uncertainties of the science, for example different views on global warming, and the difficulty of deciding on appropriate action because replacement processes or chemicals often give rise to new problems.

Product policy

Having considered the factors which underpin the development of an **international product portfolio**, the next steps are to look first at the suitability of the existing products before embarking on the development of new or modified products. The decision about which products should be included in the range to be marketed internationally is determined by several factors:

■ The company's overall objectives in terms of growth and profits.

■ The experience, philosophies and attitude of the company to international development, and which of the company's financial and managerial resources will be allocated to international marketing.

■ The characteristics of the markets such as economic development and the barriers to trade of the firm's domestic and host countries.

MANAGEMENT CHALLENGE 8.1

Global brands – do they care what happens down the supply chain?

In 2013 shocking news spread around the world that an eight-storey factory in Bangladesh had collapsed. Immediate thoughts were that an earthquake had shaken the ground or that the factory had been a target for a terrorist attack. But this was not the case and 1134 garment workers in the factory had been killed. Many hundreds of garment workers were also injured. They were killed and injured because of a negligent construction company. The company that had constructed the Rana Plaza in Dhaka, Bangladesh, had not taken the care and attention needed to provide a safe working environment for the garment workers. The construction of the building was poor, weak and was cheaply and quickly constructed. The main reason for the hurried construction of the factory was to satisfy the pressing need of western consumers that want low cost fashionable items. To satisfy the insatiable desire for fashionable clothes Walmart, Benetton, Matalan, Primark and Mango subcontracted clothing orders to agents in Bangladesh. Their brand labels were found in the rubble after the building had collapsed. Clearly, once the contract had been exchanged between the global brand and the subcontracting agent the global brand 'washed theirs hands' of the conditions of the employees at Rana Plaza.

In fact, not only was the factory unsafe to work in, the garment making employees were:

■ abused
■ working in unsanitary conditions all day, every day
■ refused maternity leave
■ did not receive their wages on time
■ were paid incredibly low wages
■ worked extremely long hours.

The global brands insisted they had asked the subcontractors to provide fair wages and working conditions but clearly the global brands did not check the Bangladeshi employees received those basic rights.

Benetton put out a press release, shortly after the Rana Plaza had collapsed, denying that they had subcontracted work to employees working at Rana Plaza. Not long afterwards Benetton withdrew their initial press release. In the spring of 2015, two years after the factory at Rana Plaza had collapsed, Benetton announced they would give a donation of US$1.1 billion to a trust fund set up for killed or injured employees and their families.

Sadly in May 2015 another Bangladeshi factory collapsed, killing and injuring more workers. The vows to ensure the workforces in Bangladesh are safe seem to have fallen on deaf ears.

Questions

1 How should a marketing company manage insatiable customer demand as well as ethical concerns?

2 What promotional activities should Benetton do to improve its poor reputation following the deaths of employees at Rana Plaza that were subcontracted to produce fashion garments for their stores?

Source: Burke, J. (2015) Bangladesh garment workers suffer poor conditions two years after reform vows, published 22 April theguardian.com (accessed 8 May 2015).

■ The requirements, expectations and attitudes of the consumers in the market.
■ The products and services themselves, their attributes, appeal and perceived values (their positioning), the stage that they are at in the life cycle and economies of scale.
■ The ease of distributing and selling them.
■ The support the products require from other elements of the marketing mix and after-sales services.
■ Environmental constraints (such as legal or political factors) which must be overcome.
■ The level of risk that the company is prepared to take.

Illustration 8.4 shows how disposal of products should be a matter of concern for businesses.

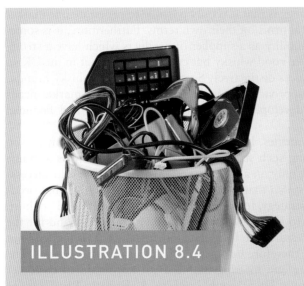

ILLUSTRATION 8.4

Recycling services: Dealing with the world's waste

Many organizations send old and out-of-date computers, mobile phones and electrical equipment to India. The organizations pay India to dispose of the waste on their behalf. The majority of the waste ends up on waste dumps, which are where thousands of homeless people live. The people that live there and their children, known as collectors, try to find items amongst the waste that they can sell to make money. One of the prized finds on dump sites is e-waste. E-waste includes computer circuit boards. The collectors dismantle e-waste computers to get to the prized circuit board which contains precious metals such as gold or copper. However, the next step in the process is to extract the gold and copper from the circuit board. This process is extremely hazardous. The process involves collectors using cyanide to breakdown the circuit board connectors, thus extracting the gold and copper. The fumes from the cyanide sometimes kill collectors. Additionally, cyanide waste contaminates the surrounding soil and local water systems.

Nitin Gupta, and his brother Rohan, love e-waste. They have built, thanks to international financial aid, a state-of-the-art factory that recycles old and broken computers. They actively encourage organizations around the world to use their factory to recycle old and broken computers – instead of sending the e-waste to dumps. Over two-thirds of Nitin's business comes from organizations that want to use their recycling services. One-third of their business comes from the 'unregulated' collectors. Nitin pays the collectors more money than they would get for circuit boards 'on the street'. He also takes the complete circuit board so the collectors do not have to use cyanide to extract the precious metals.

There are many service organizations like Nitin's that recycle waste. Indeed, e-recycling computer and mobile phone e-waste is big business. And the disposal of e-waste is on the political agenda in many countries, which means many organizations will have to pay more attention to the disposal of their products and electronic goods.

Questions

1 Who should be responsible for disposing of or recycling e-waste?

2 What should organizations do to promote their recycling policies?

Source: Ives, M. (2014) In developing world, a push to bring e-waste out of the shadows, published 6 February, Via Environment360, www.e360.yale.edu (accessed 6 May 2015).

Product strategies

Against the background of so many variables, it is inevitable that companies adopt a very wide range of **product strategies** in international markets. In formulating product policies, Mesdag (1985) postulated that a company has three basic choices:

SWYG   Sell What You have Got.

SWAB   Sell What people Actually Buy.

GLOB   Sell the same thing GLOBally disregarding national frontiers.

All three strategies have been used for a long time. Heinz, Mars, Heineken and Johnnie Walker have been international brands for decades using global product and brand strategies to enable them to clearly position their products as global brands. The Danes have long dominated the UK bacon market by following a SWAB strategy. The disadvantage of the SWAB strategy is that it is only possible to penetrate one market at a time. It may be also difficult to compete with local firms on their own terms. Furthermore, it is sometimes difficult for a foreign company to establish credibility as a supplier of products which have a strong domestic demand; for example, Suntory of Japan make good whisky but could not market it in the UK so it acquired Morrison Boxmore Distillers, which produces distinctively Scottish single malt whisky brands.

The SWAB approach is the classic differentiated approach, but while it is responsive to market needs it does make considerable demands on the firm's development, manufacturing, logistics and financial resources and is often impractical for these reasons.

SWYG are the most common form of export strategies, but they are also the most common reason for failure. The key objective for most firms following such strategies is to fill production lines at home rather than meet a market need, but by concentrating only on a few markets, many companies do successfully implement this kind of strategy. Mesdag argues also that some of the most successful global products started off as domestic products with a SWYG strategy, for example pizza, hamburgers and yoghurt. Success has been the result of the company's ability to meet new international emerging demand for the convenience of fast foods. The products may not necessarily be formulated identically across markets but they appeal to a pan-regional or global need and can therefore be positioned as cross-frontier brands. The success of the strategy has been based on identifying and meeting the needs of transnational customer segments. Heineken, the Dutch brewing firm, took over Egypt's only brewery, Al Harham Beverages, in 2002 and in so doing acquired Fayrouz, a fruit flavoured non-alcoholic malt drink popular in Egypt and certified Halal by Al Azhar, a leading Sunni Islam religious institution. Heineken then had the opportunity to market Fayrouz in the Indian subcontinent and to Muslims in the UK, Germany, Netherlands and France. In 2011 they strengthened the authenticity of the Fayrouz brand when they changed the flavours of their drinks and updated the packaging to something much more fun and trendy for their target audiences.

Keegan and Green (2014) have highlighted the key aspects of international marketing strategy as a combination of standardization or adaptation of product and promotion elements of the mix, and offer five alternative and more specific approaches to product policy.

One product, one message worldwide   These are the truly global brands. Since the 1920s, Coca-Cola have adopted a global approach, which has allowed them to make enormous cost savings and benefit from continual reinforcement of the same message. While a number of writers have argued that this will be the strategy adopted for many products in the future, in practice only a handful of products might claim to have achieved this already. A number of firms have tried this and failed.

Product extension, promotion adaptation   While the product stays the same, this strategy allows for the adaptation of the promotional effort to target either new customer segments or appeal to the particular tastes of individual countries; for example, Yoplait yoghurt (US) attempts to capture the mood of the country in its various television adverts.

Product adaptation, promotion extension   This strategy is used if a promotional campaign has achieved international appeal, but the product needs to be adapted because of the local needs. Many suppliers of capital goods, IT management and consultancy, promote the idea of providing technical solutions rather than selling industrial plants or computer hardware; and IBM have used 'solutions for a small planet'.

Dual adaptation   By adapting both products and promotion for each market, the firm is adopting a totally differentiated approach. This strategy is often adopted by firms when one of the previous three strategies has failed, but particularly if the firm is not in a leadership position and, instead, must react to the market or follow the competitors. This is closest to a multidomestic strategy.

Product invention   Product invention is adopted by firms, usually from advanced nations, who are supplying products to less well-developed countries. Products are specifically developed to meet the needs of the individual markets. European innovators and IBM worked together to create a drone that delivers medicine or food to remote areas. The "flying donkeys" as they have been named are a simple engineering answer to a big logistical problem.

Managing products across borders

The product life cycle

In the domestic market models such as the product life cycle and Boston Consulting Group's (BCG) portfolio matrix are used to manage a portfolio of products. The concepts can be applied in international markets to the management of a product, brand or product range across a portfolio of countries.

The life cycle concept is used as a model for considering the implications for marketing management of a product passing through the stages of introduction, growth, maturity and decline, and can be applied to international marketing.

The **international product life cycle** suggests that products in international markets can have consecutive 'lives' in different countries. Soon after the product was launched in its domestic market it was introduced into another developed country, A. Later it was introduced to other developed and newly industrialized countries, B and C, and only recently to a less developed country, D. In the domestic market and country A, a replacement product is required, while considerable growth is still possible in the other countries. This illustrates the dilemma that firms often face: they must decide how to allocate scarce resources between product and market development (Figure 8.3).

In some high technology markets it is now possible to accurately predict when new technology will force a new product's introduction. As a result it is now necessary for the product to be project managed for a limited and specific lifetime to ensure that by the end of its life the product has been profitable, recouped the initial investment and a replacement new innovation is ready for launch. Illustration 8.5 shows how Gillette is addressing this situation.

The most significant change for life cycle models is that global communications lead to global companies having to launch new products into many markets simultaneously to meet customer expectations, and so the sequential approach to marketing and manufacturing that is encapsulated in the original model applies less frequently. However, as we established earlier, not all companies operating internationally are global corporations, nor based on leading edge technology and it is therefore important not to ignore the model altogether. The concept of phases in the life cycle is still useful for a company that is not in a fast-changing market, perhaps simply exporting specialist engineering components and tools from an advanced economy or rolling out a service into new country markets as the opportunity arises.

FIGURE 8.3 The international product cycle

ILLUSTRATION 8.5

Gillette planning a close shave

In the late 1970s and 1980s the change to disposable razors by many consumers in the US and Europe meant that shaving products appeared to be turning into a commodity market. For Gillette, which had a 65 per cent share of the market, this was extremely serious. Gillette in the US cut advertising by a quarter and appeared to have almost given up on razors.

In Europe, however, Gillette started to spend on a pan-European campaign featuring the slogan 'Gillette – the best a man can get' to promote the top-of-the-range Contour Plus brand, and this led to a gain in market share and an increase in margins.

Gillette's mission statement over the past 25 years has been 'There is a better way to shave and we will find it', and Sensor, launched in 1989, spearheaded Gillette's fightback. Sensor was shown to be significantly better than anything else on the market and user tests showed that 80 per cent of men who tried it kept on using it. Gillette decided to centralize its marketing by combining the European and US sections into one group, headed by the previous European head, to ensure an effective launch of Sensor. Previously, marketing had been carried out by brand managers in each local country.

Sensor helped Gillette to a 70 per cent share of the world razor market, but by 1997 the sales growth was flattening, signifying the need for a new product. The successor, Mach 3, cost well over US$1 billion to develop but sold at a premium of 25–35 per cent over the price of Sensor, which Gillette retained as it does not withdraw older products.

The competition started to fight back: Schick, recently taken over by Energiser, using the Wilkinson Sword brand in some markets with its four-blade Quattro, followed by Schick Hydro, and a South Korean company, Dorco, which developed a Mach 3 competitor with prices 30 per cent cheaper than Gillette. Men and women do not shave more often, so the only way to increase sales and profits is to increase prices in developed countries, persuade customers to buy more products and win new customers in emerging markets. The Fusion range was the last new product to be introduced before Procter and Gamble bought Gillette in 2005. Five years passed before the Fusion ProGlide Series became the first introduction under P&G. With its five blade razor and range of skincare products, Gillette's aim was to 'address every aspect of interaction with hair and skin' claiming in tests involving 30 000 men there was a 2:1 preference for ProGlide over Fusion. Gillette sells in over 75 countries.

Questions

1 How should Gillette keep its technological lead?

2 Will technology be the only factor in its future success in the global shaving market?

On balance, therefore, although the validity of the product life cycle has at various times been attacked by a variety of writers, it does have a role to play for certain types of company insofar as it is a model that provides a framework for thinking in detail about product policy, NPD, product introduction and product elimination.

Product portfolio analysis

The use of portfolio approaches in international product management centres around the Boston Consulting Group's growth–share matrix, the General Electric/McKinsey screen and the Arthur D. Little business profile matrix. They are designed primarily to clarify the current strategic position of a company, its products and those of its competitors, and to help identify any future strategic options.

The complexity of the analysis increases as the competitive positions occupied by a product and the intensity of competition differ significantly from one market to another. Comparing the strength of a

FIGURE 8.4   The portfolio approach to strategic analysis (BCG matrix)

portfolio across a variety of markets becomes difficult as the analytical base constantly changes. For these reasons, the BCG matrix, for example, might be based on one product range or on one brand with the circles in the matrices representing country sales instead of different product sales, as shown in Figure 8.4. This then provides a basis for analyzing the current international product portfolio, assessing competitors' product/market strengths and forecasting the likely development of future portfolios both for itself and its competitors. The key decisions will be whether to use cash generated in 'cash cow' countries to maintain the position by introducing new products or to build positions in emerging markets (stars and question marks) where growth will be higher.

Introduction and elimination activities

While the major focus of product policy is upon new product and service development, the increased pace of the activity has a number of consequences for product management at both ends of the product life cycle. The factors that need to be taken into account in managing the product portfolio are:

- The firm's objectives.
- The profitability of the company's existing range of products and services.
- The stage in the life cycle that the products and services have reached.
- The manufacturing and service delivery capacity available.
- The likely receptiveness of the market to the new product or service.
- The competitive structure of the market.

These factors have a number of implications for the product policy. Too many product and service introductions can risk overburdening the firm's marketing system. There is a constant need for a regular review of the range and for elimination decisions to be made where a product or service is either in its decline stage or simply failing to generate sufficient profit. The international perspective, however, means that decision making is more difficult, since a product may be manufactured principally in a plant in one country but exported to many countries, be a 'cash cow' in one market and a 'dog' in another. Careful analysis is therefore needed before the product elimination decision is taken. The identification of overlaps in the product range or poor performance of specific products may necessitate elimination of products if they are in the declining stage of the product life cycle, have been duplicated or have been replaced by a newer product.

The complexity of managing a wide portfolio of products is discussed in Illustration 8.6 and it raises some fundamental issues about the product strategy alternatives.

Image, branding and positioning

Of all the elements of the product or service offer, it is the image of the brand which is the most visible and it is the perceived value which consumers attach to this that is the central factor in positioning the products in the various markets.

The image and reputation of products, companies and countries can confer different values to consumers in different countries. Research by a number of writers has shown that products from particular countries have a stereotyped national image for such attributes as quality, price and reliability. Individual corporate brands either benefit from positive country of origin perceptions or must overcome negative perceptions to succeed in international markets.

Country of origin effects

Buyers evaluate the products that they may wish to purchase based on their assessment of intrinsic (taste, design, performance and quality) and extrinsic cues (brand names, packaging and country of origin).

Where the buyers' knowledge about the product is limited, for example because they do not understand the technology, country of origin perceptions influence their buying decisions. The consumers' perceptions of companies are usually based on national stereotypes. For example, Japanese products tend to be regarded as high quality, reliable and 'miniaturized', whereas US products are seen as big and 'brash'. German products are perceived as well engineered and of high specification, whereas products from developing countries are often seen by western consumers as low quality, unreliable, inexpensive and usually copies of products from developed countries. This was the perception of Japanese products some decades ago, and shows that it is possible to change consumer attitudes.

There are significant differences between countries in the willingness of consumers to buy locally produced products. Usually this appears to be related to the feeling of nationalism that exists in the country at the particular time the assessment is made. As countries develop there is often a greater satisfaction with home produced products and services.

The **country of origin effect** does extend further. For example, the stereotyping relates just as much to developed countries, and there are strong associations between countries and the products that they are known for: Italy and pizza, and Germany and machine tools. Overcoming these stereotypes is often the first challenge for international marketers who must prove that their product does not reinforce negative stereotypes. This is particularly important as customers become more knowledgeable. For example, many new car buyers know where their car has been designed and manufactured as well as the country of origin of the brand. Increasingly, of course, the MNE's headquarters, the brand's perceived 'home', the location of product design and places of manufacture may all be in different countries. Many MNEs such as Nike are marketing, not manufacturing, companies and source products from many countries. Their brand becomes the 'badge of quality' that overlays the country of origin effect.

Product image: As we have already emphasized, product image is one of the most powerful points of differentiation for consumers. The aspirational and achiever groups of purchasers wish to belong to particular worldwide customer segments and are keen to purchase products associated with that group. This is a major buying factor that has driven the sales of Apple's iPhones, iPods and iPads. An interesting example of this is that the sales of luxury goods remained buoyant during recent recessions due to increased sales to emerging countries as the 'new' rich sought to buy similar products and services to the 'old' rich.

Company image is becoming increasingly important in creating a central theme running through diverse product ranges. It reinforces the vision and the values of the company, which can be recognized by employees and customers alike. For this reason many companies have spent considerable effort and resources on controlling and enhancing the corporate identity through consistent style and communications, discussed in more detail in Chapter 9.

Image can be equally important at the other end of the product spectrum to luxury goods. Aldi (Germany), Netto (Denmark) and Lidl (Germany) use a no-frills approach to retailing by reinforcing their message of low prices with simple decor, warehouse-type displays and single colour understated packaging.

The image of a company also plays a vital role in business-to-business marketing, for example, when quoting for international capital projects. Decisions are likely to be made on the grounds of the perceived reputation of the company as, without a strong international presence, it can be quite difficult to break into a small elite circle of international companies, even if very low prices are quoted.

Connections too can be important. Reconstruction projects following tsunamis, hurricanes and wars are extremely lucrative and are usually awarded to global companies. For example, Samoa was devastated after the tsunami in 2012, and the Post-Tsunami Reconstruction Project was established so that global companies could help in rebuilding damaged roads and seawalls. In 2014 Hurricane Sandy hit New York City and there are still hundreds of reconstruction contracts available under the Build it Back Reconstruction Project.

International branding

The image and reputation of an organization and its products and services are increasingly important differentiators from competitors' offers in international markets and the management of **international branding** is vital in adding value. The role of branding, important as it is in domestic markets, takes on an additional dimension in international markets as it is the most visible of the firm's activities, particularly for global companies, as we discussed in Chapter 6. Brands allow customers to identify products or services which will 'guarantee' satisfaction by providing specific benefits, such as performance, price, quality or status. Brands have the potential to add value to the organization by providing the following benefits:

Price premium: They should allow higher prices to be charged than for products that have an equivalent specification but no brand.

Higher volumes: Alternatively branded products can generate higher volumes than non-branded products if they are priced at market rates, rather than at a premium.

Lower costs: Higher volumes should lead to cost reduction from the economies of scale and the experience effect, so improving competitiveness.

Better utilization of assets: The predictably high level of sales should lead brand managers to make effective use of assets such as equipment, the supply chain and distribution channels.

The constituents of the brand can include both tangible benefits, such as quality and reliability, and intangible benefits which may bring out a whole range of feelings, such as status, being fashionable or possessing good judgement by purchasing a particular brand. Very young children are now fully aware of which fashion label is 'cool' at the moment and advertisers are equally alert to the effects of 'pester power' on all the family purchasing decisions.

Brand categories

Three brand categories are identified (Doyle 2000):

1 *Attribute brands* are created around the functional product or service attributes, such as quality, specification and performance, to build confidence among customers in situations where it is difficult for them to evaluate the difference between competitive products. The brand provides a 'guarantee'. Examples include Volvo for safety, Walmart for everyday low prices and Intel for computer processing.

2 *Aspirational brands* create images in the minds of customers about the type of people who purchase the brand and convey the standards and values that the brand is associated with. Such brands do not simply deliver the customer's functional requirements of the products and services, such as high specification and quality, but also recognize the customer's status, recognition and esteem that can be associated with the brand. Examples include Ferrari, Louis Vuitton or choosing to take a holiday at a high-end hotel, such at The Royal Penthouse Suite at Hotel President Wilson in Switzerland, which is currently $65 000 per night.

3 *Experience brands* focus on a shared philosophy between the customer and brand and on shared associations and emotions, but not necessarily on claims of superiority. Examples include Nike, Virgin and Mini Cooper. Coca-Cola won the Best Brand Experience Event following the launch of its 'Share a Coke' campaign where Coca-Cola bottles were personalized with names from Alex to Oleg to Zak, all names appropriate for customers in 34 countries.

The appeal of these different types of brand varies according to the context of the purchasing decision. In luxury product markets aspirational brands are likely to be most successful, whereas in consumer markets, where there is little to distinguish between the attributes and performance of products, experience branding is more appropriate. Attribute branding would be more appropriate in business-to-business markets where the purchasing process should be more rational, objective and based on specifications.

In global markets, too, because of different culture, customer expectations and market sophistication, the appeal of a particular branding approach might be more relevant for a similar product. For example, in some cultures, such as in Germany, the attributes, functionality and specification may be more important, whereas in others, such as emerging markets, aspirational branding might be more appealing.

The brand value equation (Figure 8.5) draws attention to the offer to consumers of the intangible benefits that the brand adds over and above the tangible, functional benefits of a commoditized product or service. The challenge for international branding, of course, is to what extent the intangible benefits from branded products and services vary between countries, cultures and individuals.

Apple products are the 'must haves' for the teenage and young adult generation not just because of their functionality and design but also because of peer pressure for some and 'being part of the Apple club' for others.

Rappa and Hirsh (2007) found that superb service was the indispensable ingredient of successful high-end brands and identified four principles to deliver customer satisfaction:

■ Create a customer-centred culture.

■ Use a rigorous staff selection process.

■ Constantly retrain employees.

■ Systematically measure and reward customer-centric behaviour.

Tangible and intangible benefits must also be valued against the background of the total cost of ownership of the branded product by the customer. The total cost of ownership and the tangible and intangible benefits are accrued over the lifetime of the product. For example, car ownership offers different benefits

FIGURE 8.5 The brand value equation

Tangible and intangible benefits

$$\text{Brand value} = \frac{\text{Benefits received by customers}}{\text{Costs to customer of brand purchases}}$$

Total cost of ownership

and costs in different markets, especially when considering the longer-term implications of, for example, warranty and servicing costs, car resale value and changing car fashions. Brand strength for cars is, to some extent, determined by the second-hand car values, with car marques such as BMW and Mercedes holding their value exceptionally well and some cars, such as Ferrari, even increasing in value.

Brand value

It has been suggested that the strongest brands convey a core value to all their customers by the associations that are made with their name. By adding '-ness' to the brand names consumers instantly associate values which are globally recognized – 'Pradaness', from 'Gucciness', and 'Appleness' from 'Sonyness'. Traditionally the great brands (Table 8.1) have achieved their global status through high levels of investment and consistent management across their country markets of the dimensions used to value the brand over a long period of time. Usually the investment includes a large commitment to advertising but other factors, such as understanding their customers' needs and wants, totally consistent quality, reliability and continuous innovation are just as important to achieve widespread customer loyalty and recommendations. To illustrate this point the value of Google (+15 per cent) and Apple (+21 per cent) have increased; the highest brand value increase is Facebook at 86 per cent, whereas the IBM brand decreased by 8 per cent and the Gillette brand by 9 per cent due to increased competition.

Table 8.1   The 30 best global brands 2014

Rank 2014	Change in brand value (%)	Brand	Sector	Brand value (mn)
1	+21	Apple	Technology	$118 863
2	+15	Google	Technology	$107 439
3	+3	Coca-Cola	Beverages	$81 563
4	−8	IBM	Business Services	$72 244
5	+3	Microsoft	Technology	$61 154
6	+3	GE	Diversified	$45 480
7	+15	Samsung	Technology	$45 462
8	+20	Toyota	Automotive	$42 392
9	+1	McDonald's	Restaurants	$42 254
10	+8	Mercedes-Benz	Automotive	$34 338
11	+7	BMW	Automotive	$34 214
12	−8	Intel	Technology	$34 153
13	+14	Disney	Media	$32 223
14	+6	Cisco	Technology	$30 936
15	+25	Amazon	Retail	$29 478
16	+8	Oracle	Technology	$25 980
17	−8	HP	Technology	$23 758

Table 8.1   Continued

Rank 2014	Change in brand value (%)	Brand	Sector	Brand value (mn)
18	−9	Gillette	FMCG	$22 845
19	−9	Louis Vuitton	Luxury	$22 552
20	+17	Honda	Automotive	$21 673
21	+16	H&M	Apparel	$21 083
22	+16	Nike	Sporting Goods	$19 875
23	+11	American Express	Financial Services	$19 510
24	+7	Pepsi	Beverages	$19 119
25	+4	SAP	Technology	$17 340
26	+15	Ikea	Retail	$15 885
27	+5	UPS	Transportation	$14 470
28	+9	Ebay	Retail	$14 358
29	+86	Facebook	Technology	$14 349
30	+8	Pampers	FMCG	$14 078

Source: Best Global Brands 2014 www.interbrand.com (accessed 7 May 2015).

Brand valuation is inevitably subjective to some degree, but the dimensions indicated in Figure 8.6 suggest that building the brand requires dedicated management of the complete marketing mix across the various markets, and there is evidence of this in all the successful brands. Brands can, of course, also decline in value from time to time due, for example, to failure to understand changing customer expectations (some fast food brands), to inappropriate brand stretching (a number of the top fashion brands), to failure to respond to market problems (banks and financial institutions) or product and service problems (Toyota) or failure to respond to new competition (formerly state-owned airlines and telecoms businesses and many of the developed world car manufacturers at some point in their recent history).

Branding strategies

Branding strategies and the brand portfolio   The first decision is to choose between the alternative branding strategies that can be applied to the brand portfolio. The alternatives are:

- *Umbrella brands*: occurs when one brand supports several products, as is the case with Google (see Management Challenge 8.2).
- *Product brands*: occur when, for example, Unilever, Procter & Gamble and pharmaceutical firms give each product a unique and distinctive brand.
- *Line brands*: occur where a company has a number of complementary products sharing the same brand concept, for example, L'Oréal sells haircare products under the Studio Line name.
- *Range brands*: are similar to line brands but include a broader range of products. Heinz uses Weightwatchers and Nestlé uses Findus for frozen foods.

FIGURE 8.6   Brand valuation

The most basic criteria for brand evaluation include:

- Title to the brand has to be clear and separately disposable from the rest of the business.
- The value has to be substantial and long term, based on separately identifiable earnings that have to be in excess of those achieved by unbranded products.

MANAGEMENT CHALLENGE 8.2

Google: The number 2 umbrella technology brand

Google's Googlers (their employees) create and design a range of products and services under the worldwide 2nd highest ranking brand.

There are over 40 000 Googlers who ask the question "what can Google develop for you?". By asking this question every day Google stays in touch with the consumers and gives them solutions to their problems and of course products that consumers didn't know they needed.

The main products, familiar with Google and non-Google consumers are:

1 Web-based products: These include the very simple and easy to use Google search engine. The fun thing about the search engine is the Google doodle logo – which has hundreds of different images showing Mother's Day, An Earth Day quiz, and doodles of dancing Shamrocks for St. Patrick's Day and a special Google logo for Martin Luther King Jr Day.

2 Google Chrome – a super fast web-browser for consumers and businesses.

3 Google Bookmarks – a filing system to help consumers organize and keep their favourite topics, videos or fashion pages at their finger-tips.

For businesses there are also Google products:

1 Google Adsense, which is a free service for businesses that publish a webpage. If a business has a webpage, they can earn money by simply allowing other web-based publishers to post an advertisement on their site.

2 Google Hangouts – rivalling Skype for businesses that want to connect face-to-face with employees that are remote or have meetings with colleagues overseas.

3 Google Adwords – for businesses that want to attract more customers to their website or telephone number. A coffee shop in Leeds using Adwords can pay a small fee to have an advertisement viewed on Google. A consumer search for 'coffee shop in Leeds' will increase business by attracting more customers either globally or locally.

And for leisure there are:

1 Google books – which enables consumers to download books from the classics to children's books to academic text books. Some books are free and some have a small fee.

2 Google play – is another fun platform for consumers on the go. Games, music and TV can be accessed and downloaded. There are also hundreds of magazines and newspaper articles available straight to PCs and Android phones.

Other Google products and services under the umbrella brand include Google Maps, Google Translate, Google Drive, Google Scholar and YouTube. Google has something for everyone. Their Google products and services are provided under a range of subcategories which are:

Web, mobile, business, media, geo, specialized search, home and office, social and innovation.

Questions

1 Which target markets are Google appealing to?

2 Why did Google choose the umbrella brand strategy?

3 What are the weaknesses of using an umbrella brand strategy?

Source: www.google.co.uk

- *Endorsing brands*: is a weaker association of a corporate name with a product brand name and is often used after acquisition. Over time, Nestlé has gradually increased the size of 'Nestlé' on the packaging of its acquired brands, such as Kit-Kat. This may be one step towards umbrella branding.

- *Source brands*: occur where products are double branded with a corporate or range name and a product name, for example, Ford Mondeo.

Essentially the decision about which strategy to use is determined by whether the benefits of a shared identity outweigh the importance of differentiation between the individual product brands.

A further branding strategy, private branding, is the practice of supplying products to a third party for sale under their brand name. The two South Korean companies, Samsung and LG, achieved success initially by being original equipment manufacturers (OEM), but have rapidly developed internationally to the point where they now have high shares of certain product categories by building their own brands.

Private branding is used widely in retailing and as the major retailers become more powerful, so the private brand share of the market has increased significantly, especially during times of recession. This is because the consumers perceive private brands as providing value for money, and this has been supported as retailers have promoted their own label products and continually improved the quality too.

Brand piracy

One of the most difficult challenges for brand management is dealing with **brand piracy**. Research suggests that the problem of forgery of famous brand names is increasing, and many but by no means all fake products have been found to originate in developing countries and in Asia. It is important to recognize the differences between the ways in which forgery takes place. Kaitiki (1981) identifies:

- *Outright piracy*: In which a product is in the same form and uses the same trademark as the original but is false.

- *Reverse engineering*: In which the original product is stripped down, copied and then undersold to the original manufacturer, particularly in the electronics industry.

- *Counterfeiting*: In which the product quality has been altered but the same trademark appears on the label. Burberry, Levi Strauss and LaCoste have all been victims.

- *Passing off*: Involves modifying the product but retaining a trademark which is similar in appearance, phonetic quality or meaning – for example Coalgate for Colgate and Del Mundo for Del Monte.

- *Wholesale infringement*: Is the questionable registration of the names of famous brands overseas rather than the introduction of fake products. This might be considered brand piracy but it is entirely within the law. This has been very prevalent in e-business with the registration of dotcom sites by individuals hoping to sell the site later, at substantial profit, to the famous name.

There is a vast trade in pirated brands and copied products. It has been estimated that 90 per cent of the software used in India and China is counterfeit. However, some cultures do not accept that individuals should gain from ideas which ought to benefit everyone, so there are substantial differences in the perception of the importance of counterfeiting. Others believe that the development of many underdeveloped economies would have been set back considerably if they had paid market rates for software, which raises the ethical question of whether oligopolistic companies such as Microsoft should be allowed to make fortunes for certain individuals by charging very high prices, while effectively excluding customers in underdeveloped countries who cannot afford to pay.

The issue of brand piracy clearly is costing MNEs vast revenues, and the US has led the way in insisting that governments crack down on the companies undertaking the counterfeiting. However, such firms have sophisticated networking operations, with much of their revenue coming from sales to consumers in developed countries. Trying to reduce or eliminate their activities is costly and time-consuming and unlikely to be a priority for governments in less developed countries. Moreover, pursuing legal action in foreign markets can be expensive, particularly for small companies, and can result in adverse publicity for larger firms.

The music industry has particularly suffered from illegal practices. The myth of music piracy was of a victimless crime, but the International Federation of the Phonographic Industry (IFPI) claims that billions of dollars goes to support criminal gangs as well as sucking out money from the legitimate music industry (IFPI, 2003).

Positioning

Closely related to brand strategy and at the heart of its implementation is positioning. Positioning is largely concerned with how a product or service might be differentiated from the competition. However, it is important to stress that it is the customers' perceptions of the product or service offer that will indirectly confirm the positioning and so determine its success. Firms can only seek to establish and confirm the positioning in the consumers' minds through their management of the marketing mix. In countries at different stages of economic development the customer segments that are likely to be able to purchase the product and the occasions on which it is bought may be significantly different. For example, while KFC and McDonald's restaurants aim at everyday eating for the mass market in the developed countries, in less developed countries they are perceived as places for special occasion eating, and out of reach of the poorest segments of the population. A Mercedes car may be perceived as a luxury car in many countries but as an everyday taxi in Germany.

Unilever has a different approach. It introduced a new logo for its ice cream so that while the familiar names stay the same, for example Wall's in the UK and Ola in the Netherlands, the background design and font are being standardized around the world.

There appears to be an increasing demand for standardized products among market segments that are mobile and susceptible to influence by the media and through travel, and there is a strongly emerging demand for the same products among consumers in the less developed countries, too. Achieving unique positioning for a product or service must come from the creative dimensions of positioning rather than resorting to simple price positioning.

In confirming the positioning of a product or service in a specific market or region, it is necessary, therefore, to establish in the consumers' perception exactly what is the value proposition and how it differs from existing and potential competition.

Innovation and new product development

A recurring theme of discussions of international marketing issues is the increasing need for companies to have a dynamic and proactive policy of innovation for developing new products and services in order to satisfy the apparently insatiable demand of consumers for new experiences and to reinforce and, where necessary, renew, their source of competitive advantage. Some companies have **new product development (NPD)** as a corporate objective. Today, Johnson & Johnson generates 35 per cent of its sales from products that are less than five years old, compared to 30 per cent in 1980. Lim, Sharkey and Heinrichs (2006) argue that faster NPD capability is essential for firms striving for a higher degree of export involvement. At the outset, however, it is important to stress that the most competitive firms encourage innovation in every aspect of their marketing activity. The space in which innovation takes place includes new products and services; new processes; position innovation which includes creativity in brand identity and communication; and paradigm innovation, which changes the underlying mental models that frame what the organization does. For example, IBM has reinvented itself from being a hardware company (International Business Machines), to a software and solutions provider, to a business process outsourcing company. Nestlé's new medical nutrition division aims to create a new industry between food and pharmaceuticals, in which foods are developed for people suffering, for example, from metabolic disorders. An increasing trend among online businesses is architectural innovation (Tuschman and Anderson, 2004) and the adoption of innovative business models. For example, Google does not charge for search but generates income from advertisers. Mobile phone companies give away expensive phones for free and generate income from monthly rental contracts and connection.

While product or technological innovation is quite obvious, for example the average person knows that Edison invented the light bulb, getting the bulbs into houses and schools and setting electricity is service innovation. However, due to the increase in personal economic circumstances in both the developed and developing countries, and of course increased global knowledge, consumers expect and demand more, particularly for services such as healthcare, education, leisure and entertainment. One of the key aspects that is helping services innovate and grow is technology. Barrett *et al.* (2015) state that technological innovation is particularly useful in advancing consumer self-service opportunities, such as telephoning a doctor for a diagnosis, popular in developed countries and rural areas in Peru. Additionally, mobile payments and delivery services enhance the consumer's opportunity to shop online from any device. IBM, Oracle and other tech companies have formed a non-profit consortium www.thesri.org to advance the concept using an open web social networking community and public archive. It maintains that innovation is about culture and values rather than processes and notes that the best ideas are, at first, laughable. If an innovation is truly and substantially new, it must by definition carry with it uncertainty and ambiguity.

The most innovative companies

Deciding which are the world's most innovative companies rather depends on which measure you use. Jaruzel, Staack and Goehle, B. (2014) (from Strategy&; formally Booz and Company) show that annual study of the world's biggest R&D spenders note that automobiles, computing and electronics, and healthcare were the biggest industries for R&D spending and the top five companies were Volkswagen, Samsung, Intel, Microsoft and Roche. By contrast, a survey of innovation executives to explore the relationship between innovation capabilities, corporate strategy and financial performance resulted in overwhelming votes for Apple, Google, Amazon, Samsung and Telsa Motors as the world's most innovative companies.

Patent filing is used by some as another measure of the innovativeness of firms. Huawei Technologies, China's largest telecoms equipment maker, was the world's top international patent seeker followed by Panasonic and Philips Electronics which had dominated for a decade. Next come Japan's Toyota and Fujitsu, Germany's Robert Bosch and Siemens, Finland's Nokia, South Korea's LG Electronics and Sweden's Ericsson. China was the sixth-largest patent filer by country, behind the United States, Japan, Germany, South Korea and France.

The nature of new product development

Few new products and services are actually revolutionary and Figure 8.7 shows the various categories of new products in terms of their newness to the market and company. Innovative firms encourage their staff

FIGURE 8.7   New product categories

ILLUSTRATION 8.6

New brand development – for men

Unilever has seen a change in male behaviour. For a number of years the amount of money men spent on facial care, body lotions and antiperspirant/deodorants was increasing at a much faster rate than that spent by women on similar products. Unilever recognized the trend and began investigating which of their branded products men were buying. They discovered that 40 per cent of men were using Dove soap. So . . . they did a quick and easy experiment. Unilever simply added Dove: Men+Care to their existing packaging of Dove products. They saw an amazing 31 per cent increase in sales.

Unilever decided to go further and investigate why more men were purchasing grooming and beauty products. Their research was conducted with men in the US, UK, Brazil, China and Germany. It was discovered that gender roles in many households were becoming more equal with more men doing the 'weekly supermarket shop', getting more involved in bathing their babies, cooking food for the family and general household cleaning. At the same time men were becoming more individual. Additionally, Unilever's research showed that men were more optimistic, confident and want to feel good about themselves. And whilst the 'stay at home dad' numbers had doubled in recent years and dads were posting many family photos on social media . . . at the end of the day men still wanted to be 'one of the guys'. In fact, "losing their masculinity' was something Unilever found men were worried about. Yet they were not worried about showing their caring side for others or themselves; in fact men felt this was a strength.

Taking the research findings into account Unilever felt they should go further than just changing the packaging on their existing Dove range. Therefore, they developed a new product range, which like Dove products includes conditioning products for the skin, but was specifically crafted for guys. The new product range is called Axe-White Label. The packaging is smart, with silver writing and logos. The grooming products are antiperspirant/deodorant spray, antiperspirant/deodorant solid gel, 2-in-1 shampoo and conditioner and hair styling cream. The product range comes in very outdoorsy scents: Night, Forest, Island and Air. One of the TV advertisements shows a man walking through a hotel. Women and men are guessing who he is ranging from a James Bond-like spy, a movie star, a comedian, a surgeon. All suggestions are linked to the final strapline of the advertisement: 'How you feel says it all'.

Questions

1 How did Unilever identify a new target market?

2 Why did they choose to develop new products and not re-package their existing product range?

Source: Precourt, G. (2015) 'How Unilever builds brands', WARC (World Advertising Research Centre) Event Reports, ANA Brand Masters www.warc.com.

---

to undertake incremental innovation in every aspect of business activity as a continual improvement process intended to refresh and reinforce the product range by complementing the existing company and brand image, rather than causing a change of direction.

Periodically step change innovation occurs as a result of a technological breakthrough, such as the mobile phone, or groundbreaking creative ideas often related to marketing that achieve a change of industry direction. Renewable energy innovations require technological and business innovations, step change and incremental. However, as Illustration 8.6 shows, Unilever decided to innovate rather than simply take an incremental brand change for their Dove product.

Usually, developing new technologies is hugely expensive. For example, it is estimated that the cost of developing a new drug is estimated to cost between US$800 million and $2 billion and takes over 15 years.

In order to recover the research and development costs it is necessary to market new ideas simultaneously in all developed countries, as the time taken by competitors to copy or improve products and circumvent patents is shortening. Moreover, when pharmaceutical products come out of the patent period, they can legitimately be copied as generic drugs – companies such as Ranbaxy in India and Aspen in South Africa have grown fast and built a strong global business doing this.

Even the largest companies do not have sufficient resources on their own to achieve rapid diffusion of a new product or service into all world markets, so this is at least as important a part of the process as the initial idea. This leads to the use of different market entry methods, such as licensing, franchising and strategic alliances, to secure cost-effective diffusion.

The new product development process

In its simplest form, developing products follows a similar process for international markets to that in domestic situations:

- idea generation
- initial screening
- business analysis
- development
- market testing
- commercialization and launch.

Particular emphasis must be placed upon the quality of the information system, as it is essential that the product or service meets the needs of the customers and is positioned accurately in each market from the outset. With this in mind, the international development process should incorporate the following elements.

Idea generation must ensure that ideas worldwide are accessed so that duplication is avoided and synergy is optimized by effectively using all available internal and external resources to generate new ideas, including employees, R&D departments, competitors, sales people, customers, distributors and external experts.

Initial screening involves establishing rigorous international criteria, including both production and marketing factors, to test the ideas for suitability in all world regions so that opportunities and limitations are not overlooked. Ideas that may, for example, be inappropriate for Western Europe might be appropriate for South America. In doing this an assessment should be made of the degree of adaptation that will be necessary for individual markets.

Business analysis must involve establishing criteria for potential success or failure of the product and linking the criteria with regions and/or markets. It must make provision for contingencies such as environmental and competitive situations and unexpected events which might adversely affect the business case.

Product development must include ensuring that all relevant functions such as production, design and packaging become involved in the process. The most appropriate R&D centres for the development process should be selected, with particular attention being paid to such factors as access to technological expertise and location near prime target and lead markets.

Market testing must involve ensuring the test area is representative of the prime target markets, an adequate infrastructure in terms of the necessary services such as advertising and market research agencies, and an appropriate distribution network. It should also take account of potential competitor response both in the test market and globally.

The launch must be planned either to be sequential, with an initial concentration upon prime markets or lead markets, or to be a simultaneous launch. Allowance must be made for aggressive competitive responses, as few competitors will give up market share without a fight.

To protect the firm's competitive advantage the company needs to pay particular attention to defending its intellectual property and anticipate the ability of competitors to copy a new product and launch it in a separate market. There are a number of actions that companies might take to protect their intellectual property, such as taking strong patent protection, or entering into licensing arrangements to ensure fast, widespread penetration of the world or regional markets.

Timing is perhaps the most critical element of the process, not only in terms of exploiting an opportunity or competitive weakness at the right moment but also minimizing the time to market – how long it takes from when the idea was first generated to making it available commercially and the time it takes to achieve the desired level of diffusion.

Approaches to technology transfer and the benefits for marketing

This traditional, sequential and largely internal approach to NPD has considerable disadvantages because of a number of factors, including:

- The shortening of product life cycles.
- The cost and risk of funding development internally.
- The time needed to get the new product to market.
- 'Non-core' activities such as product and packaging design and process development, as part of the in-house development process.

In an attempt to resolve these problems, many firms are adopting a more interactive approach in which new product and service developments are carried out jointly between the manufacturer, component maker, designer and technology supplier. Chesbrough (2003) explained that open innovation is an approach in which a variety of specialist organizations including design companies, R&D companies and universities might be used by a lead firm to increase the speed, effectiveness and quality of innovation. The main benefits of an interactive approach to NPD for the company are the concentration of skills and expertise on core activities, the ability to condense timescales and access to the best knowledge available on a particular topic. Increasingly web-based firms are involving their customers in innovation in their business, as we discuss in Chapter 12.

It can be difficult to obtain contributions to the innovation process from staff around the world. Eppinger and Chitkara (2006) note that companies in many industries have engineering teams located in different parts of the world, but that without frameworks to support collaboration, managers find it difficult to achieve the necessary cohesion in the operation to drive efficient growth and innovation. The authors highlight Hyundai, Hewlett Packard and Alcatel as firms that have achieved this.

To further speed up the NPD process the stages can be regarded as simultaneous rather than linear. For example, testing the concept on customers around the world, carrying out the detailed analysis for the business case and designing the product packaging, could go ahead at the same time.

Research and development strategies

No matter which approach is adopted, major international companies must still decide upon the aims of their own R&D, the exact nature of the activities undertaken and where they should be located. They must take decisions on:

- The location of their own internal R & D facilities.
- The extent to which they embrace open innovation and contract out certain parts of their research and development programme, as large pharmaceutical companies do.
- Whether they might acquire a company which can provide either the required new technology or a new product.
- Licensing the technology and process from another company.
- Funding joint ventures or strategic alliances with companies that have complementary technology.

In general, the R&D activities of international companies tend to follow an evolutionary path, but for many the major question is whether or not they should move away from the dominance of their domestic country R&D location and if so, where should their R&D facilities be located.

FIGURE 8.8　The arguments for and against centralization of R&D

Arguments for centralization	Arguments against centralization
■ economies of scale	■ pressure from subsidiaries
■ easier and faster communication	■ pressure from governments
■ better coordination	■ benefits of public relations
■ greater control over outflow of information with implications for secrecy	■ use of wider range of skills and abilities
■ greater synergy	■ benefits from comparative advantage
■ avoiding duplication	■ greater sensitivity to local tastes
■ overcoming problems of ownership	■ better monitoring of local competitive activity
	■ closeness to possible acquisitions
	■ access new technology wherever it is located

Many companies still concentrate a large proportion of R&D activity in their country of origin, but as they move increasingly towards transnational operations so the concept of the home country becomes increasingly meaningless. It is, however, useful to consider the arguments for and against the centralization of R&D activities, and these are shown in Figure 8.8.

Success and failure in new product development

One of the most difficult aspects of NPD is to reduce the high levels of risk (and therefore the cost) of new product failure. The classic studies of success and failure of new products in developed countries, particularly the US and UK, emphasize that for success it is necessary to place greater emphasis upon marketing rather than technical factors. The key to success is an effective NPD strategy which includes the development of the central and supporting processes, in order to generate a flow of new products that might vary in market impact, but will include some high revenue or high-margin generators. In emerging markets the key is to develop products and services that meet the needs of customers for more basic items and the concept of 'frugal engineering', has been introduced. The aim of the innovation is to completely re-engineer products and services rather than simply try to reduce the costs of the established processes. These new products created are not inferior quality and will find new markets in developed countries too.

Griffin (2003) suggests three fundamental requirements of the innovation process:

- Uncover unmet needs and problems.
- Develop a product with competitive advantage.
- Shepherd the products through the firm.

Tzokas, Hart and Saren (2003) suggest that market information is central to achieving success in NPD, and summarize the research studies that have highlighted its role within the strategic success factors:

- Ensuring product performance improvements over what is already available.
- Achieving synergy with existing firm technologies and manufacturing capability and learning new capabilities quickly.
- Achieving marketing synergies, such as channels and promotion, often because of the need to target a new segment.
- Integrating the contributions of marketing and R&D.
- Identifying attractive markets with growth potential.
- Effectively carrying out the NPD process, including pre-development activities, such as idea generation, screening, concept and business case investigation.
- Obtaining support from top management.
- Speed in development.

MANAGEMENT CHALLENGE 8.3

Meeting emerging market needs with frugal engineering

Over many years, innovation has (and still is) mainly concerned with improvements that embrace new technology and typically add value for those customers that can afford to pay for increasingly sophisticated products and services. In Chapter 6 we introduced the concept of customers at the bottom of the pyramid highlighting the huge number of people particularly in markets such as China, India and Brazil that are moving out of poverty, enjoying prosperity for the first time and shopping for basics, rather than 'nice to have' features.

The term 'frugal engineering' has been coined not to describe stripped down engineering – removing features to enable products to be sold at lower prices – but to take a 'clean sheet' approach, where cost discipline is an intrinsic part of the process and avoids needless costs in the first place. In developed nations expansion of features has contributed most to the profitability of firms so, for example, many car manufacturers make profit on the top-of-the-range models and little or no profit on the low specification models. But this means that production lines are not geared to producing basic items, for example, manual car windows are virtually extinct in the US. Firms in emerging markets, such as Tata with its Nano, are showing how 'frugal engineering', a term coined by Renault CEO, Carlos Ghosn, can create products with costs that are unimaginable in the developed nations.

It is not just cars that are fit for purpose in emerging markets but also 'Little Cool' refrigerators with a fan rather than a compressor, basic function laptop computers, unsophisticated X-ray machines and mobile phones that just make calls. Western firms are beginning to wake up to the opportunities, so after watching customers using mobile phones in India, Nokia developed its best selling phone costing between \$15–\$20. It sends and receives calls and texts, has a monochrome display, lacks complex software so extending battery life, and is designed to cope with high humidity and dust.

Its one added feature is an energy efficient flashlight, popular where blackouts are common.

Some customers in developed countries also see the value in frugally engineered products. Deere from the US started selling small, lower powered tractors in India but did not sell them into the US until an Indian company, Mahindra and Mahindra, beat them to it. Now Mahindra and Mahindra are competing for Deere's large tractor market. By contrast GE is selling its low cost electrocardiogram machine in the US, which was developed for India.

Another innovation for Kenyan people was provided by MPESA, a company that enables people in remote villages to save, spend and transfer money using their mobile phones without having a bank account. Additionally, Kenyan SteamaCo, a supplier of renewable energy, provides kit for Kenyan people to fully charge their mobile phones from the sun.

Questions

1 How can firms such as Tata, Nokia and GE manage their portfolio to include 'frugal engineering' but also include top-of-the-range models for more demanding customers?

2 SteamaCo. and MPESA use frugal engineering. However, these companies are not global companies. What can local and global companies learn from each other?

Sources: Radjou, N. and Prabhu, J. (2013) Frugal innovation. A new business paradigm, INSEAD Knowledge, published 10 January 2013; V. Sehgal, K. Dehoff and G. Panneer (2010) The importance of frugal engineering, *Strategy and Business*, Summer: 59 www.strategy-business .com (accessed 25 May 2010); Maina Waruru (2015) 'Microgrids and mobile tech bring solar power to rural Kenya', Reuters 16 April. Available from www.reuters .com/article/2015/04/16/us-kenya-energy-solar -idUSKBN0N70TK20150416 (accessed 11th May 2015).

Key to success in technology sectors is generating a continual flow of new product introductions, but success is by no means guaranteed. Even for technologically leading edge companies, not every idea will make it to the market and be a commercial success, so risk-taking and tolerating failure must be accepted by the firm's management. The main focus, however, should be to add value to meet the needs of customers wherever they are in the world.

SUMMARY

- In many business sectors product and service strategies are being affected by the increased globalization of consumer tastes, communications, technological advances and the concentration of business activity. At the same time, however, given the level of competition and choice available, there is an increasing expectation among customers that their individual needs will be met.

- Product managers are balancing the efficiency benefits of standardization in terms of economies of scale and the experience effect with the need and cost of adapting products and services to meet the needs of local customers, regulations and usage conditions.

- The growth of international services is a feature of international marketing and it is being driven by low labour costs and increasing demand in developing countries and the increased possibilities for transferring information through information technology and communications.

- As more products are reaching the mature phase of the life cycle they are becoming commodities, and there is a need to use additional services to differentiate them from competitor offerings. However, services are often difficult to standardize globally because they are affected significantly by the different expectations of service delivery that exist in different cultures.

- The product or service strategy is usually at the centre of international marketing operations. Branding is a key part of product and service management, particularly in international markets, but it is difficult to establish global brands that are truly distinctive and have images that appeal to cross-cultural customer segments.

- New product and service development and innovation throughout the marketing process are essential for growth and the renewal of the international portfolio and, particularly for culturally sensitive products and services, it is vital to obtain input from the different stakeholders around the world in order to ensure that they will be successful.

KEYWORDS

intangibility	adaptation	international branding
perishability	international product portfolio	branding strategies
heterogeneity	product strategies	brand piracy
inseparability	international product life cycle	new product development
international product offer	country of origin effect	
standardization	services	

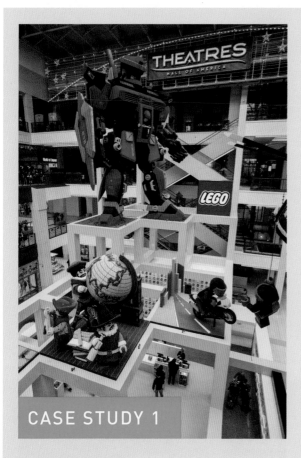

CASE STUDY 1

Lego playing with its strengths

According to Brand Finance (2015) Lego is the world's most powerful brand ahead of Ferrari and Apple. Lego sells its colourful, interlocking toy bricks in 130 countries, claiming that on average everyone on earth has 86 bricks. Lego is still owned by the family of Ole Kirk Christiansen, the Danish carpenter who founded the company in 1932, since then it has manufactured 600 billion parts and promotes learning and development through play by explaining that play is 'nutrition for the soul'.

By 2015 the company was highly profitable with an operating profit margin of around 35 per cent and return on equity rate of nearly 60 per cent, amazing for what is essentially commoditized plastic toy parts. However, in the mid-2000s Lego almost went bankrupt after making huge losses. Lego recognized that children were growing up more quickly in an age dominated by digital games and media, but they lost their way in trying to address the problem. They created many new, stylized models that were attractive to look at but did not encourage the open-ended imaginative play that the Lego brand was known for, and Lego became too dependent on licensing agreements with Disney and the Harry Potter and Star Wars movies. Sales slumped when no blockbuster films were released. Lego phased out the Duplo brand, leaving parents thinking Lego no longer made larger sized bricks for children aged 18 months to 5 years. Poor forecasting in the US resulted in overstock on some products and out of stock on more successful products. There were worldwide complaints that colours did not match. With the aim of becoming a lifestyle brand, Lego diversified into clothes, watches and video games and co-produced a kids TV show.

The problem, too, was that Lego had given product designers whatever pieces they asked for in the belief it would unleash their creativity, but the designers came up with ever more complex models and the number of components increased, hugely increasing production costs.

Lego achieved the turnaround by returning to its unique selling proposition, tightening its management, reducing the number of components back from over 12 000 to around 7000 and focusing on growth markets. They ensured their product range was right for each customer segment. Although Lego does not make gender distinctions, traditionally the core segment was 5–15-year-old boys attracted by ranges like Lego City and the large range of licenced products. To attract more girls Lego developed Lego Friends – girl models with individual personalities and interests, living in a town. Lego is strong in the pre-school group with its re-introduced Duplo range and for older groups interested in technology with ranges such as Mindstorms. Lego faces competition from other major toy manufacturers, such as Mattel and Hasbro (US), Bandai Namco and Takara Tomy (Japan) and in the construction sector, specifically from MegaBloks (Canada).

Lego is strongest in developed North American and European markets, where its market share of the construction toy market is above 70 per cent, but falling birthrates and low cost copies threaten future growth rates. In some Eastern European markets, too, Lego performs well and its future sales growth opportunities should come from the emerging toy markets, but the individual markets perform very differently. Lego sells well in Russia, but less well in China and India. India's 0–14 year-old population is 366 million but Lego's share of the toy market is very small. Indeed over the last ten years there has been little growth in construction toys whereas, for example, sales of dolls has increased fourfold during this time. Mattel has been particularly successful with its Barbie line of dolls, localized in the likeness of Bollywood actress, Katrina Kaif. Lego is now focusing more marketing effort on China, and has a production facility there to help compete against cheaper, local construction toymakers.

A particular problem for specialist toy retailers entering emerging markets is the retail market fragmentation. For example, in countries such as Vietnam, India, Indonesia and Philippines, modern retailers have a very small market share, compared to street markets and bazaars, which means that Lego cannot rely on an efficient, existing retail channel, but instead must create one. One solution could be online purchasing but consumer acceptance of this style of purchasing varies considerably between country markets.

There is a degree of nostalgia in toy purchases with parents wishing to buy quality toys for their children that are familiar and have local character. Whilst Lego has

focused on quality and innovation it must also find ways to engage with children and parents in markets where it has lower market penetration to continue its success.

Questions

1 Learning from their previous mistakes critically evaluate the branding strategy that Lego is pursuing.

2 Identify the critical success factors for Lego in its newer markets.

3 What are the key requirements for the product ranges aimed at (a) pre-school children, (b) 5–15 year old boys and girls?

Sources: Brandfinance (2015) www.brandfinance.com/news /press_releases/lego-overtakes-ferrari-as-the-worlds-most -powerful-brand; Euromonitor International (2013) Toys and games: corporate strategies in emerging markets, www .euromonitor.typepad.com/files/sampledeck-corporate -strategies-in-emerging-toy-markets.pdf.

CASE STUDY 2

Accor inseparable services: Online and face-to-face

Accor, an umbrella brand, is known for its excellent service and hospitality around the world. Accor are present in 92 countries, have 3600 hotels, 460 000 rooms and 17 000 employees. Their business model includes both owned/leased and external owner/investor. This means that 27 per cent of their hotel portfolio are franchised, 32 per cent managed and 41 per cent owned/leased. Under the Accor umbrella brand are 14 hotel brands that satisfy different customer needs.

International brands	
Brand category	**Sub-brands**
Luxury and upscale	Sofitel Sofitel Legend So Sofitel Pullman Hotel and Resorts M Gallery Memorable Hotels by Accor
Mid-scale	Novotel Hotels Suite Novotel Mercure Hotels Adagio City Aparthotel
Economy	Ibis Hotels Ibis Styles Hotels Adagio Access City Aparthotel
Regional brands	
Brand category	**Sub-brands**
Upscale	Grand Mercure The Sebel
Economy	Hotel F1

The Accor umbrella brand and its sub-brands are one of the tangible elements that employees need to know the values and working practices of. The brand names are also useful for consumers to recognize and associate with different levels of service, quality and price.

The customer experience is of paramount importance to Accor, and because of their worldwide portfolio (that is growing, particularly in Indonesia and Russia) they are keen to offer a heterogeneous, but superior, customer experience. Accor knows that inseparable moments occur both online and face-to-face along the customer's journey. They have been working hard on two particular contact points.

1 **Online:** At least 280 million inseparable moments occur each year when consumers visit Accor websites. Accor ensure the inseparable moments include tangible elements that consumers find both useful and enjoyable. Geo-location software identifies where customers are situated. Therefore, if someone visits Accor's website in France, the website text will be in French; or if located in Brazil the website text will be in Portuguese. Currently, Accor accommodates 16 languages through geo-location technology, making this inseparable moment easy for consumers to navigate around the website and book accommodation. With people booking rooms directly through Accor websites every six seconds this inseparable moment is certainly very helpful in driving consumers to purchase. Social media also shows intangible elements of Accor hotels. Sofitel's website exudes luxury and identifies with upscale consumers; especially the artistic photographs of concierge services. Whilst for the busy, budget-conscious customer Accor provides dedicated mobile applications for Hotel F1 so consumers can geo-search for a hotel, SMS a booking query, book and send payment within seconds. Accor's online connections; web or mobile, are excellent ways to ensure inseparable moments are useful and engaging.

2 **Face-to-face:** 'Welcomers' are a new innovation of face-to-face service at Accor Pullman Hotels and Resorts. Welcomers move fluidly around the hotel's floor areas speaking to guests, answering questions, inspiring ideas and making special, individual relationships with each guest. These inseparable moments make Accor guests feel delighted and special. In other Accor hotels the barrier of the reception desk has been banished. Reception desks have been replaced with 'Host pods'. Hosts, carrying mobile tablets check guests in, check train timetables, show local street maps and book guests into a local ice-hockey game. This innovative service also provides a more informal, personal inseparable moment that Accor guests enjoy. Consumers can use digital smartphone technology to check-in and out of Accor hotels – thus giving Accor Welcomers and Hosts the opportunity to do what they do best: provide outstanding hospitality service.

Questions

1 How has Accor used technology to improve inseparability moments?

2 What tangible changes have Accor made online and in hotels to improve intangible guest experiences?

3 What other service organizations could learn from Accor and improve their inseparability moments?

Source: Accor (2013) A New Voyage Begins: Business Review. Available from www.accor.com/uploads/static/ra2013/en/1.html (accessed 8 May 2015).

DISCUSSION QUESTIONS

1 Identify the major macro-environmental trends in world trade. Using examples from one product and one service sector explain how these trends have affected product and service portfolio management across international markets.

2 In an ideal world companies would like to manufacture a standardized product. What are the factors that support the case for a standardized product and what are the circumstances that are likely to prevent its implementation?

3 Examine the ways in which a major company operating in many countries around the world can use new product development and commercialization to enhance its ambitions to become a global company.

4 What challenges would you expect to face in marketing products and/or services from:

(a) A developing country to a developed country?

(b) A developed to a less developed country?

5 How might these challenges be overcome? Illustrate your answer by focusing on a product or service of your choice.

6 International services marketing is a major growth area. Using one service sector as an example, explain what the main barriers to success are and what strategies might be used to overcome them.

REFERENCES

1. Barrett, M., Davidson, E., Prabhu, J. and Vargo, S.L. (2015) 'Service innovation in the digital age: Key contributions and future directions', *MIS Quarterly*, 39(1), 135–54.

2. Chesbrough, H. (2003) 'The new imperative for creating and profiting from technology', Harvard Business School.

3. Doyle, P. (2000) *Value Based Marketing Strategies for Corporate Growth and Shareholder Value*, Wiley.

4. Eppinger, S.D. and Chitkara, A.R. (2006) 'The new practice of global product development', *MIT Sloan Management Review*, 47(4): 22–30.

5. Griffin, A. (2003) 'Marketing's role in new product development and product decisions', in *Marketing Best Practice*, Thomson South-Western.

6. IFPI (2003) *Commercial Piracy Report*, July, London. Available from www.ifpi.org.

7. Jaruzel, B., Staack, V. and Goehle, B. (2014) The top innovators and spenders. Available from www.strategyand .pwc.com/global/home/what-we-think/innovation1000 /top-innovators-spenders (accessed 11 May 2015).

8. Kaitiki, S. (1981) 'How multinationals cope with the international trade mark forgery', *Journal of International Marketing*, 1(2): 69–80.

9. Keegan, W.J. and Green, C. (2014) *Global Marketing*, 8th edn, Pearson Education.

10. Kotler, P. and Armstrong G. (2014) *Principles of Marketing*, 15th edn, Pearson Electronic Copy

11. Lim. J., Sharkey, T.W. and Heinrichs, J.H. (2006) 'Strategic impact of new product development on export involvement', *European Journal of Marketing*, 40, 44–60.

12. Mesdag, M. van (1985) 'The frontiers of choice', *Marketing*, 10 October.

13. Rappa, R. and Hirsh, E. (2007) 'The luxury touch', www-strategy-business.com, (accessed 3 April).

14. Stone, A. (2006) 'Profits save the world', *Sunday Times*, 10 December.

15. Tuschman, M.L. and Anderson, P. (2004) *Managing Strategic Innovation and Change*, 2nd edn, New York: Free Press.

16. Tzokas, N., Hart, S. and Saren, M. (2003) 'New product development, a marketing agenda for change' in S. Hart, *Marketing Changes*, Thomson.

17. United Nations (2014) Environment www.unglobalcompact .org/Issues/Environment/index.html updated 22 January 2014 (accessed May 2015).

INTERNATIONAL MARKETING PLANNING: STRATEGY DEVELOPMENT

Introduction

In Directed Study Activity 1, against the background of information on the market structure and customer needs, a segmentation approach was developed. In this activity we focus on possible strategic alternatives and the development of a global marketing strategy by companies from emerging markets who are becoming global players in the industries within which they operate.

Arguably the most significant change in international marketing over recent years has been the changing competitive landscape globally, as major players who were previously national champions in their own countries in emerging economies, ranging from China and Taiwan to Korea and Brazil, have developed as potential global players.

These companies have not really developed their global strategies through the traditional multinational route, but they are becoming global by developing global brands, either organically or by buying western companies to aid their global growth. However, as they develop, considering the possible alternative approaches to transnational development is valuable, given the very different contexts in which they operate. In this activity we consider a number of companies from emerging markets who are highly competitive and who are aiming to become truly global. You are able to choose one to investigate, but essentially the activity is about analyzing the basis of the competitive capability of the firms involved and thinking through how this has to develop and shift if they are to build and sustain a global competitive advantage. This gives you the opportunity to consider how a changing global competitive landscape modifies the competitive behaviour of companies in their struggle for a global competitive advantage. It is these issues and how the company you choose should resolve them that are explored in this activity.

Learning Objectives

On completing this activity you should be able to:

- Critically appraise the global marketing strategy that a company is following and evaluate the potential for their success or failure
- Understand the role and value of global marketing planning and its implications for the organization structure
- Understand the concept of globalization and how it affects the strategies of organizations

The scenario: The future global players from emerging markets

Boston Consulting Group (BCG) have identified 100 newcomers (called the RDE 100) from developing economies, such as China, India, Brazil, Mexico and Russia – firms who are cash rich and hungry for global growth. BCG have also identified 40 fast growing and globalizing companies from Africa.

Previously newcomers from emerging markets have focused on building their competitive advantage through marketing low-value manufacturing and service activities. These firms, however, are building the capability to compete with the established firms by the use of much more sophisticated marketing approaches: for example, by using their success in meeting customer needs in their huge and rapidly growing domestic markets as a platform for global expansion. The question for all of these companies is whether they can compete on a more sustainable basis in the global marketing environment.

Not too many years ago companies such as Toyota, LG and Samsung would have been regarded as 'newcomers' from emerging markets and, more recently, companies that have been discussed in earlier editions of this book have rapidly become quite established global operators in their particular sectors in a period of 20 years. These companies include Mittal, a previously unknown steel producer in Indonesia; now as ArcelorMittal it is the world's largest steel producer. Lenovo, which bought IBM's personal computer division is the fourth largest PC maker, and South African Breweries, a local brewer in South Africa is now one of the three largest beer companies. Which companies will be the stars of tomorrow?

The following ten firms are typical of the firms identified by BCG

1   Concha y Toro: www.conchaytoro.com

Concha y Toro from Chile is the largest Latin American wine producer and seventh largest in the world with vineyards in Argentina, Chile and the US. Exports account for over 70% of revenue and are growing rapidly. The company has demonstrated its desire to become a global brand through its sponsorship of Manchester United Football Club.

2   Marcopolo: www.marcopolo.com

Founded in 1949 in Brazil, Marcopolo is one of the biggest manufacturers of bus bodies in the world and recently initiated activities in the Light Commercial Vehicles sector, parts and components and also in the plastic products sector. It has factories in Brazil, Colombia, Argentina, Mexico, India, Egypt and South Africa.

3   Etisalat: www.etisalat.ae

Etisalat is one of the largest telecommunications companies in the world and the leading service provider in the Middle East. The company operates in 19 countries across Asia, the Middle East and Africa and has 170 million customers.

4   Jollibee: www.jollibee.com.ph

Jollibee started in 1975 as an ice cream stand in the Philippines but its move into burgers and Filipino fast food accelerated its growth. Through internal growth and acquisitions it now has over 2000 outlets in Brunei, China, Indonesia, Taiwan and the US. A quarter of its revenues come from its overseas restaurants.

5   Aspen Pharmacare: www.aspenpharma.com

Aspen Pharmacare of South Africa is Africa's largest pharmaceutical manufacturer and a major supplier of branded pharmaceutical, health care and nutritional products to 47 countries. The group has 26 manufacturing plants at 18 sites on 6 continents.

6   Embraer: www.embraer.com

A Brazilian company listed is Embraer (the Empresa Brasileira de Aeronáutica S.A.), a Brazilian aircraft manufacturer. They produce commercial jets up to 120 seats, military and corporate aircraft, are the fifth largest manufacturer of executive jets in the world and are one of the top three Brazilian exporters. They have a workforce of 19 000 and compete with Bombardier to be the third largest aircraft manufacturer behind Boeing and Airbus.

7   Tencent: www.tencent.com

Tencent is a wholly online based company. Its base is in China but already 100 of the 600 million users of its WeChat social messaging service are located outside China. Through heavy investment overseas, more than half its revenues are generated from gaming and this appears to be where growth will be generated. It owns Riot Games that created the popular League of Legends video game.

8   Infosys: www.infosys.com

Infosys Technologies was started in 1981 by seven people with $250. Today, the company is a global leader in 'next generation' IT and consulting with revenues of US$8.7 billion in 2015.

Infosys defines, designs and delivers technology-enabled business solutions for major companies offering business and technology consulting, application services, systems integration, product engineering, software development, IT infrastructure services and business process outsourcing.

9   EuroChem: www.eurochemgroup.com

EuroChem Mineral and Chemical from Russia is in the top ten producers of fertilizer and is growing rapidly through having a vertically integrated business model from extracting raw materials through to distributing the final product. It has built a production plant in the US and has a joint venture in China. 80% of its revenues are generated from exports.

10   Yildiz: https://english.yildizholding.com.tr

Yildiz from Turkey has long been successful in selling packaged food in Africa, Central and Eastern Europe and the Middle East. In 2007 it acquired Godiva, a premium chocolate company with outlets in Asia, Canada, Europe and the US. The company is the largest in its sector in Turkey and it is expected to grow its international revenues, currently 20%, rapidly over the next few years.

Developing a strategy for a global challenger from an emerging market

You are required to select one of the companies listed, all of whom come from emerging markets and are embarking on global expansion. Your brief is to develop an outline global marketing strategy to enable it to challenge the existing competitors in the market.

You should prepare a report of approximately 3500 words.

The task

1 Critically and briefly evaluate the trends in the international market sector in which the company operates.
2 Against the background of your answer to Question 1, comment on how well your chosen firm is placed to develop globally.
3 Advise the company on how to develop a sustainable long-term global marketing strategy.

The report should include the following sections:

Section 1

■ Trends in the environment and market for the sector.
■ The market structure for the sector, including the geographic spread of products, customer segmentation, competitive positioning of key global players.

Section 2

■ Summary of product and market focus, including reasons for the company's domestic, regional and international success to date.
■ Basis of current competitive advantage.
■ The strategic marketing challenges it is likely to face as it aims to improve its international competitive position.

Section 3

■ Recommendations on how to build sustainable competitive advantage in the future.
■ Implementation actions that will be critical in building competitive advantage.

Useful websites

Concha y Toro: www.conchaytoro.com

Marcopolo www.marcopolo.com

Etisalat www.etisalat.ae

Jollibee: www.jollibee.com.ph

Aspen Pharmacare www.aspenpharma.com

Embraer www.embraer.com

Tencent: www.tencent.com

Infosys www.infosys.com

EuroChem: www.eurochemgroup.com

Yildiz: https://english.yildizholding.com.tr

www.businessweek.com

www.telegraph.co.uk

www.oecd.org/statistics

www.ft.com/markets/emerging

www.businessmonitor.com/risk

Getting started

In this section the Directed Study focuses on the companies from emerging markets that are developing global competitive positions. You should use the information outlined above to obtain an understanding of who the companies are, where they come from and why they may be interesting to examine, as well as for general background information. It is important of course to use the information to decide which company you are going to use as a basis for this learning activity. To complete the learning activity, however, you will need to access a range of research material from libraries and web-based sources as well as perhaps external sources of information.

In Task 1 we build on the skills developed in DSA 1. However, in this task it is important to pay particular attention to the key trends affecting the development of the company you have chosen, their competitive positioning and how the trends in the market are impacting on the way the global market is structured.

In considering Task 2 you will need to carry out some research to understand the company background, its activities and progress to date and you will also need to gain an understanding of the competition and the market environment.

Given that your company may be relatively unknown, you should not expect to obtain very detailed information on the company and you should not try to carry out a critical evaluation of its strategy.

You are, however, required to demonstrate your understanding of the global challenges (threats and opportunities) that a firm from an emerging market faces and you are encouraged to be creative in your response to the questions asked.

The starting point for Task 3 is articulating an overall vision and setting appropriate corporate objectives for the firm in terms of developing globally. The global marketing strategy that is developed should be based on a relevant response to the analysis you have developed in answering questions 1 and 2. Against the background of the firm's capabilities, existing and potential future competition, the firm should consider the strategic options it has and develop a positioning statement that will ensure the firm can build a global competitive position in which its products and services are clearly differentiated from the competition.

Key decisions in the strategy development will relate to the degree to which the firm wishes, and is able, to standardize its product and service offerings or needs to adapt them to the requirements of the local markets. Market entry methods need to be selected if it is to enter new markets and the products and services that will be the portfolio need to be chosen. You also need to consider how the recommendations made contribute to the development of a long-term global competitive advantage across the region and the implications your recommendations have for resource allocation and portfolio management for the specified company. In summary, in completing the task you need to ensure you consider the key factors listed in the key pointers below.

Key pointers for directed study activity 2

Task 1

- The key international trends impacting on the development of the market.
- An evaluation of how the global market is structured/segmented.
- The competitive positioning of the key global players.
- The ability to analyze and synthesize material from a variety of sources.
- Relevance and coherence of analysis.

Task 2

- Assessment of current competitiveness of the specified company.
- Identification of the key strategic marketing issues the company needs to address to compete effectively in the global market.

Task 3

- Clearly stated recommendations.
- Ability to contextualize.
- Clear and logical link between analysis and response.
- Innovation and creativity in your response.
- Coherence and justification of your recommendations.
- Appreciation of the contribution to a long-term global competitive advantage.

The way forward

The task in this activity shows how the diversity encountered in developing a global marketing strategy makes it a difficult activity to carry out satisfactorily. After studying Part III of the text you may wish to revisit the solutions you have recommended in this activity, and consider how your recommendations could be successfully implemented.

In doing so you may wish to consider such aspects as:

- What is an appropriate organization management structure for delivering your strategy?
- How can you ensure a systematic planning system throughout the globe that will enable the company to satisfactorily implement the strategy, organize the diverse operations and ensure the managers around the globe respond to the challenges you have identified?

All of this is hard to achieve in a global marketing strategy. For senior managers, the problem is how to maintain cohesion between all staff in order to ensure uniform standards, a coherent worldwide strategy, retain a unique vision and purpose and yet at the same time create an operation which has empathy with consumers in each host country.

For most firms the international planning process is concerned with managing a number of tensions and ambiguities. It is how you would resolve such tensions that you may wish to consider on completion of Part III. There is a need to adopt a regular, thorough and systematic sequence, but at the same time provide the flexibility which allows more junior managers to realize opportunities and address problems when and where they occur. While detailed analysis is necessary to fully appreciate the complexities of a situation at the host country level, there is also a need for a clear uncluttered vision, shared by all staff, of where the company intends to go.

References

Aguiar, M., Bradtke, T., Erica Carlisle, D. Khanna, D. Lee, Michael, D.C., Nettesheim, C., Pai-Panandiker, R. and Ullrich, P., Meet the 2014 BCG Global Challengers, September 10, 2014 accessed at https://www.bcgperspectives.com/content/articles/globalization_growth_meet_2014_global_challengers/ Accessed 22 September 2015

PART III: IMPLEMENTATION

AIMS AND OBJECTIVES

Having defined the international marketing strategy and determined the market entry method and product policy in Part II, we now turn to implementation. The aim of this, Part III of *International Marketing Strategy*, is to examine the implementation issues and determine the activities that will ensure that the strategies are competitive and sustainable, and the products and services are effective in meeting the needs of the customers. While we address the elements of the marketing mix in turn, throughout the section we emphasize the need to integrate the various elements of marketing activity, as they are mutually reinforcing. Where possible, many firms seek to standardize their marketing activities but recognize too that they need to be adapted to the needs of the specific markets in which they are operating. In this respect, market entry and product and service management are also considerations in both strategic development and implementation.

The first chapter in Part III, Chapter 9, is a broad examination of the importance of integrating communications. International communications is not only concerned with the promotion of products and services and differentiating them from those of competitors: it is also about achieving effective communications internally, establishing a corporate identity that is understood worldwide and building long-term relationships with customers.

In Chapter 10, we turn to the more operational aspects of the marketing mix, involving the distribution of goods and services that make up a significant proportion of costs and contribute to customer satisfaction. This includes the different retailing infrastructures around the globe and the challenges of physically distributing products.

For most firms pricing is a complex area, especially so when pricing across international markets. Firms face currency risks, transaction risks and the risks of not being paid at all. In Chapter 11 we examine the problems companies face when pricing across foreign markets and look at some of the tools and techniques used by companies to combat these problems.

Finally, in Chapter 12 we explore the increasing role technology plays in providing a source of growth and enabling managers to implement their international marketing strategy efficiently and effectively. Technology is expected to provide the solution for many global sustainability problems and we discuss corporate social responsibility in this chapter too.

CHAPTER 9

INTERNATIONAL COMMUNICATIONS

LEARNING OBJECTIVES

After reading this chapter you should be able to:

- Appreciate the nature and role of communications in implementing international marketing strategies

- Understand the challenges faced in the successful management and effective integration of international marketing communications

- Be able to explain the use of the elements of an international communications strategy, including corporate identity, products and services promotion, and the development of relationships with customers

- Identify the use and the limitations of the communications tools in international marketing

- Recognize the value of integrating the communications to meet the requirements of different audiences offline and online

INTRODUCTION

The geographical and cultural separation of a company from its marketplaces causes great difficulty in communicating effectively with its stakeholders. In this chapter we take a broad view of communications and include not just the traditional promotional mix of personal selling, advertising, sponsorship, sales and public relations, but also other methods of communications which have the objective of developing better and more personalized relationships with global customers, often using online media. In our discussions we acknowledge the fact that the target audience extends beyond existing and potential customers and includes other stakeholder groups that have a potential impact on the global development of firms and their international reputation.

In doing this, the development of internal relationships between staff from different strategic business units within the global organization and with close business partners is vital in influencing overall performance. Some remote strategic business units often appear to have a closer relationship with their customers and competition than they have with the parent organization, and ensuring good communications seems to be particularly important as firms embark on joint ventures and strategic alliances.

Building a convincing value proposition for stakeholders and achieving cost-effectiveness requires the integration of marketing communications and the distribution channel. Success in this depends upon building good relationships with all of these interested parties.

The role of marketing communications

Marketing communications are concerned with presenting and exchanging information with various stakeholders, both individuals and organizations, to achieve specific results. This means not only that the information must be understood accurately but that, often, elements of persuasion are also required. In a domestic environment this process is difficult enough, but the management of both offline and online international marketing communications is made particularly challenging by a number of factors including the complexity of different market conditions, differences in media availability, languages, cultural sensitivities, regulations controlling advertising and sales promotions, and the challenge of providing adequate resourcing levels.

A variety of approaches have been taken to define and describe the marketing mix area, which is concerned with persuasive communications. Some writers refer to the 'communications mix', others to the 'promotional mix' and others, for example Kotler and Armstrong (2014) use the two terms interchangeably to mean the same thing. Communications, embracing as it does the ideas of conveying information, is the most helpful term and implies the need for a two-way process in international marketing and is at the core of the digital media. It also includes internal communications between the organization's staff, especially as organizations become larger, more diverse and complex. In addition 'internal staff' might include collaborative partners that add value to the organization's offer and are part of the supply chain. Some online organizations encourage greater involvement of customers in the business and these situations redraw the boundaries between internal and external staff.

Figure 9.1 shows the external and internal marketing communication flows and emphasizes the need to consider three dimensions: external, internal and interactive or relationship marketing.

Internal marketing

For a large diverse multinational firm it is a key task to ensure that all staff employed in its business units around the world are aware of the strategies, tactics, priorities and procedures to achieve the firm's mission and objectives. Increasingly organizations form closer collaborations with supply chain and

FIGURE 9.1   External, internal and interactive marketing

Internal marketing
(How well communicated to the staff around the world are the missions, values, objectives, priorities and procedures?)

External marketing
(How appropriate is the range of services, pricing structure, promotional effort and distribution channels to the different consumer groups around the world?)

The firm

Staff

Customer groups

Interactive marketing
(How effectively – and appropriately – do staff around the world deal with each of the customer or stakeholder groups?)

distribution channel members, franchisees, joint venture and strategic alliance partners, all of whom participate collectively in marketing networks. Organizations are dependent on staff in the extended organization working to a common set of objectives and they need to be informed about the appropriate marketing strategies.

Staff in remote locations are often overlooked in communications or receive messages that become unclear as they cross cultural and language boundaries, in the same way that external audiences may misunderstand the firm's external communications. Therefore, internal communication is vital with employees in locations overseas or in remote locations so they understand the brand, regularly receive helpful information about their brand's strategy, as well as being reminded of the organization's standards and values.

Interactive marketing

As many customers of MNEs are MNEs themselves it is essential for staff around the world to deliver consistent service. This includes service delivery staff, call centre operators, service engineers and salespeople in each location. Staff are trained how to communicate with stakeholders in a consistent way, take appropriate decisions that fit with the strategy and deliver a standardized service, so that the reputation of the organization is enhanced.

Consistent and effective two-way interactive communication is at the heart of online marketing businesses, where the Internet provides the underpinning link between the staff undertaking the various business functions and their customers. As we discuss later it is this process that creates the nature of the relationship that online businesses strive to build and maintain.

External marketing

The traditional role of international marketing communications is largely concerned with providing a mechanism by which the features and benefits of the product or service can be promoted as cost effectively as possible to existing and potential customers in different countries. Details of the features and benefits are communicated through the promotion mix, which includes online and offline communications, personal selling, advertising, sales promotion and public relations with the ultimate purpose of persuading customers to buy specific products and services. International marketing communications, however, have now become much more important within the marketing mix and the purposes for which marketing communications might be used externally in international markets are now more diverse. They include the need to communicate with a more diverse range of stakeholders, including supply chain partners, industry regulators, pressure groups and the community in general, and build higher levels of customer service through interactive or relationship marketing. International marketing communications could now be considered to include the three distinct strategic elements shown in Figure 9.2.

Communicating product and service differentiation

As we discussed in Chapters 6 and 8, increased competition and the maturation of markets have led to many firms offering largely similar core product and service specifications, with the result that in addition to its traditional role of promoting products and services, international marketing communications is increasingly used to provide the firm with an important source of differentiation. For example, by providing customers with an easily recognizable and distinctive brand image, or by explaining the unique positioning of the product.

Online and mobile communications have contributed to the vast increase in the range and volume of communications to which consumers are exposed as they go about their-day to-day lives. And, with the communication messages being delivered across multiple platforms 24/7, making one product or service distinctive becomes an ever-increasing challenge. There are a wide variety of promotional tools that might

FIGURE 9.2   The dimensions of external marketing communications

be used to persuade customers to buy the firm's products and services, and the newer information and communications technologies are increasing this choice all the time. The challenge for the firm is to use these tools as cost-effectively as possible to reach out to consumers – wherever they are in the world.

Communicating the corporate identity to international stakeholders

As stakeholders in general have become more aware of how they are affected by international organizations – both good and bad – companies have found it necessary to justify their international activities by constantly and more widely communicating their core values and standards to their internal and external audience. This is essential in order to demonstrate their responsibility to shareholders, trustworthiness to customers and care and concern for the local community, environment and local employees. The corporate image or logo is the most visible part of the identity and, in some firms, is the only standardized element of the marketing mix, because it constantly reminds stakeholders of the organization's reputation. The **corporate identity** of the firm should be deeper and more pervasive and reflected in a clear and distinctive message supported by appropriate and proactive public relations activity. Illustration 9.1 shows how a brand's identity can be increased by understanding and using consumer behaviour.

More intense global competition has provided consumers with greater choice of products and services which they perceive to be capable of satisfying their needs and providing new experiences. Customers also feel that there is less risk of dissatisfaction in switching to alternative products and services, and so are becoming less likely to stay loyal to one supplier or brand.

With the increasing cost of marketing communications and the need to reach an ever wider international audience, organizations are becoming much more aware of the high costs of winning new customers and the relatively lower costs of retaining existing customers. Attention has been drawn to how much a single customer of one product might purchase over his or her lifetime. Readers might like to calculate how much they buy from a food retailer, car manufacturer or a travel company if they stay loyal to that supplier for 5, 10 or 20 years. Food retailers offer incentives for customer loyalty, such as bonus cards and money-off vouchers for other products and services they offer, such as petrol and insurance services. They routinely communicate with consumers using direct mail, email, tweets and online banner advertisements to inform them of new product offers.

The concept of **relationship marketing** has taken on greater significance with e-commerce where communications, promotion and delivery of services have been integrated with **customer relationship management (CRM)** systems to enable firms to communicate in a much more intelligent, efficient and effective way by basing their messages on a better knowledge of the characteristics and responses of their existing

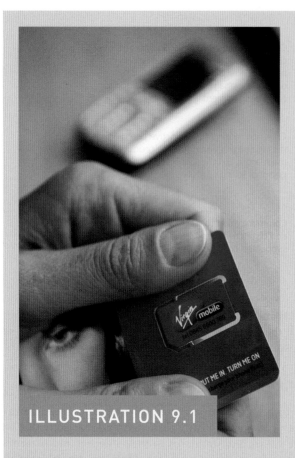

ILLUSTRATION 9.1

FoodSnapping uploads feed Australia's needy

The brand managers of Virgin Mobile Australia had a number of challenges on their hands. They wanted to (a) improve awareness of the Virgin Mobile brand and (b) increase their mobile phone market share. However, Virgin's mobile phone market share in Australia is only 6 per cent. With 7 in 10 Australian online consumers already owning a Smartphone, the chance of organic growth for Virgin Mobile was non-existent.

Virgin Mobile knew that the only opportunity for growth was through brand switching. However, this was also a major challenge as many mobile phone consumers are 'nomophobic' (a phobia against *not* having a mobile phone; including 'symptoms' of feeling disconnected, lonely and worried of 'missing something'). Nomophobic consumers may be reluctant to brand switch as they fear during the 'switching period' they will feel disconnected.

Therefore, the brand managers of Virgin Mobile Australia turned to mobile phone behaviours to seek ways to increase awareness of their brand; thus increasing market share.

It was discovered that approximately 60 million pictures are uploaded to Instagram from mobile phones each day. Of those, around 32 500 are pictures of food that come from 'FoodSnappers' and because of Australian's love of food, 'FoodSnapping' is general mobile behaviour. Despite their love of food, personal Australian's food waste amounts to A$8billion dollars each year. This is a great shame as there are many Australians that rely on food relief.

The brand managers of Virgin Mobile decided to combine these behaviours into something positive to not only improve the Virgin Mobile brand but also prick the 'social conscience' of Australian consumers.

Virgin Mobile Australia worked in partnership with OzHarvest, the leading charity that provides food relief for Australians in need. Their joint aim was to make the world a better place for people that are in need of food. To do this Virgin Mobile set up #MealforaMeal. For every FoodSnap that was hashtagged #MealforaMeal, be it on Instagram, Facebook or Twitter, Virgin Mobile would donate a meal to Australians in need of food relief via their partner OzHarvest.

PR and celebrity endorsements certainly encouraged the #MealforaMeal campaign to go viral. Actress Jane Lynch, the Virgin brand entrepreneur Richard Branson, and celebrity chefs Jamie Oliver and Adriano Zumbo, also hashtagged, blogged and 'Foodsnapped' thus encouraging Australian consumers to get involved. These activities raised awareness of a very worthy charitable cause and also raised awareness of the Virgin brand. Therefore, this campaign certainly helped the Virgin brand managers to overcome one of their challenges. Many Australians joined as 250 000 meals were donated by OzHarvest thanks to the hash-tagged 'FoodSnaps'. There were 51.4 million social interactions with many positive posts about Virgin Mobile. More importantly, to monitor their second challenge, post campaign research showed that the 'intention to stay' with Virgin Mobile and the 'consideration to choose' Virgin Mobile increased.

Questions

1 How did Virgin Mobile build brand awareness in Australia?

2 Who and what helped the campaign be successful?

3 How did Virgin Mobile overcome some of their challenges?

Sources: Caley, C. and Philipp, A. (2015) 'Virgin Mobile: Making mobile better', Warc Prize for Social Strategy, Issue: Shortlisted 2015 WARC.

and potential customers, and a better understanding of what they might wish to hear. In this way firms are able to be sensitive to different cultures and environmental contexts and develop better relationships with their customers and other influential stakeholders, irrespective of their location in the world. It is useful to reflect on the key characteristics of the Internet communication, see Table 9.1. The key drivers for communicating via the Internet are similar to the general communication strategies shown in more detail later in this chapter, with the added characteristic that social media marketing communications actively encourage stakeholders (including consumers and employees) to respond, comment upon and engage directly with the communication message.

Table 9.1 Drivers for online communications

To increase brand equity
To increase brand awareness
To increase sales
To create a buzz online
To stimulate word of mouth
To reach key influencers
To increase market share
To drive web traffic to sales
To reach stakeholders and influencers

The fundamental challenges for international marketing communications

All forms of international marketing communication have a fundamental purpose, which is to ensure that the intended messages (those which are part of the firm's international marketing strategy) are conveyed accurately between the sender and the receiver, and that the impact of unintentional messages (those which are likely to have an adverse effect on the firm's market performance and reputation) are kept to a minimum. The communications process should be two-way and the sender should always make provision for feedback to ensure that the receiver has understood the message as it was intended and has responded positively to it as Figure 9.3 shows.

In practice this apparently simple process poses considerable challenges for firms trying to manage their international marketing communications. This is often discussed in the business press, which contains many serious but frequently amusing anecdotes about the failed attempts of major firms to communicate in international markets. Mistakes in the use of language, particularly using messages which do not translate or are mistranslated are a particular problem; more serious is a lack of sensitivity to different cultures among international communicators. Management Challenge 9.1 also shows how product advertising can meets customer needs but can be seen as unethical and controversial.

Many of the **failures of communications** are unintentional, of course. Following negotiations with the Council on America–Islamic Relations, Nike had to scrap almost 40 000 pairs of sports shoes because the flame design which was used bore a resemblance to the Arabic for Allah. Two years earlier Nike was forced to withdraw a billboard showing a basketball player above the caption 'They Called him Allah' when it caused an outcry among Muslims.

FIGURE 9.3   Model of communication

MANAGEMENT CHALLENGE 9.1

Skin care: It's more than black and white

The Unilever umbrella brand has a range of sub-brands within its skin care and cosmetic range. Ponds is one of its international brands. Recently Ponds posted an advertisement on Asian Facebook promoting a soap called White Beauty. The strap line for White Beauty is '... Dark Out, White In'. The special feature of Ponds' face wash soap is that it whitens skin. Facebook viewers were asked to click LIKE for fairer skin.

This product has high sales in Pakistan, but some consumers, especially in the West, find the advertisements distasteful.

Nevertheless, Unilever and their competitors sell a range of skin whitening soap, face creams and powders for markets across Asia. P&G and L'Oreal make, sell and profit from skin whitening products named Real Beauty and Moisture White. Whilst selling products to change a person's skin colour is controversial the products are big sellers in India, Korea, Thailand, Malaysia as well as Pakistan. In fact, sales of skin whitening products have grown by 12 per cent between 2010 and 2013. One of the latest skin whitening products to hit the Malaysian

market was in 2015. Qu Puteh (translated as Qu White) is ingested. Qu Puteh's unique selling proposition is that within 7 days of ingestion skin is lightened by 45 per cent. The product gained major attention and has the potential to become an international product within the Asian region.

Face whitening creams are not just for women. The top ten whitening creams for men include Unilever's Fair & Lovely MAX Fairness for Men, Garnier's Men PowerLight Intensiv Fairness FaceWash and Olay White Radiance UV Whitening day cream.

India's government has considered the complaints and controversial discussions of products that offer to change a person's skin colour. The Advertising Standards Council has provided guidelines for India's skin care and advertising industry. Advertisements promoting face whitening products must not portray people in the commercial with darker skin to be unattractive, unlucky in love, overlooked for a job promotion or indeed discontent because of their skin tone.

Question

1 Do you consider skin whitening commercials to be racist?

Sources: Lee, A. (2015) Mirror, Mirror on the Wall. Who is the Fairest of them All? Mintel, published 12 May 2015 www. Mintel.com (accessed 21 May 2015); Top10for (2014) Top 10 Best Fairness Creams For Men in 2014. Available from www .top10for.com/top-10-best-fairness-creams-men-2014/ (accessed 21 May 2015).

Besides the often highly visible failures which make firms appear to be incompetent and insensitive there are many examples of wasted effort and resources which are not so widely publicized. There are a number of reasons for international marketing communications' failure, including:

- Inconsistency in the messages conveyed to customers by staff at different levels and from different countries and cultures.

- Different styles of presentation of corporate identity, brand and product image from different departments and country business units which can leave customers confused.

- A lack of coordination of messages, such as press releases, advertising campaigns and changes in product specification or pricing across the various country markets.

- Failure to appreciate the differences in the fields of perception (the way the message is understood) of the sender and receiver. The field of perception tends to be affected significantly by the self-reference criteria of both parties. This is, perhaps, where the greatest problems arise because, as we have already discussed, avoiding this requires knowledge of different market environments, cultural empathy and the willingness to adapt the communications programmes and processes to local requirements.

While this last area is influenced by knowledge, attitudes and empathy, the other three areas of potential communications failure are concerned with the effectiveness of the firm's strategy and planning and the degree to which the staff within the organization understand and are involved in the communications planning process. It is almost inevitable that some communication failures occur from time to time and it is vital that firms learn from their mistakes.

While it can be argued that the majority of these failures are ultimately within the control of the company, a number of situations arise where the firm's communications can be affected by factors which are outside its control or are extremely difficult to control. Examples of these are situations where:

- *Counterfeiting or other infringements* of patents or copyright as discussed in Chapter 8 take place. Not only does the firm lose revenue, but it may also suffer damage to its image if consumers believe the low-quality goods supplied by the counterfeiter are genuine. Even if the customer knows the product is counterfeit the brand name might still be subconsciously associated with a poorly performing product.

- *Parallel importing*, which is discussed in greater detail in Chapter 11, communicates contradictory messages that do not reflect the image of the brand and thus confuse consumers. This can be particularly problematic if the parallel importer seriously undercuts the prices charged by the official channel, leading customers to feel they have been 'ripped off'.

- *Competitors, governments or pressure groups* attack the standards and values of the MNE by alleging, fairly or unfairly, bad business practice. Despite their huge resources, some of the largest firms are not very effective in responding to allegations from relatively less powerful stakeholders. Companies such as Shell, Coca-Cola, KFC and McDonald's have suffered following criticism of their lack of concern for the environment or animal rights. Stakeholders are also powerful enough in some cases to change government policy. China is known for a history of animal issues, particularly animal testing on drugs and cosmetics. Until recently all cosmetics had to be tested on animals – testing on animals is law to avoid products being launched that irritate and/or cause damage to human beings. The *Be Cruelty-Free China* campaign; launched by Humane Society International, has held many events, conferences and demonstrations with the sole purpose of changing the law. Now cosmetics can be tested for skin and eye-irritation using non-animal testing mechanisms. Consumers, as stakeholders, were successful in their battle.

Customers increasingly believe reviews posted on websites rather than more rigorous and independent assessments, perhaps not realizing how much these informal reviews can be manipulated. The most significant challenge is that anyone can now comment on a firm's product and service through social media and this is increasingly at the expense of formal communications. The firm has less control or even influence over the identity, image and reputation created in the media.

International marketing communications, standardization and adaptation

The most obvious tactic for reducing instances of international communications failure might appear to be to adopt a strict policy of standardization in the implementation of communications plans. Firms adopt this principle, for example, in their use of corporate identity and global advertising campaigns. However, given the need to also demonstrate cultural sensitivity and empathy with a wide range of international customers *and* to avoid the type of mistakes referred to earlier, it is necessary to adapt the international communications to local market needs with sensitivity.

Towards standardization

The drivers for **standardization of international marketing communications** come first from the organization's desire to improve efficiency. Cost-saving activity in marketing communications includes benefits from economies of scale, for example, in advertising creative work, media buying, making better use of staff time and from the experience effect, by achieving efficiencies through replicating successful marketing communications programmes and processes in different countries.

Customers believe that they gain additional benefit and value from a consistent and widely recognized brand image that reflects their own self-image; for example, teenagers (as well as rather more elderly sports enthusiasts too) gain peer recognition, credibility and prestige from wearing branded sportswear which has strong associations with international sports stars. A company may use a top international business consultancy or advertising agency with a prestigious image just as much because the association is perceived positively by the company's suppliers and customers rather than for the cost-effectiveness of the work that is carried out.

Consistency in the corporate identity and branding, reinforces awareness in stakeholders' minds and provides the familiarity with the company which leads to a feeling of confidence, trust and loyalty. For example, it may be reassuring for a visitor to see the familiar logo and appearance of a fast food outlet, hotel chain or bank in a foreign country that they are visiting.

Over the years changes have led to greater prosperity and thus greater buying power – at least for some people – resulting in greater acceptance of imported products. Consumers and business-to-business customers often prefer internationally available products with which they have become familiar through increased travel, Internet, radio and television communications and the written media. Satellite and cable television have created worldwide customer segments for many more globally standardized products and services.

The Internet allows customers to access products from organizations from very distant locations. It allows specialist suppliers to make their standard products and services globally available to customers, and enables smaller companies to compete essentially on equal terms with their much larger competitors, so 'punching above their weight'. Of course, companies that only communicate using the Internet are limiting their customer base to those customer segments that can access the Internet or buy online.

At an operational level, advertising standardization is possible when:

- Visual messages form the main content of the advertisement.
- Well-known international film stars, popular celebrities and sports personalities are featured.
- Music is an important part of the communication.
- Well-known symbols and trademarks are featured. For example, the Grand Canyon in the US can be used to symbolize certain types of outdoor American values.

Advertisements do not travel well to other countries:

- When the use of spoken and written language forms an important part of the communication;
- If humour is used – humour is often *very* specific to certain cultures.
- If personalities are used who are well-known in one country but are not known internationally.
- If campaigns are used that rely on specific knowledge of previous advertising.

Towards adaptation   The principal drivers of international marketing, communications adaptation, are the cultural differences that must be managed when communicating with customers in different countries. As we have already seen in this book, there are some fundamental differences in the ways that consumers from different cultures respond to different communication approaches. More specifically, however, in a comparison between the US and Chinese responses to advertising, Zhang and Neelankavil (1997) observe that, overall, US subjects preferred the individualistic appeal (self-orientation, self-sufficiency and control, the pursuit of individual gains) whereas Chinese subjects favoured the collective appeal (subordination of personal interests to the goals of the group, with emphasis on sharing, cooperation and harmony, and a concern for the group's welfare). It is these differences which must be recognized, but there is also likely to be continuing convergence across cultures and moves toward standardization.

Advertisers believe that advertising is most effective when it is relevant to the target audience – one area where there are significant differences is in the portrayal of women in advertising.

Siu and Au (1997) report that research studies of advertising suggest that:

- Over 80 per cent of voiceovers are male.
- Women are depicted as housewives, mothers and/or sex objects.
- Females are shown as product users whereas males are shown in the roles of authority.

However, the role of women is changing rapidly as many more women are entering the workforce. In research carried out by Siu and Au in China and Singapore, they found that sex-role stereotyping was more apparent in China – women were depicted as product users and men as having product authority – whereas in Singapore women generally appeared as the spokesperson for the product, to have product authority and be the providers of help and advice. Positive stereotypes of women are also being shown in Indian newspapers and magazines.

Kataria's (2014) study shows that the historical portrayal of women as weak and powerless is changing and advertisements show women to be assertive and financially independent; which in turn shows the different roles that Asian women now engage in.

There are many local reasons why firms may need to adapt their communications strategy. Many companies have to change their brand names because of different meanings they have when they move to new markets. The New Zealand Dairy Board, a large exporter of dairy foods, uses the brand name Fern for its butter in Malaysia, although Anchor is the flagship brand well known in Western Europe. In Malaysia, Anchor is a widely advertised local beer, and Malaysian housewives are unlikely to buy dairy products for their children which they would subconsciously associate with alcohol.

When Johnson & Johnson entered the Hong Kong market they used the name *zhuang-cheng* which means 'an official or lord during feudal times'. This upper-class association was seen as inappropriate for China, and the more upbeat modern tone of '*qiang-sheng*', meaning 'active life', was used instead, to better reflect the drive for modernization.

The differences in appeal between Western and Asian communications are more fundamental than simply changing brand names. Chan and Huang (1997) suggest that brands can be enhanced if names and/or symbols of favourite animals and flowers and lucky numbers are used. In Asia written figures may be perceived as potent symbols; thus, as Schmitt and Pan (1994) point out, in Asian countries the emphasis may be heavier on the distinctive writing and logo of the brand than on the jingles that Western marketing communications favour.

Illustration 9.2 shows the importance of appreciating the subtlety of language, particularly when launching brand names in new countries.

Firms use a variety of ways of becoming more sensitive to cultural differences. Unilever has set up innovation centres in Asia in order to bring together research, production and marketing staff to speed up development of international brands which have a local appeal. In Bangkok there are innovation centres responsible for ice cream, laundry detergents and hair care. Asian Delight is a regional brand of ice cream – between the Magnum brand and local brands – and uses English and Thai on its packaging in Thailand, but English only in Malaysia, Singapore and Indonesia. It is sold from Wall's mobile units and cabinets in convenience stores and supermarkets. The flavours have a local appeal and include coconut-milk based ice cream mixed with fruits and vegetables traditionally used in desserts or chewy strings of green flour, black beans and sago.

ILLUSTRATION 9.2

The sweet smell of success: When global brand names cannot be used

Previous chapters in this book have shown that marketing managers must research cultural diversity, history and traditions when launching new products and services in different countries. This is particularly important when introducing an existing brand to a new market. Often marketing managers introduce a brand using the brand's existing name; to (a) form a globally recognized brand, (b) standardize the brand, and (c) benefit from associated costs. However, some brand names cannot be used throughout the world.

Yves Saint Laurent (YSL) launched a new perfume named Opium in their home country of France. The Opium brand became a 'must have' perfume. The Opium perfume was acclaimed to be the fragrance of sensual spirits that searched for the mystical and the 'unknown'. The Opium brand, therefore, was heralded as the ultimate temptation. The perfume was popular in many countries around the world. However, when YSL launched their Opium brand in China the government ordered it to be removed from all retail outlets because it may pollute the spiritual minds of young people and remind its citizens of humiliating times.

Opium, the drug, stirs extremely negative associations linked with Chinese citizens and their history. Opium was a drug used in China by nobility. However, it soon became used by the masses – so much so that the first opium prohibition was proclaimed in 1729. Banning the sale of opium in China continued at various points in its history. Addiction of opium in China, particularly in the opium dens, showed a deeply troubled side of China. Therefore, the YSL's perfume brand was seen as wholly inappropriate for China's young people. Further, the opium wars between China and Britain were seen as a humiliating period of Chinese history, thus the introduction of a brand carrying that name was considered to bring negative feelings to the minds of Chinese citizens. The Chinese government decree meant YSL could no longer sell its Opium brand in China. The controversy did however raise awareness of the global brand.

Question

1 How can managers responsible for cross-border campaigns ensure that they will convey the message effectively?

Source: Liu, J. (2015). 'Name selection in international branding: Translating brand culture', *International Journal of Business and Management*, 10(4), 187.

International marketing communications strategy

So far in this chapter we have highlighted the need to consider the nature and role of international marketing communications more broadly than was the case in the past, by focusing upon both internal and external communications and a wider range of communications tools. In thinking about developing strategy there are two significant issues to address. First, there is a need to state clear and precise objectives for the international marketing communications strategy and, second, how the various communications activities might be coordinated to maximize their cost effectiveness.

The promotional objectives can be categorized as sales-related and brand/product communications-related, which might be stated in terms of increasing sales by:

- Increasing market share at the expense of local and/or international competitors.
- Identifying new potential customers.

- Obtaining a specific number of responses to a promotional campaign.
- Reducing the impact of competitors in the market.

And brand/product communications-related by:

- Increasing the value of the corporate brand and product image.
- Helping to establish the position or to reposition the product or brand.
- Increasing awareness levels especially in new country markets.
- Changing consumers' perceptions of products, brands or the firm.

These objectives must be set for each country or region in order to fit with the firm's international development ambition.

The options that are available for a generic marketing communications strategy centre on the extent to which a **push** or **pull strategy** could and should be adopted (Figure 9.4). A push strategy means promoting the product or service to retailers and wholesalers in order to force the product or service down the distribution channel by using promotional methods, such as personal selling, discounts and special deals. A pull strategy means communicating with the final consumer to attract them to the retailer or distributor to purchase the product. In this case mass advertising, sales promotions and point of sales promotions are the most obvious promotional methods. In domestic markets, firms realize the need to have a combination of push and pull strategies, including both encouraging the intermediaries and retailers to stock the products and attracting end users to buy.

In international markets the nature of the market structure that already exists may well affect the degree to which push and pull strategies are used; for example, how well the distribution channel is established, how powerful the retailers or distributors are, how well established the competitors are and whether the firm marketing its products or services wishes to, or has the power to, challenge the existing 'route to market' by setting up a new channel.

Frequently, the international marketing communications strategy of a firm has to be adapted because of the variation in the market structures and distribution channels from country to country (for example, some are highly fragmented, while others are very concentrated). More often than not, however, it is the lack of resources, expertise and local knowledge of the firm in the target country markets that limits its communications strategy options. It may well not be able to transfer its successful domestic strategy to the new market. The firm may be forced into making use of and relying heavily upon established intermediaries to do the promotion for them through existing channels. For this reason it is possible to find organizations that have a pull strategy in their domestic or other established markets and a push strategy in their newer markets.

FIGURE 9.4   Push and pull strategies

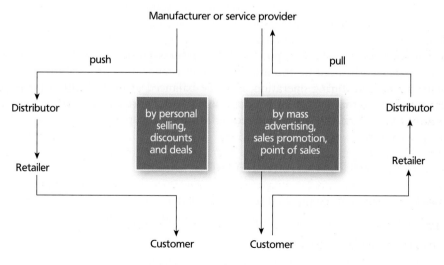

Having determined the objectives and decided upon the degree to which a push and pull strategy might be used, the dimensions of the international marketing communications implementation strategy can be defined. These are:

- The message to be communicated.
- The target audience to which the message will be directed.
- The media that will be used to carry the message.
- The ways in which the impact of the communications will be measured.

As we said at the start of this chapter, continually evaluating the impact of the communications is vital, not only in improving the effectiveness of the communication but also in assessing the degree to which each of these dimensions can be standardized across international markets.

Communicating with existing and potential customers

Given that the primary objective of international marketing communications is to persuade customers to buy products and services which will meet their requirements, it is appropriate to consider how international marketing communications are used strategically to influence each of the stages of the buying process and to help customers to complete their purchase.

A number of writers have developed models of buying behaviour which tend to vary according to the context of the study, but all acknowledge that there are a number of stages in the buying process. A simplified version of these stages (AIDA) includes:

- Awareness of the firm, its products and services and their reputation.
- Interest in the products and services, because they may be suited to the consumers' needs and worthy of consideration for potential purchase.
- Desire to buy the product or service, in preference to that of the competitor, after consumers have become better informed about its performance.
- Action by the customer in overcoming any remaining reservations or barriers and purchasing the product or service.

Illustration 9.3 provides an example of raising awareness for parents whose children play hard and come home in dirty clothes.

Different messages must be prepared and the most appropriate promotional tool selected for each part of the buying process in order to persuade customers to move to the next stage. There are significant differences between consumer markets, business-to-business and institutional market purchasing. For example, in fast-moving consumer goods marketing, advertising can be used to raise awareness, create interest and encourage consumers to purchase, but only if the messages are sensitive and appealing and the customers have access to the media used for advertising. Other tools such as point of sale promotion can be used to support the strategy, provided it is possible for the firm to maintain some level of control over the displays used by local retailers.

Capital equipment usually depends more on personal selling and providing technical service to a buying committee. This would typically be supported by awareness-raising in the trade press, using PR and corporate advertising. Here the need for monitoring the consistency of approach, and ensuring good communications with the manufacturing operation, must be balanced against the need for sensitivity to the way that business is done in that particular country. Institutional purchasing is often undertaken through competitive tenders which often, directly or indirectly, favour local suppliers.

The integration of communications

Stakeholders receive messages, both intended and unintended, from every part of the organization's activities. Davidson (2002) explains that an organization communicates in eight ways:

1. Actions: what it does.
2. Behaviour: how things are done, for example, how the telephone is answered.

ILLUSTRATION 9.3

Targeting parents: Dirty clothes are a consequence of play

Unilever, a major global brand, needed new ideas to sell their Persil/Omo clothes laundering products. Previous research showed that mums and dads the world-over want their children's clothes to be clean, fresh and pristine. And where white clothes are concerned their children's clothes need to be 100 per cent white: not 'off-white', not grey, but white. All parents know to get their children's clothes perfect is a 'big ask' as children play and paint themselves dirty day after day. Unilever's brand managers wondered what communications messages they should include to convince parents that Persil/Omo could change dirty children's clothes into fresh, dirt-free clothes better than their competitors.

In the past, brands like Unilever and its competitors, Procter and Gamble and Colgate-Palmolive, advertised laundry washing powders, tablets and soaps that use molecule technology such as cellulases to get clothes white or proteases to remove grass or meat and fat. Alternatively, advertisements showed how laundry brands provided biotechnologies that encapsulate exotic perfumes or have low-suds technology to reduce environmental damage. Whilst these product enhancements were interesting, Unilever did not feel they resonated with the issues that parents have with children's clothes.

Unilever talked to 267 mothers, grandmothers and great-grandmothers and 409 children in 10 countries, from Pakistan to US to Brazil, about their everyday lives. Their research findings showed that parents teach their children life-long values and opportunities during play-time. The values and opportunities included creativity, exploration, sociability, caring and sharing. And children certainly enjoyed playtime particularly painting, sport, making 'things', and playing on slides and swings. Both parents and children proclaimed that during playtime children got dirty!!! Children got paint on their clothes, brought home specimens of soil, flowers and even worms in their pockets, came home covered in grass-stains from football games and gymnastics and had mud engrained in their socks, shorts, tops and even hair from their 'adventures' in puddles and streams. It was clear that getting dirty was part of playtime.

With these findings in mind communication campaigns entitled 'dirt is good' were formed. The 'dirt is good' football campaign aired in South Africa, South East Asia, Pakistan, Bangladesh and Sri Lanka, shows children playing football on the streets or in a park (dependent upon country); the children kick the football onto a post and the football bursts. The children make their own football from their t-shirts, which become covered in mud and grass stains. The advertisement finishes with a mother washing her child's clothes in Persil/Omo.

The 'dirt is good' Garage Band campaign shown in UK and Brazil shows children forming a Garage Band and singing 'We will rock you'. The Garage Band advertisements show children making drum kits from old pots and pans, using lamps as a microphone and different sized spanners as a keyboard. The dust and grease makes their clothes dirty but when they take the final bow at the end of their singing debut the children's clothes 'magically' become perfect white and pristine.

The 'dirt is good' campaigns have increased market share and added €1bn turnover (between 2010 and 2014).

Questions

1 Why was Unilever's cross-cultural research effective?

2 Why do Unilever use the same 'dirt is good' football commercial filmed in the street and filmed in a park?

Sources: Arkwright, D. (2014) Dirt is good. How storytelling gave Persil a boost, published 1 April 2014. Available from *Marketing Magazine* www.marketingmagazine.co.uk (accessed 20 January 2015); ARF Ogilvy Awards (2015) 'Unilever: Dirt is good', Gold, Household.

3   Face-to-face by management: through talks, visits and meetings it shows what the management thinks is important.

4   Signals, from the organizations' actions, facilities and objects, including executive bonuses, dress, buildings.

5   Product and services, and particularly their quality.

6   Intended communications, such as advertising, which is not always received as the organization expects.

7   Word of mouth and word of Web (including email).

8   Comment by other organizations, such as pressure groups, competitors and the media.

As the number of communications has increased dramatically and customers have become more critical and sceptical, the importance of integrated marketing communications has been emphasized in order to avoid conflicting messages and instead communicate consistent and mutually supporting messages. Fill (2006) points out that traditional mass-communication strategies have given way to more personalized, customer-orientated and technology-driven approaches. To be successful the firm requires a completely different approach, focusing on the individual customer and Kotler *et al.* (2014) say that companies must integrate many communication channels, be they personal selling, social media, TV/press advertising, PR, sales promotion and direct marketing (via mail and/or online). They go on to say that the communication messages need to be interesting and compelling messages that are clear and focused for their target market and remain consistent regarding the organization's brand and values (*ibid.*, 2014).

Shimp (2006) provides a definition of integrated marketing communications which puts the customer at the centre:

1   Start with the customer or prospect.

2   Use any form of relevant contact.

3   Achieve synergy through consistency across the communication elements.

4   Build relationships.

5   Affect behaviour.

The emphasis of Shimp's approach is on marketing promotion whereas digital media encourages a two-way communications process and interactivity between the organization and its customer is a key component of integration. For example, seeing the comments of customers in social media can help a firm reduce the gap between its intended image and that perceived by customers.

The benefits of integration   Given the fact that individual messages on their own have little overall impact on customers it follows that the effect of communications will be significantly greater if the many messages are consistent, uniform and mutually supporting in the way that builds the image of the brand, product and service and reinforce the reputation, standards and values of the organization around the world.

It is easier to justify the cost and control communications activities if they are integrated so that the cumulative effect, rather than individual effect, is assessed. Measurement of individual actions is difficult, given the 'noise' in the environment, and so it is more sensible to measure the effects of the combined actions.

Integration with the global strategy   Although usually considered to be a part of the marketing mix, in many organizations communications takes on a much more important role. It is essential in explaining the organization's corporate business unit and marketing mix strategies to stakeholders, including shareholders. Global integration is needed so that the consistency of internal and external communications across borders is maintained.

Business unit integration   At business unit level, managers in charge of communications must work closely with colleagues responsible for development, operations, key account management, sales and customer service centre management to develop a highly integrated global approach that offers a seamless service to customers.

Marketing mix integration Customers continually receive communications from the organization that are the result of marketing mix actions. Every element of the marketing mix communicates with customers.

It is important to remember that non-verbal communication in many markets has a greater impact than verbal communications or written words, especially given the amount of time (milliseconds!) that a customer concentrates on one communication. For example, the colours and styles used in creative packaging or signage work communicate non-verbally with the customers, reinforcing the images and customer perceptions, but this differs between cultures. Customers can pick up small errors in colour matching and design, so discipline in the use of the corporate identity is essential. In different cultures the significance of colours, symbols and numbers is so great that they alone could deter customers from buying a product.

Coordination and planning of the international marketing communications strategy

To achieve its objectives, the communications strategy will almost certainly include a variety of promotional tools. The key to success is integrating the various promotion elements in a cost-efficient way and adding value through choosing the communications methods that will have the most impact on the customers. The actual mix chosen will depend upon a number of issues surrounding the context of the purchasing situation, including:

- The market area and industry sector.
- Whether it is consumer, institutional or business-to-business marketing.
- The customer segment to be targeted.
- The participants in the purchasing process, their requirements and expectations and the best methods to reach and influence them.
- The country or region, the culture, the communications infrastructure and the preferred methods of communicating.
- The resources made available by the organization and the implications for the level of involvement and control it wishes to exert over the communications process.

The value of different promotional methods varies according to the context in which the marketing communications are being used and the degree to which they are integrated within a marketing communications strategy, as shown in Figure 9.5.

The critical issue is the extent to which they must be adapted so that they can be effective in international markets. Management Challenge 9.2 shows how difficult it is for managers to make decisions that require them to go against their instincts and self-reference criteria.

The marketing communications tools

There are a number of offline and online marketing communications tools for the external market and it is to these that we now turn. For convenience we have grouped these tools within broad categories. In practice there is some flexibility in the way the tools are used within a coordinated strategy but the tools are listed as follows:

- Communicating **product and service differentiation**. This group includes personal selling and word of mouth communications, exhibitions and trade fairs, trade missions, advertising and the use of agencies, sales promotion and direct marketing.
- Communicating with a wider range of stakeholders. This includes corporate identity, sponsorship and public relations.

Online communications are used in all areas of communications, both complementing and replacing offline communications.

FIGURE 9.5   Internal and external international communications programmes

Marketing programmes influencing communications	International communication aims
Internally focused programmes	
Corporate identity	Consistency in all aspects of company logo, signs and image
Internal marketing communications	Reinforce motivation through telling staff what is happening
Sales force, dealer and distributor training and development	Training through conferences, manuals and brochures
Retailing merchandising	Point of sale persuasion through displays and shelf facings
First contact customer service	Welcoming first contact through telephonist and receptionist training
After-sales service	Customer retention and satisfaction through staff training and brochures
Quality management	Assuring a continuous quality approach in all programmes
Brand management	Achieving common brand standards and values
Externally focused programmes (marketing mix)	
Product attributes	Offering innovative, high-quality products
Distribution channel	Ensuring easy access to products and frequent customer encounters with the products
Price	Messages about quality and status
Product/service promotion	Managing customer expectations through the integration of the marketing mix communications
People	Using staff–customer interactions to reinforce the aims, standards and values of the firm
Customer service process	Providing a satisfactory total experience through the service offer
Physical evidence for the service delivery	All contacts with the facilities reinforce the firm's messages

Personal selling and word of mouth

For many companies the first proactive communication tool to promote exports is personal selling. Selling is often used to gain the first few orders in a new market and as the main component of a push strategy to persuade distribution channel members, such as agents, distributors or retailers to stock the product. It is expensive, however.

The use of personal selling tends to be limited to situations in which benefits can be derived from two-way information flows, negotiation is required and when the revenue from the sale is sufficiently high to justify the costs. This is typically the case with business-to-business marketing and in consumer markets where the purchase price and complexity of negotiations justifies the high cost of personal selling, for example for cars, holidays, homes and consumer durable products. Even here the need for personal selling is being challenged as direct marketing, particularly using the Internet, is now being used routinely to purchase these products.

In countries where labour costs are very low, personal selling is used to a greater extent than in high cost countries. This ranges from street and market trading to quite sophisticated multilevel distribution chains for business-to-business products. In high labour-cost countries personal selling of low unit cost products is used rarely, except for illegal trading, for example of drugs.

MANAGEMENT CHALLENGE 9.2

Self-reference criteria in advertising decisions

Advertising managers who are involved in cross-border campaigns face the problem of self-reference criteria. A European brand manager for Heinz, based in the UK, was responsible for approving advertising campaigns that had been developed by local agencies for the local country subsidiary as part of a pan-European campaign. In Germany the local agency produced a television advertising campaign. The European brand manager, his boss and his boss's boss, all English, turned down the agency's creative work.

The advertisement was meant to be humorous but they did not find it at all funny, and they were concerned that it would devalue the brand and the campaign. The agency insisted that they had tested the ad on consumers and the humour would work in Germany. After various delays the manager had to make the decision whether or not the ad should go ahead on the following Monday. However, it was the weekend and he could not reach his bosses for help with the decision. The campaign would cost £1 million which would be lost if it did not go ahead. If the campaign adversely affected the product it would be a greater disaster – his job could be on the line! Against his better judgement, and overcoming his self-reference criteria, he decided the advert should be broadcast. The campaign was a great success!

Western firms also realize that it is important to appreciate the levels of intelligence and sophistication of emerging markets. When Heinz first launched tomato ketchup in Russia they used an existing TV ad from the UK with minor modifications. Now it would be unacceptable as the Russian audience is more sophisticated. Russian actors would be needed on the advertisement. Heinz is particularly sensitive to the need to adapt to local markets and this is part of their strategy.

Consumers are very knowledgeable and well aware when some big brands are behaving in an arrogant manner and telling them what to buy. They can become annoyed when firms insult their intelligence. A number of firms have seen their reputation and share price suffer because of insensitive promotion and PR.

Question

1 Should a firm insist on standardization and consistency of its communications approach, and when should they trust partners with local knowledge?

Effective selling in international business-to-business and consumer markets involves a wide range of tasks and skills, including product and market knowledge, listening and questioning skills. However, it is in the core selling activities of negotiation and persuasion discussed in Chapter 3 that higher-order expertise is required. It is likely that local people will be more effective than home-based representatives in understanding the subtleties of the negotiation process as they apply within the local business culture. They will have fluent language skills and an intimate knowledge of the culture of the country.

However, negotiation of high-value contracts may well require specialist technical knowledge, an understanding of the processes and systems and strict adherence to the firm's standards and values. For these reasons the company may well prefer to use staff from its head office to ensure that the sales people are well informed about the firm's capabilities and that their activities can be controlled.

This is particularly the case if the opportunities to make a sale are very infrequent (e.g. with capital goods) when high levels of technical skill and an understanding of the company's systems are needed but not easily learnt by new people. For example, Rolls-Royce use a complete team of UK-based engineers, accountants and sales people to sell aero engines to customers in foreign markets. Some of the team will make frequent visits, others will be based in close online and offline contact with the customer for a period of many months. The sheer complexity of the contracts means that only Rolls-Royce employees could understand the detail sufficiently to handle the negotiations. The high contract price provides sufficient revenue to pay for the costs of the UK-based sales team.

An alternative to employing local or head office sales staff (both have their advantages and disadvantages) is to employ expatriates, staff from the domestic country to work for extended periods in the host country in order to bridge the culture and company standards gap.

In practice the expatriate is likely to experience a culture shock caused by living in a foreign culture where the familiar symbols, cues and everyday reassurances are missing, often causing feelings of frustration, stress and anxiety. The expatriate can respond to the situation in one of three ways. At one extreme, adjustment is made to the expatriate culture only. In effect the expatriate adjusts to the way of life of a ready-made cultural island within the host country and makes little attempt to adjust to the host culture. At the other extreme the expatriate completely embraces the host culture and minimizes contact with the expatriate community – and the firm too. Ideally the expatriate adjusts to both the local culture and the expatriate culture. In this way the expatriate retains the home country and firm's system of values and beliefs, but is considerate and respectful towards the people of his or her host country and to their culture. It is this last option that is usually most beneficial for the firm's sales effort.

Whichever approach to selling is adopted, it is through relevant training that firms aim to manage their sales staff's involvement with the firm and the market, and maintain their enthusiasm for selling. Multinational companies (MNC) are excellent at ensuring that sales staff are trained in product knowledge, 'soft skills' and cross-cultural understanding (Subramanian 2015). However, Attia *et al.* (2014) state that training sales staff is not universal. They researched Egyptian domestic firms and found that in comparison with international firms Egyption companies gave little attention to even basic training on customer relationship management (CRM), supply chain management and 'soft skills'. This may put Egyption firms at a disadvantage as 'soft skills' such as quality customer service, leadership, decision making and listening are high on the agenda for MNC companies as they see skills such as these, together with positive personality traits, to be essential in the global market.

Exhibitions, trade fairs and experiential marketing

Exhibitions and trade fairs are an effective way of meeting many existing and potential customers from different countries. The cost of exhibiting at international trade fairs is very high when the cost of the stand, space rental, sales staff time and travelling expenses are taken into account. It is for this reason that the selection of the most appropriate fairs for the industry is critical. Also important are the creative work for the stand, preparation of sales literature and selection of suitable personnel for the stand, bearing in mind the need for cultural and language empathy.

> Conferences and conventions are about bringing people together to communicate by sharing information and ideas, to motivate and inspire, to launch new products and disseminate the latest research, to negotiate to reach a consensus on the different challenges facing our world (Rogers, 2008, p. xvii).

Exhibitor benefits from being at a trade fair or exhibition conference include generating high-quality leads, increasing awareness and perception of the corporate brand, and of course the benefit of gaining contact with existing and potential customers (Verma 2014). And for delegates the benefits of visiting an exhibition or tradeshow are to network, gain new knowledge about products and services and listen to research findings from keynote speaker and experts. It is important, therefore, for exhibition and trade fair marketers to promote the benefits. Both exhibitors and delegates also want information regarding the security and safety at the venue, ease of access via efficient and effective transport, good accommodation, dining facilities, shopping and sightseeing opportunities. These attributes encourage more exhibitors and delegates and must also be communicated clearly to further encourage participation at trade fairs and conferences (Whitfield *et al.* 2014). An additional benefit of exhibitions is that they can provide experiential marketing, a rapidly growing communications approach also called customer experience marketing, in which customers obtain an engaging, entertaining and interactive brand experience. There are of course other ways of providing experiential marketing. For example, Apple operates stores in which customers can try out their products and Harley Davidson provides opportunities for visitors to ride its bikes. Therefore, experiential marketing is gaining in importance, not just at events and conferences but for all service organizations that want to enhance the consumer's enjoyment and engagement with their product offer.

Trade missions

Trade missions are organized visits to a country or region by a group of senior business managers from a number of firms, perhaps from the same geographic region or the same industry. They are often subsidized by national or local government. Discussions with potential customers are arranged in advance in the host country.

Trade missions are usually associated with exporting, and may be used to carry out introductory talks with prospective clients or to negotiate a contract. As with trade fairs, good preparation work before the visit is essential to ensure that meetings are arranged with appropriate customers where there is a genuine possibility of business being generated. Usually the home country's local embassy staff will provide support for trade missions and often, too, depending on the importance of the mission, there will be discussions with the host government, civil servants and politicians about how trade between the two countries can be developed.

Advertising

Online and offline advertising are usually the most visible forms of communication and are often considered the most important part of the whole strategy for consumer products in countries with a well-developed media industry. Traditionally offline advertising has disadvantages because it is essentially a one-way method of communication and in international marketing, for example, it can be difficult to control the reach of TV (the geographic area in which consumers are exposed to the messages and specific customer segments). The objective is to obtain the maximum exposure of the product or brand to the largest possible target audience.

In most business-to-business markets advertising tends to be used as a supporting activity, for example, to increase awareness or interest in the company as a whole or in a new concept. In business-to-business markets the number of important customers is often comparatively small and it is essential that advertising is precisely targeted, using appropriate specialist trade media.

Together with the increased harmonization of consumer demands for some products and the benefits of standardized products and services to firms, there is a strong move to pan-regional advertising campaigns. Consumers increasingly share common values and characteristics but there are differences: for example, consumers in developing markets are still developing their habits as consumers.

There are considerable differences in the availability and usefulness of other advertising media such as radio, cinema and posters. These differences make it essential to obtain data about media effectiveness in order to make informed decisions about international media schedules. For instance, in remote regions exposure to certain media is prevented because of the poor transmission output quality from radio stations, lack of electricity to power TVs or computers, the target audience having insufficient disposable income to afford television or radio, and low adult literacy levels preventing significant numbers of adults from reading printed advertising.

Mass communications are becoming less effective for reaching target segments, particularly in developed countries, because of the increasingly fragmented nature of the national press and television. Many households have access to multiple TV channels, films and TV on-demand, and alternative leisure activities such as gaming and social media. The traditional channels have lost audiences, particularly in the 16–24 age group. Indeed, major changes are taking place online and offline.

In these situations it may be necessary to develop a campaign based upon a multitude of individual media activities, but this does mean that the measurement of the cost-effectiveness of the campaign is extremely difficult, given that individual components of the campaign may produce different effects.

Mass marketing is still valuable in emerging markets and to help organizations create a global brand. Increased spending has led to Coca-Cola becoming the best-selling soft drink in China and overtaking Pepsi in a number of Central and Eastern European republics. Pepsi's response to this has been to embark on diversification by buying a stake in Russia's largest food group, Wimm-Bill-Dann. Conglomerates from emerging countries such as Hyundai, HTC and Huawei, recognize the value of moving from product orientation to marketing orientation and have built substantial brands through global advertising.

Table 9.2 shows the top ten advertising spenders worldwide.

Table 9.2 Top 10 global advertisers

Advertiser	Product Categories	Location	Campaigns in top 100	Points
1 Unilever	Household Goods, Food	Netherlands/UK	6	785.1
2 Procter & Gamble	Household Goods, Food	US	3	576.1
3 Coca-Cola Company, The	Soft Drinks	US	3	454.6
4 PepsiCo	Soft Drinks, Food	US	3	384.0
5 Mondelēz International	Food	US	1	258.3
6 McDonald's	Retail	US	1	190.1
7 Nestlé	Food, Soft Drinks	Switzerland	–	182.9
8 Mercedes-Benz	Automotive	Germany	3	172.5
9 Heineken	Alcoholic Drinks	Netherlands	–	167.7
10 Toyota	Automotive	Japan	1	150.6

Source: Reprinted with permission from *Advertising Age* (2006). Copyright Crain Communications Inc.

Television advertising

The main influence on television advertising expenditure is the size of the economy in gross domestic product per capita, but the regulatory environment also affects spending, particularly television which tends to be more closely regulated than other media.

Cable and satellite television have contributed to a proliferation of television channels so that viewers can receive a rapidly increasing number of programmes. This means that there is a greater capacity for television advertising but, of course, there is greater competition for prime television advertising spots (and much higher costs) if there is likely to be a large audience. Both satellite and cable television have the potential to cross country borders and attract large audiences for programmes of common international interest, for example major sporting events.

It is not only overt television advertising in large amounts that sells. The prominent placing of products on television shows, or sponsorship of programmes that are likely to be transmitted in other countries, can also become an important part of the advertising campaign, particularly as placements and sponsorship cannot be removed by viewers 'zapping' between channels. More often than not consumers will have at least two 'screens up' at one time whilst they are watching TV. 'Screens up' devices are mobile smartphones, laptops and tablets where consumers catch up on Facebook, YouTube and Twitter plus emails from work and of course downloading films which are then beamed directly onto the television screen. At the same time friends and family may be Skyping them. This behaviour shows just how important an integrated marketing communications message is across many social media platforms, in addition to traditional media. An interesting development is shown in Illustration 9.4 which shows how offline and online communications can embed a local message on national television through integrated communication. With a more sceptical and knowledgeable audience, advertisers are adopting different, more inclusive approaches that will certainly win over customers.

Press advertising

Media availability and effectiveness are particularly important in deciding the nature of campaigns, because they can vary from country to country. The lack of mass-circulation national titles might cause distribution

ILLUSTRATION 9.4

Budweiser's integrated marketing communication: Thanks to cold and wet football fans

Television viewing figures on the last day of the UK's football leagues (Premiership, Champion's League, Division One and Division Two) are extremely high as football results signify teams that have won their division, been promoted to a higher division or been relegated to a lower division. In 2015, the winner of the Dream Goal was announced on 22 May.

Roll back now to March 2015 when Budweiser launched the Dream Goal #ToTheDream campaign. The integrated marketing campaign started with Budweiser realizing there is a great deal of football talent in the UK. A lot of it happens on a cold and wet Sunday morning in front of between 10 and 50 equally cold and wet but avid fans. Welcome to amateur league football. Budweiser and ABInBev UK Limited set a competition to find the best amateur league football goal. The competition required fans to video their local amateur team's football game and upload it to Budweiser.co.uk. Calls to football fans came through different media channels. First, the budweiser. co.uk website, a dedicated Facebook page, Twitter, Google+ and youtube.com/BudweiserDreamGoal. Second, calls to fans were made through press releases where newspapers like the *Daily Mirror* championed the competition.

Talksport (radio) also supported the Budweiser competition both live on air and through their website www.talksport.com/budweiser.

Budweiser then joined forces with two well-known Sky Sports commentators and sports writers – Jamie Rednapp (retired English footballer and Premiership player for Liverpool FC, Tottenham Hotspurs, Southampton and Bournemouth) and Gary Neville (retired England footballer and Premiership player for Manchester United).

The videos from the amateur teams are shown to Jamie Rednapp and Gary Neville and critiqued in front of a studio audience. This event is made into an advertisement and shown regularly on UK television. The advertisements last between 60 seconds to 1 minute 30 seconds; making it an expensive advertisement campaign. Neville comments on the organization of the team and how the players know exactly which positions to be in. Jamie Rednapp discusses the amateur team's performance and how 'big Dad's' attention to the old-fashioned techniques is amazing. The commentators have a lot of fun analyzing the game just as they do on national television for Sky Sports Saturday Night Football and Monday Night Football.

From March to May advertisements for the Dream Goal #ToTheDream campaign took place. All other communication channels were also active in promoting the Dream Goal, recruiting fans to video amateur football goals and of course promiting Budweiser. The Facebook page has 12 million followers, Twitter has 12 000 followers and the YouTube videos have over 300 000 views.

Questions

1 How have Budweiser used integrated marketing communications for the Dream Goal campaign?

2 What benefits have links to celebrities brought to the advertisement?

3 How could Budwieser engage with consumers?

4 How could Budweiser use this integrated marketing communications format in different countries?

Source: Budweiser (2015) www.budweiser.co.uk

difficulties too, as it is easier to distribute quickly in small compact countries than in much larger ones such as France or Spain. Vast countries like the USA have a regional press. Newer publishing and printing technology has allowed many more local and free newspapers and specialist magazines to be introduced to both consumer and business-to-business markets. By their very nature they tend to be highly targeted at specific market segments and can be useful to niche marketers. Sales of mass audience newspapers in many countries are declining as readers turn to the Internet for general and specialist news coverage. For mass marketers the resulting fragmentation of readership means that national campaigns are more difficult to coordinate.

The use of agencies and consultancies

Most companies in which marketing communications are an important part of the marketing mix use agencies and consultancies. The reasons why this is so can be explained by financial considerations, specialist knowledge, creative input and external perspective.

Financial. Advertising agents that are recognized by the media are eligible for a commission based on booked advertising space. The agency can, therefore, perform the advertising services of creation, media planning and booking more economically than the client.

Agencies and consultancies can use specialist people and resources, such as a database for media planning, with a number of clients. This helps spread costs for both the agency and client.

Specialist knowledge. By concentrating on one particular area, agencies and consultancies can become experts in specialized techniques, for example international database marketing or training sales people. Client companies might have an infrequent need for these services and so find it more cost-effective to subcontract the work.

Creative input. Creativity is very important in marketing communications. The organization culture of client companies is unlikely to encourage true creativity in external communications. The challenge of new and different projects for different clients contributes to the creativity of agencies.

External perspective. The external view of agencies reduces some of the myopia of the client company. This might be particularly valuable at times of major transition, for example in moving from international marketing towards global marketing.

The selection of agencies and consultants is an important business decision. If the agency is going to be involved over a long period and be trusted with large expenditures of time and money, the decision process will be significant. A dilemma for global marketers is whether they should select one central agency or many local agencies in their target countries, both of which approaches have advantages and disadvantages.

Sales promotions

Sales promotions are used as an extra incentive for the purchaser at the point of sale. In some markets there may be no meaningful differences between a number of companies or brands, except for the degree of attractiveness of the sales promotion offer. The customers' perception of the relative value of the alternative promotions depends to a great extent on their cultural values and differences, which lead to certain types of sales promotion being very successful in one country but failing in another.

Legal restrictions also affect the opportunity for firms to standardize sales promotions across country borders. There are limitations on the amount of cash discounts and special sales promotions in some countries in Europe. Different legal definitions of the rules for lotteries, too, prevent some competition-based promotions being operated across borders.

Direct marketing

In the past, direct marketing has usually taken the form of direct mail or telephone selling, but in markets with high computer ownership the Internet has taken the lead. The key elements of direct marketing are an accurate up-to-date database, the ability to purge the database of incorrect data and to merge the database with a firm's promotional message. Usually firms subcontract direct marketing to specialist agencies which provide the various services, such as list brokering, purging and merging.

Communicating with the wider range of stakeholders

At the outset we said that the principal objective of the international marketing communications strategy was to sell products and services. However, customers in a host country are unlikely to even contemplate buying from a foreign firm that is unknown, or worse still, perceived to be exploiting its local workers, bribing government officials, showing little regard to environmental protection issues, offering poor or variable product quality or is likely to pull out from the country at any moment and thus be unable to fulfil its guarantees and obligations. A foreign firm can build increased loyalty among its customers at the expense of local firms if it is perceived to offer better quality and value for money, to be a more reliable supplier, more caring about the local community and, in some cases, through association, to be respected by world personalities.

Firms need to build their reputation with all their influential stakeholders, pressure groups and the community in general as well as customers. They do this in a number of ways:

- Corporate identity.
- Sponsorship.
- Public relations and lobbying.

Corporate identity

Corporate identity is concerned with consistently communicating not just what business the firm is in and what image it wishes to project in the market, but also how it does its business. It must reflect the standards and values it aims to uphold in its dealings with all its stakeholders. Corporate philanthropy is a key factor as Illustration 9.5 shows, but the aims of the organization and recipients of corporate giving may not always coincide. For this reason there are two distinct elements. For many MNEs the focus is upon the image it wishes to create, which is reinforced by consistency in the way the company name and logo is presented and applied to the vast range of physical outputs and assets of the company including signs, staff uniforms, letterheads, visiting cards, gifts, annual reports, packaging specification and promotional literature.

In principle, while these can all be controlled by the firm, there are many challenges in applying them consistently in all the countries where the firm operates, especially where it develops alliances with partners who might also wish to maintain their corporate identity in joint communications.

Arguably of more importance is the underlying identity of the firm and its beliefs, standards and values, which will show through in everything it does. These may pose more difficulties in the firm's attempts to achieve consistency and a favourable impact throughout the world because of the different cultural values of its staff and stakeholders in different countries.

Sponsorship and celebrity endorsement

Sponsorship involves a firm (the sponsor) providing finance, resources or other support for an event, activity, firm, person, product or service. In return the sponsor would expect to gain some advantage, such as the exposure of its brand, logo or advertising message. Sponsorship of music, performing arts and sporting events provides opportunities for:

- Brand exposure and publicity.
- Opportunities to entertain and reward customers and employees.
- Association between brands and events, with the events often reinforcing the brand positioning.
- Improving community relations by supporting community-based projects.
- Creating the opportunity to promote the brands at the event, either through providing free products or gifts such as T-shirts carrying the brand logo.

Expenditure on global sponsorship has expanded rapidly over the past two decades, and it is being used much more for the following reasons:

- Restrictive government policies on tobacco and alcohol advertising make sponsorship the most effective way of communicating the brand imagery to a mass market, for example in Formula 1 car racing.
- The escalating costs of media advertising.
- Increased leisure activities and sporting events.

ILLUSTRATION 9.5

Red carpet treatment enhances Nestlé's corporate identity

'Good Food, Good Life' is the promise that Nestlé communicates on every channel. Positioned as the 54th Best Global Brand (2014) they are certainly popular with stakeholders and consumers, particularly for much loved brands such as KitKat (confectionery), Shredded Wheat and Cheerios (breakfast cereal) Carnation Milk and Nescafé coffee (beverages).

In 2015 Nestlé won the prestigious Corporate Registers 2015 Global Winners Award for the Best Corporate Social Responsibility Report. The accolade certainly boosts the corporate identity of Nestlé with all stakeholders including investors, consumers, employees, supply chain managers and of course the communities which Nestlé works in and/or engages with.

Nestlé certainly cares, and this is communicated through Nestlé's Corporate Social Responsibility Report, their Annual Report, press releases and leadership on many international sustainability and environmental boards and committees. The facts, figures, case studies and clear objectives provide details on how Nestlé will create a shared conscience, worldwide, in humanitarian, environmental, workforce and regional communities.

This corporate identity is shown in their company vision, which is to be the leader in nutrition, health and wellness. Chief executive officer Paul Bulke states that in addition to their vision, Nestlé are actively engaging and leading on the health and well-being issues. They are working to ensure improved regional community networks and reductions in environmental

damage that future employees and consumers, and of course their children, will benefit from.

One area Nestlé is driving forward is water scarcity. Nestlé's chairman Peter Brabeck-Letmathe states that everyone in the world has a right to drink water. Yet water is scarce. Therefore, Peter Brabeck-Letmathe leads on multistakeholder initiatives on water scarcity, its challenges and ways to provide water efficiencies across the globe.

Nestlé also participate in the United Nations Global Compact (UNGC). One of Nestlé's commitments to UNGC is to ensure they adhere to human rights policies and eradicate child labour in all sectors along their supply chain. At the same time Nestlé are committed to providing rural development in and around communities where products are sourced or manufactured. Their Rural Development Framework ensures local people are given employment opportunities, training and education. Currently there are 300 000 farmers receiving training and capacity building including rice farmers in Indonesia, dairy farmers in Mexico and sugar farmers in Cote D'Ivoire, China and Vietnam.

Overall Nestlé is also championing sustainable solutions. Creating and reporting on water scarcity solutions, human rights policies, eradication of child labour and rural developments are just some of the advancements that helped Nestlé receive the Corporate Registry Award. To gain such an award Nestlé have to show clear content in their communications, communicate their actions, not just through PR but through active engagement at an international as well as at a local level, and be committed for the long term which is shown through goals, objectives targets and investment.

Questions

1 Why do Nestlé create shared values around the world?

2 How does the PR from winning the Corporate Registry Award enhance the Nestlé brand's reputation?

3 Who benefits from Nestlé's involvement in corporate social responsibilities?

Sources: Nestlé (2015) What is Creating Shared Value? Available from www.nestle.com/csv/what-is-csv (accessed 23 May 2015); Corporate Responsibility (2015) CR Reporting Awards 2015–The Winners (announced 21 May, 2015) Available from www.corporateregister.com/crra (accessed 23 May 2015).

- The cost effectiveness of sponsorship of successful events.
- Endorsement of the product or service through association with the event.
- Greater (free) media coverage of sponsored events.
- The reduced efficiencies of traditional media advertising because of clutter and zapping between television programmes, especially during advertising breaks.

Masterson (2005) explains the need to achieve a fit between the sponsor and the activity being sponsored, introduces the concept of integrated product relevance and explains the ways in which this can be used to affect the consumers' responses to the sponsor's products, by focusing on function and image similarity.

There has been an increase in the amount of broadcast sponsorship in film, television and radio programmes. This can result in the benefit of the event sponsorship being reduced. For example, Heinz sponsored a Rugby World Cup only to find that Sony sponsored the national commercial television coverage in the UK, resulting in most viewers thinking that Sony had sponsored the whole event.

Product placement and celebrity endorsement

As many television viewers record programmes and are able to fast-forward through advertising, product placement within the programmes is becoming more attractive. Those films that will gain a global TV audience, such as James Bond, offer the most potential from product placement for global firms.

Sponsorship of individuals such as sports stars and the use of celebrities to endorse brands are very beneficial because of the perceived shared values and image association between the celebrity and the brand. The problem is that individuals can be unpredictable and this can lead to unfortunate and undesirable associations. Celebrities are increasingly advertising their own merchandise on TV shopping channels.

Global brands ambassadors need to be leaders in their field and recognizable by global consumers. As David Beckham came towards the end of his footballing career, he was replaced as the face of Gillette by Tiger Woods, Thierry Henry and Roger Federer. Woods attracted unfavourable media comment because of his behaviour in his private life, which adversely affected his sporting performance. However, as Management Challenge 9.3 shows, Tiger Woods still receives money from big brand names and up and coming brands.

Public relations

Public relations is concerned with communicating news stories about the firm, its people, standards and values – particularly its attitude to social responsibility – products and services through the media and, without charge, to develop relationships, goodwill and mutual understanding between the firm and its stakeholders. The press is always hungry for stories in order to fill their ever-expanding programmes and newspapers, and are grateful for interesting and newsworthy stories that are inexpensive to obtain.

The purposes of PR are as follows:

- Helping to foster the prestige and reputation of the firm through its public image.
- Raising awareness and creating interest in the firm's products.
- Dealing with social and environmental issues and opportunities.
- Improving goodwill with customers through presenting useful information and dealing effectively with complaints.
- Promoting the sense of identification of employees with the firm through newsletters, social activities and recognition.
- Discovering and eliminating rumours and other sources of misunderstanding and misconceptions.
- Building a reputation as a good customer and reliable supplier.
- Influencing the opinions of public officials and politicians, especially in explaining the responsible operation of the business and the importance of its activities to the community.
- Dealing promptly, accurately and effectively with unfavourable negative publicity, especially where it is perceived to be a crisis which might damage the firm's reputation.
- Attracting and keeping good employees.

MANAGEMENT CHALLENGE 9.3

Tiger Woods back in the branding business

Celebrity endorsements are another communication tool for businesses to use to promote their brand. One of the highest earners from celebrity endorsements is Tiger Woods.

During Tiger Woods' phenomenal professional career, starting in 1996, he has earned more brand endorsement money through sponsorships than any other golfer; indeed any other sportsperson.

Tiger's first golf major was won in 1996. That year alone he earned US$67 million from Nike and Titleist for wearing Nike polo-shirts, caps, golf shoes and sweaters and playing each round with Titleist golf balls. For Nike and Titleist their brands were endorsed by the youngest and most amazingly talented golfer ever seen, and with their brands worn by this golf star being seen on television hour after hour, during tournaments their brand reach encircled the world. Tiger became unstoppable and won tournament after tournament. This brought further sponsorship deals for Tiger with Accenture, AT&T, American Express, Chevron, EA Sports, Gatorade, Gillette, PepsiCo and General Motors. The endorsement deals brought Tiger US$100.9 million on top of the US$21 million that he earned from winning golf tournaments.

Then came the sex scandals. Tiger, once the loving husband and amazing father of two beautiful children, revealed his dark side. It was discovered that Tiger had 14 mistresses and was heralded as a sex addict,

and when celebrities 'go bad' sponsors run a mile. His main brand sponsors such as Accenture, AT&T, PepsiCo and Gillette were the first to leave Tiger as they did not want their brands tainted because of their celebrity's personal antics. Not long after Tiger was plagued by injury. Those brands that still supported Tiger were not getting value for money as Tiger was no longer on the golf circuit promoting their brands.

However, in 2014 Tiger made his comeback. As stated earlier many major sponsors had left him but other sponsors found Tiger to be a good investment to promote their brand. Hero MotorCorp was one of those brands. Hero MotorCorp is little known outside India where it sells motorcycles and scooters. However through Tiger they hope to increase sales outside India by 10 per cent as they begin their international expansion. Hero plan expansion into Europe in 2015 and US and Brazil in 2016. Tiger's celebrity endorsement days are not over. In addition to Hero MotorCorp the following brands are investing in Tiger: MusclePharm (a sports-nutrition brand), Kowa (a Japanese textile company), and NetJets (private jet hire). These are not as glamorous as some of Tiger's earlier sponsors, although Nike never left Tiger and one of his newest sponsors is Rolex.

Questions

1 What are the benefits of using a celebrity to promote a brand?

2 Why do brands choose to abandon a celebrity like Tiger Woods?

Sources: *Golf Digest* (2015), 'Tiger's still no. 1 in making money (but just barely)', March, 66: 3, 138; Badenhausen, K. (2014) 'Tiger Woods inks huge sponsorship deal ahead of return to golf', Forbes.com (accessed 2 December 2014).

An important aspect of PR is explaining the corporate social responsibility policy of organizations and dealing with the cynicism of pressure groups and individuals communicating online and using traditional media. Public relations is concerned with a wide variety of activities in order to deliver these objectives, including:

- Dealing with press relations.
- Arranging facility visits.
- Publishing house journals and newsletters.
- Preparing videos, audiovisual presentations, printed reports and publications describing the firm's activities.
- Training courses.
- Arranging community projects.
- Lobbying governments.

From a communications perspective the effect of public relations-generated stories in the media is different from advertising. The viewer, listener or reader will perceive the information differently. Editorial material in the media is perceived by consumers to be factual and comparatively neutral whereas advertising material is expected to be persuasive and present a positive statement for the advertisers' products. Whereas the firm controls every aspect of advertising, a press release covering a firm's news story will be interpreted by the journalist who writes the story for the press or edits the videotape for television.

Crisis management

In international marketing one of the most important responsibilities of public relations is to manage unexpected crises which occur from time to time. Over the past few years there have been a number of examples of good and bad practice in managing information when dealing with a crisis such as environmental pollution, unethical promotion, exploitation of labour and health scares caused by food contamination. The golden rule is that the firm should be seen to act, before the media or government forces it to do so, in order to show that it is sorry that an incident has occurred. However, it should neither accept responsibility nor apportion blame until the evidence is investigated and the real cause of the problem identified.

Many MNEs consider government lobbying an essential part of international communications, with the aim of influencing foreign governments both directly and indirectly through asking the home country government to help. Recent examples of lobbying have been US firms seeking to reduce Chinese piracy of products and services, and allowing greater access to Japanese markets.

As government lobbying becomes increasingly important it raises issues for the company about how high profile it should be in pressing its case, particularly where it is seen to be exerting undue pressure on politicians or civil servants to behave unethically or reverse policy.

Some firms go one stage further by making donations to political parties. This, of course, can have the effect of alienating other stakeholders. There is little doubt that firms are increasingly making lobbying a major responsibility of senior management, given the pivotal role of governments in making decisions which might affect MNEs.

Online communications

In Chapter 12 we will discuss the use of technology in shaping the international marketing strategy of firms at greater length and, clearly, facilitating communications is at the heart. Here, however, we discuss the tactical use of online integrated marketing communications.

The nature of online communications

A number of online tools are used by marketers to create brand awareness, product and service associations and drive users to their websites, where customers might obtain further information, purchase an item from an online store or direct the customer to a traditional store. One significant advantage of online communications is that it is easier to measure the actions of customers and their response and so marketing metrics are more accurate.

Advertising is placed on partner sites that charge a 'click-through' fee in return for providing the sales lead and link. Search engines and comparative pricing sites provide sales leads by listing websites based on brand searches or brand associations with key words. Being listed on the first page of a key word search is essential and firms pay heavily and also manage their web content carefully to ensure that this happens in all their international markets.

Websites Some websites are clearly defined as marketplaces either owned by one specific organization or where links to commercial sites should be expected, for example, financial services supermarkets, online travel agents or insurance brokers.

Email Organizations use email to convey their marketing messages directly to their customers. However, many customers have been irritated by the large volume of spam they receive. Godin (2002) found that customers were bombarded by up to 500 marketing messages per day from traditional communication sources but today customers can expect to see up to 3000 messages, because of the rise in online communications. This means that the effect of individual messages is diluted among this volume of what he refers to as interruption marketing (spam). He has introduced the term 'permission marketing' to suggest that the communications will be more effective if customers agree to receive more communications from the firm. This opt-in approach is preferable to an opt-out, in which the customer would have to take the initiative in asking a firm not to send messages.

Viral marketing has extended the effectiveness of online communications by encouraging recipients of email messages to pass them on to others to create a 'buzz' in the marketplace. As discussed in Illustration 9.6, social networking sites provide a platform for sharing informal views about products and services that can have considerable effect on the success of marketing campaigns; researching consumer online behaviour, therefore, is essential.

Mobile communications For some time it has been predicted that mobile communications would be valuable and, as we saw in earlier chapters, multifunctional mobile devices, such as smartphones and tablets now provide more comprehensive services and interactive communications.

ILLUSTRATION 9.6

Social media marketing: International brands advertise in consumer social spaces

It is essential that international brands understand the behaviour of their target audiences. This is particularly true where social media is concerned as online behaviour in different countries varies. What international brands definitely know is social media activity is growing day-by-day. Therefore advertisers need to ensure their communication messages are shown to target markets via the most appropriate social media channel.

Currently (2015) there are 7.2 billion people in the world. Over 3 million of those people are active Internet users. The most important statistic that advertisers are reviewing is the usage of active **social media** accounts, currently over 2 billion, and active **mobile social** accounts, currently over 1.7 billion. Advertisers know that their communication messages must reach the online social consumers, grab their attention

and raise brand awareness and/or increase sales potential.

The dynamics of online and social media activity vary around the world. For instance, worldwide, the number of hours spent per day on the Internet is 4.4 hours (via desktop/laptop) and 2.7 hours (via a mobile device). Table 9.3 shows the number of hours spent on the Internet by consumers from different countries.

The amount of Internet activity, both work and leisure time, is growing, and advertisers realize the potential for communicating with consumers via Internet channels. And as familiarity and usage of the Internet grows, Internet brand presence online is essential.

Table 9.3 Number of hours spent on the Internet by consumers from different countries

	Device	
Country	Desktop/ laptop (hrs)	Mobile (hrs)
Philippines	6.3	3.3
Saudi Arabia	4.2	4.2
Japan	3.1	1.0
France	3.9	1.3
UK	4.0	1.9
Mexico	5.0	4.0
Canada	4.6	1.9

Table 9.4 M-commerce activity 'bought something' as a % of the country population

South Korea	37%
UAE	27%
Turkey	19%
UK	18%
Mexico	14%
Indonesia	9%
Japan	6%

E-commerce over the Internet is big business, but more in some countries than others. Sixty-four per cent of UK consumers stated they had 'bought something' online in the month before GlobalWebindex's survey (Mander 2014). E-commerce activity is also high in Germany (63 per cent) and South Korea (62 per cent). However, e-commerce activity is low in other countries: Philippines 21 per cent, Indonesia 16 per cent and India 14 per cent. Thus online advertisements will have different strategies, even for the same brand. Brands advertising to UK, German and South Korean consumers will heavily promote a 'call to action' to improve sales, whilst in the Philippines, Indonesia and India online advertisements will have strategies for brand awareness building, loyalty and brand switching.

The opportunity to use social media is not the same worldwide. In East Asia, North America, South America and Europe over 45 per cent of the population have active social media accounts, whilst in South Asia, Africa and Central Asia less than 10 per cent of the population have active social media accounts. Therefore, advertisers for international brands will direct their efforts through traditional and social media marketing channels that are available to the consumer.

Like e-commerce; m-commerce (mobile device used to purchase goods/services) varies. Consumers were asked by GlobalWebIndex to advise if they had used a mobile device in the last month to 'purchase something'. The table shows the mobile device behaviour in different countries.

The m-commerce activity again shows that consumers worldwide behave differently. Advertisers for international brands must provide functionality compatible to mobile devices when offering purchase opportunities for consumers in South Korea and the UAE. However, for consumers in Indonesia and Japan international brands should offer different purchase opportunities for potential consumers.

Questions

1 Why is social media marketing essential for international brands?

2 Why is it important for advertisers to know about the online behaviours of consumers from different countries?

3 Highlight some of the different behaviours of e-commerce consumers and what this means to an international brand.

Sources: Simon Kemp (2015) Digital, Social & Mobile in 2015, *We are social: News*, published 21 January 2015. Available from www.wearesocial.sg (accessed 23 May 2015); Mander, J. (2014) *Global Web Index*. Available from www.slideshare.net/globalwebindex (accessed 2 May 2015); cited in Simon Kemp (2015) 'Digital, Social & Mobile in 2015 We are social News', published 21 January 2015. Available from www.wearesocial.sg (accessed 23 May 2015).

Privacy There is a conflict between the interests of the firm and customer in developing databases. In order to offer more individually targeted, personalized and relevant communications, the firm requires ever more detailed and potentially sensitive information from the customer. However, the customer is reluctant to give firms personal information. They appreciate that certain firms such as insurance companies might need the information in order to process a transaction, can be trusted and will respect local country privacy laws, such as the 1998 Data Protection Act in the UK. They have more concern over the possibility of the firms passing on the sensitive information – deliberately or accidentally – to other firms that will not be so scrupulous in its use. It is very easy to pass information electronically to other companies or countries.

Developing profitable, long-term marketing relationships

So far in this chapter we have focused upon the communications strategies that might be used to ensure that the firm's broad base of stakeholders around the world are aware of the company's standards and values, the distinctiveness and quality of its brands, products and services and that customers are exposed to the messages that will encourage them to buy the firm's products and services rather than the competitor's. Once customers have been won over, usually at a considerable cost, firms increasingly realize that it is less costly if they can persuade them to stay loyal to the firm rather than lose them to a competitor and so face the cost of winning them over again.

Customer retention is particularly important for B2B marketing, where the number of opportunities to win over new customers may be very limited and the loss of a major customer could have a disastrous effect on the firm. The lifetime value of the customer is considerable, but the cost to the customer of changing to a new supplier can be considerable too. Both supplier and customer have something to gain from the relationship marketing (RM) concept, which is concerned with developing and maintaining mutually advantageous relationships between two or more firms in a supply chain and using their combined capability and resources to deliver the maximum added value for the ultimate customer. It involves a more holistic approach to understanding the market dynamics and developing implementation strategies to respond to the changes in the market needs that have been identified.

The concept of relationship marketing

There are significant differences between adopting a traditional marketing approach based on individual transactions, in which the emphasis is placed on the 4Ps of the product marketing mix (particularly the product P) and an approach based upon building relationships by emphasizing the three extra Ps of the service mix (particularly the people P). At the core of relationship marketing is the idea that rather than simply trying to add customer service onto a predetermined product offer, based on a rigid marketing mix, the firm should provide customer satisfaction by using the marketing mix flexibly to meet the customer's evolving needs.

Horovitz (2000) suggests that in relationship marketing the 4Ps of the traditional marketing mix are changed altogether and replaced by the 4Cs of relationship marketing: customer needs and wants; costs; convenience and communication. Clearly given the need to meet diverse cultural requirements, relationship marketing makes sense for high-involvement B2B purchases where value can be added and sales generated by RM, but less so for low-involvement purchases of consumer packaged goods. It is important to recognize that consumers do not want a relationship as such but do want interactivity, 1:1 marketing and more personalized communications, and this can be done by replacing conventional offline with online communications.

Throughout the firm the objectives of relationship marketing are to:

■ Maintain and build existing customers by offering more tailored and cost-effective business solutions.

■ Use existing relationships to obtain referral to business units and other supply chain members that are perhaps in different parts of the world and not currently customers.

■ Increase the revenue from customers by offering solutions that are a combination of products and services.

■ Reduce the operational and communications cost of servicing the customers, including the work prior to a trading relationship.

Relationships must be built with those that might influence the final purchase decision, and include internal staff as individuals and groups, experts, celebrities and other influential individuals that have the power to connect the organization with the market.

The power and influence of the organization's stakeholders in these markets will vary considerably around the world and their relative importance depends upon the specific context of the firm's activity. In the technology sector, for example, key influencers and high profile, lead customers may be located in a particular country market but their decisions might influence purchasing decisions across the world.

Database development

Managing and influencing potentially millions of interactions between staff, customers and partners requires a systematic approach. Chaffey *et al.* (2003) explain that the key objectives are: customer retention, customer extension (increasing the depth and range of customers) and customer selection (segmenting and targeting).

The starting point is to build an information technology system that will integrate the RM activity. Central to the system is a database that will identify those customers with which it is worthwhile developing a relationship. The database can best be built from the company records of its interactions with customers and then supplemented with purchased lists of possible customers. Chaffey *et al.* (2003) explain that the details about the customer should include:

- Personal and profile data, including contact details.
- Transaction data including purchase quantities, channels, timing and locations.
- Communications data, including response to campaigns.

Wasserman, Khermouch and Green (2000) explain that data mining is used to 'discover hidden facts contained in databases'. Identifying trends in behaviour and attitudes from data provides a basis for targeting prospective customers cost-effectively, developing cooperative relationships with other companies and better understanding the patterns of customer purchasing behaviour.

Customer relationship management

International consumer markets are characterized by their sheer size and the relative anonymity of their customers. Even small retailers cannot possibly know their customers' individual behaviour, attitudes, intention to purchase and experiences (good or bad) in dealing with the firm, whereas an industrial marketer with only a few customers possibly can. As we have discussed in the section on databases, technology has been developed to try to integrate RM activity and manage the vast amounts of supporting information. Customer relationship management (CRM) is effectively computer software coupled with defined management processes and procedures to enable staff throughout organizations to capture and use information about their customers to maintain and build relationships. Companies such as Siebel (US) have built their business around such concepts.

Although CRM should play a decisive role in integrating communications and developing relationships with the customer as the focus, Kotler (2003) points out that in practice, many firms have embraced the concept and spent between US$5 million and US$10 million on CRM systems, but been less than satisfied with the results. He quotes the CRM Forum research that suggests less than 30 per cent of companies are satisfied with their systems. The problems that companies identify in establishing the systems tend not to be associated with software failure (2 per cent) but rather organizational change (29 per cent), company politics/inertia (22 per cent), lack of CRM understanding (20 per cent), poor planning (12 per cent), lack of CRM skills (6 per cent), budget problems (4 per cent), bad advice (1 per cent) and other (4 per cent).

The problems arise when firms see CRM systems as a quick fix to try to manage vast amounts of data. They make broad generalizations about customer segments and are often too insensitive to different consumer cultures and concerns. Too often CRM is not adopted on an organization-wide basis and instead is adopted by individual departments for very specific reasons. It also gets modified because of the need to interface it with existing legacy systems and so becomes fragmented and, rather than reducing cost, actually increases it. The introduction of CRM leads to raised expectations of service levels among customers and staff and if this is not delivered CRM can have a detrimental effect on the business.

The opportunities for relationship marketing to offer benefits are increasing because of improvements in communications, IT and increased cross-border purchasing. However, it is important to understand that the consumer is not necessarily a willing participant in the relationship mission and, unless this is recognized, relationship marketing will prove to be of limited value. Indeed the question must be asked whether the majority of consumers will derive any benefit from a relationship with an MNE – the benefits will be mainly with the firm.

For relatively low purchase price items there is a danger that the costs to the firm of building customer loyalty might outweigh the costs of a more traditional approach to marketing products and services. It is difficult to measure the relative merits of short-term costs against longer-term revenues and few companies are willing to take a long-term view based upon their assumptions of what might happen in the future.

In practice the methods of relationship marketing in the consumer markets are diverging from relationship marketing in the business sector. In consumer markets relationship marketing will become more concerned with making one-to-one connections with customers through interactivity and promoting and placing products and services in the appropriate media at just the right moment.

SUMMARY

- To be effective in global markets external international marketing communications are driven by the need to have a uniform corporate identity, clearly differentiated product and service offers supported by consistent promotion and strategies in place to build long-term customer relationships.

- Firms also need to focus on internal and interactive communications and ensure that their staff and partners' staff in remote locations deliver consistent and integrated international marketing communications.

- There are benefits to the firm of standardizing the promotion processes and programmes to benefit from economies of scale and the learning effect, wherever possible, but communications are extremely sensitive to local culture and conditions and, without attention to detail, they can be the source of problems worldwide for firms.

- The communication tools must be used appropriately to suit the context of the markets being served, different customer needs and the firm's objectives. Media availability, cultural and legislation differences and the nature of the products and services being marketed will influence the communications strategy decisions and choice of tools.

- Customer perceptions can be damaged by poor communications management within the firm and by external factors over which the organization may have no control. The international firm must concentrate on communicating consistency in its image, standards and values to a diverse range of stakeholders, as well as making its direct appeal to existing and potential customers. It must also integrate the traditional communications with online communications to further develop interactive, one-to-one customer relationships.

- Due to the high cost of winning and losing customers, firms, particularly in the business-to-business market, must build relationships to retain their most valuable customers in the long term. They must also measure the impact of their marketing communication investment as far as possible to ensure value for money.

KEYWORDS

communications mix

promotional mix

corporate identity

relationship marketing

customer relationship management

failures of communications

standardization of international marketing communications

communications adaptation

push strategy

pull strategy

communications tools

product and service differentiation

transactions

CASE STUDY 1

Etihad Airways: Scoring global brand recognition

Etihad Airways is a global player in more ways than one. With a fleet of 117 aircraft, travelling to over 96 destinations, equating to over 1000 flights per week, Etihad certainly has presence in many counties around the world. However, Etihad Airways are not just a global brand in the travel world. The marketers of Etihad Airways have helped to promote and raise awareness of the brand in many other sectors, one of which is the sport and leisure sector.

Etihad Airways sponsors Manchester City Football Club (FC). Links with an internationally known football club is just one way to gain brand recognition outside the travel industry. Manchester City FC was chosen by Etihad Airways as a team to sponsor. The main reason for this is that Etihad Airways can combine their own well-known, international quality brand with Manchester City FC's equally well-known, international brand. Manchester City FC are an extremely popular club and Etihad Airways' logo is printed on the football shirts of the players and all merchandising materials be it calendars, scarves, hats, keyrings and even 'baby-grows'. They have been *the* winning team of the Barclays Premier League, the highest award in the English and Welsh football league. Although that is not all; Manchester City have been so successful that year on year they play in the UEFA (Union of European Football Associations) Champion's League, where teams from across Europe try to win the title of being the best team in Europe. This means that Manchester City FC regularly feature on television, across the world, be it 'live' matches, replays and news features. In addition, international sports celebrities such as Joe Hart, Yaya Touré and Sergio Agüero are wearing Manchester City players football shirts, the Etihad brand is seen by millions of sports and news fans around the world, every day.

The stadium that Manchester City FC play at is now called the Etihad Stadium, but the Etihad Stadium is not just available for football matches. At the end of 2015 AC/DC held a music concert there; prior to that the Royal Military Edinburgh Tattoo and the 2015 Motorcycle Speedway were held at the stadium. Thus the Etihad brand reaches out to over 2 million spectators at each event and millions of other spectators that watch these 'mega events' on television.

The strong partnership between Etihad and Manchester City FC goes further. Etihad Airways launched the 'Blue Moon Rising' liveried planes. The branded fleet showed the colours and logo of Manchester City FC. In the first instance the Blue Moon Rising planes took Manchester City players to and from their international football games. Not long after, a fleet of passenger planes had the Manchester City FC livery especially for flights between Abu Dhabi Airport and Manchester Airport. When the passenger planes touch down the message from the flight crew reads . . . 'Welcome to Manchester, the home of Manchester City Football Club'. Now the dual branded Etihad Airways and Manchester City FC fleet is used for many local and international flights – again promoting both brands around the world.

The branded partnership of Etihad Airways and Manchester City FC also works with children to improve their knowledge and football skills. Each year coaches from the Manchester City FC Soccer School enable over 600 Middle Eastern children, aged 7 to 14 years of age, to participate in an academy. The ultimate goals are to improve the passion for the sport in young people and of course to find the next international football superstar.

Questions

1 How has Etihad Airways used football sponsorship to raise brand awareness around the world?

2 How might Etihad Airways use sponsorship in other sports to raise brand awareness around the world?

3 Etihad Airways now sponsors Melbourne City FC, Australia and New York City FC in the US. Why have the marketing managers of Etihad Airways chosen to do this?

Sources: Etihad (2015) Etihad About Us www.etihad.com/en/about-us (accessed 18 May 2015).

CASE STUDY 2

Greenpeace – global campaigner

Competition in global markets continues to intensify and the charity sector is no different. For a campaigning charity such as Greenpeace it is essential not only to compete for donations but also to recruit new members committed and prepared to give their time to its various causes. Moreover, with limited funds, getting heard is challenging for a charity in an environment that is full of social media and heavily funded advertising, and so creative communications strategies are essential for success.

Greenpeace campaigns to change attitudes and behaviour, in order to protect and conserve the environment and to promote peace in a number of areas, such as energy conservation; reducing waste of resources and use of hazardous chemicals; promoting sustainable agriculture; protecting the world's great forests; the animals and plants and people that live in them; and its oceans; working for disarmament; elimination of nuclear weapons and tackling the causes of conflict.

Fund raising

Among its various stakeholders it is governments and large commercial organizations that are its primary targets as it is the politicians and policy makers that Greenpeace must influence if it is to achieve its objectives. Given their primary targets and need to take an independent stance, Greenpeace only raise funds from individual donors and do not accept donations from any commercial or politically-based organizations.

Although it is a global operation with branches in 41 countries, 3 million donors and more than US$350 million in annual contributions, Greenpeace's

international strategy is based on a franchise system in which each country-based Greenpeace operation contributes 17.5 per cent of its income to Greenpeace International to fund global campaigns but is also responsible for local management, campaigns and fund raising. This reflects the fact that different cultures and geographically based audiences may place a different emphasis on the relative importance of Greenpeace's campaigns. In the US the national group followed a locally focused strategy based on street canvassing and did not fully participate in Greenpeace's global campaigns, resulting in donations declining almost to the point of the US group going broke. The international body of Greenpeace, based in Amsterdam, had to take control to bring the US group back into line and focus on the global as well as the local campaigns and developing its online presence.

Getting heard

Greenpeace adopts professional marketing strategies and management but most of its activities are controversial. Greenpeace's main marketing weapons are high profile actions that make dramatic news items in the worldwide broadcast and social media. To support these public relations campaigns Greenpeace uses targeted marketing communications strategies to get its message across. Greenpeace has realized that trying to persuade governments to take action on promoting ethical behaviour has been largely ineffective. There is also little point in using its limited funds to highlight unethical practice in companies that consumers have not heard of, as this is unlikely to result in a change of behaviour. Instead Greenpeace focuses on the global brands that are supplied by companies that are using illegal or unethical practices. For example, to force Asia Pulp and Paper to cease its deforestation activity, Greenpeace publicized the fact that their customers, toymakers Mattel (makers of the Barbie doll), were buying cardboard traced back to the destruction of precious rainforests. With persuasion from Mattel, APP started discussions with Greenpeace. As an Asian company APP initially found the harsh criticism of Greenpeace difficult to take, but have since adopted a zero-deforestation policy. In this way the global brands force their suppliers to behave ethically. Greenpeace can claim many successes with major brands including Nike, McDonald's, Yum Brands, Unilever, Coca-Cola, and Nestlé pledging to end deforestation. Tech companies such as Google,

Apple and Facebook are promising to use renewable energy in their data centres, resulting in Duke Energy, the largest US power provider, being encouraged to provide clean energy to try to secure their business.

To maintain and grow their level of funding from donors over the longer term and develop cost effective communications strategies, Greenpeace recognizes that different segmentation strategies are required for each market, campaign and stakeholder. Individuals, for example, cannot just be divided into 'donors' and 'members'. As people go through life, their charity giving, their contributions to the causes and their political and economic influence also go through different stages, so Greenpeace must build their communications strategies to respond to this. Direct mail used to be an important tool in the communications armoury of Greenpeace, however, CRM and social media strategies to develop viral marketing campaigns are more cost effective. The challenge they face is how to make better use of the information they have to cost effectively change the behaviour of governments and business, and maximize the lifetime value of individual donors.

Questions

1 Advise Greenpeace on the strategic marketing decisions they need to consider if they are to maintain and grow their level of donations and increase their membership over the longer term.

2 In light of your answer to question 1, recommend to Greenpeace how they can develop an integrated communications strategy that would help them to achieve their long term objectives.

3 Which communications methods do you consider to be the most effective for Greenpeace, as they implement their integrated communications strategy?

DISCUSSION QUESTIONS

1 Communications are becoming increasingly fragmented. Why is this so and what are the critical success factors in planning, executing and controlling an integrated international communications strategy?

2 Critically examine the case for and against using one advertising agency to create and implement an international advertising campaign.

3 How might a small firm with few resources use online communications to build its international business? Using examples show how this might be done (1) in the business to consumer market and (2) in the business-to-business market.

4 Select an economic region. Identify the advantages and disadvantages of pan-regional advertising. How would you manage a pan-regional campaign for a product or service of your choice?

5 A key element of communications for a global company of your choice is maintaining relationships with all its international stakeholders. Identify the various stakeholders and prepare an outline international communications plan to promote the company's values reputation, and increase its profile.

REFERENCES

1. Attia, A.M., Asri Jantan, M., Atteya, N. and Fakhr, R. (2014). 'Sales training: comparing multinational and domestic companies', *Marketing Intelligence & Planning*, 32(1): 124–138.

2. Chaffey, D., Meyer, R., Johnston, K. and Ellis-Chadwick, F. (2003) *Internet Marketing: Strategy, Implementation and Practice*, FT/Prentice Hall.

3. Chan, A.K. and Huang, Y. (1997) 'Brand naming in China: a linguistic approach', *Marketing Intelligence and Planning*, 5(15): 227–34.

4. Davidson, H. (2002) *Committed Enterprise: How to Make Values and Visions Work,* Butterworth-Heinemann.

5. Fill, C. (2006) *Marketing Communications: Engagement, Strategies and Practice,* FT/Prentice Hall.

6. Godin, S. (2002) *Permission Marketing: Turning Strangers Into Friends and Friends Into Customers*, Free Press.

7. Horovitz, J. (2000) 'Using information to bond customers', in D. Marchand (ed.) *Competing with Information*, Wiley.

8. Kataria, M. (2014) 'Presentation of women ads in print advertisements', *Asian Journal of Multidisciplinary Studies*, 2(10).

9. Kotler, P. (2003) *Marketing Insights from A To Z: 80 Concepts Every Manager Needs to Know*, John Wiley.

10. Kotler, P. and Armstrong, G. (2014) *Principles of Marketing*, 15th edn. Pearson Electronic Copy.

11. Kotler, P., Bowen J.T. and Makens, M. (2014) *Marketing for Hospitality and Tourism*, 6th edn. Essex: Pearson Education Limited.

12. Mander, J. (2014) *Global Web Index* Available from www.slideshare.net/globalwebindex (accessed 23 May 2015). Cited in Simon Kemp (2015) Digital, Social & Mobile in 2015 We Are Social News. Published 21 January 2015. Available from www.wearesocial.sg (accessed 23 May 2015).

13. Masterson, R. (2005) 'The importance of creative match in television sponsorship', *International Journal of Advertising*, 25(4): 471–88.

14. Rogers T. (2008) Foreword. In *Conferences and Conventions: A global industry*, Rogers T (ed.). Oxford: Butterworth Heinemann, pp. xiii–xvii.

15. Schmitt, B.H. and Pan, Y. (1994) 'Managing corporate and brand identities in the Asia Pacific Region', *Californian Business Review*, 36(4): Summer.

16. Shimp, T.A. (2006) *Advertising, Promotion, and Other Aspects of Integrated Marketing Communications*, Thomson South-Western.

17. Siu, W. and Au, A.K. (1997) 'Women in advertising: a comparison of television advertisements in China and Singapore', *Marketing Intelligence and Planning*, 15(5).

18. Subramanian, R. (2015). Soft-skills training and cultural sensitization of Indian BPO workers: A qualitative study. *Communications of the IIMA*, 5(2): 2.

19. Verma, R. (2014). 'Why attend tradeshows? A comparison of exhibitor and attendee's preferences', *Cornell Hospitality Quarterly,* 55(3): 239–251.

20. Wasserman, T., Khermouch, G. and Green, J. (2000) 'Mining everyones' business', *Brandweek*, February.

21. Whitfield, J., Dioko, L.D.A., Webber, D. and Zhang, L. (2014). 'Attracting convention and exhibition attendance to complex MICE venues: Emerging data from Macao', *International Journal of Tourism Research*, 16(2): 169–179.

22. Zhang, Y. and Neelankavil, J.P. (1997) 'The influence of culture on advertising effectiveness in China and the USA: a crosscultural study', *European Journal of Management*, 31(2): 134–49.

CHAPTER 10

THE MANAGEMENT OF INTERNATIONAL DISTRIBUTION AND LOGISTICS

LEARNING OBJECTIVES

After reading this chapter you should be able to:

■ Strategically evaluate potential foreign distribution options for a given situation

■ Discuss the complexities of efficiently managing intermediaries in an international marketing context

■ Appreciate the difference in retailing infrastructures across the globe

■ Advise and recommend potential solutions to developing a logistics strategy in foreign markets

■ Understand the export documentation process

INTRODUCTION

In Chapter 7 we examined strategies for international expansion and the options available for firms entering foreign markets. In this chapter we will build on the issues discussed in Chapter 7, but focus on managing the distribution and logistics within foreign markets.

The management of foreign channels of distribution is a key area in a firm's efforts to gain competitive advantage. As products become more standardized across the world, the ability to compete on customer service becomes more vital. In order to be effective in this area, a firm must have a well-managed **integrated supply chain** within foreign markets and across international boundaries.

International marketing involves companies operating in countries other than their own. The trend to a more globalized world implies an interconnected and interdependent world where capital, goods and services are freely transferred across national frontiers. As companies continue to pursue global strategies and operate in more and more countries, customers in every corner of the world expect to be served better, faster and by whatever channel suits them. To meet those expectations, organizations need to give a global, holistic view of their customers and really understand how to develop a globally integrated distribution system.

The ultimate goal may be to have a single system that offers all global customers a streamlined efficient service. For many companies in many markets in order to achieve that they first have to develop a real understanding of the mechanics of the operations of the distribution systems of the countries in which they operate.

In this chapter, we will examine the strategic issues in managing distribution channels and discuss the issues of selecting intermediaries and how to build long-term effective relationships in international markets. We will also examine the developments in retailing and the differences in retailing across markets at different levels of economic development.

Finally, we will examine the logistics of physically moving goods across national boundaries and the importance of efficient distribution management to minimize costs in international markets.

The challenges in managing an international distribution strategy

Recent events that have affected international marketing include the global recession and its recovery, austerity measures and emerging economies, all of which have changed the distribution channels for products and services. This chapter is dedicated to the challenges and opportunities around international distribution strategies.

Distribution channels are the means by which goods are distributed from the manufacturer to the end user. Some companies have their own means of distribution, some only deal directly with the most important customers but many companies rely on other companies to perform distribution services for them. These services include:

- the purchase of goods;
- the assembly of an attractive assortment of goods;
- holding stocks or inventory;
- promoting the sale of goods to the end customer;
- the physical movement of goods.

In international marketing, companies usually take advantage of a wide number of different organizations to facilitate the distribution of their products. The large number is explained by considerable differences between countries, both in their distribution systems and in the expected level of product sales. The physical movement of goods usually includes several modes of transport – for example, by road to a port, by boat to the country of destination and by road to the customer's premises. The selection of the appropriate distribution strategy is a significant decision. While the marketing mix decisions of product and marketing communications are often more glamorous, they are usually dependent upon the chosen distribution channel. The actual distribution channel decision is fundamental as it affects all aspects of the international marketing strategy; therefore the whole channel (also referred to as the supply chain) relies on each part of the distribution channel performing its task perfectly and on time.

The key objective in building an effective distribution strategy is to build a supply chain to your markets. In fact, as Kotler and Armstrong state (2014) the distribution channel . . . 'performs better if it includes a firm, agency or mechanism that provides leadership and has the power to assign roles and manage conflict.' (p. 367).

To achieve this across international markets is a daunting task and will mean the international marketing managers have to meet a number of important challenges in order to ensure they develop a distribution strategy which delivers the effective distribution of products and services. The major areas they will need to consider are as follows:

- *Selection of foreign country intermediaries.* Should the firm use indirect or direct channels? What type of intermediaries will best serve their needs in the marketplace?
- *How to build a relationship with intermediaries.* The management and motivation of intermediaries in foreign country markets is especially important to firms trying to build a long-term presence, competing on offering quality services.

■ *How to deal with the varying types of retailing infrastructure across international markets.* Achieving a coordinated strategy across markets where retailing is at varying stages of development and the impact of the growth of retailers themselves globalizing are important considerations in the distribution strategies of firms competing in consumer goods markets.

■ *How to maximize new and innovative forms of distribution.* Can be achieved particularly through opportunities arising through the Internet and electronic forms of distribution.

■ *How to manage the logistics of physically distributing products across foreign markets.* Firms need to evaluate the options available and develop a well-managed logistics system.

In the following sections of the chapter, we will examine the issues in each of these areas of international distribution and logistics.

Selecting foreign country market intermediaries

A distribution decision is a long-term decision, as once established it can be difficult to extract a company from existing agreements. This means that channels chosen have to be appropriate for today and flexible enough to adapt to long-term market developments.

In some instances, difficulties may arise because of legal contracts, as in the case of the termination of an agency; in other situations they result from relationships that need to be initiated and then nurtured. For example, the development of sales through wholesalers and distributors might be substantially influenced by the past trading pattern and the expectation of future profitable sales. Therefore, a long-term relationship needs to be developed before a firm is willing to invest significantly in an intermediary.

The long-term nature of distribution decisions forces a careful analysis of future developments. If new forms of distribution are emerging, for example, TV and mobile phone shopping, interactive media and e-retailing, this has to be considered early in the planning stage of the distribution channels for your market.

Another important challenge is the comparative inexperience of managers in the channel selection process in international markets. In domestic marketing, most marketing managers develop marketing plans which will usually be implemented within the existing arrangement of the company's distribution channels. This is quite a different proposition to the pioneering process of establishing a distribution channel in the first place and then achieving a well-supported availability through channel members in different country markets.

Furthermore, if foreign market channels are being managed from the home market, there may be preconceived notions and preferences that home market systems can operate elsewhere. As they are unfamiliar with the market, managers may underestimate the barriers to entry erected by local competitors and even government regulations. For instance, in both France and Japan there are restrictive laws which inhibit the growth of large retailers. In Japan no one can open a store larger than 5382 square feet without permission from the community store owners: thus it can take eight to ten years for a store to win approval.

Indirect and direct channels

One of the first decisions to make in selecting intermediaries for international markets is: should the product be distributed indirectly? In other words, using outside sales agents and distributors in the country. Or should the product be distributed directly, using the company's sales force, company-owned distribution channel or other intermediaries in a foreign country? The former option is an independent channel which is non-integrated and provides very little or no control over its international distribution and affords virtually no links with the end users. On the other hand, direct distribution, which is an integrated channel, generally affords the supplier more control and, at the same time, brings responsibility, commitment and attendant risks. As we have discussed, distribution decisions are difficult to change and so it is important for firms to consider the alternatives available and the differing degrees of commitment and risk, evaluate the alternatives and select the most appropriate type of distribution.

Integrated (direct) channels of distribution are seen to be beneficial when a firm's marketing strategy requires a high level of service before or after the sale. Integrated channels will be more helpful than independent channels in ensuring that high levels of customer service will be achieved.

Indirect channels on the other hand require less investment in terms of both money and management time. Indirect channels also are seen to be beneficial in overcoming freight rate, negotiating disadvantages, lowering the cost of exporting and allowing higher margins and profits for the manufacturer. An independent channel, therefore, allows the international firm to tap the benefits of a distribution specialist within a foreign market, such as economies of scale and pooling the demand for the distribution services of several manufacturers.

The advantages and disadvantages of indirect exporting were discussed in Chapter 7. In this section we will focus on issues facing firms who have made the decision to involve themselves with intermediaries in foreign country markets, either through the use of agents or distributors or using their own company-owned sales force. These intermediaries offer a wide range of services.

- *Export distributors* – usually perform a variety of functions including: stock inventories, handling promotion, extending customer credit, processing orders, arranging shipping, product maintenance and repair.
- *Export agents* – responsibilities often include: buyer/seller introductions, host market information, trade fair exhibitions, general promotional activities.
- *Cooperative organizations* – carry on exporting activities on behalf of several producers and are partly under their administrative control (often used by producers of primary products – e.g. bananas, coffee, sugar).

A company-owned sales force may be one of three types:

1 *Travelling export sales representatives.* The company can begin by sending home-based sales people abroad to gather important information, to make the necessary customer contacts and to conduct the negotiating and selling process.
2 *Domestic-based export department or division.* An export sales manager carries on the actual selling and draws on market assistance as needed. It might evolve into a self-contained export department performing all the activities in export and operating as a profit centre.
3 *Foreign-based sales branch or subsidiary.* A foreign-based sales branch allows the company to achieve greater presence and programme control in the foreign market. The sales branch handles sales and distribution and may also handle warehousing and promotion. It often serves as a display centre and customer service centre as well.

The choices available to a firm may well be determined by whether they are operating in the business-to-business (B2B) or business-to-consumer (B2C) sector. Figure 10.1 illustrates the choices for a supplier in the business-to-business market internationally.

The main channels in the B2B market tend to be agents, distributors and companies' wholly-owned sales force. The main distribution channels in the B2C market are shown in Figure 10.2.

Over the past few years there have been considerable developments in retailing across national boundaries. In a later section in this chapter, we will examine these trends and other new forms of retailing. First, however, we will look at the factors to consider in selecting channels of distribution and then building effective relationships with intermediaries.

Channel selection

In selecting appropriate channel intermediaries, a firm has to consider many factors. Czinkota and Ronkainen (2012) suggested the 11C model to explain the factors a firm should consider in their selection process. Figure 10.3 shows the 11C elements split into elements that are external to the organization and internal to the organization.

Customer characteristics and culture

Channels of distribution have usually developed through the cultural traditions of the country and so there are great disparities across nations, making the development of any standardized approach difficult.

FIGURE 10.1 Distribution channels for business goods

FIGURE 10.2 Distribution channels for consumer goods

The distribution system of a country can vary enormously. In Finland the main sectors of the Finnish economy are dominated by oligopolies. Consumables for everyday use are marketed by an integrated system of distribution dominated by three big groups: Kesko, the S Group (SOK) and Tradeka which control more than 90 per cent of the markets in the country. In Japan, the entire distribution system is based on networks with lots of wholesalers selling to other wholesalers. There are over 300 000 wholesalers and over 1.2 million retailers. Due to the price of land being so high in Japan, many wholesalers cannot carry stock in the traditional sense, so may order on a daily basis. This means that there are many layers between the foreign company entering the market and the final consumer.

FIGURE 10.3   The 11 Cs

11 Cs

External
- Customer
- Culture
- Competition

Internal
- Company objectives
- Character
- Capital
- Cost
- Coverage
- Control
- Continuity
- Communication

Source: Czinkota, M. and Ronkainen, I. (2012). *International Marketing.* Cengage Learning.

The Japanese system centres on distributor linkages to *dainyo* manufacturers, where the distributor accepts a subservient social status in return for economic security. From this interaction emerges vertical distribution networks called *Ryūtsū keiretsu*, in which units are arrayed in hierarchical layers and power resides at the 'commanding heights' of large *keiretsu*.

Keiretsu refers to a uniquely Japanese form of corporate organization. A *keiretsu* is a grouping or family of affiliated companies that form a tight-knit alliance to work toward each other's mutual success. It can best be understood as the intricate web of relationships that links banks, manufacturers, suppliers and distributors with the Japanese government.

Distributors at 'lower' layers in the structure are tied to the *Ryūtsū keiretsu, (Distribution Keiretsu)* system by bonds of loyalty, mutual obligation, trust and power that extend throughout existing distribution structures. While this arrangement guarantees members some degree of security, it also deprives them of economic freedom. Distributors that choose to deal with firms outside of the established group risk severing their ties with the group.

While distributors lack the freedom to transact with whomever they wish, they are also relieved of many costs associated with being independent – for example, smaller distributors in the system need not shoulder the risk of carrying inventories of products that will not sell and can depend on reliable delivery and financial help where necessary.

In the past decade the power of the *keiretsu* has started to diminish. Many faced debts through bad loan portfolios and were forced to merge or go out of business. Furthermore, companies from outside the *keiretsu* system, such as Sony and new international retailers entering Japan such as Toys'R'Us and McDonald's, have managed to grow by circumventing the system and outperforming their counterparts within the *keiretsu* networks, and this has led to an overall loosening of *keiretsu* alliances. The changes in automotive distribution have also had a major impact on the power of the *keiretsu* as can be seen in Illustration 10.1.

Sometimes non-Japanese businesses are described as *keiretsu*. The Virgin Group (UK) and Tata Group (India), and airline alliances such as Oneworld and the Star Alliance (USA), are seen to have similar characteristics to those of the Japanese *keiretsu*.

Thus, the characteristics of the customer and the cultural traditions of the country have a major impact on the choices available to a firm. A Belgian shopper may buy groceries from huge hypermarkets,

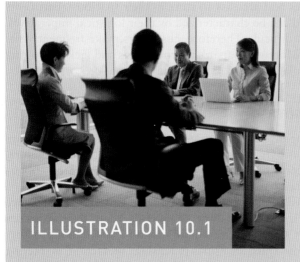

ILLUSTRATION 10.1

Japanese *keiretsu* and the automotive industry

Toyota, the global automotive brand, has used many distribution channels to move their cars from the manufacturer to the consumer. Toyota have traditionally moved their cars by ship, rail and other large road transport vehicles. Cars have moved from Toyota's manufacturing plants in Japan to London, Washington, Jakarta, Paris, in fact anywhere where there is a consumer market. Traditionally, Toyota has also used Japanese suppliers to provide parts for their cars, from steering wheels to seats, engines to headlight bulbs.

However, Toyota and their suppliers are facing a crisis. First, both are facing problems due to the recent economic changes brought on by the global recession, recession recovery and emerging markets. Second, the huge migration of Japanese citizens means their home market for cars and parts is diminishing year on year. And third, the *keiretsu system* has broken down.

The *keiretsu system* in Japan embodies a 'trust system' which brings with it a *favoured and guaranteed* distribution and purchasing system. Therefore, organizations in Japan, such as Toyota and their suppliers, have a further partnership system. An example of the partnership system comes in the format that Toyota invests money in their 'favourite suppliers' and the suppliers provide their best, most innovative products for Toyota. The age-old tradition of the bonded relationship between a car manufacturer,

such as Toyota (the *father*) and their 'favourite *son*' (the supplier of automotive parts) is at a turning point. Neither *father* nor *son* can continue solely within their *keiretsu system*. In fact both partners **must** find new partners to succeed.

Why the son needs to go beyond the *keiretsu system*

Automotive parts suppliers need to grow their business internationally because they too see their market shrinking due to the migration of Japanese citizens. Therefore, suppliers must seek new markets overseas, form new relationships (that do not have and/or know the *keiretsu system*) to survive. The markets that suppliers seek are other car manufacturers coming to set up business in Japan or they must go outside their country's borders to surrounding areas such as Indonesia and Thailand. This means the 'favourite *son*' is going outside the *keiretsu system* in order to grow their business.

Why the father needs to go outside the *keiretsu system*

Major Japanese car manufacturers including Toyota, Nissan Motor Corporation and Honda Motor Company are no longer making all their automobiles in Japan. All three are choosing to change their distribution model from manufacturing cars in Japan and distributing them around the world, to investing in new manufacturing plants nearer new consumer markets; indeed Mexico is one such country that large manufacturers see as a place to do business. Manufacturing plants in Mexico will need suppliers to provide steering wheels, seats, engines and headlight bulbs. However, to save distribution costs, the Japanese automobile brands manufacturing cars in Mexico are no longer asking their 'favourite *son*' in Japan to supply the parts. Thus the *keiretsu system* from the *father's* side is also breaking down.

Question

1 What are the strengths and weaknesses of the *keiretsu system*?

Source: Griemal, H. (2014) Japan's keiretsu suppliers: At risk in a new reality, published 29 November 2014 in *Automotive News* 89 (6640), 3–49. Available from www.autonews.com /article/20140929/OEM10/309299984/japans-keiretsu -suppliers-at-risk-in-a-new-reality (accessed 13 June 2015).

concentrating on purchases which have long shelf lives and are easy to store in their spacious apartments and houses. The Japanese customers on the other hand can be characterized by their logistical imperatives, as confined living space makes storage of goods very difficult. Therefore, customers make frequent visits to shops and rely on stores to keep their inventories. Moreover, Japan's narrow roads and lack of parking space (except for suburbs) predispose most of its population to do its shopping on foot.

Company objectives and competitive activity

The channel choice will also be determined by the company's objectives and what the firm's competitors are doing in a particular market. The distribution policy is part of a firm's international direction. Therefore, the distribution system developed will depend on the company's objective, i.e. whether their strategic objective is long term or short term and how quickly they need to realize their investment.

Most firms operating in international markets will endeavour to maintain a cost-effective balance between direct and indirect channels of distribution. Firms will use direct channels, perhaps their own sales force, in foreign country markets where their company's objective is to deliver high-value solutions to buying problems in order to maximize customer satisfaction. Thus, the firm is practising 'interaction' marketing as opposed to 'transaction' marketing. A firm whose objective is to build long-term, stable relationships with its foreign customers will have quite different objectives in the building of relationships throughout the supply chain than a firm with relatively short-term objectives in foreign country markets who purely wishes to complete the transaction before moving on to the next customer.

Character of the market

The characteristics of the market will also determine the choice available. Products often are introduced later into international markets than to the home domestic market; the company's image and awareness is normally lower, in many cases much lower, than in the domestic market and the market share attainable in the market is lower, at least initially. This makes it a much less profitable business proposition for distribution channel intermediaries. Furthermore, distribution channels are already being used by other companies who will have built up relationships with the intermediaries. This provides less space and opportunity for firms newly entering the market.

Developing countries are characterized by distribution systems consisting of a myriad of intermediaries and retail outlets. Such fragmentation results in cost inefficiencies as large volumes of product cannot be centralized and moved quickly from manufacturers to wholesalers to retailers.

Fragmented and circuitous channels also diminish possible competitive advantage by reducing the abilities of firms to get their products and services quickly and efficiently to masses of buyers. This is particularly the case for time-sensitive products. For example, overnight package couriers in some markets have failed in some cases to live up to delivery promises due to flight cancellations, poor road conditions and insufficient phone lines.

Often in emerging markets, the problems of fragmented distribution are compounded by legal restrictions as to which channels of distribution can be used by foreign importers.

The World Trade Organization is working towards the opening up of participation in distribution systems by foreign firms in a number of countries. India and Indonesia have eased restrictions, making it much easier for international companies to develop their own distribution systems. Previously foreign companies had not been allowed to set up their own distribution networks. Thailand has welcomed foreign investment, but then Tesco (UK) faced severe restrictions in Thailand when Thailand's ruling military council restricted their expansion plans in the country. However, many regions are actively encouraging the development of a global retailing industry. Illustration 10.2 gives an example in the Middle East.

Capital required and costings

In assessing the financial implications of channel selection, a firm needs to assess the relative cost of each channel, the consequences on cash flow and the capital required.

ILLUSTRATION 10.2

The Great Exhibition: Dubai's World Expo 2020

In 1851 London held the first WorldExpo named 'The Great Exhibition'. The Great Exhibition showcased amazing innovations, exotic flora and fauna, works from industry and inventions in the purpose-built Crystal Palace pavilion. Business people and consumers from around the world marvelled at the 'Koh-i-Noor' diamond (the largest cut diamond in the world), were mesmerized by the world's precursor to the fax machine, the telegraph, and 'spent a penny' to try out George Jennings' public toilet. WorldExpos like The Great Exhibition occur every five years and it is a great honour and benefit for a country to be awarded the opportunity to host a WorldExpo.

Dubai is hosting the WorldExpo 2020. In the past Dubai made its money from oil reserves, however, when the oil was running out they turned their attention elsewhere. Dubai invested in banking, hospitality, tourism and retail. Therefore, Dubai and the other emirates in the Middle East are actively seeking new markets. To do this, Dubai has opened its distribution channels to foreign investors and Dubai promotes itself as *the* place in which to do business. Distribution channels, and the accompanying rules and regulations,

have been improved in many ways, one of which is in and around the seaport of Jebel Ali, the busiest port in Dubai. The port deals with around 12 per cent of all cargo that comes to the Middle East and Dubai has plans to make Jebel Ali the biggest port in the world by 2030. One of the reasons the port receives such a high percentage of container loads of food, electronic equipment, steel, cars, concrete, buses and clothes is because it is a 'free zone'. The 'free zone' means that overseas businesses can operate without having to sign an agreement with a local business in Dubai, very different from many countries around the world. Additionally, the mountains of paperwork and bureaucratic red-tape often needed when importing and exporting goods via a seaport is very low. On top of that, taxes that businesses have to pay are lower at Jebel Ali port than other ports in the Middle East.

The port of Jebel Ali will play a crucial role in Dubai's WorldExpo 2020. Like The Great Exhibition in London; and all other WorldExpos, there will be a Pavilion that hosts some of the many exhibits. The Pavilion and all the ancillary buildings will have to be constructed. Additionally, there will be investment and improvements to roads and rail links including an extension to Dubai's Metro Red Line. To get exhibitors and consumers to the WorldExpo Pavilion, ExpoRider buses will be needed. Therefore, the Jebel Ali port will be incredibly busy before, during and after the WorldExpo. So much so, a new container dock will be built at this distribution hub.

Questions

1 How will the Jebel Ali seaport contribute to the success of the 2020 WorldExpo?

2 What are the business benefits of using Jebel Ali seaport compared to other ports in the region?

Source: Expo 2020 Dubai (2015) World Expos. Available from www.expo2020dubai.ae/en/world_expos (accessed 14 June 2015).

The relative costs of each channel   It is generally considered that it may be cheaper to use agents than set up a firm's own sales force in international markets. However, the firm has little control and may have little commitment from the agent. Also, if the company has long-term objectives in the market, then as sales develop the use of agents may be more expensive than employing the company's own sales force. A break-even analysis is necessary to evaluate the relative cost of each channel alternative over time.

Consequences on cash flow   If a firm uses wholesalers or distributors then traditionally they take ownership of the goods and the risks. This has a positive impact on cash flow. If the firm wishes to circumvent such channels and deal direct with the retailer or even the consumer, it means they have to be prepared to take on some of the traditional wholesaler services, e.g. offering of credit, breaking bulk, small orders. This means the firm will have capital and resources tied up in managing the distribution chain rather than developing the market.

Capital required   Direct distribution systems need capital injected to establish them. Non-recurring capital costs, as well as the recurring running costs when evaluating expected return in the long term, have to be taken into account.

A company also needs to evaluate whether it can raise the finance locally or whether borrowing restrictions are placed on foreign companies, what grants are available and what the regulations on earnings capital repatriation will be.

The coverage needed

Required coverage will also be a determining factor. In some markets, to get 100 per cent coverage of a market, the costs of using the company's own sales force may be too high making indirect channels more appropriate, especially in countries which are characterized by large rural populations. However, firms who rely on sparse retail outlets can maximize the opportunities that fragmented distribution channels afford. Avon has recruited and groomed armies of sales representatives to sell its cosmetics directly to millions in all reaches of Brazil, Mexico, Poland, China and Argentina. Altogether Avon is successfully operating in 26 emerging economies and targeting more, e.g. India, South Africa, Russia and Vietnam. They now have over 6 million Avon representatives in over 100 countries worldwide achieving sales of over US$10.7 billion.

Control, continuity and communication

If a firm is building an international competitive advantage in providing a quality service throughout the world then channels that enable the firm to achieve rapid response in foreign markets will be important, as will the development of a distribution system which gives them total control in the marketplace and effective direct communication to their customer.

It is the drive to achieve high levels of quality of service that, to some extent, has led to the breakdown of conventional barriers between manufacturers, agents, distributors and retailers, as firms strive to develop effective vertical marketing systems. Such firms will be selecting intermediaries which will enable them to be solution-orientated service providers operating on high margins across a multitude of international markets.

To achieve this, some manufacturers have bought themselves into retailing and other parts of the supply chain, while others, such as Benetton, have pursued similar results by franchising. From small beginnings Benetton now operates in 120 countries and has over 6200 franchised stores in the Benetton network.

The selection and contracting process

Having evaluated the criteria discussed above, a firm must select intermediaries capable of helping the firm achieve its goals and objectives. The intermediaries chosen must provide the geographic coverage needed and the services required in the particular international market(s). It is often desirable to select intermediaries that are native to the country where they will be doing business as this will enhance their ability to build and maintain customer relationships.

The selection process for channel members will be based upon an assessment of their sales volume potential, geographic and customer coverage, financial strength (which will be checked through credit rating services and references), managerial capabilities, the size and quality of the sales force, any marketing communications services and the nature and reputation of the business. In some countries, religious or ethnic differences might make an agent suitable for one part of the market coverage but unsuitable in another. This can result in more channel members being required to give adequate market coverage.

Before final contractual arrangements are made, it is thought wise to make personal visits to the prospective channel member. The long-term commitment involved in distribution channels can become particularly difficult if the contract between the company and the channel member is not carefully drafted. It is normal to prescribe a time limit and a minimum sales level to be achieved, in addition to the particular responsibilities for each party. If this is not carried out satisfactorily, the company may be stuck with a weak performer that either cannot be removed or is very costly to buy out from their contract.

Building relationships in foreign market channels

Management of sales activities and business relationships across international boundaries is a particularly complex and often overwhelming task. The combination of diverse languages, dissimilar cultural heritages and remote geographic locations can create strong barriers to building and maintaining effective **buyer–seller relationships**. Further, in international settings, communications are often complicated by a lack of trust – a critical dimension in any business relationship. Non-verbal cues, product origin biases, sales force nationality issues and differences in intercultural negotiation styles add even more complexity to the international business environment. Added to the traditional responsibilities of a sales manager, these factors make managing international relationships in distribution channels a unique and challenging task. Thus, it is crucial for firms and their sales managers both to understand and be able to work within various international markets throughout the world.

Motivating international marketing intermediaries

International marketing intermediaries can pick and choose the products they will promote to their customers. Therefore, they need to be motivated to emphasize the firm's products. As difficult as it is for manufacturers to motivate their domestic distributors or dealers, it is even more difficult in the international arena. The environment, culture and customs affecting seller–intermediary relationships can be complicating factors for the uninitiated.

Motivation, whether in the context of domestic or international channels, is the process through which the manufacturer seeks to gain the support of the marketing intermediary in carrying out the manufacturer's marketing objectives. Three basic elements are involved in this process (Rosenbloom 2009):

1 finding out the needs and problems of marketing intermediaries;
2 offering support that is consistent with their needs and problems;
3 building continuing relationships.

First, the needs and problems of international marketing intermediaries can be dramatically different from those at home. One of the most common differences is in the size of the intermediary. In emerging economies in Asia, Africa and Latin America, dealers may be family businesses with little desire to grow larger. This may also be true for more developed economies in Eastern Europe, Japan and Italy. Thus, they may not aggressively promote a foreign manufacturer's product.

Second, the specific support programme provided by the manufacturer to its international intermediaries should be based on a careful analysis of their needs and problems. Factors to be included are:

■ the adequacy of the profit margins available;
■ the guarantee of exclusive territories;
■ the adequacy and availability of advertising assistance;
■ the offer of needed financial assistance.

In light of the cost structures faced by many foreign market distributors and dealers, the need to provide them with good margin potentials on the imported products they handle is even more important. Doing so, however, may force manufacturers to change their ideas of what constitutes a 'fair' or 'reasonable' margin for foreign market distributors.

Territorial protection or even the guarantee of exclusive territories sought by many distributors in the domestic market can be even more desirable in foreign markets. On some international markets distributors, many of whom may have quite limited financial resources, will not want to assume the risk of handling and promoting a foreign manufacturer's product line if other distributors will be competing in the same territory for the same customers.

Advertising assistance for distributors and dealers is another vital form of support. A foreign manufacturer, especially a large one, can have an advantage over indigenous firms in providing advertising support because of its often greater financial resources and experience in the use of advertising. For example, firms such as Johnson Wax (with extensive distribution in Europe) and 3M (in Asia) have used their considerable resources and advertising expertise to support distributors to very good advantage in those markets.

Financial assistance in countries where intermediaries are small and fragmented is essential. Levi-Strauss found in Russia that they needed to give a six-month credit period to persuade intermediaries to stock their products. Their usual credit period was 30 to 60 days. Such constraints do not mean that manufacturers selling through foreign market intermediaries cannot build strong relationships with them; it is certainly possible to do so. However, the approach used may have to be quite different from that taken with intermediaries in their home market. Companies from the USA predominantly motivate distributors through financial incentives. However, in many other cultures motivating factors such as status, personal recognition and, in some cases management support, are much more important.

It is important to keep in regular contact with intermediaries. A consistent flow of all relevant types of communications will stimulate interest and sales performance. The cultural interface between the company and the channel member is the essence of corporate rapport. Business people from low context cultures may be thought to be insensitive and disrespectful by agents in high context culture countries. The problem can be compounded if sales performance is discussed too personally. According to Usunier and Lee (2005), precise measurement of sales people's performance, for example of the agent or the distributors, may be considered as almost evil in some countries. In South East Asia the ethic of non-confrontation clearly clashes with an objective to review performance. Various types of motivation need to be considered. In some cultures, intrinsic and group-related rewards work best. In the US, a country in which individualism and rationalism are the foundations of its society, individual and extrinsic rewards work best. In the UAE relationships and feedback are important; businesses need to understand that UAE intermediaries are not motivated by negative feedback, but are motivated by positive feedback; therefore, delivery of on-site training, on-site visits and joint agreement on objectives and task are beneficial.

Controlling intermediaries in international markets

The process of control is difficult. Control problems are substantially reduced if channel members are selected carefully, have appropriately drafted contracts which have been mutually understood and agreed and are motivated in a culturally empathetic way.

Control attempts are often exercised through other companies and sometimes through several layers of distribution intermediaries. Control should be sought through the development of written plans with clearly expressed performance objectives. These performance objectives would include some of the following: sales turnover per year, number of accounts, market share, growth rate, introduction of new products, price charged and marketing communications support. Control should be exercised through a regular report programme and periodic personal meetings.

Evaluation of performance and control against agreed plans has to be interpreted against the changing environment. In some situations, economic recession or fierce competition activity prevent the possibility of objectives being met. However, if poor performance is established, the contract between the company and the channel member will have to be reconsidered and, perhaps, terminated. In an age in which relationship marketing is becoming more important in the western world, the long-term building of suitable distribution relationships provides something of the eastern flavour of obligation and working together.

Channel updating

In managing distribution channels, firms need to ensure that as they increase their involvement in global markets they are able to adapt and update their channel strategy accordingly. Thus, the management monitoring and control mechanisms a firm puts in place should give them the ability to develop their presence in the marketplace. In China, Kodak ensured this capability was in place in their early negotiations when setting up their local manufacturing and distribution operations by taking over three lossmaking Chinese companies. They also offered a package to all their distributors offering help including marketing assistance to corner shops in exchange for becoming a Kodak Express and evicting competing film brands from the stores. Dell built a global brand by focusing on a direct sales model. However, they too have adapted their strategy in response to customer needs and have introduced a retail presence.

Developing a company-owned international sales force

Firms with expansion plans and an interest in becoming more involved in global markets will eventually take control of implementing their own marketing strategies and establish and manage their own international sales force. Generally, the firms begin to gradually move from indirect exporting to direct exporting via marketing intermediaries to a company-owned sales force (Kotler *et al.* 2009). The company can do this in several ways, including travelling export sales reps, a domestic-based export department or division and a foreign-based sales branch or subsidiary.

The advantages of using a company-owned sales force include:

- it provides far greater control over the sales and marketing effort because the sales force is now directly employed by the company;
- it facilitates formation of closer manufacturer–customer relationships;
- once established, the company-owned sales force can be helpful in identifying and exploiting new international marketing opportunities.

The disadvantages of developing a company-owned sales force include:

- a relatively larger resource commitment;
- somewhat higher exit costs should the firm decide to no longer serve a particular market;
- increased exposure to unexpected changes in the political/social environment of the host country.

One common strategy is to begin export operations by establishing a domestic-based export department and/or using home-based travelling salespeople. Then, as sales reach a certain volume in the new market, the decision is made to set up a foreign-based sales branch or subsidiary in the country.

The new unit may be strictly a marketing/sales arm or may also involve a production or warehouse facility. In either event, the firm must make a commitment of resources to develop its own direct sales force to sell the firm's offerings and build relationships with the firm's customers in that market.

It may well be that a firm uses its own sales force for key accounts and agents and distributors for small accounts. Equally, its own sales force may work in conjunction with international intermediaries, building links directly with customers but always with and through the intermediaries. This has the advantage of enabling the firm to build relationships with the customer and the intermediaries while not having to make the capital investment required to run a wholly-owned subsidiary.

However, for many multinationals, managing international operations is an issue of 'does the company control operations centrally or allow sales subsidiaries around the world a high degree of autonomy?' In some countries they may have little choice, due to the strength of local competition and the loyalty of local distributors to locally made brands.

Trends in retailing in international markets

Retailing structures differ across countries, reflecting their different histories, geography and politics. Retailing varies across the different levels of economic development and is influenced by cultural variations. The cultural importance attached to food in France provides the opportunity for small specialist food retailers to survive and prosper. In other developed countries, for example the US, the trend is towards very large superstores which incorporate a wide range of speciality foods. The French approach relies on small-scale production by the retail proprietor. The US approach encourages mass production, branding and sophisticated distribution systems to handle inventory and freshness issues.

In this section, our discussion will be concerned with three important issues for international marketers. First, the differences in the patterns of retailing around the world with particular reference to emerging markets and developing countries. Second, the internationalization of retailers and its impact on **distribution channel structures** and, third, the emergence of new forms of retailing which are particularly relevant to firms competing on international markets.

The differing patterns of retailing around the world

The concentration of the retailing industry varies significantly between markets. Low concentration ratios of retailer ownership give more power to the manufacturer. A 'no' decision from any one retailer does not make a big impact on total sales. While the low concentration ratios to be found in Japan and Italy and in many lesser developed countries increase the relative power of the manufacturer, there are problems. First, low concentration ratios in retailers might be counterbalanced by powerful wholesalers. Second, the costs of the sales force in calling on a multiplicity of very small retailers and the logistics of delivering products to them can reduce the manufacturer's profitability. If economies are sought by using wholesalers, the power balance might tilt away from the manufacturer to the wholesaler.

The main differences between traditional retailing structures found in lesser developed countries and the advanced retailing structures in more developed economies are illustrated in Table 10.1.

Retailing in developing countries is characterized by low levels of capital investment. The large size, purpose-built retail outlet, full of specialist display shelving and electronic point of sale equipment, is rarely found in less developed countries (LDCs). The more likely picture is of a very small space with goods sold by the counter service method and technology limited to a cash register or a pocket calculator. That does not mean to say that there are not innovations or exciting things happening in these markets. As you can see in Illustration 10.3 Nina Interiors, an East African retailer, is changing the way retailing business is done in that region.

Retail stores are often managed by the owner/proprietor and staffed by the extended family. The lack of capital input is partially offset by large quantities of low-cost labour and the management style is usually based on limiting risks. The retailer will seek to stock goods with a proven demand pattern. In addition, the retailer will try to obtain interest-free credit from the interface channel partners: the wholesaler and the manufacturer.

Table 10.1 Retailers – typical differences between developing and developed countries

Retailing issues	Traditional retailers in developing countries	Advanced retailing structures in mature economies
Concentration of retail power	Low	Often high
Site selection and retail location	Limited to the immediate locality	Very important, often sophisticated techniques to pinpoint the most valuable sites
Size of outlet	Limited	Large and tending to get larger
Retailer initiation of product assortment	Limited to the buy/no buy decision	Wide range of stock possible. Use of own-label and store-specific sales promotions
Retail concepts, images and corporate identity	Rarely used	Very important
Retailer-initiated sales promotion	Rarely used. Reliance on manufacturer and wholesaler-developed sales promotion and point of sale material	Very important
Use of retail technology	Limited	Vital e.g. EDI, EPOS
Service	Mainly counter-service	Mass customization, sophisticated CRM systems

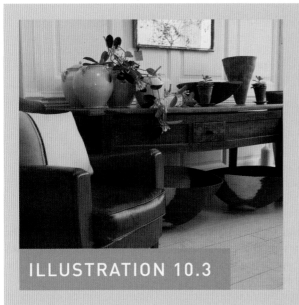

ILLUSTRATION 10.3

Nina Interiors: East Africa's High-End Superbrand

One of the SuperBrands of East Africa is Nina Interiors. Mrs Alice Karugaba worked as a secretary for the East African Development Bank in Uganda during the early 1980s. She also had a creative side and in 1981 she started to bake her favourite (and her customer's favourite) cakes and buns. Baking cakes and buns supplemented her income but also helped Mrs Karugaba become an international entrepreneur. In 1989, Mrs Karugaba partnered with McCrae's who made high quality interior furniture such as beds, sofas, cupboards, wardrobes, tables and chairs. However, McCrae's did not make soft furnishings; such as cushions, curtains and bed spreads and to provide their consumers with a full package of goods they employed Mrs Karugaba. The McCrae and Karugaba partnership was successful but in 1991 they parted company. At that time Mrs Karugaba stopped working for the bank and set up her own business called Nina Interiors. Her company was set up using only Mrs Karugaba's personal savings, one domestic sewing machine and one part-time seamstress.

Mrs Karugaba also wanted to offer her customers a full package of goods but she could not make interior furniture and as she and her part-time seamstress could only make soft furnishings Mrs Karugaba decided to import high quality interior furniture. Mrs Karugaba researched potential manufacturers and found that Malaysian companies provided the highest quality furniture. Therefore, Mrs Karugaba decided to import and subsequently retail interior furniture from Malaysian manufacturers in her retail store in Uganda. Later, when Mrs Karugaba became established she imported interior furniture from London and Dubai as well as Malaysia.

Being a woman doing business in East Africa had its challenges; particularly when trying to access finance from a Ugandan bank to fund the import activity. Additionally, the process of getting a special foreign exchange rate application, from the Central Bank of Uganda, was extremely time-consuming for her. However, Mrs Karugaba persevered and because she has kept Nina Interiors at the high quality-end of the furniture/soft furnishing market her customers include government and diplomatic corporate institutions, banks and oil companies, together with individual consumers that want something luxurious in their home.

Currently, Nina Interiors distributes products to two retails stores based in Kampala in Uganda and Kigali in Rwanda. Products are also displayed and shown on their retail store's website where orders can be placed online. Products now include home and office interior furniture and accompanying soft furnishing.

The Awards and Certifications confirm Nina Interiors' superiority:

2007: Established Nina Interiors Rwanda

2010: Best exhibitor, thirteenth Rwanda International Trade Fair

2009: Top 100 Medium sized Companies

2010: Top 100 Medium sized Companies

2011: Top 100 Medium sized Companies

2012: Top 100 Medium sized Companies

2012: First runner up Best Exhibitor Bride and Groom Expo

2013: People's Choice Award for Best Home and Office Furniture Products

2012: Full registration with UNGM (United Nations Global Marketplace)

2013: Superbrands (East Africa)

Nina Interiors has been recognized by the International Trade Centre to be a successful company that is exporting from Uganda, especially when it comes to the gender dimension of trade from Uganda. There are 40 staff, mainly women, making soft furnishings. The store in Uganda was also the first furniture store in Uganda that had a large store format (2000 sq m). This paved the way for other retailers to showcase their products in an open, design-led format.

Question

1 What do think were the main challenges and successes of Nina Interiors retailing business?

Sources: Superbrands (2014) East Africa's Superbrands – sub chapter: Nina Interiors. Available from www

.superbrandseastafrica.com/new/wp-content/uploads /downloads/Superbrands-EAST-AFRICA-Volume-IV.pdf (accessed 13 June 2015); International Trade Centre (n.d.) Case story on gender dimension of aid for trade. integrating gender into the National Export Strategy (NES) – A case for Uganda. Available from www.intracen.org/uploadedFiles /intracenorg/Content/About_ITC/Where_are_we_working /Multi-country_programmes/Women_and_trade /Integrating%20Gender%20into%20the%20National%20 Export%20Strategy.pdf (accessed 13 June 2015).

Distribution channels in developing countries depend on manufacturers and wholesalers for their sales promotion ideas and materials. In developed countries retailers often take the initiative regarding sales promotions and will develop their own schemes. The opportunities for the manufacturer to influence the retailer in advanced countries are becoming fewer and fewer.

Small-scale retailing limits the opportunities to follow own-label strategies. The minimum economies of scale cannot be reached by the small urban and rural retailer in developing countries. The balance of power lies with the manufacturer to innovate and adapt products.

The proliferation of very many small-scale retailers means that the retail market is widely dispersed. The levels of concentration of ownership are much lower than are found in mature economies with relatively structured levels of retailing.

These differences give rise to principally four stages of retailing around the world: traditional, intermediary, structured and advanced.

Traditional retailing

'Traditional retailers' are typically found in Africa, Asia, Latin America and Japan. The concentration of operators is weak, segmentation is non-existent and the level of integration of new technology is very low. These are often small-scale family retailing businesses employing few people and with a low turnover. Traditionally the retail market in India fell into this group and was largely unorganized; however with changing consumer preferences, organized retail is gradually becoming popular. Unorganized retailing in India consists of small and medium grocery stores, medicine stores, Subzi Mandi, Kirana Stores, Paan shops, etc. More than 90 per cent of retailing in India falls into the unorganized sector, the organized sector is largely concentrated in big cities. India's organized retail trade has generated a lot of interest among domestic and global retailing operators as it is viewed as being on the brink of change and poised for substantial growth. Organized retail in India is expected to grow 25–30 per cent yearly and is currently worth (2015) in the region of US$24 billion. This divergence in the sector brings particular challenges to global operators (see Illustration 10.4).

Intermediary retailing

Retailing in Italy, Spain and Eastern Europe is in the process of transformation, being both modern and traditional, and so examples of intermediary retailing. Most businesses are independent with a turnover lower than the European average. However, there is a marked tendency towards concentration, particularly in the food sector, where the number of food retailing outlets per 1000 people is dropping. The importance of wholesalers and voluntary chains is still very strong, particularly in Italy, where there are 192 000 whole-sale businesses.

In the major cities of China there have been huge developments in the retail structure of the country, taking retailing in the major cities to a very advanced status. China is encouraging mergers and partnerships between indigenous retailers to reduce costs and improve competitiveness and ensure they have the

MANAGEMENT CHALLENGE 10.1

Government and e-Choupal – Farming in the Wardha District

Agriculture in India is big business and accounts for 66 per cent of the workforce. This group of workers produce 23 per cent of the GDP for India. However, the distribution channel for farmers of smallholdings may be unfair. The vertical distribution channel is shown in Figure 10.4.

The distribution channel is flawed as the farmers are often unaware of global agricultural pricing trends. Additionally the farmers may be exploited as the price given at auction may be fixed between the purchasing agent and the national and international traders. Finally, farmers often have to wait for hours, if not days, to sell all their produce.

ITC Ltd are an exceptionally successful business in India and one of their core values is to generate economic value for the nation. They do not mean just their business should bring value to India, which is why when they saw the plight of rural farmers in India they decided to help. ITC Ltd developed an agricultural

Internet platform called e-Choupal for rural farming communities in India.

Choupal is Hindi for village meeting place. The e-Choupal provided a kiosk through which there is a virtual meeting place for rural farmers and a process for selling produce.

Farmers pay a very small fee to have ITC Ltd which includes hardware, such as a PC and Internet wireless hub, and software such as the agro farming package. The e-Choupal provides rural farmers with the opportunity to discover crop prices, soil-testing services, scientifically proven farming practices and weather reports, as well as informal chat with other farmers throughout the world.

There are two special services available via the e-Choupal kiosk:

1 Spot quote system: A farmer brings a small bag of produce, it is weighed and an on-the-spot price is given.

2 Produce handling system: The farmers arrange for all the produce they want to sell, following the spot price of course, to be collected. The collected produce is delivered to an ITC Ltd collection centre. Upon arrival of the produce at the collection centre the farmer is paid within 2 hours.

An unexpected benefit of e-Choupal is that school children have used the PC and wireless Internet system to help them with their homework.

FIGURE 10.4   Vertical distribution channel

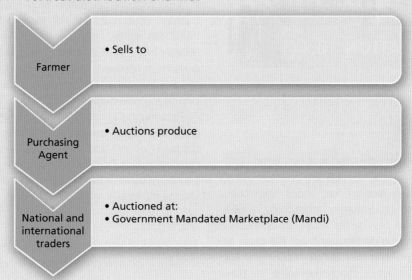

Farmer
• Sells to

Purchasing Agent
• Auctions produce

National and international traders
• Auctioned at:
• Government Mandated Marketplace (Mandi)

Questions

1 For an emerging market discuss disadvantages of the vertical distribution system shown in Figure 1.

2 What benefits has the Internet brought to rural farmers in India?

Source: Admane, R.A. (2014) 'ITC's e-Choupal: a marketing strategy for rural transformation – A case study of Wardha District', *Maharashtra International Journal of Management Research and Business Strategy* 3(1) January 249–257.

capacity to compete against such global operators as Walmart and Carrefour, who are fighting for a share of the US$1.8 trillion retail market. Shanghai Bailian Group Co. Ltd, China's largest retailer, is a vertical-integrated organization that manages the entire operation process from product design, to production, to sales. At present, products under the brand name of 'Bailian' are sold in more than 300 direct outlets throughout China. However, like India, outside the major cities of Shanghai and Bejing, China's retail sector is still dominated by small neighbourhood stores and local markets.

Countries with intermediary retailing structures are obviously attractive locations for retailers expanding internationally as they are seen as latent markets ripe for expansion. The level of economic development and the intermediary structure of retailing has historically meant that these countries are not host to large domestic retailers, making entry into the market relatively easy.

Over the course of the past decade, the entry of foreign operators into regions such as Latin America have altered the retailing landscape. There are now hypermarkets, variety stores and non-food specialists which have stimulated competition and greatly modernized retailing across the continent.

ILLUSTRATION 10.4

Comparative retailing traditions

In the UK, consumers are used to shops being open 7 days a week and in the US 24–7. In Germany, however, it is only recently that shops have been allowed to open on Saturday afternoons: a new federal law allows city centre shops to open until 8 pm. However, outside the city most still close at 4 pm for the weekend and Sunday opening is still highly restricted. This is much the same as New Zealand where stores close at 5.30 pm except for one night each week when they are open until 9.00 pm. Stores are also closed on Sundays and many are closed on Saturday afternoons.

In India, opening hours are unrestricted but most retail stores are family owned and are much smaller in size. With the exception of a few (small) super bazaars, consumers are not allowed to walk freely inside the stores, examine and compare labels of different brands before making the selection. Instead, consumers approach shops with a predetermined list of items to purchase, which are then pulled out of the bins by the salesperson.

Retailing in Greece has until recently been small-scale and highly traditional. The majority of stores are family owned and small in size and shopping for pleasure is less popular. However, the entry into the country of some of the big global retailers is starting to change the face of retailing there.

Question

1 How can a company achieve a global distribution strategy when retailing infrastructures vary so much?

Structured retailing

Retailing in the north of Europe tends to be fairly structured, reflecting the level of economic development. Denmark, Luxembourg, the Netherlands and France have enterprises larger in size, have a higher level of concentration and a greater level of productivity per employee than Southern European retailers.

In these markets, retail competition is fairly well developed and there is a mature relationship between suppliers and retailers.

Retailers also have introduced fairly sophisticated technologies facilitating more elaborate competitive strategies. They are also finding growth through opportunities overseas and new retailing formats.

Advanced retailing

The US, Germany and the UK are all examples of countries in which retailing is the most advanced in terms of concentration, segmentation, capitalization and integration. Retailer strategies are advanced and are very market focused, and generally incorporate five important dimensions.

Interactive customer marketing. Targeting of customers as individuals, developing strategies to improve retention and increase sales per shop visit.

Mass customization. Retailers are looking for improved margins through higher volumes, reduced costs and achieving low levels of returns.

Data mining. Retailers are using technology and electronic point of sale (EPOS) information to improve knowledge of customers, ensure the ability to make targeted offers which are timely and clearly differentiated. Data mining is beginning to be used by retailers in emerging and developing markets where previously there has been little reliable data on which to base decisions as can be seen in Illustration 10.3 in the case of Nina Interiors.

Category management. Retailers are aiming to achieve improved levels of customer satisfaction through reducing costs, reducing mark downs and optimizing product assortment.

Effective consumer response. Retailers are establishing permanent links with manufacturers, establishing electronic data interchange (EDI) systems for efficient inventory replenishment and ensuring a continuous just-in-time delivery of supplies.

In these markets the balance of power in the supply chain, for the present at least, seems to lie firmly with these large retailers, who are increasingly dictating the trends in their home markets and as these reach maturity are seeking growth opportunities by expanding internationally.

The globalization of retailing

One of the key trends in international distribution over the past few years has been the aggressive strategies employed by many major retailers as they have pursued global marketing objectives. Tesco, the French hypermarket groups Auchan, Carrefour and Promodes, and the German discount food retailers Aldi, Lidl and Swartz have all expanded globally. The e-commerce sector, a distribution system that has grown exponentially in recent years, is now dominated by huge global retailers and Table 10.2 gives the top ten in the world. However, it is not just in food that retailers are going global; the US retailer Walmart and specialists Toys'R'Us, Home Depot, Staples, Benetton, Body Shop and Hertz are all now global retailers. Hong Kong retailers A S Watson and Dairy Farm have entered neighbouring countries with supermarkets and pharmaceutical chains, and Japanese department stores Takashimaya and Isetan have established outlets across Asia. More recently this trend has accelerated, with German retailers Metro, Rewe and Tengelmann expanding into the Czech Republic, Hungary and Poland, often using joint ventures with former socialist cooperatives. Three western European retailers, Tengelmann (Germany), Ahold (Netherlands) and Delhaizae Le Lion (Belgium), now generate more sales and profit from their foreign activities, which include the US, Central Europe and Asia, than they do in their home markets. The smaller high-growth economies such as Ireland have also been generating the particular interest of the expanding globals.

The expansion of international activity of retailers around the world has given rise to four different types of international retailers: the hypermarket, the power retailers, the niche retailer and the designer flagship stores who target particular global cities for their stores. Examples of these cover a range of product

Table 10.2 Top 10 global powers of retailing

Top e-retailer sales rank FY$_{13}$	Name of company	Country of origin	FY$_{13}$ e-commerce retail sales (US$ mil)	FY$_{13}$ e-commerce retail sales % of total retail revenue	FY$_{13}$ e-commerce growth rate
1	Amazon.com Inc.	US	$60 903.00	100.0%	17.7%
2	JD.com Inc.	China	$10 826.75	100.0%	66.2%
3	Walmart Stores Inc.	US	$10 000.00	e 2.1%	29.9%
4	Apple Inc.	US	$9 000.00	e 30.8%	n/a
5	Otto (GmbH & Co KG)	Germany	$8 188.94	e 61.3%	7.0%
6	Tesco PLC	UK	$5 250.54	e 5.3%	11.0%
7	Liberty Interactive Corporation	US	$4 884.00	47.4%	10.9%
8	Casino Guichard-Perrachon S.A.	France	$3 952.82	6.2%	19.4%
9	Suning Commerce Group Co., Ltd.	China	$3 100.00	e 11.1%	37.8%
10	Macy's Inc.	US	$3 100.00	e 11.1%	37.8%

Source: National Retail Federation (2015) Top 250 global powers of retailing, published 11 January. Available from www.nrf.com/news/2015-top-250-global-powers-of-retailing (accessed 13 June 2015).

categories including fashion, jewellery, food and beverages, home furnishings and speciality stores. Alberta Ferretti, Joseph, Alexander McQueen, Manolo Blahnik, Agent Provocateur, Galliano, Tom Ford and Lanvin are leading names in the global high fashion niche retailing.

As well as the growing sophistication of the industry and the opening up of new markets around the world, the globalization of retailers can be attributed to a number of 'pull' and 'push' factors.

The 'push' factors are:

- saturation of the home market or over-competition;
- economic recession or limited growth in spending;
- a declining or ageing population;
- strict planning policies on store development;
- high operating costs – labour, rents, taxation;
- shareholder pressure to maintain profit growth;
- the 'me too' syndrome in retailing.

The 'pull' factors are:

- the underdevelopment of some markets or weak competition;
- strong economic growth or rising standards of living;
- high population growth or a high concentration of young adults;
- a relaxed regulatory framework;

- favourable operating costs – labour, rents, taxation;
- the geographical spread of trading risks;
- the opportunity to innovate under new market conditions.

Marketing implications for development of international distribution strategies

The internationalization of retailing has meant a new era of distribution is developing. This new competitive landscape in distribution has a number of implications for the development of the distribution strategies of international firms. The most important of these are:

- power shifts in supply chains towards retailers;
- intense concentrated competition with significant buyer power across country markets;
- rapidly advancing technology facilitating global sourcing and global electronic transactions;
- unrelenting performance measures being demanded of suppliers by international retailers;
- smart, demanding consumers expecting high levels of customer service.

Thus, power in many international markets is moving from the supplier down the supply chain to the consumer. This means effective management is critical to suppliers competing in international markets. It again highlights the importance of ensuring the distribution strategy across international markets is driven by an understanding of the target market segments, both within each foreign country market and across national market boundaries.

This intensive growth in the size and power of retailers in countries with advanced retailing structures and retailers internationalizing means there is now tremendous pressure on suppliers to improve the quality of service to them. Retailers are demanding:

- streamlined and flexible supply chains;
- suppliers who can guarantee quality and reliability across global markets;
- the ability to supply high volumes and close relationships with intermediaries in the supply chain;
- suppliers who can meet the global sourcing requirements of large-scale retailers who wish to buy centrally across the globe.

It could mean, therefore, that the firms who are successful are the firms who develop the capability to compete effectively in the supply chain activities compared to their international competitors. It is for this reason that the distribution strategy of the international company has taken on such an important dimension in recent times.

Internet retailing

Multimedia technology has provided a number of opportunities for interactive shopping which offer particular opportunities in international markets. Tele-shopping and the Internet offer suppliers the retailing opportunities for direct contact with consumers throughout the globe. What is more, they can achieve this without the problems and expense of having to establish infrastructures in foreign country markets. For example, Amazon.com, the bookshop which sells purely over the Internet, carries no books as they are directly shipped from the publishers' or distributors' warehouses. This means Amazon have few inventory or real estate costs. They offer 2.5 million titles including every English language book in print, whereas even the largest bookstore would only stock 170 000. EToys, the Internet competitor to Toys'R'Us, has no retail outlets but a higher market capitalization than Toys'R'Us. EToys and Amazon proactively trap individual information on consumer purchases and then flash messages back telling consumers of other products bought by consumers making similar purchases. The diffusion of the Internet is increasingly challenging the traditional channels of distribution. It has the capacity to bring together buyers and sellers around the world through the creation of an online marketplace. However, despite exponential growth in access to the Internet, consumers are still limiting their purchases to relatively few product lines. It is esti-mated that nearly 40 per cent of all Internet purchases are for travel, another 26 per cent for the purchase of tickets for events and concerts, and 25 per cent is spent on books and CDs.

In international marketing the major impact, as we will discuss in Chapter 12, has been the ability of the Internet to enable small- and medium-sized companies to access niche markets around the globe that were previously too logistically difficult for them to access. By simply setting up their own sites, a company in effect becomes global and can sell goods and services throughout the world. However, there has also been the development of market sites which have impacted on the way business transactions take place internationally, such as:

- *Auctions.* Online marketplaces where negotiations of price between independent buyers and sellers are implemented through a standard auction open to all participants (e.g. eBay, Dabsexchange, On Sale).
- *Single buyer markets.* Where a large buyer establishes an online intranet market for its own suppliers (e.g. GE Trade Web), usually for them to gain access to the site the suppliers will have achieved the status of approved supplier.
- *Pure exchanges.* Where individual buyers and sellers are matched according to product offers and needs.

The most promising products are often those where existing intermediaries do not perform many of the traditional 'wholesaler' functions for a broad market owing to the high cost of servicing small diverse and geographically or functionally dispersed players. There are several market characteristics in international markets which favour the development of Internet-based distribution:

- *Inefficiencies in traditional distribution channels,* as in Japan where it is difficult for international operators to penetrate the market so sellers cannot gain access to customers.
- *Market fragmentation.* Niche market players where customers are geographically dispersed across the globe and are not concentrated in any one country.
- *Minimum scale barriers.* Smaller exporters have traditionally been restricted from operating globally because of the costs and difficulties of exporting, and therefore lose out to larger players who reap economies of scale and exploit distribution relationships.
- *Commodity-type products.* Products with well-known technical specifications, or manufacturer brands that can easily be price-compared across countries and do not require substantial after-sales service.
- *Short life cycle products.* Product-markets with short life cycles create large quantities of obsolete and discontinued items. Customers may experience difficulty finding spare parts or compatible accessories for earlier generations of product.

The management of the physical distribution of goods

Physical distribution management (PDM) is concerned with the planning, implementing and control of physical flows of materials and final goods from points of origin to points of use to meet customer needs at a profit (Kotler *et al.* 2009).

In international physical distribution of goods the total distribution costs will be higher than domestic distribution. The extra activities, increased time taken and the need to adapt to special country require-ments will all increase costs. The extra costs centre around three areas:

1 *Increased distance;* this means, in terms of costs, increased transport time, inventory, cash flow and insurance.
2 *New variables to consider;* new modes of transport (air, sea, rail, road), new types of documentation, packaging for long transit times.
3 *Greater market complexity;* language differences require the translation of documents, the extra costs of bureaucracy and longer lines of communication.

MANAGEMENT CHALLENGE 10.2

The Philippines: Growth potential but distribution headaches

If a country is to be successful in the current business environment it must have a good infrastructure. There are four elements that when combined together make a good infrastructure. The elements are 1. Power supply; 2. Transport network; 3. Telecommunications; and of course 4. Water and sanitation. If any of the elements are poor or inadequate the quality of life for the country's citizens, and also the potential for growth, is severely affected.

The Philippines has the potential to grow. It is also a country which many global franchise brands are eager to do business with. However, there are some infrastructure issues in the Philippines. For example, around only 50 per cent of the population (20 per cent in rural areas) have piped water supplied to their homes. Open sewers and solid waste is commonplace in cities due to deterioration of pipes and sanitation systems. Adequate sanitation and power supplies of electricity cannot keep up with the growth in urbanization and city living. Clearly investment in power and sanitation is needed.

Investment in roads has also been limited in the Philippines. Distribution of products or building materials for hotels, restaurants, office blocks and housing is problematic. Of the 11 000 kilometres of paved roads around 50 per cent is considered to be of poor quality. This means distribution of products is slow and the pot-holes can seriously damage the vehicles that transport products.

The Philippines has many seaports, with Manila being one of the busiest seaports in the world. However, cargos and containers full of produce, cars or building materials are often delayed or hampered by inadequate logistics from many of the seaports.

The market entry rules and regulations for telecommunications companies are slow, bureaucratic and very expensive. All telecommunication service providers have to have a franchise agreement and a certificate from the National Telecommunications Commission (NTC). Further, some telecommunication service providers are reluctant to complete the franchise agreement and get the certificate from the NTC as both are seen to be politically driven and corrupt processes.

Question

1 What should the Philippines do to be successful in the global business environment?

It is important for the firm to take full account of all these extra costs when evaluating alternative distribution strategies. In taking the **total distribution cost** approach, firms will include the costs of transport, warehousing, inventory, order processing, documentation, packaging and the total cost of lost sales if delays occur. Companies find that changes to one element of distribution influence the performance and the costs of other elements. Management Challenge 10.2 shows that infrastructure problems can also make the physical distribution of products difficult.

The logistics approach to physical distribution

Many writers on physical distribution use logistics and physical distribution as terms meaning the same thing. Kotler and Armstrong (2014) make the distinction between physical distribution as a more traditional activity and logistics as being more market-orientated. In this way, physical distribution thinking starts with the finished product at the end of the production line and then attempts to find low-cost solutions to get the product to the customer. Logistics thinking, on the other hand, considers the customer and then works back to the factory. In this section we will use the market-oriented view. We will use the term logistics to mean an integrated view of physical distribution management in which customer demand influences are at least as important as cost-cutting forces. More and more companies are integrating their physical distribution strategies and linking their operations in different countries with more common processes, thus rationalizing their manufacturing and distribution infrastructure to make more effective use of business resources and so taking a logistical view of their distribution operations.

In Europe, 75 per cent of businesses operating across European markets have a pan-European **logistics or distribution strategy** in place. McKinsey Consultants estimate the European logistics market to be worth about US$400 billion. The logistics function is having an increasing influence in many parts of the business, especially in inventory planning, information technology, purchasing and manufacturing.

There are a number of factors influencing this change:

- Customers demanding improved levels of customer service.
- **Electronic Data Interchange (EDI)** becoming the all-pervading technology for firms to build links with customers, suppliers and distribution providers.
- Companies restructuring their physical distribution operations in response to the formation of regional trading blocs.

In the following sections, we will briefly examine the developments in each of the above areas.

Customer service

The main elements of customer service will revolve around:

- order to delivery time;
- consistency and reliability of delivery;
- inventory availability;
- order size constraints;
- ordering convenience;
- delivery time and flexibility;
- invoicing procedures, documentation and accuracy;
- claims procedure;
- condition of goods;
- salesperson's visits;
- order status information;
- after-sales support.

In developing customer service levels it is essential to use the elements of service that the customer regards as important. Delivery reliability might be more important than a quick order to delivery time that is unreliable in meeting delivery schedules. Understanding the way in which the international customer perceives service is important. There will be considerable differences. Customers who are distant might be more concerned about the guarantees of reliable rapid availability than customers much closer to the production source. The corporate capability to meet widely differing customer requirements in different countries needs to be managed.

In all countries, customers are becoming increasingly demanding. Partnership arrangements are becoming significant in many sectors as supply chains become more integrated. These developments are usually driven by customer-led demands for improved service. Consumers are demanding ever-quicker delivery and ever more added value from their products that increasingly require just-in-time distribution. Companies increasingly allow customers to track the progress of products through the distribution system via the Internet. The websites which allow customers to track the progress of their packages are attracting 1 000 000 hits a day. The other major area of IT involvement is in stock control and buying. Despite having 600 stores in 14 countries and using 12 different own labels, C&A is still able to deliver nine times a day to its stores due to its efficient centralized buying operation for men's and children's wear in Brussels and women's wear in Düsseldorf.

The restructuring of physical distribution operations

In mature trading regions such as the US and Europe, a large number of firms have restructured their distribution networks in response to changes in the trading structures in the region. Cross-border deliveries have increased and the number of factories and warehouses has decreased. The number of distribution centres serving more than one country has increased whereas there has been a decrease in the number of warehouses dedicated to within-country movements.

Lucent Technology dispatches all its products from its factory in Spain to a test and assembly centre in Singapore before final delivery. It might go back to a customer sitting 10 kilometres away from the factory in Spain, but it will still go to Singapore. The company gives a 48-hour delivery guarantee to customers anywhere in the world, posing demanding logistical challenges.

The physical movement of goods is a high-cost activity. Companies often incur 10 to 35 per cent of their expenditure on physical distribution. As distribution is so expensive, it is now receiving close attention from general management and from marketing management.

The logistics approach is to analyze customer requirements and to review what competitors are providing. Customers are interested in a number of things: deliveries to meet agreed time schedules, zero defect delivery, supplier willingness to meet emergency needs, supplier willingness to replace damaged goods quickly, and supplier willingness to engage in just-in-time (JIT) delivery and inventory holding.

If a company is to achieve a logistically effective system of distribution it will become involved in a highly complex and sophisticated system and will, therefore, need to:

- clearly define areas of responsibility across foreign country markets;
- have a highly developed planning system;
- have an up-to-date and comprehensive information support system;
- develop expertise in distribution management;
- have a centralized planning body to coordinate activities and exercise overall control.

Thus, a logistical system helps the company to pay attention to inventory levels and think through market relationships, to minimize costs of stock out and maximize distribution efficiency across a large number of markets.

In developing an efficient logistical system of physical distribution across international markets there are a number of important considerations:

- how intermediaries such as freight forwarders can enhance our service;
- what modes of transportation should be used;
- how the firm can make effective use of export processing zones;
- what documentation is required;
- what are the packaging requirements for transit and the market;
- how should the export sales contract be organized.

In the following sections, we will briefly discuss some of the important issues in each of these areas.

The use of intermediaries

Traditionally, intermediaries such as forwarders and freight companies simply offered transportation by land, sea and air. There are now many types of intermediaries which offer global logistical services. FedEx, UPS and DPWN (Deutsche Post World Net, which absorbed DHL) have global networks to offer express-delivery services which they also use to offer customized logistics solutions. Brokering houses such as Kuehne & Nagel offer their skills in tying together different modes of transport. Other companies offer specialized services, for instance transport and warehouse-management firms which organize the physical movement and storage of goods. Still others are dedicated contract carriers and freight forwarders, who buy capacity on ships and cargo planes, and put together loads from different companies to fill them. Most freight forwarders will offer services such as preparation and processing of international transport documents, coordination of transport services and the provision of warehousing. (See Illustration 10.5).

However, as we have seen in the above section, recent trends such as just-in-time delivery, outsourcing of non-core activities, cutting inventories and the trend to build to order (BTO) have meant international firms have had to build a comprehensive but flexible logistical operation to ensure goods reach their customers

ILLUSTRATION 10.5

Freight forward 900m tins of baked beans

A freight forwarder is a company that dispatches shipments via carriers and books or otherwise arranges space for shipments. Carriers could include vessels, aeroplanes, trucks or railroads.

Freight forwarders arrange cargo to an international destination and have the expertise that allows them to prepare and process the documentation *and* perform activities that are needed for international shipments.

During 2014 European freight business saw a positive growth in business. Overall 46.9 million 'twenty-foot equivalent units' (TEUs) passed through European seaports alone. This is an increase of 5.4 per cent on the previous year. Whilst it is difficult to imagine something of this scale, a container is 20 ft (length) × 8 ft (width) × 9 ft (height). There are around 6000 'very large' container ships that carry around 16 000 TEUs. Therefore, an enormous number of products are imported and exported via the sea. Some container ships will commence their voyage and take a week to deliver their cargo; often calling at a number of seaports along their journey. The world's biggest container ship, called the *CSCL Globe* made its maiden voyage and docked at Felixstowe

in Suffolk, UK on 7 January 2015. The owner of the port of Felixstowe, Paul Davey of Hutchison Ports (UK) Limited, was extremely proud the *CSCL Globe* docked. He stated that 30 000 local people are employed in the transport industry so getting mega container ships to dock in Felixstowe is positive news economically. He and the hundreds of spectators who saw the *CSCL Globe* dock were amazed at the size of the ship. She carries 19 100 containers.

Four thousand of the containers held food, drink, clothing, electrical goods and furniture which equates to 57 000 tonnes of cargo. The actual ship measures 400 m (1312 ft) from stem to stern which is slightly longer than four football pitches placed end to end. Instead of carrying 900 million tins of baked beans it is estimated the *CSCL Globe* could carry 156 million pairs of shoes or 300 million tablet computers.

Not all seaports could dock the *CSCL Globe* because (a) it is too large, or (b) the cranes or lifting-gear to load and unload the ship is inadequate. The port of Felixstowe invested £300 million in their port to accommodate the mega cargo ships. So much so that in March 2015 the *MSC Oscar* docked in Felixstowe. The *MSC Oscar* is slightly smaller than the *CSCL Globe*, but can carry 124 more containers than the *Globe*.

Question

1 What are the benefits, of using container ships as a distribution channel?

Sources: BBC News (2015) *CSCL Globe*: Felixstowe arrival for world's largest container ship, published 7 January. Available from www.bbc.co.uk/news/uk-england-suffolk-30700269 (accessed 18 May 2015); BBC News (2015) World's largest container ship *MSC Oscar* in Felixstowe, published 9 March 2015. Available from www.bbc.co.uk/news/uk-england-suffolk-31798664 (accessed 18 May 2015).

around the world in the right place at the right time. This is such a challenging task that companies are no longer able to do it all themselves, so more of them are using intermediaries and outsourcing the logistical functions. This has meant the global freight-transport industry itself has had to reshape, as manufacturers seek service suppliers with global reach. Manufacturers want custom-designed delivery systems, using all types of transport – land, sea and air. Many of the larger firms now offer a whole range of options beyond their original specific function. This has meant that distinctions between the various intermediaries, such as freight forwarders, transport companies, express couriers and logistics services are blurring.

All intermediaries deal with three parallel flows: physical goods, information and finance (leasing, lending and brokerage). What is happening now is that while previously intermediaries specialized in one of the flows they are now offering the full range of services. Even global manufacturers are entering the logistics business. Caterpillar, which makes construction equipment, uses the global distribution network it has already developed as a channel for the products of other manufacturers.

There have been two driving forces for this. First, global competition has meant a downward pressure on costs. This has spawned the phenomenon that began in the logistics sector with outsourcing, but has extended to the whole range of other services now regarded as legitimate logistics tasks. Indeed, many of the multinational logistics companies such as DPWN, FedEx, UPS and TNT, the so-called integrators, themselves outsource the functions they take on to small specialist suppliers. See Management Challenge 10.3 for innovative ways logistics are handled in the air.

Second, the technological advances discussed earlier mean that logistics specialists are able to offer increasingly sophisticated services to exporters that firms cannot provide in-house. For example, a firm's products might once have passed from factory to national warehouse and then on to a foreign regional warehouse, then to a local depot, before delivery to the end consumer: a wasteful process in terms of time and cost. Today, using state-of-the-art systems, a logistics specialist taking responsibility for the warehouse function will deliver to the customer direct from the main warehouse, cutting out three of four links in the chain.

At the more advanced end of the logistics services spectrum, companies are handing control of more and more roles to their logistics partners. This is partly driven by the sheer geographical complexity of many exporters' operations where, for example, head office, factory and customer may be separated by thousands of miles.

As more companies attempt to develop the newly opened emerging markets where they have little knowledge or understanding of the distribution system, the use of third party intermediaries to organize logistics is becoming an essential part of a global marketing strategy.

Transportation

The physical handling and movement of goods over long distances will practically always have to be performed by third parties.

Transportation is the most visible part of the physical distribution strategy. The main options are:

- *Ocean transport:* capacity for large loads of differentiated products, raw materials, semi-finished goods, finished goods. Handling of goods in bulk, in packaged or unitized form, pallets, containers.
- *Inland waterway transport:* heavy and bulk products. Growing container transport. Restrictions because of need for suitable loading/unloading terminals.
- *Air transport:* urgent shipments, perishables, low-density light/high value, relatively small shipments.
- *Road transport:* most flexible door-to-door transport for all kinds of products but mostly finished goods. Container transport.
- *Rail transport:* long distance heavy and bulk products. Container transport.

Ocean and inland waterways   Sea and inland waterways provide a very low-cost way to transport bulky, low value or non-perishable products such as coal and oil. Water transport is slow and is subject to difficulties caused by the weather; for example, some ports are iced over for part of the winter. Water transport usually needs to be used with other modes of transport to achieve door-to-door delivery.

One of the policies used to encourage growth in South Korea, a newly industrialized country, has been the stimulation of its shipping and shipbuilding industry.

Ocean shipping can be **open market**, i.e. free ocean where there are very few restrictions, or it can be organized in conferences which are essentially cartels that regulate rates and capacities available on routes.

As in other areas of distribution, the containerization of ports and the impact of information technology have meant sea transport has become a capital-intensive industry where there is high pressure to achieve full capacity utilization.

The costs of ocean freight, as a result, have declined over the past decade and so it is still the most cost-effective method of transporting goods to distant markets.

The average cost for a six-metre dry cargo container to be shipped from the UK to Shanghai in China will be £1000–£1550 and the approximate transit time would be 20–25 days.

MANAGEMENT CHALLENGE 10.3

Amazon Prime Air

Some products take weeks to arrive if the manufacturer chooses to use freight as their distribution channel. Music can be purchased and downloaded within minutes. The twenty-first century young consumer is more inclined to want their products and services quickly. Amazon understand this, especially when so many consumers pre-order Harry Potter and Batman: Arkham Knight for PS4 or the latest version of Kindle because they want to be the first to have the new product. Additionally, the speedy delivery postal option for products is on the increase and the delivery of products within five days is on the decline. Amazon has devised a way to deliver products usually delivered by post, to customers within 30 minutes. Amazon promote the fact that their Prime Air will deliver products anywhere within 30 minutes. The Amazon Prime Air is a drone which takes to the sky from an Amazon Depot and it will deliver products to consumers at home, their office, on a boat in a lake, or even to a person hiking across the Yorkshire Pennines. Consumers are at the heart of this logistical operation. And it is through the consumers GPS signal on their Smartphone that the Amazon Prime Air will locate the consumer and deliver the parcel. The drone has been fitted with flight sensors, sonar, cameras and radars to ensure the drone avoids any obstacles that may damage the product it is delivering.

The non-manned machine-2-machine air delivery service is also being used by DHL who use drones, called parcelcopters, to deliver health parcels to a remote island off the German coast. Google is also using drone-based delivery services to deliver cattle vaccines to farmers in Australia.

Question

1 What are the benefits of the non-manned machine-2-machine air distribution channel used by Amazon, DHL and Google?

Source: BBC (2015) Amazon details drone delivery plans, published 8 May 2015. Available from www.bbc.co.uk/news /technology-32653269 (accessed 13 May 2015).

However, a number of hidden costs can arise in overseas shipping:

- overseas warehousing costs due to having to send large inventories in container loads;
- inventory losses from handling spoilage, theft, obsolescence and exchange rate charges in manual time;
- cost of time in transit;
- lost sales from late arrival.

Inland waterways are very important in countries with poor infrastructures. In Vietnam the most popular mode of transportation is by water. A dense network of waterways exists, although even this system will suffer the vagaries of both flood and drought conditions.

Air   Air freight is considerably more expensive per tonne/kilometre than the other modes of transport. Air freight is particularly appropriate for the movement of high-value low-bulk and perishable items. For example, diamonds, computer software, specialist component parts and cut flowers use air freight. Air freight is extending its market through promoting its advantages. The higher freight charges can often be offset. Packing costs and insurance rates are significantly less by air. Storage en route, overseas warehousing and inventory losses may all be less by air as will the actual cost of the time in transit. In addition, the development of larger and more flexible aeroplanes for air freight has helped reduce costs.

Road   Very flexible in route and time. Schedules can deliver direct to customers' premises. Very efficient for short hauls of high-value goods. Restrictions at border controls can be time-consuming, however, and long distances and the need for sea crossings reduce the attractiveness of freight transport by road. In some parts of the world, particularly in LDCs, road surfaces are poor and the distribution infrastructure indequate. In Vietnam, an attractive emerging market for many international firms, the majority of the road network is beaten track which, during the wet season (six months of the year), makes transporting anything by road very difficult and there are often problems of transporting goods across African countries due to poor road infrastructure.

Rail   Rail services provide a very good method of transporting bulky goods over long land distances. The increasing use of containers provides a flexible means to use rail and road modes with minimal load transfer times and costs.

In Europe, we are seeing the development of the use of 'Bloc Trains' as a highly efficient means of rail transport. In the US they use 'Double Bloc' trains to transport goods across the vast plains. In a number of markets, rail transport is fraught with difficulties. In China, a shipment from Shanghai to Guangzhou, a distance of approximately 2000 kilometres, can take 25 days. Across the interior it is even slower. Shanghai to Xian, 1500 kilometres, can take 45 days. Much of the rail capacity is antiquated and many of the rail lines are old, leading to frequent derailments. See Illustration 10.6 for further details about train transportation issues along the 21st Century Silk Road.

ILLUSTRATION 10.6

A slow train to China?

Distribution channels come in many forms: road, rail, air, ship and of course clouds for internet-based products and services. Choosing which channel to use is often based on two variants:

1 Time and

2 Cost.

The longest rail track now spans between China and Spain. The train track, the longest in the world, is called the 21st Century Silk Road. The first major trading journey carried a 30-carriage train from Yiwu; a manufacturing distribution centre in China to Madrid in Spain. The journey broke all speed records for a trading journey; however, it still took 21 days to travel the 8000 miles between China and Spain. The first delivery from China brought thousands of toys and goods for Christmas 2014. The return cargo

from Spain to China was full of traditional Spanish produce, including olive oil, wine and ham. To make the 16 000 mile round trip the train goes through Kazakhstan, Russia, Belarus, Poland, Germany and France. However, in some areas of Kazakhstan, temperatures often drop to around –7 degrees Celsius (20 degrees Fahrenheit). Products like the Spanish ham and wine can freeze which will ruin the produce. There are trains that have containers which keep temperatures inside warmer than –7 degrees Celsius and these are used for more sensitive hardware such as laptops, smartphones and computer equipment. The temperature controlled train containers cost more money than *general* containers.

Another long train container journey is between China and Poland which takes around 14 days and costs $10 000 for a 10-ton 40-foot load. A similar load going by air takes around four days (including passage through customs and delivery-time at each end of the journey) would cost $40 000. If a manufacturer chooses to send a similar cargo of products by boat the cost would be $5000. The cargo of products sent by sea would take around six weeks.

Questions

1 Which is the cheapest distribution channel and which distribution channel takes the longest?

2 What are the strengths and weaknesses of train transportation?

Source: Mount, I. (2014) 'Spain to China by rail: A 21st Century Silk Road riddled with obstacles', *Fortune*, published 24 December 2014.

The final decision on transport   The decision concerning which transport mode to use is discussed by Branch (2005). He identifies four factors as decisive in choosing transport: the terms of the export contract, the commodity specification, freight and overall transit time.

In the terms of the export contract, the customer can specify the mode(s) of transport and can insist on the country's national shipping line or airline being used. In considering different modes of transport, the specification of the commodity will have a strong influence on modal choice. For example, transport of fresh food will have requirements to prevent spoilage and contamination. The cost of transport is of major importance: it creates extra costs above the normal domestic cost. It is important, therefore, that transport options are researched thoroughly so that the best value arrangements can be made for both the buyer and the supplier.

Export processing zones

The principle of the export processing zone (EPZ) started with the opening of the world's first EPZ at Shannon in the Republic of Ireland. Since then there has been a proliferation in the establishment of EPZs worldwide, with notable examples being Jebel Ali at Dubai in the UAE and Subic Bay in the Philippines. The principle of the EPZ has been embraced as a worldwide instrument for national economic development by the United Nations.

The concept of the EPZ concerns the duty-free and tax-free manufacture or processing of products for export purposes within a customs-controlled ('offshore') environment. Components may be imported into the zone duty free and tax free to be processed or manufactured into the finished product, or stored for onward distribution and then re-exported without any liability of import duties or other taxes. The purpose of the EPZ is to ensure that at least 70 per cent of the zone-produced articles are re-exported. The remaining percentage of items produced within the zone may be imported into domestic territory upon payment of the appropriate import duty and tax for the finished article.

Companies trading from within the export processing zone can be wholly-owned by foreign-based enterprises and, in most cases, all profits may be repatriated to the home country. Foreign direct investment by overseas-based companies is encouraged in zone operations, since normal national rules regarding profits or ownership do not apply. It is also possible for locally based companies to engage in zone operations as long as they are involved in import and export operations.

It is also likely that the workforce used will cost the zone company less than for home-based operations, since the majority of the EPZs are located in developing countries, especially East and South East Asia and Central America.

The benefits for companies in taking advantage of EPZs are:

- All goods entering the EPZ are exempted from customs duties and import permits.
- Firms can use foreign currency to settle transactions.
- EPZs can be used for assembly of products and so help reduce transportation costs.
- EPZs give a company much more flexibility and help avoid the unwanted bureaucracy of customs and excise.

China has developed 124 export processing zones in the coastal regions and special economic zones (SEZs) in the interior of China to help develop export sea trade. Examples of EPZs in China are Hong Kong, Shenzen, Shanghai and Tianjin.

Administrative problems resulting from the cross-border transfer of goods

For many companies, particularly those that are infrequent exporters or that have insufficient resources for effective export administration, the process of ensuring that goods reach their ultimate destination is beset with difficulties: goods held in customs warehouses without apparent reason, confusing paperwork, high and apparently arbitrary duties, levies and surcharges and the need to make exorbitant payments to expedite the release of goods. The UN Conference on Trade and Development (UNCTAD) believe these additional costs to world trade could be as much as 10 per cent of the US$12.5 trillion total world trade. UNCTAD also believes that those costs could be cut by US$250 billion by improved efficiency. It is unlikely, however, that such changes as these will happen quickly, and so companies face a series of decisions about how to manage their own risks and costs, while still providing an effective service to their customers.

Documentation

A number of different documents are required in cross-border marketing. These include invoices, consignment notes and customs documents. SITRO, the Simpler Trade Procedures Board, has been involved in developing simpler documentation and export procedures with the aim of encouraging international trade. EDI is expanding and now provides a fast integrated system which is reducing documentation preparation time and errors.

The process of documentation has more importance than its rather mechanistic and bureaucratic nature would suggest. Errors made in documents can result in laws being broken, customs regulations being violated or, in financial institutions, refusing to honour demands for payment. Country variations are considerable with regard to export documentation procedures. Different documents are required in different formats. Figure 10.5 shows a typical export order process.

Documentation problems have five main causes: complexity, culture, change, cost and error. Complexity arises from the number of different parties requiring precise documents delivered at the correct time. In addition to the customer, banks, chambers of commerce, consulates, international carriers, domestic carriers, customs, port/terminal/customs clearance areas, insurance companies and the exporting company or freight forwarding company are being used by the exporter.

Different countries require different numbers of copies of documents, sometimes in their own language and sometimes open to official scrutiny that is strongly influenced by the culture of that country. Document clearance can, therefore, be slow and subject to bureaucratic delays.

Errors in documentation can have serious consequences. The definition of an 'error' is open to interpretation. Errors can result in goods being held in customs or in a port. Clearance delays cause failure to meet customer service objectives. In extreme cases, errors result in goods being confiscated or not being paid for.

The development of regional trading blocs is reducing some of the complexity of documentation. Previous to the single European market, a firm transporting goods from Manchester (UK) to Milan (Italy) would

FIGURE 10.5   The export order and physical process

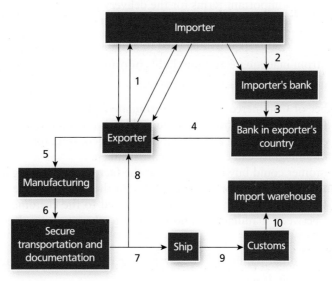

require 38 different documents. Now, theoretically, none are required! Some companies seek to minimize their exposure to documentation problems by using freight forwarders to handle freight and documentation. Other companies develop their own expertise and handle documentation in-house.

Packaging

Packaging for international markets needs to reflect climatic, geographical, economic, cultural and distribution channel considerations. In this section we will concentrate on the specific requirements that particularly relate to transport and warehousing.

The main packaging issues of interest for the exporter are: loss, damage and the provision of handling points to cope with the range of transport modes and the levels of handling sophistication and types of equipment used throughout the entire transit.

- *Loss.* The main concerns of loss of goods relate to misdirection and to theft (pilferage). The use of containers has reduced some of the opportunities for theft. Misdirection can be minimized by the appropriate use of shipping marks and labelling. High-value consignments need to be marked in such a way as to avoid drawing them to the attention of potential thieves. Marking needs to be simple, security-conscious and readily understandable by different people in different countries.

- *Damage.* The length of transit and variations in climate and physical movement give rise to many opportunities for damage to occur. Goods stowed in large ships might be contaminated by chemical odours or corroding machinery. Goods might be left out in the open air in equatorial or severe winter conditions. Walmart found that local Brazilian suppliers could not meet their standards for packaging and quality control.

A good balance needs to be achieved between the high costs of the substantial export packing required to eliminate all or almost all damage and the price and profit implications that this has for the customer and the exporter; see Case Study 2 at the end of this chapter for more details about packaging.

Over the years, export packaging has been modified from wooden crates and straw, etc., towards fibreboard and cardboard cartons. Different countries have different regulations about what materials are acceptable. In addition, export packaging influences customer satisfaction through its appearance and in its appropriateness to minimize handling costs for the customer.

The export sales contract

The export sales contract covers important terms for the delivery of products in international trade. There are three main areas of uncertainty in international trade contracts which Branch (2005) identifies as:

- uncertainty about which legal system will be used to adjudicate the contract;
- difficulties resulting from inadequate and unreliable information;
- differences in the interpretation of different trade terms.

The International Chamber of Commerce (ICC) has formulated a set of internationally recognized trade terms called Incoterms. The use of Incoterms will reduce these uncertainties. However, because there are many different ways in which the customer and the supplier could contract for the international delivery of products, the possibility of ambiguity can exist unless care is taken.

At one extreme the customer could buy the product at the factory gate, taking all the responsibility for permits, arrangements and costs of transport and insurance. At the other extreme the supplier can arrange and pay for all costs to the point where the product is delivered to the customer's premises. There are a variety of different steps between manufacture and delivery to the customer. Keegan and Green (2010) identify nine steps:

- obtaining an export permit, if required. For example, for the sale of armaments;
- obtaining a currency permit, if required;

- packing the goods for export;

- transporting the goods to the place of departure. This is usually road transport to a seaport or to an airport. For some countries, for example within continental Europe, transport could be entirely by road;

- preparing a bill of lading;

- completing necessary customs export papers;

- preparing customs or consular invoices as required in the country of destination;

- arranging for ocean freight and preparation;

- obtaining marine insurance and certificate of the policy.

There are a number of Incoterms specifying many variations of responsibility for the required steps in the delivery process. The main terms are defined below:

- *Ex-works (EXW)*. In this contract the exporter makes goods available at a specified time at the exporter's factory or warehouse. The advantage to the buyer in this arrangement is that of obtaining the goods at the lowest possible price.

- *Free on board (FOB)*. In this contract the exporter is responsible for the costs and risks of moving the goods up to the point of passing them over the ship's rail. The FOB contract will specify the name of the ship and the name of the port. The benefit to the buyer in this arrangement is that the goods can be transported in the national shipping line of the buyer and can be insured using a national insurance company. In this way the amount of foreign currency needed to finance the contract is reduced.

- *Cost, insurance, freight (CIF)*. This contract specifies that the exporter is responsible for all costs and risks to a specified destination port indicated by the buyer. The buyer benefits from receiving the goods in the home country and is, therefore, spared the costs, risks and management of the goods in transit. The exporter can benefit from a higher price for the contract. Whether the contract is more profitable will depend on the extra total distribution costs associated with the CIF contract. From a national point of view, the use of CIF contracts by a country's exporters is preferred as invisible earnings through extra freight and insurance services are increased when CIF contracts are used rather than FOB contracts.

Governments of all types of political and economic persuasion sometimes develop policies to favour their own national companies, and they can try to influence the availability of transport modes. In addition, the extra incentive to increase foreign currency earnings can change the export sales contract and with it the specification of the Incoterms.

SUMMARY

- The management of international distribution channels and logistics is challenging because it is frequently determined more by the available infrastructure and host country channel structure than by what the firm would like to do.

- The lack of experience in distribution decision making is exposed further by explicit and implicit cultural differences. It is important to understand and manage cultural differences among different members of the variety of distribution channel arrangements in different country markets.

- Cultural differences add to control difficulties. Typically, companies have less control over international channels than they have in their domestic market. The usual pattern is to have a smaller market share and to use longer distribution channels, that is, using more layers of distribution intermediaries. Both of these factors reduce the power of the manufacturer. Less channel power usually results in less control over other channel members.

- The changing nature of retailing patterns influences distribution planning. The long-term commitments that form the basis of successful distribution need to be nurtured. However, change also implies some adapting of distribution channel arrangements. It is a considerable challenge to add new types of distribution intermediaries while holding on to long-established accounts.

- Successful management of international distribution channels and logistics represents a significant challenge to the international marketer. The proximity of the company, the distribution intermediaries and the customer make cultural interactions an important influence on success.

- Success in international distribution channel and logistics management has to be based on high-quality strategic decisions and consistent and efficient tactical implementation.

KEYWORDS

integrated supply chain	mass customization	electronic data interchange
foreign market channels	data mining	build to order
indirect channels	category management	open market
direct channels	effective consumer response	export processing zone
buyer–seller relationships	interactive shopping	export administration
distribution channel structures	total distribution cost	
interactive customer marketing	logistics or distribution strategy	

CASE STUDY 1

Distribution channels in the Asian insurance market

Insurance companies in many Asian markets have traditionally depended on individual agents as their main sales channel. However, the market share of this channel is decreasing. According to a report by Celent, Asian insurance companies are moving away from a sales model that is built around agents, and developing a diverse model that encompasses various channels such as agents, banks, direct sales and financial advisers. Although Asian insurance distribution channels are diversifying, the potential share of each channel across Asian markets does vary.

According to Wenli Yuan, senior analyst with Celent's Asian Financial Services Group, a growing number of insurance companies in Asia are collaborating with organizations with huge customer databases, such as banks and public utilities departments, to reach out to their customers through database marketing.

Previously consisting mainly of tele-marketing and direct mailing, database marketing is today considered an important channel by most insurers, in view of the new possibilities enabled by the high levels of Internet penetration and proliferation of mobile devices such as smartphones and tablets. Social media has become a vital platform for business to engage with consumers and build their brand as well as being a rich data source in its own right on today's fast moving consumer trends.

Another new important channel is banks. According to Mr Jaganathan, assistant governor at the Asia Conference on Bancassurance, using banks as a primary distribution channel presents a unique proposition for insurers. By leveraging on a bank's existing branch network and customer base, which are well-established throughout most markets in Asia, insurers are able to scale up very quickly into geographical areas and customer segments that might not be accessible by existing channels. It is therefore not surprising that bancassurance is the fastest growing channel for insurance across Asian markets.

However, in Asia, because of the complex nature of life insurance products, insurers are also starting to go through personal financial advisers. Intermediaries such as financial advisers are seen to have the advantage of providing advice to consumers on overall financial planning by growing, managing and protecting personal wealth to meet specific financial goals. With increasing affluence, a growing segment of consumers with more complex financial needs and goals require the sort of comprehensive service that is delivered by financial advisers. In addition, financial advisers may be perceived to be more independent than tied agents, which will be important as consumers become more discerning. As a relatively new channel in most of Asia, the primary focus currently is to establish public confidence through raising professional and ethical standards of financial advisers.

Given the growth of the new distribution channels, increased use of technology, mobile and social media, there is a need for insurers to consider what distribution strategies are most appropriate in this new digital age.

Questions

1 Evaluate the advantages and disadvantages of the alternative distribution channels in the Asian insurance market.

2 Develop an outline distribution strategy which would help an insurer achieve the optimum mix of distribution channels.

Sources: Keynote address by Mr Donald Joshua Jaganathan; assistant governor at the 15th Asia Conference on Bancassurance & Alternative Distribution Channels: 'Nailing down the winning strategies in bancassurance' www.uk.capgemini.com and www.celent.com (accessed April 2015).

CASE STUDY 2

Poor packaging = damage = lost profits

Correct transportation packaging is a priority for every business; be it a rural Bangladeshi farmer or a global soft drinks giant like Coca-Cola, particularly during transportation. If a rural farmer does choose poor quality or inappropriate cloth bags in which to transport their rice, flour or wheat, there is a good chance the cloth bags will split. Split bags spill produce which means less produce can be sold. Similarly if Coca-Cola choose incorrect packaging, their bottles could be punctured or broken when being lifted on or off ships or trains, which again means stock losses during transportation. Philip Luijckx, the marketing manager of industrial and consumer packaging for Dow Performance Packaging states that it is important for businesses to choose packaging that is sustainable and 'fit for purpose'. In fact, many businesses underestimate the stresses that products go through during the transportation process. Products can be vibrated constantly when packaged and transported on trains. Equally, products receive regular 'shocks' when the transportation lorry goes over a pot-hole or when train containers are connected/disconnected from the engine. The consequences of choosing packaging which is not 'fit for purpose' and does not protect the valuable products contained within are:

- loss of sales for the manufacturer
- loss of profit for the supply chain
- environmental cost as damaged products will be dumped or recycled.

Packaging has become more environmentally friendly over the years. Innovation has made packaging more sustainable whilst still being robust enough to get products to the end-user intact.

What is interesting is end-users such as Lockheed Martin Corporation, a global security and aerospace company, who insist that their suppliers delivering product to them do so with environmentally friendly packaging. Lockheed Martin Corporation go so far as to provide details of the types of packing they want their products wrapped and boxed in. Suggestions include:

- Biodegradable bags that are air cushioned to "absorb shock" and protect hard-edged products during transportation.
- Bubble wrap, also biodegradable, which like air-cushioned bags absorb shock and vibration which is especially useful for fragile products.
- Recycled moulded cardboard boxes and sheets particularly useful for absorbing constant vibrations experienced during long train transportation.

Lockheed Martin Corporation, the end-user (customer) of products request their suppliers use environmentally friendly packaging to reduce landfill waste. In the past a high majority of landfill waste came from product packaging. In this way the consumer is driving businesses to ensure their transportation packaging is robust and sustainable.

Questions

1 What problems occur when businesses decide to save money by choosing cheap packaging?

2 Why should manufacturers use sustainable packaging?

3 How should transport packaging companies market their products?

Sources: LePree, J. (2014) Finding the balance in packaging chemical engineering, published 1 July 2014. Available from www.chemengonline.com/finding-the-balance-in-packaging/?printmode=1 (accessed 17 June 2015); Lockheed Martin Corporation (2010) Sustainable packaging guidelines for suppliers Lockheed Martin Corporation. Available from www.lockheedmartin.com/content/dam/lockheed/data/corporate/documents/suppliers/LM-Sustainable-Packaging-Guidelines.pdf (accessed 17 June 2015).

DISCUSSION QUESTIONS

1 How might companies use the Internet to increase the competitiveness of their international distribution strategy?

2 How might the analysis of the retailer infrastructure and retailer marketing practices in advanced economies influence the development of marketing plans for retailers based in less-developed countries?

3 Discuss what factors contribute to the increasing complexity of global logistics operations. Explain why cooperative relationships are so important in this aspect of international marketing operations.

4 The arrival of the global village has had a major impact on companies' distribution methods. Identify four factors involved and explain how each has influenced distribution.

5 Fully evaluate the statement: 'Distribution and logistics are increasingly becoming the battleground in international markets as companies seek to gain global competitive advantage.'

REFERENCES

1. Branch, A.E. (2005) *Export Practice and Management*, 5th edn. Thomson Learning.
2. Czinkota, M. and Ronkainen, I. (2012) *International Marketing*. Cengage Learning.
3. Keegan, W.J. and Green, M.J. (2010) *Global Marketing Management*. 6th edn. Pearson.
4. Kotler, P., Keller, K.L., Brady, M., Goodman, M. and Hansen, T. (2009) *Marketing Management*, Pearson.
5. Kotler, P. and Armstrong, G. (2014) *Principles of Marketing*. Toronto: Pearson Prentice Hall. p. 367.
6. Rosenbloom, B. (2009) *Marketing Channels, a Management View*, 8th edn. FT/Prentice Hall.
7. Usunier, J.C. and Lee, J.A. (2005) *Marketing Across Cultures*, 5th edn. Prentice Hall.

CHAPTER 11

PRICING FOR INTERNATIONAL MARKETS

LEARNING OBJECTIVES

After reading this chapter you should be able to:

- Discuss the issues that affect international pricing decisions

- Evaluate different strategic options for pricing across international markets

- Differentiate between the problems facing companies engaged in foreign market pricing and those faced by companies trying to coordinate strategies across a range of global markets

- Find solutions to the problems of pricing in high-risk markets

INTRODUCTION

Many organizations believe that pricing is the most flexible, independent and controllable element of the marketing mix and that it plays a major role in international marketing management. This is largely based on the fact that pricing changes appear to prompt an immediate response in the market. However, despite the apparent simplicity of using pricing as a major marketing tool, many managers find pricing decisions difficult to make. This is in part due to the fact that while most firms recognize the importance of pricing at a tactical level in stimulating short-term demand, far fewer recognize the importance of the strategic role of pricing in international marketing.

In this chapter, we focus upon both the internal and external factors that affect international pricing decisions, the role that pricing plays in developing strategies to meet corporate objectives, and the relationship between pricing and other aspects of the firm's activities. In addition to considering the stages involved in developing a comprehensive international pricing policy, we discuss the specific problems associated with pricing in international marketing which do not affect the domestic business. We then go on to explore the financial issues in managing risk in pricing and of non-payment of debts.

Domestic vs international pricing

For many companies operating in domestic markets, pricing decisions are based on the relatively straightforward process of allocating the total estimated cost of producing, managing and marketing a product or service between the forecast total volume of sales, and adding an appropriate profit margin. Problems for these firms arise when costs increase, sales do not materialize or competitors undercut the prices. In international markets, however, pricing decisions are much more complex, because they are affected by a number of additional external factors, such as fluctuations in exchange rates, accelerating inflation in certain countries and the use of alternative payment methods such as leasing, barter and countertrade. The global financial crisis of 2008 still affects the complexities of pricing in a global market. Additionally, where there is economic and political uncertainty pricing decisions become even more difficult for many companies who are often now trading in countries with high levels of inflation, high levels of debt, high unemployment and political tensions.

In recent years, too, it has become more apparent that customer tastes have become much more sophisticated, and that purchase decisions are made less frequently on the basis of price consideration, but are increasingly influenced by wider expectations of product performance and perceptions of value. This has particular implications for international products, which are often perceived to be of significantly different value – higher or lower – than locally produced products. Pricing strategies are also strongly influenced by the nature and intensity of the competition which exists in the various local markets.

For these reasons, it is important to recognize at the outset that the development and implementation of pricing strategies in international markets should go through the following stages:

1 Analyzing the factors which influence international pricing, such as the cost structures, the value of the product, the market structure, competitor pricing levels and a variety of environmental constraints.

2 Confirming what impact the corporate strategies should have on pricing policy.

3 Evaluating the various strategic pricing options and selecting the most appropriate approach.

4 Implementing the strategy through the use of a variety of tactics and procedures to set prices at strategic business unit (SBU) level.

5 Managing prices and financing international transactions.

The factors affecting international pricing decisions

A firm exporting speculatively for the first time, with little knowledge of the market environment that it is entering, is likely to set a price based largely on company and product factors. Due to its restricted resources, the firm places particular emphasis on ensuring that sales revenue generated at least covers the costs incurred. However, while it is important that firms recognize that the cost structures for production, marketing and distribution of products and services are of vital importance, they should not be regarded as the sole determinants when setting prices. Sarathy, Terpstra and Russow (2006) identify many other factors that firms should take into consideration – environment, market, company and specific product factors – these are summarized below. It is by giving full recognition to the effect of these factors on pricing decisions that the company can develop a strategic rather than a purely tactical approach to pricing.

Factors influencing the pricing strategy

Company and product factors

- corporate and marketing objectives;
- firm and product positioning;
- product range, life cycle, substitutes, product differentiation and unique selling propositions;
- cost structures, manufacturing, experience effect and economies of scale;

- marketing, product development;
- available resources;
- inventory;
- shipping costs.

Market factors

- consumers' perceptions, expectations and ability to pay;
- need for product and promotional adaptation, market servicing, extra packaging requirements;
- market structure, distribution channels, discounting pressures;
- market growth, demand elasticities;
- need for credit;
- competition objectives, strategies and strength.

Environmental factors

- government influences and constraints;
- currency fluctuations;
- business cycle stage, level of inflation;
- use of non-money payment and leasing.

Companies operating internationally must consider all the above factors detailed for each specific country market. However, as with all the other marketing mix factors, the individual country pricing policies need to be integrated and coordinated within a wider regional or global strategy in order to enable corporate objectives to be met.

While it is important that companies consider all the factors listed, some of them, such as corporate objectives, market and product factors, consumer perceptions, competitor responses and cost structures are of particular significance.

Company and product factors

Corporate objectives   The short-term tactical use of pricing such as discounts, product offers and seasonal reductions is often emphasized by managers, at the expense of its strategic role. Sometimes firms will use export markets if they have excess production capacity to dump excess products. This means they use marginal pricing strategies, pricing at really low prices so they cover only the variable costs. Yet pricing over the past few years has played a very significant part in the restructuring of many industries, resulting in the growth of some businesses and the decline of others. New global brands from emerging markets such LG (Korea) and Haeir (China) have approached a new international market for a specific product with the intention of building market share over a period of years, through maintaining or even reducing pricing levels, establishing the product, the brand name and setting up effective distribution and servicing networks. As a result of this strategy they are now beginning to dominate a whole range of market sectors especially in markets such as consumer electronics. This has usually been accomplished at the expense of short-term profits, as the company will have a long-term perspective on profits.

By contrast, US firms have relied in the past more on international corporate strategies with greater emphasis on factors such as advertising and selling, believing that these reduce the need to compete on price. The reason for this is that the cost base of US manufacturing is usually much higher than that of its foreign competitors. However, the rapid growth of brands from China, Korea and the Asian economies has led to a change in the priorities of US firms. In a recent survey US firms ranked pricing as more important than any other element of the marketing mix, whereas Asian firms, which have been aggressively reducing their cost base for years, now place greater emphasis upon other factors as they seek to build global brands. The move of many Asian manufacturers from being contract manufacturers to marketing their own brands globally has seen them placing much more emphasis on innovation and marketing as they upgrade and develop their products and differentiate themselves by building their own distinctive brands.

The international nature of competition leads to the question of whether firms should aim for a broadly standardized price structure, or whether prices should be adapted in each country.

Product and service factors

While in theory standardization in pricing might appear easier to manage and therefore be preferable, in practice the different local economic, legal and competitive factors in each market make it rarely achievable. The occasions when price standardization is achievable are more usually related to the nature of the product and its stage in the life cycle – for example, standardized pricing can be adopted for certain hi-tech products where limited competition exists. Cavusgil *et al.* (2014) in their examination of export pricing, state that exporting goods can be problematic as changes in tariffs, exchange rate fluctuations and differing trade barriers can affect business dramatically and quickly. They go on to say that SMEs are affected more that MNCs as they are less likely to make plans years in advance (*ibid.* 2014). Aircraft makers, for example, because of the relative uniqueness and complexity of the technology, tend to charge the same price regardless of where the customer is based. However, in contrast, shipbuilders, with products in the mature phase of the product life cycle, adapt prices to meet each particular purchase situation.

In developing pricing strategies, a company needs to be aware of the price dynamics of specific products in the various markets. Five characteristics of the product are important in pricing:

■ *Frequency of purchase.* Frequently purchased products, for example baby food, petrol, tea and bread, tend to be very price-sensitive in all international markets, whereas occasional purchases are not.

■ *Degree of necessity.* If a product is essential for its users, price changes are unlikely to affect the market size, except in countries where extreme poverty exists and people cannot afford even the most basic necessities.

■ *Unit price.* High-priced products such as holidays and cars are evaluated in greater detail in terms of the consumer's perceptions of value for money, and so, for example, reliability, style and features of cars are extremely important to consumers besides price.

■ *Degree of comparability.* Consumers are less price-conscious about insurance policies than grocery products, because the alternatives are more difficult to compare. Price-setting is particularly difficult in certain services, such as advertising, consultancy and accountancy, which have a different perceived value from country to country.

■ *Degree of fashion or status.* The high prices of luxury goods are seen as establishing their quality and it is usually the goods that have a prestige.

Developing pricing strategies for services across international markets is difficult for several reasons. Services are highly perishable, and human resource constraints often restrict the capacity to grow a service business in foreign country markets, and so companies are restricted by the high costs of expansion and managing short-term capacity issues. Likewise the intangibility of services compared with goods may lead to higher marketing costs because the company has to build the market reputation on the actual service experience of consumers rather than building a brand image in anticipation of the consumer experience. This means positioning optimum prices in foreign country markets can be difficult to judge. In business-to-business marketing, where the growth of international services predominates, managers are often tasked with developing effective global pricing strategies for B2B customers that are characterized by different cultures and differing perceptions as to the value of the different service attributes they are buying. The intensive customer contact, extensive customization requirements, and the costs of building a service quality reputation in the market, make the challenge of formulating international pricing strategies for services across international markets particularly problematic.

The characteristics of the product or service, particularly the high unit price items, lead international marketers to adopt local pricing strategies which are broadly similar for individual markets, so that the positioning of specific products remains consistent from country to country. Marks and Spencer sell basic

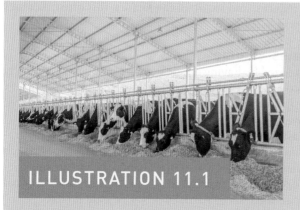

ILLUSTRATION 11.1

Milk: Global pricing and politics shake the UK dairy farmers' profits

Over the last 20 years, dairy farms in the UK have reduced in number. Of those that are left, 50 per cent of milk is sold directly, mainly to wholesalers or retailers, whilst the other 50 per cent is sent to manufacturers to make into cheese, yoghurt and butter. However, a high percentage of these products are also made from milk imported from overseas.

UK farmers are affected by international pricing, which sometimes can make their profits go down. Huge farms in America and New Zealand (with average herds three to four times bigger than the average herd owned by a UK dairy farmer) have recently benefited from fantastic weather. The yields from their cows has grown to such a high level that the price milk is sold for is reduced. This is bad news for the UK dairy farmer as milk prices are dictated globally. Therefore, a reduction in milk prices in one country affects dairy farmers worldwide.

Recently, politics has impacted on British (and European) dairy farms. The milk supplied to manufacturers to make cheese, yoghurt and butter was left standing in factories and ports. Russia's recent (2015) import ban on products from Europe meant cheese from the UK could not be sold in Russia. Russia had previously imported a lot of cheese from Europe. This created a 'cheese mountain' which in turn reduced cheese prices. British and European dairy farmers saw their profits reduce again for issues outside their control. Most businesses are in control of the key elements of the marketing mix. However, this is not the case for the UK dairy farmer.

Questions

1 What are the main factors that affect the price of milk?

2 What factors can farmers control and which can they not control?

Source: *The Guardian* Editorial (2015) 'The Guardian view on milk prices: dairy farmers are being driven out of business. The groceries regulator should find out why', published 12 January 2015.

foods at higher prices than other food retailers in the UK, by guaranteeing extremely high consistency of quality. This difference is not perceived to be so great in other countries, however, where consumers feel that the general quality is not significantly different to justify a substantially higher price.

Price plays an important role in product differentiation by enhancing the perceived value of the product and helping consumers to distinguish between offers from different competitors in order that their needs can be met. Watch prices, for example, range from very little for a child's watch, to a high premium price for a Rolex. Within this range, individual manufacturers normally confine specific brands within particular pricing bands which are linked to the positioning of the brand and the profile of the watches within the range, and to the characteristics of the target segment.

The key role of price in differentiating products within a category and within a particular market can be used as an offensive strategy. This is demonstrated by the South Korean car manufacturer, Kia, which entered the US car market knowing that its brand name had little credibility there and that the market was already saturated with broadly equivalent products. It targeted its Japanese equivalents, the Honda Civic and Toyota Corolla, by offering a similar car at a 25 per cent lower price.

The influence of cost structures on pricing

There is a close relationship between prices, costs and sales volume of a product, because the price charged affects sales volume by increasing or decreasing the overall demand. As a result of producing or marketing larger volumes the unit cost of an individual product reduces, and so, of all the factors, this often becomes the initial stimulus for firms taking the decision to export.

The relationship between demand and sales volume   The way price affects demand is influenced by many factors. Some products are characterized by having **elastic demand** and being extremely price-sensitive, so that sales volumes increase significantly as prices are reduced. In underdeveloped markets, where there is low penetration but considerable desire for western products such as soft drinks or fast food, sales will increase rapidly if the price is reduced relative to consumers' ability to pay.

By contrast, other products are characterized by **inelastic demand**. For example, suppliers of power generation equipment cannot significantly stimulate demand in individual markets by reducing the price. For such firms, an increase in business revenue is largely determined by changes in external factors, such as an improvement in the economy. The potential market for the European power generation equipment suppliers National Power and ABB was increased by the political decision in Malaysia to partially privatize state utilities.

The relationship between cost and sales volume   A second situation of inelastic demand occurs if a firm finds that it has reached saturation in its home market so that even if prices were reduced, there would not be significant extra sales to offset the loss of profit. The firm might conclude that exporting would provide an alternative method of increasing sales and thereby generate additional profit.

This is especially so when firms can increase sales by entering an export market, make use of existing spare production capacity and so price purely to cover their variable costs. Consider the situation shown in Table 11.1 where all the fixed costs are absorbed by the sales in the domestic market, but in addition, 10 per cent extra sales are obtained in export markets at the same prices. Provided there are no increases in fixed costs, there would be recovery of the fixed costs because of the additional 10 per cent export business. This recovery of fixed costs by the export business would be shown as an additional contribution to the general overheads of the business. The contribution from the export business would all be additional profit.

The **fixed production cost** of the product includes depreciation of equipment, building rental and business rates. General overheads include advertising, selling, distribution and administration.

The example shows that in practice the additional £100 000 sales have generated an additional £40 000 profit (6.3 per cent on total sales) – far greater than the $30 000 profit generated on the £1 million domestic sales (3 per cent profit on total sales). The firm could, therefore, afford to reduce its export price considerably and still make a profit, provided that no extra general overhead costs were incurred, as long as there was spare production capacity and no extra investment had to be made.

Table 11.1   The effect of additional export sales on contribution

	Domestic sales (100 000 units) £000	+ 10% Export sales	Domestic + 10% export sales (110 000 units) £000
Sales	1000	100	1100
Fixed production costs	300		300
Variable production costs	500	50	550
Total costs	800	50	850
Contribution to general overheads	200	50	250
General overheads	170	10	180*
Profit	30	40	70

Note: *General overheads are higher due to additional exporting costs

In export markets, the firm might choose one of the following four alternatives, setting the selling price at:

- Production cost plus general overhead plus added profit (this would normally be the list price).
- Production cost, but without general overhead or profit added.
- Below production cost.
- Production cost with specific export costs added.

The choice of alternatives will depend on the firm's objectives in entering international markets. The first leads to the safest, albeit least competitive, price and is frequently the approach adopted by new exporters who are unwilling to take any significant risk. The firm might even take the list price, including the domestic gross margin, and add to it all the costs of exporting such as marketing, distribution and administration, resulting in the export price being far greater than the domestic price. In most international markets, however, a list price calculated in this way is unlikely to gain significant market share, and so a lower selling price is required.

The arguments for using the second option, to set a lower export selling price, are based on the belief that export costs should not include domestic sales costs such as advertising, marketing research, domestic and administration costs. While this option has some merit, it might well fail to take account of high specific export costs.

The third option is clearly quite risky as it is designed to substantially increase volume. The danger, of course, is that if the increased volume generated does not absorb the fixed and general overhead costs, the product will be unprofitable and losses will result. This approach is often used in overseas markets and is based on **marginal costing**, whereby unused production capacity or extended production runs can provide extra goods for sale with little or no change in fixed costs, so that the extra production can effectively be produced at a lower cost than the original production schedule. Another risk with this strategy is that the firm could be accused of **dumping** excess capacity in foreign markets. This sometimes is exacerbated as a result of government policy, particularly in declining industries, for example, if governments continue to subsidize their own inefficient industries by providing various incentives such as subsidies.

The fourth option begs the question of whether or not export pricing should reflect the entire costs specific to export sales, and if so, which costs can be directly attributable to exports. It can be argued that, particularly if a firm intends ultimately to commence manufacture in foreign markets, it is vital to know exactly what the realistic costs for foreign markets are. Allocating costs such as research and development accurately and appropriately, however, can be difficult. See Illustration 11.2 for details of hidden costs.

Specific export costs

While export volumes are small in comparison to the domestic market, some experimentation in export pricing is possible, but as exporting becomes a more significant part of the activities of the company, perhaps requiring the allocation of dedicated equipment or staff, it is necessary to reflect all costs that are specific to export sales. These costs include tariffs, special packaging, insurance, tax liabilities, extra transport, warehousing costs and export selling as well as money transmission, hedging and foreign exchange costs.

However, often when operating across international markets cost elements can frequently be overlooked or under-estimated by companies. These include:

- Additional freight and handling costs due to a misunderstanding of trading terms.
- Last-minute product modifications to meet an export standard.
- Packaging and labelling requirements (language, ingredients, use-by dates).
- Documentation requirements such as certificates of origin and invoices.
- Insurance (including credit insurance), finance and banking charges.
- Delays in customs clearance if documentation, packaging and labelling is not in order.
- Vaguely worded contracts or agreements.

The most immediate and obvious result of all these costs being passed on is that the price to the consumer in an export market is likely to be much greater than the price to a domestic consumer. An example of this is shown in Table 11.2.

ILLUSTRATION 11.2

KINECT
for Xbox

Fruit Ninja – Extra costs for online gaming success

The Australian government encourages businesses to export goods and services by providing loans, grants, education packages, regular road shows and guidance on Free Trade Agreements. In conjunction with the Australian Trade Commission and Australian Chamber of Commerce and Industry, the Australian government plays host at an award ceremony entitled the Australian Export Awards. Winning such an award not only puts Australia on the map for innovation, creativity and business excellence but it is an excellent PR opportunity for the winners. Halfbrick won the Online Sales Award 2014. Halfbrick is a B2B and B2C company that develops software for online games.

Their most famous gaming character is the Fruit Ninja. Fruit Ninja software was exported B2B to Apple via their iOS platform for iPod Touch and iPhone devices. The game became Halfbrick's first export, it was an instant success with 500 million copies downloaded onto Apple platforms. When the game became available on non-Apple platforms its popularity increased further as it was downloaded 1 billion times! The game also became a B2C export so gamers can download the software onto Windows platforms, or purchase it for X-Box and Gameboy Advance. During the research and development stage of Fruit Ninja, Halfbrick completed a competitor analysis of games to explore gaps in the market that their chosen target market would want. The target

market for Fruit Ninja is game-loving children. To reach their target market, Halfbrick had to set up a range of social media platforms which included a lot of time and effort in staff; but the ongoing (daily) posts on social media keep the target market interested in their brand. In fact on Facebook the Fruit Ninja has 6.6 million fans and on Fruit Ninja's Twitter page there are 24.9K followers. In 2015, Halfbrick has launched the Fruit Ninja Academy. This is a way to encourage parents to keep in touch with the Fruit Ninja brand. On Facebook and Twitter parents are regularly encouraged to enrol their children to the Fruit Ninja Academy to help them improve their mathematics skills whilst having fun. In 2014, new privacy measures were put in place so that children and parents understand that data captured by Halfbrick is used to improve the gaming experience but details of children that interact with the games are private.

The film industry also became a fan of the Fruit Ninja. Dreamworks decided Fruit Ninja should join forces with their animated character Puss in Boots. Therefore, *Fruit Ninja: Puss in Boots* was revealed to coincide with the launch of the Puss in Boots film. To take part in the venture, Halfbrick dedicated a number of employees to re-skin the game; so instead of a sword-wielding Fruit Ninja the Halfbrick/Dreamworks game starred a sword-wielding Puss in Boots!

New games from Halfbrick have also been launched and exported. To do that employees of Halfbrick visited certain countries and set up networks around the world. In some countries Halfbrick pay agents, distributers or provide office space for employees (Los Angeles, San Franciso, Madrid and Bulgaria) as they understand the local market better than Halfbrick employees based in Australia. To localize even further they set up a partnership with iDreamSky, a Chinese games publisher.

Future exports are planned for India and Brazil where new research activities are needed to understand the needs of this new market of gamers (and their parents).

Question

1 What are the other hidden and extra costs that Halfbrick have had to pay?

Source: Halfbrick (2015) www.halfbrick.com

Table 11.2   Escalation of costs through exporting using the 'cost plus' export pricing model

FOB	Free On Board	
	EXW price plus	100
+	Transport to carrier (eg wharf, airport)	17
+	Customs clearance	8
+	Additional packaging/labour for transport	5
+	Agent's commission	13
	FOB	143
CFR	**Cost And Freight**	
	or	
CPT	**Carriage Paid To**	
	FOB price plus	143
+	Sea/air freight charges to wharf/airport	32
+	Sea/air document fees (e.g. airway bill, B/L)	11
+	BAF (bunker adjustment factor)	2
+	Transport contingency	2
	CFR or CPT	190
CIF	**Cost, Insurance, Freight**	
	CFR or CPT price plus	190
+	Marine insurance premium	2
	CIF	192
DDP	**Delivery Duty Paid**	
	CIF price plus	192
+	Import duty/tax (calculated as 20% of CIF price)	39
+	Customs clearance fees	8
+	Delivery charge from airport to customer	10
	DDP	249

Source: www.austrade.gov.au, *Austrade Guide to Export pricing*.

This raises the question of whether foreign consumers will be prepared to pay a higher price for imported rather than locally produced goods. Justifying the cost of the product on the basis of its added value might be possible in the short term, but is unlikely to provide the international marketer with a basis for long-term viability in each local market. A strategy must be developed to deal with this situation in which the cost to the ultimate consumer is reduced. The main options available to the exporter include:

- aggressively reducing production costs, modifying the product if necessary and sourcing overseas;
- shortening the distribution channel, for example, by selling direct to retailers;
- selecting a different market entry strategy, such as foreign manufacture, assembly or licensing to avoid the additional costs of exporting.

The implications of changing the market entry and distribution strategy have been dealt with in earlier chapters of this book; here we discuss strategies for reducing cost.

Top down pricing is another way for businesses to decide how much they will charge for goods and services when they export them to countries. During the research and development stage; an important stage that businesses go through when deciding to export goods and services overseas, it is highly recommended that businesses complete a competitor price analysis. By completing a competitor price analysis businesses will understand:

1 What the consumer is prepared to pay for goods and services, and
2 An indication of what price to sell goods and services to an agent or distributor.

This process is called the 'top down' export pricing model.

Table 11.3 provides an example of how the 'top down' export pricing model works. The example provided is for a case of wine being sold from an Australian vineyard to a retailer in Hong Kong. A case of wine contains 12 bottles. The marketer from the Australian vineyard will need to complete a number of calculations to decipher the price they will sell wine for in Hong Kong retail outlets. See Table 11.3 for details of the calculation and Management Challenge 11.1 for top down pricing of sugar.

Cost reduction

The rationale behind any firm's decision to enter international markets is usually to increase profitability, and this is based upon a recognition of the fact that the size of the firm's actual market share is a primary determinant of profitability. Thus the argument goes that firms with a larger market share normally have lower unit costs, and they are perceived by customers to market higher-quality products, leading to relatively higher market prices. Both of these factors result in higher profits for the firm.

Most companies in international markets have the potential to benefit from driving down costs through achieving **economies of scale**, exploiting the benefits of the **learning curve** and making strategic decisions on the location or relocation of manufacturing plants within the context of worldwide operations.

Economies of scale

Economies of scale are obtained as a result of manufacturing additional products with the same or only slightly higher fixed costs, so that, in practice, for every additional product produced, the unit cost reduces. This is a slight over-simplification of the situation as, for example, installation of new plant might in the short term increase unit costs during the period when the plant is running at below its economic capacity. While in domestic markets the benefits from economies of scale follow directly, in international markets these economies must more than offset savings achieved by having local plants, which result in reduced transport costs and the avoidance of import tariffs.

Learning curve

Some authors have suggested that, although it is less well-known than economies of scale, the learning curve has potentially greater benefit for cost reduction. Its origins lie in the production of aircraft in the

Second World War. The observation that the time needed to perform a specific task reduced as the operatives become more familiar with it was made. Since then a series of studies by the Boston Consulting Group have found evidence that the effect was much more widespread than this, and covered all aspects of business, including high and low technology, products and services, and consumer and industrial products. They point out that there is a direct relationship between the cumulative volume of production and the costs incurred in producing the same product benefits. The major sources of savings from the experience gained through the learning curve are:

- greater labour efficiency;
- task specialization and method improvement;
- new production processes;
- better performance of existing equipment;
- changes to the mix of resources;
- greater product standardization;
- improved product designs.

Table 11.3 'Top down' export pricing model – wine sold from an Australian vineyard for retail outlets in Hong Kong

	Per Bottle	Quick Tips
Similar wine per bottle at retail store	**HK $305**	
Deduct VAT	HK $0	
Consumer Price per bottle Excluding VAT[1]	**HK $305**	
Deduct retail margin of 60%	HK $183	305 × 0.60
Retailers Buying Price Per Bottle	**HK $122**	**305 − 183**
Importers Buy Price per bottle HK $ – Deduct Importers margin of 30%[2] + Clearance & Warehouse Allowance of 3% + Advertising & Promotion Allowance of 5% = total of 38%	HK $88	122/1.38
Importers Buy Price per case with duty HK $	HK $1056	88 × 12
Importers Price per case before duty – Deduct Duty (80%) of CIF	HK $587	1056/1.8
Convert to AUD $[3]	AUD $146.00	587/4
CIF per case	**AUD $146**	
Deduct Freight[4]	AUD $1.00	
Deduct Marine Insurance	AUD $1.00	
FOB per case	**AUD $144**	

[1]VAT and sales taxes are applied in many overseas markets. In this example there are no VAT or Sales Taxes in Hong Kong.
[2]Retailers take a full margin on the selling price not the buying price.
[3]Assumes an exchange rate of AUD $1 to HK $4.
[4]Assumes a freight rate of AUD $1200 for 20 foot FCL sea freight container that packs 1200 cases.

Source www.austrade.gov.au Austrade Guide to Export pricing

MANAGEMENT CHALLENGE 11.1

Top down pricing model for sugar exports

Australia's largest export market is China (27 per cent of total exports). China is also the largest country that Australian imports from. China consumes about 4 million tonnes of sugar per year; Australia supplies are 250 000 tonnes of sugar to China. Therefore, any new sugar business that wants to export their products to China will need to calculate the price they are willing to sell their sugar for.

Question

Using the 'top down' export pricing model shown in Table 11.3 what is the FOB of a bale of sugar that Australian sugar growers should price up for retailers in China?

Use the following information within your calculations.

1 VAT and sales taxes are applied in many overseas markets. For this example there are no VAT or sales taxes in China.

2 Retailers take a full margin on the selling price not the buying price.

3 Assumes an exchange rate of 1 AUD = 4.76036 CNY.

4 Assumes a freight rate of AUD $1200 for 20 foot FCL sea freight container that packs 1200 bales.

5 Bales contain 25 bags of sugar.

Use the following table to complete your calculation.

Top down pricing model for sugar exports	Bag of Sugar	Quick tips
Similar bag of sugar at a retail store in China	CNY	
Deduct VAT	CNY	
Consumer price per bag of sugar excluding VAT **(1)**	CNY	
Deduct retail margin of 60%		
Retailers buying price per bag of sugar	CNY	
Importers buying price per bag of sugar CNY − deduct importers margin of 30% **(2)** + clearance & warehouse allowance of 3% + advertising & Promotion allowance of 5% = total 38%	CNY	
Importer buy price per bale with duty CNY	CNY	
Importer price per bale before duty − deduct duty (80%) of CIF	CNY	
Convert to AUD$ **(3)**	AUD	
CIF per bale	AUD	
Deduct Freight **(4)**	AUD	
Deduct marine insurance	AUD	
FOB per bale of sugar **(5)**	AUD	

1CNY = 0.21 AUD

Thus, the learning curve provides an opportunity for cost reductions, although if managers do not make a concerted effort, costs will rise.

The combined effects of economies of scale and the learning curve are seen in the electronics market, where aggressive firms slash prices to gain market share, knowing that cost reductions will follow. For example, Apple launched their iPad Air product and made 129 per cent mark-up. This means Apple make £225 profit on a product that costs them just £174 to produce (Woollaston 2013) on the basis that the volume generated by increased demand would force component and assembly costs down, through a combination of these two effects, and of course the desirability of Apple products. A key issue in international marketing is how best these effects can be exploited, particularly as the skills and experience are spread throughout the world. The efficient transfer of these skills and knowledge between different strategic business units then becomes paramount.

Location of production facility

Driven by the continual need to reduce costs, companies have increasingly considered selective location or relocation of production facilities. As firms increasingly market their products globally, so their choice of manufacturing locations is determined by many considerations other than simply being close to particular markets. They might choose to locate a factory in a less developed country in order to take advantage of lower labour costs, but also they may well develop specific skills and areas of specialization in those locations. For example, a large proportion of televisions, radios, calculators and jeans are manufactured in China and South East Asia. Bangladesh is another country which is becoming a location for production in televisions, mobile phones and refrigerators. Due to the skills of its employees, location and price advantage, Walton's the manufacturing arm of WALTON Group headquartered in Dhaka, Bangladesh, has a stated mission to lead the field in technology advancement and innovation. So much so that Walton's 2020 vision is to show to the world that 'Made in Bangledesh' is a sign that means aspiration and quality in the minds of consumers.

India is another country with an excellent location which attracts organizations eager to do business. India has over 1 billion inhabitants, 125 million of whom are considered to represent a financially aware middle class, thus presenting not only a highly skilled but cheap workforce for multinationals but also a growing consumer market for the goods India produces. The Indian government has a range of incentives that encourage Foreign Direct Investment such as stamp duty exemption for land acquisition and exemption of value added tax. These incentives will certainly attract global brands who can adapt their prices accordingly. India's government is so confident in its ability to provide products and services they have set up their own website entitled www.makeinindia.com, together with a guidance team to encourage more brands to invest.

Thomson-CSF (France), Coca-Cola, Motorola, IBM and Hewlett Packard have invested heavily in the Indian region. During 2014 new brands such as ThyssenKrupp Aerospace the German-based conglomerate, chose India to produce aerospace materials. Twitter, a San Francisco-based company; investing outside the US for the first time, chose India to be their new research and design (R&D) centre.

Problems associated with manufacturing in western countries have helped to accelerate this transfer of manufacturing to South Asia. Lagging productivity, reluctance to source materials and parts globally, strong unions and high standards of living were the causes of the decline in the US manufacturing base. Therefore, many regions and countries, like India, are responding to this opportunity for inward investment by marketing a variety of incentives and attractions to companies wishing to relocate.

It is not only in manufacturing that relocation of activities can benefit from lower labour costs. For instance, the introduction of fibre optic cables allows considerably more information to be transferred quickly and accurately by telecommunications, and so can lead to high labour-content jobs such as data input, order processing and invoicing being carried out in other countries. It is on this foundation that India has built a global advantage in offering high tech services such as data processing, call centres and software application.

Market factors

Consumers' response   Perhaps the most critical factor to be considered when developing a pricing strategy in international markets, however, is how the customers and competitors will respond.

There are nine factors which influence the sensitivity of customers to prices and all have implications for the international marketer. Price sensitivity reduces:

- the more distinctive the product is;
- the greater the perceived quality;
- the less aware consumers are of substitutes in the market;
- if it is difficult to make comparisons, for example in the quality of services such as consultancy or accountancy;
- if the price of a product represents a small proportion of total expenditure of the customer;
- as the perceived benefit increases;
- if the product is used in association with a product bought previously so that, for example, components and replacements are usually extremely highly priced;
- if costs are shared with other parties;
- if the product or service cannot be stored.

The issue with all these factors is that it is customer perceptions and purchasing behaviour which are most important in setting prices. In France, Disneyland Paris suffered considerably from weaknesses in its financial structure. The fundamental problems were that customer perceptions and demand for Disneyland Paris were out of step with forecasts. The explanation for the weaknesses in their offer was found to be in the factors affecting price sensitivity. High interest rates and high labour costs in France were underestimated and the availability of disposable income of potential consumers overestimated; particularly during and following the global financial crises. This means after 22 years Disneyland Paris still runs at a loss. In 2014 Walt Disney provided a US$1.5 billion bailout for their French resort and it is hoped that, following the launch of the Star Wars attraction in 2017, Disneyland Paris will make a profit (Possebon 2014). Customers' perception of credit can also influence purchasing behaviour. In Central Europe and Asia consumers have been reluctant to borrow money to buy goods.

Competitors' response   As competition increases in virtually every product and market, the likely response of the competitors to a firm's pricing strategy becomes increasingly important. An attempt should be made to forecast how competitors might react to a change in pricing strategy by analyzing the market and product factors which affect them, consumer perceptions of their product offers and their **internal cost structures**. Competitors' pricing strategies will be affected by such issues as their commitment to particular products and markets, and the stance that they might have adopted in the past during periods of fierce competition.

Before implementing pricing strategies and tactics, therefore, it is essential to estimate the likely consumer and competitor response by evaluating similar situations which have arisen in other international markets or countries. The responses of competitors who adopt a global strategic approach are likely to be more easily predicted than a competitor adopting a multidomestic strategy.

Developing pricing strategies

Having discussed the factors which firms should consider in the pricing process, we now turn to the development of international pricing strategies. The first question to be addressed is to what extent prices should be standardized across the markets. There are three approaches to international pricing strategies.

Standardization, or **ethnocentric** pricing, based on setting a price for the product as it leaves the factory, irrespective of its final destination. While each customer pays the same price for the product at the factory gate, they are expected to pay transport and import duties themselves, either directly or indirectly, and this leads to considerable differences in the price to the final consumer.

For the firm, this is a low-risk strategy as a fixed return is guaranteed and the international buyer takes all the exchange rate risk. However, no attempt is made to respond to local conditions in each national market and so no effort is made to maximize either profits or sales volume. This type of pricing strategy is often used when selling highly specialized manufacturing plant.

Adaptation, or **polycentric** pricing, allows each local subsidiary or partner to set a price which is considered to be the most appropriate for local conditions, and no attempt is made to coordinate prices from country to country. The only constraints that are applied when using this strategy relate to transfer pricing within the corporate structure.

The weakness with this policy is the lack of control that the headquarters have over the prices set by the subsidiary operations. Significantly different prices must be set in adjacent markets, and this can reflect badly on the image of multinational firms. It also encourages the creation of grey markets (which are dealt with in greater detail later in this chapter), whereby products can be purchased in one market and sold in another, undercutting the established market prices in the process. Firms marketing on the Internet find it very difficult to pursue such strategies, because of the free flow of information across markets. Gap customers soon discovered they could save up to 40 per cent of the price of a garment by buying online rather than in their local store, leading to a speedy change in their pricing strategy.

Invention, or **geocentric** pricing, involves neither fixing a single price, nor allowing local subsidiaries total freedom for setting prices either, but attempts to take the best of both approaches. While the need to take account of local factors is recognized, particularly in the short term, the firm still expects local pricing strategies to be integrated into a company-wide long-term strategy. The benefits of this approach are shown in the following example. A firm which intends to establish a manufacturing base within a particular region may need to rapidly increase market share in order to generate the additional sales necessary for a viable production plant. In the short term, the local subsidiary may be required to sell at what for them is an uneconomic price, so that by the time the new plant comes on stream, sufficient sales have built up to make the plant and the individual subsidiaries profitable.

The objectives of pricing

The objectives of the firm's pricing strategy are directly related to the various factors which have been discussed, but it should be emphasized that they will be affected as much by the prevailing company culture and attitudes to international marketing as by market and environmental conditions. The most common pricing objectives for companies are listed below, but it must be recognized that firms also adapt or add other specific objectives according to their own specific and changing circumstances. The alternative approaches are:

- *Rate of return.* Cost-orientated companies set prices to achieve a specific level of return on investment, and may quote the same ex-works price for both domestic and international markets.
- *Market stabilization.* A firm may choose not to provoke retaliation from the leader, so that market shares are not significantly changed.
- *Demand-led pricing.* Prices are adjusted according to an assessment of demand, so that high prices are charged when demand is buoyant and low prices are charged when demand is weak.
- *Competition-led pricing.* In commodity markets such as coffee and wheat, world market prices are established through continual interaction between buyers and sellers. Selling outside the narrow band of prices that have been mutually agreed will either reduce sales or unnecessarily reduce profits.
- *Pricing to reflect product differentiation.* Individual products are used to emphasize differences between products targeted at various market segments. Carmakers, for example, charge prices for the top-of-the-range models which are far higher than is justified by the cost of the additional features which distinguish them from the basic models, but problems arise in different international markets, as consumers' perceptions vary as to what is considered to be a basic model.
- *Market skimming.* The objective of market skimming is for the firm to enter the market at a high price and lower the price only gradually, or even abandon the market as competition increases. It is often used by companies in recovering high research and development costs.

■ *Market penetration.* Low prices can be used by a firm to rapidly increase sales by stimulating growth and increasing market share, but at the same time discouraging competition. Japanese companies have used this strategy extensively to gain leadership in a number of markets, such as cars, home entertainment products and electronic components.

■ *Early cash recovery.* Faced with liquidity problems, products in the mature or declining phase of the product life cycle, or products with an uncertain future in the market because of changes in government policy, a firm may aim for early cash recovery, to increase sales and generate cash rapidly. A variety of mechanisms are used, including special offers, discounts for prompt payment and rigorous credit control; all this type of pricing is a form of **marginal cost pricing.**

■ *Prevent new entry.* Competitors can be discouraged from entering a market by establishing low prices which will indicate to potential competitors the prospect of low returns and price wars. Domestic firms have used this strategy to attempt to prevent entry by international competitors; however, the danger is that the other firm might successfully enter the market with a quite different positioning, such as higher specification or quality, or with improved service levels. The defending firm, due to its low-price strategy, may not have the income to make the necessary investment to compete with the new entrant.

Setting a price

Having determined suitable strategies for pricing in international markets, a company must then consider the options available in setting individual prices. Companies can decide on the basis of their knowledge, objectives and situation to take either a cost, market or competition-orientated approach.

Cost-orientated approaches are intended to either:

■ achieve a specific return on investment; or
■ ensure an early recovery of either cash, or investments made to enter the market.

Market-orientated pricing approaches give the company the opportunity to:

■ stabilize competitive positions within the market;
■ skim the most profitable business; or
■ penetrate the market by adopting an aggressive strategy to increase market share.

Competition-orientated approaches are designed to:

■ maintain and improve market position;
■ meet and follow competition;
■ reflect differences in the perceived value and performance of competitive products; or
■ prevent or discourage new entrants in the market.

No matter which of these broad strategies are adopted, the process for determining export pricing is essentially the same:

■ determine export market potential;
■ estimate the price range and target price;
■ calculate sales potential at the target price;
■ evaluate tariff and non-tariff barriers;
■ select suitable pricing strategy in line with company objectives;
■ consider likely competitor response;
■ select pricing tactics, set distributor and end-user prices;
■ monitor performance and take necessary corrective action.

Problems of pricing and financing international transactions

There are a number of specific problems which arise in setting and managing prices in international markets. Problems arise in four main areas:

1 *Problems in multinational pricing.* Companies find difficulty in coordinating and controlling prices across their activities sufficiently to enable them to achieve effective financial performance and their desired price positioning:

 - How can prices be coordinated by the company across the various markets?
 - How can a company retain uniform price positioning in different market situations?
 - At what price should a company transfer products or services from a subsidiary in one country to a subsidiary in another?
 - How can a firm deal with importation and sale of its products by an unauthorized dealer?

2 *Problems in managing foreign currency and fluctuating exchange rates.* Considerable problems arise in foreign transactions because of the need to buy and sell products in different currencies:

 - In what currency should a company price its products in international markets?
 - How should the company deal with fluctuating exchange rates?
 - How can a company minimize exchange rate risk over the longer-term transactions?

3 *Problems of obtaining suitable payment in high-risk markets.* Obtaining payment promptly and in a suitable currency from the less developed countries can cause expense and additional difficulties:

 - How might/should a company deal with selling to countries where there is a risk of non-payment?
 - How should a company approach selling to countries which have a shortage of hard currency or high inflation?
 - How can a company obtain payment upfront on long-term transactions?

4 *Administrative problems of cross-border transfer of goods.* Problems of bureaucracy and delays arise as a result of simply moving goods physically across borders:

 - At what point should an exporter release control and responsibility for goods?
 - What steps can be taken in the export order process to minimize delays?

These four major problem areas will now be dealt with in the following sections.

Problems in multinational pricing

Coordination of prices across markets

The pressure on companies to market truly global products backed by globally standardized advertising campaigns is caused by three major trends: the homogenization of customer demand, the lowering of trade barriers and the emergence of international competitors. At the same time these largely undifferentiated global products can be sold at very different prices in different countries, based on factors such as purchasing power, exchange rate changes and competition and consumer preferences.

Until recently this has been a perfectly acceptable practice. However, in the past decade it has become increasingly difficult for companies to maintain a differentiated pricing strategy across international markets when they are marketing similar if not standardized products. Readily available information on worldwide prices through modern data transfer and the Internet have greatly increased price transparency.

Advances in telecommunications systems have also greatly reduced international transaction costs. Global companies who obviously follow differentiated pricing policies are often threatened, first by an erosion of consumer confidence as customers learn of the more attractive pricing policies in other markets and second by **grey marketing** which can result in the cannibalization of sales in countries with relatively high prices and damaging relationships with authorized distributors.

European Monetary Union   The issue of achieving **price coordination** across markets has become particularly pertinent in the European Union (EU) since the establishment of the European Monetary Union (EMU). The EMU, sometimes called the Eurozone or Euro area, is the name given to the union of countries using the euro as a domestic currency.

National price levels across the EU are far from uniform. Among the Eurozone countries, Austria and Finland are viewed as high-priced markets, France, Belgium and Germany are seen as average, Portugal and Spain as having much lower prices. Price levels in Scandinavia can be 40 per cent higher than in southern parts of the Eurozone. This has caused some difficulties for companies who have tried to differentiate prices as in the case of the scandal around European envelope manufacturers in Management Challenge 11.2.

Differences in taxation and excise duties as well as disparities in **production costs** and wage levels lead to price differentials and difficulties in managing problems in the economy. Firms in product markets have tended to adapt their prices to the buying power, income levels and consumer preferences of national

MANAGEMENT CHALLENGE 11.2

Envelope scandal: Are your purchases fair?

The envelope business has been under pressure recently due to consumers and organizations reducing their use of postal services. However, that is no excuse for breaking EU law by breaching Anti-trust Competition rules. Five envelope manufacturers: Bong (Sweden), GPV (France), Hamelin (France), Mayer-Kuvert (Germany) and Tompla (Spain) did just that when they formed a cartel and manipulated the prices charged for envelopes.

Under the EU anti-trust competition rules it is prohibited for two or more organizations to join forces and restrict competition. There are two particular rules brought forward in the envelope scandal:

Horizontal agreements (agreements with other competitors within the same marketplace) cannot join forces and restrict competition.

Vertical agreements (agreements with distributors and manufacturers) cannot be made to restrict competition.

Additionally businesses must not charge unfair (uncompetitive) prices.

The European Commission found that the envelope manufacturers mentioned had abused their position and they were all fined under the aforementioned anti-trust competition rules. The envelope manufacturers were corrupt because they had internal, high-level discussions about the prices they would sell their envelopes for. Therefore, when envelope 'bids to tender' were announced each manufacturer would share their bid price with the other envelope manufacturers. The purpose of sharing the bid price was to raise envelope prices, and to distribute 'fairly' the number of bids each business was awarded. This behaviour manipulated prices and was recognized as corrupt.

The five envelope manufacturers were fined €19.5m in total.

Many consumers and distributers consider this behaviour to be an indirect way of robbing the consumer; who after all bore the brunt of the inflated prices.

Questions

1 Discuss the advantages of the anti-trust competition rules on pricing.

2 Should envelope manufacturers always control the price aspect of the marketing mix?

Sources: Nais, S. (2015) European Commission fines envelope cartel €19.5m. Available at www.printweek.com /print-week/news/1148964/european-commission-fines-envelope-cartel-eur195m (accessed 23 May 2015).

markets. However, in the service sector and particularly the tourism industry, it is not very easy to differentiate prices to reflect the differences in buying power and consumer preferences of the variety of national and international consumers that a company may be targeting.

Prior to the formation of the EMU these differences were largely concealed from the European consumer, despite the formation of the Single European Market. The formation of the EMU and the introduction of the euro has changed all that. Now prices are no longer distorted by fluctuating exchange rates. This means companies competing on the European market need to consider the implications of the **price transparency** in the Eurozone. The onset of price transparency impacts on firms in different ways. Highly specialized products with few direct rivals are largely immune to the risk of price transparency generating more intense competition. However, companies marketing goods that are supplied direct to the consumer have come under increasing pressure from retailers to reduce margins if retailers themselves have had to cut prices to meet new price points set in euros. Furthermore, more retailers and businesses have moved to a policy of European-wide sourcing and using the Internet to search for the lowest prices for products. It has, therefore, become virtually impossible for companies to operate on the European market without a sophisticated strategy to effectively coordinate prices across the EU. It is this that has led to so many companies revamping their approach to managing their European marketing strategies.

Firms who have failed to meet this challenge have left themselves open to the threat of grey market goods cannibalizing their sales in high-priced national markets.

Economic and Monetary Union and the euro were introduced to help achieve the goal of a single European market. One particular objective was to create a single market where currency could move as freely and cheaply in the Eurozone as it could within national markets. However, to achieve a truly single market, integration of payment facilities across borders was needed to create a single financial services market across the Euro zone. This is known as the Single European Payments Area (SEPA).

The key problem SEPA resolves for companies marketing across the Eurozone is the differences they face between the way domestic and cross-border payments operate and are priced. With the SEPA in place, companies can execute any payment within the euro area as easily and at the same cost as they could in their existing domestic markets.

The objective of SEPA introduced in 2008 was to create a single payment area where consumers and businesses can make cross-border payments as easily, safely and efficiently as they can within their own countries and perhaps most importantly, as cheaply. Cross-border euro payments are treated exactly like domestic payments whatever their amount. It could still take three business days from order to receipt for cross-border payments, as opposed to a single day within a country, and it still means companies face cross-border pricing difficulties with customers outside the SEPA (see Illustration 11.3 for the latest information on SEPA improvements). In the SEPA there has been a consolidation of the cross-border payment infrastructure which means there are now common rules for clearing and settlement, which means costs are minimized and processes quicker. The harmonized European payments infrastructure also makes it possible to implement efficient e-solutions. According to GTnews.com, e-payments will soon account for 95–99 per cent of the total volume of payments.

What is grey marketing?

As said above, grey marketing has become a particular problem for companies operating across Europe where there are huge price differentials and trade barriers so goods are able to flow freely across borders. Grey marketing is a business phenomenon that has seen unprecedented growth in the past few years as information on prices has flowed across countries and consumers have discovered how varied prices can be when companies try to pursue highly differentiated pricing strategies across markets that can no longer be kept separate.

Grey marketing occurs when trademarked goods are sold through channels of distribution that have not been given authority to sell the goods by the trademark holder. This could occur within a country but more and more it is becoming common across countries. This becomes problematic, especially for global marketers trying to manage a coordinated marketing strategy across different markets. Coca-Cola had to bring forward the European launch of Vanilla Coke after it found the product was already being sold in the UK by a distributor who had imported it directly from Canada, where it had been launched several months

SEPA: Fast, efficient and cost effective

Out of the 28 Member States of the European Union, 19 countries are in the Eurozone. The countries in the Eurozone are Austria, Belgium, Cyprus, Estonia, Finland, France, Germany, Greece, Ireland, Italy, Latvia, Lithuania, Luxembourg, Malta, the Netherlands, Portugal, Slovakia, Slovenia and Spain have the euro as their official currency.

The Single Euro Payments Area (SEPA) was formed in 2008 between the countries of the Eurozone. The aim was that banks dealing with transfers in euros between members of the Eurozone (SEPA Credit Transfers) would charge no more for such cross border transfers than they charged for domestic transfers. In practice, this means no charge at all in several countries where domestic transfers are free of commission. Banks outside the Eurozone still charge substantial commissions for cross-border transfers of funds. Typical remitting costs from the UK are £9 per transaction for small personal payments, and £20 and upwards pro rata for commercial payments. This means that non-euro payments made to SEPA destinations attract charges at the remitting end, and then are often charged commission of €30 or more by the receiving bank within the SEPA for converting the received funds into euros. This meant that pricing decisions made by non-Eurozone businesses trading in Europe would have to factor these costs into their prices, possibly affecting their competitiveness in their European markets.

Since 2008, non-Eurozone businesses wishing to transfer funds to SEPA beneficiaries can save by ensuring that the funds are converted into Euros by the remitting bank, as SEPA rules now forbid the receiving bank from levying commission on incoming euro transfers as long as IBANs (International Bank Account Numbers) and BICs (Bank Identifier Codes) of the beneficiary are correctly quoted on the transfer.

To improve SEPA further a Direct Debit Scheme was introduced in November 2009 to enable euro payments to be collected by creditors more quickly and cost efficiently than was previously possible. Clients using this scheme will need to operate a euro account with a bank in a SEPA country.

SEPA has had some problems. Harmonization across so many countries and businesses is bound to cause upheaval. Therefore, from 2016 SEPA transaction compliance is mandatory.

Mandatory compliance will continue to improve SEPA and will be beneficial to over 20 million businesses and European public authorities. SEPA provides an 'open door' to new European distributors, markets and suppliers, because it is now cheaper to do business with all countries across the SEPA zone.

This means it is no longer necessary for a UK organization, or any other non-Eurozone organization, to open local bank accounts for payments and collections in the European countries in which they do business. With this type of money management system a UK organization can lower their costs and move money speedily as some member states move money within the hour (and not three days as it was previously). UK retailers are particularly happy with SEPA as they will now be able to have lower-fee one card-payment terminals for all consumers with a SEPA compliant card.

Question

1 What are the benefits of using SEPA?

Source: EU (2014) Questions and Answers on SEPA Last updated 11.11.2014. Available from www.ec.europa.eu/finance/payments/sepa/faq/index_en.htm (accessed 20 May 2015).

previously. Typically, however, grey market goods are international brands with high price differentials and low costs of arbitrage. The costs connected with the arbitrage are transportation, tariffs, taxes and the costs of modifying the product, i.e. changing the language of instructions.

It is perhaps important to point out that there is nothing illegal about grey market goods; it is purely the practice of buying a product in one market and selling it in other markets in order to benefit from the prevailing price differential. Grey markets tend to develop in markets where information on prices for basically the same product in different countries is cheap and easy to obtain (e.g. cars, designer goods, consumer durables). Sadly, despite the wonders that the Internet brings for marketers in terms of global consumers, extensive 24/7 promotional opportunities and innovative distribution/place channels, the Internet is a breeding ground for grey market activity. Just like all the positive things that the Internet brings, the downside of the Internet grey market is often products are sold at as much as 25 per cent less than the authorized price (and have the biggest influence on pricing, product availability, and movement of products across borders). KPMG estimates the revenue generated by international grey marketing activities to be about US$25 billion a year. While grey marketing is seen by its critics as a free-riding strategy, it is being increasingly seen as a viable international strategy by smaller firms who, with limited resources, can use it to compete against larger firms in international markets.

There are three types of grey markets (see Figure 11.1):

1 *Parallel importing*. When the product is priced lower in the home market where it is produced than the export market. The grey marketer in the export market will parallel import directly from the home market rather than source from within their own country; for example, there is a strong parallel import trade in Levi jeans between the USA and Europe. Levi Strauss took out a lawsuit against the retail chain Tesco for selling Levi jeans they sourced directly from outside the EU. Levi insisted that jeans in Europe should only be sourced from authorized dealers within the EU. The judgment by the court, which shocked consumer rights groups everywhere, was that Tesco should not be allowed to import jeans made by Levi Strauss from outside the EU and sell them at reduced prices without first getting permission from the jeans maker. The high-end market in particular suffers from grey marketing which is why Louis Vuitton are worried about their increased sales figures (see Illustration 11.4).

2 *Re-importing*. When the product is priced cheaper in an export market than in the home market where it was produced; re-importation in this case can be profitable to the grey marketer.

3 *Lateral importing*. When there is a price difference between export markets, products are sold from one country to another through unauthorized channels.

A disturbing example of this can be found in the pharmaceutical industry, where it is estimated that US$18 million of reduced-price HIV drugs intended for African markets were diverted back to Europe to be sold at much higher prices on the grey market.

FIGURE 11.1   Three types of grey market

Note: Price in Country B < price in Country C

Source: Assnus, G. and Wiesse, C. (1995) 'How to address the gray market threat using price coordination', in I. Doole and R. Lowe, *International Marketing Strategy: Contemporary readings,* International Thomson Business Press.

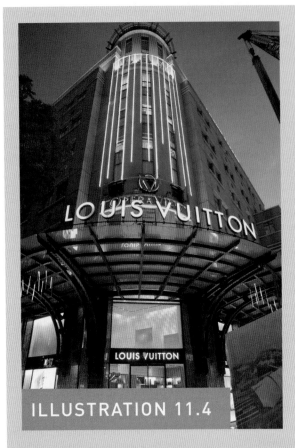

ILLUSTRATION 11.4

Louis Vuitton sells to 'retailer tourists'

LVMH Moet Hennessy had an excellent start to the year 2015. LVMH's overall sales figures had increased by 16 per cent during the first quarter (Q1) compared to those shown during the same period in 2014. Their sales in fashion and leather goods certainly contributed to this increase as sales in Q1 2014 were €2639 million rising to €2975 million in Q1 2015. LVMH state that it is product innovation and fashion shows that keep their clothes and handbags *alive* and *desired*; particularly by the fashionable elite in Japan, US and Europe. It is for this reason their sales have increased. However, LVMH are worried that they are *competing with themselves* as grey markets are creeping in.

Their main fear is the Chinese grey market. The average wealth of Chinese citizens has grown in recent years. The number of Chinese millionaires has grown to 3 per cent of the world's total number of millionaires. With the increase in wealth Chinese consumers are a major force behind the increased sales of many luxury items. The desire for global, luxurious but discerning brands is unabated. What is interesting, but worrying to LVMH, is that 50 per cent of luxury items that are bought by Chinese consumers are bought outside China.

LVMH's products, such as handbags, are sold for higher prices in China than they are sold in Europe. The reason for this is that import duties on luxury goods to be sold in China can be as high as 25 per cent, VAT 17 per cent and Consumption Tax can be as much as 45 per cent; Consumption Tax is especially high for luxury items. Chinese consumers are aware of this and flock to Europe or the US to 'snap up a bargain' LVMH handbag. Chinese 'holiday retailers', who do not declare themselves as retail buyers, buy LVMH handbags in bulk at lower prices in Europe or the US. Upon return to China 'holiday retailers' resell LVMH handbags at inflated prices or worse still below the price of LVMH handbags sold through official distribution channels.

LVMH could of course reduce the price of handbags in China to stop the 'holiday retailer'. Or they could increase the price of handbags in Europe and the US to reduce the price gap between China and Europe/US.

Question

1 Do you think large international companies should manage grey marketing in the distribution channels through legal or pricing means or let the market itself act as a regulator?

Sources: Atsmon, Y., Ducarme, D., Magni, M. and Wu, C. (2012) Luxury without borders: China's new class of shoppers take on the world, McKinsey and Company. Available from www.mckinseychina.com (accessed 13 September 2014); Brinnded, L. (2015) LVMH is cannibalising itself in China, published 14 April 2015. Available from www.uk.businessinsider.com/lvmh-q1-revenue-analyst-call-on-pricing-policy-luxury-goods-arbitrage-and-the-grey-market-2015-4 (accessed 13 May 2015); Credit Suisse (2014) Global Wealth Report 2014 CREDIT SUISSE AG: Switzerland.

Price coordination strategies

Typically firms try to defend themselves against grey market activities by calling for government intervention or legal protection. As seen in the previous section, companies may resort to imposing restrictions or even threats on retailers. In the US, Walmart sourced products through grey markets and suffered the resultant threats from firms such as Adidas and Levi jeans. Other reactive measures have included the refusal to issue warranties in certain markets, or even buying out the grey marketer.

Companies competing in international markets who wish to develop more effective strategies to deal with the problem of price coordination across increasingly interdependent markets and the threat of grey market goods have four options open to them:

1 *Economic measures*. The company can influence the country manager's pricing decision by controlling the input into those decisions. A multinational can do this through transfer pricing (see the later section in this chapter). By raising the price by which it transfers products to the low-priced country the headquarters essentially imposes a tax on that market. Closely related to transfer pricing is rationing the product quantities allocated to each country or region and so limiting the number of units sold in the diverting country.

2 *Centralization*. The company can move towards more centralization in the setting of prices. Traditionally many multinational companies have given country managers a high degree of decision-making autonomy. Usually they are in the best position to assess consumer response to any given pricing decisions and they are able to react swiftly to competitor activity. A centralized approach, however, could overcome difficulties with grey market goods although it does usually result in dissatisfaction among country managers. A compromise approach is to shift the decision-making authority in pricing from a country to a regional level; however, increasingly grey market goods are becoming a global issue.

3 *Formalization*. The company can standardize the process of planning and implementing pricing decisions. Thus the company influences prices at the local level by prescribing a process that is followed by country managers when establishing pricing policy.

4 *Informal coordination*. A number of companies have moved towards a more informal system of coordination without either a high degree of centralization or formalization. This thinking is usual in the transnational company where international subsidiaries make differentiated and innovative contributions to an integrated worldwide operation. While this approach may incorporate a variety of techniques, the essential asset is that there are common shared business values across the subsidiaries that are backed by compatible incentive systems.

In a proactive approach to coordinating its pricing decision across international markets, a company has to select the appropriate strategy which will in effect be determined, first, by the level of local resources available, and then by the level of environmental complexity, as illustrated in Figure 11.2.

FIGURE 11.2 A framework for selecting a coordination method

Source: Assnus, G. and Wiesse, C. (1995) 'How to address the gray market threat using price coordination', in I. Doole and R. Lowe, *International Marketing Strategy: Contemporary readings,* International Thomson Business Press.

Transfer pricing in international markets

Transfer pricing is an area that has created complications for many international marketing firms. It is concerned with the pricing of goods sold within a corporate family, when the transactions involved are from division to division, to a foreign subsidiary or to a partner in a joint venture agreement. While these transfer prices are internal to the company, they are important externally because goods being transferred from country to country must have a value for cross-border taxation purposes.

The objective of the corporation in this situation is to ensure that the transfer price paid optimizes corporate rather than divisional objectives. This can prove difficult when a company internationally is organized into profit centres. For profit centres to work effectively, a price must be set for everything that is transferred, be it working materials, components, finished goods or services. A high transfer price, for example from the domestic division to a foreign subsidiary, is reflected in an apparently poor performance by the foreign subsidiary, whereas a low price would not be acceptable to the domestic division providing the goods. This issue alone can be the cause of much mistrust between subsidiaries – at best leading to fierce arguments, and at worst leading to loss of business through overpricing.

There tend to be three bases for transfer pricing:

1 *Transfer at cost.* In which the transfer price is set at the level of the production cost, and the international division is credited with the entire profit that the firm makes. This means that the production centre is evaluated on efficiency parameters rather than profitability.

2 *Transfer at arm's-length.* When the international division is charged the same as any buyer outside the firm. Problems occur if the overseas division is allowed to buy elsewhere when the price is uncompetitive or the product quality is inferior, and further difficulties arise if there are no external buyers, making it difficult to establish a relevant price. This is the strategy most preferred by national governments and the agreed general principle of the OECD. The OECD say this principle should govern transfer pricing transactions and has published detailed guidelines to guide companies.

3 *Transfer at cost plus.* Is a compromise, where profits are split between the production and international divisions. The actual formula used for assessing the transfer price can vary, but usually it is this method which has the greatest chance of minimizing executive time spent on transfer price disagreements, optimizing corporate profits and motivating the home and international divisions. Often a senior executive is appointed to rule on disputes.

However, the real interest of transfer pricing is how it is used strategically by companies either to act as a barrier to entry, or to marshal resources around the world.

To create barriers to entry

Most oil companies are vertically integrated, from oil exploration right through to selling petrol at the pumps, and use transfer pricing as part of their strategy to maintain barriers to entry. The major cost for oil companies is at the exploration and refining stage and so, by charging high transfer prices for crude oil, profits are generated at the refining stage of the process, rather than in distribution, where it is relatively easy to enter the market. Oil companies, therefore, attempt, by the use of transfer pricing, to make petrol distribution unattractive to potential competitors. Supermarkets and hypermarkets, with their huge purchasing power, have managed to challenge the dominance of the oil companies by using low-priced petrol as a loss-leader to entice customers to stores.

To avoid domestic tax liabilities

When countries have different levels of taxation on corporate profits, firms try to ensure that profits are accumulated at the most advantageous point. Companies operating in countries with high corporation tax may be tempted to sell at low transfer prices to their subsidiaries in countries with lower corporate taxation.

To avoid foreign tax

Foreign tax authorities wish to maximize the taxable income within their jurisdiction, and there are a number of strategies a company might use to avoid tax – for example, by charging lower transfer prices if there is high customs duty on goods. The impact of such avoidance strategies is diminishing, as customs authorities become more aware of this practice. Recently the US government demanded huge taxes from Sony when it discovered that it generated 60 per cent of its global sales in the USA but very little profit due to Sony's management of transfer pricing. Japan then retaliated by doing the same to Coca-Cola. However, it can be argued that as the general level of import duties is reducing as international trade agreements come into effect, so the need to take avoiding action is declining.

To manage the level of involvement in markets

If a firm has both a wholly owned subsidiary and a joint venture in a particular country, it will wish to sell at a higher price to a company with which it has a joint venture than one that is a wholly-owned subsidiary. Selling at a low price to foreign partnerships or licensees has the effect of sharing more of the profit with the partner.

Transfer pricing is an area where profit objectives, managerial motivations and government regulation interact and so the expertise of many people – accountants, legal counsel, tax advisors and division managers – is needed to achieve an agreement. The international marketing manager's contribution is primarily concerned with two aspects of the problem:

- achieving an effective distribution of goods to world markets;
- ensuring that the impact of the transfer price does not affect foreign market opportunities.

Problems in managing foreign currency transactions

Perhaps the most critical issue for managers is how to deal with the various problems involved in managing transactions which involve currency exchange; a second difficulty is what action to take when selling to countries where there is high inflation.

What currency should the price be quoted in?

In any international marketing transaction, the exporter has the option of quoting in either the domestic or the local currency. If the exporter quotes in their own domestic currency, then not only is it administratively much easier, but also the risks associated with changes in the exchange rate are borne by the customer, whereas by quoting prices in the **foreign currency** the exporter bears the **exchange rate risk**. However, there are benefits to the exporter in quoting in foreign currency:

- it could provide access to finance abroad at lower interest rates;
- good currency management may be a means of gaining additional profits;
- quoting in foreign currency could be a condition of the contract;
- customers normally prefer to be quoted in their own currency in order to be able to make competitive comparisons and to know exactly what the eventual price will be.

Furthermore, customers in export markets often prefer quotations in their own currency to enable them to more easily compare the tenders of competitors from a range of countries.

Often the choice of currency for the price quotation depends partly on the trade practices in the export market and the industry concerned. Suppliers competing for business in the oil industry, wherever in the world they may be supplying, may well find they are asked to quote in US dollars. In the airline industry things are more complicated. EADS, the European group manufacturing the Airbus plane, has all its costs in euros, but on the global market, planes are priced in US dollars. This gives the US company Boeing an

MANAGEMENT CHALLENGE 11.3

Can we avoid the currency risk without losing our customers?

Management Development Ltd (MDL) is a small firm specializing in management training and development. The firm delivers training programmes using a combination of self-study material and study weekends and operates in the UK, Middle East and the Far East.

Ten years ago the firm took a strategic decision to enter the Malaysian market. They appointed an agent in Malaysia to market the courses and recruit students. To encourage students to join training, course payment could be made in stages.

The majority of the firm's costs, developing study material, tutoring, etc. were incurred in sterling.

The income from selling in Malaysia would normally be in ringgits. Income in ringgits and costs in sterling meant MDL faced a currency risk. Traditional methods for avoiding currency exposure (hedging) were not considered appropriate due to the small scale of the operation.

Over the last ten years the financial results from the contract have been poor. Prices have been going up by 5 to 10 per cent per year and recruitment has been good but still the firm is failing to make a reasonable return. MDL's accountant says you only need to look at the HM Revenue and Customs exchange rate database to find the reason (www.hmrc.gov.uk/exrate/malaysia.htm).

Question

1 How should MDL resolve their dilemma?

Source: Fiona Elspeth.

---

advantage competing on international markets, because they do not have the same exchange risk as EADS and can forecast their costs and prices with much more certainty than their arch rival Airbus.

When exporters experience a period of strong home currency it reduces their competitiveness on international markets and makes them vulnerable to price-cutting pressures from international customers, as happened to MDL (see Management Challenge 11.3).

Thus, as well as the decision as to what currency to quote in, the main worry for both suppliers and customers on international markets is fluctuating exchange rates and how to deal with them.

The introduction of the euro has effectively eliminated exchange rate risk in the Eurozone countries. Even countries like the UK, who have decided not to enter the EMU for the present time, increasingly find that companies selling goods into Europe are pressurized to quote prices in the euro.

Should prices be raised/lowered as exchange rates fluctuate?

One of the most difficult problems that exporters face is caused by fluctuating exchange rates.

Sarathy, Terpstra and Russow (2006) identified three types of risk affecting firms, arising from exchange rate fluctuations:

1 *Transaction risk*. This occurs when the exporter quotes in a foreign currency, which then appreciates, diminishing the financial return to the firm. US hoteliers in Hawaii experienced a noticeable decline in Japanese tourism when the dollar rose in value from ¥90 to ¥120 in just over a year.

2 *Competitive risk*. Arises because the geographic pattern of a firm's manufacturing and sales puts them at a disadvantage compared to their competition. If, for instance, the firm is manufacturing in a country with an appreciating currency but trying to compete in a marketplace where currencies are depreciating, it could lose out to a local manufacturer. Firms may then try to maximize their expenditure in the market place. This is why Mercedes and BMW are now manufacturing in the USA.

3 *Market portfolio risk*. This risk occurs because a company with a narrow market portfolio will be influenced to a much greater extent by changes in exchange rates than a diversified firm that is better able to balance changes in exchange rates through operating in many countries.

Various tactics can be adopted to deal with currency fluctuations. When the domestic currency is weak, the firm should:

- compete on price;
- introduce new products with additional features;
- source and manufacture in the domestic country;
- fully exploit export opportunities;
- obtain payment in cash;
- use a full-cost approach for existing markets, but use marginal costs for new more competitive markets;
- repatriate foreign-earned income quickly;
- reduce expenditure and buy services (advertising, transport, etc.) locally;
- minimize overseas borrowing;
- invoice in domestic currency.

When the domestic currency is strong, the firm should:

- compete on non-price factors (quality, delivery, service);
- improve productivity and reduce costs;
- prioritize strong currency countries for exports;
- use countertrade for weak currency countries;
- reduce profit margins and use marginal costs for pricing;
- keep the foreign-earned income in the local country;
- maximize expenditures in local country currency;
- buy services abroad in local currencies;
- borrow money for expansion in local markets;
- invoice foreign customers in their own currency.

Problems in minimizing the risk of non-payment in high-risk countries

The international marketing manager increasingly needs to be knowledgeable about the various complexities of financing international marketing transactions and sources of finance to support international marketing strategies, especially when trading with markets is seen to be high risk due to adverse economic and political conditions, high inflation or perhaps lack of hard currency. For a company exporting goods to such markets there is a considerable risk of non-payment for a variety of reasons, such as:

- the buyer failing or refusing to pay for the goods;
- insolvency of the buyer;
- a general moratorium on external debt by the host;
- government political and legal decisions;
- war;
- failure to fulfil the conditions of the contract;
- lack of hard currency;
- high inflation.

Traditionally managers will seek financial support to help reduce the risk of non-payment due to these factors through home governments, commercial banks or some kind of cooperation agreement.

Government-sponsored finance   Governments are often willing to financially support companies in financing international trade transactions in the hope that increased exports will generate economic growth at home and boost employment. National governments approach such support in a variety of ways but in most countries there is an export–import bank or perhaps export bank or, as in the UK, a government department (Trade Partners UK) who fund a variety of support packages to help companies finance export strategies. Governments will also provide low-cost export guarantee insurance to protect their exporters against non-payment by foreign buyers. However, such protection may not be available in particularly high-risk markets.

Commercial banks   Commercial banks compete intensively to offer international trade services to companies operating in international markets. However, they tend only to be willing to support low-risk activities, which sometimes makes it difficult for companies expanding into emerging markets. Commercial banks may also be more interested in short-term financing, and so potentially not such a good source for companies making a long-term investment decision in incipient markets where it may be several years before a full return on investment can be achieved. Many banks who made long-term loans to developing markets have suffered losses when countries not experiencing the growth rates expected have been unable to meet debt repayments. This has led to a number of banks being less willing to exposure in long-term high-risk markets.

One of the ways banks can help against the risk of non-payment is by forfaiting.

Forfaiting   This is a way of financing without recourse. It means that companies selling products essentially transfer the transaction risk to a forfaiting house. A bill of exchange, usually requiring a bank guarantee or, as in the US, a back up letter of credit, is drawn up to the value of the contract and the seller transfers the claim resulting from the transaction to the forfaiting house. The seller immediately receives the full amount of the contract minus the discount agreed for the period of the contract. This discount will vary depending on the length of the contract, the level of country risk and whether the invoice is guaranteed by a commercial bank. For the company it provides a source of finance to support medium-term contracts in a market and a means of reducing the risk of non-payment.

Cooperation agreements   These agreements are special kinds of countertrade deals (see below) that extend over long periods of time and may have government involvement. They may be called product purchase transactions, buyback deals or pay as you earn deals. For instance, a company may obtain finance to help set up a factory in a particular country if they then agree to buy back the output of the plant.

Countertrade and leasing

So far in this chapter we have focused upon largely conventional approaches to international pricing; however, over the past two decades there has been a dramatic increase in the use of leasing and countertrade deals, which are used as a response to the lack of hard currency, particularly among less developed countries.

Counter trade deals are more prevalent when companies are trying to enter emerging or less developed markets. The reason for this is threefold:

■ It is sometimes difficult to obtain finance commercially to enter such markets.

■ The markets themselves may have limited access to hard currency which means the finance of joint ventures or strategic alliances has to be sought through less traditional means.

■ Emerging markets may see such deals as a way of encouraging job creation in their own countries and so actively encourage such financing deals.

What is countertrade?   Countertrade covers various forms of trading arrangements where part or all of the payment for goods is in the form of other goods or services, and price-setting and financing are dealt with together in one transaction. The original and simple barter system has been developed in order to accommodate modern trading situations. Estimates of countertrade activity range from 20 to 30 per cent of world trade, and it is predicted to grow further due to its ability, first, to overcome market imperfections and, second, to provide opportunities for extraordinary profits to be made.

There are many variants of countertrade, resulting from the need to adapt arrangements to meet the needs of individual transactions. The following are the basic forms:

Barter. This is a single exchange of goods with no direct use of money, and does not require intermediaries. It is the simplest form, but has become unpopular because, first, if the goods are not exchanged simultaneously then one participant is effectively financing the other, and second, one of the parties may well receive unwanted goods as part of the deal. Coca Cola has entered several barter deals in Eastern Europe. Russia paid Coca-Cola in vodka, Poland did the same with Coca-Cola but paid in beer.

Compensation trading. This involves an agreement in which payment for goods is accepted in a combination of goods and cash.

Counter-purchase. This involves the negotiation of two contracts. In the first, the international marketer agrees to sell the product at an established price in local currency. In the second, simultaneous contract, the international firm buys goods or services for an equivalent or proportionate cash payment from another local supplier.

Offset. This is similar to counter-purchase, but in this case national governments cooperate to support the deal. Sometimes called a product purchase transaction, it is a way in which the international firm is able to obtain more saleable goods from the country in exchange. For example, Boeing sold AWACS aircraft to the British Ministry of Defence on the basis that the purchase price would be spent on British goods.

Switch deals involve a third party (usually a merchant house), which specializes in barter trading, disposing of the goods. For example, if an Eastern European company importing western products can only provide in return heavily discounted relatively low-quality products, which may not be saleable in the West, a third country will need to be found in order that a switch deal can be set up in which these lower-quality goods can be exchanged for other products that are more suitable for the original western markets.

Cooperation agreements. These can cover buyback deals, pay-as-you-earn deals or a range of other beneficial arrangements made between two parties. It is an arrangement whereby part or all of the cost of purchase of capital equipment might be paid for in the form of production from the equipment supplied, either over time or in the form of some other benefit. See Illustration 11.5.

In Japan and South East Asia compensation and offset are the most frequently used forms of countertrade. Barter and counter-purchase tend to be more common in lesser developed countries.

So far, the examples of countertrade have involved deals of products, but many other less tangible elements such as know-how, software and information can be included in agreements. Many of the deals set up are complicated and in some cases have stretched over many years.

Advantages and limitations of countertrade

The advantages of countertrade are as follows:

- New markets can be developed for a country's products, as marketing and quality control skills are often 'imported' with the deal, and it can lead to gaining experience in western markets.
- Surplus and poorer quality products can be sold through countertrade whereas they could not be sold for cash. Moreover, dumping and heavy discounting can be disguised.
- Countertrade through bilateral and multilateral trade agreement can strengthen political ties.
- Countertrade and contract manufacture can be used to enter high-risk areas.
- Countertrade can provide extraordinary profits as it allows companies to circumvent government restrictions.

ILLUSTRATION 11.5

B2B cooperation between Diageo and pension trustees

Diageo is the owner of global brands including Smirnoff, Baileys and Johnny Walker. Despite continued success in expanding their business internationally, recently they had a big problem. The big problem was the fact Diageo had a pension deficit. The pension deficit meant that Diageo did not have enough money in the pension pot to pay employees when they retired. Diageo were very innovative and organized a cooperation agreement between themselves and Trustees of Diageo's pension plan. Diageo transferred ownership of £430 million worth of Johnny Walker whisky to the Trust. The 2.5 million barrels of whisky did not physically move to the Trustees. This was because

the barrels of whisky had not actually matured. However, the barrels of whisky were a physical asset that Diageo had that would be turned into cash at a future date. The future date would be when the whisky had matured and sold on the open market. The B2B cooperation agreement was accepted between Diageo and the pension Trustees, which in turn meant Diageo could pay retiring employees their pension.

Diageo is not the only company in the UK that has had a pension deficit. M&S and Sainsbury's also had a pension deficit and like Diageo they engaged in a cashless cooperation exchange. M&S and Sainsbury's did not use stock (such as whisky barrels), they used their high-street retail stores as an asset for collateral. British Airways also were in a similar situation and they used aeroplanes in their cooperation exchange. Cooperation exchanges like these are often known as an asset-backed funding (ABF) arrangement.

Question

1 What are the advantages and disadvantages of the cooperation arrangements?

Sources: Kaikati, A.M. and Kaikati, J.G. (2013) 'Doing business without exchanging money: The scale and creativity of modern barter', *California Management Review* (55), 46–71; Mistry, B. (2013) Plugging the pension blackhole, published November 2013, The Treasurer. Available from www.treasurers.org/ACTmedia/Nov13TTtowerswatson38-39.pdf (accessed 31 May 2015).

However, there are disadvantages and limitations in using countertrade:

- There is a lack of flexibility, as the transactions are often dependent on product availability, and countertraded products are often of poor quality, overpriced or are available due to a surplus.
- Products taken in exchange may not fit with the firm's trading objectives, or may be difficult to sell.
- Dealing with companies and government organizations may be difficult, particularly in locating and organizing countertrade products.
- Negotiations may be difficult, as there are no guide market prices.
- Countertrade deals are difficult to evaluate in terms of profitability and companies can, through countertrade, create new competition.

It is likely that in the future, countertrading will develop further in the form of longer-term rather than shorter-term partnerships as multinationals seek permanent foreign sources for incorporation in their global sourcing strategy. LDCs offer the benefits of low-cost labour and materials, as well as relatively untapped markets for goods. This has resulted in multinationals reversing the traditional countertrade process by first seeking opportunities, and then identifying potential countertrade partners with which to exploit the opportunities. For an example of countertrade please see Illustration 11.6.

Leasing

Leasing is used as an alternative to outright purchase in countries where there is a shortage of capital available to purchase high-priced capital and industrial goods. Usually the rental fee will cover servicing and the costs of spares too, and so the problem of poor levels of maintenance, which is often associated with high technology and capital equipment in LDCs, can be overcome. Leasing arrangements can be attractive, too, in countries where investment grants and tax incentives are offered for new plant and machinery, in which case the leaser can take advantage of the tax provisions in a way that the lessee cannot, and share some of the savings. It is estimated that leased aircraft account for about 20 per cent of the world's aircraft fleet.

Deciding at what stage of the export sales process the price should be quoted

Export price quotations are important, because they spell out the legal and cost responsibilities of the buyer and seller. Sellers, as previously mentioned, favour a quote that gives them the least liability and responsibility, such as FOB (free on board), or ex-works, which means the exporter's liability finishes when the goods are loaded on to the buyer's carrier. Buyers, on the other hand, would prefer either franco domicile, where responsibility is borne by the supplier all the way to the customer's warehouse, or CIF port of discharge, which means the buyer's responsibility begins only when the goods are in their own country.

Generally, the more **market-orientated pricing** policies are based on CIF, which indicates a strong commitment to the market. By pricing ex-works, an exporter is not taking any steps to build relations with the market and so may be indicating only short-term commitment. The major stages at which export prices might be quoted are articulated through internationally agreed terms called Incoterms. The main ones are as follows:

- Ex ws: ex-works or ex point of origin.
- FAS: free alongside ship.
- FOB: free on board.
- C. and F.: cost and freight.
- CIF: cost, insurance freight.
- DAF: Delivered at Frontier
- DDP: Delivered duty paid to destination point.

In deciding at what stage of the export sales process to price in a company has to be clear about the responsibilities and the costs it is including in its price and what responsibility they wish to pass onto the buyer. Table 11.3 illustrates these costs for each of the main stages in the export sales process.

The export order process

To further emphasize the complexity of managing international pricing, a major task of the marketer is to choose payment terms that will satisfy importers and at the same time safeguard the interests of the exporter. The transactions process for handling export is illustrated in Figure 11.3.

In the process, the customer agrees to payment. The customer begins the process (1) by sending an enquiry for the goods. The price and terms are confirmed by a pro-forma invoice (2) by the supplier, so that the customer knows for what amount (3) to instruct its bank on the method of payment (4). The method of payment is confirmed and arranged. If this is by letter of credit this will be opened by the issuing bank (5) in the supplier's country.

When the goods are shipped (6) the shipping documents are returned to the supplier (7), so that shipment is confirmed by their presentation (8) together with all stipulated documents and certificates for payment (9). The monies are automatically transmitted from the customer's account via the issuing bank. The customer may only collect the goods (10) when all the documents have been returned to them.

ILLUSTRATION 11.6

IKEA's buy back strategy?

IKEA is a Swedish home products retailer that sells ready-to-assemble furniture, accessories and bathroom and kitchen items in their retail stores around the world. The company, which pioneered flat-pack design furniture at affordable prices, is now the world's largest furniture retailer.

The chain has 313 stores in 37 countries, most of them in Europe, North America, Asia and Australia. The IKEA Group itself owns 276 stores in 25 countries and the other 37 stores are owned and run by franchisees.

Central to its marketing strategy is the standardization of its core concept of Swedish democratic designs. However, its competitive prices are the mainstay of its competitive edge, and IKEA manages its supply route specifically to ensure it can keep prices down. It has suppliers in 50 countries, roughly two-thirds of its products are sourced from Europe with about one third from Asia. A small amount of products are produced in North America. In Eastern Europe an essential part of their procurement strategy is the buyback contract, a form of countertrade in which machinery and equipment for increasing and upgrading production is leased to Eastern European companies in exchange for an export contract. In this way the suppliers are able to meet IKEA's high-quality standards and specifications. The repayment period is between three and five years, and in return, IKEA usually buys three to four times the value of the equipment supplied.

IKEA has now expanded into the Russian market with similar deals and they successfully developed IKEA MOS, a shopping centre located on a site adjacent to one of IKEA's two existing stores in the Moscow region of Russia. The objective for IKEA was to introduce into Russia a totally new concept of retail and provide local customers with an innovative, customer-orientated retail environment. However, IKEA's developments of the Russian market have been beset with difficulties. They have been campaigning vigorously against corruption and indeed last year froze their investments in the country in protest at the bureaucratic hurdles they faced. They also had huge difficulties with the unspoken rule that you needed to pay bribes to get things agreed with local government officials. However, in spite of its high-profile anticorruption stand, IKEA has had to sack two senior executives in Russia for allegedly turning a blind eye to bribes paid by a sub-contractor to secure electricity supplies for its St Petersburg outlets.

Questions

1 Evaluate the pros and cons of countertrade strategies in helping IKEA to sustain its competitive advantage across international markets over the longer term.

2 How would you respond to the demand for payment from officials in return for agreements needed to run your business in a country?

While letters of credit and drafts are the most common payment method, there are also several other methods of payment:

- A *draft* is drawn by the exporter on the importer, who makes it into a trade acceptance by writing on it the word 'accepted'. A *sight draft* is an unconditional order to pay a sum of money on demand or to the order of a specified person. Drafts which are payable at a future date are called *term drafts*.

- A *letter of credit* is similar to a draft, except it is drawn on the bank and becomes a bank acceptance rather than a trade acceptance. There is greater assurance of payment, as an unconditional undertaking is given by the bank that the debts of the buyer will be paid to the seller.

- A *bill of exchange* is an unconditional order in writing which is signed by one person and requires the person to whom it is addressed to pay a certain sum of money on instruction at a specified time.

Table 11.4   Incoterms stages and services at each stage of the export sales process

Services	EXW Ex Works	FAS Free Alongside Ship	FOB Free Onboard Vessel	C&F Cost and Freight	CIF Cost Insurance and Freight	DAF Delivered At Frontier	DEQ Delivered Ex Quay Duty Unpaid	DDP Delivered Duty Paid
Warehouse Storage	Seller	Seller	Seller	Seller	Seller	Seller	Seller	Seller
Warehouse labour	Seller	Seller	Seller	Seller	Seller	Seller	Seller	Seller
Export packing	Seller	Seller	Seller	Seller	Seller	Seller	Seller	Seller
Loading charges	Buyer	Seller	Seller	Seller	Seller	Seller	Seller	Seller
Inland freight	Buyer	Seller	Seller	Seller	Seller	Seller	Seller	Seller
Terminal charges	Buyer	Seller	Seller	Seller	Seller	Seller	Seller	Seller
Forwarder's fees	Buyer	Buyer	Seller	Seller	Seller	Seller	Seller	Seller
Loading on vessel	Buyer	Buyer	Seller	Seller	Seller	Seller	Seller	Seller
Ocean/Air freight	Buyer	Buyer	Buyer	Seller	Seller	Seller	Seller	Seller
Charges on arrival at destination	Buyer	Buyer	Buyer	Buyer	Buyer	Buyer	Seller	Seller
Duty taxes and customs clearance	Buyer	Buyer	Buyer	Buyer	Buyer	Buyer	Buyer	Seller
Delivery to destination	Buyer	Buyer	Buyer	Buyer	Buyer	Buyer	Buyer	Seller

Source: www.austrade.gov.au, *Austrade Guide to Export pricing.*

FIGURE 11.3   The export order process

- *A documentary collection* is when a bill of exchange is presented to the importer via the banking system or alternatively the exporter can present the bill direct. If the importer pays the bill of exchange on presentation, usually by authorizing the bank to transfer funds to the exporter's bank account, then no further action is required.

- *Open account* is when the sales terms are agreed between buyer and seller, but without documents specifying clearly the importer's payment obligations. There is less paperwork but greater risk of non-payment, so it is only used when a trusting relationship has been developed between the trading parties. In countries where foreign exchange is difficult to obtain, drafts and letters of credit will be given priority in any currency allocation.

- *A consignment note* is when the exporter retains title of the goods until the importer sells them. Exporters own the goods longer in this method than any other, and so the financial burden and risks are at their greatest. In addition, the recovery of either goods or debt could be very difficult, and it is for this reason that consignments tend to be limited to companies trading with their subsidiaries.

The credit terms given are also important in determining the final price to the buyer. When products from international competitors are perceived to be similar, the purchaser may choose the supplier that offers the best credit terms, in order to effect a greater discount. In effect the supplier is offering a source of finance to the buyer, and in some countries – for example Brazil – government support is given to firms to help them gain a competitive advantage through this method. There has been a variety of international agreements to try and stop such practices, but it is still quite prevalent in some countries.

SUMMARY

- In international markets pricing decisions are much more complex, because they are affected by a number of additional external factors, such as fluctuations in exchange rates, accelerating inflation in certain countries and the use of alternative payment methods such as leasing, barter and countertrade.

- Many factors and problems contribute to making effective pricing management one of the most difficult aspects of international marketing to achieve. As well as the market factors associated with pricing decisions in each country it is necessary to deal with the complexities of financing deals based in different currencies and trying to maintain cross-border consistency of pricing.

■ While there are cost benefits in standardizing products, services and processes, local factors affect the cost base in individual countries and make it difficult to maintain similar prices in different markets.

■ In addition to this strategic role, there are a number of issues relating to the detailed operational management of international transactions. These particularly relate to the reduction of risk in carrying out international trade transactions, especially when trading in high-risk countries.

■ There are also areas of specific management expertise in pricing that exist in international marketing. These include, for example, the management of transfer pricing between business units within an MNE, grey marketing and countertrade and the administration of cross-border transfers of goods.

■ What becomes quite clear in developing international pricing is that there is a need not only to use pricing in a key role in achieving a company's financial objectives, but also as part of an integrated strategy, for example along with other marketing mix elements, to respond positively to the opportunities and threats of the various markets in which it operates.

KEYWORDS

price standardization	internal cost structures	production costs
elastic demand	ethnocentric	price transparency
inelastic demand	polycentric	transfer pricing
fixed production cost	geocentric	foreign currency
marginal costing	marginal cost pricing	exchange rate risk
dumping	exchange rate	eurozone
economies of scale	grey marketing	countertrade
learning curve	price coordination	market-orientated pricing

CASE STUDY 1

Countertrade and bartering

Bartering and trading without money is a centuries-old way of doing business. It is now an up and coming way of doing business and it is not just individuals that barter. Global brands are also in on the act. Indeed, global bartering transactions, often known as moneyless or no money transactions, account for approximately US$3.7 trillion annually. On its own this is meaningless, but when compared with the fact that global business transactions account for US$16 trillion annually it is easy to see that money-less transactions account for a high number of business transactions.

This means A LOT of business is done without money exchanging between the two parties involved in the transaction. One of the benefits of using no money transactions is that it takes care of the risks of foreign exchange problems, fees and some restrictions of trade. The three mini case studies below provide an outline of some of the ways in which moneyless transactions can take place.

Case Study 1 Education

There are many interesting ways in which counter-trade/bartering takes place. Lindenwood University saw that students were not returning to complete their studies. Upon investigation they discovered that some parents in rural areas could not afford to pay for their child's tuition fees. The university and parents bartered and it was accepted that farmers could pay for their child's tuition fees with a pig. The campaign 'Pork for Tuition' was launched and became a great success, especially as students were able to return to university which prior to the 'Pork for Tuition' campaign they would not have been able to do. The pigs received in the non-money transaction were slaughtered and used in the university's cafeteria.

Case Study 2: Hotel product placement

Advertising and product placement fees are very expensive. Therefore Hilton Hotels linked with film makers Paramount Pictures during the award-winning production of 'Up in the Air'. George Clooney was the star attraction in the film but so was Hilton Hotels. George Clooney's character Ryan Bingham stayed in Hilton Hotels, he wore a Hilton Hotel bathrobe, used Hilton's amenities and suggested to one of the other characters in the film that they should sign up for the Hilton Hotels Loyalty scheme. The advertising and product placement for Hilton Hotels was very good for their brand. In return for 'being in the film' Hilton Hotels provided rooms and hospitality for the cast and crew of the 'Up in the Air' film. Additionally Hilton Hotels posted details of the film on their social media spaces and placed 'Up in the Air' film details on the millions of hotel bedroom key cards and promoted it on their hotel bedroom film channel. The bartering system shown here benefited both Hilton Hotels and the 'Up in the Air' film.

Case Study 3: Gossip

BzzAgent is all about gossip. They are a word of mouth (WOM) organization that provides a platform for organizations such as Tesco, Garnier, Douwe Egberts and Phileas Fogg to name but a few, to receive honest feedback from consumers. Consumers received products and services from international brands and they are asked to review them, rate them, like them, share them and answer surveys about them. The consumer is a BzzAgent and they are asked to gossip about the products through social media about different brands. Therefore, the bartering system is between consumers and brands. The consumer provides time and gossip (BzzAgent) for WOM marketing and the international brand exchanges that for products.

Questions

1 What pricing benefits are there for international brands to use non-money transactions?

2 What are the benefits for each mini case study?

3 What other ways could organizations use bartering and counter transactions to do business?

Source: Kaikati, A.M. and Kaikati, J.G. (2013) 'Doing business without exchanging money: The scale and creativity of modern barter', *California Management Review* (55), 46–71.

CASE STUDY 2

Torque PLC

Torque PLC develops and manufactures pneumatic anti-lock braking systems, electronic braking systems, automated manual transmission systems and an array of conventional products, such as actuators, air compressors and air control valves. In addition, it provides replacement parts, diagnostic tools, training and other services to vehicle distributors, repair shops and fleet operators. Its customers also include a commercial vehicle distributor network that provides replacement parts.

The company markets its products primarily in America, Asia and Europe through its global sales force.

Global challenges

To maintain its global market presence Torque faces a number of challenges. With its focus on bespoke design, new products are generally developed in response to the performance specification of the customer. Although Torque drives a best cost strategy, the ability to exploit economies of scale and design efficiencies is limited. The sustainability of providing such a high level of solution service also make it difficult to compete in a market where customers are looking for cost effective solutions. This means efficient and effective solutions are needed for the company to be sustainable.

Another challenge they face is calculating a sales price across the global markets. Traditionally, Torque used a full absorption costing approach to their pricing. The fixed costs, material costs, labour and process and full export costs, and a defined margin would be included in a bottom up approach to building the price for all quotation requests across the global markets. However, this gave the global sales force little flexibility when negotiating in different country markets and meant they were often unable to respond to local market conditions. It also meant they found it problematic when pitching themselves against competitors with a much lower cost base.

The company responded to this challenge by the initiation of a value-based pricing approach to its global markets. The aim was to focus the engineering resources to those developments which clearly built value to the customers and for which the customer was therefore willing to pay. This enabled the company to achieve higher value margins in targeted areas and focus resources on those areas which delivered a high margin. The aim was to avoid setting prices that were either uncompetitive for customers or lower than they were willing to pay.

An example of the value-based approach to pricing is the method used to price a new brake disc. This brake consists of a turning disc which is mounted to the axle and on top of a brake caliper, carrying the brake pads and the adjuster unit. Torque developed a monobloc brake caliper, which reduced the weight. The better distribution of the forces within the single bloc used less material than in the previous version of two halves screwed together.

By using the value-based pricing approach it was possible to justify a higher added value price for the monobloc solution than the previous cost-plus approach. By communicating and explaining these commercial advantages, the customer was willing to pay for the clear added value and the delivery contract was extended over a five-year period. This generated additional sales with a higher margin and improved customer satisfaction.

Questions

1 Critically evaluate the global pricing strategies pursued by Torque PLC.

2 Discuss how far the value-based approach to pricing meets the global challenges outlined.

3 What other market-based approaches to pricing could they take?

DISCUSSION QUESTIONS

1 What are the arguments for and against using price and non-price factors when competing in international markets?

2 What pricing problems might a multinational company face in marketing to less developed countries, and how might they be overcome?

3 Increasingly competing on global markets requires substantial investment, often undertaken by two or more firms in a joint venture or strategic alliance. Consider the implications of such ventures in developing a strategic approach to coordinating pricing strategies across international markets.

4 Why should a domestic supplier invoice export goods in a foreign currency? What are the advantages and disadvantages of foreign currency invoicing?

5 The Internet is increasing price transparency across international markets. Fully evaluate the problems and opportunities this brings to the company trying to build a global competitive advantage.

REFERENCES

1. Cavusgil, S.T., Ghauri, P., Knight, G. and Riesenberge, J. (2014) *International Business*, Global Edition, 3rd edn, Pearson: London.

2. Possebon, M. (2014) Why Euro Disney is a 22-year money-losing failure Business Insider (UK), published 7 October 2014. Available from www.uk.businessinsider .com/euro-disney-announces-1-billion-crisis-plan-2014-10 (accessed 28 May 2015).

3. Sarathy, R., Terpstra, V. and Russow, L. (2006) *International Marketing*, 9th edn, Dryden Press.

4. Woollaston, V. (2013) Apple's astonishing 129% mark-up, published 6 November 2013. Available from www.dailymail .co.uk/sciencetech/article-2488524/Apples-astonishing -129-mark-iPad-Air.html (accessed 28 May 2015).

CHAPTER 12

TECHNOLOGY ENABLED SUSTAINABLE INTERNATIONAL MARKETING

LEARNING OBJECTIVES

After reading this chapter you should be able to:

- Understand how technology presents opportunities and poses challenges for international marketing strategy development

- Appreciate the role of the enabling technologies in the international marketing strategy process

- Identify the approaches to achieving sustainability and corporate social responsibility

- Understand the integration of solutions to international marketing strategy problems through the use of enabling technologies

- Identify the opportunities and challenges posed by the use of enabling technologies now and in the future

INTRODUCTION

Technology is at the forefront of economic development as it drives business growth in most business sectors and connects the increasingly global marketplace. Many of the changes taking place in global marketing, such as global sourcing, social networking and mobile access to the media, have been accelerated because of advances in technology. New technology has also generated new products, services and processes that have contributed in no small part to the unsustainability of the world today. Technology is expected by many to solve the global problems, such as the generation of renewable energy and making better use of resources. International marketing is at the heart of many of these new initiatives.

As we saw in the first section of the book, technology is a major driver of both the pace and magnitude of change in international marketing. It provides more immediate methods of gathering marketing information from around the world, quicker and more effective methods of analysis and prediction of future customer needs and wants. It is revolutionizing individual and organizational communications and so provides the enabling mechanism by which effective and integrated responses can be made to changing marketplaces. It is, therefore, an essential element in the development of the international marketing strategy. Technology underpins the choice of implementation strategies of the marketing mix, facilitates the process of learning and sharing best practice, and enables more effective control of a firm's diverse international activities.

In this chapter, therefore, we focus upon the ways in which technological, business and marketing innovation facilitate further development of international marketing, in providing solutions to international marketing problems and the mechanisms to exploit opportunities. The technology tools that are available to develop appropriate strategic responses are identified. As we shall see, this involves integrating separate elements of international marketing into a cohesive approach. We then discuss how firms can pull together the various aspects of corporate social responsibility discussed throughout this book into a cohesive sustainable strategy. Finally, we focus on the challenges and opportunities faced in international markets in the future and consider the role enabling technologies will play in them.

The enabling technologies

Down the centuries, advances in technology, business and marketing innovations have provided solutions for business problems, such as in design, manufacturing, operations, internal and external communications, inventory control, managing finances and so on. Technological advances have enabled innovative firms to make product and service developments that provide distinctive benefits to customers. The technology is either industry sector specific or generic in nature. Of course, a specific industry technology may sometimes start off being used in one sector and over time be transferred to others. For example, the **Internet** was initially developed for use in the defence industry and Facebook was initially built for college students.

Marketing and business innovations have often built on and enhanced technological inventions, for example, in the mobile phone sector, marketing pay-as-you-go and monthly contracts, which included 'free' sophisticated phones, provided the impetus for global growth. Technological platforms provide opportunities for many and varied new developments, for example, the Internet has generated many social media developments and Apple iPhones and iPads provide a platform for hundreds of thousands of apps.

The Internet has had the effect of 'shrinking the world' and has facilitated the worldwide integration of the different technologies, systems and processes in supply chains that are used locally by different parts of the organization and its partners. It enables experts around the world to be accessed virtually and instantly. When some advanced GE medical equipment being used to treat a child broke down in the middle of the night in the US, the customer was not able to get hold of a local engineer. However, it was normal working hours for the call-centre in France. The problem could be diagnosed online and expert help provided from France to solve the problem.

We refer here to **enabling technologies**, because there is no single technology that supports international marketing. The major steps forward in recent years have been associated with the integration of many technologies, such as those that support e-commerce, information management and search, mobile communications and social media, customer relations management, computer-aided design, process, inventory and logistics management. So, enabling technologies in international marketing provide the solutions to old problems, such as:

- How can customers in remote locations around the world contribute to the design of a new global product as much as the customer next door?
- How can an organization use the advocates for its products to share their good experiences with potential customers around the world? and
- How can a ten-person business market its products or services to its potential customers in 40 or 50 countries, when managing market entry in so many countries through agents and distributors would probably be beyond the resources of most small businesses?

Technology does not remove the elements, challenges and dilemmas associated with the international marketing process, such as the need for cultural sensitivity, the need to make products and services available to customers worldwide with minimum investment, or the need to be both efficient and effective by achieving an appropriate balance between the standardization and adaptation of the international marketing process and programmes. It does have a major impact on the nature of the international marketing strategy that is used and enables creative solutions to be found which will increase the organizations' competitive capability.

Technological innovation

In considering the application of technology it is useful to focus specifically upon how technological advancement both creates new marketing opportunities and poses new challenges for firms, for example, in energy generation, conservation and waste recycling discussed in previous chapters. For international marketers, timing of the introduction of innovations is critical. Energy Saving Trust (2015) explain how the future is available now for businesses premises, roads/highways, cruise ships, tourist attractions and even for individuals that want to use alternative energy sources. Alternative energy comes in all shapes, sizes and budgets from advanced biofuels, ground source heat pumps, concentrated solar power, wind turbines, hydro technology from small streams to rivers. Technological innovations that help reduce carbon dioxide emissions are highly saleable as multinational companies and individual business entrepreneurs want to reduce their carbon footprint and demonstrate they care for our planet's future. Decision making by governments is built around the necessary support infrastructure to reduce carbon (CO_2) emissions in the hope that this will slow down climate change. Details of government commitment are shown in the Kyoto Protocol. The Kyoto Protocol is the international agreement between 37 industrialized countries and the European Community to ensure businesses consider the effects their organization has on the world's atmosphere. With this is mind sales of products and services that promise environmentally friendly solutions will certainly grow. See Illustration 12.1 to see how the Boston Consultancy Group advised China on how to make its buildings green.

ILLUSTRATION 12.1

B2B: The Boston Consultancy Group advise China on turning grey buildings into green ones

When countries like China, Indonesia, Turkey or Brazil emerge and grow, so does their need for more roads, factories and office blocks. This causes a strain on the country's natural resources. Growth has consequences, therefore it is important that all stakeholders responsible for the growth of a country use energy efficient and cost efficient technology when building the infrastructure. China committed itself to the Kyoto Protocol, however, at the last global meeting China was still the highest emitter of CO_2 gases. This is partly due to the increased number of commercial and residential buildings being constructed and rapid urbanization. It is anticipated business growth will continue and around 270 million Chinese citizens will leave rural areas and move to the growing number of mega cities.

Commercial (shops, schools, offices, hotels etc.) and residential buildings consume 25 per cent of China's energy; contributing to a high proportion of the CO_2 gases emitted into the atmosphere. The Boston Consultancy Group provided advice to help China's grey buildings become green. They calculated that if the existing inefficient grey buildings reduce their emissions by just 5 per cent and new buildings be 'built green' to ensure emissions be reduced by 60 per cent, the energy saved would be equivalent to:

1 All lights in the US being turned off for one month

2 All cars in Sweden, Norway and Denmark being removed from use

3 All air traffic ceasing to fly for 4 months.

Central and local governments in China rose to this challenge and set targets to reduce energy emissions.

The office building for the Ministry of Science and Technology includes some green technology, e.g.:

■ Rooftop heat-recycling systems.

■ Mirrors that reflect daylight into the building.

■ An irrigation system for a rooftop garden that breathes oxygen into the city, is a habitat for wildlife, keeps the building warm in winter and cool in the summer.

China is also installing thousands of solar powered installations to reduce energy and thus CO_2 emissions. During the first quarter of 2015 China announced she had connected 5.04 gigawatts of solar capacity to the grid. This is equal to the total solar power energy for all of France.

Questions

1 How does the office for the Ministry of Science and Technology benefit from using the technology outlined above?

2 How does China benefit from using the technology outlined above?

Sources: Asia Green Buildings (2015) China: Impressive solar capacity installed in three months, published 21 April 2015. Available from www.asiagreenbuildings.com /china-impressive-solar-capacity-installed-in-three-months/ (accessed 4 June 2015); The Boston Consultancy Group (2009) 'From grey to green. How energy efficient buildings can help make China's rapid urbanization sustainable', Boston Consultancy Group.

It is important to emphasize that technology is of no value until it has a practical application, as illustrated in Figure 12.1. Those firms that are first to embrace a new technology and find a practical application, for example in creating a new product or service, a new route to market or a lower energy consuming process, will gain a new source of competitive advantage.

This sets new standards for the industry sector and means competitors also have to achieve those standards if they wish to compete in the future. Global communications make customers worldwide aware of the latest products and create new stakeholder expectations so all competitors in the sector, wherever they are in the world, have to catch up by embracing the new product and service offers and industry standards if they wish to survive.

FIGURE 12.1   The vicious circle of technology and competitive advantage

Disruptive technologies

From time to time technological advances make existing products and services redundant, and sometimes challenge the very existence of businesses if they fail to react quickly enough. For example, the conventional worldwide photography sector was virtually destroyed by digital camera technology, severely damaging companies such as Kodak. Traditional fixed line telephony was the cornerstone of the former state-owned telecommunications firms for over a century, but the introduction of mobile and Internet systems, such as Skype, HipChat and Google Hangouts has completely changed the economics of the sector. Often it is entrepreneurial born global firms that exploit the disruptive technology if a new competence is required that the organization that previously led the sector does not have. However, as discussed in Illustration 12.2, technology that is becoming old can move businesses to reinvent their products and re-launch them as 'retro' but hi-tech.

ILLUSTRATION 12.2

Hi-tech and retro: The old and new converge

Technological innovations are giving life to 'old tech'. In 1982 Clive Sinclair launched one of the first games computers named the ZX Spectrum. Games included the Football Manager and Galaxia. This year it has been relaunched by Steve Wilcox of Elite Systems – who was a big fan of the ZX Spectrum in the 1990s. The new and improved Sinclair ZX Spectrum games computer has over 1000 games pre-loaded, it has Bluetooth connectivity and any apps people want can be downloaded from the app store onto the computer. The games look and sound exactly the same. Therefore, for £99.99 the target market (over 30 years of age) are buying nostalgia and the feel of controlling the game through keyboards rather than 'touch screen and swipe'. There is a fan base as Steve raised over £64 000 by online crowd-sourcing.

Also this year Sony launched a Walkman at the Consumer Electrics Show, Las Vegas. The original Walkman, which played music from one cassette tape, debuted in 1979 and since then 220 million copies

of the original Walkman, and its updates, have been sold. Over the years the Walkman has been shown in many films as an accessory for heroes or heroines. The new Walkman can store 1700 songs and has Wi-Fi compatibility. Its quality (and price) make it a high-end piece of music kit. Especially if, as recommended, consumers purchase the headphones at £549 and the USB headphone amplifier which costs £719. The Walkman is twinned with Android compatible apps, therefore music can be downloaded from Google play. The downside to the new Walkman is it takes 4 hours 30 minutes to charge up. However, unlike the designers of the Sinclair ZX Spectrum, the Sony Walkman is high tech, sleek and beautiful to look at and hold. The new Sony Walkman is all about enjoying a supreme listening experience; and whilst the name has nostalgic undertones, the new kit is for music aficionados.

Questions

1 What are the benefits of relaunching old kit with new technology?

2 What other 'old brands' have been relaunched/revamped/re-engineered?

3 What 'old brands' could be relaunched/revamped/re-engineered; and why?

Sources: Newsbeat (2015) Sony launches new £949 Walkman at the Consumer Electronics Show, published 6 January 2015. Available from www.bbc.co.uk/newsbeat /article/30696416/sony-launches-new-949-walkman-at -the-consumer-electronics-show (accessed 4 June 2015); Wallop, H. (2015) First look at relaunched ZX Spectrum, *The Telegraph* published 13 Mar 2015 Available from www .telegraph.co.uk/technology/video-games/11471430/First -look-at-relaunched-ZX-Spectrum.html (accessed 4 June 2015).

MANAGEMENT CHALLENGE 12.1

Technological convergence: One phablet controlling many machines

Consumers of smartphones consider their phone to be more important than their wallet or purse stating "my life is on my phone". Which is of course true for many. Smartphones are indispensable especially as many consumers are choosing to use a 'phablet' – such as the Samsung Galaxy Note 2, OppoN1, Nokia Lumia or the Google Nexus 6. They are nicknamed 'phablets' because of their at least 5 inch screen (measured diagonally) and their inclusion of all things that can be done on a mobile phone *and* a tablet.

Through cloud storage and apps, consumers can upload and download photographs, read books, convert currencies, pay for online purchases from Amazon or Skype loved ones. However, the more recent technologies enable consumers to use their phone on an M2M (Machine 2 Machine) basis.

M2M and the IoT (Internet of Things) gives consumers the opportunity to join the *technology connected* revolution by interacting with their phablets, which in turn interact with other technology/ machines that consumers have at home. This M2M has happened because many consumers do not have 9am to 5pm jobs, therefore, cost-conscious and environmentally aware consumers only want to turn on their heating devices when they return home.

Through apps on their phablets consumers can use smart technology to control their central heating device in their home from anywhere in the world; or 30 minutes from home! This means consumers can turn on the heating device so that their home is lovely and warm when they arrive.

Belkin WeMo is a cooking pot that can also be linked to a consumer's home Wi-fi system. Again the cooking pot can be switched on via an app on a phablet to ensure the consumers' evening meal is ready upon their arrival at home. To ensure the consumer's journey home is stress-free M2M technology, developed by Cisco, will change traffic lights and redirect traffic through cities more effectively. So when the consumer arrives home they can kick off their shoes and Bluetooth their favourite music from their phablet to their beautiful, sleek speakers.

Technology converging with other technology via the mobile phone is predicted to ensure brands stay connected with their consumers on a regular basis during their day-to-day lives.

Questions

1 What are the arguments for and against businesses including M2M technology in their products as part of their marketing strategy?

2 What are the benefits for the consumer to engage with M2M technology on their phablet?

Sources: Belkin (2015) Setting up the WeMo slow cooker (Crock-Pot®). Available from www.belkin.com/uk/support -article?articleNum=101177 (accessed 10 June 2015).

Cisco (2014) AGT and Cisco traffic incident management solution: Improving traffic safety and efficiency. Available from www.cisco.com/web/strategy/docs/agt-s-cc-city-tim-aag .pdf (accessed 10 June 2015).

A more recent trend, frugal engineering discussed earlier, has challenged the assumption that innovation should focus on adding additional features for wealthy customers. Technological innovation is being applied to address the needs of cost conscious customers in emerging markets. Potentially this could be disruptive for many established companies. Companies, when expanding internationally, often choose cities that are ranked high on the City Competitive Scale which are places that attract talent and are spaces that thrive on innovation and are often creative industry clusters. Currently the top five cities are New York, London, Singapore, Paris and Hong Kong.

Convergent technology

An important trend is the integration of technologies and technology gadgets for business and consumer markets so, for example, the mobile phone has became a mobile communications and computing device that embraces not just voice, text and games but also downloaded music, video, television and Internet access, particularly to social media. As the functionality increases so mobile computing is replacing 'fixed position' computing. In the same way traditional home television and recording devices are being wirelessly connected with personal computers; notebooks/tablets and global communications. Integration goes further because revenues can be generated by products (such as the hardware, including mobile devices and tablets, services (e.g. streaming downloads)) and content (e.g. music, podcasts, films, games, and social media).

Major players such as Apple, Microsoft and Google are trying to establish themselves as dominant, branded players at the centre of this convergence, while other less powerful firms are seeking to connect a more open and inclusive network. Management Challenge 12.1 shows just how convergent smartphones are.

The Internet and international business communications

The Internet is the central pillar of the economies of developed countries, and the growth of emerging economies is increasingly dependent on the Internet too. A report by Boston Consulting Group (2010) ranked Sweden, Denmark, South Korea and the UK as the 4 highest countries on its 'e-intensity index', a measure of the reach and depth of the Internet. The report noted that Britain was a net exporter of e-commerce goods and services, exporting £2.80 for every £1 imported, whereas in the 'off-line economy', only 90p was exported for every £1 imported. Boston Consulting Group's (2013) latest report shows South Korea has moved to the top of the list; followed by Denmark, Sweden and the UK.

In the business-to-business market the development of the Internet external networks and extranet internal organizational networks has revolutionized demand and customer information management, supply and value chain management, distribution channel management and control. It has speeded up the process so that real time decisions can be made in virtual, global market places or 'hubs' that manage supply and demand. To support high speed decision making mobile technology is essential.

In consumer markets communications technology is regarded as a utility, similar to power and water. It has helped people around the world to become more aware of changes in the market environment and exciting new products and services that are introduced anywhere in the world. Customers have changing lifestyles, are more easily bored with their existing products and services and are always looking for innovative new products and services that will regain their interest. They are less brand-loyal, so if one firm does not meet the needs of international customers then a competitor will. Customers find out online about new products and services, have new ways of assessing their suitability and likely performance, believing online peer reviews more than company advertising, becoming deeply sceptical of the communications of multinational organizations and suspicious of the motives of the most powerful. Information must be available in two or three clicks and the products must be accessible to purchase quickly and more cost-effectively and delivery should only take a day. Customers live on their phones now and seem to prefer to lose their wallet or purse rather than their mobile phone!

The key function of the Internet is provided by search engines (such as Google, Bing, Yahoo! and Ask) enabling users to find the information and services they need. This is critical for international marketers who want potential customers to be able to find them. Customers are impatient so it is vital for organizations that they appear high in the list of results of search. Many would argue that the current search functions can be highly frustrating and little progress has been made over the last ten years by the dominant providers to satisfy the needs of average users. However, there is evidence to suggest that the search providers are at last aiming to improve. Google suggests that there are three layers of search: content, social and local and the firm is aiming to capture the market for location based search with Google's automatic Location Search function that enables consumers to get a satisfactory answer. It should also provide new sources of revenue by attracting local advertisers. Given that the number of mobile phone connections is in excess of 7.5 billion and the world population (2015) is approx. 7.3 billion, the market for efficient search continues to grow. Therefore, Google, Bing, Facebook and Twitter see huge potential for advertising income as more businesses promote their products and services across a range of social media platforms.

All businesses must respond to these opportunities and threats, so they must embrace new methods of communicating in order to gain more customer insights, retain and connect better with their customers. Many people in emerging economies do not even have access to old technologies, such as reliable electricity, fixed line telecommunications, radio and television, let alone the latest information and telecommunications technology, but increasingly these markets are being recognized for their potential. It is possible to leapfrog existing technology with innovations that are appropriate to the specific situation, such as the developments for remote areas of Africa of the wind-up radio, solar energy systems to power communications equipment and recharge mobile phone batteries and mobile phones as a tool for making online payments. The cost of a fixed line telecommunications structure would be prohibitively expensive in most of the largely rural countries of Africa; with in excess of 500 million mobile subscriptions there is a high level of demand. With 14 per cent of the world's population, Africa accounts for only 2 per cent of Internet use. Of the 20 countries with the most expensive broadband subscription fees (over US$1000 per month in some countries) 14 are in sub-Saharan Africa. The technological leap will be interesting. Cable systems are being laid around coasts, so bandwidth increase will become huge and costs will fall sharply. The challenge will be to connect the rural broadband users with wireless technologies through 3G/4G networks to the communications provider. For international marketers to and from Africa this will bring about another industrial revolution, discussed in Illustration 12.3.

Email and text messaging can become frustrating for users, particularly in some of the emerging countries such as Nigeria and Indonesia where there are millions of Internet devices but connectivity is not

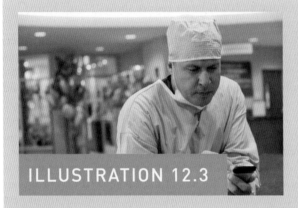

ILLUSTRATION 12.3

mHealth and text-baby

Health care in South Africa is at breaking point. This is particularly acute in rural areas where there is often only one health care worker per 1000 people. Many diseases, such as malaria, kill an African child every 30 seconds. Diseases such as Lassa fever, polio and leprosy, virtually eradicated elsewhere in the world, are still debilitating and/or fatal in Africa.

Simon Spurr, the Chief Executive of FOLUP saw this problem and is one of many technology-driven organizations that have provided a helpful solution. FOLUP web and mobile platforms can help South African patients get a real-time diagnosis from expert doctors. Using smartphones/phablets or PCs patients in remote parts of Africa can upload their symptoms, provide readings of their blood pressure or feedback on their reaction to medicines provided. Patients take an active part in their health care with a medical expert through wireless interaction and together the patient

and doctor come to a collaborative decision. Mobile technology is high in Africa. Two-thirds of people in Africa own a mobile phone and ownership, due to its low cost, is predicted to grow very quickly in future years. FOLUP technology not only provides connections to expert doctors there are also mHealth apps for communities. The apps are community forums for people with similar diseases to share information, motivate each other and to not feel isolated. Therefore, FOLUP's connection to health care experts and a supportive community is a fantastic enable for African citizens.

A further development of mHeath is available to Tanzanian women who are pregnant or caring for babies and young children. The *Healthy Pregnancy, Healthy Baby Text Messaging Service* provides a free text messaging advisory service. The text messages include advice about morning sickness, breast feeding, dietary care and for mothers that have their babies at home there are text details of how to cut and clean the umbilical cord.

Question

1 What advice regarding investment in information and communications technology would you give to an African company seeking to develop and improve current mHealth and mBaby businesses?

Sources: Mulligan, G. (2015) Good prognosis: The rise of e-health in Africa, *New African*, published 17 March. Available from www.newafricanmagazine.com/good-prognosis-rise-e-health-africa/ Accessed 1 June 2015; Our Africa (2015) Health. Available from www.our-africa.org/health (accessed 11 June 2015).

country-wide, not secure and often not available. Other communications mechanisms, such as Twitter which limits message size to 140 characters, work differently but are preferred by many users for social and increasingly business networking. When consumers sign up to Pinterest and Instagram the suggested number of pins and photographs can become overwhelming. However, technology platforms enable customers around the world to continually develop more efficient and effective integrated communication of word, stationary and video imagery, sound and complex data.

Online strategies

The advances in communications technology enable internationally trading firms to develop new international marketing strategies. No longer is international marketing limited by the physical boundaries of the media footprint or the salesperson's or distribution company's territory. At a local level new developments in hand-held devices allow connection between users that is almost unlimited, offering opportunities for promotions close to location and point of sale (for example, of restaurants, entertainment and shops) but few of these opportunities have yet been exploited.

The Internet provides a global marketplace that is open to everyone. It is also:

- a method of collecting, searching for and exchanging marketing and business information;
- an alternative route to market to traditional distribution channels;
- a means of building customer relationships;
- a device for the digital delivery of certain information services;
- a networked system for managing the supply chain; and
- a virtual marketplace, trading floor and auction house.

The Internet also provides a mechanism for social networking through dedicated websites. The relevance of social networking for international marketing, which will be discussed in more detail later, is that it provides the opportunity for individuals and groups to discuss new products and services, problems encountered in dealing with organizations and dissatisfaction with the behaviour of organizations.

The purpose of websites

Websites are created by individuals and organizations as a shop window or for facilitating activities. While they are used for many purposes, their relevance for international marketing falls into the following main categories:

- organization sites
- service online
- information online
- business transactions online (E-commerce websites also used for M-commerce transactions).

Organization sites

Many organizations use their website to provide information to their stakeholders about the organization, ranging from its origins, business mission and areas of activity, standards and values, brands, financial performance, job opportunities and contact points, through to quite specific information about products and their applications. Firms appealing to global customers must consider the degree to which their website should build much closer relationships with customers by providing a site in the local language.

There are, of course, dangers too in just translating web content without addressing the need for it to be sensitive to cultural needs.

As well as providing information about products, some sites take customers through the purchasing process. For example, BMW help customers to design their new car from a range of options, such as whether to have cruise control, petrol or diesel, metallic paint and alloy wheels, but when the customer has designed the car they are then referred to their local dealer to complete the purchase.

Service online

Online banking puts customers more in control of their accounts, enabling them to obtain information from anywhere in the world and make transactions any time of the day or night. The saving to the bank is automation and being able to reduce the resourcing of bank branches and service centres and cut the cost of individual banking transactions.

Firms delivering packages, such as Federal Express, have been able to make huge savings on staff employed to answer queries from customers about where their package is, by providing an online tracking service around the world. The system involves applying a barcode to the package, which is then scanned each time it progresses past a key point on its journey. This information can then be transferred to the website and accessed by customers worldwide. Another example is real-time in-flight information that can be accessed online by those that are going to meet a flight, letting them know if the plane is going to be late.

Information online

Organizations in the business of providing information, such as Wikipedia or the *Financial Times*, provide websites that enable customers to access current and archived past files of news, data and images. Often, such sites provide one level of access free, but may charge a subscription for heavier users or may require payment for more valuable information. As this information is in digital form it can be accessed and delivered online anywhere in the world.

Sites of media organizations, such as the BBC or CNN are used to maintain and build the relationship with their consumers considerably beyond the scheduled content.

Business transactions online

These websites typically include elements of the previous categories but in addition enable customers to complete a transaction and purchase products or services online. The websites comprise two parts, the first providing the shop window, which must be eye catching for the potential customer and an easy-to-use check out process, that also assures the buyer of its security, particularly important where the purchase is cross-border.

Social networking

The disadvantage of websites is that consumers have to go to them to receive the information they want, whereas it is suggested that platforms and networks will become more important for sharing information. One example is Digg which aggregates social media news and provides links to interesting stories that are voted on by users.

Social networking has always been a feature of the Internet and, for example, people recorded web logs before the term 'blogs' was coined. As early as 1995 Amazon allowed users to write reviews and consumer guides. The phrase Web 2.0 was coined to indicate a second generation of Web services including social networking websites and online communications tools and emphasizes collaboration using the Web as a platform, users owning and exercising control over the data rather than hierarchical control being exercised.

Weblogs, chat rooms and community websites, such as Taobao, MySpace and Ibibo provide a platform for millions of consumers to air their views. Blogs are updated thousands of times an hour. Many of the comments relate to product, services and opinions about companies and it is essential for organizations to know what is being said about them. This requires intelligent search engines, such as Attentio, that can dig deeper than general searches and aggregate the data to provide a fuller picture of the trends and conversations that are taking place.

Businesses increasingly see the benefit of some involvement in other types of websites, even if the purpose is only to hear what is being said about the company, its competitors and their products. Blog and Forum websites, such as Google's Blogger, enable people to meet others with common views and thus enable firms to quickly hear about dissatisfaction. They can also be used by companies to inform and keep their staff around the world up-to-date. Social websites, such as Facebook, are effectively member groups or communities with common interests. File sharing websites, such as Flickr and YouTube, have on numerous occasions been used to share both photo and video files that have either enhanced the reputation of a company and its staff or proved embarrassing. Perhaps the most significant developments are likely to come from mobile device websites that support smartphones.

International e-markets and e-marketing

There are a number of e-marketing business models and e-marketplaces that originally started as digital extensions of physical marketing models. These business models focus on **business to business marketing** discussed next and **business to consumer marketing**, and other models are discussed later.

Business to business (B2B)

The interactions involved in B2B marketing are much more complex because they involve the exchange of significant amounts of information between the seller and customer before, during and after any transaction. The information includes such things as specifications, designs and drawings, purchase contracts, supply chain management, manufacturing and delivery schedules, inventory control, negotiation of price, distribution channel management and delivery. The information comes from different departments within the firms and is exchanged between the firms involved in the value chain.

For many years firms have been using **information technology** to improve the efficiency and effectiveness of the internal firm processes, for example, demand forecasting, inventory control, computer-aided design and manufacturing. The Internet enables this to be linked with external organizations and customers. The Internet has enabled a far wider range of data to be exchanged without restriction on the number of participant organizations. The mechanisms by which the exchanges take place and business can be transacted are Web portals. These are 'hubs' where all the interested participants congregate. Typically there are two types of hubs:

- industry-specific hubs, such as automobile or aerospace manufacturing; and
- function-specific hubs, such as advertising or human resource management.

Using e-hubs, firms improve the efficiency of the processes of transactions and thereby lower costs. The hubs can reduce the transaction cost by bringing together all the purchasing requirements of many hundreds of customers worldwide (Kaplan and Sawhney 2000). E-hubs attract many buyers who are able to negotiate bulk discounts on behalf of a range of smaller, individual buyers.

If the products are commodities with no need to negotiate specifications then dynamic pricing enables buyers and sellers to negotiate prices and volumes in real time. In sectors such as energy purchasing the peaks and troughs of supply and demand can be smoothed.

The US originally dominated B2B and much of the innovation in B2B came from the US, but firms around the world recognize that the potential savings can be quite significant with the increasing internationalization of sourcing and **supply chain management**. A culture change in the attitude of firms is needed as companies that may normally be competing can cooperate for the mutual benefit of reducing costs. Illustration 12.4 shows how Jack Ma has helped millions of Chinese entrepreneurs to access global business markets.

The benefits of **e-procurement**, such as convenience and cost saving through group purchasing, appeal to governments for public sector and private–public sector purchasing. However, often progress is much slower than in private business.

Disintermediation and re-intermediation

The Internet offers the possibility for an organization to efficiently handle many more transactions than was possible previously. With the benefit of the enabling Internet technology, many organizations have reassessed the value contribution of the intermediaries (distributors and agents) with the intention of

ILLUSTRATION 12.4

Jack Ma creating Chinese entrepreneurs

To thousands of Chinese people, Jack Ma has achieved rock star status to the point where he needs bodyguards to hold back the adoring fans. He is listed in *Time* magazine's top 100 most influential people in the world and has achieved this status by enabling many Chinese to become their own boss – a dream ingrained in the Chinese culture. Ma set up Alibaba which is now the world's largest B2B market place and, through the acquisition of Yahoo! China, enables the company to challenge US global online giants, Google, eBay, Yahoo! and Amazon. Alibaba has become a leader in its own right though its own innovations that deliver value to users.

Alibaba has two B2B websites at its heart, alibaba.com, a marketplace for firms across the world to trade in English, and china.alibaba.com, a domestic Chinese service. While the aim of rival western sites, such as Ariba and Commerce One, was to cut the procurement costs for multinationals, Alibaba's was to build markets for many Chinese SMEs, which make a vast array of manufactured goods available to western traders, who might resell on eBay.

Ma has led the Chinese development of online communities and social networking with a consumer auction site, Taobao, that has an innovation that reflects a cultural difference. Whereas eBay transactions are between largely anonymous buyers and sellers, Taobao facilitates instant messaging, voicemail and allows personal photographs and details to be posted, creating a community of 'friends' in a country where there is still a lack of trust. By 2010 Taobao claimed it had 190 million customers in China and transactions worth £19 billion. Ma has also addressed the problem of settlement risks in online payments in China, where there are no credit cards, by introducing AliPay, which holds cash in an escrow account until the goods are delivered. AliPay is effectively an online bank that is able to maintain many thousands of supplier and customer credit histories.

Alibaba International claims to be the world's largest B2B marketplace for global trade with 500 000 people visiting the site every day and Alibaba China is the largest site for domestic China trade with 16 million registered users. Taobao has 30 million registered users and is the largest e-commerce website in Asia.

The interesting aspect of Ma is that he is a business entrepreneur rather than a computer geek like the founders of Yahoo! and Google. He believes that 'someone as dumb as me should be able to use technology'. He will not accept a new feature unless he can understand it and use it.

Question

1 What are the critical success factors in creating a successful B2B and C2C electronic market place?

Sources: 'Jack Ma is attracting a following among entrepreneurs in China and Internet companies worldwide', *The Economist*, 21 September, 2006. 'Taobao's Alipay will charge fees', 16 March, 2007, www.chinatechnews.com: and 'Alibaba IPO would touch US$1 billion', 1 June 2007, accessed at: www.chinaeconomicreview.com/it/category /services/.

managing the distribution themselves and cutting out the intermediary. The benefits to the organization are the removal of channel infrastructure costs and intermediary margins and the opportunity to develop a direct relationship with the final customer. 'Cutting out the middleman' is described as disintermediation. Chaffey *et al.* (2006) observe that at the start of the e-business boom it was expected that there would be widespread disintermediation. While it has happened in some sectors, in others there has been little change and the results of disintermediation is some sectors have been disappointing with the marketing organization incurring substantial additional IT, order management and logistics costs, offsetting the forecast savings. This idea of 'cutting out the middleman' has grown into Bring-Your-Own-Device (BYOD), Bring-Your-Own-Apps (BYOA) and BringYour-Own-Network (BYON). Many businesses enable their employees to Bring-Your-Own-Apps (BYOA) by synching their work email via a mobile platform so they can read emails on the go without having to go through their organization's website. Additionally, travellers such as those travelling with Etihad can store their flight booking form via an Etihad app for faster boarding. Additionally, many consumers Bring-Their-Own-Cloud and have many gigabytes of data from word documents to photographs available to them through their Google Drive or Dropbox app.

The counter to disintermediation is re-intermediation and the creation of new firms that add value in the purchasing situation, such as travel and household goods. While many financial services products and offers from utilities lend themselves to online selling, it is a laborious task to compare the many offerings from competing companies. Consequently many brokers have set up websites such as Uswitch and moneyextra to allow customers to compare many different financial product offerings. Of course this means that the Internet marketer must ensure that they are represented on key sites where there are high volumes of potential customers and ensure that they are offering competitive prices.

The alternative strategy is for the marketer to set up his own intermediary to compete with the existing intermediaries; this is referred to as counter-mediation. A group of airlines set up an alternative to www.expedia.com to offer airline tickets.

Business to consumer

In the B2C sector, well designed websites, whether from small or large companies, provide a satisfying experience for the online shopper and this means customers are able to browse through the information that is available about the products and services they are seeking to buy, and do so at their leisure. The best websites offer potential customers the choice of which language they wish to communicate in and are sensitive to the local culture and legal frameworks. Having selected the product they enable customers to easily purchase and pay for the product online, using credit cards to make payment. In practice, many more customers are prepared to use the Internet to carry out their information search on companies, products and services, but are still unwilling to pay online because of fears about the security of online payment and the potential for fraud, or, in emerging markets, unable because of the lack of a suitable payment method such as a credit card. Firms that have both virtual and physical stores allow customers to find out information and then choose whether to buy online or go to the store.

Some services can be supplied as digital services online over the Internet. For example, information, software, financial advice, ticketless travel and music can be downloaded direct to the customer's computer. For physical products, however, the supplier still needs a suitable distribution method to deliver the goods to the consumer. Fulfilment of the order depends on more traditional distribution, with its associated limitations of the country's existing infrastructure and the availability of appropriate logistics in each customer's country. Small items such as cosmetics or books can be posted, but delivering valuable bulky goods such as furniture, or goods that require special storage conditions such as food, directly to the door also require arrangements to be made for the customer to receive them. However, to accommodate for the fact that many people work, Amazon has drop off zones which hold much bulkier items that cannot be left at a PO Box or posted through a letter box. The drop off zones are often placed at petrol stations or supermarkets.

Using the Internet simply to transact business underutilizes its potential, however, and does little to build competitive advantage, or improve the overall effectiveness of the operation in winning global customers and developing their loyalty. Moreover, without building competitive advantage and unique selling propositions, firms using the Internet to sell their products are vulnerable to lower priced offers from other global competitors, because sophisticated search engines identify the cheapest offers of comparable products or services. Many companies believe they can survive and grow by offering the lowest priced products direct to customers, but inevitably new entrants will always offer lower prices, even if they are not sustainable in the longer term.

E-business operations are expensive to establish and maintain, given the large outlay for information technology, systems, management and website development. Moreover, e-commerce firms require sophisticated systems to fulfil orders promptly and accurately and need to innovate constantly to retain customer interest and loyalty. The challenge for a business is therefore to maximize income. Chaffey *et al.* (2006) identify a number of opportunities for generating income from a website, for example, by charging for sponsorship, advertising and 'click-through' fees for sales generated by a second firm that has a direct link to its own site.

Consumer to consumer (C2C)

Timmers (1999) has identified other Internet business models involving exchange between supplier and customer. These include C2C in which consumers sell to each other through an online auction. One of the most successful sites for trading between individuals by online bidding is eBay. This type of buying and selling tends to become almost a hobby in itself for customers. They take a fee to insert the advertisement and a fee based on the final value. It has been successful internationally but has had problems competing in certain markets. As stated earlier, it pulled out of Japan and failed to compete with Alibaba, partly because it did not really understand the Chinese culture.

New models of international business are being developed that incorporate a number of aspects of business, consumer and social networking websites and an example of this is discussed in Management Challenge 12.2 which provides an example of a business that shares its knowhow on an international ticketing website that can be used for local needs.

MANAGEMENT CHALLENGE 12.2

Secure ticketing B2B

It seems a long time ago for the five friends from Munich who organized a party in their back garden for hundreds of people to watch Germany's opening match of the 2006 World Cup, on the understanding that everyone would contribute 20–23 euros for food and drink. After the event it occurred to them that they had a business opportunity and formed Amiando, now Europe's leading online service for on-demand event organization and ticketing. The original idea was to create a platform for selling tickets to an event, initially e-invites for private parties, but this was soon followed by a payment and ticketing system, promotion and demand management attendee registration. The parent company Amiando has a spin-off company called Xing Events which is a B2B offer for organizations that would like a safe and secure network from which to sell tickets for an event. Xing Events provides the opportunity to create an online ticket website for free. Xing Events provide the platform and the secure money transfer facility. However, it does not stop there. The advice and expertise is shared and for a small fee (and sometimes for free) Xing Events enables organizations to create a special customized website that requests additional information from the attendees to be used for future communication opportunities. Take for example a charity that wishes to organize a music event. The charity could ask attendees their age, gender and the band they are most looking forward to watching. This data would provide the charity with a social map of their attendees. Data collected on the website could be analyzed and processed through Xing Events who provide a feature called people2meet. People2meet enables the charity to match like-minded people together and send special messages to different groups. For example, attendees could be grouped by band preference and they could be notified of special information about band merchandise or places to meet up after the concert. Xing Events also provides an Events Planner app that the charity could use to show attendees details of the music event opening time and a running order of the bands.

Question

1 How might viral marketing be used by international firms to create a new business model or to promote their business?

Source: Xing Events www.amiando.com.

International marketing solution integration

The most significant international marketing strategy development that is facilitated by technology is business solution integration. As competition increases, so firms must seek to find new sources of competitive advantage, secure ever-lower costs, increase their speed of action and responsiveness, demonstrate their adaptability to new situations, and flexibility in offering new innovative products and services perceived by customers to be valuable. They must also develop better relationships with their customers and business partners in order to retain their business. The strategy to achieve these outcomes is based on the effective integration of the elements of the marketing and business processes.

Knowledge management

The move to an increasingly global market served by e-business has prompted firms to redefine their sources of competitive advantage. In a global market the traditional sources of competitive advantage can be easily challenged. A company that operates in a small number of countries or within a restricted business sector may believe that its competitive advantage comes from low-cost manufacturing, design capability, sales expertise and distribution efficiency. However, when exposed to global competition it may find that its own competitive advantage cannot be transported to new countries and discover, instead, that regional or global competitors have even greater competitive advantage in their own domestic market as well as in the target country market.

By contrast, knowledge, expertise and experience have the potential to be transferable if they can be effectively collected, stored, accessed and communicated around the world (hence the term knowledge management). Below we discuss the processes for managing knowledge to support the customer–client interface, but **knowledge management** is essential to maximize added value throughout the supply chain. There is a danger in building competitive advantage through knowledge management, of course, because the knowledge assets of a firm are locked into their staff and their records, typically contained in their computers. Staff are becoming increasingly mobile, computer systems are still notoriously insecure and the potential loss of knowledge to a competitor is an ever greater problem for firms. Business espionage is growing in many countries.

Supply chain management

Technology-enabled supply chain management has helped firms to grow through exploiting market development opportunities, reducing investment by buying rather than manufacturing components, and enabling small firms to have similar costs to large firms through e-procurement. It is vital that each part of the supply chain of the product maximizes the added value and this is made possible by integrating the activities. A supply chain for a complex product might typically involve such distinctly different activities as design, manufacture of raw materials, component assembly, advertising, logistics and local servicing. It is highly unlikely that one company could be the leader in each of these areas of activity, particularly when the most efficient members of the supply chain will increasingly be located around the world.

The implications, of course, are that through using e-commerce for procurement, partnerships can be set up and dissolved instantly. Suppliers need to have huge flexibility and excellent systems to manage the rapid changes that are necessary to survive in this type of market. Suppliers are in completely open competition with other firms around the world.

Cost savings can be made in all areas of the supply chain, such as inventory reduction and just-in-time sourcing. Amazon is able to offer millions of books and music titles and other items by quickly obtaining stocks held anywhere in the world, whereas an average traditional bookstore might physically hold only 170 000 titles. Savings can be made in evaluating suppliers, specifications and delivery times and arranging scheduling. Marketing costs can be reduced because it is easier, quicker and cheaper to make alterations to Web content than incur the design and printing costs of a new brochure.

Advantest America Inc. supplies measuring instruments, semiconductor test systems and related equipment. It outsourced delivery of its replacement parts, e-commerce and supply chain management services to FedEx Corporation, which provides transport. Using FedEx's sophisticated, integrated systems it was able to reduce its delivery times by more than 50 per cent, to 48 hours in Asia and 24 hours for customers in America and Europe. Previously, starting from the time the order was taken, it could take between 25 and 42 hours even to get through customs and onto a commercial aeroplane. Extending the system to the firm's customized printed circuit boards would avoid the need for the customer to hold stock on site, thus considerably reducing their inventory.

Every element in the logistics process must be tackled in order to improve performance. In service call centres the cost of employing a person capable of dealing with service calls in India is about one-tenth of the cost of employing a person in the UK for an equivalent level of performance. Very often service centre calls are routine and technology can be used to make further savings by replacing people-based transactions with 'intelligent' computer-based responses.

Value chain integration

The key question is how effectively the individual supply chain members around the world work in partnership to maximize the effectiveness of their contributions towards improving efficiency and adding value across the entire value chain, so-called value chain integration. Success is then likely to be dependent on the effectiveness of the working relationship between the members of the supply chain, the speed and openness of information sharing and the degree of collaboration between each company, its suppliers and customers, with the objective of adding value and removing transaction costs.

So, for example, a supermarket chain will allow its hundreds of suppliers to have access to its data warehouse, so they will know how their particular product is selling in each individual store, and to the inventory system to ensure that the supermarket never runs out of stock. This system makes it easier for additional suppliers to be included and managed at low additional cost, allowing consumers more choice and more competitive prices. Hagiu (2013), however, explains that although multi-sided platforms (MSPs), such as PayPal, Microsoft, Google, Facebook and Apple, can lower costs, there are dangers with online collaboration as firms cede too much power to the MSPs. Toys'R'Us signed a ten-year 'exclusive' agreement with Amazon with the intention of creating an online retail business to dominate its category and paid them US$50 million annually, plus a percentage of sales, but not long afterwards Amazon recruited small third party merchants to sell toys and games directly through its website. Toys'R'Us lost money and successfully sued Amazon for US$200 million in damages. As the name implies, multi-sided platforms (MSPs) are only as good as those that engage in it. A recent MSP success is AirBNB, a platform where consumers can rent out space in their house or apartment usually to holidaymakers. If AirBNB was not populated by people that rent their houses and apartments, and reviews of happy holidaymakers, then the multisided platform would not be successful.

Virtual enterprise networks

The possibility for Internet technology-supported collaboration between supply chain members is being extended and applied to SMEs and individuals with complementary expertise that form themselves into a virtual enterprise network to bid for and carry out projects and routine business. Snyder (2005) explains that the Internet has reduced transaction costs and outsourcing risks, enabling the individuals and organizations to form a more efficient form of organization, based on virtually integrated collaborative networks rather than hierarchical bureaucracies. Virtual enterprise networks are expected to become more common, international in nature and focused on international marketing opportunities.

Customer relationship management

Customer relationship management (CRM) is the process of identifying, attracting, differentiating and retaining customers (Hoffman 2003). It allows a firm to focus its efforts on its most lucrative customers, no matter where they are from, and is based on the 'rule' that 80 per cent of a firm's profits come from 20 per cent of its customers. It is also designed to achieve efficient and effective customer management. As pressures on costs and prices increase, firms must manage customers as inexpensively as they can without losing customer loyalty. To answer a customer query with an automatic Web or text-based service can be less than a tenth of the cost of a person handling it by telephone through a service call centre, but the question is whether it can be as responsive to customer queries.

CRM allows customers to be categorized on the basis of their past profitability. The most profitable customers will be recognized and will be routed to the area that will handle calls fastest. For example, this can be done automatically by transferring telephone calls with a particular number. The profitable customers can then be targeted with attractive deals. The information is shared throughout the company to ensure integration of the firm's activities so that profitable customers get priority service throughout the firm and also from partner firms.

To deliver a CRM strategy the key component is the database of customer information. Techniques and systems are used to manage and extract data (data mining) to identify trends and analyze customer characteristics that enable the targeting to be carried out. Building and sustaining a competitive advantage using a consumer-centric approach, coupled with CRM technology; often on a global scale, should be at the heart of every business. Richardson, James and Kelly (2015) also argue that businesses no longer provide goods and services for consumers; there is a partnership where the consumer and the business co-create products and services both seeking value from a transaction.

The system involves the retention of large amounts of detailed information about individual customers in a firm database. Customers often resent firms holding information about them and in some countries it would infringe privacy laws. Companies analyze the data that they have but only past behaviour has been recorded and so this data may not be an accurate predictor of future behaviour. There is an assumption that customers want a 'relationship' with suppliers and that in some way they will benefit from it. If the benefit is not clear, then customers will not remain loyal.

Customization

As we have suggested on a number of occasions, customers increasingly want to be treated as individuals and not simply be the unwilling targets of mass market advertising. The Internet allows companies to mass customize their offering and a variety of firms are exploiting the flexibility of online mobile communication. A number of firms are providing software applications that are designed to personalize or more individually target the firm's interactions. For example, Lindgren (2003) explains how Poindexter (US) uses statistical analysis to identify the shared characteristics of online advertising viewers, and be able to cluster those customers who respond to websites and online advertisements in a similar way. The clusters can then be offered a customized marketing mix and customized promotions and product offers. For example, an online shopper who puts products in an online basket but does not go through with the purchase immediately, might be offered a discount by the online retailer as an incentive to go through with the purchase. As more viewers are analyzed the system learns the best response and so delivers better performance.

Customers can be targeted and made aware of special deals being offered in their own neighbourhood, perhaps on travel, at a restaurant or at the wine shop. Global positioning systems coupled with mobile telephony enable firms to text consumers about deals available in the shop that they are just passing.

The impact on international marketing strategy

Having discussed the central role of the Internet as a technology enabler of international marketing and highlighted the various elements of the electronic marketplace, we now turn to how these can both influence and support the much more dynamic approach to international marketing strategy development that we mentioned at the start of this chapter.

The impact of technology on analysis

Demand patterns are now changing more quickly because of changes in the environment, customer needs and wants and competition, and so it is increasingly vital for firms to be able to track changes through an effective marketing information system. Much of the data that must be gathered from around the world can be more effectively collected, managed and communicated through integrated web-based systems. Firms can track political, economic and legal changes and new product launches by competitors as they are announced by using search engines and sites that provide up-to-date expert analysis. Point of sale information can be collected and analyzed by retailers on a daily basis to provide information about what products are selling and not selling so that appropriate action can be taken to avoid unnecessary inventory, and build a supply chain that is flexible and responsive. For example, for clothing products sourced from Asia to sell in the US, the fabric production, garment making and logistics must be fast, flexible and quickly adaptable to changing fashion needs to avoid stock write-offs or write-downs.

In the past, fashion magazines and newspaper articles provided information about the latest trend and images of celebrities wearing the next 'cool' brand or 'must have' product. Now social networking websites provide the responses from customers that are likely to affect their purchasing habits. Because of the informal, non-regulated nature of the websites, firms can influence their perceptions of the products as we discuss later in this section.

The Internet provides not only general information about the firm's products but also makes it easier and faster to apply questionnaires to existing and potential customers around the world by using the Internet. Customer behaviour can be monitored on websites by tracking navigation through the site to provide new insights, thought processes and predict likely purchasing intentions. Egol, Clyde and Rangan (2010) explain how online shopping behaviour can lead to six consumer segments:

- *Shoppers* 2.0, the most technologically advanced group, price sensitive with little brand loyalty.
- *Deal hunters*, are price sensitive but although they gather information online they get the best deal in store.
- *Online window shoppers*, again gather information online and in store, but are less price sensitive and less likely to switch brands.
- *Channel surfers*, hunt out the brands they love and try to source the brands at reasonable prices.
- *Loyalists*, are least likely to switch brands or retail formats.
- *Laggards*, are least likely to change behaviour and carry out little online research.

The Internet provides some negative information as well, from blogs and social networking sites. Firms can suffer considerable damage at the hands of such sites.

As we discussed in Part I, organizations are collecting this type of information in a much more systematic way. For example, Procter & Gamble and Unilever have a database of observed behaviour accessible to staff worldwide through an intranet.

Radian6 is an organization which uses algorithms to understand what consumers feel about products and services; they do this by analyzing comments shared on Facebook, Twitter, websites, blogs and so on. All happy consumers that say they enjoyed their visit to a theme park, or compliment a receptionist, or shout out about a chef's fabulous food, are analyzed as providing a positive sentiment to the brand. However, consumers that share bad experiences and comment that a product was terrible or service staff were not courteous are analyzed as providing a negative sentiment to the brand. There are hundreds of companies like Radian6 that help businesses analyze and understand internet 'chatter' so they can understand and customize their products and services to different customer needs identified through social media. Social media comments can be highly customized. A consumer who complains, via Twitter, they are waiting in a queue to check-in at a hotel can be identified immediately. The team tracking social media comments will advise the hotel that a person in the queue is complaining. Extra staff can be brought to reception to help alleviate the situation and give refreshments to all people who are waiting as an apology.

It seems therefore that a huge amount of micro and big data can be generated and analyzed. However, Ofek and Wathieu (2010) observe that while managers recognize major social, economic and technological trends, their focus is often on short term goals and they often fail to realize the significance of these trends in reshaping the business.

The impact of technology on international strategy development

For some firms their international marketing strategy is inextricably linked to technology either because of the nature of the business, in the case of firms such as IBM, Microsoft and Acer, or because it is the route to market in the case of Expedia, Dell and Bloomberg.

For firms in most industry sectors technology, business and marketing innovations are a major source of international competitive advantage. As we discussed earlier, organizations in developed countries cannot compete against the low labour and other associated costs, operational scale benefits and lower research and development costs of firms from developing countries, such as India and China.

Their source of competitive advantage in the future, therefore, is likely to come from technological, business process and marketing innovation, from knowledge management of the organization's intellectual property and assets, its ability to manage effectively and the contributions of the supply chain to maximize the customer value. For these reasons technological competence and capability, understanding the competitive market position and gaining in-depth customer insights will become key success criteria in the future.

Internet-based market entry

The Internet provides a market entry method that is particularly suitable for smaller, widespread niche markets. While the website might be accessible worldwide, the firm may need to select markets to focus on, possibly excluding those where there may be particular barriers, such as language, legal, payment and over-fulfilment problems. The cost of organizing to serve certain markets might outweigh the possible benefits. For firms that already have a strong presence in many markets the Internet supports all aspects of their activity.

Web-based services will be successful if firms develop a global strategy based upon the integrated value chain. As this is a pervasive method of entry, based on global communications, it can facilitate lower-risk access to difficult markets. By building online delivery capability it is possible to serve markets profitably where there might be limited demand. Of course, an e-commerce strategy is limited in scope simply because it appeals to a very specific transnational segment – those that are able to gain access to the firm's website – but as Internet access, particularly high speed access, continues to grow this is a diminishing problem.

The impact of technology on strategy implementation and control

Product and service management   Technology supports the delivery and control of all the elements of the augmented product and service offer (see Chapter 8, Figure 8.2) and integrates the worldwide members of the supply chain, as discussed earlier in this chapter. It is also used to speed up innovation and facilitate worldwide contributions to new product and service development activity.

In doing this, technology is increasingly supporting, on the one hand, the standardization of the components of the product, and creating worldwide product 'platforms'. For example, car firms such as VW, and household appliance manufacturers such as Whirlpool, use a common platform and make minor adaptations for different models and markets. On the other hand, it is enabling firms to offer increased customization of products and services and one-to-one marketing. Illustration 12.5 shows how customers can be encouraged to provide innovative ideas for new products and communications, using so-called crowd funding.

Pricing   As we discussed earlier in the chapter, technology is driving down costs and prices through supply chain efficiencies, economies of scale, the experience curve effect and greater price transparency. Price transparency for customers and other stakeholders is created because of the ease with which it is now possible to compare prices offered by competing potential suppliers across borders by searching through the information on their websites. Some sites such as Expedia in travel, Kelkoo on a range of products in B2C markets, and the sector and function e-hubs in B2B provide the opportunity for customers to compare prices on one site. The sophistication and usefulness of web search activity is improving as competition between firms such as Google and Microsoft increases.

ILLUSTRATION 12.5

Crowd sourcing: Funding the perfect road

Julie and Scott Brusaw are engineers; one has a creative streak and the other applies the creative ideas! Julie suggested to Scott that roads should be made of solar panels so that electricity can be generated from the sun for everybody and not just individuals that have solar panels on the roofs of their houses. Scott, the inventor said it was not possible. But . . . three days later he changed his mind.

However, they had a problem which so many inventors have: they did not have enough money to put their idea into practice. To design, create, engineer and take their product to market would cost a lot of money – US$1 000 000. Julie and Scott could go to the bank or get sponsorship. For such a huge amount of money they did not think they could persuade the bank. Therefore, they chose to go to indiegogo.com which is a crowd-funding website. Julie and Scott promoted their idea to strangers. They asked strangers to fund their creative idea to make solar panelled roads that would generate electricity and reduce carbon emissions by 75 per cent when compared with other road making processes.

Currently there are 49 603 strangers, known as funders, that contributed to their solar panelled road. The funders come from 165 countries and together they have contributed US$2 255 697.

Julie and Scott were overwhelmed with the response and support. Clearly, like Julie and Scott there are many people that think they needed to 'do something' to reduce carbon emissions that contribute to global warming. The solar panelled roads do that. They also have a special added value feature. The special feature is that the solar roadways can be warmed up at any time. Therefore, the solar panelled roads can melt the snow and ice – making driving conditions easier and safer during the winter months.

Question

1 What are the advantages and disadvantages of international crowd funding for small businesses and inventors?

Source: Indiegogo (2015) www.indiegogo.com/projects /solar-roadways#/story.

The Internet makes grey marketing easier and also makes it much more difficult for firms to operate specific geographic territories and price differentials across country borders, so grey marketing may become less of an issue in international markets as firms give up hope of trying to control it. Price transparency has the effect of driving mature products towards commoditization in which products become less differentiated and competition is based largely on price. When there are many competitors, price transparency forces down prices as suppliers have to respond by cutting the costs of their products and services. This usually forces them to find ever-lower cost sources. The alternative is to innovate and develop new products and services or add additional services, many of which, such as loyalty reward schemes, are operated online. However, these strategies will only work if customers around the world perceive the additional services to be valuable and of additional benefit over the commodity product alternative.

Customization is clearly the opposite of commoditization and, therefore, can be used partially to counter price transparency. As international pricing embraces both pricing and financing the transaction, technology allows pricing to be customized. It can enable complex calculations to be made to facilitate the negotiation of mutually beneficial deals between supplier and customer with flexible pricing and financing and also control non-standard repayment schedules that ensure that the transaction is ultimately profitable. An example of this from personal finance is that it is possible to offset longer-term loans, such as a mortgage to buy a house, against savings in a current account and pay interest daily on the balance outstanding.

Channel management Electronic marketing has encouraged disintermediation, or the removal of intermediaries from the supply chain, as suppliers market directly to customers. Technology now enables firms to efficiently manage thousands of small transactions that previously would have been left for a local intermediary to undertake. This is possible because e-marketing has typically lower transaction costs and is capable of managing large inventories, logistics, ordering and payments but also allows the virtual bundling of products that might be sourced from different partner suppliers. Disintermediation provides the manufacturer with stronger control of its activities in the market and avoids being so reliant on third parties. It also enables the distribution channels to be customized to the specific needs of the customers.

For those firms that are maintaining intermediaries within their distribution channel, technology allows much closer cooperation through sharing of market information but also greater control of intermediaries by making it easier to check on a daily basis that they are fulfilling their commitments to the supplier.

Communications The main advantage of e-marketing communications is that they are targeted and are often based on one-to-one communications. The most important aspect is that they are interactive. Customers are required to do something rather than being passive recipients of untargeted advertising or other promotion. As customers become more involved, so they are more likely to buy.

Marketing through websites, even interactive ones, is reactive, because potential customers must take the initiative and locate the site first, typically by using search, which is critically important. It is essential that the firm features high on the list of search results. Word of mouth referral or viral marketing is important in building traffic to the website, but to gain a large market in unexciting business sectors it is not enough just to have a website. It is also necessary to proactively market and promote the brand and the site in the traditional media. The fundamental questions of marketing need to be asked, such as who are we targeting, where will we find the target customers on the Internet, and how will we get them directed to our site? How best can we then communicate our message to them globally and at low cost? The key is to deliver the right message to the right people at the right time in the right place using the right e-based communication channels.

Control, evaluation and learning Technology enables firms to collect, transfer and analyze vast amounts of data from anywhere in the world. Using Enterprise Resource Planning (ERP) software they are able to control the use of resources and improve the efficiency of their operations. Financial management and control can be more immediate and more detailed. Firms use other processes and systems to control the supporting operations to ensure quality and efficiency of the manufacturing, distribution operations, and measure the effectiveness of the marketing processes and programmes.

These techniques can be applied in worldwide operations because they can be supported by information technology and systems. Underpinning all these techniques is the need to develop a learning organization that follows good practice, shares new ideas and creates greater confidence in the abilities of its staff so that they can be empowered to take decisions in their own area of expertise and knowledge.

Some limitations of e-commerce for international marketing strategy

There are some disadvantages in operating e-business globally, including the high cost of providing a global website with 24-hour service for customers who expect interactive capability, wherever possible, in their own language and culture and adapted to their own environment. There are also some significant perceived and real dangers associated with e-commerce. Customers are concerned with data security and the risks, for example, of credit card fraud. Customers are also concerned with identity theft, data protection and the use, storage and passing on to third parties of personal information to firms anywhere in the world. Of course technology is being continually developed and improved to try to overcome these difficulties.

Firms basing their business on e-commerce must recognize that there are typically low entry barriers and competitors have greater and easier access to information that can be used to challenge the existing supplier. For example, Yell the business directory company, blamed a decline in profits on a rival business set up by ex-sales staff made redundant in the US by the company. Computer systems are still prone to system failure and corruption and it is still alarmingly easy for computer hackers and computer viruses to cause severe damage to multinational enterprises. Often MNEs, particularly banks, do not publicize such difficulties as it may well deter customers. There is also a proliferation of anti-MNE websites and social networking sites that can publicize damaging stories – true or not – virtually without challenge. This is possible, of course, simply because of the relatively uncontrolled nature of the Internet.

International e-business marketing businesses face some challenges:

1 The decisions of customers in e-commerce are strongly affected by cultural issues. Customers from some countries, typically low-context countries, embrace the Internet in different ways to those in high-context cultures, because of the lower emphasis placed on implicit interactions when building relationships and purchasing products.

2 Brand values often depend on the different communication methods that people use, both explicit and implicit, such as image, reputation, word of mouth and continual exposure online and offline. This emphasizes the need for an integrated communications approach involving virtual and physical media.

3 By being global, e-commerce still favours global players. Consumers expect high quality of performance and image but these can be severely tarnished by a low-cost, poorly performing website and slow or inaccurate order fulfilment.

4 The effectiveness of websites is influenced by such factors as the ease of navigation, company and products information, shipping details and sensitivity to language and culture.

5 The barriers to entry must be significant if the defenders of domestic or limited country niches wish to retain their market share. It must be recognized by marketers that the marketing skills to ensure success in e-business are different from traditional skills, in that success depends on attracting consumers to sites and this is typically more difficult because of the increased media 'noise'.

6 The development of intelligent agents that search for specific pieces of information on markets and potential suppliers means that marketers cannot base their appeal to customers on traditional marketing-mix factors but must find a new sustainable competitive advantage.

Legislation

The aspect of the Internet that seems to raise most concern is the fact that there is very little control exerted and consequently the Internet is used for unethical and illegal purposes and to circumvent the law. The Internet has grown extremely rapidly and the application of existing law and introduction of legislation to control activities has lagged behind. Governments do not want to stifle development and so legislation is being developed not in anticipation but only as problems arise.

Problems of application of existing law to the Internet

The Internet removes traditional geographic boundaries, so that virtually anyone anywhere in the world can access a website. Zugelder, Flaherty and Johnson (2000) explain that a particular difficulty is the fact that websites are subject to the laws of individual countries, both home and host country, where customers are based. Websites are also subject to regional trade agreements (e.g. EU and NAFTA) and regulations of organizations such as the WTO, the World International Property Organization (WIPO) and the Berne Convention on copyright law. Many countries either do not conform or interpret many conventions differently.

The result is a chaotic situation in which multiple and contradictory laws apply to the same transaction, leaving a marketer open to the possibility of unintentionally violating the laws of a foreign country. A whole series of issues arise in e-marketing, including what constitutes a contract in cyberspace, how international tax can be harmonized and how tax should be collected for online transactions.

There are many issues of intellectual property protection, including copyright infringement, inappropriate linking to information from another website and trademark infringement, such as the registering of existing trademarks as domain names for the website. Because of the demand for domain names, second-level (for example .co, .org and .com) and third-level country names (.uk and .de) have been added. Countries including the UK, Mexico and Russia, have taken a 'first come, first served' approach to this, and companies such as Nike, Chrysler and Sony initially failed to register as widely as they should have and have suffered as a consequence.

Consumer protection for international consumer clients must be provided to avoid unfair and deceptive trading practices, such as unsubstantiated advertising claims and false endorsements. Relationship marketing is based, especially for small firms, on building substantial data on customers in order to retain their loyalty, but in a number of countries gathering such information is illegal as laws exist to protect consumer privacy. Marketers must also know the difference between what is considered free speech and what is defamation and disparagement.

Other Internet problems

The problems discussed so far have related to the application of largely existing legislation to the new medium and the fact that the Internet crosses country borders indiscriminately. Other issues are the ease of access and lack of control of illegal activity. It has been estimated that a large percentage of international consumer e-commerce is devoted to pornography and a worrying part of this traffic is illegal and supporting paedophilia. It requires close cooperation between country law enforcement agencies to catch the culprits.

The ease of communicating with many recipients makes it easy to send out 'junk mail' (spam). Millions of messages can be sent out worldwide in the hope of getting just a few responses. Many firms sell to potential customers through emails and text messages. However, if this is overused it degenerates into spam. Spam is the intrusive, offensive and often pornographic junk email that fills up the inboxes of email systems. It threatens to create gridlock on the Internet if it is not controlled. The US has proposed opt-out legislation so that spam would be legal unless the receiver has opted out of receiving it. The EU legislation is opt-in – spam could not be sent unless the receiver had given consent to receive it – and would be more effective in controlling spam.

Moving to a customer-led strategy

The Internet and developments in the media have revolutionized business communications and transactions and changed marketing forever by allowing anyone anywhere in the world to buy online from anyone else. The range of communication methods has increased significantly as a result of technological advances and entrepreneurialism. The growth in social networking has transformed communications. Sometimes blogging is well informed and sometimes it is completely incorrect and often malicious, but it strongly influences consumer purchasing and usage decisions. The technology advances were expected to level the playing field between small and large firms so that the most innovative firms, small or large, would become the winners. It was thought that the technologists rather than the marketers would be in control. In reality, consumers have become more sophisticated in their use of technology and media, and used it to their advantage. As a result, consumers are increasingly in control of events and so even greater customer insights are needed and marketing expertise has never been more vital. Illustration 12.6 provides one example of how the current generation of teenagers might be consuming media.

At the start of the chapter we put forward the idea that technology is an enabler, and Hamill and Stevenson (2003) suggest that technology facilitates cost-effective relationship building, but does not automatically achieve a customer-focused approach. Ritter and Walter (2006) examine the impact of information technology on customer relationships in the B2B context. They conclude that while IT competence can replace parts of relationship management, it cannot do so totally.

Technology has shifted the balance of power from suppliers to customers. Consequently, customer dominance must be accepted and those arrogant firms that take customers for granted will suffer. Organizations must adopt a customer-led approach in order to achieve sustainability. This means that they must develop innovative approaches to sales, marketing and overall corporate strategy that are driven by what customers need and want.

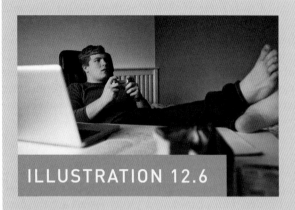

ILLUSTRATION 12.6

How teenagers consume media

When Morgan Stanley in the UK asked Matthew Robson, a 15-year-old schoolboy, to write a report on how he and his friends consume media they were surprised to see the results. We have included some of the points made here to illustrate some differences between the generations and prompt a discussion about how teenagers consume media in different countries. The changing preferences for media consumption have major implications for marketers to this segment now and in the future, and to those that wish to communicate with them. One example is discussed in the end-of-chapter Case Study 1.

Teenagers do not regularly listen to music on the radio and instead rely on online sites streaming music for free. They prefer sites that allow users to listen to their choice rather than that of the radio presenter. They watch TV selectively, boys generally watch more during the football season and choose regular programmes, such as soap operas, but they have less time available to watch TV. Services that allow you to watch what you want are more popular and teenagers switch to other channels or do something else while the adverts are running. Teenagers cannot be bothered to read newspapers, except free sheets while travelling and they only like compact size papers, which are easier to read.

The Wii has increased the interest in gaming of girls and younger players, and teenagers tend to game in longer sessions over one hour, rather than in short bursts. Connection to the Internet allows voice chat between users for free over the console, which teenagers prefer, whereas they would be unwilling to pay to use the phone.

Teenagers are heavily active on social networking sites, with the most common being Facebook, which allows wide scale interactions. Teenagers do not use Twitter although most sign up to the service. They would prefer to text friends rather than tweet, which they see as pointless as no-one views their profiles. They use YouTube to watch videos and use it as a background music player. Google is the favoured search tool.

While teenagers enjoy and support viral marketing because of the often humorous and interesting content, they see website ads (pop ups and banners) as irritating, annoying and pointless.

Teenagers listen to a lot of music while doing something else but are reluctant to pay for it and instead download illegally. They prefer to have a 'hard copy' of the music they like in order to share it as they wish. iTunes is unpopular with many because of the cost. Going to the cinema is common among younger teens aged 13–14, not because of the film, but because of the opportunity to get together with friends, but when they can no longer go to the cinema at children's prices it becomes less popular.

Almost all – 99 per cent – of teenagers have a mobile phone on pay-as-you-go and usually only use the phone for texting and calling. Other features are considered too expensive, such as Internet features and mobile email – as they can use the PC when they get home. They use mobile phones to send songs and videos even when it is illegal. Every teenager has access to a basic computer with Internet availability and has Microsoft Office installed to help them do their homework, but most do not have sophisticated computers.

They like anything with a touch screen, phones with large capacities for music, portable devices and really big TVs. They don't like anything with wires, clunky phones and devices with a short battery life.

Question

1 What patterns of media consumption by teenagers do you detect and how do these differ between cultures and countries?

Sources: M. Robson, 'Teenager causes city sensation with research on media', *Daily Telegraph*, 13 July 2009.

MANAGEMENT CHALLENGE 12.3

Rethinking watches and time

Traditional watchmakers are worried about the launch of Google, Apple and Samsung's smartwatches as they feel it will erode their market share. As always, when competition is strong, watchmakers begin to innovate.

What Watch has launched a watch that freezes 'a moment in time'. Many people experience many 'moments in time' during their lives, such as when they get married, when they pass their driving test, graduation day, receiving a sports award, doing a bungee jump, or dying their hair blue. Consumers that wear a What Watch merely tap a button on the side of their watch that captures that 'moment in time'. A microchip inside the watch records the date, time and second, and sends the information through a Bluetooth connection to the What Watch app stored on the wearer's Android or iOS devise. The What Watch app enables wearers to add a picture to that 'moment in time'. This means consumers can share their 'moments in time' with friends and family and/or keep a lifetime diary of 'life-time' moments. What Watch wearers will be able to create a timeline of events backed up with photographs or video clips of 'the moment'. Watches are always personal and What Watch want to create a relationship and an emotional link between their watch and its wearer.

Question

1 How are What Watch using the concept of customer relationship marketing through the technology inside the watch, the Watch Watch app and the watch wearer?

Source: What Watch www.whatwatch.com/howitworks.php.

The objective of being customer-led is to identify, acquire, retain and grow 'quality' customers. Nykamp (2001) suggests that organizations must achieve competitive differentiation by building impermeable customer relationships and the challenge is to use the interactive power of the Internet to facilitate this by helping the organization to build close one-to-one relationships with their most valuable and growable customers. Management Challenge 12.3 shows how a new watchmaking company is trying to form a relationship with watch wearers during the important times in their lives.

Many firms have recognized the need to be customer-led and have responded by implementing sophisticated and expensive customer relationship management systems. Hamill and Stevenson (2013) suggest that many of these systems have failed to produce the expected return because they have been technology-driven rather than customer-led. The term CRM has been hijacked by software vendors promising 'out-of-the-box' solutions to complex strategic, organizational and human resources problems. They claim that technology has a part to play but customer-led is not about software, database marketing, loyalty programmes, customer bribes or hard selling. It is about building strong one-to-one relationships with quality customers, achieving customer loyalty, maximizing customer lifetime earnings and re-engineering the firm towards satisfying the needs of 'quality' customers on a customized and personalized basis. The most convincing reason for a customer to buy from any company in the world is that they are totally satisfied, have no reason to complain about the service they receive and are surprised and delighted by some of the firm's innovative actions.

To deliver this requires a more fundamental reinvention of the firm if it wishes to really succeed in the future. A new mindset is needed together with an innovative approach to the strategy. In practice firms will need to:

- Focus not on markets but on quality customers from anywhere in the world. By quality customers it is the strategically significant, most valuable and 'growable' customers that should be given the highest priority. The suggestion is that, over time, firms have moved from supplying markets to serving market segments, and are now focusing on serving individual customers one at a time.

■ Focus on one-to-one relationships. To do this firms must learn about customers and deliver personalized and customized products, services and support in order to maximize the up- and cross-selling opportunities. The implications of this are that at one level firms must be sensitive to the customer's business and social culture and the customer's business dynamics. At another level the firm must be able to form supply and value chain alliances that enable the up- and cross-selling to be developed for the customer's benefit.

■ Increasing both lifetime and short-term revenue from customers. Firms must focus on the delivery of exceptional value by developing an effective worldwide supply chain, building ever-closer relationships both with customers and partners and finding ways to erect barriers to entry by competitor firms.

■ Win–win. The long-term business relationships must be valuable for both supplier and provider and so long-term value for the customer and firm must be maximized. Some compromises by both parties may be required to achieve this.

■ Integrated and coordinated approach. The success of a customer-led relationship building approach is that it requires commitment at all levels, creating, communicating and delivering value. For all businesses, but particularly global businesses, this is clearly a major challenge.

Most firms would claim to be customer-led, but the real test for them is whether they would be willing to change their strategy radically because of the trends that are being perceived in the marketplace. Lindstrom and Seybold (2003) report on research that suggests that marketing strategies in the future may need to be changed radically in order to be customer-led. Very young, computer literate child consumers have a large influence on family purchasing decisions. They are extremely well-informed through online networking sites that influence their behaviour. It is necessary to ask just how far firms should change their international marketing strategy to respond to these changes.

Sustainability and corporate social responsibility

Sustainability is the topic of ever more intense public attention and debate, and we have discussed various aspects of sustainability and corporate social responsibility in this book. Much of the public debate has centred on the green environment, reduction in the consumption of the world's non-renewable energy and other resources, the dumping of waste and pollution of the landscape and sea, and so on. It is becoming increasingly important for global firms to address these issues responsibly as they will affect the reputation of the company and its brand value. However, for some firms the failure to secure viable energy and resources, minimize waste and develop a sustainable, competitive cost base will put at risk the future of the business. Technological solutions from renewable sources of energy, recycling and using recycled components, and improved processes are essential.

Corporate social responsibility covers many areas: from treating staff well and paying them a living wage, not using child labour, paying suppliers a fair price and treating customers fairly, to adopting fair competition practices, and not resorting to bribery, fraud or other illegal practices. Berns *et al.* (2009) found from a survey of 50 global Thought Leaders that the barriers that impede decisive corporate action include:

■ a lack of understanding of what sustainability is and means to the enterprise;

■ difficulty modelling the business case; and

■ flaws in execution after a plan has been developed.

The growing awareness of consumers of the issues and their ability to access information about company practices worldwide means that more firms will come under pressure to provide answers. The Gulf of Mexico oil spill was a major problem for BP, one of the largest companies in the world, so all companies will have to address these issues. Along with technological advances, marketing will need to provide the answers.

SUMMARY

- Technology is creating new market opportunities and continually changing the way business is done in international markets. New technology provides solutions to solve old problems but also sets new challenges for international marketing management. Firms will underperform or even fail if they are not able to exploit the global opportunities offered by the new technology or if they take the wrong decisions about how new technology might affect their industry sector.

- Consumer e-marketing, and especially innovative business models attract the interest of global consumers and facilitate new routes to market. Consumers are enthusiastically embracing new ways of communicating, through mobile devices and social media, collecting information about products and services, sharing opinions and making purchase and usage decisions.

- Although the Internet and advances in telecommunications have had the most dramatic effect on international marketing, other technologies and software to support integrated marketing solutions, particularly in B2B marketing, have been part of this change. For example, e-procurement through e-hubs enables purchasing to be more efficiently managed worldwide.

- Greater cooperation because of improvements in communication and the ease of information sharing make supply chains more effective. However, excess capacity and increased competition mean that the power in the supply chain is increasingly favouring the customer.

- Technology will provide some of the solutions to achieve sustainability of resources and strategies, and companies will have to take a more responsible attitude to the green environment, but they will also have to adopt greater corporate social responsibility as communications increasingly enable the community to scrutinize their actions.

- Because of this, firms will need to work ever harder to find new customers, gain deeper insights about the behaviour and opinions of different global segments and retain the loyalty of existing customers. Their international marketing strategies will have to be customer-led to develop compelling added value offers.

KEYWORDS

Internet	information technology	knowledge management
enabling technologies	industry-specific hubs	customer relationship management
e-commerce	function-specific hubs	
websites	supply chain management	mass customize
business to business marketing	e-procurement	legislation
business to consumer marketing	online auction	customer-led

CASE STUDY 1

Heart problems? Wearable Tech could save your life

The Internet of Things (IoT) was introduced in Management Challenge 12.1 showing the benefits for consumers that are *technology connected*. Technology can also help consumers improve their health and save their life. The technology referred to in this case study is a Wireless Body Area Network (WBAN). Converging WBANs and the Internet can make significant improvements in a patient's health and well-being. Patients that have a heart condition are finding the WBAN particularly beneficial. Figure 12.2 shows the different layers of technology needed to keep a heart patient healthy.

The person in Figure 12.2 suffers from heart problems. They have a WBAN microchip implanted in their body. The data monitors and collects the person's temperature, blood pressure and heartbeat. The data is transferred from the WBAN microchip onto the person's smartphone app which is then sent immediately to a cloud database. The person's data can then be downloaded by a medical doctor or clinician. The positive benefits for both the person who suffers from heart problems and their doctor is that data is transmitted in real-time and is transmitted constantly. If the person's heart begins to beat irregularly or the person has a heart attack the cloud data will provide alerts. Should the person call for an ambulance or go to hospital their heart data before, during and after the irregular heartbeat or heart attack will be transmitted to the ambulance or hospital. This enables medical staff to attend to their patients' needs and save lives.

The technology that enables life-saving opportunities has two layers; the product layer and the service layer.

Technology for the product layer includes the WBAN microchip, IoT, medical cloud computing data storage facility and of course the laptops/desktops etc that medical doctors and clinicians use.

The service layer of technology includes software to read and store data in the implanted microchip and the software that stores and/or analyzes the data.

The benefit of WBAN technology is immeasurable for both patients, doctors and clinicians.

However, there are many people that argue that medical data should remain as private as possible between the patient and their doctor. Therefore, it is necessary for any business that develops WBANs or medical cloud computing data storage facilities to ensure the patient's name, medical details, their address and details of past diagnoses and medical treatment are secure. As shown in the chapter, privacy

FIGURE 12.2   Layers of technology

laws are not consistent or robust in some countries. This means it is important for WBAN business to choose carefully which cloud computing data storage facility they will use. WBAN businesses may choose not to use a cloud computing data storage facility in their own country as they feel better, safer facilities are available in different countries.

Questions

1 What are the strengths and weaknesses of WBAN shown in this case study?

2 What recommendations would you make to businesses interested in eHealth?

3 In addition to heart sufferers what other uses are there for wearable devices?

Source: Sawand, A., Djahel, S., Zhang, Z. and Nait-Abdesselam, F. (2015). Toward energy-efficient and trustworthy eHealth monitoring system. *Communications, China*, 12(1): 46–65.

CASE STUDY 2

Unilever: Redefining product policy for a global future

Unilever illustrates many of the challenges faced in developing and managing a global strategy. Its product portfolio ranges from food, to household goods to personal care products, and brands such as Ben & Jerry's ice-cream, Lipton tea and Dove soap.

In 1930 Lever Brothers, a British soap maker, merged with Margarine Unie of the Netherlands to form Unilever, but the global business started in the nineteenth century when the two companies sent out young men on ships from Rotterdam and Liverpool to various parts of the world to build businesses, set up plantations, build factories and establish distribution and supply systems. This early colonization meant that Unilever had a more established position in many emerging markets than its rivals and so had greater opportunities, but because of the long communication lines the chief executives of the country operations became used to being self sufficient and gained a high level of independence. They were responsible for managing everything from the local supply chain to advertising and human resources.

While the old structure encouraged entrepreneurship in the national businesses it inhibited exploitation of new products in other countries because of a 'not invented here' effect – any local innovation would have only a 50 per cent chance of being adopted in one more country.

Unilever operated as a federation of national businesses and this led to complexity and fragmentation. For example, the company had three operating companies in China, each of which had its own chairman, who reported to two regional presidents, who answered to two members of the executive committee. Unilever undertook a rationalization of its structures and cut out many small volume products and brands that resulted in a loss of over 50 000 jobs worldwide, the closure of 50 of its 300 factories and 75 of its 100 regional centres.

The company rationalized the 64 variants of tomato soup in Europe. The 64 pieces of advertising for the Pond's range of beauty products in Asia were reduced to four. Two or three adverts were created for Axe (Lynx in the UK) where previously there were 30 or 40. However, cultural differences still needed to be respected, particularly in advertising. For example, in the Dove ads women in Brazil hug one another, but that is not acceptable in the US where they stand slightly apart.

Focus on growth

After the 2007/2008 recession, Unilever's emerging markets had become 'decoupled' from the developed economies. Sales growth in developed markets lagged behind but Unilever benefited from the high rates of sales growth of up to 10 per cent per annum in the emerging markets in Asia, Africa and Latin America. Now, around 60 per cent of Unilever's sales are generated there.

Unilever is the largest manufacturer of deodorants in the world with brands such as Rexona, Shield, Lynx, Axe and Sure and has, for example, a 70 per cent market share in Argentina. However, only 7 out of 100 Asians use deodorants and many Russians only use them for special occasions, such as weddings, so there is huge potential.

Unilever's 'jewel in the crown' is Hindustan Unilever, India's biggest consumer goods company and biggest advertiser. It caters for all segments by adapting products and prices, for example, offering Surf Excel for the affluent, Rin for the 'aspiring class' and Wheel for poorer people, who generally live in the countryside. One-use sachets amount to 70 per cent of shampoo sales as India's poor cannot afford to buy a bottle.

However, it is now becoming harder for Unilever to find growth, especially in developed markets. The era of 'continual consumption' seems to have ended as consumers seek to pay as little as possible for what they need by substituting the branded products for own label alternatives. Unilever must respond to perpetual low prices offered by some retailers and can no longer rely on sales promotions and discounts (two for one and 20 per cent free) to maintain loyalty, but instead must find new ways to communicate with consumers. In emerging markets, value-for-money global, regional and local competition is intensifying too and a recognizable, heavily promoted brand is no longer a guarantee of success.

Company integrity

Unilever recognizes the need to further build its reputation with its stakeholders and balance its desire for growth with addressing the needs of the communities by working to address global warming, poverty, water shortage, population growth and obesity, for example, by producing detergents that use less hot water, making healthier ice cream and reducing the environmental impact of its packaging. Unilever has produced concentrated versions of its laundry products, minimizing packaging usage and reducing the need for so many delivery lorries, saving vast areas of shelf space and achieving significant CO_2 reduction. The company opposes deforestation and rain forest clearance to produce palm oil, which it uses in half its best selling foods, such as Kit Kat and Flora margarine and in its Dove range of toiletries.

Questions

1 Carry out a full analysis of the environment in which Unilever is operating and identify ten key challenges it faces.

2 What do you consider to be the main competitive advantages that Unilever have in developing a global strategy for developed and emerging markets?

3 What competitive capabilities do Unilever need to enable them to continue to grow successfully?

4 What are the key features of Unilever that should be highlighted in promotional activities? Create promotional messages for a range of B2B target markets.

DISCUSSION QUESTIONS

1 The fundamental concerns of international marketing strategy analysis, development and implementation are to add stakeholder value and remove unnecessary costs. How can innovation in information and communications technology assist in this process of global consumer marketing?

2 For a company providing international consultancy to major multinationals in the use of renewable energy identify the key areas for decision making in the marketing process.

3 How might mobile computing change international marketing?

4 Write a report to the chief executive of a small company supplying gaming software to be used by the global gaming hardware brands, analyzing the use of social and business networking sites in marketing the business.

5 As the marketing manager of a global, fast moving consumer goods company of your choice identify the key decisions that will be needed to ensure the company has a sustainable future.

REFERENCES

1. Berns, M., Townend, A., Khayat, Z., Balagopal, B., Reeves, M., Hopkins, M.S. and Krushwitz, N. (2009) 'The business of sustainability, what it means to managers now', *MIT Sloan Management Review,* Fall, 51(1): 20–26.

2. Boston Consulting Group (2010) The connected kingdom: How the Internet is transforming the UK economy. Available from www.bcg.com (accessed 28 October 2013).

3. Boston Consulting Group (2013) The 2013 BCG e-Intensity index. Available from www.bcgperspectives.com (accessed 3 June 2015).

4. Chaffey, D., Mayer, R., Johnston, K. and Ellis-Chadwick, F. (2006) *Internet Marketing*, FT/Prentice Hall.

5. Egol, M., Clyde, A. and Rangan, K. (2010) 'The new consumer frugality', www.strategy+business.com, 15 March.

6. Energy Saving Trust (2015) www.energysavingtrust.org.uk

7. Hagiu, A. (2013) Strategic decisions for multisided platforms: Winter 2014 research feature, published December 19, 2013. *MIT Sloane Management Review*. Available from www.sloanreview.mit.edu/article/strategic-decisions-for-multisided-platforms/ (accessed 11 June 2015).

8. Hamill, J. and Stevenson, A. (2003) 'Customer-led strategic Internet marketing', in S. Hart (ed.), *Marketing Changes*, Thomson Learning.

9. Hoffman, K.D. (2003) 'Services marketing', in *Marketing Best Practice,* Thomson Learning.

10. Kaplan, S. and Sawhney, M. (2000) 'E-hubs: the new B2B marketplaces', *Harvard Business Review*, 78(3): 97–103.

11. Lindgren, J.H.E. (2003) 'Marketing', in *Marketing Best Practice*, Thomson Learning.

12. Lindstrom, M. and Seybold, P. (2003) *BRAND child*, Kogan Page.

13. Nykamp, M. (2001) *The Customer Differential*, AMACOM.

14. Ofek, E. and Wathieu, L. (2010) 'Are you ignoring trends that could shake up your business?' *Harvard Business Review,* July/August 2010, 88(7/8): 124–131.

15. Richardson, N., James, J. and Kelley, N. (2015). *Customer-Centric Marketing: Supporting Sustainability in the Digital Age*. Kogan Page.

16. Ritter, T. and Walter, A. (2006) 'Matching high-tech and high-touch in supplier-customer relationships', *European Journal of Marketing*, 40(3/4): 292–310.

17. Snyder, D.P. (2005) 'Extra-Preneurship', *Futurist,* 39(4): 47–53.

18. Timmers, P. (1999) *Electronic Commerce Strategies and Models for Business to Business Trading*, Wiley.

19. Zugelder, M.T., Flaherty, T.B. and Johnson, J.P. (2000) 'Legal issues associated with international Internet marketing', *International Marketing Review*, 17(3).

PART 3

INTERNATIONAL MARKETING PLANNING: IMPLEMENTATION, CONTROL AND EVALUATION

Introduction

In the previous two Directed Study Activity sections on planning we explored the dimensions of analysis and strategy development. We now turn to the implementation of the plan through the application of the marketing mix that has been covered in the chapters in Part III. In practice, of course, some of the content of the previous chapters needs to be revisited because there is no clear distinction between what might be considered strategy development and implementation. This is especially true of product and service strategy, where many decisions can be regarded as operational, and market entry, where many decisions are closely associated with distribution.

The starting point for implementation is planning the international marketing mix. This includes completing the product and service plan and preparing communications, distribution and pricing plans. The plan should explain how relationships with key partners can be built and managed within the supply chain, how customer relationships can be developed and how technology can be used to facilitate the firm's international marketing plan implementation.

The success of the implementation plan is dependent on the planning ability, management capability and motivation and effectiveness of the firm's staff. The global market environment is constantly changing and competition from existing and new companies is intensifying. As we saw in DSA 2, while organizations may perceive themselves to have competitive advantage, such as a new product idea, low cost manufacturing or a strong brand, this can be quickly eroded by a new competitor, so the key to successful implementation is having competitive capability – the ability to continuously compete internationally – no matter what challenges are faced. In the implementation stage this means being able to quickly assess situations, develop innovative solutions, make strategic decisions when necessary and implement new plans.

Management need to anticipate and plan for potential problems that might arise in managing the implementation stage. Of course, these problems may well originate in topics that were considered in the first two parts of the book. We also consider how to establish appropriate performance standards and measurement techniques that can be used to maintain control over the plan and the evaluation that will enable corrective action to be taken whenever the firm's performance deviates from the plan (as it surely will).

In this activity the focus is on developing the skills of decision making in a local business unit at an operational level, while still keeping in mind the implication of the firm's global strategy on these local decisions.

Learning Objectives

On completing this activity you should be able to:

- Appreciate the opportunities for growth in an international business sector and how they are influenced by the strategy implementation

- Use appropriate concepts and an analysis of market factors to develop marketing mix implementation strategies

- Appreciate the benefit of developing better customer relationship management

- Identify the methods that should be used for the management and control of the business

The scenario: Multinational organizations

This directed study activity can be applied to any multinational organization, but we have chosen to provide a short case study of Yum! Brands, which is the largest restaurant business in the world, slightly ahead of McDonalds. The company has reached an interesting point in its history as its growth opportunities now exist in emerging rather than traditional markets. In developed countries the debate about healthy eating has intensified; in emerging markets, as the demand grows for branded fast food, so local competitors have begun to emerge. A lot of information and comment is available online and in the media to support the activity and so the information presented is there merely to present the scenario to start your study.

Yum Brands – eating into new markets

Yum Brands is the world's largest restaurant group with 41 000 restaurants in 125 countries and revenues of over $13 billion. It was spun off from PepsiCo which owns and franchises the KFC, Pizza Hut and Taco Bell brands worldwide. Seventy per cent of the profits are generated outside the USA but in 1997 the figure was only 20 per cent. Sales have declined in the US as consumers seek what they consider to be healthier, fresher and less standardized food, whereas outside the US the demand for global fast food brands has grown rapidly.

KFC was the first quick service restaurant chain to enter China in 1987. It is the market leader with over 5000 units in 1000 cities, and is still opening new KFC restaurants at a rate of around 700 per year. The development of the Chinese market was much faster than the company originally anticipated. As it owned the outlets Yum Brands was able to exert tight control over operations and learn quickly about the Chinese market. Typically the initial investment was repaid out of profits in two to three years. Success was attributed to the establishment of an effective and efficient local supply chain and distribution infrastructure, based on what seemed to be a strong network of partners.

However, in 2013 customer confidence was adversely affected by a report that highlighted excessive levels of antibiotics in some chicken supplied to KFC and a government investigation found that a KFC supplier, a division of OSI, was altering expiry dates on the chicken it was supplying. The market is still expected to expand rapidly as the middle class grows from 300 million to 800 million over the next 25 years. KFC is growing again

and Yum China has the opportunity to exploit its other brands and meal formats, such as Pizza Hut, so long as it maintains the confidence of its customers. Looking to the future, India is expected to become the largest consuming country by 2030 and promises to provide Yum Brands with further growth but so far it has only 500 outlets in the country.

Yum Restaurant International (YRI)

Yum divides its remaining markets into three types of region, where different strategies might be needed: developing; developed – underpenetrated (for example, France, Italy and Germany); and developed – established. Sales are split: Europe 30 per cent, Asia 27 per cent, Americas 19 per cent, Middle East/South Africa 13 per cent and Australia/New Zealand 11 per cent.

Future growth in both outlets and profitability will come from the developing and the underpenetrated developed markets. Yum mainly uses a franchise model in these markets and has over 1000 franchisees. Franchising has the benefit of leveraging additional investment and local management expertise. Building on the familiarity of travellers with the brand, Yum has opened restaurants in many locations sometimes using strategic partners, for example in Myanmar with Yoma Strategic Holdings of Singapore. A key partner for Yum throughout the Middle East is Americana Group established as a trading company in 1964 in Kuwait. Americana manufactures food products for the Middle East and North Africa as well as operating many international franchises, and this has led to it creating six home grown brands, Chicken Tikka, Fish Market, Samadi, Maestro, Grand Café and Fusion, which it claims are as successful with Middle East consumers as its international franchises. By franchising Yum has perhaps indirectly helped to create new competition.

Each new territory presents local challenges that are often best understood by a local partner. The third restaurant planned in Mongolia was designed to be a drive-thru, but deciding which side to place the delivery window was a problem as half the cars have left-hand drives, and the other half right-hand drives!

In the developed world (underpenetrated) the aim is to narrow the gap against the competition, for example, in France and Germany, where the company has huge potential given that KFC has far fewer outlets than McDonalds.

In the developed world (established) the aim is to capture the remaining development potential and improve margins. In the UK, for example, following underperformance Yum Brands sold its 330 Pizza Hut outlets to Rutland Partners in a franchise arrangement. In this way they retained control of the brand and secured investment from their master franchisee to refurbish the stores and restructure the operation.

One of the reasons that Yum Brands has been successful has been its willingness to adapt its menu and customer experience to fit with local needs and culture, but there is always the problem of controlling different business models to ensure quality and profitability. Moreover, given that Yum Brands needs to build the loyalty of the next generation of consumers it must make decisions on the best ways to communicate with them. The traditional model of promotion using TV advertising at the heart of the strategy will not be enough to win over these consumers. Yum Brands spends over $500 million globally on marketing.

In the media there has been considerable discussion about the fast food operators' approach to sustainability and corporate social responsibility, including topics ranging from encouraging child obesity, ill treatment of staff, overuse of packaging, questionable sourcing of food products and cultural insensitivity. Yum Brands will also have to work hard to maintain its corporate reputation.

The task

1 Critically evaluate the global marketing implementation strategy of Yum! Brands, paying particular attention to whether the company is responding to the changing nature of expectations of customers and consumer purchasing behaviour in markets around the world, not forgetting that in a franchising model the company has multiple levels of customers and some powerful global and well entrenched local competitors.

2 Having identified the challenges Yum! Brands faces, develop an international marketing implementation strategy in outline both for the consumer and franchisee market that both leverages and builds competitive advantage. Focus on the marketing mix implementation issues, including an assessment of the key brand, product, service and communications issues. Identify, too, the factors that will influence the pricing strategy.

3 Prepare a plan for the control, management and continuous improvement of the operations, including appropriate measurement, and outline the processes that are required to achieve sustained success. Explain particularly the key dimensions of the marketing culture that is needed and how consistent that is across the global markets.

Getting started

This section focuses on the global consumer markets but you also need to consider the importance of managing relationships with the franchisees and supply chain. You should use this case study not only to focus on the implementation issues of the strategy process but also to study in greater depth the particular issues involved in managing this service sector model.

Clearly the effective marketing of services requires an understanding of customer requirements and service expectation as well as staff motivation and management, customer relationship building and the cultural issues that underpin much of this.

Task 1 requires an analysis of the factors that have led to the growth in fast food in international markets, particularly in emerging markets over recent years and of the factors that will determine the nature of consumer purchasing in the future – and consequently how important relationship-building with global customers will be in the future. By now you should have a very good understanding of how you can access and analyze research material from libraries and online sources to complete this task. There is a huge amount of information and comment about the fast food market and the competition in the literature and business press to help you complete Tasks 2 and 3, but you must also include your own creative approaches. You require an understanding of the sector and how it differs in the markets around the world.

Customer satisfaction is very dependent on the customers' perception of the brand but also the suitability of the product in appealing to local taste and service expectations. Consequently, setting realistic customer expectations, motivating and training staff, managing the supply chain effectively and managing a cost-effective fast food service are all critical for success. Task 3 requires you to think about how you would organize and manage this on a global basis.

In completing the tasks you need to consider the issues highlighted in the following framework shown in Table II.

The way forward

Strategy development and planning is a continuous process. Having completed the tasks in this section, you will have gained a better understanding of the fast food market and the perceived value that consumer and franchisee customers are able to obtain. You should now be well informed to revisit the strategy development process.

You should return to the Part 1 planning framework to review the current market environment for Yum! Brands as the basis for their ongoing strategy. The most important issue is to decide where and how the firm can further build its strong global position, using an assessment of the market environment, customer demands and competitor activity. Given the fast growth of the sector you should review the firm's ambitions particularly in developing markets, and focus on the market factors in these countries and use the market information and research framework to identify further growth opportunities. You should also consider the more traditional markets that are still significant to assess the opportunities to increase market share. Finally, you might reassess the company capability and expertise that will be expected to underpin its continued expansion.

You should review the firm's apparent vision and objectives from the material that is contained on its website. You should reevaluate and restate the firm's competitive advantage and assess how this informs the international positioning of the various Yum! Brands. Using the recent data available online you should assess the market entry methods used and the effectiveness of these methods in delivering the strategy.

Checklist for success

Having completed the directed study activities you should think about how comprehensive your work is and whether you really have addressed the fundamental issues that could well make the difference between a failing and a successful strategy. To help you do this we have identified some of the issues you should consider. Clearly you may not be able to answer these in detail because you will not have sufficient detail about the firm's operations, but you should have thought about how you would address the issues given access to the information.

Does the plan contain:

- Assumptions about the world economy and the environmental trends in the principal markets?
- Details of historical performance (sales, costs, profitability)?
- Forecasts of future performance based on (a) an extrapolation of the past, (b) alternative scenarios?
- Identified opportunities and threats?
- Analysis of the company strengths, weaknesses and future capabilities in comparison with local and international competition?
- Long-term aims and objectives and the strategies to achieve them?
- One-year marketing objectives and individual strategies (for example, budgets, brand objectives and development of personnel)?
- Country-by-country forecasts and targets?
- Country-by-country plans for all marketing activities and coordination with other functions (for example, supply chain management)?
- An explanation of how country plans will be integrated regionally or globally if appropriate? It might be useful to comment on the current structure of the company.
- A summary of the critical factors for success?
- An assessment of the likely competitor response?

If your objective is to increase market share in some markets, your competitors will not simply lie down and let you take their business without fighting back!

- A contingency component for when the unexpected happens and things do not go to plan?
- A control process for feedback, evaluation and taking corrective action?

Table II Key factors to consider in evaluating the implementation of the strategy

The element of the plan	Some concepts, models and issues to be addressed
Environmental analysis	• Identify the global trends that have provided the opportunity for growth in the sector
	• Analyze the nature of customer needs and the nature of competition in the sector
	• Evaluate the firm's strategy and its regional focus

Table II Continued

The element of the plan	Some concepts, models and issues to be addressed
Marketing mix	• Building the corporate identity and managing the brand
	• Product differentiation and the three service Ps
	• Communication to customers and other stakeholders
	• Managing the delivery to achieve customer satisfaction
	• Managing cost and the pricing strategy
	• The use of technology
Relationship marketing	• The methods of identifying current and potential high value customers
	• Knowledge and database management
	• Customer relationship management
Control and management	• The organization and management structure using the 7S framework
	• Internal communications with its own staff
	• Financial and marketing measures and controls
	• Performance management and improvement processes, including benchmarking, balanced scorecard and self-assessment and improvement
	• Technology-enabled systems

GLOSSARY

7S framework Framework devised by consultants McKinsey & Co for analyzing how well the organization is positioned to deliver its objectives

Acquisition A market entry strategy in which the firm invests in assets outside the home country

Adaptation Flexible approach to marketing that aims to vary the marketing mix programmes to meet the local conditions in each country market

Asian Free Trade Area (AFTA) As of 2015 the ASEAN members are Brunei Darussalam, Cambodia, Indonesia, Lao PDR, Malaysia, Myanmar, Philippines, Singapore, Thailand and Vietnam.

Association of South East Asian Nations (ASEAN) A free trade area of 580 million across Thailand, Indonesia, Singapore, Brunei, Malaysia and the Philippines, Vietnam, Myanmar, Cambodia and Laos

Attitude A complex mental state involving beliefs and feelings and values and dispositions to act in certain ways

Balance of payments A system of recording all of a country's economic transactions with the rest of the world over a period of one year

Barrier to entry Real or perceived reason why a firm might be prevented from marketing its products and services in a new market

Beliefs The psychological state in which an individual holds a proposition or premise to be true

Born global A business who, from the very start, chooses its target market and sales outputs to be in several countries; most often with a drive to grow internationally, as opposed to expanding in their home market

Brand piracy Naming a product in such a way that it confuses customers, or enables the pirate firm to sell forgeries and fake products

Branding strategies The alternative approaches to applying names (or brands) to a product and groups of products to achieve the desired positioning

Build to order When a product is scheduled and built in response to a specification and confirmed order received from a final customer

Business-to-business marketing Marketing products and services to other organizations

Business-to consumer-marketing Marketing products and services to people who will consume them

Buyer–seller relationships Collective term for the categories of relationship between a buyer and seller. These can be categorized into transactional relationships, collaborative relationships, alliances and reciprocal relationships

Category management Category management is a retailing concept in which the total range of products sold by a retailer is broken down into discrete groups of similar or related products; these groups are known as product categories

Communications adaptation Marketing communication strategies that are flexible, allowing variation in the use of the mix between countries to meet local conditions

Communications mix Often used interchangeably with promotions mix, the communications mix implies a broader range of uses of offline and online interactive tools

Communications tools The range of tools a marketer can use, including personal selling, advertising, sales promotion, public relations, sponsorship and online media

Comparative advantage The advantage a nation has by being able to produce products or services more efficiently and at lower cost than a competitor nation

Comparative research Comparative research is a research methodology in the social sciences that aims to make comparisons across different countries or cultures

Competitive advantage Competitive advantage is something which organizations provide to consumers to make them seem more interesting, better value for money, are more engaged on social media or provide better offers than their competitors.

Consumer behaviour The behaviour of individuals when buying goods and services for their own use or for private consumption

Contract manufacture Arrangement in which a subcontractor undertakes manufacturing (or service provision) under licence

Control The management responsibility for measuring performance and taking corrective action when deviation from the standards set occurs, so that the goals of the organization are achieved

Corporate identity The corporate personality demonstrated in branding and other communications to reflect the values and culture of the organization

Countertrade Exchanging goods or services which are paid for, in whole or part, with other goods or services, rather than with money

Country of origin effect The perceptions and attitudes that exist towards the products or brands on the basis of their country of origin, design or manufacture

Cross-cultural Dealing with or comparing two or more cultures

Cross-cultural research The conducting of a research project across a number of nations or culture groupings

Cultural identity Cultural identity is the identity of a group or culture, or of an individual, as far as one is influenced by one's belonging to a group or culture

Cultural paradoxes A terms used to describe the cultural sensitivities in a market where there is evidence both of the westernization of tastes and the assertion of ethnic, religious and cultural differences

Cultural sensitivity Cultural sensitivity is the quality of being aware and accepting of other cultures. This is important because what seems acceptable in some countries can be rude or derogatory in others

Customer relationship management The process of storing and analyzing data relating to customers, to enable the organization to serve their needs efficiently and effectively

Customer-led Adopting marketing approaches that primarily focus on the needs and expectations of customers

Customs The overt forms of behaviour and significant events which symbolize the particularistic characteristics of a particular culture

Data mining A technique for searching large-scale databases for patterns; used mainly to find previously unknown correlations between variables that may be commercially useful

Differentiated marketing Strategy whereby a company attempts to appeal to two or more clearly defined market segments with a specific product and unique marketing strategy tailored to each separate segment

Direct channels Distribution channel in which a producer supplies or serves directly an ultimate user

Direct marketing Online or offline communication with potential consumers or business customers designed to generate a response, such as an order or request for more information

Distribution channel structures Path or 'pipeline' through which goods and services flow from vendor to the consumer. A distribution channel may include several interconnected intermediaries such as wholesalers, distributors, agents, retailers

Distributors Firms that buy and stock products from a manufacturer before adding a margin and selling them to the final customers

Doha Round Commenced 2001, the name given to the current negotiations being undertaken by members of the WTO who are attempting to liberalize trading rules in a number of areas, including agricultural subsidies, textiles and clothing, services, technical barriers to trade, trade-related investments and rules of origin

Domestic purchasing International trade in which a foreign firm approaches a non-exporter, buys the product 'at the factory gate' and takes the responsibility for all aspects of exporting, without involvement from the seller

Dumping When a manufacturer in one country exports a product to another country at a price which is either below the price it charges in its home market or is below its costs of production

E-commerce The exchange of goods, services and cash using the Internet

Economic and Monetary Union The creation of a single currency bloc within the European Union which began on 1st January 1999

Economies of scale Unit cost reductions which result from increasing total output

Effective consumer response Supply chain partnerships which work together towards making the retail sector more responsive to consumer demand and promote the removal of unnecessary costs from the supply chain

Elastic demand Demand for a product that changes substantially in response to small changes in price; when demand is elastic, a small decrease in price may substantially increase total revenues

Electronic commerce Exchange of goods and services using the Internet or other online network

Electronic data interchange (EDI) refers to the structured transmission of data between organizations by electronic means. It is used to transfer electronic documents from one computer system to another, i.e. from one trading partner to another trading partner

Emerging economies Emerging markets are nations with social or business activity in the process of rapid growth and industrialization

Enabling technologies The use of a variety of largely integrated technologies that facilitate fast and effective international marketing processes

Enculturation Enculturation is the process by which a person learns the requirements of the culture by which he or she is surrounded

E-procurement The use of the Internet or other online services to manage the purchasing and delivery of services and products

Ethical challenges Challenge of setting the ethical values in international marketing strategies and then driving those through long distribution channels across geographical markets with different ethical values

Ethnocentric Centred on a specific ethnic group, usually one's own

Eurozone The eurozone, officially the euro area, is an economic and monetary union (EMU) of 19 European Union (EU) member states which have adopted the euro currency as their sole legal tender

European Union An international organization of European countries formed after World War II to reduce trade barriers and increase cooperation among its members

Exchange rate Rate of exchange: the charge for exchanging currency of one country for currency of another

Exchange Rate Mechanism The European Exchange Rate Mechanism (ERM) was a system introduced by the European Community in March 1979, as part of the European Monetary System (EMS), to reduce exchange rate variability and achieve monetary stability in Europe, in preparation for economic and monetary union

Exchange rate risk The potential to lose money because of a change in the exchange rate

Existing markets Product/service markets where customers demands are served from a number of suppliers and the infrastructure to support the market is established

Export administration The management of the processes that allow an export transaction to take place

Export houses (also export management companies) Specialist firms that act as the export department for a range of companies and take on the role and responsibilities that would normally be done by those companies

Export marketing Marketing of goods and/or services across national/political boundaries

Export processing zone Designated area or region where firms can import duty-free as long as the imports are used as inputs into the production of exports

Exporting Selling abroad products produced in the home country, typically without significant adaptation to foreign market needs

Failures of communications When the recipient does not receive the marketing messages as intended

Fixed production cost Costs of production that are fixed and unrelated to the volume of production

Foreign currency Any currency that is in use in a foreign country, but not in one's own

Foreign market channels Channels of distribution within countries outside a firm's domestic operations

Franchising A contractual arrangement whereby a parent company (the franchisor) allows another firm (the franchisee) to operate a business that it has developed in return for a fee, provided that it adheres to the stated policies and practices

Function-specific hubs Electronic marketplaces where buyers and sellers meet using the Internet to trade in business services, such as HR services or business process management

Generic marketing strategies Marketing strategies that can be applied to all market contexts, based on segmentation, targeting and positioning and underpinned by Porter's generic growth strategies (cost leadership, focus and differentiation)

Geocentric Having the earth as the centre

Global appeal The attraction of certain products and services to a global customer segment

Global brand A brand that has a similar name, similar distinctive image and positioning around the world

Global marketing The process of conceptualizing and then conveying a final product or service worldwide with the hopes of reaching the international marketing community

Global presence Ensuring that the company has assets and operations located in all (major) country markets

Global reach The ability of the marketing efforts of the firm to connect with customers around the world, where appropriate using third parties

Global segments Through research and analysis global segments can be identified into homogeneous entities that are categorized by psychographic and behavioural similarities.

Global sourcing The process of arranging goods and services to be supplied irrespective of geographic location

Global System of Trade Preferences among developing countries (GSTP) A trade agreement established in 1988 to encourage and increase trade with and between developing nations. The trade agreement is supported by the United Nations.

Global youth culture Contemporary 15–24-year-olds combining local and international culture and identities through technology and social media

Globalization The process of progressing towards trading in all major regions and most country markets

Grey marketing The trade of a commodity through distribution channels which, while legal, are unofficial, unauthorized or unintended by the original manufacturer

Gross national income National income plus capital consumption allowance

Gross national income per capita The GNI per capita is the gross national income divided by the country's population, thus becoming the GNI per person living in the country.

Hard currency A currency that is not likely to depreciate suddenly in value

Heterogeneity Because services are delivered and received by individual people the concept suggests that each interaction will be unique

High-context cultures Cultures in which the context is at least as important as what is actually said

Incipient markets Markets where economic conditions suggest a market may develop but the market as yet does not exist

Indirect channels The selling and distribution of products to customers through intermediaries such as wholesalers, distributors, agents, dealers or retailers

Indirect exporting Market entry methods in which firms commit few resources to international marketing and largely rely on third parties to build their international business

Individualism Individualism is the moral stance, political philosophy, ideology or social outlook that stresses the moral worth of the individual

Industry-specific hubs Electronic market places where buyers and sellers meet using the Internet to trade components and services required in particular industries, such as aerospace manufacture

Inelastic demand The demand that exists when price changes do not result in significant changes in the quantity of a product demanded

Information technology The organization's management process for creating, storing, exchanging and using information

Inseparability In services marketing, the service is created, delivered and consumed at the same point whereas in product marketing there is usually separation between manufacture and consumption

Intangibility Whereas products are physical entities, services are characterized by being intangible – they cannot be touched, smelled or seen

Integrated supply chain The optimization and control of the supply chain network of suppliers, factories, warehouses, distribution centres and retailers through which materials are acquired, transformed and delivered to the customer

Interactive customer marketing Ability to address an individual and the ability to gather and remember the response of that individual leading to the ability to address the individual once more in a way that takes into account his or her unique response

Interactive shopping Allows the consumer to play an active role in the selection and customization of his/her order

Internal cost structures Cost elements that correspond to the specific internal operations of a company

International branding A brand that is known in a region of the world or in a cluster of countries

International Development Association (IDA) An agency of the United Nations affiliated with the World Bank

International manager A member of staff with the responsibility of managing across country borders

International marketing The process of planning and conducting transactions across national borders to create exchanges that satisfy the objectives of individuals and organizations

International Monetary Fund A United Nations agency to promote trade by increasing the exchange stability of the major currencies

International niche marketing Marketing a differentiated product or service to different countries, usually to a single customer segment (a group of customers with a distinctive, common characteristic)

International product life cycle A concept that enables the firm to describe the stages (introduction, growth, maturity, decline) that its product portfolio has attained in different country markets

International product offer The bundle of benefits for international customers that are presented in the total product 'package'

International product portfolio The firm's chosen range of products and services that provide a complete and satisfactory offer to customers

International trade International trade is exchange of capital, goods and services across international borders or territories. It refers to exports of goods and services by a firm to a foreign-based buyer (importer). In most countries, it represents a significant share of gross domestic product

Internationalization Pursuit of market opportunities outside the home country

Internet The network of computers that enable digital files, such as emails to be sent

Joint ventures A market entry approach whereby two or more companies share ownership of a newly created firm

Knowledge management Strategies and practices used by organizations to identify, share and enable adoption of the insights and experiences that constitute knowledge

Latent markets A group of people who have been identified as potential consumers of a product that does not yet exist

Learning curve A learning curve is a line graph displaying opportunities across the x-axis, and a measure of performance along the y-axis

Legislation The legal framework enacted by governing bodies that determines how business can be carried out. The Internet is subject to the laws of many governing bodies

Less developed economies The name given to a country which, according to the United Nations, exhibits the lowest indicators of socioeconomic development, with the lowest human development index ratings of all countries in the world

Licensing A market entry strategy in which a firm makes assets, such as an image or know-how, available to another firm in exchange for royalties

Logistics The management of the flow of goods, information and other resources, including energy and people, between the point of origin and the point of consumption in order to meet the requirements of consumers

Logistics or distribution strategy Management's plan for moving products to intermediaries and final customers

Low-context cultures Are those where people are more psychologically distant so that information needs to be explicit if members are to understand it

Management contracts Service projects undertaken by partner firms in conjunction with a supplier, typically of major infrastructure installations

Marginal cost pricing The outcome of perfectly competitive markets in which the price of each good is equal to its marginal cost

Marginal costing An accounting technique whereby the effect on costs of a small increment or decrease in output may be estimated. Assuming that the change in output does not affect the elements comprising fixed costs, the marginal cost will be the variable cost per unit of output

Market access The opportunity for firms to enter sectors, from which they were previously barred

Market concentrators Typically smaller firms that focus their internationalization on a small number of geographic markets

Market entry The approach that a firm uses to pursue market opportunities outside its home market

Market expanders Typically larger firms that focus their internationalization on a large number of geographic markets

Market involvement The degree to which a firm commits resources to a specific market, enabling it to directly control its marketing activities, rather than rely on third parties

Market-orientated pricing Determining the initial price of a product by comparison with competitors' prices

Market profile analysis An analysis that draws a marketing profile of a country

Market segmentation A market segment is a sub-set of a market made up of people or organizations sharing one or more characteristics that cause them to demand similar products and/or services based on qualities of those products such as price or function

Marketing information A system in which marketing information is formally gathered, stored, analyzed and distributed to managers in accord with their informational needs on a regular basis

Marketing research Research that gathers and analyzes information about the moving of goods or services from producer to consumer

Mass customization The use of flexible computer-aided manufacturing systems to produce custom output

Mass customize The use of flexible computer-aided manufacturing and service systems to produce output that is designed to meet the individual requirements of the customer

Mercosur Regional common southern market integrated by the full members Argentina, Brazil, Paraguay, Uruguay and Venezuela.

Mergers of equals Firms with similar market power merge their operations in the belief that to succeed globally, scale advantages are required

Micromultinationals Small- to medium-sized companies that invest time and effort in a constellation of different countries; enabled through the technological advances of the twenty-first century.

Multi-country study A market research study that is carried out across a number of countries

Multinational enterprise (MNE) An international or transnational enterprise which has productive capacity in several countries

Multimedia technology The knowledge and use of tools, techniques, systems or methods of organization of media and/or content that uses a combination of different content forms

Network A collection of individuals that are willing to share information

New product development The process of ensuring that new products and services are created to meet changing customer needs, and replace those that are no longer satisfactory

Next Eleven The Next Eleven (or N11) are eleven countries identified as having the potential to become among the world's largest economies in the twenty-first century

Non-tariff barriers Trade barriers that restrict imports but are not in the usual form of a tariff

Non-verbal communication Gestures, body language, facial expression, sign language are all ways of communicating without the spoken word

North American Free Trade Area (NAFTA) Formed between Canada, Mexico and the United States of America

Omnibus studies An omnibus study is completed via a quantitative survey. The questions in the survey are provided by different companies and the questions are often about different products and/or services.

Omnibus surveys A survey covering a number of topics, usually for different clients. The samples tend to be nationally representative and composed of types of people for which there is a general demand

Online auction Participants are able to bid to purchase products and services using the Internet

Online databases An electronic collection of information

Open market A competitive market where buyers and sellers can operate without restrictions

Organization structure Explanation of how tasks are allocated, activities coordinated and staff supervised in the delivery of the organization's strategy

Outsource Obtaining supplies or services from another firm (typically in a lower cost country), rather than carrying out the work within the firm

Pareto Law Also known as the 80–20 rule, states that for many events, 80 per cent of the effects come from 20 per cent of the causes. In marketing, 80 per cent of the sales often come from 20 per cent of the customers

Perception of risk The subjective judgment that people make about the characteristics and severity of a risk

Perishability Services cannot be stored and, hence, if an opportunity for a sale is missed, then it is lost for ever

Piggybacking A market entry approach based on riding on the back of an already successful international marketer by persuading the firm to carry non-competing products

Piracy A contemporary security concern for shipping; annual cargo crime losses are estimated at US$30–50 billion internationally

Polycentric Having many centres, especially centres of authority or control

Price coordination The attempt to coordinate prices across dispersed geographical markets with the objective of achieving a consistent pricing policy across those markets

Price standardization Setting a standard, identical price in all markets, regardless of whether they are foreign or domestic

Price transparency The accessibility of information on the order flow for a particular stock, allowing knowledge of the quantities of stock being offered and the bids at the various price levels

Primary data Data observed or collected directly from firsthand experience

Product and service differentiation The process of distinguishing a product or service offering from competitive offerings to make it more attractive to a particular target market

Product strategies The approach adopted to selection and positioning of products and services, and the marketing support provided to satisfy customer needs

Production costs The cost-of-production theory of value is the theory that the price of an object or condition is determined by the sum of the cost of the resources that went into making it. The cost can compose any of the factors of production (including labour, capital or land) and taxation

Promotional mix The mix of communications tools used to persuade customers to buy and use products or services

Pull strategy Pull strategies involve promoting the product or service to the intended consumer, who will demand supplies from the intermediaries

Purchasing power parity (PPP) The situation where the exchange rate between two currencies represents the difference between the price levels in the two countries

Push strategy Push strategies involve promoting the product or service to intermediaries, who will then promote them to the final consumers

Qualitative research A set of research techniques in which data is obtained from a relatively small group of respondents and is not analyzed with statistical techniques

Reciprocal trading Trading in which the supplier also purchases products or services from the customer

Relationship marketing The creation of mutually beneficial long term value through building customer relationships rather than relying on converting customers through advertising and sales promotions

Research question Formed by researchers around which they centre their research project. Research questions are written after researchers have gathered sufficient secondary information to understand a subject area, what is already known about that subject area and how they would like to investigate the subject area further.

Research process The ordered set of activities focused on the systematic collection of information using accepted methods of analysis as a basis for drawing conclusions and making recommendations

Risk and control The necessary balance to be struck in entering new markets, which involves accepting risk of failure, set against committing sufficient resource in an attempt to exert control in the market and 'guarantee' success

Secondary data Data collected and recorded by another

Self-reference criterion The assumption that a product can successfully be sold abroad on the basis of its success in the home market

Services Intangible, largely experience-based economic activity

Silent language Non-verbal signals in a communication

Single European Market The complete integration of the economies of member states of the European Union

Small- and medium-sized enterprises Small (typically up to 50 employees) and medium (from 50–250 employees) firms that have a different approach and mindset to large multinational organizations

Social and cultural factors Customs, lifestyles and values that characterize society

Spoken language Spoken language is a form of communication in which words are derived from a large vocabulary

Stages of internationalization An international marketing concept in which firms progress through a series of steps as they develop from a domestic to a global company. Each step has distinctive characteristics

Standardization Approach to marketing that aims to reduce marketing mix variation between countries and regions of the world

Standardization of international marketing communications Where possible, reducing variation in the use of the communications mix between different countries and regions

Strategic alliance A contractual arrangement whereby two or more firms form a partnership to exploit a market opportunity together, so that they reduce risk

Supply chain A group of firms that undertake support activities in the manufacture and supply of materials and components,

conversion into finished goods and making them available to buyers

Supply chain management The management of a group of firms that contribute to the development, manufacture and delivery of a final product to maximize efficiency and effectiveness

Tariff barriers A government tax on imports or exports

Total distribution cost The total cost incurred by an exporter in the distribution of merchandise internationally including transport, warehousing, inventory holding, order processing, documentation, taxes, packaging, etc.

Trade deficit A negative balance of trade

Trading blocs A trade bloc is a type of intergovernmental agreement, often part of a regional intergovernmental organization, where regional barriers to trade (tariffs and non-tariff barriers) are reduced or eliminated among the participating states

Trading companies Organizations involved in the exchange of products, services and cash that were particularly important in opening up new markets in underdeveloped countries

Transactions The exchange of items of value, including information, goods, services and money

Transfer pricing The price that is assumed to have been charged by one part of a company for products and services it provides to another part of the same company, in order to calculate each division's profit and loss separately

Transnational segmentation Entering foreign markets with a solid marketing plan that helps a company create a positive brand presence and resonates with residents of the foreign country

Transnationality The pursuit of opportunities in all parts of the world by integrating and coordinating sourcing of products and services from all parts of the world and serving multiple country markets across all world regions

Values Monetary or material worth, as in commerce or trade

Websites Collections of related webpages containing images, videos or other digital material

Wholly-owned subsidiary Independent business unit in a foreign location owned by a parent firm with headquarters in the home country

World Bank An international banking organization established to control the distribution of economic aid between member nations, and to make loans to them in times of financial crisis

World trade The value of the trading of goods and services across the globe

World Trade Organization The World Trade Organization (WTO) deals with the rules of trade between nations at a global or near-global level

World Wide Web Global network of computers connecting the sites that supply a variety of data, audio and visual resources

CREDITS

Page 9 - ©Gideon Mendel/Corbis; Page 10 - ©Jenna Blake/Corbis; Page 16 - ©Roel Smart/Thinkstock Photos; Page 20 - ©Barnie Rabbit/Demotix/Corbis; Page 30 - ©Bruce Connolly/Corbis; Page 31 - ©ivosar/Thinkstock Photos; Page 37 - ©AndreaWillmore/Thinkstock Photos; Page 41 - ©shalamov/Thinkstock Photos; Page 45 - ©Aurora Photos/Alamy; Page 57 - ©Horacio Villalobos/Corbis; Page 59 - ©Erik Tham/Corbis; Page 60 - ©TongRo Images/Thinkstock Photos; Page 62 - ©africanpix/Thinkstock Photos; Page 64 - ©shujaa_777/Thinkstock Photos; Page 70 - ©Faisal Puksi. Reproduced with kind permission; Page 72 - ©Iain Masterton/Alamy; Page 74 - ©Alex Hinds/Alamy; Page 76 - ©Maria Teijeiro/Thinkstock Photos; Page 84 - ©Jeff Blackler/REX; Page 90 - ©Monkey Business Images/Thinkstock Photos; Page 93 - ©RUBEN GUTIERREZ/Thinkstock Photos; Page 96 - ©ihsanGercelman/Thinkstock Photos; Page 101 - ©EDB Image Archive/Alamy; Page 112 - ©TongRo Images/Thinkstock Photos; Page 119 - ©payphoto/Thinkstock Photos; Page 123 - ©AndreyPopov/Thinkstock Photos; Page 126 - ©Atlantide Phototravel/Corbis; Page 132 - ©MichaelJay/Thinkstock Photos; Page 146 - ©michaeljung/Thinkstock Photos; Page 149 - ©JAG Images/Corbis; Page 153 - ©Olivier Polet/Corbis; Page 157 - ©Richard Levine/Demotix/Corbis; Page 162 - ©Kim Kulish/Corbis; Page 179 - ©hessbeck/Thinkstock Photos; Page 181 - ©srgktk/Thinkstock Photos; Page 182 - ©Anatolii Babii/Alamy; Page 191 - ©B Christopher/Alamy; Page 194 - ©Percy Feinstein/Corbis; Page 197 - ©Amit Bhargava/Corbis; Page 204 - ©picturesbyrob/Alamy; Page 209 - ©Riccardo_Mojana/Thinkstock Photos; Page 218 - ©bbsferrari/Thinkstock Photos; Page 221 - ©Chen Chao/Thinkstock Photos; Page 222 - ©Purestock/Thinkstock Photos; Page 229 - ©Gideon Mendel/Corbis; Page 232 - ©DC_Colombia/Thinkstock Photos; Page 241 - ©Robert Harding Picture Library Ltd/Alamy; Page 242 - ©Juan Carlos/Corbis; Page 243 - ©Wavebreakmedia Ltd/Thinkstock Photos; Page 250 - ©moodboard/Thinkstock Photos; Page 252 - ©Richard Levine/Alamy; Page 259 - ©incamerastock/Alamy; Page 262 - ©Blue Lantern Studio/Corbis; Page 264 - ©ventdusud/Thinkstock Photos; Page 269 - ©Gewoldi/Thinkstock Photos; Page 272 - ©Home Bird/Alamy; Page 283 - ©Imaginechina/Corbis; Page 289 - ©Richard T. Nowitz/Corbis; Page 290 - ©Newscast/Alamy; Page 302 - ©Newscast/Alamy; Page 308 - ©SafakOguz/Thinkstock Photos; Page 311 - ©Carolyn Jenkins/Alamy; Page 319 - ©Peter Muller/Cultura/Corbis; Page 322 - ©Bob Pardue - Signs/Alamy; Page 326 - ©gpointstudio/Thinkstock Photos; Page 331 - ©imageBROKER/Alamy; Page 332 - ©Matt Mawson/Corbis; Page 341 - ©Ryan McVay/Thinkstock Photos; Page 343 - ©jamaln/Thinkstock Photos; Page 349 - ©Ingram Publishing/Thinkstock Photos; Page 352 - ©JasonBatterham/Thinkstock Photos; Page 360 - ©dpa picture alliance/Alamy; Page 363 - ©gk-6mt/Thinkstock Photos; Page 368 - ©anek_s/Thinkstock Photos; Page 369 - ©nakornkhai/Thinkstock Photos; Page 375 - ©semakokal/Thinkstock Photos; Page 378 - ©Guo Haipeng/Xinhua Press/Corbis; Page 390 - ©marcoscisetti/Thinkstock Photos; Page 392 - ©Tibor Bognar/Corbis; Page 400 - ©PSL Images/Alamy; Page 402 - ©Chris Hellier/Corbis; Page 405 - ©Fuse/Thinkstock Photos; Page 406 - ©BartekSzewczyk/Thinkstock Photos; Page 411 - ©nextlevel/Thinkstock Photos; Page 413 - ©Stephen Cooper/Alamy; Page 416 - ©Jupiterimages/Thinkstock Photos; Page 420 - ©LAN/Corbis; Page 428 - ©Huntstock/Thinkstock Photos; Page 432 - ©monkeybusinessimages/Thinkstock Photos; Page 436 - ©alexey_boldin/Thinkstock Photos; Page 437 - ©Art Directors & TRIP/Alamy

INDEX